Pelican Book A809
Political Leaders of the Twentieth Century

Lenin: A Biography

David Shub was born in Russia in 1887 and educated there.
Over a period of more than fifty years he has had intimate
contact with the leaders of every faction in the Russian
revolutionary movement, both as a revolutionary and as a
close student of Russian affairs.

Mr Shub became a member of the Russian Social Democratic
Party in 1903, at a time when Lenin was one of its leaders.
From 1904 to 1905 he lived in the western European centres
of Russian revolutionary activity (London, Paris, Geneva),
where he often met Lenin and the other leaders of the Social
Democratic Party – Bolshevik and Menshevik.

In September 1905 Mr Shub returned to Russia and
participated in the Russian Revolution of 1905–6. Late in
1906 he was arrested for revolutionary activity and sentenced
to exile in Siberia, whence he escaped a year later.

He arrived in the United States in 1908. Since then he has
maintained close contact with the leading figures of the Russian
revolutionary movement and has written extensively on
Russian affairs. He was personally acquainted with many of
the Bolshevik leaders, including Lenin, Trotsky, and Bukharin,
as well as with the outstanding liberals and socialists.

For many years he has edited and contributed to liberal,
labour and socialist publications in several languages.

Political Leaders of the
Twentieth Century

Lenin: A Biography

David Shub

Penguin Books

Penguin Books Inc., Baltimore, Md.
Penguin Books Ltd, Harmondsworth, Middlesex, England
Penguin Books Pty Ltd, Ringwood, Victoria, Australia

First published by Doubleday & Company Inc. 1948
Published in a revised edition in Pelican Books 1966
Copyright © David Shub, 1948, 1966

Reprinted 1967

Printed in the United States of America

In Memory of My Son, Boris Shub (1912–1965)

Contents

Preface

When I first began work on this book, shortly after Lenin's death, 'Marxism-Leninism' was just being invented by the rising Stalin. Communism had achieved power only in Russia; its future development was not at all clear; and both Russia and the International Communist Movement appeared to be characterized by a good deal of spontaneity and variety.

By the time the original edition of this book was published, in the spring of 1948, 'Marxism-Leninism' had hardened into a 'monolithic' creed which Stalin had authoritatively defined for two decades in Russia and extended at war's end into Central Europe and East Asia.

Today, 'Marxism-Leninism' appears to be a rather flexible and ambiguous set of ideas, variously interpreted by contending Communist factions in Moscow, Peking, Belgrade, Bucharest and elsewhere; utilized by each to prove its own points; and increasingly irrelevant to the needs of modern society.

Yet it seems to me that, throughout these four decades and all the vicissitudes which Russia and world Communism have undergone, certain elements of the Leninist heritage have remained relatively constant. These elements have been common to Stalin and Trotsky, and later to Khrushchev and Mao, and continue to separate Communists as such from democratic Socialists and radicals. They are, by and large, the same elements which separated Lenin from Russian democrats long before he won power: the idea of tutelage by an intellectual *élite* of professional revolutionaries ('the leading role of the party'), the organization of a political movement along lines of military hierarchy and discipline ('democratic centralism'), the primacy of ends over means and of ideology over empirical fact, the pretension to unique insight into the historical process, the suspicion of all outsiders to the movement as enemies or potential enemies, and so on. The evolution of these and other characteristically Leninist ideas is described in this book.

There has been much scholarly discussion as to how much of

the Leninist heritage derives from Marxism and how much from peculiarly Russian traditions. While it is indisputable that Lenin evolved his theory and practice in Russian conditions, and based it on Marxism as he understood it, my own view is that Communism is inseparable from the unique character and personality of Lenin himself and is therefore somewhat of a historical mutation. Russian conditions, after all, bred Mikhailovsky, Korolenko, Berdyayev, Miliukov and Kerensky as well as Lenin; as for Marxism, the more obvious intellectual line of descent is through Engels, Kautsky and Bernstein to various forms of modern social democracy; and even the Russian Marxism of the turn of the century produced Plekhanov, Struve, Axelrod, Potresov and Martov as well as Lenin.

The historical circumstances which gave Lenin his moment on the world stage have complex roots, to be sure; but it was Lenin the man who stamped events from the moment he arrived in Petrograd in April 1917. Neither Trotsky, Stalin, Zinoviev, Bukharin nor any of the others could have done what he did over the next four years; nor would they, at a dozen critical turning points, have done quite the same thing in quite the same way. Since it is precisely Lenin's approach to the problems of war, peace, revolution and freedom in the years 1917–21 which constitutes the basis of the Communist movement today, a study of his ideas, actions and personality remains relevant, I believe, to an understanding of contemporary developments.

This revision of the original edition has been necessitated by the copious flow of new material relating to Lenin and the Russian Revolution which has been published since 1948. The new material comes from four main sources. First, the publication by the Soviet Communist Party since 1956 of materials suppressed in Stalin's time. Second, the memoirs, reminiscences and documentary collections published by a number of Russian democratic leaders, notably Kerensky, Tseretelli, Woytinsky, Dan and Abramovich. Third, the publication of Imperial German and Austro-Hungarian state documents captured by the Western Allies after World War II. And finally, the growth of an impressive British and American scholarship in the field of Russian studies since 1948, which has in recent years produced literally scores of interesting and valuable works.

To include all the new material available since 1948 would have meant a book perhaps thrice the size of the original – and therefore of diminished interest to the intelligent, non-specialist reader to whom this book is primarily addressed. Nevertheless, some revisions or additions have been made in nearly every chapter – and substantial new material has been added on such subjects as Lenin's relations with Imperial Germany, with Stalin, with Inessa Armand, with the Russian radicals Peter Kropotkin and Vladimir Korolenko, and so on.

In some respects the new material has merely confirmed the accuracy of the original edition. Such was the case with Khrushchev's release in 1956 of Lenin's 'Testament', which had appeared in this book eight years earlier although its existence was still being officially denied at that time in the Soviet Union. In other respects, however, the new material has permitted a deepening of the portrait of Lenin originally drawn and the unravelling of various historiographical mysteries. Finally, the painstaking criticism of such authorities as the late Professor Michael Karpovich of Harvard University, as well as of less friendly critics, have enabled me to rectify a number of errors in the first edition.

It is my hope that this new Pelican edition will stimulate, in Britain and the Commonwealth, the same sort of discussion and re-evaluation of Lenin and the Russian Revolution as has taken place in other countries in which this book has already appeared.

DAVID SHUB
New York, 1965

Prologue
Bitter Heritage

Vladimir came running home from school, breathless and frightened.

'What is it?' his mother demanded.

'Alexander! He's been arrested.'

Maria Alexandrovna clutched the table. 'Alexander arrested! What for?'

'He's charged with plotting to assassinate the Tsar.'

'How do you know?'

'Kashkadomova told me. She asked me to step out of the classroom – showed me a letter she had just received from her father's friend in St Petersburg.'

Maria Alexandrovna decided to take the next train to the capital. She knew it would not be an easy journey. No railway passed through the provincial town of Simbirsk. Even steamers plying the Volga could only dock there during the navigable months; in winter the sole highway was the fast-frozen river. The first part of her journey would have to be made on horseback.

She hoped, however, that she would not have to travel alone. The Ulyanovs were a highly respected family in Simbirsk. Ilya Nikolayevich, her husband, who had died a year before, had been an 'active state counsellor', had taught mathematics and physics in Penza and Nizhnii Novgorod, and, a few months before Vladimir's birth, had been named school inspector for the entire province. But Maria Alexandrovna was disappointed. Friends and neighbours would have nothing to do with the mother of a political prisoner. She left for the capital alone.

At Sizran she boarded the St Petersburg train. On the long, dismal journey she thought of her son about to be tried for high treason.[1] Alexander, twenty-one years old, was the eldest of her six children and young Vladimir's idol. Outwardly he was soft, but where principles were concerned she knew him to be adamant. Slow and cautious, he had wanted to be sure before joining the revolutionary movement. Only a year before he had said: 'It is absurd, even immoral, for a man who has no understanding of medicine to cure the sick. How much more absurd and immoral it is to seek to heal social ills without understanding their cause.'[2]

At that time Alexander's chief interest had been zoology. He had written a prize paper on the subject and even Vladimir had been deceived by his brother's preoccupation with natural science. He had explained to friends: 'Alexander will never be a revolutionist. On his last summer visit home he spent his time preparing a dissertation on Annelides and worked constantly with his microscope. A revolutionist cannot possibly devote so much time to the study of Annelides.'

But a few months later Alexander, the scientist, was making bombs. As a member of the revolutionary party, *Narodnaya Volya* (the People's Will), he became a leader of a group of St Petersburg student terrorists. In secret meetings at his apartment plans were laid to kill Alexander III on 1 March 1887, the sixth anniversary of the assassination of his father, Alexander II.

Ulyanov also prepared a manifesto to the Russian people, to be published immediately after the Tsar's death. Couched in the revolutionary language of the time, it began: 'The spirit of the Russian land lives and the truth is not extinguished in the hearts of her sons. On —, 1887, Tsar Alexander III was executed.'

The date was advanced several days when the terrorists learned that the Tsar was planning to leave for his summer palace in the Crimea. Assassins were planted in the square before St Isaac's Cathedral. But the Tsar did not appear and at twilight the conspirators returned to their underground headquarters. Ulyanov then heard that on 28 February the Tsar was to drive along the Nevsky Prospect, probably to attend memorial services at his father's crypt in the Cathedral of St Peter and St Paul. Once more the terrorists waited, but no Tsar's carriage appeared. The secret police, suspecting an assassination plot, had warned the monarch to remain in the Winter Palace.

Hours later the terrorists left their stations along the Nevsky and met in a tavern. One of them, Andreiushkin, had been shadowed for days by detectives. They followed him to the tavern, where he and his comrades were seized.

Ulyanov and his lieutenant, Lukashevich, after waiting impatiently all day, proceeded to their headquarters. The police were there to meet them. In Ulyanov's possession they found a code-book with a number of incriminating names and addresses, including those of the Polish revolutionary leaders Josef and Bronislaw Pilsudski.

Within the next few days hundreds of suspects were picked up in various cities and towns throughout Russia, the police having obtained the key to the code by torturing one of the terrorists. They singled out fifteen men, including Alexander Ulyanov, for trial. The charge: conspiracy to assassinate the Tsar.

Maria Alexandrovna reached St Petersburg seven days after her son's arrest. For weeks she tried to see him. In despair, she wrote a letter to the Tsar, in the margin of which Alexander III made this note: 'I think it would be advisable to allow her to visit her son, so that she might see for herself the kind of person this precious son of hers is.'

Maria Alexandrovna met her son. Alexander embraced his mother, wept, asked her to forgive him for the suffering he had brought her. But his first allegiance, he insisted, was to the revolutionary movement. As a revolutionist, he had no alternative but to fight for his country's liberation.

'But your way of achieving this liberation is so terrible,' Maria said.

'There is no other way,' Alexander replied.

At the preliminary hearing Ulyanov refused to talk. But when he realized that many of his comrades faced execution, he decided to shoulder the main responsibility himself.

In a heavily guarded St Petersburg courtroom Alexander and fourteen of his co-conspirators went on trial before a special panel of the Senate, Russia's highest tribunal. Refusing to be represented by counsel, Alexander was his own advocate. It was a curious defence. In order to save his comrades Alexander confessed to acts he had never committed. To Lukashevich, sitting at his side, he kept whispering, 'Blame everything on me.'

In his concluding address, Ulyanov cried: 'My purpose was to aid in the liberation of the unhappy Russian people. Under a system which permits no freedom of expression and crushes every attempt to work for their welfare and enlightenment by legal means, the only instrument that remains is terror. We cannot fight this régime in open battle, because it is too firmly entrenched and commands enormous powers of repression. Therefore, any individual sensitive to injustice must resort to terror. Terror is our answer to the violence of the state. It is the only way to force a despotic régime to grant political freedom to the people.'

Speaking for himself, and for his comrades beside him, he declared that he was not afraid to die, because 'there is no death more honourable than death for the common good'.[3]

Alexander Ulyanov was sentenced to die on the gallows. Frantically his mother pleaded with him to ask for imperial clemency. Alexander refused, although some of his co-defendants petitioned the Tsar and their death sentences were commuted. He did make one last request – for a volume of Heine's poetry.

In the early morning of 8 May 1887, Alexander and four of his comrades were hanged in the courtyard of the Schlusselburg fortress.

When the St Petersburg newspaper carrying the news of Alexander's execution reached Vladimir in Simbirsk, he threw the paper to the floor and cried:

'I'll make them pay for this! I swear it!'

'You'll make who pay?' asked a neighbour, Maria Savenko.

'Never mind, I know,' Vladimir replied.[4]

The world knows Vladimir Ulyanov as Lenin.

Chapter 1
Seeds of Revolution

Thirty years were to elapse from the death of Alexander Ulyanov to the day when his· brother Vladimir Ilyich Ulyanov-Lenin changed the course of history by establishing the Soviet régime. During that turbulent period Lenin was to create and lead to power a new type of political organization, a party of professional revolutionists devoted to a secular creed with the power of a universal religion. He was to found an international revolutionary order which today – nearly half a century after his death – still struggles to remake the world in his image.

Alexander Ulyanov, the martyred idealist who dreamed of freedom through assassination, and his brother Vladimir, who took a more pragmatic road to reach another goal, drew their inspiration – each in his own way – from the same source. They were both bred in a revolutionary tradition whose physiognomy was uniquely Russian and whose spirit contained incredible contradictions of nobility and baseness, saintlike virtue and underworld criminality, boundless love and unbridled hate.

When Alexander Ulyanov died on the gallows, the ingredients that were to shape the destiny of his brother had already been prepared by two generations of Russian revolutionists – and by centuries of Russian historical experience.

The Russian revolutionary movement dates back to the close of the Napoleonic era, when Russian officers returned from western Europe infected with the ideas of the French Revolution. The first conscious revolutionists were, for the most part, army officers who banded together in secret societies. The earliest overt act against autocratic power was the attempt by a group of these officers, known as the Decembrists, to deny the throne to Grand Duke Nicholas, on the death of Tsar Alexander I, and to install his brother Constantine as a constitutional monarch.

On 26 December 1825, the day Nicholas was to ascend the throne, a regiment of the Guards, supported by several companies of Imperial Marines, marched to Senate Square in St Petersburg, refused to swear allegiance to Nicholas, proclaimed Constantine the lawful Emperor, and demanded a constitution for Russia. The emissaries sent by Nicholas to negotiate with the rebel leaders were fired upon; in the meantime the populace began to join the insurgents. Before the revolt could gain momentum, Nicholas ordered a battery to open fire on the rebels. The Decembrists were quickly put to flight, leaving many dead and wounded on the streets of the capital. Five of their leaders were hanged, thirty-one were sentenced to long terms of hard labour, others were exiled to Siberia.[1]

At the time of the Decembrist revolt Russia was still an agrarian country whose economy rested on serfdom; the faint beginnings of capitalism were just emerging. While western Europe had for centuries been the scene of struggle between kings and cities against feudal lords, and then of the third estate against the absolute power of the king, in Russia those centuries saw only the ever-greater subjugation of the people.

The peasants harboured smoldering hatred against their oppressors which exploded from time to time in violent uprisings. Some, like Stenka Razin's revolt in the seventeenth century and Pugachev's rebellion during the reign of Catherine the Great, assumed vast proportions. But these insurrections were not motivated by a conscious desire for political freedom and social progress; they were inchoate uprisings of illiterate slaves, marked by incredible savagery and crushed with equally incredible brutality. After every such defeat, the peasants went back crawling at the feet of their masters.

As a result Russia in the early nineteenth century was sharply divided into two opposing camps: the Tsarist Government, its powerful bureaucracy and nobility on the one hand and the multi-million-headed servile peasantry on the other.[2]

With the development of commerce and industry, a class of merchants and entrepreneurs began to appear, recruited mainly from the gentry, though some stemmed from the ranks of peasants who had bought their freedom.

In 1833, eight years after the Decembrist revolt, Pushkin remarked that Moscow's 'aristocratic glitter' was giving way to 'flourishing industry', and that 'wealthy merchants were settling in the palaces abandoned by the nobility'.

The French Revolution of 1830 gave fresh impetus to revolutionary ideas in Russia. In St Petersburg, Moscow, and the larger cities of the provinces, clandestine circles were organized, whose members met secretly to discuss political, literary and social problems. The pioneers of the democratic movement were members of the nobility, professors, writers and students. Their most vivid figure was Alexander Herzen. Herzen and his friends wanted, above all, the end of serfdom and autocratic rule. Few among these men welcomed the rise of the bourgeoisie as the potential bearer of political freedom. The majority, including Herzen himself, were hostile towards the merchant class and towards capitalism as such. Uniquely, Russian democratic thought from its inception was steeped in Socialism. Political protest against autocracy went hand in hand with social protest, not only against the economic order based on serfdom, but against rising capitalism as well.

The early Russian rebels adopted Fourier, Saint-Simon and other French Socialists as their teachers. But they realized that they had no large social group to lean on for support. The educated landowners, fearing peasant uprisings, supported the Tsar, while the masses of the people lived in abysmal ignorance.

'The people have a desire for potatoes,' wrote Byelinski, the illustrious literary critic, in 1847, 'but none whatsoever for a constitution; the latter is wanted by the educated urban classes who are powerless to do anything.'

The European revolutions of 1848 were greeted by these intellectuals with enthusiasm and great hope, but the subsequent collapse caused even stronger reaction against the bourgeoisie. A German scholar, Baron Haxthausen, who travelled in Russia during this period, wrote that since Russia had no working class and since the peasant commune (*obshchina*) really secured land to each peasant, revolution was impossible in Russia. Herzen picked up his observation but drew the opposite conclusion. Precisely because of the weakness of Russian capitalism and the existence of the peasant communes, he wrote, Socialism could be introduced more easily in Russia than anywhere else. And he continued: 'What can be accomplished only by a series of cataclysms in the West can develop in Russia out of existing conditions.'

The growing popularity of heterodox political thought led to a tightening of Tsarist censorship and to increased persecution of intellectuals. Turgenev was arrested in 1852 for displeasing the censor. The members of a literary circle, whose main crime consisted of nightly discussion of Fourier's theories, were condemned to death in a body. Among them was Dostoyevsky. The prisoners were forced to go through final preparations for execution before their sentences were commuted to hard labour in Siberia.[3]

When Nicholas I died in 1855 there was no immediate change in policy. But after Russia's defeat in the Crimean War, Tsar Alexander II instituted some halting reforms. Yielding to persistent agitation, he appointed a committee to draw up a decree for the abolition of serfdom. Encouraged by the apparent turn towards liberalism, the press not only took up the agrarian problem, but began a bold discussion of all political questions. Herzen was the leading spirit of this awakening. His magazine, *Kolokol*, or *The Bell*, published in London, had a tremendous influence among the aristocracy, as well as among radicals and liberals.

The Tsar's Act of Liberation abolishing serfdom in 1861 proved a disappointment. The peasants, who expected to receive land free and clear, were saddled with such heavy mortgages and taxes that they could not hope to redeem their land within a reasonable period. But the peasants could not conceive that the Tsar had given them freedom under such heavy disadvantages. Blaming the landowners, their dissatisfaction expressed itself in arson and riots. In reprisal, the government sent punitive expeditions against the peasant villages.

The most influential figure among the radical intelligentsia in this period was Nikolai Chernyshevsky, publicist, economist, novelist and critic, who translated John Stuart Mill into Russian and whom Marx described as 'the great Russian scholar and critic who has in a masterly way exposed the bankruptcy of bourgeois economics'. Chernyshevsky was not a Marxist, however; his vision of the future society was based largely on the ideas of the French Utopians Fourier and Louis Blanc.

Although as late as 1858 Chernyshevsky still had high hopes for Alexander II, within a few years he was thoroughly disillusioned. In a letter to Herzen, he protested against *Kolokol*'s praise of the Tsar: 'What does this mean? Instead of fierce denunciations of falsehood there are borne to us from the banks of the Thames hymns of praise for Alexander II. The liberal landowners, liberal writers, liberal professors lull you with hopes in the progressive aims of our government ... but this is how the matter really stands. At the end of the reign of Nicholas I, everyone sincerely loving Russia came to the conclusion that only by force could human rights be seized by the people from the Tsar's grip, that only those rights which are conquered are stable, for whatever is given as a gift can also be taken away.'

Herzen printed the letter anonymously in *Kolokol*, and replied: 'We will not call for the axe as the *ultima ratio* so long as there remains one vestige of reasonable hope for a solution without the axe. The further I look into the western world, into the chain of events which brought Europe to us Russians, the more there arises in me a disgust for all bloody revolutions.'

However, a few months after the promulgation of the Act of Liberation illegal pamphlets were distributed in Moscow and St Petersburg. One of these pamphlets accused the government of provoking a new Pugachev rebellion by its agrarian policy. The 'educated classes' were called on to take power 'out of the hands of the incompetent government in order to establish the rule of law in the country'. If they failed to do so the 'patriots' would be forced to summon the people to revolt. Another leaflet demanded the convocation of a Constituent Assembly to give Russia a democratic régime. A third concluded with the warning that if the government did not remove the causes of popular discontent, Russia would see an insurrection by the summer of 1863.

During the same year came a proclamation 'To the Young Generation', which argued that the 1848 defeat of Socialism in western Europe proved nothing as far as Russia was concerned. For, in contrast to the West, Russia had peasant communes 'and enough land to last 10,000 years. We are a retarded people, and therein lies our salvation. . . . We believe that we are destined to bring a new principle into history, to say our own word, and not to ape Europe's outlived ideas.'

In the winter of 1862 illegal proclamations urging revolution appeared. One called for armed uprising and ruthless extermination of the enemies of freedom. The author was Zaichnevsky.

'Soon the day will come', this proclamation declared, 'when we shall unfurl the great banner of the future, the red banner, and with the battle cry, "Long live the Social and Democratic

Republic in Russia ", march upon the Winter Palace to exterminate everyone there. It is quite possible that the affair will end with the extirpation of the Imperial family alone, *i.e.* some one hundred people in all. But it is also possible that the entire Imperial Party will rise as one to defend its Emperor. In that case, fully confident of ourselves, of our strength, of the sympathy of the people with our cause, and the glorious future of Russia thus destined to be the first to realize the great ideal of Socialism, we shall utter the cry, "Use the axe", and then crush the Imperial Party, dealing with it as mercilessly as it is now dealing with us.

'The outcry will be: "Kill them! Kill them in the public squares, in their homes, in the streets of the cities, in the villages and the hamlets!" Remember that when that time comes, whoever is not with us is against us! We are convinced that the revolutionary party which is to assume power must maintain its present centralized organization so that it may build the foundation for a new social-economic order in the shortest possible time. This organization must usurp government power through a dictatorship and must stop at nothing. Elections to the National Assembly must be directed by the government which shall immediately make certain that its members include none of those who are in favour of the present order, should any such persons still be found alive.'[4]

Herzen sharply condemned proclamations of this violent character on the ground that their effect was to tighten the bonds between the autocracy and the propertied classes and to force the régime to take further repressive measures. And, as a matter of fact, wholesale arrests and new political restrictions usually followed the appearance of such leaflets.

Playing upon the Emperor's fear of revolution, his advisers induced him to sign one reactionary measure after another. The new Minister of Education changed the high-school curriculum; natural sciences were eliminated; history, geography and modern language courses were slashed down. A spy system was introduced among the students to report the slightest evidence of 'sedition'. Again students took the lead in demonstrations of protest. Punishment was swift and summary. Many were expelled from the universities and banished to Siberia.

A new leader of revolt became known – a nobleman and former artillery officer named Michael Bakunin. Bakunin regarded the repudiation of religion as the first step towards progress. He preached the abolition of hereditary property, advocated the transfer of land to agricultural communes and factories to labour associations. He urged equality for women, the abolition of marriage and the family, and free education for all children. The abolition of the state, according to Bakunin, was the keynote. No social or economic freedom was possible under any régime, he argued, because all government was founded on force and class domination.

Bakunin, who commanded a large following among students, told them to leave the universities and go 'to the people' to lead their revolt against the social order. His credo was that the entire structure of society must be demolished before a new and better one could be built.

Bakunin's most remarkable disciple, Sergei Nechayev, was the son of a priest. Young Nechayev passionately embraced the cause of social revolution. In 1869 he organized a secret society in Moscow for the purpose of preparing a mass insurrection. In his zeal, Nechayev went far beyond Bakunin. He shrank from nothing to attract followers, resorting to deceit, terrorism and murder.

Implicated in the student riots of 1869, Nechayev fled to Switzerland, where he issued an appeal to Russian students to join his revolutionary organization. Here he was befriended by Bakunin, whom he impressed with his strong character and revolutionary fanaticism. Together with Bakunin, Nechayev published a periodical called *The People's Justice* which advocated the most desperate acts of terrorism, not only against the Tsar's representatives, but also against liberal writers and journalists. In their *Catechism of a Revolutionist* Nechayev and Bakunin wrote:

'The Revolutionist is a doomed man. He has no private interests, no affairs, sentiments, ties, property nor even a name of his own. His entire being is devoured by one purpose, one thought, one passion – the revolution. . . . Heart and soul, not merely by word but by deed, he has severed every link with the social order and with the entire civilized world; with the laws, good manners, conventions, and morality of that world. He is its merciless enemy and continues to inhabit it with only one purpose – to destroy it. . . . He despises public opinion. He hates and despises the social morality of his time, its motives and manifestations. Everything which promotes the success of the revolution is moral, everything which hinders it is immoral. . . . The nature of the true revolutionist excludes all romanticism, all tenderness, all ecstasy, all love.'

Bakunin issued a paper certifying Nechayev as leader of the Russian branch of the 'Revolutionary Union of the World'. With this document, Nechayev returned to Russia and began to recruit members, weaving fantasies about the 'Revolutionary Union of the World', and the 'Society of the People's Justice', neither of which existed in fact.

He persuaded his comrades to assassinate a student named Ivanov, by telling them that Ivanov was a spy. The real reason for the murder was that Ivanov was an independent young man who promised danger to the 'cause'. Nechayev's slogan was 'Everything for the Revolution – the end justifies the means!'

The murder of Ivanov was the beginning of the end of Nechayev's career. It led to the unearthing of his secret organization in Moscow and to the arrest of some three hundred persons. Again Nechayev fled to Switzerland and continued to issue proclamations, but his methods, described by Dostoyevsky in the novel, *The Possessed*, finally cost him his following, including Bakunin.

Bakunin wrote to his friend Talandier that Nechayev 'knows no hesitation, stops at nothing, and is as ruthless with himself as he is with others. He is a fanatic, a loyal fanatic; but at the same time a very dangerous one, association with whom may be fatal to all concerned. . . . He has come to the conclusion that in order to create a workable and strong organization one must use as a basis the philosophy of Machiavelli and adopt the motto of the Jesuits: "Violence for the Body; lies for the Soul."

'With the exception of a small group who are to be the chosen leaders, all the members should serve as blind tools in the hands of those leaders who must be united and loyal. It is permissible to deceive these members, compromise them in every way, rob them, and even murder them if necessary. . . . When all of us came together and exposed him, he had the audacity to say: "Well, that is our method. We consider all those who disapprove of this method and refuse to apply it our enemies and we think it our duty to deceive and discredit all who refuse to go with us the whole way."'[5]

Nechayev was eventually extradited for the murder of Ivanov and sentenced to twenty years at hard labour. In 1883 he died in the fortress of St Peter and St Paul, but not before he had managed to win a following among the prison guards.

Another guiding spirit among the Russian student colony in Switzerland, and one who drew his inspiration from the same general current as Herzen, was Peter Lavrov, a former officer and St Petersburg professor. Unlike Nechayev and Bakunin, Lavrov favoured the gradual education of the masses to an understanding of the moral aspect of revolution.

'The reconstruction of Russian society', wrote Lavrov, 'must be achieved not only for the sake of the people, but also through the people. But the masses are not ready for such reconstruction. Therefore the triumph of our ideas cannot be achieved at once, but requires preparation and clear understanding of what is possible at the given moment.'[6]

According to Lavrov, the role of the intellectuals was to imbue the people with the knowledge that would help them to attain 'the moral ideal of Socialism' through their communes and artisans' cooperatives (artels).

To Bakunin, the true revolutionaries were Stenka Razin and Pugachev, and the only sure path to revolution was by unleashing the elemental fury latent in the Russian people. Both Lavrov and Bakunin called on the youth to 'go to the people'. But while Lavrov's followers preached 'the moral ideal of Socialism', the Bakuninists went among the people to appeal to their 'instinct', their passion for vengeance, in the assurance that this would generate 'a new popular ideal of freedom, equality, and justice'.

A man of similar ideas, with a somewhat smaller following, was Peter Tkachev, who came to Switzerland in 1874, after several years in Tsarist prisons. Like the pamphleteer Zaichnevsky, Tkachev believed in the dictatorship of a revolutionary minority. He advocated the forcible seizure of political power for the purpose of reorganizing society on a Communist basis.

'When he was released from the Kronstadt Fortress,' Tkachev's sister wrote in 1913, 'he maintained that to rejuvenate Russia it would be necessary to liquidate everyone over twenty years of age. Somewhat later he abandoned this misanthropic plan, but he still believed that, for the sake of the common good, one not only could, but should, sacrifice individual persons. He always regarded the majority as a sluggish mass, unable either to understand or to defend its interests. The conscious revolutionary minority would have to create a new and better system for the majority, and compel it to accept that system.'

Tkachev drew the following picture of the peasant paradise that would come into being after the social revolution:

'The peasant would live a life of ease and joy. His purse would be filled not with copper pennies, but with gold coin. His cattle and fowl would be uncounted. All sorts of meats and birthday pies and sweet wines would stand on his table from sunrise to sunset. And he would eat and drink all his belly could hold, and would work only when he had a mind to, and no one would dare to force his will on him: if it pleases you – eat, if it pleases you – lie on the stove. A wonderfully happy life!'

Lavrov indignantly refused to print this article, on the ground that 'no desire to hasten the revolution can justify such attempts to inflame the people to passions of greed and sloth.'

'A revolutionist', Tkachev wrote in 1875, 'always has the right and should regard himself as having the right to call the people to an insurrection. He should regard the people as always ready for a revolution. Every people that is oppressed by an arbitrary government (and such is the condition under which all peoples live) is always able and willing to make a revolution. It is always ready for it. Why wait?

'A real revolution can be brought about only in one way: through the seizure of power by revolutionists. In other words, the immediate and most important task of revolution must be solely the overthrow of the government and the transformation of the present conservative state into a revolutionary state. The capture of a government power in itself does not yet constitute a revolution. It is only a prelude. The revolution is brought about by the revolutionary government, which, on the one hand, eradicates all the conservative and reactionary elements of society, eliminating all those institutions which hinder the establishment of equality and brotherhood among men, and, on the other hand, introduces such institutions as favour the development of these principles. . . .

'The revolutionary minority, having freed the people from the yoke of fear and terror, provides an opportunity for the people to manifest their revolutionary destructive power. Supported by this power and skilfully directing it towards the elimination of the enemies of the revolution, the minority demolishes the bulwarks of the old government and deprives the latter of its means of defence and counter-action. Then, utilizing its authority, the minority introduces new progressive and Communist ideas into life. In its work of reformation, the revolutionary minority need not rely upon the active support of the people. The revolutionary role of the people ends the instant they have destroyed the institutions which oppressed them, the instant they have overthrown the tyrants and exploiters who ruled over them. By utilizing the revolutionary destructive power of the people, by eliminating the enemies of the revolution, and by basing its constructive acts upon the character and urgency of the people's wants (that is to say, upon the conservative forces of the people), the revolutionary minority will lay the foundation of a new and more sensible social order.'[7]

Lavrov, who also advocated popular revolution, completely rejected the dictatorship of the minority:

'History has shown us, and psychology proves, that the possession of great power corrupts the best people,' he stated, 'and that even the ablest leaders, who meant to benefit the people by decree, failed. Every dictatorship must surround itself by compulsory means of defence which must serve as obedient tools in its hands. Every dictatorship is called upon to suppress not only its reactionary opponents but also those who disagree with its methods and actions. Whenever a dictatorship succeeded in establishing itself it had to spend more time and effort in retaining its power and defending it against its rivals than upon the realization of its programme, with the aid of that power. The abolition of dictatorship assumed by a party can only be dreamed about before the usurpation takes place. In the struggle of parties for power, in the clash of open or concealed ambitions, every moment furnishes an added reason and necessity for maintaining the dictatorship, creates a new excuse for not relinquishing it. A dictatorship can be wrested from the dictators only by a new revolution.'

Lavrov was only echoing the beliefs of Herzen, who years before had written:

'Social progress is possible only under complete republican freedom, under full democratic equality. A republic that would not lead to Socialism seems an absurdity to us – a transitional stage regarding itself as the goal. On the other hand, Socialism which might try to dispense with political freedom would rapidly degenerate into an autocratic Communism.'

He wrote further, in 1869:

'Violence and terror are employed to spread religious and political creeds, to establish autocratic empires and indivisible republics. But force can merely destroy and clear the place – no more. With the methods of Peter the Great the social revolution will never attain beyond the slave-labour equality of Gracchus and Babeuf and the Communist serfdom of Cabet.'

'Falsehood', wrote Lavrov in the middle seventies, 'can never be the means for spreading truth. Exploitation or the authoritarian rule of individuals can never be the means for the realization of justice. Triumph over idle pleasure cannot be attained by the forcible seizure of unearned wealth, or the transfer of the opportunity for enjoyment from one individual to another. . . . People who assert that the *end justifies the means* should keep in mind the limitation of their rule by the rather simple truism; *except those means which undermine the goal itself*.'

And further: 'The contemporary Russian active in public life should, in our opinion, discard the antiquated notion that it is possible to impose upon the people revolutionary ideas developed by a small, ideologically more advanced minority, that socialist revolutionaries, having overthrown the central government by a successful blow, can step into its place and legislate a new order into existence, heaping its blessings upon the unprepared masses. We do not wish a new coercive government.'[8] . . .

Many Russian students studying in Switzerland heeded these revolutionary doctrines, and brought them back to Russia.

To check the influence of the *émigré* revolutionists, the Tsarist Government ordered all students who were abroad to return to Russia by January 1874, endeavouring at the same time to draw women students back to Russia by opening institutions of higher learning for them. Most students complied with the decree as a welcome opportunity for going out among the Russian people to preach the theories of Socialism.

In 1876 the revolutionists, under Bakunin's influence, formed a society called 'Land and Freedom'. Its programme called for a social revolution from 'below', through uprisings and passive resistance among the peasants, as well as strikes among the workers. 'Fighting units' were formed to lead the coming insurrection.

A split occurred in the Land and Freedom group in 1879, when an executive committee was set up to organize terrorist acts. A small faction, headed by George Plekhanov, rejected the policy of terrorism and became known as the 'Black Repartition'. The larger group called itself *Narodnaya Volya* (the People's Will).[9] Both believed that the Russian peasant was by nature strongly inclined to Socialism. Contrary to the Marxist notion that only the industrial working class could bring Socialism, they believed that in Russia the peasant could play the same role as the industrial proletariat in other countries.

But the People's Will believed that Socialism could not be realized for some time; the immediate goal was the expropriation of the estates in favour of the peasantry and the establishment of civil liberty. In its programme, the party stipulated that after the fall of Tsarism, a Provisional Government would be set up to govern Russia until an elected Constituent Assembly gave the Russian people a system of their own choosing; the only road to democratic freedom in an autocratic state was through political assassination, the party asserted.

On Sunday 13 March 1881, Tsar Alexander II was assassinated by members of the People's Will.

If the terrorists thought that their act would strike fear into the heart of the new Emperor, Alexander III, their hopes were soon shattered. In a manifesto dated 13 May 1881, Alexander III proclaimed: 'In the midst of our great grief the voice of God commands us to stand bravely at the helm of the state, to trust Divine Providence, with faith in the power and truth of Absolutism.'

Five participants in the assassination were executed, most of the party leaders were sentenced to long prison terms and Siberian exile. A score, including Vera Figner, the 'Madonna of the Schlusselburg', were immured for decades in the dungeons of the famous fortress, where some died and others went insane.

But the People's Will, despite its belief in terrorist acts against the Tsar and his reactionary Ministers, had little in common with Bakunin, Nechayev or Tkachev.

'None of us', wrote Vera Figner in 1918, 'was a Jacobin. We never thought of forcing upon the majority of the people the will of the minority, and we never planned a government which would bring about revolutionary, socialistic, economic, and political changes by decree. If we had thought so, we would not have called our party the People's Will. How remote we were from the Jacobin theory can be seen from the open letter which the Executive Committee wrote to Emperor Alexander III immediately after the assassination of his father.

'While demanding the formation of a Constituent Assembly the Executive Committee at the same time promised to abide by the will of the people which was to be expressed through chosen representatives. Should the people's representatives favour some measure that is directly opposed to the demands of the revolutionary party, this party would under no circumstances resort to acts of violence and terrorism to enforce its programme, but would limit itself to peaceful propaganda. . . .'[10]

The best evidence of the moral attitude of the People's Will towards terror came a few months after the death of Alexander II, when President Garfield was assassinated. The Executive Committee of the People's Will sent this message to the United States:

'While expressing our deepest sympathy with the American people in connexion with the death of their President James Abram Garfield, the Executive Committee considers it its duty to protest in the name of the Russian Revolutionaries against acts of violence similar to the assault of Guiteau. In a country in which individual freedom makes possible every honest ideological combat, in which the free popular will determines not only the laws, but also the personality of the Executive – in such a country a political murder as a means of combat is an expression of exactly the same spirit of despotism which we seek to abolish in Russia. Personal despotism is as abominable as party despotism, and violence is only justified when directed against violence.'[11]

And from their fortress dungeons the members of the Executive Committee sent a message to the Russian people in June 1882, called 'From the Dead to the Living', which stressed even more clearly their moral repudiation of violence and bloodshed.

'Brethren and sisters,' said the message, 'out of our graves we send you what may be our last greeting, our testament. On the day of our triumph do not soil the glory of the revolution by any acts of cruelty or brutality against the vanquished foe. May our unhappy lot not only be the price of Russian freedom, but also serve to bring a more beautiful, more humane society. We salute our country, we salute all mankind.'[12]

After the decimation of the People's Will leadership, a few revolutionists succeeded in eluding the Tsarist police and escaping abroad. Among them were George Plekhanov, Paul Axelrod, Vera Zasulich, and Leo Deutch of the Black Repartition. Reviewing their past theories in the light of the doctrine of Karl Marx and of the experiences of the European labour movement, Plekhanov and his associates turned to Social Democracy. In 1883 they organized the 'Group for the Emancipation of Labour', in order to propagate Marxism in Russia. This organization published books and pamphlets rejecting the notion that Russia was destined to follow a unique path to Socialism either through a peasant uprising or a *coup d'état* by a revolutionary minority.

The members of the Group for the Emancipation of Labour maintained that the struggle for Socialism could be successful only when the revolutionary parties were supported by an organized and class-conscious working class. They pointed out that Russia was gradually becoming a capitalist country. To attain the final objective of a socialist society, political freedom was the necessary stepping-stone.

The leader of the Marxists was Plekhanov. Under his guidance Marxist works were printed in Switzerland and smuggled into Russia, and in the mid-eighties the first clandestine Social Democratic circles were formed.[13]

But all over Russia there still existed young revolutionists' organizations which tried to revive the People's Will. One of these was the terrorist group headed by Alexander Ulyanov.

The programme of the St Petersburg terrorists as drawn up by Ulyanov contained the following revealing passage:

'Convinced that terror results wholly from the absence of a minimum of freedom, we can state with complete confidence that terrorist activities will cease, if the Government grants this "minimum of freedom".'

When Alexander Ulyanov became convinced that the Tsar would not grant them the 'minimum' he turned to the terrorist action which led him to the gallows in May 1887. His younger brother, Vladimir, did not take the path of terror. He soon embraced Marxism instead. But although he turned to the teaching of Karl Marx, his whole being was profoundly influenced by the conflicting cross-currents of the Russian revolutionary movement. At the time of his brothers' death – and before he had read a word of Marx – Lenin was already drawing from both the humanitarian teachings of Herzen and Lavrov, and the demoniac visions of Bakunin, Tkachev and Nechayev.

The current of thinking that ran from Herzen and Lavrov through the People's Will to Alexander Ulyanov probably produced greater idealism and self-sacrifice than any other political movement in history. The theories of universal destruction propagated by men like Nechayev were still to be tested in life.

The apostles of enlightenment looked towards the liberation of man. Even when they resorted to individual terrorism, they sought moral justification for their acts, never masking their true aims, and always preferring to sacrifice their own lives rather than send others to their death.

Nechayev and his followers, on the other hand, frankly advocated the use of deception, calumny and murder for the attainment of their objectives. They regarded the Russian people mainly as a means towards their apocalyptic end, envisaging either ideal anarchy or the dictatorship of a revolutionary minority ruling by means of unlimited force and terror.

The early revolutionary parties contained adherents of both schools. But by the time Lenin's brother was executed the humanitarian current dominated the Russian revolutionary movement. And Herzen's precept of 1867 – 'Socialism which would dispense with political freedom would soon degenerate into autocratic Communism' – was accepted as a truism by all who called themselves revolutionists. The doctrines of Nechayev seemed to be buried forever. No one, except perhaps Dostoyevsky, foresaw that only a few decades later they would be revived to play a decisive role in the history of Russia and the world.

Chapter 2
Youth

Vladimir Ilyich Ulyanov was born in Simbirsk, a provincial town on the Volga, on 22 April 1870. His mother, Maria Alexandrovna, was the daughter of a physician named Alexander Blank, who left his St Petersburg hospital to settle on a small estate in the village of Kokushkino, in the province of Kazan. According to Maria Ulyanov, Vladimir's younger sister, their maternal grandmother was German and their mother was 'reared to a certain degree in German traditions.'[1] The Blank household was run along spartan lines and the children were largely self-educated. Maria Alexandrovna taught herself German, French, English and the piano.

She married Ilya Ulyanov in the summer of 1863, and went to live with him in Penza. Ilya, according to a friend, was 'a strong man of firm character who was very stern in his relations with his subordinates.' He was conservative in his politics and a devout member of the Russian Orthodox Church. In 1866 Maria bore him the first of their six children, Alexander, or Sasha as the family called him. In September 1869, when Ilya was appointed provincial school inspector, they rented the house in Simbirsk where Vladimir was born the following spring.

Vladimir – little Volodya – was a boisterous child with lively grey eyes and a top-heavy body. He learned to walk at about the same time as his younger sister Olga. Toddling through the house, he would often fall on his head, his screams alarming the entire household. 'Mother', writes his sister Anna, 'was always afraid that he might fracture his skull or grow up to be defective.'

Olga was his playmate, Alexander his hero. With gleeful imperiousness he would order Olga to hide under the couch and to come out on his command. When their game became too noisy, Maria Alexandrovna would pick up the two children and deposit them on their father's black chair in the library, where they were told to sit in silence until released.

When Vladimir was five his mother taught him to read and gave him piano lessons. At eight he was playing simple pieces and doing four-handed *études* with his mother. On entering school the following year, he gave up the piano, because, according to his brother Dmitri, he thought it was 'an unbecoming occupation for boys'.

He was always imitating Alexander, says Anna. 'Whenever Volodya was asked what he wanted to play, did he wish to go walking, take his *kasha* with butter or milk, he never answered directly, but looked first at Alexander, who generally turned aside and kept his brother in suspense. The older children used to make fun of him because of this, but that never prevented Volodya from answering "like Sasha".'[2]

The brothers played chess, went skiing and skating in winter, fishing and swimming at their maternal estate in Kokushkino in summer. By studying textbooks on chess, they sometimes managed to beat their father, who fancied himself an expert in the game.

Vladimir was a model student who mastered his lessons with almost disconcerting thoroughness. When Ilya Nikolayevich, from his heights as provincial school inspector, quizzed him on the day's lessons, Vladimir always seemed to know the answers. Dmitri recalls the meticulous care that young Vladimir put into his classroom compositions.

'He never wrote them on the eve of the day when they were to be handed in, as most students did. On the contrary, on being assigned the subject, Vladimir Ilyich set to work immediately. On a quarter of a sheet of paper he would make an outline together with the introduction and conclusion. He would then take another sheet, fold it in half, and make a rough draft on the left side of the paper, in accordance with his outline. The right side or margin remained clear. Here he would enter additions, explanations, corrections, as well as source indications – "see there and there, page so and so."

'Gradually, as the days progressed, the right side of the sheet became filled with a series of notes, alterations, quotations, etc. Then, shortly before it was necessary to hand it in, he would take some new clean sheets of paper and write the composition, but *not* in its final form, referring to his notes and sources in various books.'

In this early capacity for systematic work an essential facet of the coming man reveals itself for the first time. And system went hand in hand with complete concentration. Schoolboy friends who interrupted him while he was studying were greeted with, 'Would you kindly favour me with your absence?'

From all that the reminiscences of his family and early friends reveal, his childhood and adolescence were almost idyllic. In their summer rambles through the countryside the parents and children joined together in reciting the poetry of Pushkin, Nekrasov and Lermontov, and singing popular ballads. With his mother or Olga at the piano, Vladimir sang melodies from Vertovsky's opera *Askold's Grave* and Valentine's aria from *Faust*, 'God Almighty, God of Love'.

Alexander was editor of a family weekly, to which every member of the household contributed. The essays were collected and bound and read aloud on Saturday evenings. Vladimir also had no fewer than twenty cousins – rarely mentioned in official biographies because none ever became a Communist. Nevertheless, the Ulyanov children spent considerable time with their cousins, particularly during the summers at Kokushkino.

Although the Ulyanovs were not wealthy, their style of life compared favourably with that of the minor nobility, in whose ranks Ilya Nikolayevich was enrolled by virtue of his official position. His death, when Vladimir was sixteen, was the first blow, followed within a year by the tragic death of Alexander. But Maria Alexandrovna was a strong woman who rallied with determination, drawing the children closer to her, and the family always remained intimately bound to one another.

Ilya Nikolayevich bequeathed a substantial legacy, which his widow managed ably for many years, together with other bequests. This family fund included the moneys left by Lenin's father and his uncle Vasily; the widow's pension of 1,200 rubles a year; a large house and garden in Simbirsk, which was later profitably sold; and part of the Kokushkino estate which Lenin's mother had inherited. The family fund made it possible for Lenin to postpone earning a livelihood until the age of twenty-seven, his brother Dmitri until the age of twenty-eight. The family was also enabled to undertake several trips abroad – such as the four months Lenin himself spent travelling in 1895, when he was twenty-five. Lenin continued to receive money from his mother years later, after he had settled abroad.

A month after Alexander's death, Vladimir graduated from

the Simbirsk gymnasium with a gold medal as the school's best student 'in ability, development, and conduct'.

But his admission to Kazan University seemed unlikely because he was the brother of an executed terrorist. It is an ironic commentary on Tsarist absolutism that, despite inevitable doubts of Vladimir's loyalty to the throne, he was admitted to the university. And it is an even greater irony that the man who made this possible was the father of Alexander Kerensky, whose Provisional Government he was to overthrow in 1917.

Fyodor Kerensky was not only the director of the Simbirsk gymnasium; he had also been named guardian of the Ulyanov family by Ilya Nikolayevich's will.

'Neither in nor out of school', wrote Fyodor Kerensky in his letter of recommendation, 'has a single instance been observed when Ulyanov by word or deed caused dissatisfaction to his teachers or the school authorities.'

And he gave as the foundation of Vladimir's unimpeachable character the sound religious environment of his home.

'His mental and moral instruction', he continued, 'has always been thoroughly looked after, first by both his parents, and, upon the death of his father, by his mother, who concentrated all her care and attention on the education of her children. Religion and discipline were the basis of this upbringing, whose fruits are apparent in Ulyanov's exemplary conduct.'[3]

What Vladimir thought of this document at the time is not known, but many years later, in reply to a Bolshevik Party questionnaire asking when he ceased to believe in God, Lenin wrote: 'At the age of sixteen.'

He described his 'emancipation' from religion to Krzhizhanovsky, a companion of his early revolutionary days. 'When he perceived clearly that there was no God,' writes his friend, 'he tore the cross violently from his neck, spat upon it contemptuously, and threw it away. In short he freed himself from religious prejudices in typical revolutionary Leninist fashion, without prolonged hesitation or timid consideration, without mental struggle with the spirit of doubt.'[4]

It was at the age of seventeen that Lenin developed the fervent admiration for Chernyshevsky which he was to retain throughout his life.

When Vladimir entered Kazan University, in the fall of 1887, he found himself drawn almost at once into student disorders. Professors were being expelled for mildly liberal opinions and students who were suspected of engaging in any political activity were being sent into exile. These measures only stiffened student resistance. On 4 December 1887, the assembled student body of Kazan University presented the dean with a programme of their demands.

Vladimir, who was observed standing in the front row with clenched fists, was arrested that very night with forty other students and expelled from Kazan. The police officer who escorted young Ulyanov to the city limits asked him:

'Why did you engage in this revolt, young man? Don't you realize you're up against a wall?'

'Yes, a wall, but a rotten one; one kick and it will crumble,' Vladimir is said to have replied.[5]

At his mother's request, he was permitted to live under police surveillance at the Kokushkino estate. Here the family spent the winter in virtual isolation. But Vladimir was not particularly unhappy. The house was filled with books belonging to his late uncle, and for recreation there were skiing and hunting. Anna was not very impressed with his marksmanship. When a hare crossed their path one day she remarked dryly, 'That must be the animal you have been hunting all winter.'

In the autumn of 1888 Vladimir was permitted to reside in Kazan once more, but his application for return to the university was denied. The family rented a two-storey house with a balcony and pleasant garden. A spare kitchen, providing him with the privacy he desired, became his study.

It was in this kitchen, at the age of eighteen, that he began reading Karl Marx. In the evenings he expounded Marx's principles to his sister Anna, seeking to convey the sense of new horizons which these writings gave him. Soon he was trying to convert friends and organizing discussion groups in their homes. Out of consideration for his mother, the meetings were not held in his house.

The following year the family moved to Samara, where Vladimir organized a small Marxist group. In the meantime his mother was making repeated efforts to have him readmitted to the university.

The matter was referred to the warden of the Kazan school district, who turned in an unfavourable report.

'During his short stay in the university', the warden wrote, 'he was conspicuous for his reticence, lack of attention, and even rudeness. Only a day or two before the students' meeting he gave grounds for suspicion that he was fomenting trouble. He spent a great deal of time in the smoking-room conversing with the most suspicious of the students, went home, and returned, bringing something with him that the others had requested, and generally behaved in a strange manner.'[6]

Maria Alexandrovna then took her son's case to the Ministry of Education in St Petersburg, and through her persistence he was finally allowed to take his law examinations at the St Petersburg University.

During the summer before going to the capital, Vladimir studied intensively. He set up a table in a solitary spot in the woods near Samara, where he went every morning, loaded with legal treatises. No one ever ventured near this den. In the afternoon he swam in the river, and at night he resumed his law studies at home.

His first stay in St Petersburg was brief. He passed his law examinations with honours in 1891 and was admitted to the bar. But his moment of success was marred when Olga, his childhood playmate, who was studying in the capital at the same time, contracted typhoid fever and died.

Probably for his mother's sake he returned to Samara and went through the motions of starting a law practice. Actually the clandestine Marxist club he had started was soon consuming most of his time. His first real disciples were his sisters, Anna and Maria, and his brother Dmitri.

The two younger Ulyanovs, Dmitri and Maria, were of much the same cast as their late brother Alexander – deep-set eyes, high foreheads, pale, handsome. Vladimir, with his small thick nose and broad high cheekbones, had a rather plain face, except for the piercing intelligence of his eyes. At twenty-one he was rapidly losing his hair.

Early in 1892 a famine hit the province of Samara, and when the peasants flocked to the city in search of bread, a committee of citizens was organized to aid the destitute. But Vladimir took an unexpected stand.

'The famine', he asserted, 'is the direct consequence of a particular social order. So long as that order exists, famines are inevitable. They can be abolished only by the abolition of that order of society. Being in this sense inevitable, famine today performs a progressive function. It destroys the peasant economy and throws peasants from the village into the city. Thus the proletariat is formed which speeds the industrialization of the nation. . . . It will cause the peasant to reflect on the fundamental facts of capitalist society. It will destroy his faith in the Tsar and in Tsarism and will in time speed the victory of the revolution.

'It is easy to understand the desire of so-called "society" to come to the assistance of the starving, to ameliorate their lot. This "society" is itself part of the bourgeois order. . . . The famine threatens to create serious disturbances and possibly the destruction of the entire bourgeois order. Hence the efforts of the well to do to mitigate the effect of the famine are quite natural. . . . *Psychologically this talk of feeding the starving is nothing but an expression of the saccharine sweet sentimentality so characteristic of our intelligentsia.*'[7]

The authentic voice of Lenin had spoken for the first time.

In the autumn of 1893 Vladimir Ulyanov left Samara for St Petersburg and joined an underground Social Democratic circle called the 'Elders' (*Stariki*). He arrived on the scene during the period of Russia's great industrial awakening, with new plants in all parts of the country and peasants flocking into the cities to become factory hands. The Social Democrats of St Petersburg and other large cities were concentrating their propaganda on small groups of workers, whom they secretly instructed in the Communist Manifesto, the elements of political economy, and natural science. But this was propaganda on a fairly high plane, with the result that these groups remained isolated from the mass of the people.

Workers who 'graduated' from the propaganda seminars were ordered to stay out of trouble; they practically never took part in strikes and other labour disturbances.

Ulyanov at once suggested proceeding from select propaganda to mass agitation. His scheme was opposed by the more conservative members, but by 1895 those who remained with him agreed to start a campaign of mass agitation among the workers.

Ulyanov became the leader of the Elders. He was the author of its first proclamation addressed to the workers of a St Petersburg factory, the first broadside written out in longhand, copied four times, and handed out among workers. Later, when the resources of the organization improved, proclamations were hectographed and distributed more widely.[8]

To the autocracy, writings of the Marxist school were at first not unwelcome. 'A small clique', said Police Director Zvolianski. 'Nothing will come of them for at least fifty years.' The revolutionary organization which the régime still dreaded was the terrorist People's Will. Marxists, the authorities calculated, could do more to counteract the influence of the People's Will than the Tsar's secret police. Furthermore, their writings were so ponderous and scientific that the revolutionary implications seemed too remote to be dangerous. At this time two such works were published with the censor's approval. One was Plekhanov's *An Outline of the Monistic Conception of History*, developing the Marxist theory of the class struggle as the vital force in history. The other was Peter Struve's *Critical Notes on the Economic Development of Russia*.

At a meeting in a St Petersburg suburb on Christmas Day 1894 Ulyanov read a paper on these two works. Praising Plekhanov's work almost reverently, he severely criticized Struve's departure from orthodox Marxism. It was at this meeting that an early Social Democratic associate, Alexander Potresov, first spoke with Ulyanov.

'I remember to this day', Potresov wrote many years later, 'the vigour and acuteness of Ulyanov's criticism. . . . My opinion was that he undoubtedly represented a great force. . . .

'His face was worn; his entire head bald, except for some thin hair at the temples, and he had a scanty reddish beard. His squinting eyes peered slyly from under his brows.' At twenty-four he was already known as the 'old man'.

The illusion of precocious maturity became even more pronounced when he spoke. For 'his voice sounded old and hoarse'. To Potresov he represented 'a typical middle-aged tradesman from northern Russia'.

This impression was shared by Ulyanov's other comrades.

They jested that Ulyanov must have been born old and bald. 'There must have been an inner reason, springing from his emotional make-up,' says Potresov, 'that was responsible for the complete suppression of youthfulness in the man.'

Overwork was a contributing cause to a severe attack of pneumonia in the early part of 1895. In the spring, Ulyanov went abroad for medical treatment. On 2 May, he wrote his mother from Salzburg:

I have been travelling abroad now for the last forty-eight hours and have been practising the language. I have turned out to be weak; I understand the Germans with the greatest of difficulty or, better still, I don't understand them at all. I don't even understand the simplest words – so unusual is their pronunciation and so quickly do they talk. You ask the conductor some question, and he answers. I don't understand. He repeats it more loudly. I still don't understand, and he gets angry and goes off. In spite of this disgraceful fiasco, I am not discouraged and keep dislocating the German language with much zeal.

This trip abroad at last gave Ulyanov an opportunity for first-hand contacts with Plekhanov and Axelrod, the founding fathers of Russian Marxism, as well as with foreign Socialist leaders. Thus he acquainted himself more intimately with the problems of the Western Socialist Movements.[9]

In Paris he met Paul Lafargue, Marx's son-in-law. Ulyanov spoke of the enthusiasm of Russian workers for Marx's teachings. The French Socialist was sceptical. 'They study Marx! But do they understand him?'

'Yes.'

'Pooh! They understand nothing. No one here understands him and our movement is twenty years old.'[10]

When Plekhanov and Ulyanov – the two men who were later to epitomize the struggle between moderate and insurrectionary Marxism in Russia – met near Geneva early in 1895, Plekhanov was the teacher, Ulyanov the disciple. In the quiet mountain village of Ormoni they spent many hours together.

Plekhanov was a man of deep humanist roots, at home in all fields of knowledge. His most casual conversations were studded with brilliant comments on art, literature, the theatre and philosophy. His was the temperament of the philosopher. Yet, not satisfied with the power of the written word alone, he became a political leader. When unable to cope with the ruthlessness of the man of action, he retreated to the written word.

'A noble desire', wrote Lunacharsky, first Soviet Commissar of Education, 'to defend culture and its further progress from Tsarist and bourgeois barbarism led him to assume the role of a political fighter. Lenin, on the contrary, was above all a political fighter. Plekhanov was bound by a thousand ties to the culture of the past; Lenin cast aside every vestige of nationalism. From basic divergence, evident in their work, their manner, their physiognomy, came the difference in tactics and political destiny.'

Another well-known Bolshevik, Nicholas Semashko, saw the same contrast between the two men. Of Plekhanov he wrote: 'I was struck by his extraordinary alert eyes, his nervous and mobile features. His eyes seemed to bore from under the heavy black brows. . . . His speech was accompanied by broad and often theatrical gesticulation. . . . I have never met a more brilliant conversationalist in all my life. . . . His knowledge fairly weighed down his opponent. At every debate he appeared with a large pile of books. He quoted Hegel from memory and would translate on the spot with pungent commentaries. . . .

'Lenin, our own Slavic product born on the border of Europe and Asia, had in him the blood of both Europe and Asia. . . .'[11]

Plekhanov and Ulyanov talked a great deal about their own lives. Once Plekhanov told Ulyanov that as a youth he had enjoyed playing soldiers, imagining himself as a great Russian general, an all-conquering 'Russian Napoleon'. Ulyanov laughed and said: 'I also played soldiers until a comparatively late age. My companions always wished to be Russians and represent Russian arms exclusively, but I never had any such desire. In all the games I found it more pleasant to imagine myself as the commander of an English army who beat the Russians, "his opponents", with severity and without mercy.' To which Plekhanov jokingly remarked: 'Evidently, since childhood you have had more cosmopolitanism in your guts than I.'

When the conversation turned to literature or art, Plekhanov found the young man unimaginative and uninspired. But no sooner did Ulyanov return to politics than, in Potresov's words, 'he became a changed man, thoroughly aroused and revealing a mind of great brilliance and power. Every remark showed deep reflection. One felt that his opinions were backed by life experience, and while his life experience was quite simple and not extensive, it was sufficient to make him an expert in revolutionary work.'

Plekhanov felt he had found the practical leader so badly needed by the party. Here was the man, he thought, with the fire and force to turn strikes into a revolutionary struggle against absolutism. Plekhanov was enthusiastic; Ulyanov seemed to remind him of his old friend, Alexander Mikhailov, the great leader of the People's Will. Like Mikhailov, Ulyanov was a master of organizational detail. Yet Potresov had 'a vague feeling that the two men who apparently believed in the same goal spoke different languages.'

From Geneva, Ulyanov went to Zurich to see Axelrod with Plekhanov's introduction. Their first meeting was brief. Axelrod knew little of the young man and talk did not flow freely. Ulyanov handed him a recently published volume of Marxist articles of which only a few copies had escaped destruction when the St Petersburg censor had ordered the book burned.

Turning to the volume Ulyanov had left, Axelrod soon became engrossed in one article, which revealed an original and forceful mind. But he was disturbed by the author's animosity towards liberals. The article was signed 'K. Tulin'.

'Who is Tulin?' Axelrod asked Ulyanov the following day.

'That is my pseudonym.'

A warm debate followed at once. 'We believe', said Axelrod, 'that at the present moment in history the immediate interests of the Russian workers are identical with those of the other progressive forces in society. In Russia, the workers and Liberals are faced with the same task, the overthrow of absolutism.'

Ulyanov smiled. 'Plekhanov said the same thing, you know. He expressed his opinion figuratively. "You", he said, "turn your back upon the Liberals. We turn our faces towards them".'

They devoted the better part of a week to arguing the question. Finally Ulyanov declared that he was convinced. These first talks impressed Axelrod as deeply as they had Plekhanov. The movement had had no one who combined a grasp of Marxist theory with practical organizing ability.

'Now we have that man,' said Axelrod. 'He is Ulyanov, future leader of the labour movement.'[12]

In September 1895 Ulyanov returned to Russia, bringing with him a store of illegal literature in a double-bottom valise – the conventional device for smuggling revolutionary documents. This luggage was manufactured skilfully but the secret police were not unacquainted with the article. The only hope of success was that customs would not go through every piece of luggage carefully. At the frontier, however, Ulyanov's valise was singled out for careful examination, was turned upside down, and the bottom sounded. But nothing was said. Ulyanov was permitted to proceed, and he delivered the valise to the proper contact in St Petersburg.

In St Petersburg, Ulyanov became acquainted with Jules Martov, who in the years to come was to be one of his main political antagonists. The grandson of a prominent Jewish editor and publicist, Martov, whose real name was Jules Tsederbaum, was then twenty-two years old. He studied at the University of St Petersburg, where he had become a revolutionist and a Marxist. He was later expelled from the university for participating in revolutionary demonstrations. Exiled for a number of years from the capital, he played an important part in the rise of the labour movement in Vilna. The two young men used to meet in the public library under the watchful eyes of the secret police. 'At that time', says Martov, 'Ulyanov was not so sure of himself, nor of the role which history was to call on him to play.'

He was modest enough, in view of his position at twenty-five as a leader among the sophisticated young Marxists of St Petersburg. 'Vladimir Ulyanov', says Martov, 'was in that stage of development when a man of high calibre seeks to learn rather than teach others. The future Lenin was then still imbued with respect for the leaders of Social Democracy. Towards Plekhanov and Axelrod he felt like a pupil. Even towards political opponents he showed a considerable modesty.'

During that winter and autumn he was closely watched by the secret police. Anticipating possible trouble, he warned his sister Anna to restrain his mother from coming to St Petersburg in the event of his arrest. Prison would only bring back sombre memories of Alexander.

Ulyanov had to live a very frugal existence in St Petersburg. He still practised law, but his clients were few, and he was forced to turn to his mother for help.

'I beg you,' he wrote on 5 October 1895, 'please send me a little money, because my funds are almost completely gone. They write me from Samara that the money for the Grafov case, which I handled, will be forthcoming in November. That will give me (if they fulfil their promise, for I don't know how binding it is) about seventy rubles. They also promise me a position as assistant to a legal counsellor. But when this will materialize I don't know.'

In the same letter Vladimir wrote: 'Lately I have been keeping accounts of my receipts and expenditures in St Petersburg in order to find out how much I really spend to live. In the month from 28 August to 27 September it seems I spent fifty-four rubles, thirty kopecks, not counting the money I spent for buying things (about ten rubles) and expenses involved in a certain court case (also about ten rubles) which I may handle. True, part of these fifty-four rubles represent an expense which may not be repeated every month (galoshes, clothes, books, etc.). But even if you deduct this much (sixteen rubles) my expenses are too large – thirty-eight rubles a month. It is clear that I did not properly figure how to live. I spent one ruble, thirty-six kopecks on carfare alone during this month. In all likelihood I will spend less when I get settled.'[13]

Unfortunately his living quarters left much to be desired. 'I am not very satisfied with my room', he wrote. 'In the first place, my landlady is a nagging woman. In the second place, the adjoining room is separated from mine only by a thin partition, so that everything that happens can be heard in my room, and sometimes I must run away from the balalaika with which my neighbour amuses himself at the expense of my ears.'

The game of hide-and-seek with the police continued. One day his mind's eye told him that a few paces back a man was strolling too casually, too bored with the afternoon gaiety of the street. He turned sharply into a nearby courtyard. Here his friend dropped his masquerade and did the obvious – hid beyond the gate. Ulyanov slipped suddenly into the vestibule unnoticed. 'I sat down in the doorman's chair where no one in the street could see me. But I could see through the window and I laughed at the spy's bewilderment. Someone came down the stairs and looked with astonishment when he saw me sitting on the doorman's chair – a man all alone, laughing heartily.'

The game continued for several months, and still the secret police groped blindly. It seemed impossible to get a clear picture of what the man was doing or who his co-conspirators were. The Okhrana (Secret Political Police) tried another tack: surely there was one potential Judas in the organization. In due time he was found; a few rubles gave him eloquence. On 20 December 1895, Ulyanov and Martov were arrested; the proofs for the first issue of the clandestine newspaper they were to publish were seized.

Chapter 3
Prison and Siberia

Regulations of the St Petersburg prison where Ulyanov was confined were not very harsh. Visitors were allowed twice a week, once in the prisoner's cell, the other time in the general anteroom. The first, in a guard's presence, lasted a half hour; the second, a full hour with one file of guards standing behind the visitors and another behind the prisoners. But there was so much noise, with everyone talking at once, that anything could be discussed. Relatives were allowed to bring books and food several times a week. The reading matter was only carelessly checked. Actually it was possible to slip through almost any publication, including the latest works on the banned list. Thus the prisoners could maintain contact with political affairs outside. And for many inmates the splendid prison library served as an institution for higher learning.

Despite Ulyanov's protests, Maria Alexandrovna visited him regularly. She came with his sister Anna as often as regulations allowed, bringing bundles of books which in time crowded Ulyanov's cell. Ulyanov had taught Anna to write in a dot-dash code, minute enough to pass unnoticed in the books she brought. By this and other means Ulyanov carried on an active correspondence with his party comrades outside.

After his arrest, the various Social Democratic groups banded together in the 'League for the Liberation of Labour'. This was a ruse aimed at persuading the government that those in prison were not the actual Social Democratic leaders. It didn't work. A month later many members of the League, including Potresov, were arrested. But new men took their places and revolutionary propaganda continued among the St Petersburg workers.

While in prison Ulyanov became recognized as the real head of the League, directing many of its activities, and turning out from his cell pamphlets written in invisible ink. He remembered that as a boy he used to write between the lines of books with milk and that when the page was held before a flame it became legible. From black bread he kneaded inkwells, which could be swallowed in any emergency. One day he was forced to consume six inkwells.

But he was proud of his ingenuity, and told Anna that there was no cunning in this world that could not be outwitted by still greater cunning.

In 1896 he wrote a pamphlet on strikes which became effective propaganda for the League, in connexion with the walk-out of 35,000 textile workers under its leadership. He also began his first major work, *The Development of Capitalism in Russia*. To prepare the documentation for this book he read everything he could find on economics and finance. Many books were sent to him by Struve who, despite their polemic a year earlier, remained a good friend.

At the same time he did not neglect his physical well-being. He exercised regularly, joining his fellow inmates in chopping wood and other manual tasks. Thanks to the food brought by his mother, he managed to follow the diet that had been prescribed for him by a Swiss physician. Apart from losing some weight, he emerged from the St Petersburg prison, after fourteen months, in excellent health.

In letters to his mother and sister later, Lenin reminisced about his régime in prison. '. . . I did gymnastics every day before sleeping and did so with great pleasure and profit. Loosening up, I would feel warm even in the severest cold when the cell was freezing, and I would sleep so much better after that. I can recommend . . . a convenient gymnastic exercise (though it may look comic) – fifty bows to the ground. I used to set myself this exercise – and was not embarrassed by the warden peering through the slit and wondering where all this piety came from in a man who did not once express the wish to attend the prison church! But the exercise should be done no fewer than fifty times at one go, and should be done so as to touch the floor with one's hands without bending one's knees. . . .'

As far as mental work was concerned, Lenin 'especially recommended doing translations both ways, that is, first from a foreign language into Russian, and then from the Russian translation again into the foreign language. I have concluded from my experience that this is the most rational method of learning a language. . . . After the evening meal, in order to relax, I would apply myself to *belles lettres* and nowhere have I enjoyed them better than in prison.'[1]

Upon being released, Ulyanov was banished for three years to the village of Shushenskoe in eastern Siberia. He arrived there in May 1897 under the armed escort of two gendarmes and was turned over to a police guard, who had been an army sergeant major. From the government he received an allowance of seven rubles and forty kopecks a month, enough to pay for room, board and laundry.

Ulyanov soon became a familiar figure in the streets of Shushenskoe. Ermakov, a local peasant, remembers his daily walk, always 'pacing with his arms folded behind his back, head down, and seemingly lost in deep thought.'

Ulyanov did not find existence in Siberia intolerable. His life was tranquil, his health good. Hunting, fishing and swimming were enjoyable pastimes; forced isolation an excellent setting for study and writing. In the evening, when tired, he played the guitar of his peasant neighbour. Except for the initial absence of newspapers, he scarcely missed civilization. His relative contentment with life was mirrored in his letters home.

'Shushenskoe', he wrote to his mother, 'is quite a nice village, though it is situated on a stretch of bare ground. About a mile and a half or so away is a forest. . . . There is no outlet to the Yenisei River, but the Shushensk flows past the village, and about a mile and a half off there is a broad tributary of the Yenisei where one can swim. In the distance are the Sayansk Mountains. Some of them are quite white, since the snow on them seldom melts. So that even from an artistic viewpoint there is something to be said for our place, and it's not without reason that while at Krasnoyarsk I wrote some poetry starting with "In the village of Shushensk, beneath the mountains of Sayansk". Unfortunately I never got beyond the first stanza.

'. . . Hunting isn't bad at all. Yesterday I went about twelve miles out without a dog and for a poor shot like me, hunting is not easy. There are even wild goats in the woods, and in the marshy forest, about thirty or forty miles away where the local peasants go hunting there are squirrels, sables, bears, and deer. . . .'

To his sister he presented the seedier side of the picture: 'The village is surrounded by piles of manure, which are not carted away into the fields, but are dumped on the outskirts, so that before getting out one must pass by heaps of manure.'

But life was by no means unbearable, he continued. 'In an inner sense one day differs from another only in that today you read one paper and tomorrow another; one day you stroll out to the right of the village and the next day to the left; today you write one kind of article, tomorrow another. Just now I have put aside my main work in order to write an article. Of course I am quite well. . . . The weather is now beastly – wind, cold, autumn showers, so that most of the time I stay indoors, although we may have some nice weather even in September. I am getting ready to go to Minusinsk to do some shopping; buy a lamp, some supplies for the winter. . . .'[2]

Food was simple – plenty of milk and a steady diet of mutton. A ram would be slaughtered and there would be meat for the week. When the stock was depleted another week's supply was laid in. The meat was chopped in a large cattle trough, made into hamburgers, and served twice a day. There were scraps enough for Ulyanov's hunting dog Jenka.

Chess was an effective escape from boredom. In lieu of a better partner, he taught the game to Stroganov, a peasant with whom he often went hunting. 'Stroganov played very well, but of course Vladimir Ilych always won', is the testimony of another peasant. Chess was a passion with most political exiles. Ulyanov played by correspondence with a comrade named Lepeshinsky. For a time he became so engrossed in the game that he would mutter in his sleep: 'If he moves the knight here, I'll move my rook there.' Because of this avid interest he gave up the game when he left Siberia. And even during his long years as an *émigré* in western Europe he could rarely be persuaded to play. 'It absorbs one too much and interferes with work,' he said.

Most of the simple townsfolk became very fond of him. Even the local constabulary succumbed to his personality. Zarvertkin, a peasant, relates that he was having tea one day with Ulyanov when he noticed men in uniform prowling around the windows. No sooner had he seen this when three men burst into the house – the local assistant district attorney, the captain, and sergeant of gendarmes. Without a word of greeting or removing his hat, one of the men arrogantly demanded, 'Where is Ulyanov's study?'

Ulyanov pointed to the table littered with books and papers and to the few shelves filled with books. The search began, followed by a cross-examination. But in a few minutes the roles were reversed; caps were removed, and Ulyanov was the commanding officer.

In May 1898, Nadezhda Krupskaya arrived in Shushenskoe. She had first met Lenin at a meeting of St Petersburg Marxists in 1894. She had already heard of the arrival from the Volga region of 'a very educated Marxist, who was extremely serious and who never read *belles lettres*'. Krupskaya was teaching in an evening school for adults, and many of her students frequented a study group which Lenin was conducting. He often came to see her at the school. When he fell ill, Krupskaya often visited him, and their friendship gradually ripened into love.

After Lenin's arrest, Krupskaya would send letters to him through his relatives who were permitted to visit the prison. In his notes sent out of prison, Lenin inquired: 'Is there a book in the library about Minoga?' Minoga was the party name for Krupskaya, and this was Lenin's way of finding out whether or not she had been arrested.

From the prison corridor through which the prisoners were conducted for their daily exercise, Lenin could see a section of the sidewalk on Shpalernaya Street. He wrote Krupskaya a coded message asking her to come to that place at an appointed hour (she recalled years later that it was 2.15 p.m.). For three days in a row she came, and stood on the street for about an hour and a half. But Lenin was unable to catch sight of her at that distance.

It was from Shushenskoe that Lenin wrote Krupskaya asking her to come and be his wife. She replied simply, 'If I'm to be a wife, so be it' – an answer of which Lenin often reminded her.

Years later, Krupskaya was asked to read a play about Lenin's life – in which it was written that, upon her arrival to join him in exile, the two began to translate the Webbs together. According to her secretary, Krupskaya became indignant: 'Just think what this looks like! We were young then, we had just got married, we loved each other passionately. For a time nothing else existed for us. And he would have us doing nothing but translating the Webbs!'

In a review by Krupskaya of one of Lenin's works, she later wrote of their life in Siberia: 'We were young then – and that enhanced our exile. The fact that I don't write about this in my memoirs does not at all mean that there was no poetry, no youthful passion in our life.'

In Krupskaya, Ulyanov found the ideal comrade and secretary who subordinated herself completely to his work. Their marriage was to last for life.

Of their reunion in Siberia, Krupskaya writes prosaically. She arrived with her mother in the evening; Vladimir was out hunting; the peasant's house was very neat, the floors covered with bright home-spun rugs, the walls whitewashed, and the rooms decorated with fir plants. Vladimir Ilyich's room was very clean, although not large.

'The hosts offered us the use of the rest of the house', Krupskaya writes; 'the place was soon filled with people, members of the household and neighbours, who regarded us curiously and asked us all sorts of questions. At length Vladimir Ilyich returned from the hunt. He was surprised to find a light in his room. The owner of the house told him that it was because Oscar Alexandrovich, an exiled worker from St Petersburg, had come into his room drunk and flung his books about. Ilyich quickly ran to the front porch. At this moment I, too, came out of the house. We talked for a long time that evening.' The only personal touch Krupskaya permits herself is that 'Ilyich looked fine; he exuded health and vigour.'[3]

Once the honeymoon days were over, the couple spent mornings translating Sidney and Beatrice Webb's *Theory and Practice of Trade Unionism*. For two hours each afternoon they copied the text of the *Development of Capitalism in Russia*. Published in St Petersburg in 1899, under the pseudonym of Vladimir Ilin, this work established Ulyanov's reputation among Russian radicals as an important Marxist theoretician.

'The Russia of the wooden plough and the flail,' he wrote, 'of the watermill and hand loom, rapidly began to be transformed into the Russia of the steel plough and the threshing machine, of steam-driven flour mills and looms.'

The development of capitalism in Russia 'rouses the worker to think, transforms a vague, dull discontent into a conscious protest, transforms a petty, fragmentary, and senseless revolt into an organized class struggle for the liberation of all the toiling people.'

Krupskaya quickly learned to share Ulyanov's love for hunting. 'Vladimir Ilyich', she relates, 'made himself a pair of hunting breeches out of leather and ventured into all kinds of bogs. When I came in the spring, I often marvelled at their excited talk about some quarry. Prominsky, smiling happily, would tell us that he had seen some ducks. Then Oscar would appear with similar news about the ducks. Hours were spent talking about them. The following spring I learned to do the same thing.'

The only other political exiles in town were two workers: a Polish Social Democrat with his wife and six children, and a Finnish mechanic who had worked in the Putilov plant of St Petersburg. With these two Lenin was on very friendly terms. But when he tried to make the acquaintance of the local schoolteacher, he was rebuffed. The teacher preferred the company of the local aristocracy – the priest and several shopkeepers who spent their days playing cards and drinking vodka.

On Sundays, Ulyanov ran a legal information bureau, which soon gave him the reputation of being a great lawyer, particularly after he helped a gold miner win a case against his employers.

After his marriage Lenin's home became the general headquarters for exiled politicals of the region. Correspondence was extensive. Books, newspapers and magazines, Russian and foreign, were exchanged. Although meetings were forbidden, conferences were arranged on one pretext or another. Some visitors stayed overnight; others for weeks at a time.

Mail arrived twice a week, bringing letters, papers and books from European Russia. Lenin's sister Anna wrote them frequently, as did several St Petersburg friends. There was mail from Martov in Turukhansk, Potresov in Orlov, and fellow-exiles closer to Shushenskoe. They corresponded about events in Russia, made plans for the future, discussed new movements in philosophy.

'Vladimir Ilyich was the central figure in the community of exiled Social Democrats', according to Z. Krzhizhanovskaya, an old friend. 'His busy, cheerful mode of living, full of inner meaning, acted as a stimulus, set the pace for all of us, kept us from lapsing into indolence.'[4]

Under his influence, 'there was neither the boredom of idleness, nor the feeling of dejection, nor intrigue. Everybody was busy, preparing himself for the future, instructing the workers, following

Russian events. Everybody felt alive, alert, happy.' Not even the bitter Siberian cold kept visitors away. One such winter day, Krzhizhanovskaya and her husband set out for a visit to the Ulyanovs. Using fleet Siberian ponies, they made fifty-five *versts* across the Minusinsk steppe in a single day, arriving in Shushenskoe in the evening. They found Ulyanov's study stocked with books, newspapers and statistical reports.

During the visit of the Krzhizhanovskys, the 'old man' was full of youthful zest. 'The morning following our arrival we held a skating race on the frozen river', writes Krzhizhanovskaya. 'Prizes were offered for fancy skating and speed. Vladimir Ilyich would bow to others in the matter of fancy skating, but he was reluctant to be beaten in speed. Straining every effort, he outdistanced us all and came in first.'

Nor was Ulyanov's bounding energy confined to ice skating. It needed an even more vigorous outlet. In the mornings, when he felt particularly active, 'he wanted to wrestle with somebody', says Krzhizhanovskaya's husband. 'For this reason I was often drawn into a sort of wrestling match with him that lasted until he became tired; it required all my power of resistance.'

All this play was the prelude to the day's work. After a short walk the visitors got down to work. A definite amount of time was assigned to writing, to the study of philosophy, to compiling statistical reports, to reading Russian and foreign works on economics.

When large bundles of newspapers arrived after long delays, Ulyanov read them in sequence, according to their date, beginning with the oldest issues. He would allow no departure from this system. Krzhizhanovsky tried it just once. When he grabbed some of the more recent papers and read the news aloud, Ulyanov shut his ears.

As relaxation, they were supposed to read fiction. 'In those days, Vladimir Ilyich was not a great admirer of good literature and patiently bore with my jeering remarks about his undeveloped literary tastes', the same friend reports.

Occasionally Ulyanov obtained permission to leave Shushenskoe on a short trip, but these excursions were bound up with red tape. A special permit was necessary for every departure beyond the village limits. Technically this regulation applied to hunting beyond the village confines, but this formality was generally overlooked. In fact, the police guard was so well disposed towards Ulyanov that he did not censor his correspondence.

During his final year of exile Ulyanov developed the ambitious plan which he later elaborated in *What Is to Be Done?* and *Letter to a Comrade*. He proposed the establishment of an official Social Democratic newspaper outside of Russia. This central organ would be no ordinary publication. From abroad it would direct Marxist political action throughout Russia by means of an underground network of smugglers and party agents. He became so completely absorbed in working out the technique for this scheme that he went for days without food or sleep. He talked over the project night after night with Krzhizhanovsky, corresponded with Martov and Potresov, discussed the prospects for going abroad as soon as his term of exile was over.

Ulyanov received disturbing news from Potresov several months before leaving Siberia. The magazine published by the 'legal Marxists' in St Petersburg, *Zhizn*, had published articles by Peter Struve and Professor Tugan-Baranovsky which challenged some of the revolutionary tenets of Marxism. Struve called for a critical revision of the whole of Marxist economic theory; he considered the very term 'scientific socialism' to be just 'one big utopia'.

Socialism did not emerge from the facts which Marx observed, according to Struve. 'Marx thought that socialism would inherit all the material and cultural achievements of the bourgeoisie. And at the same time he counted on socialism taking over as a result of a crisis, economic disruption and impoverishment! The only realistic conclusion from such assumptions would be pessimism and "destructive socialism".'

Along with Nicholas Berdyayev, Struve denied the existence of a 'class morality', holding that good and evil were independent of the class struggle. He also held that Marx's historical materialism had little connexion with philosophical materialism. In these and other respects, Struve anticipated the leading German Social Democrat, Eduard Bernstein, whose book *The Premises of Socialism* helped further to stimulate the forces of Russian 'revisionism'. An important work in this direction was *Capitalism and Agriculture*, by Sergei Bulgakov, published in 1900; it demonstrated that small farming had shown amazing vitality and that there was not, as yet, any natural process of concentration going on in agriculture.

Ulyanov reacted to these ideological developments first with suspicion, then with a declaration of war. On 22 April 1899, he wrote Potresov: 'In general, the whole of this "new critical current in Marxism", with which Struve and Bulgakov are so taken up, seems extremely suspect to me; blatant phrases about criticism "against dogma", and so on – and no positive results of criticism at all.'

Later, he wrote again that if Struve 'ceased being a comrade, so much the worse for him. This is a loss for all comrades, because Struve is a very gifted and educated man. All the same, friendship is friendship and duty is duty, and nothing can prevent the conflict.'

With Potresov and Martov also completing their terms of exile, the three men planned their future campaigns together. For the moment it was agreed that Ulyanov and Potresov would proceed to Pskov – pending their departure for western Europe.

The largest problem ahead was organization. 'It is absolutely essential', wrote Ulyanov, 'that we improve our revolutionary organization and discipline, and perfect our conspiratorial methods. We must frankly admit that in this respect we lag behind the old Russian revolutionary parties, and we must put forth every effort to overtake and surpass them.'

The period of exile was ending, but not before Ulyanov had completed *The Aims of Russian Social Democrats* which was to appear in Switzerland under the signature of N. Lenin – his first use of that name. In March 1900, before the lingering Siberian winter was over, the long and arduous journey back to European Russia began. The first three hundred miles along the shore of the Yenisei River were covered by horse.

'We rode day and night', relates Krupskaya. 'Fortunately the moon lighted our way. Vladimir, who travelled without a heavy fur coat, claiming that he felt too warm, but keeping his hands concealed beneath my mother's muff, let his thoughts outstrip us as we sped on joyfully towards remote Russia, where the great work was to begin.'

They stopped in Ufa, where Lenin entrusted his wife and mother-in-law to the care of local comrades. Then he continued on alone to Pskov. His appeal to the Director of State Police to permit Krupskaya to join him in Pskov was rejected, but he was allowed to spend a week with his mother in Moscow.

'Why did you write that you've improved in health? How thin you are!' were Maria Alexandrovna's first words. Lenin muttered an excuse, then before so much as removing his coat quickly asked: 'Has there been a telegram from Martov?' When told that no word had come he began to pace the room nervously. 'We must send him a telegram at once! Mitya,' he called to his brother, 'please take this to the telegraph office.'[5]

The family had expected the first moments of Vladimir's home-coming to be theirs. But Martov was the key to his plans. A week later he left for Pskov, where Potresov joined him. Not until the end of the year could he visit his wife in Ufa.

The Social Democratic movement had gathered considerable momentum during Lenin's absence. At the same time, however, conflicting trends were developing within its growing ranks of adherents. Influenced by impressive strikes in St Petersburg and other cities, a new faction, known as the 'Economists', maintained that workers would achieve better results by fighting for their economic interests than by revolutionary action. The Social Democrats, they argued, should champion the practical demands of labour, namely higher wages, shorter hours, and better factory conditions. Some Economists went so far as to assert that providing political leadership was the business of liberal intellectuals; that the workers needed no party of their own; that their sole political function was to support the middle class in its struggle against absolutism.

As against this conservative current, the same period saw the rise of a Social Democratic mass movement. In 1897 the secret Jewish Social Democratic cells of Russian Poland and Lithuania held a clandestine conference in Vilna and organized the General Jewish Workers' Alliance. This organization, which became known as the 'Bund', was Russia's first Social Democratic mass organiza-tion. Its members were mainly factory workers and artisans, in contrast to the earlier circles of intellectuals, students, and a sprinkling of proletarians.

In March 1898 the first all-Russian Congress of Social

Democratic organizations met in Minsk, with six delegates from the Russian organization and three from the Bund. The Congress proclaimed the birth of the Russian Social Democratic Labour Party, elected a three-man Central Committee, and published a general manifesto of Social Democratic aims. Composed by Struve and edited by the Central Committee, the manifesto claimed for the new party the revolutionary mantle of the People's Will.

'The principal and immediate goal of the Party is to achieve political freedom,' said the document. 'The Social Democrats strive for the very aim already defined by the heroic fighters of the People's Will. The ways and means of Social Democracy are, however, different. Their selection is determined by its avowed will to become and remain the class movement of the organized working masses.'

The Minsk Congress established the Social Democratic Party as the political instrument of the proletariat and whipped together the separate units which had worked independently of one another. A second party congress was scheduled to meet within six months, but a few weeks later the Minsk delegates were all arrested, imprisoned, and later exiled.[6]

In the same year – 1898 – the Economists caused a split among the Social Democratic *émigrés* in western Europe. They founded a magazine, called *The Worker's Cause*, which urged Social Democratic organizations to subordinate their Marxist propaganda to a campaign for the right to strike and for freedom of speech, press and assembly. In a famous 'Credo' written in 1899, Ekaterina Kuskova – wife of a leading economist, Sergei Prokopovich, and herself later an outstanding publicist – argued that Russian workers were relatively immature compared with those of the West; that the propagation of Socialism might provoke the sort of elemental mass upheaval which the revolutionaries could not control; that Russia needed not a revolution, but a constitution; and that, although Social Democratic leaders recognized the need for political freedom in theory, their sectarian tactics were not helping to bring it about. Lenin in Siberia had obtained a copy of this document through Struve, and organized a 'Protest' of seventeen exiled Marxists against it. At liberty, Lenin was preparing a full-scale offensive against such ideas.

In May 1900, Lenin, Martov, Potresov and other Marxists met secretly in Pskov to draw up final plans for publishing their paper abroad. It was to be called *Iskra* – the Spark. Struve and Tugan-Baranovsky came to Pskov, and an agreement for collaboration was worked out between the returned exiles and the 'legal Marxists'. Lenin and Potresov were instructed to go abroad to enlist Plekhanov's support; he was to become one of the editors of *Iskra*, but refused to recognize the 'legal Marxists' as Social Democrats.[7]

Quickly settling his affairs, Lenin prepared to leave Russia. Forbidden under the terms of his sentence to enter St Petersburg, he left his train at a suburban station. The next morning, however, when he left the tavern where he had stopped overnight, he was set upon by two men, who pinioned his arms, pushed him into a cab, and drove him off to the police station. A search revealed nothing incriminating on his person. At the police hearing he was asked: 'Why did you come here? Don't you know that you are not allowed to enter the capital? And why of all places did you choose Tsarskoye Selo [residence of the Tsar]? Don't you know that we watch every little bush here?'

From the police station he was transferred to the house of detention, where he remained for three weeks. Conditions in the prison were abominable. The vermin gave him no rest and he was kept awake by the loud talk and swearing that came from the waiting-room where police guards, spies and stool pigeons gathered every night to play cards. But he was far more troubled by the thought that the police might confiscate the exit visa he carried in his pocket. The permit to leave Russia was his most precious possession, the Open Sesame for the realization of his plans.

Following his release, Lenin went to Podolsk, accompanied by a gendarme who delivered him to the captain of the district police. The latter demanded Lenin's documents. Lenin showed his passport. After examining it, the captain pocketed the papers and said, 'You may go. I'll keep this.' Lenin's worst fears seemed to have been realized. A provincial police captain was shutting the door to Europe in his face. He determined to put on a bold front.

'I need that document. Will you please return it?' Lenin demanded.

'Didn't you hear me say that I'll keep it?'

Lenin protested vigorously, refusing to leave the room unless his passport was returned to him. The captain was equally obdurate. Finally, Lenin, moving towards the door, said, 'In that case, I'll lodge a complaint with the head of the State Police Department in St Petersburg against your unlawful action.' He made a move to leave; the captain lost his nerve.

'Hey there, Ulyanov,' he cried, 'come back, here is your passport.'[8]

A few days later Lenin crossed the frontier into Germany. Soon Potresov joined him, after conferring with Plekhanov and Axelrod in Switzerland regarding *Iskra*. A suitable printing plant and the editorial office had to be arranged as well as an underground network to distribute the paper inside Russia. Secret printing facilities would be supplied by the German Social Democratic Party. Potresov enlisted the aid of Clara Zetkin and Adolf Braun, who arranged that the paper be printed in Leipzig while the editorial board was to reside in Munich.

A final conference was held in Geneva. Plekhanov preferred printing in Switzerland with himself at the head of the editorial board, but Lenin and Potresov prevailed. Plekhanov finally agreed that *Iskra* be published in Germany. A statement announcing the forthcoming appearance of the new revolutionary organ declared that its first function would be to rally all the Party forces around it. The secret distributing agents of *Iskra* would also be the connecting links of the Party network. Uncompromising war would be waged against all 'opportunist' and wavering elements until a powerful revolutionary party was forged.

The *Spark* was ready to be ignited.[9]

Chapter 4
The Birth of Bolshevism

The first issue of *Iskra* rolled off the secret Social Democratic press in Leipzig on 24 December 1900. It was printed in small, crowded type on thin onion-skin paper, designed for convenient smuggling and distribution by underground network Party agents inside Russia.

The issues were shipped to Berlin and stored in the cellars of the *Vorwaerts*, the official organ of the German Social Democratic Party. In this subterranean storeroom a handful of trusted German Social Democrats carefully folded copies of *Iskra* in small parcels and concealed them in packing-cases. These were routed to towns close to the Russo-German frontier, where they were picked up by the professional smugglers who ran the contraband across the border to waiting *Iskra* agents.

From these border points the papers were delivered by special messengers to clandestine *Iskra* committees throughout the Russian Empire.

The men who worked for this underground chain from Berlin headquarters to the final distribution points in Russia had their hands full. They had to run the gamut of the Prussian police, who assisted undercover Okhrana agents in Germany in ferreting out Russian revolutionists, as well as the ubiquitous political police in Russia. Often large batches of papers were confiscated, and *Iskra* smugglers were arrested and exiled to Siberia.[1]

From its birth *Iskra* was more than a revolutionary newspaper. It became one of the fountain-heads of the Russian Social Democratic movement. From *Iskra* editorial headquarters in Munich radiated instructions to hundreds of Party cells throughout Russia. The Party doctrines formulated in the pages of *Iskra* became the fighting programme for groups of Party members everywhere. *Iskra* spread its gospel and stamped out heresies. Struve collaborated in the first issues of *Iskra*, but soon became editor of a liberal democratic journal *Osvobozhdenie* (Liberation) – and thereafter Lenin regarded him as a renegade.

'If we have a strongly organized party,' Lenin wrote in the first issue, 'a single strike may grow into a political demonstration into a political victory over the régime. If we have a strongly organized party, a rebellion in a single locality may spread into a victorious revolution.'

To build that 'strongly organized party' was Lenin's main objective. Although sufficiently concerned with every comma that appeared in *Iskra* to do the proof-reading himself, he allowed Martov, Potresov and Zasulich to do much of the editing, while he followed closely the workings of the *Iskra* machinery inside Russia. There the fight against the Economists and other revisionist groups was carried by *Iskra* supporters into the underground Social Democratic committees and workers' organizations. *Iskra* also conducted a strong campaign against the use of individual terrorism as a political weapon. Discussions on this subject raged for weeks on end. It was not easy to convince men bred in the tradition of the People's Will to abandon political assassination in the fight against Tsarism.

To combat all forms of heresy *Iskra* agents in Russia started an intensive campaign of propaganda and agitation among workers and students. Lenin drew this distinction between propaganda and agitation:

'A propagandist, when he discusses unemployment, must explain the capitalist nature of the crisis; he must show the reason for its inevitability in modern society; he must describe the necessity of rebuilding society on a Socialist basis, etc. In a word, he must give many ideas concentrated all together, so many that all of them will not be understood by the average person, and in their totality they will be understood by relatively few.

'The agitator, on the other hand, will pick out one more or less familiar and concrete aspect of the entire problem. Let us say the death of an unemployed worker as a result of starvation. His efforts will be concentrated on this fact, to impart to the masses a single idea – the idea of the senseless contradictions between the growth of wealth and the growth of poverty. He will strive to evoke among the masses discontent and revolt against this great injustice and will leave the full explanation for this contradiction to the propagandists.'

To carry their message home, *Iskra* agents distributed leaflets and newspapers at every opportunity. They addressed special leaflets to the intellectuals, to workers in various industries, dealing with their specific problems. Often the Social Democratic committees took the lead in organizing strikes. (There were no legal trade unions at the time.) More intensive propaganda was conducted in small clandestine groups called 'circles'.

But systematic work was impossible. It was difficult to find safe quarters, arrests were frequent, propagandizing was a dangerous business. Moreover, educated propagandists were hard to find; when one was arrested his circle usually disintegrated because there was no one to take his place. Although the curriculum of the propaganda circles called for between six and ten lectures, the course was seldom completed. In many cases the lecture consisted of reading *Iskra* to the members. Each issue gave the propagandists material for discussion, for winning new adherents. Workers to whom the propagandist read several copies often became sufficiently interested to read the paper to their comrades. Thus *Iskra* passed from hand to hand, until the newsprint was so worn it could barely be read.

Most of the early *Iskra* propagandists were university and high-school students. These young men and girls were full of enthusiasm and revolutionary romanticism, but they were short on practical experience. Satisfying the curiosity of mature, albeit poorly schooled workers was a difficult assignment for the young zealots.

Often they had little actual knowledge of the conditions under which the workers who made up their audience lived, and frequently their answers to questions of economics rang false. Later, in the large cities, propagandists drawn from the ranks of self-educated workers began to appear and to exert a larger influence among their comrades.

Agitation was carried on by various means. In some cases one trained man read the latest issue of a legal newspaper to his fellow-workers, injecting his comments. At the same time he tried to pick out those among his listeners who showed promise. These he took in hand, and furnished with 'legal' books on current problems. If the worker showed interest, he was given clandestine literature. After a probationary period he became a member of the Party.

In the summer, meetings were held in secluded woods where Cossacks and police were unlikely to appear. Along the route from the city to the secret rendezvous guides were stationed to indicate the way. The members of this patrol had prearranged signals and passwords to direct participants to the meeting place. The patrols remained at their posts throughout the meeting, watching for police or spies. If a suspicious element was noticed, word was immediately passed down the line and the meeting either broke up or reassembled elsewhere. When fast-riding Cossacks appeared so suddenly that this method of warning was too slow, the sentries gave the alarm with pistol shots.

Copies of *Iskra* leaflets were distributed not only in the factories but on the streets, in army barracks, and through the mail. In large cities they were widely scattered through the streets. In small towns and villages, to which they were brought in peasant carts on market days, they were pasted on walls. Distribution was made late at night or in the early morning. In workers' districts pamphlets were showered down in factory courtyards, or near water pumps, where workers would find them in the morning.

This dangerous operation was known as 'sowing'. Sowing was done by two men, with an advance guard as a look-out. If the street was deserted, the men went into the open courtyards and left the pamphlets in the corridors. When the advance man gave the alarm, the sowers strolled off casually until danger was past. To indicate that the mission was accomplished, a distinctive mark was left by each sower on a wall. Thus, in the morning, there was a full report on the night's work.

But the most spectacular form of paper warfare was waged in the large theatres of Moscow, St Petersburg, Kharkov, Kiev and Odessa. Here groups of three men took their seats in the gallery and as soon as the lights were dimmed, they dropped their literature out over the audience below. Sometimes this barrage was accompanied by shouts of 'Down with autocracy! Long live political freedom.' The leaflets rained down on the parquet and into the boxes of wealthy merchants and aristocrats. The penalty for those sowers who were caught was years of exile to Siberia.[2]

The systematic dissemination of clandestine revolutionary literature was by no means an *Iskra* monopoly. Other revolutionary groups were doing the same thing among workers in the cities and among the peasants in the countryside. The unique feature of the *Iskra* machine, however, was that its agents were becoming the nucleus of a tight band of professional revolutionists. And it was

Lenin himself who referred to these men as 'agents' in order to stress their special revolutionary function.

'Alas, alas!' he wrote. 'Again I have let slip that awful word "agents". . . . I like the word because it clearly and distinctly indicates the common cause to which all the agents bend their thoughts and actions . . . the thing we need is a militant organization of agents.'[3]

From the Russian factories, theatres, barracks and streets, where *Iskra* agents spread the revolutionary word at the risk of their freedom, from the 'circles' and wooded meeting places where *Iskra* teachings were debated under pain of Siberian exile, to Lenin's editorial office in Munich, was a distance that could not be measured in miles. Between the orderly South German world in which *Iskra*'s message was written and the turbulent Russian arena where it was translated into dangerous action, there existed a vast psychological gulf.

Unregistered, under the name of Meyer, Lenin took up his abode in a little room offered him by a German saloon-keeper, a Social Democrat. His food consisted of *Mehlspeise*, supplemented in the morning and the evening by tea in a tin cup, which he had to keep clean and deposit on a nail above the sink.

Engrossed though he was in his revolutionary work, he did not forget his family in Russia. He wrote to his mother on 26 December 1900:

Darling Mother,

You will probably receive this letter a short time before the holidays. I felicitate you and hope that you will spend them cheerfully. Perhaps Mitya will arrive now and you will all be together, at least those of you in Russia. We and Anna had planned to get together, but it could not be arranged. Christmas is already being celebrated here. Everywhere there are Christmas trees. The streets are unusually lively these days. I recently took a trip to Vienna and it gave me great pleasure to be on the move after weeks of being settled in one place. We are having an unpleasant winter – without snow. . . . There is a constant dampness everywhere. Luckily it is not cold, and I can do without a winter coat. This rotten weather is very penetrating and one recalls our Russian winter with pleasure, the snowy roads, the clean frozen air. This is my first winter abroad – the first that bears no resemblance to winter. I cannot say that

I am very pleased with it, although there are occasionally very lovely days like the best days of late autumn in Russia.

I live as before, quite alone, and . . . regrettably without system. I am always hoping to organize my work more systematically, but somehow I cannot get to it. . . .

On 20 February 1901, he wrote:

Darling Mother:

The carnival ended here some days ago. It was the first time I had ever seen the last day of the carnival abroad . . . a procession of masked paraders on the streets; wholesale tomfoolery; clouds of confetti thrown into the faces of passers-by; little paper kites. Here they know how to make merry on the streets! . . . Nadya's exile will soon be over. I will send a request for a passport for her one of these days. I should like to ask Maniasha to send me with her a little box of 'my' pen points. Can you imagine, I have not been able to get them here in any place. Silly people, the Czechs and the Germans. English pen points are not to be had here. Only 'their own' products. But they are good for nothing. . . .

'Nadya' was Krupskaya, whose term of restricted residence in Russia was almost over.

On her arrival in western Europe she was forced to travel from city to city looking for Lenin. For two days she did not know whether she was Modraezek, Ritmeyer, Lenina, Ulyanova, Krupskaya, or what you will. First she came to Prague, and began to search for Modraczek, the alias under which she believed Lenin lived. She had wired ahead about her coming. But when she arrived at the station there was no one to meet her.

'I waited and waited', she relates. 'In perplexity I hired a cabman wearing a silk hat, loaded my things into his vehicle, and proceeded to Modraczek's address. We came to a narrow street in the workers' quarters and stopped in front of a huge house with mattresses hanging out of the windows for airing. I climbed to the fourth floor. A blonde Czech woman opened the door. I asked for Herr Modraczek. Whereupon a workman appeared and said: "I am Modraczek." Bewildered, I muttered: "No, my husband!" Modraczek at last divined the meaning of it all. "Ah, you are probably the wife of Herr Ritmeyer. He lives in Munich but he has sent you books and letters to Ufa from my address." '

And so she set out for Munich. This time she checked her things at the station and took the streetcar to the part of the city where she hoped to locate Ritmeyer. She found the house but the address turned out to be that of a beer hall. She stepped up to the bar, behind which stood a small corpulent German, and timidly asked him about Herr Ritmeyer, feeling that there was something wrong again. The barkeeper answered, 'Yes, that is me. What is it?' Utterly confused, she murmured, 'No, it's my husband I am looking for.'

'Was there no end to this labyrinth?' she writes. At last the wife of Ritmeyer entered, and surmised who Krupskaya was. 'Ah, that must be the wife of Herr Meyer. He has been expecting his wife from Siberia. I'll take you to him.' She followed the woman into the yard of the big house.

She found Lenin seated at a table with his sister Anna and Martov.

'Why the devil didn't you write and tell me where I could find you?' were Krupskaya's first words.

'Didn't write to you?' exclaimed Lenin. 'Why, I've been going three times a day to meet you. Where have you come from?'

It developed that Lenin had sent his Munich address inside a book to a friend. The friend had forgotten to forward the information to Krupskaya.

Lenin and his wife moved into a crowded three-room apartment, two rooms of which were occupied by a worker, his wife and their six children. Their single room served as their sleeping quarters, parlour, kitchen and study.

Although Krupskaya cooked on the landlady's stove, all the culinary preliminaries were done in their room. 'I tried to make as little noise as possible', she recalls. 'When busy writing, Ilych had a habit of pacing the room and muttering to himself the thoughts he was going to set down on paper. . . . At such times I never spoke to him, never asked him any questions.'

Her discretion was generally rewarded. During their walks later in the day he would talk to her about what he had written. This became almost as much of a necessity as his whispering to himself before actually putting something down on paper.[4]

A month later, they gave up their cramped quarters and settled in a small three-room apartment in Schwabing, then the new workers' quarter of Munich. Lydia Dan, Martov's sister, recalls the atmosphere:

In one of the rooms of a scantily furnished apartment were situated the 'editorial board' and 'secretariat' of *Iskra;* it also served as a reception-room. 'The other room', as it was called, made up the living quarters where the Lenins slept and where he worked at his squalid desk. People avoided entering that room, except for a 'session' when someone needed a 'private consultation', but even then to touch Vladimir Ilyich's desk was absolutely not done. That was a taboo under all conditions. In the first room, one could feel at home. Here all the work was done and all the conversation took place, except when Krupskaya invited one into the kitchen to have tea. . . .

The editorial board met after an early lunch and stayed on till about seven or eight in the evening, when they went off to dinner and then scattered to their various rooms. Much time went into decoding the letters received from Russia – in which everyone took a hand. Krupskaya accurately copied into books or innocent letters the conspiratorial messages in invisible ink – which were never sent to Russia directly from Munich, but through various other addresses. The messages were written in code as well as invisible ink. Occasionally there were mistakes in the code, and angry letters would return from Russia that the recipients had not understood the message from *Iskra.* Lenin, according to Lydia Dan, would be furious:

I remember when I sinned once, got mixed up, and the angry letter arrived from Russia. I didn't know where to hide my head in shame. . . . And Lenin kept upbraiding me, finally ending with 'You've killed us off! With you we'll never get to the revolution!' I was terribly ashamed, but all the same – because I was young – I felt the need of cutting short the reprimand and asked him 'Have we long to wait for the revolution?' Lenin at once changed his tone, reflected and replied, 'Ach, a long time! About thirty years.' . . . That was at the end of 1901, or perhaps, at the very beginning of 1902.

On Sundays the Lenins, along with various visiting comrades, went for walks.

Usually they went to have lunch together in some large beer hall, where Lenin very attentively examined – one might say, studied! – the menu and selected a good portion of meat, such as he probably never got at home during the week, for Krupskaya was not much of a cook. He drank a stein of beer with pleasure, teasing me because I drank mineral water rather than beer in Munich. Finally, he would declare that he was at our disposal and was ready, if it pleased us, to go for a walk. However, he never forgot to make it a condition – one which we accepted with varying degrees of pleasure – that we should not discuss politics. . . .

Lenin did not like talking while he walked; he walked to relax; he may, indeed, have pondered on some serious subject or he may have given himself up to contemplating the landscape; but he was invariably in a good mood. In those days, like all of us, he loved to sing: it was a songful time! But none of us had good voices. Lenin did not seem to have a good ear and, in my opinion, he sang falsetto. He most often sang an old song, a Populist one very likely. . . . I do not recall all the words, but I remember the lines,

> '. . . your doctrine is false:
> Freedom can be fettered,
> but freedom can't be killed.'

In a letter to Lenin's mother Krupskaya wrote on 2 August 1901: 'Volodya [Lenin] is working diligently these days. I am very pleased with him. When he becomes completely engrossed in a certain work, he is in excellent spirits. That is his nature. His health is very good. Not the slightest trace of his cold lingers. Nor does he suffer from insomnia. He invigorates himself daily with a cold-water rub-down. In addition we go bathing almost every day.'

But the following spring they were on the move again. The printing plant in Leipzig had been abandoned in favour of Munich. Now the owner of the Munich plant refused to continue turning out *Iskra*. It was too great a risk. Plekhanov and Axelrod favoured transferring operations to Switzerland, but the majority voted for London.

Lenin and Krupskaya arrived in England in April 1902, in the midst of a dense fog. Their first encounter with English middle-class respectability was not pleasant. For a week or two they lived in a sublet bedroom. Then they rented an unfurnished two-room apartment in the neighbourhood of King's Cross Road. But before they could settle down to work they had trouble with their landlady. She insisted that they put curtains on their windows. They yielded. Then she wanted to know why Krupskaya wore no wedding ring. On this point she received no satisfaction. She only accepted their word that they were legally married after they threatened to bring her to court for slander. The Lenin's small flat again housed the *Iskra* editorial board and secretariat. Martov, Zasulich and another comrade formed a 'commune' in an almost unfurnished flat without any service. They set up certain rules for housekeeping and preparing communal meals, but the ill-kept 'commune' inevitably shocked new arrivals.

Very promptly Lenin and Krupskaya discovered that, although they had translated Sidney and Beatrice Webb, their knowledge of English bore only a remote resemblance to the native product. With his usual zest Lenin set to work learning the language. He went wherever he could hear English spoken, to pubs, to Hyde Park, to all sorts of meetings. Crowding up front, he listened carefully to every word, and watched the lip movements of speakers. In addition he hired two English teachers whom he taught Russian in exchange for English lessons. With these efforts his English soon became fairly proficient, if not fluent.

Lenin also had purchased a map of London and digested it so thoroughly that he astounded old-timers by his knowledge. The library of the British Museum held an inexhaustible fascination for him. Fully half of his time was spent there, in the midst of the world's richest collection of books. The library was a treasure house for his research, even as it had been for Karl Marx before him.

Lenin often studied the throbbing life of London from the top of an omnibus and in long walks through the slum districts which most tourists assiduously avoided. 'He liked the bustle of this huge commercial city', writes Krupskaya. 'The quiet squares, the detached houses, with their separate entrances and shining windows adorned with greenery, the drives frequented only by highly polished broughams, were much in evidence, but tucked away nearby, the mean little streets, inhabited by the London working people, where lines with washing hung across the street, and pale children played in the gutter – these sites could not be seen from the bus top. In such districts we went on foot, and observing these glaring contrasts of wealth and poverty, Ilyich would mutter between clenched teeth, in English! "Two nations!"'

For Lenin, London was the very citadel of capitalism, the strongest fortress of the bourgeois order. Yet when a friend, Alexeyev, poked fun at the London *Justice*, a little weekly published by the British Social Democratic Federation, for its predictions of imminent social revolution, Lenin was very annoyed.

'I myself hope to see the Socialist revolution,' Lenin told Alexeyev.

In England, as elsewhere, the countryside attracted him strongly. For several reasons his favourite haunt was Primrose Hill. For one thing the trip there cost only sixpence. From the top of the hill he could see all of London in its smoky immensity – then he would walk among the parks and shaded roadways.[5]

He wrote to his mother in Samara on 4 February 1903:

> We have fine weather; the winter is exceptionally good, mild, and (so far) little rain or fog. . . . Our life goes on as usual, quietly and modestly. The other day, for the first time this winter, we went to a good concert and were very pleased with it, especially with Tchaikovsky's Pathétique symphony. . . . How we should love to go to the Moscow Art Theatre to see Gorky's *The Lower Depths*!

On 29 March he wrote:

> It is warm here. The other day we took E. V. (Krupskaya's mother) for a long walk. We took sandwiches instead of having dinner and spent the entire Sunday *'ins Gruene'*. . . . The air intoxicated us all as though we were children, and afterwards I succumbed to sleep as if I had just returned from a Siberian hunting trip.[6]

While in London, Lenin met Trotsky for the first time. Friends in Samara had already written to him about an enthusiastic *Iskra* man who had recently escaped from Siberia. 'The young eagle' was the way they had described him. And by his prolific writings he had also earned the nickname of the 'Pen'.

Trotsky himself arrived in quite abrupt fashion, with a loud knock at the front door. 'I knew from the sound that it must be someone calling on us and hurried downstairs', says Krupskaya. 'The caller was Trotsky, and I led him into our room. Vladimir Ilyich had just awakened and was still in bed.'

When Krupskaya returned from paying the cabman, she found 'Vladimir Ilyich still in bed talking animatedly with Trotsky on some abstruse theme. The enthusiastic references to the man as a "young eagle" made Vladimir Ilyich study the caller very closely during their first conversation.' Evidently he passed muster, for thereafter 'they walked and discussed things together a great deal.' Moreover, when Trotsky received word to return to Russia, Lenin asked him to remain abroad, to familiarize himself with party matters and assist in the work of *Iskra*. And he fought for Trotsky in the teeth of opposition by other members of the editorial board.

Plekhanov regarded Trotsky with immediate suspicion. He saw him as an ally of the younger element, Lenin, Martov and Potresov. When Lenin sent Trotsky's articles to Plekhanov, the latter's comment was:

'The pen of our "Pen" does not please me.'

'Style is a matter of practice,' Lenin replied. 'The man is capable of learning and will prove very useful.' In March 1903 he considered Trotsky's apprenticeship completed and proposed his election to the editorial board.[7]

Iskra, conforming to Lenin's plan, had called into existence a group of 'professional revolutionists' whose duty it was, in Lenin's words, to 'devote not only their free evenings but their whole life to working for the Revolution'.

By the end of 1902 the majority of the Social Democratic Party committees in Russia had already been fused into the *Iskra* network. The general quickening of the social tempo of the country helped speed this process. The earlier great industrial strikes were followed by student walkouts, street demonstrations and peasant riots. In 1903 disorders among students and peasants intensified.

Meanwhile in the pages of *Iskra* and in various pamphlets Lenin was developing theories which were increasingly in conflict with the views held by the older Social Democratic leaders.

In 1902 he published his book *What Is to Be Done?*, in which he forcefully presented his views regarding the relations between the Party intellectuals and workers, between the revolutionary *élite* and the politically inarticulate mass. This work was to become a revolutionary bible to his adherents. Here the doctrine of the 'professional revolutionists' was explicitly stated for the first time.

'The history of every country teaches us', he wrote, 'that by its own ability the working class can attain only a trade-unionist self-consciousness, that is to say, an appreciation of the need to fight the bosses, to wrest from the government this or that legislative enactment for the benefit of the workers. The Socialist doctrine, on the other hand, is the outgrowth of those philosophical, historical and economic theories which had been developed by the representatives of the well to do, the intellectuals.

'By their social origin, Marx and Engels, the founders of modern scientific Socialism, were themselves members of the bourgeois intelligentsia. Similarly, in Russia, the theoretical principles of Social Democracy originated independently of the unconscious strivings of the labouring classes. They were a natural and inevitable result of the development of the ideas of the revolutionary Socialist intellectuals.'

Only revolutionary intellectuals, 'professional revolutionists', could rescue the working class from bourgeois influence and convert it to Socialism.

To this fundamental theme he returned again and again.

'Since the development of an independent ideology among the workers, as a result of their own struggle, is out of the question,' he declared, 'there is thus possible either a bourgeois ideology or a Socialist ideology, and the question is: Which of the two shall it be? The blind unfolding of the labour movement can lead only to the permeation of that movement with a bourgeois ideology, because the unconscious growth of the labour movement takes the form of trade unionism, and trade unionism signifies the mental enslavement of the workers to the bourgeoisie. Therefore, our task as Social Democrats is to oppose this blind process, to divert the labour movement from the unconscious tendency of trade unionism to march under the protective wing of the bourgeoisie, and to bring it under the influence of Social Democracy instead.'[8]

Thus Lenin was in effect preaching the ideas formulated decades earlier by Peter Tkachev.

'Neither now nor in the future', Tkachev had written in 1874, 'will the common people by its own power bring on a social revolution. We alone, the revolutionary minority, can and should do that as soon as possible.

'We should not deceive ourselves', said Tkachev, 'that the people, by its own might, can made a social revolution and organize its life on a better foundation. The people, of course, is necessary for a social revolution. *But only when the revolutionary minority assumes the leadership in this revolution.*'

Where Tkachev had spoken of 'the people', Lenin now substituted the term 'proletariat'; Tkachev looked to the 'critically thinking individual' as the saviour; Lenin preferred the 'professional revolutionist'.[9]

In the articles Lenin wrote during this period, as well as in *What Is to Be Done?*, in his letters to the revolutionary workers in Russia, he was consistently advocating and gradually building up a party apparatus of the 'professional revolutionists'.

This departure from the prevailing Marxist line slowly prepared the ground for the split that was to come in 1903. Potresov and Martov felt that Lenin was returning to the sectarianism which had characterized him at the time of their first meeting. 'At first', Potresov later recalled, 'it seemed to us that we were a group of comrades: that not just ideas united us, but also friendship and complete mutual trust. . . . But the quiet friendship and calm that had reigned in our ranks had disappeared quickly. The person responsible for the change was Lenin. As time went on, his despotic character became more and more evident. He could not bear any opinion different from his own. It was foreign to his nature to be just to someone with whom he was in serious disagreement. His opponent would then become a personal enemy, in the struggle with whom all tactics were permissible. Vera Zasulich was the first to notice this characteristic in Lenin. At first she detected it in his attitude towards people with different ideas – the liberals, for example. But gradually it began to appear also in his attitude towards his closest comrades. . . . At first we had been a united family, a group of people who had committed themselves to the Revolution. But we had gradually turned into an executive organ in the hands of a strong man with a dictatorial character.'

Lenin, on the other hand, was becoming increasingly sceptical of the revolutionary single-mindedness of his colleagues. Frictions in the editorial office of *Iskra* were mounting. Some were of a personal nature. Among other things, Plekhanov could not tolerate Lenin's manner of writing.

'His articles', said Plekhanov, 'are not written in the sense that the French use the term. It is not literary work. It is nothing.'[10]

But Plekhanov, the cultivated man of letters and sparkling political essayist, gave misplaced emphasis to this so-called lack of style. Plekhanov measured his sentences for their prose effect. Lenin wrote only to influence the actions of men. If his writing was often repetitious and over-simplified, he nevertheless hammered out what he wanted to say very effectively. And if his words did not always appeal to refined intellects, they carried power for the larger mass at which they were aimed. In a debate the same was true. Before a highly sophisticated audience he was no match for Plekhanov's erudition. But the words that left the party intellectuals cold stirred the masses, whom he swayed through invective and the constant reiteration of simple slogans. In other words, Lenin was a natural political leader, which his antagonists – even in the early intra-party struggle – were not.

When Peter Struve, who had written the manifesto for the First Social Democratic Congress, deserted the Marxist ranks for the Liberal camp, Lenin wrote an article in *Iskra* calling him a renegade and traitor. Takhtarev, who was then Lenin's close friend, asked him how he could permit himself to use such vitriolic language, since any worker who read the article might feel it was his duty to kill Struve as a 'traitor'.

'He deserves to die', was Lenin's calm reply. That was in 1903, and Takhtarev did not take Lenin seriously; neither did his Social Democratic colleagues. His strong, often abusive, language was merely taken for rhetoric. At the same time, Potresov and Martov failed to note what they discovered later, that Krupskaya had stopped showing them all the letters received from Russia or all the letters sent out to Russia on Lenin's instructions.[11]

Serious dissensions among the *Iskra* editors had begun in 1902, when the Party programme came up for discussion. Plekhanov's first draft, which was considered by the full board in Munich, failed to satisfy Lenin, Martov or Potresov. Lenin objected to Plekhanov's assertion that small scale production was economically viable and therefore not doomed to inevitable extinction. Lenin also considered that Plekhanov had falsely depicted the lower middle class, 'underscoring their revolutionary tendencies, while ignoring their conservatism and reactionism'. Plekhanov had written of Social Democracy at the head of 'the working and exploited masses'; Lenin argued that one could not put the class struggle of the workers into the same category as the special interests of peasants and small producers.

Plekhanov was asked to rewrite the programme, with the objections of the others in mind. His second programme, however, pleased Lenin even less than the first. For Plekhanov had substituted the phrase 'power of the proletariat' for 'dictatorship of the proletariat'.

Axelrod and Zasulich shared Plekhanov's views; Martov and Potresov were inclined more towards Lenin, although they did not concur entirely. It was Plekhanov's programme that prevailed in the end, somewhat edited by Martov, Zasulich and Theodore Dan in an effort to reconcile the differences with Lenin. The major change made at Lenin's insistence was the restoration of the clause dealing with the 'dictatorship of the proletariat'. The new text, although finally accepted, did not fully satisfy Lenin.

Other differences followed, and the breach between the London office of *Iskra* and the Plekhanov–Axelrod headquarters in Switzerland widened. Finally, in April 1903, *Iskra* was transferred to Geneva, where controversial articles were henceforth to be submitted to the vote of the six members of the editorial board, Lenin, Plekhanov, Martov, Potresov, Zasulich and Axelrod. Often this led to a 3–3 deadlock, with Lenin, Martov and Potresov lining up against the three older Social Democrats.

Leaving England behind him in April 1903, Lenin settled in a small house in Secheron, a working-class district on the outskirts of Geneva. The struggles inside *Iskra* were now growing more frequent and more explosive. Potresov, who often sided with Lenin, reported that 'it was impossible to work with him. For Lenin could not bear opinions which were contrary to his own. Because of that, the slightest disagreement with him became a serious controversy and affected our personal relations.'

The constant state of internal warfare was, according to Potresov, largely the result of 'Lenin's great cunning and his readiness to do anything to make his opinion prevail. . . . Frequently my editorial colleagues and I felt out of place in our own newspaper office.'

Lenin, he concluded, divided the world sharply between those who were with him and those who were against him. There was no middle ground.

'For him there existed no personal or social relationship outside of these two classes. When the political principle was enunciated that in the fight against the common enemy – the Tsarist government – it was desirable to present a united front by combining with other groups and parties, Lenin accepted it reluctantly and only in theory. In practice, it remained an idle phrase. He could not have acted on that principle even if he had wanted to, because he was incapable of co-operating with other people. It went against his grain.'

These *Iskra* battles wore out Lenin as much as his associates. According to Krupskaya, 'Vladimir Ilyich was greatly pained at any differences with Plekhanov. He grew restless and did not sleep at night.' When he read Plekhanov's marginal criticism of his articles 'he became greatly agitated and paced up and down, up and down'. Plekhanov still considered, however, that he and Lenin were close. He wrote him: 'Believe one thing – that I respect you greatly, and think that we are closer to one another on 75 per cent than to all the other members of the (*Iskra*) board. There is a difference of 25 per cent; but 75 per cent is three times larger than 25 per cent.'

Despite the gathering storm-clouds, the other editors of *Iskra* did not grasp the far-reaching implications of their daily tussles with Lenin. They regarded these quarrels as a family affair and did not suspect that Lenin wanted to build up a rival organization responsible to him alone. Yet that is precisely what Lenin was beginning to do. This organization, conceived by Lenin and fostered by the myopic consent of the other Social Democratic leaders, was in fact the embryo of the Communist Party machine. For even in this period Lenin was surrounding himself with men such as Gusev-Drabkin, Pavlovich-Krasikov, Liadov and Bonch-Bruyevich, men whose obedience to him was absolute and unquestioning.

Lenin, the splendid organizer, was an even more thorough disciplinarian. 'In Lenin's organization, discipline reached the point of almost military obedience.' It was, according to Potresov, 'an organization uniting the superior command and the "agents" of the Party executives. The two combined were designed to dictate their will to the obedient majority. It was an organization of the revolutionary minority; at the proper moment this minority was to seize the reins of power. . . .'

It was an organization groomed to give practical effect to Lenin's theory that in the struggle for power the masses were to be pliant instruments in the hands of a determined general staff of 'professional revolutionists'.[12]

Because Lenin's ideas of party discipline and organization were so explicitly bound up with his theory of the 'professional revolutionist', a showdown within the Social Democratic Party was inevitable. The stage was set in November 1902 when, at the initiative of *Iskra*, a committee was organized inside Russia to call a Party Congress – the first since the founding of the Social Democratic Party in 1898 and the first in which Lenin was to participate.

In the early summer of 1903 delegates of clandestine Social Democratic committees from all parts of Russia began to congregate in Geneva. To maintain secrecy, the delegates kept aloof from one another and even more from the Russian *émigrés* who lived in Switzerland.

Among the first delegates to arrive from Russia was Shotman, a St Petersburg worker. Shotman had an unusual opportunity for intimate contact with the *émigré* leaders, eager to receive first-hand news from Russia. He has recorded his impressions:

'Potresov was a broad-shouldered, ruddy-cheeked man; with his neatly trimmed beard, his well cut suit, he looked like a true European. Martov resembled a poor Russian intellectual. His face was pale, he had sunken cheeks; his scant beard was untidy. His glasses barely remained on his nose. His suit hung on him as on a clothes hanger. Manuscripts and pamphlets protruded from all his pockets. He was stooped; one of his shoulders was higher than the other. He had a stutter. His outward appearance was far from attractive. But as soon as he began a fervent speech all these outer faults seemed to vanish, and what remained was his colossal knowledge, his sharp mind, and his fanatical devotion to the cause of the working class.' Axelrod 'captured my heart at once with his loving, fatherly attitude. He joked with us for hours. . . . He was very happy when we told him that the pamphlets which he and Plekhanov wrote were avidly read by the workers. . . .'

Shotman writes of his first contact with Lenin: 'I do not remember what was discussed at the meeting. . . . But I remember very vividly that immediately after his first address I was won over to his side, so simple, clear, and convincing was his manner of speaking.

'When Plekhanov spoke, I enjoyed the beauty of his speech, the remarkable incisiveness of his words. But when Lenin arose in opposition, I was always on Lenin's side. Why? I cannot explain it to myself. But so it was, and not only with me, but with my comrades, also workers.'

Despite the simmering differences between Plekhanov and

Lenin, the preliminary caucuses pointed to substantial agreement among the delegates. It seemed as if the Congress sessions would be harmonious and brief. It was in this spirit that the delegates left Geneva for Brussels for the opening on 30 July 1903.

On their arrival in Brussels most of the forty-three delegates scattered to private homes in various parts of the city. Their rendezvous was the Coq d'Or, a hotel owned by a Belgian Socialist. Twice daily they met here to eat, drink and talk; Emile Vandervelde, the leader of the Belgian Socialist Party, lent them a helping hand in finding a meeting place.

For security reasons, the sessions moved from one site to another, mainly to local trade-union halls in the working-class districts of Brussels. One meeting ended in minor disaster. The session opened in a dark hall with practically no light or ventilation and only enough chairs for the members of the presidium. The delegates were forced to sit on rough, damp boards. The presiding 'table' was nothing more than several planks of wood carelessly nailed together.

As soon as the meeting got under way, the delegates began to fidget about. They squirmed, coughed, and looked at one another guiltily. Soon the presidium was affected with the same discomfort. Within a few minutes the delegates began sneaking out of the hall. When about half were gone, one delegate finally proposed adjournment. The motion was carried immediately. An invisible army of vermin had routed the delegates to the Second Congress of the All-Russian Social Democratic Labour Party!

The Congress was not destined to remain long in Brussels. After four or five sessions devoted to heated debates on the party programme, the police warned four delegates to leave the city within twenty-four hours. No reason was given for this action. Vandervelde's efforts to intervene bore no result. With police spies watching the movements of all the delegates, the Congress voted for transfer to London.

Sessions were resumed on the morning following the arrival of the delegation in the British capital. As in Brussels, the meetings were held in local trade-union headquarters. Once, as the Russians were leaving their meeting hall, they were pelted with wet papers and other missiles by a gang of street urchins. It was the first time the children of London had seen human beings who shouted at the top of their lungs, gesticulated with their hands, and carried their debates into the street. The following day, at the request of the local trade union, a policeman was placed on duty outside the meeting hall to protect the revolutionists from juvenile mischief.[13]

But there was far greater mischief afoot inside the meeting hall, where the delegates were trying to thrash out a party constitution and programme. Of the forty-three delegates present only three or four were workers; the rest were 'professional revolutionists' of the intellectual or semi-intellectual variety. These delegates, holding a total of fifty-one votes, represented three main trends: *Iskra*, the Jewish Socialist Bund and the Economists. The differences were substantial. The Bund and the other semi-autonomous Social Democratic groups did not want a highly centralized party with tight discipline imposed from above. The Bund preferred a loose federation. Nor did the Economists wish to bow to the will of the *Iskra* high command.

Lenin understood quite clearly that the success of his blueprint for tight party organization depended on the degree of discipline he could enforce from the start. He began, therefore, by pushing through a motion which set up a presidium consisting entirely of *Iskra* men, with Plekhanov as chairman and himself and Pavlovich-Krasikov as vice-chairmen. He won on this motion, despite the protests of Martov that the procedure was undemocratic. This was the opening skirmish in the Lenin–Martov battle which was soon to have far more serious repercussions.

Later, Lenin admitted quite frankly that the purpose of his move had been to wield the 'iron fist' against all Social Democratic groups that resisted *Iskra*'s control over the Party.

Lenin lost to Martov, however, by a vote of twenty-three to twenty-eight on the wording of the rules defining Party membership. Lenin wanted to limit membership to those who not only subscribed to the party programme but participated actively in one of its organizations. Martov, on the other hand, was willing to admit all who accepted the programme and gave the Party 'regular personal cooperation under the guidance of one of its organizations'.

To many delegates this difference seemed merely verbal. Actually the minor variation in language contained the fissionable element that was to smash the Social Democratic Party into its ultimately irreconcilable Bolshevik and Menshevik factions.

Although Martov carried the Congress by a small margin on the paragraph defining Party membership, Lenin won on almost every other important issue. And he owed his victories largely to Plekhanov's support.

The members of Lenin's 1903 majority became known as 'Bolsheviks' (after *bolshinstvo*, the Russian word for majority), Martov's group were dubbed 'Mensheviks' (after *menshinstvo*, meaning minority).

The Congress voted for the dissolution of all independent Party organizations and their fusion into a single Party apparatus. After this vote the Bund and a number of other groups walked out. This left the *Iskra* group in complete command. But the elimination of the dissident factions brought no harmony. The fight between Martov and Lenin continued, with Plekhanov lining up on Lenin's side.

Lenin won on his motion for cutting the *Iskra* editorial board to three – himself, Plekhanov and Martov. This meant the elimination of Axelrod, Potresov and Zasulich – all of whom were Martov supporters in the growing ideological war between Lenin and Martov. Lenin was confident that in this three-man board he could wield control. Plekhanov would not take an active part in the day-to-day politics of the paper and on the broad issues Lenin felt certain Plekhanov would support him against Martov.

His confidence was reinforced by Plekhanov's fateful speech at the Congress on the subject of the 'dictatorship of the proletariat'. On Lenin's insistence Plekhanov had already written in the programme draft that the concept of proletarian dictatorship includes 'the suppression of all social movements which directly or indirectly threaten the interests of the proletariat'.

A delegate named Akimov-Makhnovetz spoke against the dictatorship clause, pointing out that no such provision was to be found in the programme of a single European Socialist Party.

Plekhanov replied by telling the delegates that 'every democratic principle must be appraised not separately and abstractly, but in its relation to what may be regarded as the basic principle of democracy; namely, that *salus populi lex suprema est*. Translated into a revolutionist's language, it means that the success of the revolution is the supreme law.

'Even the principle of universal suffrage', continued Plekhanov, 'must be approached from the viewpoint of the basic principle I have indicated. . . . The bourgeoisie of the Italian Republic once deprived all persons belonging to the nobility of their political rights. The revolutionary proletariat could limit the political rights of the upper classes, just as the upper classes once limited his rights.

'The same point of view should be adopted on the question of the duration of parliament. If the people, in a surge of revolutionary enthusiasm, should elect a good parliament, we should endeavour to make it a long parliament. If the elections miscarry, we should try to disperse it, not in two years, but in two weeks.'

Lenin applauded enthusiastically. The official minutes of the Congress faithfully record: '*Applause; some delegates hiss: voices: "Don't hiss!"* Plekhanov: *"Why not? I beg the comrades not to stand on ceremony."* Delegate Egorov rises and says: *"If such speeches bring applause, I must hiss."* '

Lenin applauded, but Plekhanov, in his last years, deeply regretted his London oration. A few weeks after the Congress, when Plekhanov had already begun to backtrack on his support of Lenin, Martov tried to explain away Plekhanov's speech.

'Plekhanov's words', he said, 'evoked indignation on the part of some delegates which might easily have been avoided had Comrade Plekhanov added that it was impossible to imagine a situation so tragic that the proletariat, in order to fortify its victory, should resort to such methods.'[14]

It was a brave attempt to undo the words which justified the suppression of freedom, but Plekhanov thanked him ironically for this afterthought. In later years, when he was reminded that Leninism could be considered a legitimate offspring of that speech, Plekhanov tried to explain that he had spoken of dispersing a democratically elected parliament as only 'theoretically possible', not as desirable or necessary. Yet the record is clear that at the Congress Plekhanov stood with Lenin. His change of heart came later.

At one point during the Congress Plekhanov was so impressed with Lenin that he exclaimed to Axelrod: 'Of such stuff are Robespierres made!' Plekhanov meant this as a high compliment. And when Akimov tried to drive a wedge between Plekhanov and Lenin, Plekhanov retorted: 'Napoleon had a passion for getting his marshals divorced from their wives. Comrade Akimov is like

Napoleon in this respect. He wants to divorce me from Lenin at all cost. But I am not out to divorce Lenin, and I hope he doesn't intend to divorce me.'[15]

But the divorce was soon to come. The Congress, which began in harmony, ended after a month of debate in an uproar. On the morning following the last session Martov and his followers left for Paris, Lenin and his cohorts for Geneva. The two groups were not on speaking terms. Martov had refused to serve on the three-man *Iskra* board on the ground that he could not accept the vote of non-confidence in Axelrod, Potresov and Zasulich.

A short time thereafter another conference was held in Geneva which, if anything, widened the split. Plekhanov still stood by Lenin, although Martov tried to convince him that Lenin was seeking control of *Iskra*. In Geneva Trotsky joined Martov in the fight against Lenin. Finally Plekhanov tried to restore party harmony by reconstituting the editorial board on its old basis, with the return of Axelrod, Potresov, Martov and Zasulich. Lenin refused. When Plekhanov insisted that there was no other way to restore unity, Lenin handed in his resignation.

'I am absolutely convinced', said Lenin, 'that you will come to the conclusion that it is impossible to work with the Mensheviks. I resign from the editorship of *Iskra*. You can take in the other members and be responsible for the future developments.'

The 'divorce' between Plekhanov and Lenin had come after all. For Lenin, the decision to resign from *Iskra* rather than continue to share authority with his old Social Democratic comrades in arms was one of the most difficult of his career. He knew that for the moment he would be isolated and without an effective weapon in the propaganda war for the triumph of his ideas.

Lenin's intransigent stand brought a barrage of criticism from his former comrades. 'Autocrat', 'bureaucrat', 'formalist', 'centralist', 'copperhead', 'obstinate', and 'narrow-minded' were some of the epithets fired at him, as he himself ironically enumerated in his 1904 pamphlet *One Step Forward, Two Steps Back*.

Plekhanov now attacked Lenin vigorously in *Iskra* and other legal and illegal publications. On 1 May 1904, he prophetically predicted the future life of a party based on Lenin's organizational principles. Imagine, he wrote, that the Central Committee 'possessed the still-debated right of liquidation'. Then, with a party congress in the offing, 'the Central Committee everywhere liquidates the elements with which it is dissatisfied, everywhere seats its own creatures and, filling all the committees with these creatures, without difficulty guarantees itself a fully submissive majority at the congress. The congress, constituted of the creatures of the Central Committee, amiably cries "Hurrah!", approves all its successful and unsuccessful actions, and applauds all its plans and initiatives. Then, in reality, there would be in the party neither a majority, nor a minority, because we would then have realized the idea of the Persian Shah.'

Another vigorous attack on Lenin came from Trotsky, who described Lenin as a 'despot and terrorist who sought to turn the Central Committee of the Party into a Committee of Public Safety – in order to be able to play the role of Robespierre.'

Replying to Lenin's *One Step Forward, Two Steps Back*, Trotsky wrote that if Lenin ever took power 'the entire international movement of the proletariat would be accused by a revolutionary tribunal of 'moderatism' and the leonine head of Marx would be the first to fall under the guillotine.'

When Lenin spoke of the dictatorship of the proletariat, wrote Trotsky in 1904, he really meant 'a dictatorship over the proletariat'.[16]

No longer was this a family squabble. The early differences in the *Iskra* and the battles in Munich, London and Geneva had finally cleared the air, to reveal a profound rift between Lenin and the Mensheviks.

Back in his home in Secheron, Lenin was on the verge of a nervous breakdown as a result of the many months of tense jockeying for power. Only the arrival of a few supporters from Russia could disperse his gloom momentarily. One of them, nicknamed the 'Baron', provided Lenin with badly needed comic relief. The baron was a young man who described himself as a representative of the St Petersburg Bolshevik organization.

'We are now placing our organization on a collective basis', the baron told Lenin; 'we have collectives of propagandists, of agitators, of organizers, etc.'

Lenin listened attentively then shot this question, 'How many people have you in the propaganda collective?'

'As yet only one,' the baron replied sheepishly.

'A bit too few,' replied Lenin, 'and in the agitators' collective?'
Blushing violently, the baron replied, 'As yet only one.'

Lenin roared with laughter, and the baron could not help joining him.

A handful of other Bolsheviks joined Lenin at Secheron. They were minor characters who never figured in the later growth of the Bolshevik Party, but their presence was a tonic during this trying period. Meetings were held once a week at Lenin's home and, although nothing important was accomplished, he was encouraged by their optimism. Their songs and general tomfoolery momentarily dispelled his gloom.

By the summer of 1904, however, his nerves were almost completely shattered. Krupskaya decided to take him 'as far as possible from people, to forget for a time all work and worry.'

They spent a month tramping through the Swiss countryside, from Geneva to Lausanne to Interlaken to Lucerne, with knapsacks on their backs. 'Volodya and I have made a pact not to discuss business affairs,' she wrote to Lenin's mother on 2 July 1904. 'We sleep ten hours a day, swim, and walk. Volodya doesn't even read the papers properly.'

With their limited funds they seldom ate regular meals. In one small mountain inn a worker advised them: 'Don't eat with the tourists, eat with the coachmen, hacks, and labourers. It's twice as cheap and more satisfying.' They followed his advice. Lenin's pack was loaded down with a heavy French dictionary and other books which he never opened during his vacation from worry. 'Instead of the dictionary,' writes Krupskaya, 'we looked at mountains capped with perpetual snow, at blue lakes, and strangely wild waterfalls.' After spending a month in these surroundings, 'Vladimir Ilyich's nerves became normal again.'[17]

Lenin returned to Geneva refreshed and ready to resume the fight. He was greatly heartened by the decision of A. A. Bogdanov, a Marxist writer on economics and philosophy, to join the Bolshevik nucleus in Switzerland. Bogdanov's conversion to Bolshevism was the stimulant Lenin badly needed. They spent the month of August together in a little village near Lac de Bré, drawing up new plans. With Bogdanov's Russian contacts he mobilized a group of young Marxist writers for a new fighting newspaper to compete with *Iskra*, which was now firmly in Menshevik hands.

In the autumn Lenin called together a group of twenty-two Bolsheviks in Geneva to outline his final scheme. Among those present were Lepeshinsky – with whom he had played chess in Siberia – Olminsky, Lunacharsky, Zemliachka, Vorovsky, Gusev and Velichkina.

Lenin announced that the new paper would be 'the real organ of the working-class movement in Russia . . . without it we shall meet with certain and inglorious death.'

The first issue of Lenin's answer to *Iskra* appeared in December 1904. It was called *Vperiod* (*Forward*); later the name was changed to *Proletari* (*Proletarian*). Serving under Lenin's supreme editorial command were Bogdanov, Lunacharsky, Olminsky and Vorovsky.

With the appearance of *Vperiod* Lenin's spirits soared once again. The atmosphere in the editorial office was very different from that of the old *Iskra*. Instead of bitter fighting, good spirits and complete harmony prevailed. Lenin's eyes beamed when the first copy was ready. Around him sat men on whom he could count.

'At last we have finished with that filthy squabbling,' Lenin wrote, 'and we are working in a friendly way with those who want to work. . . . Hurrah! Don't lose heart; things are brightening up again.'[18]

But there were other, more substantial reasons for Lenin's new optimism. In February 1904 the Tsarist Government had blundered into war with Japan. Spring and summer had brought an unbroken series of military defeats and with them the rumblings of revolt. In January 1905 the Japanese took Port Arthur.

'It is not the Russian people, but the autocracy that has suffered shameful defeat', Lenin wrote. 'The Russian people gained by the defeat of the autocracy. The capitulation of Port Arthur is the prologue to the capitulation of Tsarism.'

The seeds which generations of rebels had sown in Russian soil were about to yield their first real harvest: Russia was on the verge of revolution.

Lenin, on the eve of the great upheaval of 1905, was thirty-four years old. Behind him he had put more than a decade of hard revolutionary experience – a familiar pattern of conspiracy, imprisonment, Siberian exile, and the shuttling existence of a political *émigré*. Four years of hectic life abroad, in the cafés, rooming-houses and meeting halls of Munich, Brussels, London and Geneva had not made him a western European. He learned the languages of this alien world but his outlook remained profoundly Russian.

The tough core of his political lines had firmly set; despite his Marxist and European schooling, his philosophy was conditioned by powerful ingredients of Russian revolutionary absolutism and by a sense of his own unique mission. Arbitrary and dictatorial in the eyes of his former mentors and Social Democratic comrades, he regarded them with increasing disdain for their 'bourgeois' aversion to a monolithic party of revolutionary conspirators; for their constant preoccupation with the moral aspects of revolution.

If the man had inner doubts, he did not permit himself to express them. In his writings he was becoming more and more dogmatic, more intolerant of differences of opinion. And while he was to reverse himself on many basic issues of the Russian revolution, he always managed to present these as merely 'tactical' shifts, while lambasting his opponents as 'opportunists' and 'traitors' for much less.

Within his own circle of Bolshevik followers he already commanded veneration and blind loyalty. One of his disciples of this period, N. Valentinov, who joined Lenin in Geneva after his release from prison in Kiev, leaves a vivid picture of Lenin on the eve of the First Revolution.

'When I first met Lenin', writes Valentinov, 'he was thirty-four years old. Certain of his comrades who surrounded him in Geneva were older. . . . Yet Lenin's circle seemed to regard him as the senior member . . . and called him "Ilyich". . . . Among Russian workers, peasants and townsfolk this patronymic form is applied to old persons held in high esteem. . . . "Ilyich", said many of his comrades, "has penetrated the mystery of social-economic processes as no one else in Russia. . . . Only Ilyich has found the solution of the problem of problems – a special type of structure for the Party, that organ which the highest dictates of history have charged with the mission of making and leading the Revolution".'

Whether Lenin approved of this neo-idolatry is very doubtful. Of the great political leaders in modern history none had less personal vanity, less desire to flaunt his own person rather than his ideas. But despite his personal reticence and keen sense of humour he was well aware of the enormous political value of the adulation he inspired. In 1905 it never occurred to his followers to call him the 'Leader', yet the respectful patronymic 'Ilyich' set him apart from his contemporaries.

Lepeshinsky tried to capture this feeling in a caricature of 1904, in which he depicted Lenin as a gigantic sleeping tomcat on whose body tiny mice perched themselves. The mice were labelled 'Mensheviks'. That was Lenin in the eyes of his early Bolshevik comrades.

Whether Lenin in that period saw himself as a future dictator is hard to say. He never stated it in so many words until power was in his hands. Then he put his cards on the table with remarkable frankness.

'Classes are led by parties,' said Lenin in 1920, 'and parties are led by individuals who are called leaders. . . . This is the A B C. The will of a class is sometimes fulfilled by a dictator. . . . Soviet socialist democracy is not in the least incompatible with individual rule and dictatorship. . . . What is necessary is individual rule, the recognition of the dictatorial powers of one man. . . . All phrases about equal rights are nonsense.'[19]

Although Lenin did not use such language in his Geneva days, his general approach to the coming revolution was already clear. His was a hard-headed, unsentimental outlook which placed a higher value on loyalty to himself and his party than on other considerations. During an ideological argument, Valentinov once reproached Lenin for his indifference to the behaviour of a certain Bolshevik, X, who had been given a passport and funds to return to Russia but had squandered the money in a brothel and never reached his destination. Lenin's answer was revealing:

'You very probably would never have gone to that brothel, and certainly you would never spend Party money on drink; so far as I know, you have no weakness for liquor. But you are apt to do things that are much worse. You are capable of intriguing with the Menshevik Martynov, an inveterate enemy of our orthodox, revolutionary old *Iskra*. You are capable of approving the reactionary bourgeois theory of Mach, a foe of materialism. You are capable of admiring the alleged "quest for truth" of Bulgakov. All this adds up to a brothel many times worse than the whorehouse with the naked tarts visited by X. Your brothel poisons and obscures the class consciousness of the workers; and if we are to judge your conduct and that of X from this point of view, the only correct one for a Social Democrat, we shall arrive at different conclusions. You deserve to be held up to shame for trying to substitute an obscure theory for Marxism, while the offence of X may be easily condoned. As a party man, X is a steadfast, seasoned revolutionary; he had proved himself a staunch *Iskra* man before the congress, during the congress, after the congress, and this is of primary importance. . . .

'You're right in this, you're absolutely right. All those who give up Marxism are my enemies. I refuse to shake hands with them, and I do not sit down at the same table with the Philistines'.

Valentinov was also surprised at Lenin's interest in the details of the street fighting which he had seen in Kiev in July 1903. Seeing Valentinov's perplexity with his preoccupation in the 'jaw-breaking' aspect of the Kiev disorders, Lenin declared:

'But you must understand, the moment has come when it is necessary to fight not only in the figurative, political meaning of the word, but in its simplest, most direct physical sense. The time when demonstrators unfurled the Red Flag, shouted "down with absolutism!" and then scattered in all directions, is past. It is necessary to begin its *physical* destruction by mass attack, to deal physical blows against the apparatus of absolutism and its defenders. The bullies of absolutism must receive two, or, even better, four blows for each one they deal out a worker, a student, or a peasant. Only this, not fine words, will force them to be more careful and less arbitrary. What is necessary now is not argumentation in the manner of our namby-pamby intellectuals, but learning to give proletarian punches on the jaw. We must know how and want to fight.'

Here Lenin clenched his fist and swung it, as if to show how it should be done. 'We have begun to demonstrate with fist and rocks', he said; 'when we learn to fight we'll take up something even more persuasive.'

That was Lenin the practical revolutionist, the future organizer of proletarian revolt. It was the sort of language that neither Plekhanov nor Martov understood. But combined with this tough faith in the muscular prerequisites of successful insurrection was a dogmatism that would do justice to the most fanatical Jesuit.

'Orthodox Marxism', Lenin told Valentinov, 'requires no revision of any kind, either in the field of philosophy, in its theory of political economy, or its theory of historical development.'[20]

In his writings he expressed this dogmatic faith in even stronger language. In his *Materialism and Empiro-Criticism* Lenin declared:

'Marx's theory is the objective truth. Following the path of this theory, we will approach the objective truth more and more closely, while if we follow any other path we cannot arrive at anything except confusion and falsehood. From the philosophy of Marxism, cast of one piece of steel, it is impossible to expunge a single basic premise, a single essential part, without deviating from objective truth, without falling into the arms of bourgeois-reactionary falsehood. . . .

'Efforts to find a new point in philosophy reveal the same poverty of spirit as efforts to create a 'new' theory of value, or a 'new' theory of rent.'[21]

Armed with this passionate faith in the proletarian fist and in the 'objective truth' of Marxism, Lenin was ready to return to the Russian battle front.

Chapter 5
The First Revolution

While conflict raged in Social Democratic ranks, the Revolutionary movement was not marking time in Russia. A new party had come on the scene and had stirred fresh currents in the Russian people. This was the Socialist Revolutionary Party. The leaders of the party were Catherine Breshkovsky, who had served six prison terms and spent more than twenty years in Siberia; Mikhail Gotz, son of a Moscow millionaire and a famous Siberian exile; Gregory Gershuni, whose Terrorist Brigade carried out the assassination of leading reactionary Ministers and Governors; Victor Chernov; and a number of old revolutionists of the People's Will. Terrorism was the most spectacular phase of Socialist Revolutionary action, but hardly the most important. The party founded a newspaper in Geneva and set up many illegal printing plants within Russia itself. By 1903 its pamphlets and papers were distributed in forty-two provinces.

The Socialist Revolutionaries differed in many important respects from the Social Democrats. They did not take much stock in the ramifications and niceties of Marxist theory but drew more on the ideas of Herzen, Lavrov and Mikhailovsky. Their general approach to social problems was to proceed from the bottom up; *i.e.*, from the masses of the people. Hence their emphasis on the *people*, on the *mir*, and on a cooperation between consumer and producer in the form of cooperatives. The coming Revolution, the Socialist Revolutionaries believed, had to be national in character, expressing the aspirations of workers, peasants and intellectuals. The proletariat was no sacred cow; student, teacher, peasant, scientist and writer were equally important in a democratic society. Placing a high value on the labour of the mind, they fought for complete intellectual liberty. To the new party, regarding itself as the heir of the People's Will, liberty was as much an end as a means. To build Socialism without intellectual freedom, they said, meant quartering all humanity in barracks. Their ultimate goal was the reorganization of production and the entire social order according to Socialist principles, albeit they believed that Russia was not yet ready for the complete realization of this aim. Nevertheless, in accordance with the traditions of the Russian peasantry and its conviction that the land belongs to no individual, that the right to use it is conferred only by labour, the Socialist Revolutionary programme demanded the immediate socialization of the land; *i.e.* 'the conversion of land into national property, without compensation.'

Moreover, they emphasized that they would support measures for the socialization of other branches of the national economy 'only to the extent to which the democratization of the political régime and the character of the measures would provide sufficient guarantees against increasing the dependence of the working class upon the ruling bureaucracy.' The programme of the new party warned the working class against that form of 'state socialism' which would concentrate the various branches of industry and trade 'in the hands of the ruling bureaucracy for the sake of its fiscal and political aims'.

Social Democratic reaction to the new party was hostile. The Marxist group could not accept the Socialist Revolutionary contention that the peasant communes could serve as a departing point for Socialism in the rural districts. The older party maintained that the peasants were indeed a potential revolutionary force, but not a socialist one. The Social Democrats, in fact, regarded the village *mir* as a reactionary institution 'in the bosom of which the class struggle was already developing'.

The Socialist Revolutionaries' use of individual terror against high-ranking reactionary members of the government also came in for denunciation by the Social Democrats. The Marxist group condemned these tactics, seeing only 'a means of struggle used by the petty bourgeois bound to put the masses to sleep by making them believe that the arm of a hero can bring liberation.'

Generally the Socialist Revolutionaries were more romantic and sentimental than their Social Democratic contemporaries. Moreover, they attached much more importance to the development of consumers' and producers' co-operatives. The Social Democrats scoffed at these leanings, declaring of the Belgian co-operatives: 'They seek to destroy their bourgeois capitalist régime by bombarding it with small loaves of bread manufactured in co-operative bakeries.'

While the Socialist Revolutionaries aligned themselves with the older party in demands for a Constituent Assembly and a democratic republic, they placed as great an emphasis on 'recognition of the inalienable rights of man and citizens', wide autonomy for urban and rural communities and regions, the broadest possible application of federalist principles to the separate nationalities, and recognition of the rights of self-determination of nationalities.[1]

Socialist theory did not by any means monopolize Russian political thinking. Drawing on the ranks of the middle class and the Zemstvos – the provincial assemblies – Liberalism also began to organize for political action.

When Tsar Nicholas II ascended the throne in 1894, the zemstvo of the Tver province appealed to the new monarch with 'the hope that the voice of the people and the expression of its desires will be heard on the heights of the throne and will be heeded'. To this moderate appeal the Tsar replied that the zemstvo was indulging in idle dreams, and reaffirmed his intention to maintain unaltered the principles of absolutism.

Pobedonostsev, procurator of the Holy Synod, was the Tsar's mentor, entrusted with blanket authority to appoint and remove Ministers and to promote such policies as he thought best. Pobedonostsev cracked down on the zemstvos even where previous régimes had permitted them to function, and embarked on the systematic persecution of religious and racial minorities. The Tsar, relying on his adviser's judgement, ignored the approaching storm clouds.

'The Emperor lacks real education or experience in affairs of state and most particularly any strength of character', said A. A. Polovtzev, the Secretary of State and member of the Imperial Council. 'Anyone can convince him to change his mind. The Emperor's Uncle Sergei has the greatest influence on him, but Sergei is, in every sense of the word, a worthless individual. . . .'

Pobedonostsev himself was not much kinder in his judgement of the Tsar. 'He has a naturally bright mind', said the head of the Synod; 'he is shrewd, quickly grasps the meaning of what he hears, but only understands the significance of some isolated fact, without connexion with the rest, without appreciating the interrelation of all other pertinent facts, events, trends, occurrences. He sticks to his insignificant petty point of view. This is the result of his military-school education, as well probably as the influence of the many chambermaids who surround his mother.'[2]

With the court hopelessly absorbed in petty intrigues, the Liberals began to press for constitutional changes. In 1903, under the leadership of Professor Paul Miliukov, Princes Paul and Peter Dolgorukov, Ivan Petrunkevich, Fyodor Kokoshkin, Fyodor Rodichev and Vladimir Nabokov, a Union of Liberation was founded. Its members were drawn from the liberal professions, the intelligentsia, and the zemstvos. In Stuttgart and later in Paris, the Union published a weekly newspaper, *Osvobozhdenie*, under the editorship of Peter Struve; copies were smuggled into Russia where they were widely read and circulated. Inside Russia, the Union secretly recruited members and also arranged public, apparently non-political conventions, banquets and meetings of learned societies which, as time went on, gradually took a political turn.[3]

In the midst of Russian military defeat Von Plehve, the reactionary Minister of the Interior, was assassinated by a member of the Terrorist Brigade of the Soviet Revolutionary Party; street demonstrations broke out, opposition from every side grew bolder. For the first time the Tsar retreated, summoning Prince Sviatopolk-Mirsky, a more liberal man, to Von Plehhve's post. Censorship was somewhat relaxed and reforms were pledged. In November 1904 a great congress of the zemstvos met in St Petersburg and demanded freedom of speech and press, inviolability of person, equality for national minorities, and the convocation of a representative assembly. Similar demands were advanced by many other groups.

In the meantime, the Ministry of the Interior and the political police were trying their hand at another game. In the effort to wean the workers away from radicalism, they had organized a Union of Russian Workers, whose programme called for the defence of the economic rights of labour, and loyalty to the Tsar. Father Gapon, a priest, was placed at the head of the union. But the logic of events pushed this organization far beyond the objectives intended by its police sponsors.

On Sunday, 22 January 1905, the union organized a procession to the Winter Palace to present a petition to the Tsar. The marchers, numbering many thousands of unarmed workers, accompanied by their wives and children, carried ikons and placards. They were not received by the Tsar or his Ministers. Instead, they were brought to a halt by troops ordered the evening before to keep the demonstration out of the Winter Palace square. The soldiers opened fire on the multitude as it approached the Troitski Bridge, and continued firing indiscriminately. More than seventy were killed and many hundreds of wounded were left behind by the fleeing crowd. This massacre destroyed the last particle of public faith in the régime. 'Bloody Sunday' produced universal indignation and a wave of protest strikes all over Russia.[4]

Less than a month after the massacre, the Terrorist Brigade of the Socialist Revolutionary Party assassinated the Tsar's uncle, the detested Grand Duke Sergei, then Governor-General of Moscow.

'Learn to look the coming revolution straight in the eye', Kaliaiev, the assassin, told the judges who sentenced him to death. 'Our generation will end this autocracy forever. . . .'

In May 1905 a Union of Unions was organized under the chairmanship of Professor Miliukov. This brought together all the liberal and radical groups in a renewed demand for parliamentary government and the institution of universal suffrage.

On 19 August 1905, the Tsar signed a manifesto summoning a popular assembly, the Imperial Duma, with advisory powers, but without legislative authority. This half-measure, like so many concessions the Tsar granted under duress, satisfied no one, serving only to whet the appetite of the people for political freedom.

In September 1905, forty members of the Union of Liberation and twenty zemstvo workers met in Moscow to draw up a programme for Russia's first liberal party. The programme was ratified a month later at a broader convention in Moscow, and the new group baptized the 'Constitutional Democratic Party' — soon popularly known, after its Russian initials, as *Ka-Dey* or Cadet.

Meanwhile, strikes, demonstrations, riots, disjointed and spontaneous, gained momentum and scope. In mid-September the workers of the illegal Typographical Union of Moscow went out on strike. They were soon joined by the bakers, then the telegraph and postal operators. The strike grew into nation-wide proportions without direction from any party. In this strike for liberty the leaders were legion, the people themselves without central direction.

On 22 October 1905, Count Witte, a former Minister of Finance, warned the Tsar that Russia was on the verge of a bloody revolution unless substantial concessions were granted immediately.

He wrote:

The present movement for freedom is not of new birth. Its roots are imbedded in centuries of Russian history . . . 'Freedom' must become the slogan of the government. No other possibility for the salvation of the state exists. The march of historical progress cannot be halted. The idea of civil liberty will triumph if not through reform then by the path of revolution. In the latter eventuality, the idea of freedom will rise again only from the ashes of the destroyed thousand-year-old Russian past. . . . The horrors of this Russian insurrection may surpass all records in the history of mankind. A possible foreign intervention may dismember the country. . . . The attempt to realize the ideals of theoretical Socialism – they will not succeed but they will be made – will destroy the family, organized religion, private property, and the foundation of all law.

The government must be ready to proceed along constitutional lines. The government must sincerely and openly strive for the well-being of the state and not endeavour to protect this or that type of government. There is no alternative. The government must either place itself at the head of the movement which has gripped the country or it must relinquish it to the elementary forces to tear it to pieces.[5]

Late in October the powerful All-Russian Railway Workers' Union called a general strike. On 25 October railroad transportation came to a halt throughout the Russian Empire. The general strike, now nationwide and embracing all essential services and industries, had at last paralysed the government.

At the same time a strange new 'government' appeared in St Petersburg, the Soviet Council of Workers' Deputies. Elections to the new body began in the factories on 26 October. A young lawyer named Khrustalev-Nosar was elected chairman, with Trotsky and the Socialist Revolutionary Nikolai Avksentiev as vice-chairmen of the first Soviet.

The initiative for this proletarian parliament came from the Menshevik wing of the St Petersburg Social Democratic Party. The general strike needed a central non-partisan directorate to give it political direction and this body was the answer. On 26 October the first meeting of the Soviet took place in the Technological Institute. It was attended by only forty delegates, representing 20,000 workers; not all the St Petersburg factories had had time to elect their delegates.

The Soviet's first appeal called on the entire working class to join the strike.

'In the next few days', said the appeal, 'decisive events will take place in Russia, which will determine for many years the fate of the working class in Russia. We must be fully prepared to cope with these events united through our common Soviet.'

The Soviet acted openly before the eyes of the Russian people and the régime. Overnight it became known and popular everywhere as an institution of power in the hands of the masses.

Khrustalev assumed the role of the tribune of the people, but his political leadership was jostled on the third day by Trotsky. The latter's talents as an orator immediately pushed him to the forefront.

Although the Soviet was conceived merely as a central strike committee, its leaders soon realized that it could become an effective organ for political agitation – an organ to pave the way for a revolution. Within a few days it became an instrument of revolutionary power.

Every day of the Soviet's existence was packed with political excitement, as more workers joined the strike. On 28 October the Soviet ordered the shutdown of all shops; grocery stores were permitted to be open only from eight to eleven in the morning. The same day it warned factory owners and shopkeepers that they would face the 'people's vengeance' if they tried to conduct their business. Two days later, when the strikes reached their peak, life in St Petersburg was at a complete standstill. Telephone and telegraph services were suspended, electricity was cut off; only searchlights illuminated the Nevsky Prospect. Restaurants, courts, theatres and schools were closed.

Although not a shot had been fired this was Revolution, and the Tsar's advisers knew it. From Berlin, Kaiser Wilhelm advised his cousin Nicholas to grant a constitution, while at the same time offering his aid to crush the workers of St Petersburg. A number of German naval vessels actually appeared off Peterhof in the

T–D

Gulf of Finland. Wilhelm also offered to provide the Tsar with a haven. His offer caused great excitement at the Russian court. Those opposed to constitutional concessions were in favour of the Tsar's departure. Witte, on the other hand, argued that this step meant the end of the dynasty.

Realizing that further delay would be fatal, Nicholas dismissed Pobedonostsev, appointed Count Witte Premier of Russia and, on 30 October 1905, issued a brand-new manifesto. This document granted freedom of speech, conscience and assembly, the right of labour to organize, and a more liberal suffrage law for elections to the Duma. Nicholas also promised, for the first time, that no laws would be decreed without the Duma's sanction. When Trepov, the Governor of St Petersburg, heard the news, he exclaimed:

'Thank God the manifesto has been signed. Freedom has been granted; the people will choose their own representatives. A new life is beginning.'

When the first issue of the Soviet newspaper *Izvestia* appeared, Trotsky had this to say of the Czar's promises:

'We are given a Witte, but Trepov remains; we are given a constitution, but absolutism remains. All is given and nothing is given.'

The Soviet voted to continue the strike. 'The struggling revolutionary proletariat cannot lay down its weapons until the political rights of the Russian people are established on a firm foundation, until a democratic republic is established, the best road for the further progress to Socialism.'

On 31 October there was a tremendous demonstration in St Petersburg, with flags and revolutionary songs, led by three members of the Soviet. But no soldiers or sailors took part; the military was still faithful to the government.

The crowd demanded an amnesty for all political prisoners, the slogan provided by the Soviet, but their attempt to break into the prisons was foiled.

No sooner had the demonstrators left for their homes than a counter-demonstration of the Tsar's ultra-reactionary supporters, the Black Hundreds, gathered and began beating up students.

On 3 November the strike ended. But *Izvestia* continued the fight with words: 'The proletariat knows what it wants and what it doesn't want. It doesn't want the police hooligan Trepov, nor the 'liberal' mediator Witte – neither the jaws of a wolf nor the tail of a fox. It doesn't want Cossack whips wrapped up in a constitution.'

The constitutional Prime Minister, Witte, played politics with both the Right and the Left. He conferred with Khrustalev and threatened him with Trepov, and threatened Trepov with Khrustalev. While the government hesitated, the Soviet came out with the slogan 'Disarm the autocracy and arm the Revolution'. The Soviet demanded an eight-hour workday and a rise in wages for all the workers of St Petersburg. This move drove the capitalists and the middle class into the arms of the régime. The peasants remained passive.

On 8 November a mutiny broke out among the sailors of Kronstadt fortress, but it was quickly suppressed and the leaders faced possible execution. The Petrograd workers again called a strike, with the approval of the Executive Committee of the Soviet.

The demand of the strike was the abolition of courts-martial and the death penalty. At the same time the Soviet decided to start broad agitation in the Army. The strike was more successful than the authorities had expected. Count Witte had to appeal to the workers in a language never before used in a Minister of the Tsar.

'Brother workers, go back to your jobs. Stop your rebellion. Pity your wives and children', begged the Premier. 'Listen to the advice of a man who is favourably disposed to you and desires only your welfare.'

The Soviet Executive Committee promptly replied: 'The Soviet of Workers' Deputies ... expresses its extreme amazement that the Tsarist Minister unceremoniously allows himself to call the Petrograd workers "brothers". The proletarians are no relatives of Count Witte.'[6]

It was at this time, November 1905, that Lenin returned to Russia. What had he been doing since Bloody Sunday?

News of the massacre of 22 January reached him as he and Krupskaya were on their way to the Geneva library. All the Bolsheviks flocked to Lepeshinsky's *émigré* restaurant, where excitement was at such a pitch that scarcely a word was spoken. They spontaneously struck up the strains of the revolutionary Funeral March.

Lenin now felt that an armed uprising and the establishment of a 'dictatorship of workers and peasants' were immediately realizable objectives. He studied everything Marx and Engels had written on the art of insurrection; the technique of barricade warfare as described in the memoirs of General Cluseret who had suppressed the Paris uprising of 1848. And he sought out Father Gapon, who was then in Geneva. Apparently he did not trust the priest, although he expressed hope that he would 'work to obtain that clarity of revolutionary outlook necessary for a political leader'.

Believing that an insurrection was imminent, Lenin set out to wrest control of the Party from the Mensheviks. In April he summoned his followers for what he designated as the Third Congress of the All-Russian Social Democratic Party. Convening in London from 25 April to 10 May 1905, this Congress was attended only by Bolsheviks, including Litvinov, Kamenev, Rykov, Krassin and Lunacharsky.

Lenin had little difficulty getting his programme adopted in London. The Bolshevik delegates accepted him as their leader, and gave him *carte blanche*. The immediate task was to organize an armed uprising, the Congress declared. The Mensheviks were virtually excommunicated, a fact which had no practical significance, inasmuch as they did not recognize the authority of the Third Congress. As far as they were concerned, the London gathering was the first Congress of the Bolshevik Party.

One day the Bolshevik delegates wandered through the graveyard where Karl Marx was buried, lost amid endless rows of 'bourgeois' tombstones. Finally a group of masons recognized them as Russians and directed them to the spot. The headstone was partially sunk in the ground and was covered with moss.

'You see', said Lenin, 'how well the British workman knows whom we are looking for, whom we sincerely love. And yet Marx is their genius, not ours, reared and nurtured by great British industry, British technical development, British science and civilization. The British worker cares little about him. He thinks Marx is good only for the miserable Russians and Orientals chafing under the yoke of capitalism. As if these British workers do not suffer the thrall of their own capitalism!'[7]

In the summer of 1905 a young Bolshevik from Kazan came to

Lenin asking for instructions. What were the rank and file in Russia to do?

Lenin sprang to his feet, paced the room, his thumbs tugging at his vest, and began speaking rapidly.

'What is to be done? One thing – an armed uprising – an immediate armed uprising.'

The Kazan comrade hinted that Bolsheviks within Russia doubted whether an uprising at this time could bring victory. Lenin stood still for a moment.

'Victory?' he rasped. 'What do we care about victory?'

The young man gaped in astonishment. Lenin seemed to be declaiming to a large gathering. His right fist was tightly clenched as he hammered out:

'We do not live by illusions. Tell that to the comrades in my name. We are sober realists. Let no one believe that we shall necessarily win. We are still very weak, but this is by no means a question of victory alone. We want the uprising to shake the foundation of the autocracy and set the broad masses into motion. Our task then will be to attract those masses to our cause. That is the main point! *The uprising is what matters.* Talk that "we can't win" and therefore don't need the uprising is the talk of cowards with whom we must have no relations.'

The Bolshevik from Kazan left with the slogan 'armed uprising' ringing in his ears.

All the Bolshevik activities were directed by Lenin, under the slogans of armed rebellion, the formation of a revolutionary army, and the establishment of a Provisional Revolutionary Government. Lenin took energetic measures for the purchase and smuggling of arms into Russia. He established contact with the mutineers on the s.s. *Potemkin*, pointing to the lessons that could be drawn from the sailors' revolt. 'The revolutionary army', he said, 'is needed because great historical questions can be solved only by force, and in the modern struggle organized force means military organization.'[8]

In a letter to the Military Organization of the St Petersburg Committee of the Social Democratic Party he gave instructions on the struggle:

It requires furious *energy* and *more* energy. I am appalled, truly appalled to see that more than half a year has been spent in talk about bombs – and not a single bomb has yet been made. Go to the youth. Or else, by God, you will be late (I can see that from all indications), and will find yourself with learned memoranda, plans, blueprints, schemes, excellent prescriptions, but without an organization, without living work. Go to the youth. Organize at once and everywhere fighting brigades among students, and particularly among workers. Let them arm them-selves immediately with whatever weapons they can obtain – a knife, a revolver, a kerosene-soaked rag for setting fires.

Do not demand obligatory entry into the Social Democratic Party. For Christ's sake, throw out all your schemes, consign all functions, rights, and privileges to the devil. If the Fighting Organization does not have at least two hundred to three hundred squads in Petersburg in one to two months, then it is a dead committee and should be buried. Let the squads begin to train for immediate operations. Some can undertake to assassin-ate a spy or blow up a police station, others can attack a bank to expro-priate funds for an insurrection. Let every squad learn, if only by beating up police. The dozens of sacrifices will be repaid with interest by pro-ducing hundreds of experienced fighters who will lead hundreds of thousands tomorrow.[9]

The general strike came as a complete surprise to Lenin. It did not fit the slogans of his newspaper nor the resolutions of the Third Congress. But it loomed so large across the face of Russia that he was forced to recognize its importance and he was compelled to reckon with the newly established Soviet Workers' Deputies. At first the novel revolutionary institution alarmed him more than it did the Tsar. When the Mensheviks and Socialist Revolutionaries organized the Soviet, Lenin regarded this undisciplined organism as a dangerous rival to the Party, a spontaneous proletarian assem-bly which a small group of 'professional revolutionists' would not be able to control.[10]

When Lenin returned to Russia in November, the Soviet was an established force in the revolution. *Novoye Vremya*, a reaction-ary newspaper, wrote that there are 'two governments in Russia, Premier Witte's and Khrustalev's, and that it is a question which will succeed in arresting the other.'

This was a somewhat exaggerated picture of the Soviet's im-portance in 1905, but it showed clearly that its enemies sensed its potential power. Somewhat later the question posed by *Novoye Vremya* was settled by the arrest of Khrustalev, and the leadership of the Soviet went to a committee of three headed by Trotsky.

Quick to realize that his initial opposition to the Soviet had been a mistake, Lenin now became an advocate of expanding its role to that of the nucleus for a Provisional Government.

The temporary era of civil liberty had brought into the open the first Bolshevik daily newspaper in St Petersburg, *Novaya Zhizn*, and Lenin for the first time had a legal forum from which to plead his cause. In a letter, he urged Plekhanov to become one of its editors:

> I need hardly repeat to you that we Bolsheviks are most anxious to work together with you. . . . In questions of theory and tactics you and I agree nine-tenths of the way; we ought not to widen the breach because of disagreement on one-tenth. You wanted and still want to correct several – according to your view – false statements in my works. But at no time did I try especially to impose my views upon anyone among the Social Democrats. And no one, absolutely no one, of the new editorial board has been engaged because he is a 'Leninist'. A new, perfectly legal newspaper that will have tens if not hundreds of thousands of readers, including the entire morning working force of Russians right now, this at a time when your prodigious knowledge and tremendous political experience are terribly indispensable for the proletariat – all this creates *a new base* that will make it possible to forget the old, and to confer on vital tasks. . . .

> In all likelihood, you will not wish to make common cause with only one-half of the Party. As a condition for your joining the editorial staff, you will stipulate the peremptory union of the entire Party. That such a union is desirable and essential – in this you are absolutely right. But is that possible now? Can we have an editorial staff now in coalition with the Mensheviks? We are of the opinion that it can't be done; the Mensheviks also think likewise.

Plekhanov ignored the letter, and humorously compared Lenin's invitation to him to join *Novaya Zhizn's* seven Bolshevik editors to an alliance between the wolf and the lamb. Shortly afterwards, a Menshevik daily, *Natchalo*, was also begun, but Plekhanov, who was ill and could not return to Russia, was not among its editors. The policy of *Natchalo* was influenced mainly by Trotsky and Parvus (Dr A. Helphand), who together were to evolve the theory of 'permanent revolution' (*i.e.* the idea that the Russian revolution was the prelude to a socialist world revolution). Yet *Natchalo* and *Novaya Zhizn* urged essentially similar policies. As Lenin wrote later, 'the Mensheviks together with the Bolsheviks clamoured for a strike and an uprising then. They called upon the workers not to quit their fight until they had seized all power . . . . Differences arose only in regard to details in the appraisal of events. . . .'

Lenin divided his time between the offices of *Novaya Zhizn* and underground conferences to map insurrectionary plans. For a time he found it safer to live apart from his wife on a false passport under the name of William Frey. One evening while 'Frey' was dining with one of his chief lieutenants in a Tartar restaurant in St Petersburg, he saw an attractive young woman sitting alone at an adjoining table. His companion, quick to note that Lenin was interested, approached the woman, whom he knew, and said: 'If you aren't waiting for anyone, why not join us? You'll meet a very interesting man' – indicating Lenin's table. 'He is very well known, but don't ask for particulars.'

Elizabeth K, who was a rather wealthy young woman, was sufficiently curious to welcome an introduction to 'William Frey'.

'Are you British?' she asked.

'Not quite,' he replied sardonically.

They spent more than an hour in pleasant banter before parting. A few days later she dropped into the *Novaya Zhizn* office to visit one of the contributors. Mysterious Mr Frey was there greeting her with his habitual mocking smile.

'How do you do? I am very happy to see you again. Don't you patronize the Tartar restaurant any longer?'

Elizabeth quite properly understood this to be an invitation. When she told it to the Bolshevik who had introduced them, he laughed.

'My good friend "Frey" is, of course, interested in the feminine question, but primarily from a collective, social and political viewpoint. I should never have supposed that he was capable of dealing with the question on a personal plane. Allow me to add this: After our dinner that evening he asked me whether I could vouch for you. He is inclined to be suspicious and to avoid new acquaintances, so as not to run into informers. I was forced to tell him who you were, and that your apartment was excellently suited for secret gatherings.'

Two days later the three dined once more in the Tartar restaurant. Madame K consented to Frey using her apartment twice a week for meetings with comrades which could not safely be held elsewhere. On the appointed day she would send her maid away and personally admit visitors who answered to the password. She was never present in the room where the sessions took place, scrupulously retiring beyond the reach of the voices.

Several evenings Lenin came alone. He would help Elizabeth prepare the samovar and carry it into the dining-room. A warm friendship developed between them. Sometimes she played the piano for him. But she was puzzled by his interest in a particular passage in Beethoven's 'Appassionata Sonata', which he asked her to repeat time and again. Invariably as she reached that passage Lenin became animated. One evening he asked her to indicate the spot in the score where the magic passage occurred. It developed that the reason for his interest was that it reminded him of the revolutionary hymn of the Jewish Socialist Bund. Madame K, who was far more at home in the musical and literary world of St Petersburg than among Marxists, laughed scornfully.[11]

The high tide of revolution had now passed and reactionaries had begun a strong counter-offensive. Spearheading this drive were the pogroms of the Black Hundreds, the Russian Ku Klux organization supported by the Okhrana. Behind Premier Witte's back, Minister of the Interior Durnovo obtained the Tsar's approval for his plans to restore the autocratic powers of the throne.

'It's their heads or ours,' said Nicholas. 'This situation can't last. I authorize you to take all measures that you consider necessary.'

Uprisings of soldiers and sailors, badly planned and ill-directed, were taking place in various parts of the country. A strike of postal and telegraph workers again tied up communications. The industrialists saw the spectre of social revolution and demanded that the government take drastic action. Plekhanov, from abroad, counselled both Bolsheviks and Mensheviks to be cautious. He thought they seemed 'determined to provoke an early, relentless clash' with the government, while in his view 'it is to our advantage *to temporize and to deter* the final clash. . . . At this moment, the situation favours the enemy. . . .

'If we were to lose the battle now, reaction would breathe more freely. . . . Absolutism or semi-absolutism would return only through our own recklessness.'

The Soviet nevertheless, under Trotsky's leadership, issued a manifesto to the people calling for a boycott of tax payments, the overthrow of the régime, and the convocation of a Constituent Assembly. But the response of the masses was indifferent. On 16 December 1905, the day after this appeal was published, the entire Executive Committee of the Soviet was arrested and all newspapers which had carried the text were suppressed.

The Bolsheviks meanwhile continued their own preparations, purchasing contraband arms, and organizing units of twenty-five armed men as fighting brigades. Lenin fixed his main hopes on Moscow. In St Petersburg, the centre of political activity, no other political faction favoured insurrection. But Moscow seemed ripe for revolt. The thoughts of armed rebellion were not confined to the Bolsheviks.

When a new general strike was called for 20 December, St Petersburg did not respond, but in Moscow the strike changed swiftly into an insurrection. Party fighting brigades, supported by a section of the populace, threw up barricades. The walls of Moscow were plastered with leaflets containing tactical instructions on the conduct of the insurrection: fight in groups of three and four – attack suddenly and disappear just as fast.

This type of desultory fighting might have continued for weeks. St Petersburg seemed in no hurry to send reinforcements to government forces commanded by Dubassov, the Governor-General of Moscow. The troops stationed there were insufficient. After permitting the insurrectionary stew to boil for a week, the government finally sent the crack Semionovsky Guards and artillery from St Petersburg. On the twenty-ninth Dubassov began mopping up the barricades. The last stronghold, the Presnia suburb where more than two hundred men put up a last ditch defence, fell on the morning of the thirty-first.

Lenin himself was in Finland from the twenty-fourth until the suppression of the Moscow insurrection. The collapse of the uprising brought strong intra-Bolshevik opposition to Lenin into the open for the first time. He was accused of 'Nechayevism', of 'adventurist tactics', of a deliberate policy of blood-letting. For his part, however, he regarded the abortive revolt as an important lesson to the masses and to the Party leadership. It was a dress rehearsal for 1917.

The suppression of the Moscow uprising was followed by an even swifter decline in revolutionary fortunes. As the Tsar regained self-confidence, his Ministers violated the guarantees of civil liberty given under the October Manifesto, Radical newspapers were suppressed and Socialist leaders arrested.

In this period, when absolutism was reasserting itself but the spell of the October general strike and the Manifesto was still not entirely destroyed, the decisive question was the role which the Duma would play. For although the régime had clamped down on the extremists it had not yet regained sufficient strength to rescind the Manifesto. The Liberals, particularly the Cadets, continued to hope that the Duma would be strong enough to enact the laws making Russia a constitutional monarchy.

The revolutionary Socialist parties entertained no such hope. They rejected the notion that Nicholas would bow to legislation restricting his power, but they differed on tactics for the Duma elections. The Mensheviks favoured an active election campaign as an effective way of presenting their programme to the people. And their deputies on the floor of the Duma, free to attack the régime by virtue of their parliamentary immunity, would use it as a tribune and the strategic centre of battle.

Lenin, on the other hand, branded the Duma as a complete fraud and demanded boycott of the elections.[12] And Lenin's point of view won in the councils of all Socialist parties. But Lenin did not merely recommend a boycott. He carried on a relentless campaign, speaking at scores of anti-Duma meetings. One such meeting took place in a secluded wood outside of St Petersburg. A series of orators condemned the Cadets and attacked the coming Duma. Each speaker demanded the enforcement of the rights granted by the Tsar's decree and the establishment of a democratic republic. The response of the crowd was not very enthusiastic. Finally the chairman announced that the next speaker would be Lenin.

Amid bursts of applause, he spoke effectively but without oratorical flourishes. He hammered away with greater emphasis at points which previous speakers had already made. Declaring that the defeat of the Moscow insurrection had not terminated the revolutionary struggle, he attacked the Liberals for 'haggling with Tsarism over the dead bodies of the workers'. He accused the

Mensheviks of failing to grasp the lesson of the abortive revolt. But he also said that it was impossible to introduce Socialism in Russia.

A bourgeois revolution was needed to smash the remnants of feudalism and bring radical agrarian reforms, said Lenin. With the framework of a democratic republic the working class would organize and grow strong. Proletarian revolution would come first in Great Britain and France. He was very firm on this point, stressing the Marxist axiom that such revolutions must begin in advanced capitalist nations.

Immediately after Lenin's speech the crowd unfurled a red flag, fell into ranks, and marched towards the city to the accompaniment of revolutionary songs. But the marchers had not proceeded far before they encountered a company of Cossacks who bore down upon them swiftly with their short whips. The crowd dispersed and fled.[13]

Despite the boycott proclaimed by the Socialists, the elections to the first Imperial Duma saw broad mass participation. Of the 478 deputies elected, nearly half belonged to the Constitutional Democratic party, or Cadets. Another 107 belonged to the so-called Labour Group (*Trudoviki*). There were only sixteen conservatives, and no Black Hundreds. Of the many non-party deputies elected, eighteen later formed a Social Democratic group. By profession, 111 of the deputies were peasant-proprietors, 25 mill workers, 24 retailers, 65 landowners, two mill owners, the remainder provincial and town employees or members of the liberal professions.

Just before the Imperial Duma opened, the Bolsheviks and Mensheviks held a secret conclave in Stockholm. On the insistence of his followers, Lenin had agreed to seek a reconciliation. Pre-Congress manoeuvres centred on the efforts of each side to arrive in Stockholm with a majority. Lenin frankly explained to Lunacharsky: 'If we have a majority in the Central Committee, we will demand the strictest discipline. We will insist that the Mensheviks submit to party unity. So much the worse for them if their petty bourgeois nature will not allow them to go along with us. Let them assume responsibility for splitting party unity.'

'But what if we remain in the minority?' asked Lunacharsky. 'Shall we be forced to submit to them?'

Lenin replied with a smile: 'We won't permit the idea of unity to tie a noose around our necks, and we shall under no circumstances permit the Mensheviks to lead us by the rope.'[14]

The Mensheviks went to Stockholm hoping to restore party unity. To Lenin, on the other hand, the Mensheviks were no less enemies than Tsarism and the Cadets. If he chose for the moment to show an outward spirit of *rapprochement*, it was only because of the current sentiment in his own rank and file.

When the sessions of the Stockholm Congress opened, balloting for the Duma was not over. Because of the complex electoral system, voting was still to take place in many districts where Social Democratic sentiment was strong. Incomplete returns already showed that, despite the boycott, the Cadets and other anti-government groups would command a substantial majority. The Cadets were the largest single party. Under the circumstances, sentiment in favour of running Social Democratic candidates in the remaining elections appeared strong among the convention delegates.

It also became apparent that Lenin's hopes of capturing a majority in the Central Committee were ill-founded. The Mensheviks had a comfortable margin, electing seven of the ten members on the central body. Outwardly, Lenin was bound by the Stockholm decisions and, on paper, party unity was achieved. In practice, however, Lenin was guided by what he had told Lunacharsky. By retaining his own Bolshevik Centre he made certain that formal unity would not interfere with his plans.

During his stay in Stockholm, Lenin once more saw Elizabeth K. She had followed him there according to previous arrangements with a Swedish Social Democrat. When she reached the city she communicated with the Swedish intermediary who put through a telephone call to Lenin. He agreed to meet her the following day in the automat, with the warning that if other Russians were present she was to take no notice of him until they had left. At the appointed time she went to the automat. While waiting for Lenin, she noticed two Georgians struggling with one of the vending machines. When Lenin appeared they rushed to his side and one of them said loudly: 'Comrade Ilyich, please show us how to use this infernal bourgeois mechanism. We want ham sandwiches and instead we get nothing but pastry.'

Lenin had less difficulty with the 'infernal bourgeois mechanism' and the two Georgians got their ham sandwiches. During this interlude Lenin and Elizabeth showed no signs of recognizing each other. After the two Georgians had gone, he told her: 'Those were delegates of our Caucasian organization. Splendid boys but complete savages.'

The Congress gave Lenin little leisure, but on at least one Sunday he was able to spend several hours with Elizabeth in the country near Stockholm. Along the shores of a lake they found a boat for hire. Lenin took the oars and was soon stroking with a powerful rhythm.

'You were not cut out for the role of a professional revolutionist,' mocked Elizabeth. 'You should have been a farmer, a fisherman, a sailor, or a tinsmith.' Lenin laughed heartily. As the boat turned a bend and unfolded a scene of northern beauty, Elizabeth remarked that the setting reminded her of Knut Hamsun's novels.

'Yes, indeed,' replied Lenin. 'Hamsun is an extraordinary writer. In *Hunger* he gives a remarkable picture of the physical and psychological symptoms of a person suffering from starvation – an unfortunate victim of the capitalist order.'

Elizabeth shrugged her shoulders and laughed. She had been thinking of Hamsun's more romantic works, *Pan* and *Victoria*. Again, as when she had played the 'Appassionata Sonata' for him, she realized that their worlds were far apart. As the Congress dragged on and Lenin found little opportunity to be with her, she grew restless and finally left Stockholm without notifying him of her departure.

Back in St Petersburg several weeks later she received a note from Lenin to which she did not reply. She had decided to break off her relations with him forever, she thought at that time.

But two years later, when she was in Paris, she could not resist attending a meeting where Lenin spoke. During the intermission she went backstage to see him. He was surrounded by the usual crowd of admirers. When he saw her his eyes opened wide in amazement, but he quickly checked himself and asked calmly, 'What brought you here?'

'I came to hear your lecture,' she replied; 'besides which I have a commission to you from a certain person.' Thereupon she handed him an envelope containing her address and telephone number with the hour at which she could be reached.

The next morning, instead of the expected phone call, Lenin himself appeared, looking somewhat sheepish.

'I thought you were no longer alive,' he said, and as they shook hands he reached out to embrace her. But she stopped him with, 'I'm sorry, my friend, all that is past.'

'You are quite right.' He laughed. 'All that is past. But still you are an interesting woman. It's a pity you are not a Social Democrat.'

Elizabeth's reply was quick. 'You are an interesting man. It's a pity you are *only* a Social Democrat.' Lenin roared with laughter.

The atmosphere was cleared, and all tension vanished. They chatted pleasantly for several hours. She reminded Lenin of their excursion outside of Stockholm. 'It was then I realized for the first time,' Lenin remarked, 'that you are not at all a Social Democrat. You had read all Hamsun's works except *Hunger*.'

'I, too, realized how far apart we were on that trip,' Elizabeth replied. 'It seemed to me that you had read only *Hunger*.'

They parted with the understanding that they would meet again in Switzerland. Their relationship was so discreet and so outside the normal orbit of Lenin's life that it has heretofore completely escaped the notice of his biographers.[15]

On 10 May 1906, while Lenin was still in Stockholm, the Imperial Duma convened. St Petersburg resembled a beleaguered city; the streets were filled with crack troops; military patrols guarded the squares and kept a sharp watch for demonstrations. The Duma at once addressed a petition to the Tsar, outlining a long list of proposed reforms. It called for full political freedom; amnesty for political prisoners and religious dissidents; abolition of capital punishment; equality for the various national minorities; autonomy for Poland and Finland; a broader suffrage law; democratization of the organs of local self-government; expropriation of state lands and the estates of the nobility for the benefit of the peasantry; humane labour laws and comprehensive social legislation.

For a considerable time the Tsar wavered. At one stage he went so far as to enter into negotiations with Miliukov, the Cadet leader, with a view towards establishing a constitutional government. While Miliukov himself was not convinced that these overtures were sincere, a determining factor in the Tsar's shifty calculations was the degree of united popular support behind the Duma. If the Duma was not supported by the entire nation, and especially if the city workers were divided in their attitude, there was little reason to bow to the Duma's will.

In this critical hour Plekhanov and the Mensheviks appealed to the workers to put aside their differences with the Liberals and throw the weight of their support behind the Duma. 'All of the people must unanimously support the Duma', Plekhanov wrote. 'To struggle successfully for socialism it is necessary to have political freedom. It will be your misfortune, the misfortune of the country as a whole, if you do not concentrate all your energies, all your attention, now on this to the end. The reaction will profit by your fatal mistakes and will deal a terrible blow to the cause of liberty.'

A Bolshevik resolution written by Lenin, on the other hand, declared that 'the demand to appoint a ministry responsible to the Duma only serves to fortify constitutional illusions and to debauch the revolutionary consciousness of the people'. Lenin wrote openly in the newspaper *Echo*: 'The Imperial Duma is an unsuitable institution for realizing and ensuring the victory of the revolution. Only an all-popular Constituent Assembly elected by universal, equal, direct and secret ballot of all the citizens without distinction of sex, religion or nationality, and possessed of the full extent of state power – only it is capable of bringing about complete freedom.'

After the Revolution of 1917 documents found among the archives of the secret police disclosed that the Okhrana had instructed its agents and spies to give the Bolsheviks a free hand in their campaign against the Duma. Every important mass meeting arranged during that critical period had the tacit support and the devious cooperation of Okhrana agents. Bolshevik agitation for an armed uprising no longer frightened the government. The real danger to its power was in the Duma.

Under these circumstances nothing was more useful to the Tsar than the Bolshevik assaults on the Duma. From the standpoint of the régime, Lenin's campaign was a success. It helped undermine public confidence in the Duma to such an extent that seventy-two days after its opening it was possible for Nicholas to order its dissolution without risking another general strike. New elections were ordered six months hence.[16]

During this period Lenin elaborated the theory of a 'proletarian-peasant dictatorship'. But dictatorship as conceived in 1905–6 had a vastly different meaning from the 'proletarian-peasant dictatorship' he was to proclaim in 1917.

The Russian revolution, as Lenin saw it in 1905, was to be bourgeois in character. Instead of overthrowing the bourgeois order it was to clear the ground for the swift development of Russian capitalism along western European lines.

In his pamphlet, *Two Tactics*, published in 1905, Lenin wrote:

> The Marxists are absolutely convinced of the bourgeois character of the Russian revolution. What does that mean? It means that the democratic changes in the political order and the social economic reforms which are necessary for Russia, when effected, will not undermine capitalism or the rule of the bourgeoisie, but, on the contrary, will for the first time properly clear the ground for an extensive European, not Asiatic, development of capitalism. They will, for the first time, make possible the rule of the bourgeoisie, as a class. The Socialist Revolutionaries do not understand this because they do not know the ABC of the development of capitalistic production. They fail to understand that even the redistribution of all the land available in accordance with the peasants' wishes will not in the least contribute to the destruction of capitalism, but, on the contrary, will only stimulate the development of capitalism and will accelerate the process of class cleavage among the peasants themselves.
>
> To claim that Russia could skip the period of capitalist development was sheer nonsense. Marxism had forever shaken itself loose from the nonsensical patter of the Populists and the anarchists to the effect that Russia can escape a capitalistic development.
>
> Russia suffers from an underdevelopment of capitalism. A bourgeois revolution was more beneficial to the working class than to the bourgeoisie.
>
> The broader, the more decisive and consistent the bourgeois revolution the more certain the struggle of the proletariat against the bourgeoisie for Socialism.

In the same pamphlet Lenin declared that a Provisional Government was a necessary preliminary to the establishment of a democratic republic; its duty would be to institute the widest political freedom and convene a Constituent Assembly, based on universal suffrage. 'The establishment of a democratic republic is possible only as the result of a successful popular armed uprising, whose organ will be a provisional revolutionary government', he wrote.

The complete and immediate emancipation of the working classes in Russia, he asserted, was impossible; attempting to carry out the maximum programme at the outset was irrational.

He wrote:

Only the most ignorant people can ignore the bourgeois character of the democratic revolution; only the most naïve optimists can forget how little as yet the masses of the workers are informed of the aims of Social-ism and the methods of achieving it.

We are all convinced that the emancipation of the workers can be achieved only by the workers themselves. A socialist revolution is out of the question unless the working class becomes class conscious and or-ganized, trained and educated in open class struggle. To the anarchists who object that we are delaying the socialist revolution we reply: we are not delaying it, but are making the first step towards Socialism the only possible and correct way; namely, through a democratic republic.

He who wishes to proceed to Socialism by any path other than political democracy must inevitably arrive at absurd and reactionary conclusions, both in the political and economic sense.[17]

Twelve years later Lenin was to amend these views considerably. The 'dictatorship of workers and peasants' which Lenin preached in 1905 was not intended by him to be socialist in character, but a 'bourgeois democratic dictatorship'.

'It will be able', he maintained, 'to effect the redistribution of land, to carry out a thorough and consistent democratization, es-tablish a republic, eradicate all the Asiatic features of our rural and factory life, take the first steps towards improving the conditions of the workers, raise their standard of living, and, last but not least, spread the revolutionary flame to Europe. Such a victory will not in the least contribute to turning our bourgeois revolu-tion into a socialist revolution. The democratic revolution will at no time overstep the limits of bourgeois social-economic relations.'

At the same time Lenin gave notice that when the revolution came the victors would take merciless revenge on absolutism: 'The Bolsheviks, the Jacobins of the Russian revolution, expect

. . . workers and peasants to settle their accounts with the monarchy and aristocracy in the "plebeian manner", ruthlessly destroying all the enemies of freedom, suppressing their propaganda by force, and refusing to make any compromise with the accursed heritage of slavery, Asiatic cruelty, and the disgrace of mankind.'[18]

While theorizing about the future, Lenin did not neglect the realities of the present.

After the dissolution of the Duma, the Bolshevik Centre, headed by Lenin, Leonid Krassin and A. A. Bogdanov, continued to work for an armed uprising. Krassin, a revolutionist since 1887 and a member of the Central Committee since the Second Congress, had organized a secret printing plant in Baku and had wise contacts in the upper crust of society. As a friend of Maxim Gorky, he came in contact in 1903 with Sava Morozov, a Moscow millionaire textile manufacturer who dabbled in radicalism. While acting as Lenin's 'finance minister' Krassin approached Morozov for a loan, beginning by expounding on Lenin's virtues as a radical leader. Morozov cut him short: 'I know all about that; I agree; Lenin is a man of vision. How much does he want?'

'As much as possible,' replied Krassin.

'My personal yearly income,' replied Morozov, 'is about 60,000 rubles. A third of it goes for petty things, scholarships and the like. Shall we say 1,000 rubles a month?'[19]

When Morozov committed suicide in 1905, he left a large legacy to Gorky's wife for the use of the Bolshevik Party. The following year Krassin arranged a profitable American tour for Gorky, which raised considerable additional funds for the Party. Years later, Gorky testified that 'in the period from 1901 to 1917, hundreds of thousands of rubles passed through my hands for the cause of the Russian Social Democratic party. Of these sums, my personal contribution can be counted in tens of thousands, but all the rest was scooped out of the pockets of the 'bourgeoisie'. *Iskra* was published on the funds provided by Sava Morozov, who of course gave rather than lent the money. I could name a good dozen respectable people – "bourgeois" all of them – who materially helped the growth of the Social Democratic party. V. I. Lenin and other old party workers know this full well.'

In addition to helping Gorky raise funds, Krassin personally supervised the underground ammunition plants set up by the

Bolsheviks, and assisted his close friend 'Papasha', later known as Maxim Litvinov, in smuggling arms from the Balkans.[20]

To forestall a reactionary victory in the election campaign for the Second Duma, the Mensheviks wanted to fuse with local liberal candidates in districts where reactionary candidates appeared likely to win. Most of the Socialist Revolutionaries, Trudoviks and Cadets also favoured agreement among the parties of the Left and centre to defeat candidates of the Black Hundreds.

This question proved troublesome to the newly reunited Social Democratic ranks. While approved in principle, it was still to be decided on what scale such agreements were to be concluded. To settle this issue, a conference of the Social Democratic organization of St Petersburg was called early in January 1907. Led by Lenin, the Bolsheviks insisted that the main business on hand was to define the position of the Mensheviks on the issue of fusion. Feeling insecure, the Mensheviks tried to eliminate this from the agenda. When a clash arose between the forty-two Bolshevik delegates and the thirty-one Menshevik representatives over the question of mandates, the Mensheviks withdrew from the conference.

The remaining delegates heard Lenin advocate a policy of complete independence in the elections. To the young Bolsheviks his appeal was in complete accord with their slogans of 'armed uprising' and 'dictatorship of the proletariat and peasantry'. A small group headed by Vladimir Woytinsky, however, argued that the Bolsheviks should fuse on a limited scale with the parties to the left of the Cadets.

On the appearance of this unexpected opposition Lenin abruptly reversed himself. After fifteen minutes of speculation he suddenly advocated fusion slates. The delegates were so startled by this about-face that Lenin was forced to call a special caucus for the next day. The Bolshevik delegates crowded along the walls of a tiny room and huddled on the floor to hear Lenin explain his sudden change of heart.

Pointing out that the general aim of a 'dictatorship of the proletariat and the peasants' was unchanged, he declared that it could only be achieved when the concrete conditions necessary for its realization existed. Taking off his overcoat, he spoke of the 'dictatorship of the proletariat' as a slogan to be used when victory was near. Then, with a smile on his lips, he suddenly remarked: 'Look at me now, don't I look a victor?' This note of humour was unexpected. After a short discussion his proposal was unanimously adopted.[21]

Although it was Lenin who had reversed himself completely, he charged the Mensheviks with treason in his pamphlet, *On the Hypocrisy of the 31 Mensheviks*. The Menshevik leaders, said Lenin 'had sold out to the bourgeoisie'. The Mensheviks insisted that Lenin appear before a party tribunal on charges of slander. The trial took place in February 1907 under the chairmanship of Raphael Abramovich, then a member of the Central Committee of the Social Democratic Party. At the hearing Lenin admitted that he had slandered the Menshevik leaders but claimed that he was right in resorting to calumny, in order to discredit the Menshevik policies before the masses.

Lenin explained that he understood the difference between honourable and dishonourable, friendly and hostile polemics. Although he could have said that in their desire to forestall a victory of the Black Hundreds the Mensheviks had entered into an election treaty with the Constitutional Democrats, he did not wish to use such a comradely tone. Thus he purposely wrote that the workers are being sold out, that their votes are being traded for a mere seat in the Duma:

I purposely chose that tone calculated to evoke in the hearer hatred, disgust, and contempt for the people who carry on such tactics. That tone, that formulation is not designed to convince, but to break the ranks, not to correct a mistake of the opponent but to annihilate him, to wipe him off the face of the earth. Indeed that approach evokes the worst thoughts and suspicions against the opponent, and, it is true, instead of convincing and correcting, introduces confusion into the ranks of the working class. It is not permissible to write about party comrades in a language that systematically sows hatred, repugnance, and contempt among the workers to those that think differently from us. It is *permissible* and it is *imperative* to write in such a language about an organization that split off. . . . I am told: 'You introduced confusion in the ranks of the working class.' My answer is: 'I purposely and calculatingly introduced confusion in the ranks of a part of the St Petersburg proletariat that followed the splitting Mensheviks and I will always act the same way during a split.'[22]

This incredibly frank statement of his methods was published many years later by the Soviet Government in Lenin's *Collected Works*.

Despite these internecine battles, the elections brought another defeat for the régime. Again the majority of the deputies were Liberals and Socialists. But in some districts members of the Black Hundreds were elected. They had not held a single seat in the First Duma.

The Social Democrats and Socialist Revolutionaries each elected some sixty deputies and there was a large group of Trudoviks. Of the Social Democratic delegation the large majority were Mensheviks.

Again the government was faced with either acceding to the popular demand for broad reforms or dissolving the Duma once more. Premier Stolypin began to look for an excuse to dissolve the Duma and the Bolsheviks furnished him with one. Lenin insisted that the deputies use their parliamentary immunity to agitate for an armed uprising. Unless they used their parliamentary status to organize a revolt, they were useless, he said. The Bolshevik Centre began organizing delegations of soldiers and sailors who demanded that the Duma start 'real work'. These delegations, organized by Duma deputies together with their secret revolutionary military groups, attempted to show that the people were demanding 'deeds' instead of speeches.

Years later it was discovered that these secret Bolshevik cells were infested with agents of the secret police. By keeping a sharp eye on the Social Democratic deputies, these stool pigeons were able to frame the deputies on the charges of inciting rebellion, thus giving Stolypin his excuse.

A woman agent named Shornikova, planted by the Okhrana in the Social Democratic military organization, confessed: 'I met every member of the Central Committee then in St Petersburg, and all the members of the military organization; I knew all the secret meeting places and passwords of the revolutionary army cells throughout Russia. I kept the archives of the revolutionary organization in the Army; I was present at all the district meetings, propaganda rallies, and party conferences; I was always in the know. All the information I gathered was conscientiously reported to the Okhrana.'[23]

At the next Party Congress, called in London in April 1907, Lenin won control of the Central Committee. The sessions, lasting a month, were attended by representatives of the Mensheviks, Bolsheviks, Jewish Socialist Bund, Polish, Latvian and Lithuanian Social Democratic parties. All the leading lights were present, including Lenin, Plekhanov, Axelrod, Martov, Potresov, Trotsky, Bogdanov, Krassin, Rosa Luxemburg, Irakli Tseretelli and Maxim Gorky. In addition, the Congress included many who were to be famous in the years to come: Zinoviev and Kamenev, who played leading roles in the early years of the Soviet régime; Tomsky, the future leader of Soviet trade unions; Yaroslavsky, chief of the militant atheists; Voroshilov, head of the Soviet Army; David Zaslavsky, Moscow's top propagandist; Fuerstenberg-Ganetsky, who figured so significantly in the events of 1917; and Stalin.

Shortly after the Social Democratic Duma deputies returned to Russia from London, the military organization of St Petersburg decided to make demands on them through a delegation of soldiers. Madame Shornikova, the Okhrana agent, took part in the drafting of the resolution. While the police could have arrested the members of the military organization at will, their object was to establish collusion with the Social Democratic deputies. All the threads of this frame-up led directly to Premier Stolypin, who saw the text of the resolution before it reached the Social Democratic deputies. Shornikova had made two copies, leaving one with the military organization and sending the other to the secret police.

No sooner did the delegation present the resolution than gendarmes appeared. Their search for the document, however, was fruitless. A deputy placed it in his portfolio and since the police had no right to search him, the whole frame-up was in danger of collapse. The police, however, used the copy of the resolution forwarded by Shornikova, and submitted it as evidence at the trial of the Social Democratic deputies. The deputies were charged with high treason, and on 16 June 1907, the Duma was dissolved. Tseretelli and the majority of the Social Democratic deputies were sentenced to hard labour in Siberia. The Party belonged to the Bolsheviks.[24]

Did Lenin in this period believe in the possible success of an armed uprising? According to Lepeshinsky, Lenin, in the summer of 1906, forecast defeat for the revolution and stressed the need of preparing for strategic retreat. Nevertheless, he urged sustaining the 'revolutionary mood' of the workers because he thought such a mood never did any harm. If there was any chance to score a half-victory, according to Lenin, it was only by arousing the revolutionary instinct of the masses. If, on the other hand, retreat was inevitable, then at least it could be executed in military fashion, to frighten the forces of reaction.[25]

Madame Krzhizhanovskaya, however, claims that Lenin still expected a successful armed uprising, despite the Moscow fiasco in December 1905. Lenin, she asserts, hoped that the peasants would come to the rescue of the workers and that a new revolutionary wave would sweep the country. To lead the revolting peasants, Lenin proposed setting up trained units of five to ten determined men. He expected widespread peasant disturbances to begin in the fall of 1906. But the peasants failed to rise.[26]

After the Shornikova affair, life for Lenin in St Petersburg became hazardous. Wanted by the police, he was forced to meet his wife in the Vienna Restaurant, where they would sit in silence, afraid to talk to each other. Finally they would leave, take a cab to an hotel, engage a private room, and order supper.

When he fled one night as the police were closing in he was unable to inform Krupskaya. While she kept an all-night vigil for her husband, who was supposed to be attending a meeting, Lenin made good his flight to Finland.

On 10 July 1907, he wrote his mother: 'I have returned here dreadfully tired. Now I am a little rested. Resting here is wonderful. Bathing, walking, solitude, and complete relaxation are better for me than anything else. I hope to spend two weeks more here and then return to work.'

It was in Finland that Lenin began to develop the headaches and insomnia which were to torture him intermittently for the rest of his life. Immediately after breakfast he would write for five or six hours without a break. Late at night he took long walks in an effort to tire himself to sleep. He arose late and morose after one of his sleepless nights.

Occasionally he would visit friends near by: the Krassins, the Bogdanovs, or Gregory Alexinsky, leader of the Bolsheviks in the Second Duma who had escaped the police, and his wife Tatyana.

Remaining in Finland was dangerous. With the police searching for him, he was forced to attempt escape to Stockholm. To board ship at the port of Abo was to invite certain arrest. Lenin therefore decided to cross the ice at night to a gulf island, where he would board a waiting vessel. Accompanied by two Finnish peasants, who acted as guides, he made his way at night along the ice towards the island. Suddenly the ice began to give way under their feet. They barely made the opposite shore. Lenin later recalled that when he heard the ice cracking one thought flashed through his mind:

'What a silly way to die.'[27]

Chapter 6
The Lower Depths

Lenin now faced perhaps the most difficult period of his career. The revolution had, for the time, spent itself, and prospects ahead were not bright. His capture of the party machinery had given him control of the Central Committee, but his majority was precarious, depending on the support of the Polish and Lettish factions. Moreover, the London Congress had voted to dissolve all party fighting units and strong-arm squads (*boyeviki*) and prohibited the raising of party funds by armed robberies, known as 'expropriations'.

Lenin had no intention of disbanding the Bolshevik fighting units and 'expropriation' squads. More than ever he needed large sums of money to carry on under unfavourable conditions until there was a new upward surge of revolutionary feeling among the masses. To keep the Bolshevik movement alive and vigorous required desperate measures. He could not allow squeamish men such as Plekhanov and Martov to tie his hands. The Bolshevik Centre had to be maintained at all costs – and money had to be raised by any possible means.

By mid-1907 Lenin abandoned hope for an imminent armed uprising and called on his comrades in Russia to participate in the elections for the Third Duma. But the raids of his strong-arm men continued. The money went into the private Bolshevik treasury to build up the strength of his faction in the key centres of Russia.

From the London Congress until 1910 the Bolshevik Centre subsidized the Bolshevik-controlled St Petersburg Committee of the Party to the extent of one thousand rubles a month and gave the Moscow Committee five hundred rubles a month – this at a time when the visible income of the United Central Committee did not exceed one hundred rubles a month.

Lenin secured these large sums from a number of sources. For many years Maxim Gorky supported Lenin with donations. Garin-Mikhailovsky, another writer and wealthy engineer, gave Lenin tens of thousands of rubles. This was in addition to the 12,000-rubles-a-year subsidy given to the Bolsheviks by Sava Morozov, the Moscow millionaire.

But these were not the main sources of income. The armed hold-ups of the Bolshevik *boyeviki* provided much more. The largest of these robberies was staged in Tiflis in June 1907.

At ten-thirty on the morning of 26 June 1907, the Tiflis post office received a large consignment of cash for the local branch of the State Bank. Soviet historians maintain the sum was 250,000 rubles; the Russian press then placed the figure at 341,000 rubles. Officials of the bank loaded the sacks into a stage-coach and proceeded under armed escort towards the bank, followed by a coach filled with soldiers. Both vehicles were escorted by a phalanx of armed Cossacks. As the convoy approached the heart of the city, a bomb was hurled into the street from the roof of a near-by house. It exploded with such force that window-panes within the radius of a mile were shattered. Simultaneously bombs were hurled from the street at the Cossacks, while seemingly innocent pedestrians opened fire with revolvers. The sacks of money vanished.

At the inquiry no one could say what had become of the cash. Eye-witnesses declared that the first bomb had hurled the treasurer and his accountant into the street. By some miracle the coach remained undamaged, but the terrified horses dashed madly away. A tall passer-by caught up with the stage-coach and hurled a bomb under the horses' legs. In the explosion that followed everything seemed to vanish in a cloud of smoke. One witness testified that a man dressed in an officer's uniform rode by in a carriage, stopped before the demolished coach, snatched something from inside, and escaped, firing in all directions. Scores were killed and wounded in the Tiflis robbery.

Months later a number of prominent Bolsheviks were arrested in Berlin, Munich and Paris, when they attempted to exchange five-hundred-ruble notes bearing the serial number of the money consigned to the Tiflis bank. The numbers had been broadcast abroad. In January 1908 a woman was arrested in Munich when she tried to change one of these bills. At about the same time Maxim Litvinov was arrested in Paris with twelve bills in his possession.

All those discovered with the incriminating bank-notes in their possession were arrested, but the French and German Governments refused to turn them over to the Russian authorities.

Further investigation of the Tiflis hold-up revealed that Bolshevik agents had trailed the bank convoy from St Petersburg to Tiflis;

that two women had shadowed the treasurer and given the signal
to men waiting in a restaurant. Leonid Krassin had supplied the
boyeviki with necessary bombs. The man dressed in an officer's
uniform was Ter-Petrosian, better known as Kamo. The money
seized in the 'expropriation' went to Lenin for party use.[1]

✕   The nucleus of the Caucasus strong-arm squad consisted of
seven persons, two of whom were women. Their leaders were
Kamo, Lomidze and Tzintsadze. Kamo's superior, as Lenin's
deputy in the Caucasus, was 'Comrade Koba', also known as
Joseph Djugashvili, and later as Stalin. Kamo was the field commander of these operations; Stalin represented Lenin's supreme
headquarters.

Since the London Congress of the Social Democratic Party had
outlawed these strong-arm tactics, the members of the Caucasian
boyeviki group, as well as Stalin, were expelled from the Party.[2]

The adulation of the Caucasian partisans for Lenin was fostered by Stalin and other Bolshevik delegates from the Caucasus,
who returned from the Stockholm and London Congresses with
word that Lenin personified the revolution; his word was law.

When Lomidze's comrades advised him to retire to his native
village for a rest, he answered he could not do so before he had
achieved the ambition of his life – to stage a 200,000 ruble robbery and to present the loot to Lenin with the words: 'Do with this
as you will.'

After the great Tiflis coup Lomidze went to St Petersburg *en
route* to Finland to see Lenin. He had accomplished his mission. At
the railway station in St Petersburg, however, someone betrayed
him, and he was arrested and exiled.

Kamo himself was forced to flee to Berlin. There he concocted
a plan for breaking into the home of the banker Mendelssohn,
murdering him, and carrying off his fortune. Kamo assumed
the Mendelssohn would have several million marks in his possession. This plot never materialized. Soon after his arrival in Berlin,
the vigilant Prussian police discovered a valise filled with explosives
and an infernal machine in Kamo's possession and arrested him.
Inasmuch as the Tiflis hold-up was regarded by the German
authorities as an ordinary crime, Kamo faced extradition and
probable execution. Kamo spoke no German and, as an Armenian,
pretended to understand very little Russian. Questioning him was

very difficult. The German Social Democratic Party retained a well-known Socialist lawyer as his counsel. Krassin, then employed in Berlin as an engineer, advised Kamo to simulate madness.

Kamo took his advice and, three weeks before the trial, began to play insane. For the next four years, with incredible stamina and will-power, he played the role of a violent maniac.

On the first day of his 'illness' Kamo screamed, tore his clothes, threw his food on the floor, and attacked the attendants. He was transferred to a freezing underground cell, where for nine days he was confined entirely naked. Then he was returned to his original cell. Permitted to see his attorney, he cleverly conveyed to him that he was quite normal.

At his trial in November 1907 Kamo continued to behave like a madman. The court ordered him removed to the prison psychopathic ward for observation. For four months he spent day and night on his feet, never lying down. To rest himself, he would stand in a corner, facing the wall, and in turn lift up one foot and then the other.

Later he went on a hunger strike. Fed forcibly, some of his teeth were broken in the process. His ingenuity was inexhaustible. At one stage he pulled out half of his hair and arranged it carefully in small mats on a blanket. Once he pretended to attempt hanging himself as a means of attracting the attention of the guards. So perfect was his performance that he was never suspected of dissimulation.[3]

Shortly before the Tiflis robbery the Prussian police discovered a Berlin storehouse filled with water-marked paper to be used for counterfeiting three-ruble notes. Several Bolsheviks were arrested.

This counterfeit press had been scheduled to operate in Finland, according to the plans of Lenin and Krassin. When the Russian mint officials who had promised their aid withdrew, however, the operation was transferred to Germany.

The German Social Democrats were furious because the paper to be used for counterfeiting had been shipped without their knowledge to the address of the Berlin *Vorwaerts*.

When Axelrod heard of the news, he wrote to Martov: 'If the affair is true, how can one remain in the same party with the Bolsheviks?'

And Plekhanov declared, 'The whole affair is so outrageous that it is really high time for us to break off all relations with the Bolsheviks.'[4]

Lenin was not greatly disturbed by the indignant protests of Axelrod and Plekhanov.

'When I see Social Democrats', he declared, 'announcing with pride and self-satisfaction that "we are no anarchists, no thieves, no brigands, we are above that, we reject the partisan struggle", then I ask myself – do these people understand what they are saying?'[5]

Nevertheless, many Bolsheviks demanded an investigation of the counterfeit plot. The Foreign Bureau of the Party appointed George Chicherin, later Soviet Foreign Commissar, to conduct the probe. Lenin was certain that all clues had been destroyed. Chicherin, however, showed photographs of leading Bolsheviks to the German manufacturer from whom the water-marked paper had been ordered. The latter identified Krassin as the man who had placed the order. Lenin, alarmed, induced the Central Committee to delegate the investigation to its Foreign Bureau. Here the Bolshevik majority buried the evidence.

Acting on Lenin's suggestion, the Bolshevik majority of the Central Committee also restored to good standing in the Party the Caucasian strong-arm men and Stalin. Moreover, they demanded that Martov be tried for appearing as a witness against the accused Bolsheviks at the party investigation.[6]

A memorial volume published in Moscow after Krassin's death proudly described how the plans for the 'expropriations' were formulated by Krassin and carried out by Kamo. When Krassin himself was arrested in Finland in 1907, Lenin was certain that the police of St Petersburg had enough evidence to hang him. But while the Bolsheviks were working on a scheme to spring Krassin, the latter was suddenly released without explanation. He left for Berlin, where he obtained a position with the electrical firm of Siemens-Schukert and also managed to cash in a batch of five-hundred ruble bills from the Tiflis haul by the chemical alteration of the serial numbers.

No sooner had the Krassin scandal died down when the Party was again thrown into an uproar by the Comrade Victor affair. Victor, whose real name was Taratuta, was admitted to the Bolshevik Centre, although for three years he had been under suspicion as an Okhrana informer. But no investigation was made, and Victor's undertakings remained a secret from all but a handful of Bolshevik leaders. When these charges were levelled against Victor in the *Proletari* by Bogdanov, an investigation was finally ordered, but the findings were never made public. Although Victor had not been publicly exonerated, the Bolsheviks at the London Congress named him a member of the Central Committee of the Social Democratic Party, head of the important Foreign Bureau, as well as Financial Director of the Bolshevik Centre. In this last capacity, Victor soon displayed remarkable talents.

A Moscow manufacturer named Schmidt had bequeathed a large sum of money to the Social Democratic Party. Differences arose as to who, specifically, was entitled to the money. Lenin demanded that the money go to the Bolshevik Centre rather than to the Central Committee of the united party. The executor, however, insisted that the Central Committee was the only recognized party centre. A conference was called between the members of the Bolshevik Centre – all of whom were also members of the Central Committee – and the executor and family heirs. Here the executor complained that Victor had tried to extort the money from him for the Bolshevik Centre. The Bolshevik leaders promised to defer decision until the estate was fully settled and to investigate Victor's action.

The Menshevik and Bund members of the Central Committee knew nothing of the whole affair until much later, when the question was raised by chance at the Central Committee meeting. The Bolsheviks replied that since the estate was not yet settled, the matter should remain quiet 'for reasons of conspiracy'.

A year later it was discovered that Victor had already handed over a large part of the legacy to the Bolshevik Centre; that during the settlement negotiations with Schmidt's direct heirs, Victor and other members of the Bolshevik Centre had warned Schmidt's relatives that the Caucasian strong-arm men would handle them if they contested the will.

But the Schmidt affair really went back further. Schmidt, his brother, and two sisters had inherited a furniture factory in Moscow. In January 1905, when his workers went on strike, Schmidt granted their demands and suggested that they persuade workers in other factories to follow their example. He also invested a large

sum for a school in his factory and planned to make his men share-
holders in the plant.

During the Moscow insurrection of December 1905 Bolshevik
rebels barricaded themselves in the factory, whereupon the building was destroyed by artillery fire. Schmidt was arrested and jailed.
After a year in prison he hanged himself. Before his death he willed
most of his estate to the Social Democratic Party. His sisters, although they had Bolshevik sympathies, tried to delay the transfer
of the money. When Lenin, then in Switzerland, discovered what
was going on, he sent a Bolshevik named Andrekanis to Moscow
with instructions to convince one of the sisters to relinquish her
share to the Bolshevik Centre. Andrekanis persuaded one of them,
Catherine, to marry him. After the marriage, however, he did not
deliver the money until his Bolshevik comrades threatened to kill
him. The Bolshevik Centre finally collected 100,000 rubles on this
transaction.

Lenin then sent Victor to get his hands on the other sister's
share. Victor followed Andrekanis's example. He married the
other girl, Elizabeth, but the money did not reach the Bolshevik
coffers. Bogdanov, Lunacharsky and other Bolshevik leaders again
charged that Victor was a Tsarist spy. But Lenin stood by Victor,
refusing at first to have him tried. A Party court was finally convened and Vladimir Burtzev, the great nemesis of *agents provocateurs*, was called in as an investigator. When Victor walked
into Burtzev's office to be interrogated, he was followed by Kamo.
The Georgian tried to convince Burtzev that he was wasting his
time on a stool pigeon, and pulled out a knife with which he proposed to slit Victor's throat at once. Burtzev dissuaded him with
some difficulty. But Kamo said he would wait outside and stab
Victor as soon as he emerged. Finally, Burtzev convinced him that
although Victor was certainly a scoundrel, there was no proof he
was a stool-pigeon.

The court found no proof of Comrade Victor's guilt, but ruled
he was unfit to engage in party activities. He was dropped from the
party organizations.[7]

That should have been the end of Victor's political career. But
it wasn't. After the Bolshevik Revolution, Victor was back in
Lenin's favour. Under his real name, Taratuta, he became Moscow's representative of the Communist International in France.

Later he was given a high post in the Soviet Supreme Economic Council. When he died in the twenties, the Soviet press said very little about him. A review of Comrade Victor's career would have been too embarrassing.

Still another source of income for the Bolshevik Centre came from the Lbov gang. In 1907 a notorious band of brigands known throughout Russia as the *Lbovtsy*, after their leader Lbov, were operating in the Ural Mountains. They agreed to purchase from the Bolshevik-controlled Military Technical Bureau attached to the Party Central Committee several hundred thousand dollars' worth of arms. The Lbovtsy paid in advance. As usual, non-Bolshevik members of the Central Committee were kept in the dark, although the agreement was drawn up on its official stationery. The money went to the Bolshevik Centre which, however, failed to deliver the arms to the Ural gang.

The whole affair was exposed when Sasha, one of the bandits, fled to Paris to escape the hangman's noose. He published an open letter accusing the Bolshevik Centre of double-crossing his underworld associates. Lenin's paper, *Proletari*, indignantly maintained that there was no grain of truth in Sasha's accusation. Sasha thereupon appealed to the Central Committee of the Social Democratic Party. After a thorough investigation, which included questioning members of the Bolshevik Centre, it was established that Sasha's facts were correct.

A little later the Geneva Bolsheviks charged that one of their comrades, Gertsik, was a spy. A Party court found no evidence against the man, but expelled him because of his questionable moral character. After the verdict, the 'Circle of Bolshevik Idealists' published a statement restating the charge against Gertsik. The latter then approached Lenin, threatening to expose the whole truth of the Tiflis robbery unless the charge was withdrawn. Thereupon, the Foreign Bureau of the Central Committee issued a statement warning its members against dealing with Gertsik as a spy. He then appealed to the International Socialist Bureau. Vladimir Burtzev stated that there was absolutely no evidence to support the accusation. At the meeting of the Social Democratic Central Committee it was shown that the Foreign Bureau's announcement was spurious. Lenin himself admitted that it had been issued by Victor at his behest in order to silence Gertsik.

'Revolution is a difficult matter. It cannot be made with gloves or manicured nails', Lenin often told Vladimir Woytinsky. 'A party is no girls' dormitory; party members should not be measured by the narrow standards of petty bourgeois morality. Sometimes a scoundrel is useful to our party precisely because he is a scoundrel.'

Lenin replied ironically to complaints made against the conduct of a Bolshevik with a quotation from Gogol's *Inspector General*: 'In a good household even the sweepings are sometimes useful.'

Stanislav Volsky, a prominent old Bolshevik who later edited Maxim Gorky's Petrograd newspaper, was one of those surprised when Lenin nominated Victor, despite his reputation, for the Central Committee at the London Party Congress of 1907. Lenin shrugged off these reproaches by saying, quite simply: 'A Central Committee to be effective must be made up of gifted writers, able organizers, and a few intelligent scoundrels. I recommended Comrade X [Victor] as an intelligent scoundrel.'

When Professor Rozhkov, an early Bolshevik leader, remarked that everybody knew Victor to be a scoundrel, Lenin laughed. 'That is exactly why he is useful to us. Precisely because he will stop at nothing. Now tell me frankly, would you consent to be a gigolo? To live with a Moscow heiress for her money? You would not! Neither could I bring myself to do it. But Victor did, and therefore he is a very useful man who cannot be replaced.'[8]

His opinion of many close associates who were to play a much larger role in Soviet history was no better. Of Lunacharsky, the future Soviet Commissar of Education, Lenin said in 1912: 'From his convictions and literary tastes, it is obvious that he is simply a *poseur*. I say candidly, he is a filthy type, a drunkard and profligate. His eyes are fixed on heaven, while his feet searchingly shuffle along the ground. He is a moral gigolo.'

Concerning Maxim Litvinov, Lenin declared: 'He is consistent and firm. But these are the qualities of good speculators and gamblers. They are the virtues of a clever and adroit Jew. Litvinov will never develop into a great man of action. He will always chase after millions, but will lose himself on the road for the sake of a quarter.'[9]

Nevertheless, Lenin's total disregard of 'bourgeois prejudices' as evidenced by his support of Comrade Victor, the counterfeiting scheme, and the continued underworld exploits of the Caucasian *boyeviki* boomeranged. A wave of desertions from the Bolsevikh Centre included some of its leading writers and theoreticians, among them Maxim Gorky, Bogdanov, Lunacharsky, Professor Rozhkov, Alexinsky, Professor Pokrovsky and Stanislav Volsky. These men indicted Lenin for disregarding the majority will of his own faction, for illegal seizure of party funds and the party press and for seeking to suppress all independent opinion. Krassin, who had helped organize some of the shadier activities of the Bolshevik Centre, also deserted Lenin for reasons of his own. In later years some of these men were to return to the Bolshevik camp, but in 1908 Lenin stood almost alone. The two leading Bolsheviks who remained firmly at Lenin's side throughout this crisis were Gregory Zinoviev and Leo Kamenev – both of whom were to be executed by Stalin in 1936.

In Russia itself former professional revolutionists and students alike were losing their faith and enthusiasm. Under the firm hand of Premier Stolypin, who was the ablest reactionary statesman to win the Tsar's confidence, the revolutionary tide was halted. With a revised election law imposing new class restrictions on suffrage, the Third Duma was far more conservative than its predecessors. And under Stolypin's iron-handed guidance, revolutionary and terrorist action was suppressed with ruthless efficiency. Intellectuals and workers alike deserted the revolutionary ranks. In this phase of general disillusionment some took refuge in science, religion and philosophy; others abandoned revolutionary asceticism for unbridled debauchery; many committed suicide. The revolutionary circles which had shone so brightly a few years earlier gave way to 'leagues of suicide', 'leagues of love', and other forms of cynical escape.

Back in Geneva, Lenin found it difficult to accustom himself again to the life of an *émigré*. 'All day', wrote Krupskaya, 'Vladimir Ilyich sat in the library, but in the evening we did not know what to do with ourselves. It was difficult to sit in our uncomfortable, cold room. We longed for the company of human beings. Nearly every day we either went to the cinema or the theatre, although we seldom sat through to the end.'[10]

Lenin occupied himself with editing various Bolshevik publications, especially the newspaper *Proletari*, but he was discontented with his existence.

'It's several days since we've landed in this damned hole,' he wrote to his sister Maria on 14 January 1908, 'but we can't help ourselves. We will have to get used to it. How are all doing? Are you freezing? Is Mother well? Please kiss her for me.'

He wrote his mother a week later:

We are getting acclimated by degrees and will get settled no worse than before. Soon after my arrival here I received a letter from Gorky asking me to visit him in Capri. Nadya and I had no other thought than to accept and take the trip to Italy. (In Capri narcissus are *now* blooming, according to Gorky.) But not now. I must organize matters first, and after that we'll take a pleasure trip.[11]

Walking one day along the deserted streets of Geneva in this period of doubt and pessimism, he remarked to his wife: 'I feel as if I have come here to be buried.'

In Switzerland, Lenin again met Elizabeth K. She lived not far from Geneva, and Lenin often visited her by bicycle. He always carried a spare piece of rubber from old overshoes with which to repair possible punctures in his tyres. 'This rubber,' he declared proudly, 'I have brought all the way from St Petersburg.' Sometimes he brought along a tiny chessboard to teach her the game, but she made little progress. With some impatience Lenin remarked, 'I have yet to meet a single woman who can do these three things: understand Marx, play chess or read a railroad timetable.'

In the autumn of 1909 Lenin moved to Paris, where he was to spend probably the most difficult years of his exile. He always recalled this period morbidly; the devil himself, he said, had brought him to Paris. The Lenins rented a four-room flat on the outskirts of the city. The rooms were large and light, with mirrors over the mantels. One room was for Krupskaya's mother, another for Lenin's sister Maria who was studying in Paris, a third for the Lenins, the fourth a sitting room. The spacious apartment scarcely harmonized with the shabby furniture they had brought from Switzerland. Krupskaya had to have gas installed and attend to other household details which were unnecessary in Geneva. Books could not be borrowed from the library without the landlord's endorsement, and their apparent poverty made him hesitate. The Bibliothèque Nationale was a considerable distance off and Lenin was forced to travel there by bicycle. Once he fell in the path of a motor-car, barely escaping serious injury. In the end his bicycle was stolen. He usually left it on the stairs of a house near the library, in charge of the concierge, whom he paid ten centimes for the service. The concierge claimed she had furnished parking space but had not undertaken to guard the bicycle.

There was much red tape getting a book too. And the library closed during the luncheon period. Lenin was forever cursing the Bibliothèque Nationale and Paris. He tried other libraries, but found them inadequate.

His sister's attack of appendicitis did not help matters. To his brother Dmitri in Russia he wrote:

Sister Maniusha has already written you about her illness. I want your advice. The doctors have found an inflammation of the appendix. I consulted a good local surgeon and he advises an operation. It is said that the operation is not too serious and brings a cure. This surgeon is praised by all. He recently operated on one of my wife's friends. . . . Excellent! Only one teaspoon of blood. In eight days she left her bed. . . . I beg you to answer me at once. I am inclined to favour an operation, but without your advice I am afraid to decide. Reply immediately. That the operation will be well done there is no doubt. . . .

I am not writing of this to Mother, because I do not wish to worry her needlessly. There is no danger. Maniusha is not even confined to bed all the time. I'm not writing to Aniuta either, since the letter might fall into Mama's hands. I am waiting for an answer. The advice here is to operate quickly. What do you think?[12]

A month later he wrote to his mother:

You concern yourself endlessly about Maniusha. She is recovering splendidly. She cannot walk about much yet. The operation left her with a slight pain in her right leg. . . . In the three weeks of our stay here she has improved greatly. I urge her to drink lots of milk and eat sour milk. She prepares the sour milk herself, but I don't think she eats enough, and because of that we fight continually. The rooms here are fine and the food is good and reasonable. (Ten francs a day for all four of us.) Nadya and I ride continually on our bicycles. I embrace you, dear, and wish you health.

Lenin's concern for his mother and other members of his family is constantly revealed in his letters. They are filled with personal inquiries. 'I am very uneasy,' he wrote to his mother, 'because your quarters are cold. . . . Take care not to catch cold. . . . Perhaps you can do something . . . install a small iron stove?'

'Vladimir Ilyich', writes sister Maria, 'always wanted Mother to live with him, and invited her to stay with him on more than one occasion. But that was difficult because Mother always lived with those of her children who needed her help. . . . That is why she was able to see him abroad only twice and to spend only a short time with him.'

In 1910 the Lenins moved to the quiet rue Marie Rose, not far from the Boulevard Montparnasse, where they had two rooms whose windows faced a garden. Here Lenin began to work hard, and instituted a strict régime. At eight o'clock in the morning he rose and went to the Bibliothèque, returning about two. Then he worked at home, Krupskaya making certain his comrades disturbed him as little as possible.

The monotony of existence was broken in 1911 by the unexpected arrival of Kamo. In March 1909 German physicians had ruled that Kamo was fit to stand trial. Once more he was returned to prison, where he again simulated insanity. In April he was recommitted to the prison hospital. Here he perfected a new 'illness', pretending to suffer from a destruction of the sensitivity of the skin. So masterly was his performance that the doctors were fascinated. To test him, they pricked his skin with pins and burned him with hot irons. Kamo remained impervious to it all. The physicians concluded that his illness was authentic.

The hospital officials, however, insisted that Kamo be turned over to the Russian authorities, on the ground that the burden of supporting an alien madman should not fall on German taxpayers.

In October 1909 Kamo was delivered to the Russo-German frontier and turned over to Russian gendarmes. Brought to Tiflis to stand military trial, Kamo's execution as a terrorist seemed certain. But the entire liberal press of Europe came to Kamo's defence, following the publication of an article by Kamo's German attorney in the Berlin *Vorwaerts*. Both the German and Russian Governments were severely attacked by the French Socialist and Liberal press.

For tactical reasons, the Russian Government bowed to the protests. Premier Stolypin wrote to the Governor of the Caucasus: 'Should Mirsky [the name on Kamo's passport] be sentenced to death, the attacks of the press on the German Government will no doubt increase, and that, the Ministry of the Interior has reason to fear, might have a harmful effect on the solution of the question of the extradition of the anarchists.'

Accordingly Kamo was not sentenced to death. Instead, the court, accepting affidavits by Berlin specialists, found him incurably insane and committed him to the psychopathic ward of the Metekh fortress in Tiflis.

The prison doctor also came to the conclusion that Kamo was hopelessly insane and had him transferred to a mental hospital. He soon escaped from the hospital, stowed away on a ship bound for France, and finally arrived in Paris. Lenin at once took Kamo under his wing.

Madame K, who now lived in France, frequently saw Lenin. Once he arranged an appointment with her in a small square near the Bibliothèque Nationale. He came accompanied by a swarthy man with a rather frightening appearance. One eye twinkled brightly, the other seemed lifeless. Introducing him without giving his name, Lenin said: 'This is one of my good friends. It is necessary that he rest somewhere in a village for a few days. He must not see or be seen by anyone.' With this curt explanation Lenin departed and left Elizabeth alone with this strange individual.

Speaking Russian with a strong Caucasian accent, the man said, 'Would you care to have something to drink in a café? Then we'll go where you lead me.' He addressed her with the familiar Russian 'thou', much to her annoyance. But the Caucasian continued his friendly banter: 'Don't you want anything to drink?' When Elizabeth objected to his use of the familiar form, he replied: 'You're a comrade, aren't you? You aren't a bourgeois? That's the way I address every comrade.'

After they had had coffee in a neighbourhood café, they left for her home a few miles outside of Paris. As they rode in the train, he watched the peaceful French countryside roll by. 'Not worth a damn,' he commented contemptuously. 'No forests, no mountains, everything is flat and divided into little pieces with fences everywhere. How can they treat the soil this way? In my home, the

Caucasus, there are mountains, forests, and no fences. You can go where you please, while here there is nothing like it. A bourgeois country.'

Lenin's 'good friend' spent three days at Madame K's home. During this time he visited Paris once. When he returned he declared with his usual bluntness, 'No, you are not a spy of the Okhrana. Ilyich says he vouches for you. And I myself see it. You are perhaps a little bourgeois. But you are a good comrade. Thank you for sheltering me. If you ever come to us in Tiflis, I will hide you from the Okhrana. I will hide you so well that nobody will find you. You know, they kept me in prison and watched me day and night. Still I escaped, and they could not find me. It is a good thing that they did not, for they would have hanged me or sentenced me to hard labour for life. But they could never find Kamo, because Kamo is the biggest revolutionist in the entire Caucasus. Everybody in Tiflis will tell you that Kamo is a revolutionist and a Bolshevik without equal. They are hunting for me everywhere. In Berlin they once captured me. An *agent provocateur* betrayed me. If I ever find him, I'll cut his throat. The German police delivered me to the Okhrana. But I escaped.'

Elizabeth listened to this recital with evident scepticism. 'You don't believe me?' he continued. 'You see I have only one good eye. The other is damaged. I was wounded by the splinter of a bomb, because I am a revolutionist and a Bolshevik.' The next day he left for Paris.[13]

'Kamo', relates Krupskaya, 'asked me to buy him almonds. He would sit in our kitchen and living-room eating almonds as he had done at home and would tell us about his arrest in Berlin, about the way he had simulated insanity, about the sparrow he tamed in prison, etc. Ilyich would listen and feel extremely sorry for this exceedingly brave, childishly naïve, warm-hearted man, who was capable of performing heroic feats but did not know what work to take up. The proposals he made were fantastic.'

Lenin did not contradict him, but tried to bring him gently down to earth. It was finally decided that Kamo go to Belgium for an operation on his injured eye. From there he would go by sea to the Caucasus. As a parting gift, Lenin gave him the coat his mother had presented to him.[14]

Several months later Kamo returned to Russia to raise new funds for the Bolshevik Centre. He organized another robbery which cost seven people their lives. Kamo himself was captured by the Cossacks and brought to trial. Death by hanging seemed certain. But the district attorney, touched with compassion for the man whom he regarded as a misguided fanatic, decided to stay execution of the death sentence until the Tsar's coming amnesty manifesto on the tercentenary of the Romanov dynasty. As a result, Kamo's sentence was commuted to twenty years' hard labour.

Lenin remained stubborn in his resolve not to seek reconciliation with his opponents. At the Congress of the Socialist International in Copenhagen in the summer of 1910, where the differences dividing the various factions were sharply revealed, general animosity was concentrated chiefly against Lenin. 'He is one man against the whole Party. He is ruining the Party. How fortunate the Party would be if he disappeared, vanished, evaporated, died!' were the remarks Madame Krzhizhanovskaya heard on every side during meetings of the Russian section. When she asked one of Lenin's opponents how one man could ruin the entire Party, he replied: '*Because there is no other man who thinks and dreams of nothing but revolution – twenty-four hours a day.*'[15]

After Lenin's return from Copenhagen to Paris, he asked Madame K if she had any friends with children in St Petersburg. He needed the addresses, he said, in order to send toys to Russia. Then he gave her an address in Switzerland where she could secure the toys. Lenin explained that these gifts were for children of workers who belonged to the Party: they could not be sent to the workers directly without arousing suspicion. The workers would later call for the toys. Madame K was rather dubious, but asked no questions.

In Switzerland she called for the consignment of toys, consisting of small coloured blocks which, when put up together, made a composite picture of Swiss landscapes. She noticed, however, that the blocks were made of hollow cardboard. Her curiosity aroused, she opened one and found it contained three tissue-paper copies of Lenin's organ *Proletari*. The blocks had been manufactured for that purpose. When Madame K returned to Paris, she berated Lenin for the mission he had assigned to her, pointing out that she was exposing her St Petersburg friends to arrest for sedition.

'That is nothing,' Lenin calmly replied. 'In fact, it's even useful. It's in prison that one becomes a real revolutionist.'

'That may be,' she replied. 'But you should have told me.'

'You asked me for an opportunity to serve the party,' he said. 'Now you are discontented. What cowardice!'[16]

Madame K and Lenin met for the last time in Galicia in 1914, just before the outbreak of war. By that time he was deeply involved with another woman – Inessa Armand – whom he met in Paris in 1910, when he was forty and she thirty-six. Inessa, born Elizabeth de Herbenville in Paris, was the daughter of an actor and a musician who was taken to Russia at the age of six after her father's death. She was brought by her aunt, a French governess in the house of Eugène Armand, who owned a textile factory in Pushkino near Moscow. She married the manufacturer's son Alexander at the age of eighteen and bore him five children.

Upon reading Chernyshevsky's *What is to Be Done?*, Inessa began to model her life on that of its Utopian heroine. *Pravda* and *Izvestia* in May 1964 claimed that she joined the Bolshevik Party in 1903; but Vladimir Zenzinov, a Muscovite and Socialist Revolutionary leader, has testified that she belonged to his party as late as 1904. It was in that year that Inessa broke with her husband and went to Sweden to study feminism, and there that she read Lenin's *What Is to Be Done?* and, soon afterwards, became a Bolshevik. Sent on an organizing mission to Russia, she was arrested in January 1905, released in the amnesty of October 1905; arrested again in 1907, and exiled for two years to Archangel province. She escaped two months before the end of her term and fled abroad – first to Brussels, then to Paris where she studied at the Sorbonne and met Lenin.

Inessa often visited the Lenins' apartment and could be frequently seen with Lenin at his favourite café in the Avenue d'Orléans. In 1911–12 he paid her ever-growing attention; the French Socialist, Charles Rappoport, observed that he could not take his eyes off her (*'avec ses petits yeux mongols il épait toujours cette petite française'*).

'I saw Inessa Armand twice', Ekaterina Kuskova wrote in 1957. 'Beautiful, elegant – not comparable in any way with the dowdy Krupskaya. ... When the Bolshevik school for workers opened near Paris, Lenin made Armand give lectures to the workers – he always attended them. The former wife of a rich manufacturer, she did not at once get used to the "proletarian milieu". Krupskaya never attended these lectures. To all appearances they led a harmonious family life, all three of them. It was probably Krupskaya who suffered most. . . . Alexandra Kollontai, who was very close to Lenin for many years, has told us that Krupskaya was well aware of all that was going on. She knew that Lenin was very attached to Inessa and had offered many times to make herself scarce, but Lenin always replied : "Stay!" '

The revolutionary movement continued to lose ground in Russia. Police spies and *agents provocateurs* riddled its weakened ranks. The Bolshevik Centre, sending in new reinforcements to replace the men in prison and Siberia, tried to tie together the torn threads of the organization. Herculean efforts, powered by a single will, kept the skeleton of the Party alive.

But although 1910 was ebb-tide for revolutionary Socialism, Russia had moved forward considerably since 1905. Within the limits imposed by Stolypin there was more freedom of the press; from time to time Socialist periodicals appeared. When the censor banned a newspaper, it often reappeared under a different name the following day. Workers now exercised the right to organize trade unions and mutual aid associations. As long as these organizations stayed out of politics the régime did not interfere. When a union engaged in political propaganda, it was disbanded and its leaders were seized. Nevertheless, the workers found ways of making ample use of the right to organize.

The Mensheviks, realizing the potentialities of trade unionism, now devoted their main energies to this field. But Lenin regarded this new trend as a danger to the Social Democratic Party. He noted with alarm that workers were shying away from the underground and were less inclined to accept the leadership of the professional revolutionists. The Party was in danger of becoming an emasculated auxiliary of the legal trade-union movement. Lenin accused the Menshevik leaders in Russia of treason to the revolutionary cause, charging them with seeking to 'liquidate' the Social Democratic Party. The term 'liquidator' as used by Lenin in 1910 was intended to carry the same vituperation as 'counter-revolutionary' in later years.

As the trade-union movement grew in influence, however, Lenin launched a campaign to gain control of the strategic unions, while demanding that they be subordinated to the Party. One of the strongest labour organizations was the St Petersburg Metalworkers' Union.

In 1906 a worker named Roman Malinovsky was elected its general secretary. Malinovsky had come to the capital from Russian Poland where he had belonged to a Polish revolutionary organization. His intelligence and zeal, as well as his oratorical ability, had won for him the following of his fellow metalworkers. In 1909 Malinovsky was arrested and expelled from St Petersburg. He went to Moscow, where he joined the local Menshevik organization, but in April 1910 Malinovsky and a group of his comrades were arrested. He was soon released, although the Mensheviks seized with him remained in jail. His release aroused suspicion because all had been arrested for their revolutionary speeches at the same mass meeting and Malinovsky's oration had been the most inflammatory of all. A short time later Malinovsky joined the Bolshevik faction.

Soon thereafter came a wave of arrests among the Bolsheviks in Moscow. Among those rounded up was Nikolai Bukharin (destined to become one of the top Soviet hierarchs and to be executed by Stalin in 1938). Bukharin, then a member of the Moscow Committee of the Bolshevik Party, had distrusted Malinovsky from the start, despite the latter's assiduous attempts to win his confidence. For Bukharin had noticed several times that when he arranged a secret rendezvous with a party comrade, Okhrana agents would be waiting to pounce on him. In each case Malinovsky had known of the appointments and the men whom Bukharin was to meet had been arrested.

When Bukharin himself was finally seized he was convinced that Malinovsky had betrayed him in order to eliminate him from the Moscow Committee. In jail Bukharin met several Mensheviks who also suspected Malinovsky of being responsible for their arrest. But there were no conclusive facts. With Bukharin and other Bolshevik leaders out of the way, Malinovsky began a meteoric rise in the Party organization.

Despite the lull in revolutionary action, the labour movement was making impressive gains. Tsarism was still firmly in control, but the workers, rebounding from their great defeat of 1906 and 1907, staged effective strikes in St Petersburg, Moscow and a number of provincial cities. The tribune for the reviving labour movement was the Social Democratic delegation in the Third Duma. Soviet historians admit that these deputies, through their parliamentary speeches, contributed greatly towards stirring the Russian workers to resume the fight for their political and economic rights.

The split in the Social Democratic Party, however, continued to grow more irreconcilable. When the United Central Committee of the Party met in Paris in 1910, the Bolsheviks claimed control by virtue of their 1907 majority at the London Congress. But the Menshevik and Jewish Socialist Bund members refused to submit to Lenin's leadership.

The Bolshevik Centre, then headed by Lenin, Zinoviev and Kamenev, used the large funds at its disposal for overt as well as underground activity in Russia. Through his agents in Russia, Lenin founded a large weekly in St Petersburg called *Zvezda* (Star). The paper acquired added prestige when Plekhanov consented to contribute articles. The condition he laid down was that *Zvezda* represent all Social Democratic groups opposed to liquidating the underground Party organizations. The first issue appeared late in 1910, with the official support of the Social Democratic delegation in the Duma. The editorial board included one Duma deputy, one Bolshevik and one Plekhanovite Menshevik. The newspaper suspended publication in June 1911. When it reappeared in the fall, Plekhanov and the other non-Bolsheviks were out. *Zvezda* became Lenin's personal organ and its main contributors were Zinoviev, Kamenev and Krupskaya.[17]

Lenin was now forty years old, at the very prime of his powers, but the structure he had spent years to perfect was still quite feeble. The strain was telling. He looked worn, was harassed more than ever by headaches and insomnia, but continued to work with furious energy.

For recreation he sometimes went to the theatre but, as usual, seldom remained beyond the first act.

'The comrades', said Krupskaya, 'used to mock us for not getting our money's worth.' She recalls only one occasion when Lenin remained in his seat until the final curtain. This was a performance of Tolstoy's *The Living Corpse*. He found more pleasure in visiting the bistros and cabarets of the working-class districts, listening to husky-voiced performers sing proletarian songs, but, as always, his real relaxation came in strolling through the wooded suburbs of the city.

During the summer of 1911 Lenin lived with the Zinoviev family in the little village of Longjumeau outside of Paris. This was no vacation period. A Bolshevik Party school was set up and Lenin worked every day except Sunday, when he stubbornly refused to talk shop. Instead he drove his companions about on the handle-bars of his bicycle.

By the end of 1911 Lenin was occupied with new plans for gaining control of the Party machine, hoping to win a new Congress majority which would sanction his supremacy. In his own ranks there were still some who advocated reunion with the Mensheviks, and representatives of the two groups negotiated once more in Paris; but Lenin would have no part in these talks. To forestall the opposition, he sent his agents into Russia to mobilize a 'general party convention' of his sympathizers.

The conference of Bolsheviks was scheduled to open in Prague in January 1912. After Lenin had left for that city two Bolshevik delegates arrived in Paris on their way to Prague. One of them was Brendinsky, whose chief work was distributing illegal literature in Moscow. He had been arrested in Vilna just before his departure for western Europe but was released after ten days in prison. The other delegate told Krupskaya that during Brendinsky's imprisonment revolutionaries who had come to him for literature were also seized.

Krupskaya had received word that the Bolshevik publications were not being distributed in Moscow. When she asked Brendinsky to whom he delivered his literature in Moscow he became confused declaring that it went to workers. She asked for their names and addresses. His stumbling reply showed he was lying. Under further questioning, Brendinsky broke down. It was discovered that all the literature he received from abroad had gone directly to the Okhrana.

'I was very proud that I had protected the conference from a *provocateur*', said Krupskaya. 'But I did not know that there were two other spies there.'

Many years later the Great Soviet Encyclopedia in its account of the Prague Conference admitted that two of the thirteen voting delegates were Okhrana agents. (As a matter of fact, there were three.)[18]

Lenin's hand-picked delegates in Prague proclaimed that they represented the entire Social Democratic Party and denounced the 'liquidators' and other anti-Leninists. A Central Committee was elected consisting of Lenin, Zinoviev, Ordzhonikidze, Spandarian, Goloschokin, Schwartzman and – Malinovsky.

Malinovsky was appointed chief of the Russian Bureau of the Bolshevik Central Committee, with the right to add such new members to the Central Committee as he saw fit. Soon after his return to Russia, Malinovsky appointed Stalin, who had escaped from exile in the Vologda province in February 1912.

The Prague Conference put the final stamp on the division between the two factions. Thereafter the Bolshevik Party maintained a completely separate existence from the Mensheviks, except for their limited collaboration in the Duma. But this, too, was soon to end.

Lenin had told his sister Anna when she visited him in Paris a few months before, 'I do not know whether I'll live to see a revival of the Party.' But now he felt confident that the turning point had been reached.

Stalin, for the short time that he was free, played a leading role in reorganizing the Bolshevik cells in Russia. Living under the assumed name of Ivanov in a small St Petersburg hotel, he wrote to Lenin on 10 February 1912: 'Things are going rather well. I hope they will be going very well. The frame of mind of our crowd is reassuring.'

Less than two months later a political crisis shook the Russian Empire. It started with a strike by miners in the Lena goldfields of northern Siberia. When the miners' delegates were arrested, the men gathered in a throng to demand their release. Without warning troops opened fire on the strikers and hundreds were shot down. This was on 4 April 1912. A week later, when the news reached European Russia, it produced violent reverberations. In the course of a few days spontaneous strikes swept nearly all the great industrial cities of Russia; more than 215,000 workers walked out in protest. It was the greatest demonstration of unrest since the general strike of 1905. Arrests quickly followed. Stalin, who was working in the St Petersburg office of Lenin's weekly newspaper, was seized once more and exiled in the region of Narim in Siberia.

At about this time Burtzev charged that Dr Zhitomirsky, one of the leaders of the Foreign Bureau of the Bolshevik Party and a close friend of Lenin, was an *agent provocateur*. Greatly disturbed, Lenin ordered Malinovsky to investigate where Burtzev got his evidence. But Burtzev was suspicious of Malinovsky and refused to divulge any information to him. After the Revolution of 1917, when the State Police records were opened, it was disclosed that Dr Zhitomirsky had served as an Okhrana agent from 1902 to 1917.

The Prague conference had also decided to turn out a popular daily newspaper in St Petersburg to be called *Pravda*, and Malinovsky was entrusted with publishing it.

The Mensheviks, despite their large trade-union following, were not only unable to finance a daily newspaper, but even had trouble supporting their weekly. The Bolshevik Centre, however, drawing on the large funds obtained by armed expropriations, legacies and political marriages, was in a position to foot the bill. The first issue of *Pravda* appeared in May 1912, a few weeks after the protest strike that followed the Lena massacres. In this fresh current of revolutionary agitation, *Pravda*, as the only labour daily newspaper in Russia, gained a large circulation. It published stenographic accounts of Duma speeches by Socialist deputies, reported every important labour dispute, and carried letters and first-hand accounts from leading factories. For some time the paper carefully avoided controversy with other Socialist groups, thereby gaining a solid reputation among the workers of St Petersburg. Only after *Pravda* had gained considerable prestige and influence did Lenin begin to blast his Socialist opponents in its pages.

In July 1912 Lenin, Zinoviev and Kamenev moved from Paris to Cracow, Galicia. Their purpose was to be close to the Russian frontier in order to facilitate the editing of *Pravda* and the direction of Bolshevik action in Russia. The arrangements which permitted Lenin to live in Cracow were made with the Austrian Government by Fuerstenberg-Ganetsky, a man who was to appear many times in the crucial years ahead, when Lenin needed his services most.

Most of the *Pravda* editorials and policy articles were written by

Lenin, although in St Petersburg the publisher was Roman Malinovsky and the official editor was Chernomazov.[19]

In Pronino, not far from Cracow, the Lenins and Zinovievs for a time shared an apartment. Until noon, when the post arrived, Lenin remained in his study. Then his colleagues gathered to read the mail. On the basis of their discussion of the news from Russia, Lenin assigned articles for forthcoming issues of *Pravda*. All ate together in the kitchen. Dinner and supper nearly always consisted of soup and meat balls. After a short rest, Lenin would resume work, remaining at his desk until nine in the evening.

His own work finished, he collected and read the batch of articles that were to go to St Petersburg – his own was always ready first – then he took the outgoing mail to the post office.

In September 1913, Inessa Armand rejoined the Lenins. Sent to Russia on a Party assignment, she had been imprisoned for a year and released, at the request of her former husband, after developing signs of tuberculosis.

'We were terribly glad . . . at her arrival', writes Krupskaya. 'In the autumn, all of us became very close to Inessa. In her there was much ardour and joy of living. We had known Inessa in Paris, but there was a large colony there. In Cracow lived a small closely-knit circle of comrades. Inessa rented a room in the same family with which Kamenev lived. . . .

'Ilyich, Inessa and I often went on walks together. Zinoviev and Kamenev dubbed us the "hikers" party . . . Inessa was a good musician, urged us all to go to Beethoven concerts, and played many Beethoven pieces very well. Ilyich especially loved the "Pathétique" Sonata, constantly begging her to play it.'

But Inessa found life in Cracow unsatisfying. She decided to deliver a series of lectures abroad and then settle in Paris; Lenin, together with Malinovsky, came to Paris for a month that winter.

In Cracow Lenin renewed his favourite winter sport, ice skating. Another pastime was playing with Zinoviev's young son, Stepa. Lenin, always passionately fond of children, formed a particular attachment for the child. To Stepa's mother he revealed his sorrow at having no child of his own. 'What a pity we haven't a boy like Stepa,' he sighed. When Zinoviev would not allow him to adopt the child Lenin was disappointed. While Stepa was an infant, Lenin would gaze at him for a long time and ask why he was crying.

When Stepa began to walk and talk, Lenin became his playmate, crawling under the bed to get Stepa's ball, carrying the boy on his shoulders, racing with him, obeying his every wish. The two turned the house topsy-turvy in their play. If anyone tried to interrupt, Lenin would reply with mock gravity, 'Don't interfere; we're playing.' Even Stepa, however, had to retire when Lenin was working. As soon as he saw Lenin begin to write, he would quiet down.[20]

At this time Bukharin fled from exile, crossed the Russian frontier, and reached Lenin in Galicia. As soon as he arrived, he warned Lenin against Malinovsky. Lenin ordered Malinovsky to report to him in Pronino in order to meet Bukharin face to face. Bukharin sat waiting in a small room in Lenin's house. Malinovsky had not been told anything. When Malinovsky entered the room and saw Bukharin he was terrified.

'I had the impression', Bukharin later wrote, 'that he thought I would pounce upon him with a knife.' But when Lenin entered the room, and Malinovsky realized he was in no immediate danger, he recovered his poise, walked over to Bukharin with outstretched arms, and said: 'Ah, Nikolai. How did you get here?'

Despite Bukharin's suspicions, both Lenin and Zinoviev defended Malinovsky vigorously. They explained Malinovsky's swift conversion to Bolshevism on the ground that, as a real proletarian, he saw the harm the 'liquidators' were doing. The accusations against Malinovsky were malicious, they insisted. Bukharin was not convinced. In the meantime Malinovsky had become the leader of the Bolshevik organization in Russia. He was, in fact, Lenin's deputy inside Russia. He sat in the Fourth Duma as the leader of the Bolshevik faction of five deputies and as the vice-chairman of the combined Social Democratic delegation, headed by Nikolai Chkheidze, an old Menshevik from the Caucasus. In the previous three Dumas the Social Democratic delegation had voted and acted as a unit, and had built up wide popularity among the Russian masses. At the opening of the Fourth Duma, the Social Democratic caucus picked Malinovsky to reply to the policy address of Prime Minister Kokovtzev.

In December 1912, at a Party Council held at Lenin's home in Cracow, Bolshevik delegates from St Petersburg, Moscow, the

Urals, the Caucasus and the southern provinces decided to organize revolutionary street demonstrations, strikes, and secret shop and factory committees. The council was attended by Lenin, Kamenev, Zinoviev, Krupskaya, the Bolshevik Duma deputies, including Malinovsky as well as Stalin, who had made good another escape from exile.

Another delegate who participated in the Cracow Party Council was Alexander Troyanovsky, later Soviet Ambassador to the United States.

In February 1913 Troyanovsky's wife, who had just returned from Austria with instructions from Lenin, was arrested in Kiev. She had been asked to become secretary to the Bolshevik group in the Duma. Important secret documents were found in her possession.

Very few people had known of her arrival. Both Bukharin and Troyanovsky suspected Malinovsky's hand in her arrest. To confirm their suspicions, Troyanovsky sent a registered letter to his wife's father, telling him he knew who had betrayed his wife to the police and that he was determined to square accounts with the informer. The letter brought the results Troyanovsky expected. His wife was immediately released.

Convinced now that his wife's arrest was the work of an *agent provocateur*, Troyanovsky investigated the details of her trip to Russia, whom she met there, as well as the circumstances of her arrest and release. All the evidence pointed strongly to Malinovsky.

After discussing the matter with Bukharin, both wrote to the Central Committee demanding that Malinovsky appear before a Party court. In reply, they received a severe rebuke from Lenin, who, speaking for the Central Committee, forbade them to spread these rumours about Malinovsky. Lenin called their action worse than treason, and threatened to have them expelled from the Party if they persisted. Bukharin obeyed, but Troyanovsky soon parted company with Lenin and did not rejoin the Bolsheviks until 1921.[21] But fresh evidence against Malinovsky continued to accumulate.

Late in the summer of 1913 Sverdlov, an active Bolshevik Party worker, fled from Siberia to St Petersburg, and hid in the apartment of Badayev, a Bolshevik deputy to the Duma. A few days later the janitor asked Badayev whether he was harbouring a man answering to Sverdlov's description. Badayev denied having any stranger in his apartment, but he realized that Sverdlov was no longer safe with him. After consulting Malinovsky, he decided to move Sverdlov elsewhere. Sverdlov was to stand at the window while Badayev and Malinovsky kept a look-out for spies. If the road was clear, they were both to light cigarettes as a signal for Sverdlov to come out. When Sverdlov saw the signal, he went into the street. The two men helped him over a fence, where a cab was waiting to take him to Malinovsky's flat. From there he was taken to the home of Petrovsky, another Bolshevik member of the Duma. That very night he was arrested and sent back to Siberia. And still no action was taken to investigate Malinovsky.

A few days after Sverdlov's arrest the Bolsheviks organized a concert and ball under the auspices of an innocent front to raise income for *Pravda*. Such concerts were held frequently in St Petersburg, and served as fairly safe meeting places for revolutionaries, including those living under false passports. Among those present were Stalin, who was living illegally in St Petersburg, and Malinovsky.

Before Stalin had time to warm his feet he found himself surrounded by police agents. The organizers of the concert took him into a dressing-room to change his clothes and furnish him with a disguise, but agents of the secret police broke into the dressing-room. One of them seized Stalin with the shout, 'Djugashvili, we've finally got you!'

'I'm not Djugashvili,' said Stalin. 'My name is Ivanov.'

'Tell those stories to your grandmother,' the police operative told him. He was taken away to prison and again exiled to Siberia, where he remained until the revolution.[22]

After these new arrests the conviction grew that there was an agent provocateur in the Bolshevik higher councils who was delivering Party members to the police. But no one could name him.

In August 1913 the Bolshevik leaders were summoned to a new Central Committee conference in a village near Zakopane in Galicia. There were twenty-two Bolsheviks present, including Lenin, Zinoviev, Kamenev, Troyanovsky, Shotman, Ganetsky, Malinovsky and the other Bolshevik deputies in the Duma. Five of these men later proved to be Okhrana agents. (Their reports were published in Moscow after the Soviet Revolution in the book, *The Bolsheviks According to the Documents of the Moscow Okhrana*.) Lenin pushed through his resolution to split the Social Democratic delegation in the Duma and Malinovsky was charged with the task of establishing a separate Bolshevik caucus.

Two weeks later the six Bolshevik deputies presented the seven Menshevik deputies with an ultimatum to accept Lenin's programme. When the Mensheviks refused, Lenin's followers formed their own caucus with Malinovsky as chairman.[23]

Immediately *Pravda* began a campaign to discredit Chkheidze and the Mensheviks. Most of the *Pravda* editorials continued to be written by Lenin and Zinoviev, but local policy was set by Malinovsky, who took every occasion to attack the Menshevik Duma deputies and trade-union leaders, not only in the press, but also at open meetings. He accused the Mensheviks of betraying the interests of the working class and bowing to Tsarist reaction. In the Duma itself Malinovsky delivered fiery revolutionary speeches accusing the entire liberal and radical opposition of cowardice and treason to the people.

The Bolsheviks succeeded in gaining the upper hand in several major unions, when the government suddenly began to round up all the Menshevik leaders and prominent Menshevik workers. At the time these arrests seemed part of the general policy of repression. Later they were revealed as a plan conceived by Malinovsky.

Malinovsky's bold speeches in the Duma and at labour meetings made him very popular among the workers. He became Lenin's *alter ego* in Russia, often journeying to Cracow for instructions.

When Malinovsky had first taken his seat in the Duma, Lydia Dan, wife of the Menshevik leader Theodore Dan, and sister of Martov, received anonymous letters from the secret police that Malinovsky was one of their agents. Another such letter was received by the editorial offices of the Menshevik paper in St Petersburg. But no one paid much attention to these accusations.

In April 1914 the Tsarist Government made an attack on the parliamentary immunity of the members of the Duma. The Tsar had removed Premier Kokovtsev for alleged liberal tendencies, and replaced him with the incompetent old reactionary, Goremykin, who was ordered to stamp out the revolutionary movement. Goremykin started by bringing charges against Chkheidze for a radical speech he had made in the Duma. As Goremykin began to address the Duma, the left-wing deputies pounded on their desks and shouted, 'Freedom of speech for members of the Duma!' Goremykin could not continue. Rodzianko, the Speaker, after trying unsuccessfully to restore order, apologized to Goremykin, and moved that the Social Democrats and Alexander Kerensky's Trudovik group be excluded for fifteen sessions. The motion was carried.

When the suspended deputies returned on 7 May 1914, Kerensky, on behalf of the entire Left, read a statement condemning the government. The Speaker interrupted him several times and finally ruled him out of order. Malinovsky followed Kerensky, but he, too, was ruled out of order. Malinovsky, however, continued to speak from the rostrum until the Speaker called the sergeant-at-arms, who ordered him to return to his seat.

Malinovsky demanded that all left-wing deputies resign from the Duma, charging that their continued presence there merely enhanced the prestige of reaction. When his proposal was rejected, he went to the Speaker in his chambers and delivered a sealed envelope to him with the words, 'Good-bye, Mr Rodzianko.'

'What do you mean?' Rodzianko asked in amazement.

'You'll know when you have read this,' Malinovsky replied, and added that he was leaving the country that very day.

Malinovsky went home. When Rodzianko opened the Duma he informed the members that he had just received Malinovsky's resignation from the Duma. The statement caused a commotion and everyone looked at Badayev, the only Bolshevik member present at the session. No less amazed than the rest, he immediately telephoned to *Pravda*, where the editorial workers were thunderstruck by the news.

Badayev explained that no one in the Bolshevik delegation had had an inkling of Malinovsky's plans. They considered it a flagrant breach of Party discipline. Petrovsky was sent to Malinovsky to demand that he appear before the Bolshevik deputies with a satisfactory explanation.

Petrovsky found Malinovsky, half-dressed, pacing the floor of his room. 'Don't disturb me. I'm terribly upset,' he told Petrovsky.

'Is it true that you resigned your seat in the Duma?' Petrovsky asked.

'Yes, but leave me alone now,' was the answer.

'I'm not interested in your nervousness,' Petrovsky said. 'Without permission from the Party you have taken a step which borders on treason. I was sent by the Party to demand that you come immediately to the delegation's office to explain your unprecedented action.'

'I'm not in a position just now to give any explanations,' Malinovsky answered curtly.

'Does that mean that you refuse to abide by the decision of the Party?'

'Take it any way you like!' Malinovsky shouted. 'But I tell you again I am in no position to explain.'

When Petrovsky reported to the Bolshevik Duma group they sent him back to Malinovsky with the message that unless he came immediately they would take strong measures against him. When Petrovsky returned, Malinovsky shouted at him, 'Didn't I ask you to leave me alone? What are you doing here again? I told you once I would not go, and that's all there is to it.'

Threatened with a Party trial, Malinovsky became hysterical, and ran up and down the room, shouting, 'Try me! Bring your charges! Do what you like! I won't give any explanations, do you hear? No explanations!'

'Is that your final answer?' Petrovsky asked.

'Yes, yes, that's my final answer. I am leaving the country to-night. If you don't believe me, here is my exit permit.'

Badayev declared that Malinovsky's act was not only a violation of Bolshevik discipline, but that it supplied their enemies with effective ammunition. Rumours spread of a split within the Bolshevik delegation, and the affair created a tremendous sensation.[24]

What Badayev did not say was that the Menshevik newspaper *Rabochaya Gazeta* demanded that a commission of all the left-wing parties investigate the whole Malinovsky affair. This demand came when Vice-Speaker of the Duma, Prince Volkonsky, a Conservative deputy, was reported to have told a left-wing deputy that he had been informed that Malinovsky had been a police spy all along. When pressed by Social Democrats, Prince Volkonsky refused to confirm or deny the rumour.

The Mensheviks set about investigating Malinovsky's record and came across other evidence that he was indeed an agent of the

Okhrana. Their newspaper then published an editorial demanding that he face a tribunal.

Malinovsky himself ignored the demand for some time. *Pravda*, however, published a statement signed by Lenin and Zinoviev condemning the Mensheviks as slanderers and cowards, who were afraid to come out with an open charge against Malinovsky, but were seeking to stab the Bolshevik Party in the back. Martov and Dan, the two top Menshevik leaders then in St Petersburg, published a signed statement reiterating their charges and their demand. Exposing a police agent was a penal offence, so Martov and Dan, by their signed statement, risked arrest.

Lenin, Zinoviev and Kamenev, writing in *Pravda*, replied that they refused to allow 'liquidators' and representatives of 'Stolypin's Workers' Party' to sit in judgement over a spokesman of the revolutionary proletariat. *Rabochaya Gazeta*, meanwhile, continued to print resolutions and letters demanding that Malinovsky face a revolutionary tribunal.

Malinovsky had gone to Lenin in Galicia from St Petersburg. Precisely what happened between the two of them is not known, but this is what Bukharin, who was with Lenin at the time, later wrote:

I remember the shameful time when Roman Malinovsky came to Pronino. The first night I slept in the room upstairs. I slept badly, waking up once in a while. How could it be otherwise when the matter concerned the spy activities of the leader of the Bolshevik faction in the Duma?

I heard distinctly how Ilyich paced the room downstairs. He couldn't sleep. He went out on the balcony, made some tea, and again paced up and down the terrace, stopping every once in a while. He spent the whole night pacing and thinking. A hazy slumber overcame me at times. But as soon as consciousness returned, my ear caught the steady thud below.

At last it is morning. I go downstairs. I see Ilyich carefully dressed. There are yellow rings around his eyes. But he laughs merrily; his gestures are the usual ones.

'Did you sleep well?' he asks, and laughs. 'Would you care to have some tea? Some bread? Shall we take a stroll?' Just as if nothing had happened. As if there had been no sleepless night, no pain, no suffering, no struggle, no hard thinking, no pondering. No, Ilyich simply put on the armour of his iron will. Nothing could ever break through it.[25]

Lenin found a way out. On 25 May 1914, the following letter

signed by Malinovsky appeared in *Pravda:* 'Although for personal reasons I have discontinued my political activities, I remain a Bolshevik adherent. I shall bring those reactionaries Martov and Dan to court in a free country if they have the effrontery to accuse me over their signatures.'

Along with Malinovsky's letter, *Pravda* received this telegram from Galicia signed by Lenin, Zinoviev and Ganetsky: MARTOV AND DAN ARE FILTHY SLANDERERS WHO ALWAYS SPREAD SINISTER RUMOURS ABOUT THEIR OPPONENTS. WE DEMAND OF THEM A DIRECT ACCUSATION WITH THEIR SIGNATURES. HAVING INVESTIGATED THE RUMOURS, WE ARE ABSOLUTELY CONVINCED OF MALINOVSKY'S POLITICAL HONESTY.

Editorially, *Pravda* announced that these statements by Malinovsky and Lenin put an end to the dastardly slander and called on its followers 'to march forward with closed ranks against the enemies outside and the slanderers and traitors like the Martovs and the Dans'.

In 1915 Lenin's *émigré* paper *Sozialdemokrat* carried an item that Malinovsky had been killed in the war. An obituary was published mourning the premature death of 'this great proletarian leader'. But Malinovsky was not dead by any means, neither was his case closed. He was still to plague Lenin and the Bolshevik Party.

The attitude of the non-Bolshevik factions to Lenin at this time was succinctly expressed by Charles Rappaport, the Russo-French Socialist, who later became an important Communist. Rappaport compared Lenin's position in the revolutionary movement to that of Stolypin in the Tsarist régime. No party could exist under Lenin's autocratic rule, said Rappaport in 1914:

We recognized Lenin's achievements. He is a man of iron will and an incomparable organizer of groups. But Lenin regards only himself as a Socialist. Whoever opposes him is forever condemned by him. . . . He sees in capital punishment the only means of assuring the existence of the Social Democratic Party. War is declared on anyone who differs with him. Instead of combating his opponents in the Social Democratic Party by Socialist methods, *i.e.* by argument, Lenin uses only surgical methods, those of 'bloodletting'. No party could exist under the régime of this

Social Democratic Tsar, who regards himself as a super-Marxist, but who is, in reality, nothing but an adventurer of the highest order. I do not belong to any of the contending factions, but the experience of many years led me to the conviction that Lenin's victory would be the greatest menace to the Russian Revolution. Lenin will hold it in his embrace so tightly that he will choke it.[26]

In a letter to Chkheidze, the leader of the Mensheviks in the Duma, Trotsky had previously written:

One cannot but deplore as a devilish brew the party squabble which is systematically fomented by the master of such affairs, Lenin, that professional exploiter of backwardness in the Russian workers' movement. . . . The entire edifice of Leninism at present rests on lies and falsification and carries within itself the poisonous seeds of its own disintegration.

On 16–17 July 1914 a special conference of the International Socialist Bureau was held in Brussels. Its agenda was to include the problem of unity in the Russian labour movement. Among the members of the Bureau present at the conference were Vandervelde, Huysman and Kautsky; Russian Social Democracy was represented by Axelrod, Plekhanov, Martov, Trotsky, Alexinsky, Ganetsky and Rosa Luxemburg.

The International Socialist Bureau had long been concerned by the split in the Social Democratic Party and the aggressive role of Lenin and his lieutenants. Still it avoided interfering in the Party's affairs. However, the scandal had become too great to be overlooked any longer. Lenin did not wish to submit to a reprimand by the Socialist International. Neither he, Zinoviev nor Kamenev appeared at the Brussels Conference.

Instead, Lenin sent Inessa Armand, counting on her mastery of languages, her devotion and her steadfastness. He wrote her speech and supplemented this with four sets of private notes – all of which take up forty pages in his collected works.[27] Apparently some of Lenin's lieutenants doubted her fitness for the role. Lenin reassured her:

'I stubbornly disbelieve the pessimists who say that you are hardly – Nonsense and again nonsense! With a splendid tongue you will smash them all; you will not let Vandervelde interrupt you and yell. . . .

'You must make the report. You will say that you demand it

and that you *have* precise and practical *proposals*. What can be more practical and businesslike? We go our way, they theirs – and we'll see what happens. Either a general line is accepted or we say let's report to our congress, *we to the congress of our party*. (But in fact, it is clear, we will accept exactly nothing.)'

The brunt of Lenin's argument, as presented by Inessa, was that the best way to assure the unity of the movement was to recognize Lenin's committee as the Central Committee of the entire Party. Inessa, Krupskaya writes, 'carried out her task bravely'; an Okhrana agent who was present said that 'no one had expected the impudence of the Leninists to reach such proportions'.

Plekhanov, Martov, Alexinsky and others replied by an all-out indictment against Lenin. Plekhanov charged Lenin with seizing Party property and declared that unity was impossible without curtailing Lenin's influence in the Party. Alexinsky charged that Lenin had blocked the unmasking of *agent provocateurs*. The members of the International Bureau were shocked at these charges. Vandervelde, seconded by Kautsky, proposed that the question of the schism in the Russian Social Democratic Party be put before the Congress of the International in Vienna at the end of August. That Congress, however, was fated not to convene.

But although Lenin was not popular among the elder leaders of the Social Democratic Party, his influence among factory workers of St Petersburg, Moscow and other industrial centres mounted. His simple and direct slogans for revolutionary action appealed more strongly to the average Russian worker than the complicated theories of western European Marxism and the Menshevik policy of moderation.

In June 1914 the Bolshevik Central Committee was meeting in Cracow to discuss the steps for convening a new Bolshevik congress. But these preparations were interrupted by the outbreak of war.

Chapter 7
From War To Revolution

Lenin had seen the Russo-Japanese war drive the entering wedge for the Revolution of 1905; he expected another war to be the prologue to a new Revolution. In 1913 he had written to Maxim Gorky 'War between Austria and Russia would be very useful to the cause of the revolution in western Europe. But it is hard to believe that Franz Josef and Nicholas will grant us this pleasure.'[1]

A year later they did. When news of the German declaration of war on Russia reached Lenin in Cracow the first question he asked Zinoviev was: 'How will the second Socialist International react?'

'You will see,' predicted Zinoviev. 'The Social Democratic gentlemen of Germany will not dare to vote against the Kaiser's Government on the question of the war credits. They will abstain.'

'No,' replied Lenin. 'They are not so cowardly as all that. Without doubt they will not oppose the war. But to appease their conscience they will vote against it, if for no other reason than for fear the working class will rise up against them.'

They were both wrong. Despite the fact that all Social Democratic parties of Europe were consistently opposed to militarism, the Second International took the position that the only way to stop war was to prevent its outbreak. After war started, they argued, as Marxists, a general strike would harm only the more advanced nations, while the backward, reactionary régimes, such as Tsarist Russia, would suffer least. The impracticality of general strikes or revolts among the soldiers during the early phase of actual warfare was conceded even by such left-wingers as Rosa Luxemburg.

The Conference of the International Socialist Bureau, held in Brussels late in July 1914, condemned Austria and Russia. And in Germany the Social Democrats tried hard to stave off the impending conflict. Tremendous demonstrations were staged in all the German cities, and on 25 July the Executive Committee of the German Social Democratic Party proclaimed: 'No German soldier's blood must be spilt to gratify the murderous intentions of the Austrian tyrant. We call upon you, comrades, to express at once by mass meetings the unshakeable desire of the class-conscious proletariat for peace.'

Nevertheless, when the pleas of German workers were not heeded, the Social Democrats were faced with the reality of a war they had fought against so long. Arguing that they had tried to prevent the Kaiser's Government from aggression and that to oppose the war now could mean a victory for the Tsar, the German Social Democrats, including such fiery anti-militarists as Karl Liebknecht, confounded both Lenin and Zinoviev by voting in favour of the first war credits. When Lenin picked up the Berlin *Vorwaerts* he refused to believe the news.

'It is impossible!' he cried out. 'This copy is certainly a forgery. The bourgeois German *canaille* must have published a special number.' Convinced at last, he exclaimed with finality: 'The Second International is dead!'[2]

With the outbreak of war the Austrian police began a spy hunt throughout Galicia. Every foreigner was a suspect. On the rainy night of 7 August 1914, Lenin called on Ganetsky.

'A search has just been made of my living quarters,' he said. 'It was conducted by the *Wachtmeister* of the local gendarmerie. He has ordered me to meet him in the morning at the railroad station and go with him to Nowy Targ. The search was quite superficial. The fool left the entire party correspondence intact, taking with him only one manuscript on the agrarian problem. He thought statistical tables were a secret code. Fortunately he left the correspondence alone, because it contains addresses and other conspiratory matters. . . . What do you think? Will they arrest us tomorrow in Nowy Targ or will they let us go? The prospects are not very good. It is war, you know. The stupid gendarme suspects me of spying and I will probably be arrested.'

The Cracow police, according to Ganetsky, were well aware that Lenin was an irreconcilable enemy of Tsarism. They had kept a continuous watch over him and knew that he did not concern himself with Austrian affairs. That was the attitude of Cracow. But Nowy Targ was another story. Here the worst could be expected.

Ganetsky therefore communicated with Dr Marek, the Austrian Social Democratic deputy who had helped obtain permission for Lenin to settle in Cracow. Lenin himself wired to the police director of Cracow:

The local police suspects me of espionage. I have been living in Cracow for the past two years at 57 Lubomirszca Street in the Zwenschintz district. Personally gave information to the police commissioner of Zwenschintz. I am an *émigré*, a Social Democrat. I beg you to wire the proper officials of Nowy Targ in order to prevent a misunderstanding.

The next day the local gendarmerie received a telegram from the police commissioner of Cracow stating that there were no reasons to hold Lenin. In the meantime, however, Lenin and Zinoviev had been arrested. Ganetsky then telegraphed the Austrian Social Democratic leader, Victor Adler, and the Galician Socialist deputy Ignatz Daszynski. The Socialists in Austria, like their comrades in Germany, were generally supporting the war effort and therefore were in better standing with their government than usual. Adler went to the Foreign Minister to intercede on Lenin's behalf. He assured the Minister that, in view of Lenin's attitude towards Tsarism, freeing him would be most useful to the Austro-German cause. At large, Lenin would certainly conduct active propaganda against the Allies, Adler asserted. This reasoning impressed the Foreign Minister. The conversation continued:

MINISTER: You say then that Lenin is the greatest foe of the Allies?

ADLER: Even more so than yourself, Your Excellency.

The Austrian Ministry of the Interior then issued this order:

According to statements by Deputies Dr Adler and Daszynski (the latter is now in Cracow in connexion with the organization of the Polish Legion and is in constant contact with the military authorities), they are in a position to supply information regarding Ulyanov.

It is the opinion of Dr Adler that under the present circumstances Ulyanov could be of great service. The police authorities are requested also to inform us, as soon as possible, what military court has jurisdiction over Ulyanov.[3]

Lenin was released from prison on 19 August 1914 , with permission to go to Switzerland.

In Zurich and Geneva sharp differences of opinion on the war were already developing among the Socialist *émigrés*. Martinov, a Menshevik leader, gave a series of lectures which started a debate lasting several evenings. Then a number of Germans spoke. They were followed by Karl Radek, Trotsky, Alexinsky, and finally by Lenin, Zinoviev and Martov.

Trotsky, who at that time was still not close to Lenin, held that the pro-war stand of most Socialist parties stemmed from objective causes. Despite the assumed community of interest among capitalists of all countries he maintained that the world economic structure was still largely national rather than international. International trusts were the exceptions. And the workers believed, according to Trotsky, that if their country conquered new colonies and markets they would enjoy higher living standards. In time of war, therefore, the workers still identified themselves with the cause of their exploiters.

Trotsky's slogan in 1914 was 'peace without indemnities and annexation, peace without victors and vanquished'. The only radical step he advocated was the dismemberment of the Austro-Hungarian Empire. His 'internationalism' was then directed primarily against Germany. During the first few weeks of the war, when German victory seemed likely, even the 'internationalists' were afraid of the possible consequences. But by the time Trotsky left for Paris the fortunes of war had changed. It was clear that Wilhelm would not get the kind of peace he wanted. In France, Trotsky was soon fighting against the patriotism of the French Socialist Party as he had previously attacked the German Social Democrats.

Martov, Martinov and a number of Bolsheviks then in Switzerland shared the same 'internationalist' viewpoint. But it was generally agreed that internationalism was still too weak to overcome the new flush of national patriotism which the war had produced.[4]

At a meeting of the Bolsheviks, held in the woods near Berne on the morning after his arrival, Lenin outlined his views on the war. A resolution was adopted branding the conflict as imperialist and the conduct of the leaders of the Second International as a betrayal of the proletariat. The Bolshevik Duma deputy Samoliov was instructed to take this resolution back to St Petersburg to the Central Committee and the Bolshevik Duma group.[5]

At a debate in Zurich, Lenin called Trotsky's slogan of peace 'a pious platitude'. Not peace but civil war was Lenin's programme. To go into the trenches and create revolutionary cells was the correct tactics, he maintained.

'Take your rifles and turn them against your officers and the capitalists', he said. And he quoted Engels to the effect that the workers should let the bourgeoisie shoot first. Now that the world bourgeoisie had begun shooting it was time to reply. Pounding his fist, he repeated, 'You shot first, gentlemen of the bourgeoisie.'

Litvak of the Jewish Socialist Bund says:

We were amazed that Lenin advocated cutting away Russia's peripheral provinces, the Ukraine, the Baltic provinces, and the rest. When I said that he must have been jesting, that he might have meant autonomy and federation but surely not cutting Russia off from the Baltic and Black seas, the arteries of Russian economy, he replied that he was in dead earnest.

'We great Russians,' he said, 'have always acted like boors towards subject peoples. All we can do is suppress them.'[6]

Bukharin gives this account of Lenin's early reaction to the war:

Ilyich was striding about as mad as a tiger, an untamable one. Great sage, revolutionary prophet that he was, not for a moment did he despair, not for a moment did he helplessly fold his arms. His first slogan, an answer to the declaration of war, was a slogan for the soldiers of all armies: 'Turn your guns on your officers!' This slogan was not published. Its more general form became the following: 'Turn the imperialist war into a civil war'. I recall the long arguments carried on in our small circle, when Ilyich posed the point-blank question not only of splitting the Party, but even of renouncing the very name of 'Social Democrat'! When Gregory [Zinoviev] began to talk of traditions as well as of numbers, Lenin remarked wrathfully and ferociously, not paying any attention to women present, 'Oh yes, there is plenty of dung among them' [only he used a much stronger word], and with furious energy began to expose his ideas regarding Communist parties and a new International revolutionary and insurrectionist. . . .

Word that Plekhanov was advocating support of the Allied war-effort infuriated Lenin. He was anxious to meet Plekhanov face to face. Plekhanov had published a pamphlet and delivered a series of lectures demanding that Socialists everywhere stand behind the Allies. He maintained that if Germany won, she would deprive Russia of her littoral provinces and turn her into a virtual German colony. Russia's industry would decline, and with it the Russian working class. The land-owners would gain dominance, thus strengthening Tsarism and turning back the clock for Russia by decades. Moreover, argued Plekhanov, in fighting side by side with democratic France and England, the cause of Russian democracy would be furthered. He urged Russian Socialist *émigrés* in France to volunteer for service in the French Army.

'We learned in Lausanne,' relates Bukharin, 'that Plekhanov was to make a speech at the Maison du Peuple and we immediately sent a wire to Lenin, who was then in Berne. Ilych arrived with the speed of the wind. The hall was crowded to suffocation. . . . Plekhanov, noticing Lenin, remarked jestingly that he felt "decoyed into a trap".'

His eyes flashing under his silvery brows, Plekhanov eloquently defended the Socialists of the Allied countries for their patriotism. When Plekhanov criticized the German Social Democrats, Lenin joined in the general applause. But when Plekhanov argued that the Socialist parties of France, Belgium and England had to give full support to their governments against German militarism, Lenin was furious. As soon as Plekhanov finished talking, Lenin rose, holding a glass of beer in his hand, and walked to the platform. His face was as white as a death-mask.

'Never before or after did I see such a deathly pallor on Ilyich's face,' Bukharin writes. 'Only his eyes were burning brightly, when, in a dry, guttural voice, he started to lash his opponent sharply and forcefully.'[7]

'He spoke calmly,' relates Krupskaya, 'and only his paleness betrayed his emotion. Ilyich said that the war which had broken out was not an accidental one, that it had been prepared by the entire character and development of bourgeois society. The International Socialist congresses in Stuttgart, Copenhagen, and Basle had decided the attitude of the Socialist towards the coming war. The Social Democrats would carry out their duty if they conducted a fight against chauvinistic fog in their own countries. The war must be transformed into a resolute conflict between the proletariat and the ruling classes. Ilyich spoke only ten minutes, he touched only the essentials. Plekhanov, with his well-known barbs, answered him. The Mensheviks, who were in the majority at the meeting, applauded him. It was the impression that Plekhanov had won.'[8]

Three days later Lenin lectured in the same crowded auditorium, developing his theory in greater detail.

In a letter to Shliapnikov, a prominent Bolshevik, on 17 October 1914, he wrote:

T–F

In Russia chauvinism is hiding behind the phrases of *la belle France*, unfortunate Belgium, and enmity to the Kaiser and Kaiserism. Therefore it is our absolute duty to fight against his sophistry, and in order that this fight travel along a clear and straight path, a slogan is necessary to summarize the entire question. The slogan should show that from the standpoint of the interests of the Russian working class there is little doubt that the defeat of Tsarism is the lesser catastrophe, because Tsarism is a hundred times worse than Kaiserism. The slogan 'peace' is not the right one at this moment. This is a slogan of priests and the petit bourgeoisie. The proletarian slogan should be 'civil war'. . . . We cannot *promise* a civil war and we cannot *decree* a civil war, but our duty is to conduct all our work, if necessary for a long time, *in that direction*. [Lenin's emphasis.][9]

On 1 November 1914, the *Sozialdemokrat* published Lenin's manifesto, which declared:

Under given conditions it is impossible to determine from the standpoint of the international proletariat which is the lesser evil for Socialism, the defeat of one or the other group of belligerent nations. For us Russian Social Democrats, however, there cannot exist the least doubt that from the standpoint of the working class and of the labouring masses of all the peoples of Russia the lesser evil would be the defeat of the Tsarist monarchy, the most reactionary and barbarous government which oppresses the greatest number of nations and the greatest mass of the population of Europe and Asia.

The proletarian International has not perished and will not perish. The working masses will overcome all obstacles and create a new International. The present triumph of opportunism is short-lived. The greater the war losses, the clearer it will become to the working masses that the opportunists betrayed the cause of the workers and that it is necessary to turn the weapons against the governments and the bourgeoisie of the respective countries. . . . Turning the present imperialist war into a civil war is the only correct proletarian slogan.

Germany and Austria, according to Lenin, were really victims of the predatory designs of the English, French and Russians. 'We know that for decades the three blackguards (the bourgeoisie and the governments of England, France and Russia) had been preparing to attack Germany', he wrote in the *Sozialdemokrat* of February 1915. 'Shall we evince surprise that the two other blackguards started the attack before the first three received the weapons which they had ordered?'

When a Bolshevik named Shklovsky attempted to argue that unless Germany was defeated, democracy in France would be destroyed, Lenin replied:

'Let them destroy it. France is nothing but a backward republic of usurers and *rentiers* fattening on their gold. If Germany, who has outstripped her industrially, defeats her, there will be no harm in that. For us revolutionary Marxists it makes no difference who wins. Our business is to strive everywhere to transform the imperialist war into a civil war.'[10]

Above all he despised the pacifists and conscientious objectors who wanted a premature end of the war, thereby destroying the bright prospects of revolution. 'War is no accident and no "sin"', as the Christian reverends think', he wrote on 11 November 1914. 'They, like all opportunists, preach patriotism, humanitarianism and pacifism. War is an inevitable part of capitalism. It is just as much a legitimate form of capitalism as is peace. The strikes of the conscientious objectors and similar opposition to war are nothing but pitiful, cowardly, idle dreams. What idiot believes that the armed bourgeoisie can be overthrown without a struggle? It is simply insane to talk about abolishing capitalism without a frightful civil war or without a succession of such wars. It is the duty of the Socialists to agitate for class struggle in time of war. The only duty of the Socialists, when an imperialist war breaks out between the bourgeois classes of different nations, is to transform this war between nations into a war between classes. Down with the sentimental, hypocritical slogan: "Peace at any Price!" Long Live the Civil War!'[11]

Active among the 'internationalists' in Switzerland was Karl Radek, who arrived from Germany in August 1914. His paper on imperialism, delivered in Zurich, was received with considerable interest. On the other hand, his boastful manner annoyed everyone. He would tell those who listened to him in the cafés how a German general or an Austrian minister had confided high military and political secrets to him. At the same time he had a brilliant wit coupled with an uncommon ugliness. But as he talked in his thick Galician accent his features livened and became almost pleasant.

Radek had much to say about Parvus, the Russo-German Social Democrat, who had a bad reputation because of corrupt dealings with women and money. He had been expelled from the German

Social Democratic Party for misappropriation of funds. But Radek spoke of Parvus with a great deal of warmth and with indulgence towards his faults. Parvus had a brilliant mind, Radek said, but could not stick to one thing for any length of time. At the moment, however, Parvus was serving the Central Powers. Turkey and Germany were trying to recruit Georgian war prisoners to fight the Russians on the Caucasian front as special units in the Turkish Army. They maintained an affiliated organization in Bulgaria where many Georgian deserters had fled. Unofficially, Parvus, who had lived in Constantinople for several years before the war, was the organizer of this scheme.

Now Parvus was both an ardent German patriot and a contractor for the German Army. Speculation during the war added to his earnings. He went to Germany from Constantinople and then on to Stockholm, always maintaining liaison with the German Government, and – according to Radek – with the German Army as well. One of the men who worked for him was Ganetsky. Radek, who remained in constant contact with both Parvus and Ganetsky, had no part in Parvus's commercial and financial affairs, but the Parvus–Ganetsky link and Parvus's ties with Berlin were to play an important role in Lenin's later actions.[12]

Lenin had sent word to Kamenev, in St Petersburg, to have the Bolshevik deputies make a declaration from the floor of the Duma that the Russian working class hoped for Russia's defeat; that it was the duty of every class-conscious worker, of every revolutionary Socialist, to help transform the war against Germany into a civil war in Russia. At a secret joint conference of the Bolshevik organization and the Bolshevik Duma deputies in a St Petersburg suburb, Kamenev moved for the adoption of Lenin's declaration, suggesting that one of the deputies read the declaration in the name of the entire Bolshevik faction and of the 'class-conscious proletariat'.

While Kamenev was urging the Duma deputies to accept Lenin's declaration, the police raided the conference and arrested all those present. Later it was learned that *agents provocateurs* had tipped off the State Police Department. All the participants, including the Duma deputies, were convicted of high treason and sent to Siberia.[13]

Lenin's propaganda found sympathetic response at this stage among *émigrés* who shared his hopes that Russia's defeat would hasten the revolution. Some of his supporters were pacifists who considered Lenin an apostle of peace and did not take his summons to civil war seriously. But in every nation there were small groups of anti-war Socialists. Some of these demanded that the workers of all Europe stop the war by revolutionary action. Others held that it was the task of a reborn Socialist International to bring pressure on the belligerent governments to conclude a just peace. And a militant minority agreed with Lenin that the time had come for all revolutionary Socialist parties to unite into a new International, whose task would be to transform the imperialist war into a civil war.

The Mensheviks had split into two factions. The majority, led by Potresov in Russia and Plekhanov in Switzerland, favoured support of the war; the minority, headed by Martov and Axelrod, sided with the 'internationalists', taking the same position as the left-wing Socialists of Germany, Italy and France. The Socialist Revolutionary ranks were split along the same lines. While the group headed by Victor Chernov joined the 'internationalists', a second led by Nikolai Avksentiev favoured the Allies.

Despite great difficulties Lenin carried on correspondence with the St Petersburg Bureau of the Bolshevik Central Committee and succeeded in establishing communications with Stalin, Sverdlov and other Bolshevik exiles in Siberia. He also managed to send them his 'theses' on the war.

From his exile Stalin wrote to Lenin in February 1915:

My greetings to you, dear Ilyich, hearty, hearty greetings! . . . How are you getting on; how is your health? I live as before, chewing bread, just finished half my term. Somewhat boring, but it cannot be helped. How are your affairs? Things must be more lively down your way. . . . Recently I read some articles by Kropotkin – he is an old fool, completely out of his mind. I have also read Plekhanov's little screed in *Rech* – what an incorrigible old gossip he is! . . . Send us the good news that very soon an organ will appear that will hammer their ugly mugs hard, and without stopping.[14]

The same month Lenin delivered a policy report to the Bolshevik groups abroad, and the conference adopted his resolution which formulated the main Bolshevik slogans for the duration. Lenin proposed that the 'opportunists' be presented with the following ultimatum: 'Here is the manifesto . . . of our Central Committee on the war. Are you willing to publish it in your language? No? Then, good-bye, our ways part!'[15]

Lenin also found time to correspond with Inessa Armand, who was preparing a pamphlet on feminism in which she was to demand 'free love'. Lenin urged her to abandon the idea, which, he said, was 'not a proletarian but a bourgeois conception of love', that reduced itself to 'freedom from childbirth and freedom to be adulterous'. Inessa protested that she did not 'understand how one can identify freedom of love with adultery'.

Lenin replied in a letter on 24 June 1915: 'You, forgetting the objective and the class point of view, are launching an attack against me. . . . "Even a fleeting passion and affair"', you write, "is more poetic and pure than loveless kisses of vulgar and common married couples!" . . . Is such a contrast logical? The loveless kisses of vulgar couples are *dirty*. I agree. One should set against them . . . what? It would seem to me "loving kisses". But you oppose them with "fleeting" (why fleeting?) *passion* (why not love?). Logically, it turns out as though loveless kisses (fleeting) are opposed to loveless conjugal kisses. . . . Strange.'

Within Russia, meanwhile, the war was straining a badly integrated economy, exposing the weak spots of agriculture, industry and the transportation system. On the already heavily overtaxed nation fell the added burden of war. Every day of fighting in 1915 required an expenditure of 25·7 million rubles; in 1916 this sum jumped to 41·7 million rubles. Russia itself could not pay these vast sums. The government was forced to obtain foreign loans and the external debt mounted rapidly.

Agriculture and industry were badly hit by conscription. Eighteen million men, nearly half of the adult working population, were called up. Manufacturers were compelled to petition for the return of workers from the front. Skilled labourers disappeared and were replaced by untrained hands from the villages. Nor were methods of production improved. The Russian industrial plant was badly equipped and little machinery was coming from abroad.

In addition the importation of raw materials decreased, while the output of coal shrank.

After some initial victories in Galicia and East Prussia, the poorly equipped Russian armies suffered costly defeats and were heavily bled in ill-planned operations. For the inefficient conduct of the war and the short-sighted approach to domestic affairs the responsibility fell squarely on the shoulders of Tsar Nicholas.

Nor was anything done to relieve the land hunger, which had nearly caused a peasant revolution in 1905. Contrary to the régime's expectations, the war did not relegate the agrarian question to the background. Indeed the peasants firmly believed that ownership of the land would be their reward for bearing arms for the Tsar. This was very well expressed by the conservative peasant deputies in the Duma.

'Land reform is necessary, gentlemen,' they said. 'The peasants are fighting for it at the front. We have the full right to it. We are fighting for our happiness on the field of battle. The peasants have not forgotten the words of the autocrat that they would receive additional land where land hunger was particularly keen. But where is it not keen now? On the contrary, within the last two years it has grown. Let them have additional land. They need it badly, and they are waiting for it.'

At the outset of the war the Duma had been called together for a one-day session to demonstrate that Russia was united. A 'civil peace' had been concluded between the government and the Liberals. 'Let us forget our internal quarrels,' said the Cadets. 'Let us not give the enemy the slightest opportunity to hope for dissension among us, and let us remember that the first and foremost duty before us is to support the nation's defenders who are fighting for our just cause.'

But Tsar Nicholas II was a weak and stubborn man who, instead of drawing on the support of the Liberals, relied on his German consort and Rasputin. Compared with Nicholas II, the Empress Alexandra had both brains and will-power. And she was well aware of her husband's limitations. In one of her letters she wrote: 'I know your mildness and yielding character, owing to which you are always ready to give in whenever you are not buttressed by your poor old wifie.'

Rasputin's hold over the Empress came not only from his

hypnotic gifts, which enabled him to check the bleeding of the haemophilic heir to the throne, but from his alleged powers as a clairvoyant. He became intermediary between Alexandra and God and played the same role for Nicholas. Utilizing his position with great shrewdness, he never asked for personal favours. When he wanted to free his own son from military duty he accomplished his purpose by warning the Tsar against the mobilization of the second-class reserves. 'You will save your empire if you don't call the second class', he told the Tsar. Rasputin's methods were all the more successful because neither the Emperor nor his consort had the slightest political understanding. Rasputin had no programme but he was always consulted when political appointments were made. This was his favourite domain. Here he filled his pockets without arousing the Tsar's suspicion. The popular rumours that Rasputin was a German spy were never proved. Both Rasputin and the Empress did, however, wage a vicious campaign against the Duma, as the challenger to imperial power.

'As now decided, the Duma will convene in August, whereas our Friend asked you several times to postpone the opening to a later date', the Empress wrote to her husband in the summer of 1915.

Major defeats on the Galician front forced the Tsar to reconvene the Duma on 19 June 1915. But on 3 September it was adjourned once more. These sporadic sessions did not improve the temper of the deputies, who were demanding the removal of Rasputin from the court. The so-called Progressive Bloc, formed in 1915, tried to reconcile the interests of the middle class, the nobility and the court party. Miliukov, the organizer of this alliance, acknowledged that the initiative had come from certain Tsarist Ministers. Including six conservative and liberal Duma groups, the bloc's programme called for broad political and social reforms and the creation of a united government, but it did not venture to demand a cabinet responsible to the Duma. Final authority would still rest with the Tsar. This excellent programme, however, proved to be nothing more than a catalogue of pious wishes. No reforms were enacted.[16]

Lenin wrote in the summer of 1915:

Much has been left in the world that must be destroyed by fire and iron for the liberation of the working class. And if bitterness and despair grow in the masses, if a revolutionary situation is at hand, prepare to organize new organizations and *utilize* these so useful weapons of death and destruction against your own government and your bourgeoisie.

This is not easy, to be sure. It will demand difficult preparatory activities. It will demand great sacrifices. This is a *new* species of organization and struggle that *one must learn*, and learning is never done without errors and defeats. The relation of this species of class struggle to participation in elections is the same as storming a fortress is to manoeuvring, marching, or lying in the trenches.

Attacking the formula of 'No victory, no defeat', Lenin wrote in July 1915:

The slogan, if you reflect on it, means 'civil peace', the rejection of the class struggle of the oppressed classes in all belligerent countries, because class struggle is impossible without striking against one's own bourgeoisie and one's own government, and striking against one's government during war is *treason* against the state. It means helping the defeat of one's own country.

On 5 September 1915, a conference of all European anti-war Socialist groups who called themselves 'internationalists' opened in Zimmerwald, Switzerland. Earlier, in Berne, Lenin had proposed creating a new International and appealing to the soldiers and workers of all belligerent nations to lay down their arms and go out on strike against the war.

When Italy entered the conflict in May 1915, the Italian Socialists took the lead in the international anti-war organization. The Italian Socialist Party sent Angelica Balabanov and Morgari to Berne to negotiate with the Internationalists.

Most of the foreign radicals gathered in the Maison du Peuple. Balabanov writes:

Those who visited me in Berne were not official delegates but individuals tormented by the failure of their parties and risking their liberty to bring word from groups of German, Austrian, and French Socialists who had not abandoned their principles. . . . Their hostility towards their respective governments and towards their former leaders was overwhelming. I noted that the German Socialists among them would often be more lenient in their attitude towards the French 'social patriots', the French more inclined to extenuate the failures of the German official leaders than their own.

Lenin's proposals had met a hostile reception at Berne. Merrheim, one of the French left-wing syndicalist leaders, argued that the proposed manifesto to the workers and soldiers would be a futile gesture. Other delegates pointed out that the men who signed this appeal would face the death penalty as traitors when they returned to their homes, while Lenin himself remained safely in neutral Switzerland. After an eight-hour conference, the Berne session had broken up without results.

Robert Grimm, a Swiss journalist and Socialist leader, moved to create a permanent liaison between the various anti-war groups. The Italian Socialist Party had invited all groups that accepted the principle of class struggle and voted against military appropriations. But the organizers of the Zimmerwald Conference also wanted to invite the so-called 'Centrists' of the German Social Democratic Party, led by Karl Kautsky, Eduard Bernstein and Hugo Haase.

At a pre-conference meeting Zinoviev, representing the Bolsheviks, had spoken against inviting the German 'Centrists'. A few weeks earlier Kautsky, Bernstein and Haase had published a manifesto demanding peace without annexations. When Axelrod, representing the Menshevik 'internationalists', declared that if the 'Centrists' were not invited he would not participate either, Zinoviev's recommendation was voted down.

Later it developed that the Kautsky group preferred to deal directly with the powerful French Socialist Party rather than with the splinter groups assembled at Zimmerwald.

Germany was represented by ten delegates, of whom the majority, headed by Ledebour, took a middle position between Kautsky and the extreme Left. Only the followers of Karl Liebknecht sided with Lenin.

The Bolsheviks were represented by Lenin and Zinoviev, the Menshevik internationalists by Axelrod and Martov. Trotsky spoke for his own small group. The internationalists of the Russian Socialist Revolutionary Party were represented by Chernov and Bobrov; Poland by Karl Radek, Varsky and Lapinsky (all three acting for splinter groups). There were also two delegates of the fictitious Balkan Federation, Kolarov (later President of Bulgaria) and Christian Rakovsky. Also present were delegates from splinter groups in Sweden, Norway and Holland. From France came the syndicalist Merrheim and the Socialist Bourderon, neither speaking for his organization. Only two large western European organizations were represented, the Italian and Swiss Socialist parties. In all there were thirty-five delegates.

The Zimmerwald Conference opened with a statement signed by Ledebour and Hoffmann of Germany, and Merrheim and Bourderon, declaring that 'this is not our war'. Amid prolonged cheers they pledged themselves to work for a just peace. The German delegates insisted that Germany evacuate Belgium.

The majority statement condemned the war as imperialist and called for a fight against war and for Socialism. But the Bolsheviks insisted on a more militant resolution, urging an open civil war and the organization of a new revolutionary International.

With the French and German delegations equally opposed to Lenin's proposed manifesto, the conference was on the verge of breaking up. At this point, however, Rakovsky stepped into the breach with a compromise proposal. The manifesto which was finally adopted called on the proletariat of Europe to fight for 'peace without indemnities and without annexations' on the basis of the 'self-determination of peoples'. Lenin voted against the compromise proposal when it was offered in committee and when the final vote was taken.

Out of this conference emerged the so-called Zimmerwald Union, a loose grouping of anti-war Socialists which lasted until the formation of the Communist International.[17]

A month after Zimmerwald, Lenin wrote in his *Sozialdemokrat*:

The social content of the next revolution in Russia can only be a revolutionary democratic dictatorship of the proletariat and the peasantry. The revolution cannot emerge victorious without overthrowing the monarchy and the feudal landowners, and it is impossible to overthrow them without the peasantry supporting the proletariat. The aim of the proletariat in Russia is to lead the bourgeois democratic revolution to its end, in order to kindle the Socialist Revolution in Europe.

To the question, 'What would the party of the proletariat do if the revolution placed it in power in the present war?' we answer: 'We would propose peace to all the belligerents, the liberation of all colonies and all dependencies, all the oppressed, and those peoples who do not have equal rights. Neither Germany nor England and France would accept these conditions with their present governments. Then we would have to prepare and conduct a revolutionary war; *i.e.* not only would we carry through our whole minimum programme with decisive means but we would at once systematically start to incite rebellion among all the peoples now oppressed by the Great Russians, all the colonies and dependent countries of Asia (India, China, Persia and others). And we would also raise in rebellion the Socialist proletariat of Europe against their governments and in spite of their social chauvinists. There is no doubt that the victory of the proletariat in Russia would create very favourable conditions for the development of the revolution in Asia and Europe.[18]

While these great issues were being fought over, Lenin was having trouble paying for his room and board.

Krupskaya wrote Lenin's mother on 14 September 1915:

Our old resources will soon run out and the question of earning a livelihood looms very large. It is difficult to find anything here. I have been promised some work teaching but the matter is dragging. I was promised some copy work, but nothing came of that either. I will try again and again. But all these things are very problematic. We must think of journalistic earnings. I don't like to have this side of our existence fall on Volodya's shoulders. He works too much as it is, and the question of livelihood disturbs him greatly.

Lenin himself wrote, on 4 January 1916, to the secretary of the Great Encyclopedia in Petrograd:

I take the liberty of offering my services to the editors of the Encyclopedia, if all the articles for the coming volumes have not already been assigned. I have excellent contacts with the German and French libraries which I may need to use in Berne, and am in an extraordinary bad situation with reference to my own literary employment. For that reason I should be glad to write articles on political economy, politics, labour movement, philosophy, etc.

My wife, under the name of N. Krupskaya, has written on pedagogical subjects in the magazines *Russian School* and *Liberal Education*. She has specialized in modern schools and in the study of the old pedagogical classics. She would gladly undertake to write articles on the subjects.[19]

No answer came to this letter.

In January 1916 Lenin and his wife moved from Berne to Zurich. They rented a room in the apartment of a woman who had been a cook in a Vienna hotel, but before they were comfortably settled the former tenant appeared to claim his quarters. The landlady asked the Lenins to find another room, but insisted that they continue eating at her place. The price was so reasonable that they could not refuse. For the next two months they dined with an assortment of criminals and prostitutes. Meals were served in the kitchen, coffee came in cracked cups, the conversation was of the underworld variety – and Lenin, according to his wife, enjoyed it all immensely.

The tenant who had dispossessed them turned out to be a professional criminal. 'He did not hesitate to speak frankly in our presence', writes Krupskaya. 'And it must be said that there was more humanity in his talk than in the wealthy dining-rooms of good hotels.' Another table companion was a prostitute who discussed with Lenin the details of her profession, her mother's health, and her anxieties about the kind of career her younger sister would choose.

Lenin and his wife found a small room in the ancient house of a shoemaker. The building was old, dark, located on a narrow street. Perhaps they could have found something better even for the rent they paid, but Lenin liked the owner and his fellow-tenants. The shoemaker was a sort of revolutionist, opposed to the war. His family occupied two rooms. Other rooms were occupied by the wife of a German soldier and her children, an Italian, an Austrian actor who owned a yellow cat, and the Lenins. Windows could not be opened during the day because of the dreadful stench of rotting meat coming from a sausage factory in the building.

One evening, when the women of the house were gathered around the stove in Lenin's room, the cobbler's wife cried out: 'The soldiers must now turn their guns against their own governments.'

'After that', writes Krupskaya, 'Ilyich would not even hear of moving.'

But despite these minor diversions, Lenin was quite miserable in Zurich. He felt caged, isolated from events. Communication with Russia was very bad; no emissaries were coming from abroad and the small colony of Russian émigrés did not interest him. His only visitors were a young adherent, Grisha Usyevich, who reported all the news from the émigré colony, and a demented individual who would call on him early every morning until Lenin made it a practice to leave before nine to escape his company.

Lenin's efforts to organize a following among the mixed radical groups in Zurich met with little success. A gathering was called in the Café Zum Adler, not far from Lenin's living quarters. The audience included a few Russian and Polish Bolsheviks, some Swiss Socialists, and a handful of young Germans and Italians. When Lenin outlined to them his attitude towards the war and towards Europe's Socialist leaders as a whole, he met a cool reception. One young Swiss radical told Lenin that he was beating his head against the wall in vain. Others agreed, and the gathering fizzled out. At later meetings the audience continued to shrink in size. At the final session in the Café Zum Adler, attended only by Russians and Poles, Krupskaya reports that 'we exchanged some funny stories and went home'.

Never was Lenin's isolation so complete as in Zurich in 1916. One day he ran across Nobse, the left-wing editor of the local Socialist newspaper. Nobse pretended to be in a hurry to catch a streetcar. But Lenin, according to Krupskaya, 'grabbed him by the arm and began to explain to Nobse the inevitability of a world revolution.'

Krupskaya was moved almost to tears by the spectacle. Her husband, 'with his trembling hand fastened on the button of Nobse's overcoat, trying to convince the man of the soundness of his position, looked very tragic. It made one think of how strange it was to see such colossal strength and energy going to waste, how queer that such selfless devotion to the working class was being left unused and perishing, and that such clear ideas of what was happening in the world could find no application whatsoever.'[20]

Her mind flashed back to 'a big white polar bear whom Ilyich and I once saw in the London Zoo, before whose cage we stood for a long time. "All the beasts become accustomed to their cages in time, the bears, the tigers, all of them," the keeper explained. "Only the white polar bear from the Russian north never gets used to his cage, and strains day and night against the iron bars".'

The 'white polar bear from the Russian north' was straining against the bars that confined him to Zurich.

Lenin's reaction to the assassination of Austrian Foreign Minister Stuerck by Friedrich Adler reveals the curious turn of mind which separated him from his fellow-Socialists in western Europe.

Friedrich, son of Victor Adler, the veteran Socialist leader, was the secretary of the Austrian Social Democratic Party. That party condemned terrorism as a political weapon. Yet Adler in 1916 shot and killed the Austrian Foreign Minister in a futile attempt to stir his comrades to action against the war. The news shocked and confused not only Adler's party, but Socialists throughout the world. At first none of the Russian Social Democrats in Zurich believed it. Krupskaya thought Adler was the victim, not the assailant.

Lenin ventured the opinion that Adler had been driven to the act by his Russian wife. But what concerned him more was the fact that Adler chose this course when he could have utilized the party lists at his disposal to circulate anti-war propaganda.

Meeting Angelica Balabanov, the secretary of the Zimmerwald Union and later secretary of the Communist International, in a Zurich library, Lenin asked:

'What sort of woman is Adler's wife?'

'A Russian Social Democrat,' Balabanov replied.

'A Social Democrat?' Lenin repeated with surprise. 'I thought she was a Socialist Revolutionary, a terrorist who had influenced her husband. But why should he pick on Stuerck? Wasn't Adler the secretary of the Austrian Social Democratic Party? Didn't he have the addresses of all the members of the organization? If he had printed an appeal and sent it out secretly to a hundred people it would have been more clever and useful.'

'I looked at him and waited for him to finish, unable to believe my own eyes and ears,' relates Balabanov. 'The tragedy that had driven the man, a Socialist who did not believe in acts of violence, to contradict everything which he himself had been preaching to the working class, and with one shot destroy that which it had taken a whole generation to build up, by which his own father lived and breathed, apparently did not exist for Vladimir Ilyich.

'Neither the conflict and mental anguish in Adler's soul, which drove him to rebel against his own principles, nor the consequence of his act stirred Lenin. He calculated exactly how many broadcasts Adler could have sent out, assuming that prior to his act Adler could calmly weigh and judge as to what was more useful, the death of a Minister or the issuance of a hundred secret broadcasts. . . . I laughed aloud and said to him: "You know Vladimir Ilyich, I envy you."

' "Why, Comrade Balabanov?"

' "I envy your ability to react so simply and directly, like a child, to such matters. Here is a whole tragedy, the struggle of two conflicting elements in one person, the struggle of two generations embodied in father and son."

' "Whatever it may be," Lenin replied, "Adler committed a foolish act. Just imagine the secretary of a party knowing all the addresses and making no use of them." ' [21]

This was hard-boiled pragmatism of a kind that neither Madame Balabanov nor the majority of Russian revolutionists could understand. As far as Lenin was concerned, Adler's action was a useless romantic gesture; it made no sense. Heroic gestures won no battles.

As the war continued on with no end in sight, the Zimmerwald International Socialist Committee called another conference. Held in the Swiss town of Kienthal on 24 April 1916, the forty-three delegates included three Socialist members of the French Chamber of Deputies.

At Kienthal the Zimmerwald Left, headed by Lenin, was much stronger than a half-year before and pushed through a resolution censuring the International Socialist Bureau of the Second International. While this was no clear-cut Bolshevik victory, Lenin was satisfied with the tactical gain.

'In spite of a host of drawbacks,' he wrote in May 1916, 'this is after all a step forward to a rupture with the social patriots.'

But Lenin attacked not only the right-wing Socialists and Centrists but also some of his own supporters for their attitude towards war, peace and revolution. He was particularly stern with their 'pacifist illusions'.

'There was nothing more pernicious', said Lenin, 'than the clerical, petty-bourgeois, pacifist argument that war could be abolished under capitalism. Imperialism necessarily gives rise to fierce rivalry among the capitalist states for the division and redivision of the world. Consequently, under capitalism, wars are inevitable. Only when capitalism is overthrown and Socialism triumphs all over the world will war be abolished.'[22]

Lenin poured withering scorn on those who suggested that the proletariat should refuse to bear arms. 'Our slogan', said Lenin, 'must be: Arm the proletariat in order to vanquish, expropriate, and disarm the bourgeoisie!'

Chafing because political action was impossible, Lenin plunged into writing. In the fall of 1916 he buried himself in the library from nine to six every day, collecting the material to complete his book *Imperialism, the Highest Stage of Capitalism*.

Once a week only, on Thursday, he would leave the library early for a mountain-climbing jaunt with his wife. Two chocolate nut bars were their field rations for the afternoon. In a secluded spot in the woods they would lie in the grass and read. The book he finished that year has since become the New Testament of Leninist-Marxism. Where *Das Kapital* had analysed the structure of industrial capitalism, Lenin emphasized the newer role of financial monopolies in world economy. He laid down the thesis that capitalist states, in their pursuit for new markets and colonies, would always settle their competitive differences by war. Only the destruction of the capitalist system, argued Lenin, would bring an end to the epoch of imperialist wars.

But he went still further. Until Socialism was established everywhere, it was false to advocate disarmament. Socialism could come only through revolution, according to Lenin, and revolutions could not be made by unarmed men. Before the victory of Socialism could be accomplished a war to the finish between the bourgeoisie and the proletariat was inevitable. Guns would decide that revolution, and guns in the hands of revolutionary troops spelled victory for the proletariat.

Lenin wrote in December 1916:

In many countries, especially in the small countries which are neutral in the present struggle, such as Sweden, Norway, Holland, Switzerland, voices are heard in favour of changing one of the demands in our minimum programme, namely, the demand for the arming of the people to disarming. Those who defend this attitude usually argue: 'We are against all wars, and that is why we demand disarmament.'

I have already shown how wrong this attitude is. Socialists, as long as they do not cease to be Socialists, cannot oppose war on general principles. One should not let himself be deceived by the imperialist character of the present war. It is possible to have wars and uprisings for democracy, as for example wars of oppressed people against their oppressors. Civil war between the bourgeoisie and the proletariat for Socialism is inevitable. It is possible to have war of one country, where Socialism has been victorious, against another bourgeois, reactionary country.[23]

The year 1916 was also darkened by the death of Maria Alexandrovna. Lenin had not seen his mother since their last meeting in Stockholm in 1910. It was there that she had heard him speak before an audience for the first and last time. Later he had escorted her and his sister Maria to the Russian steamer which took them home. Lenin could not risk boarding the vessel; farewells were said at the dock.

'I remember', said his sister, 'the look on his face as he stood there and gazed at Mother. How much pain was expressed in his face! It was almost as if he felt that this was his last meeting with Mother.'

It *was* the last meeting. Maria Alexandrovna's death hit Lenin hard. His letters home showed deep depression and unhappiness.

Isolated from events in Russia, deserted by many of his early followers, struggling to pay his modest living expenses, seeking in vain to rally Socialists of other lands to his slogans of international civil war, Lenin, at the end of 1916, was hitting the bottom rung of his ladder. Never did his words seem to attract fewer followers. Many looked on him as a crackpot.

When he returned from a political meeting in Geneva, he complained because he was receiving no word from the few men he had sent to Russia. One of his disciples, Comrade Filia, then suggested calling a congress of some fifty to sixty Bolsheviks in Russia to issue an anti-war manifesto in the name of the Party.

Lenin replied: 'Why fifty or sixty? That's too many. Four or five are sufficient. One from the Caucasus, one or two from Siberia, one from the Urals, one from Moscow, and one from Petrograd. If these four or five men, representing the labouring classes, came together from these centres, declared themselves delegates to a conference called in the name of the Party, and came out strongly against war, that would be a great historic event and would be a tremendous spur to the development of the revolutionary movement in Russia.'

Filia looked at Lenin with astonishment.

'Around these four or five men calling themselves a party conference,' Lenin continued, 'in the tense revolutionary atmosphere that would be created, there would crystallize the will of tens of thousands of workers hoping for a revolution.'[24]

But even these four or five were not available as the year 1916 drew to a close. Where were they to be found? The Bolshevik from the Caucasus, for example, was in Siberian exile, together with the Bolshevik members of the Duma and the members of the Central Committee of the Bolshevik Party.

Stalin was in the remote Turukhansk region on the Yenesei River. A few months before he was sent to this frozen desert, another prominent Bolshevik exile, Joseph Dubrovinsky, committed suicide by plunging into the icy river. Another revolutionist, Gallin, ended his life by locking himself within his cabin and setting it afire.

Stalin lived in the village of Kureika, located about fifteen miles within the Arctic Circle, on the banks of a stream of the same name. In the summer only a few steamers ventured that far. The remainder of the year there was practically no contact with the world.

From the warm Caucasus to Kureika was a change that few men would have survived. But Stalin acclimated himself to this brutal environment. He became an expert trapper, fisherman and lumberjack. He learned to live entirely on his own resourcefulness and inner strength during his four years of exile.

On rare occasions he attended meetings of exiles, but seldom rose to speak. When he did express an opinion it did not make him more popular. Once, when a criminal named Balanovsky robbed a peasant, the political exiles set up a court to try him for his crime. Unexpectedly, Stalin rose to defend the man.

'The thief is a product of capitalist society,' he said. 'Instead of condemning him for his act, he should be recruited, because men of this type are necessary for the fight to destroy the capitalist order.'

On another occasion Stalin himself was summoned to face a revolutionary 'court' for consorting with a police officer. Stalin assured the 'judges' that this friendship would not deter him from killing the policeman if he later found him on the opposite side of the barricades.

When war came, Stalin and about twenty other exiles were called up for military service, but the future architect of Red Army victory over Germany was rejected by army doctors because one of his arms did not bend properly. He remained in Siberian exile until the March Revolution.

Lenin had few adherents among the Bolsheviks who were still in European Russia on the eve of the Revolution. When his friend Solomon heard he was badly in need of money, he tried collecting funds among Lenin's former friends in Petrograd. He approached Krassin, who then had an excellent job as an engineer. The future Soviet diplomat shrugged his shoulders when Solomon asked him to contribute money for Lenin's support.

'George,' he said, 'you're wasting your time. You don't know Ilyich as well as I do. Let him go to the devil. Let's go out to lunch instead.'

While they were dining, Solomon renewed his plea. 'All right,' replied Krassin, 'I'll do it as a favour to you.' And he reached into his wallet for two five-ruble notes.

Angrily, Solomon threw back the ten rubles. 'We'll do without your contribution,' he told Krassin.

'That's excellent,' Krassin calmly replied, slipping the two notes back into his wallet. 'But don't be angry, George. Lenin doesn't deserve help. He is a destructive type and you can never tell what wild scheme will suddenly emanate from his Tartar skull. To hell with him.'[25]

Krassin wasn't the only Bolshevik who had grave doubts about Lenin in those days. In a Paris *émigré* newspaper *Our Echo* in July 1916 Viacheslav Menzhinsky, later chief of the Soviet secret police (in an article signed S.D.), wrote:

Lenin is a political Jesuit who over the course of many years has molded Marxism to his aims of the moment. He has now become completely confused. . . . Lenin, this illegitimate child of Russian absolutism, considers himself not only the natural successor to the Russian throne, when it becomes vacant, but also the sole heir of the Socialist International. Should he ever come to power, the mischief he would do would not be much less than that of Paul I [the half-mad Tsar who preceded Alexander I]. The Leninists are not even a faction, but a clan of party gypsies, who swing their whips so affectionately and hope to drown the voice of the proletariat with their screams, imagining it to be their unchallengeable right to be the *drivers* of the proletariat.

The year 1916 was bitter and quarrelsome for Lenin. 'Never, I think,' wrote Krupskaya, 'was Vladimir Ilyich in a more irreconcilable mood than during the last months of 1916 and the early months of 1917.' He had 'differences of opinion with Rosa Luxemburg, Radek, the Dutch, Bukharin, Piatakov . . . and Kollontai' and even with his sister Anna. When Maxim Gorky, trying to arrange legal publication of Lenin's *Imperialism* in Petrograd, asked him to omit some of the abusive epithets directed at Kautsky, Lenin wrote Inessa Armand that this was 'ridiculous and offensive'. He added: 'There you are, that's my fate. One fighting campaign after another – against political stupidities, vileness, opportunism, etc. And this from 1893 on. And the hatred of the philistines because of it. Well, all the same, I would not change my fate for "peace" with the philistines. . . .'

On 22 January 1917, Lenin told an assembly of young workers in Zurich: 'The present grave-like stillness in Europe must not deceive us. Europe is charged with revolution. The monstrous horrors of the imperialist war and the suffering caused by the high cost of living engender everywhere a revolutionary spirit; and the ruling classes, the bourgeoisie and their lackey governments, are moving more and more into a blind alley from which they can never extricate themselves without tremendous upheavals.'[26]

The 'grave-like stillness' was about to end.

Events inside Russia were heading rapidly towards the explosion that was to bring Lenin from exile in Switzerland to the limelight in Petrograd. The years of uphill struggle were drawing to a close. In January 1917 Lenin's name was still only vaguely known in Russia except among professional revolutionists. To the Socialists of western Europe he was still the café conspirator, the Russian with large theories and few followers. Three months later, installed in the palace of the Tsar's favourite ballerina, he was to become the thundering voice of a revolutionary movement such as the world had not seen since the days of the Jacobins.

Chapter 8
'The Freest Country in the World'

Long queues lined up in front of food stores in every Russian city and town. There was a critical shortage of bread, meat, oils and fat. In many cities electric powerhouses and waterworks ceased to operate. In some communities public and private bathhouses closed down. From every town came reports of impending rebellion.

The head of the Moscow Political Secret Service Bureau advised the State Police Department in October 1916: 'Privation is so great that many people are not only undernourished, but are actually starving. There is not the slightest doubt that to permit these lines when there is a shortage of food is as harmful in its influence as the holding of revolutionary meetings and the scattering of tens of thousands of revolutionary leaflets. I am sure that such bitterness and exasperation have never been witnessed before. Compared with conditions in 1905 the present state of affairs is of far graver portent to the government.'

In January 1917 the State Police Department reported: 'If the populace thus far has not engaged in food riots, that does not mean that it is not going to do so in the near future. The exasperation of the people is growing by leaps and bounds. Every day more and more of them demand: "Either give us food or stop the war." And they are the most suitable element among which to conduct anti-government propaganda. They have nothing to lose from a disadvantageous peace. Just when the thing will happen and how it is hard to tell. But events of the greatest importance and fraught with the most dangerous consequences are most certainly close at hand.'

The government chose to ignore these warnings.

The continued drafting of workers and the requisitioning of horses greatly diminished the areas of sown land. Shortage of farm hands slashed the crop yield. By January 1917 the price of commodities in Petrograd had increased six-fold and in the provinces five-fold. In Moscow signs reading 'No bread today, and none expected' were a common sight.

There was also a serious fuel shortage. Moscow was compelled to cut in half its consumption of electricity for lighting purposes.

Among the peasants still ran the thread of hope that after the war they would be given land. The most extravagant rumours spread through the villages. As the war continued and new classes were mobilized, these expectations dimmed. Soldiers writing from the front described their sufferings. They wrote of being compelled to fight without guns and on short rations. And, as casualty lists mounted, crippled veterans began to fill the villages. The second-class military reserves, who included the last bulwark of the peasant countryside, were called to the colours.

Ugly rumours of Rasputin's power, of treason and betrayal, reached the villages. The same unrest existed even more actively in the Army, whose great bulk was made up of peasants linked to their villages by common suffering and common interests. The front subsisted on rumours and reports from the village, the village on tidings from the front. The peasants in the ranks reacted much as did the peasants at home, but with greater intensity. Their resentment, aggravated by their misery and by unnecessarily cruel army discipline, took more resolute forms.

The State Police was forced to report. 'The Army in the rear and at the fighting line is full of elements, some of whom may become an active force of rebellion, while others may refuse to participate in punitive measures against the mutineers. Should the former succeed in organizing themselves properly, there would hardly be enough units in the Army to constitute a strong counter-revolutionary force to defend the government. A whole people in arms is permeated with revolutionary elements made up of class-conscious workers and peasants, to whom might be added tens of thousands of soldiers belonging to the oppressed nationalities.'

The inflammable material was rapidly approaching the point of spontaneous combustion. The government, dominated by Rasputin and his puppets, was disintegrating. No such pitiful assembly ever headed the Russian Government as during the last year of Romanov rule. The only more or less able personality was Protopopov, the Minister of the Interior. But even he was an eccentric. He picked the day for summoning the Duma by consulting his horoscope, and recommended dissolution because the Emperor of Japan had dissolved Parliament repeatedly without disastrous results.

The other Ministers were opportunists, grafters, and old men placed in high office to cover up corruption. There was Stuermer, a dotard 'fit to be led by a string', as Rasputin expressed it. Khvostov was an embezzler who had purchased his office through Rasputin. There was Shcheglovitov, whom Rasputin called a 'brazen-faced Cain'; Kurlov, a debauchee and grafter; Dobrovolsky, who made decisions of state at spiritualist séances.

Even the Empress Alexandra was aware of the utter incompetence of the Ministers. In letters to her husband she called them 'fools and idiots', and said she felt like 'giving them a good beating'. But the Tsar believed that these were precisely the kind of people he needed.

Compared with this *camarilla*, the earlier Ministers of Nicholas, men such as Witte, Stolypin, and even Plehve and Pobedonostsev, were major statesmen.

In the last month of the monarchy, with the Tsar spending much of his time at military headquarters in Mohilev, the real ruler of Russia was the Empress. Acting in her husband's name, she seated and unseated Ministers.

The Duma was powerless to influence events. Yet by the latter part of 1916 the parties of the Progressive Bloc had to make a determined bid for power. Conditions in the country were such that a drastic change was imperative. New political leadership and a new command were needed to save Russia's economic structure and the Army. Alexander Guchkov, former president of the Duma, urged a *coup d'état*. A number of plans were proposed. Someone suggested that the Empress be invited aboard a warship and taken to England. Guchkov and General Krimov favoured seizure of the imperial train, forcing Nicholas to abdicate in favour of his young son Alexis, with the Grand Duke Mikhail (the Tsar's brother) as regent, and arresting the members of the government.

On 7 November 1916, Grand Duke Nikolai Nikolayevich had an intimate talk with his nephew the Tsar and warned him that his throne was tottering. 'Come to your senses before it is too late,' he said. 'Grant a responsible ministry.' The Tsar remained silent and the Grand Duke left, convinced that 'soon we would be rolling downhill, and that sooner or later he would lose his crown.'[1]

On 30 December 1916, members of the court attempted to save the dynasty by killing Rasputin. The assassination was carried out in the home of Prince Yussupov, with the participation of the Tsar's cousin, Grand Duke Dmitri, and Purishkevich, the monarchist leader in the Duma. The elimination of Rasputin, however, came too late to save the dynasty.

From all quarters the Duma was bombarded with demands that it assume full control. The hungry and irate people; the army leaders, desperate because of the incompetent conduct of the war; the representatives of the nobility, even members of the Tsar's own family, demanded the creation of a government responsible to the Duma.

To those who demanded that the Duma seize the reigns of government, Mikhail Rodzianko, its president, replied, 'Legislative bodies cannot occupy themselves with *coups d'état*. I am neither able nor willing to arouse the people against the Tsar.'[1]

In January 1917 General Krimov, returning from the front, described the critical situation along the fighting line. Speaking at a meeting in the home of Rodzianko, attended by members of the Duma, the State Council and the various Industrial Military committees, he declared that the Army was ready to support the Duma in a palace revolution. He asserted that the officers and men no longer had faith in the command; that there was political interference with the conduct of operations, that there could be no decisive victory unless a new government was established.

'The feeling in the Army is such,' he concluded, 'that the Army will greet with joy the news of a *coup d'état*.'

But the Duma was not ready to act. Opinion was divided.

'The general is right – a *coup d'état* is necessary,' argued Deputy Shingarev, 'but who will dare to undertake it?'

Deputy Shidlovsky angrily exclaimed, 'We cannot waste pity on the Tsar if he ruins Russia.'

This sentiment was echoed by many members of the Duma, who subscribed to the words of General Brusilov, the commander on the south-western Front, 'If it comes to a choice between the Tsar and Russia, I will take Russia.'

On 3 February 1917, Grand Duke Mikhail asked Rodzianko point-blank: 'Do you think there is going to be a revolution?' Rodzianko replied that it was still possible to save the country by removing the Empress from politics and appointing Ministers in whom the country had confidence. He warned, however, that revolution was inevitable if the Empress remained in power.

'As long as the war goes on, the people realize that division means ruin for the Army,' Rodzianko stated. 'But there is another kind of danger. The government and the Empress are leading Russia towards a separate peace, to shame, and into the arms of Germany. The nation will not tolerate it, and should it prove true – and there are plenty of rumours to that effect – we shall have a terrible revolution which will carry away the throne, the dynasty, you and me.'

The Grand Duke agreed: 'Sir George Buchanan [the British Ambassador] said the same thing to my brother. Our family realizes how harmful the Empress is. She and my brother are surrounded by traitors; all decent people have left them. But what to do?'

'Describe the exact situation to the Tsar,' Rodzianko suggested. 'You, Your Highness, as his only brother, should tell him the truth. Tell him all the harm the Empress does; that the people regard her as Germanophile, working against the interests of Russia.'

The Grand Duke promised to try.

Two weeks later, on 15 February, Rodzianko warned the Tsar that Russia was approaching the breaking point. 'Your Majesty must find a way to remove the Empress from politics.'

He pleaded with Nicholas to appoint a responsible Prime Minister to work with the Duma and other public bodies in the direction of the war. Said Rodzianko: 'The idea spreads that everything is done that harms Russia and benefits the enemy. Strange rumours circulate about traitors and spies in the rear of the Army. There is not one honest man in your entourage: all decent people have either been sent away or have left. It is no secret that the Empress issues state orders without consulting you; that Ministers go to her with their reports; and that at her will those of whom she disapproves are removed and are replaced by others who are totally unfit.'

Nicholas replied: 'Produce your facts. You have no evidence to support your words.'

When, on 23 February, Rodzianko again reported to the Tsar, he found him irritable and impatient. He interrupted Rodzianko with the request that he finish his business because the Grand Duke Mikhail was waiting for tea. When Rodzianko again reminded him of the danger of rebellion, Nicholas replied: 'The information I have is quite contrary to yours, and as to the Duma, I should like to say that if it permits itself such harsh speeches as last time it will be dissolved.'

'Your Majesty,' Rodzianko replied, 'I regard it as my duty to tell you that I have a foreboding that this is my last report to you.'

'Why?' asked Nicholas.

'Because the Duma will be dismissed, and the course which the government pursues will lead to no good results. There is still time and opportunity to turn back and form a government responsible to the chambers. But this, seemingly, is not to be. Your Majesty does not agree with me and things are as they have been. The result will be a revolution and such anarchy as no one will be able to control.'

Nicholas did not reply.[2]

On 27 February 1917, the Duma was convened by imperial decree.

At its opening session, Alexander Kerensky, leader of the Trudoviks, declared: 'There are people who assert that the Ministers are at fault. Not so. The country now realizes that the Ministers are but fleeting shadows. The country can clearly see who sends them here. To prevent a catastrophe the Tsar himself must be removed, by force if there is no other way. . . . If you will not listen to the voice of warning now you will find yourself face to face with the facts, not warning. Look up at the distant flashes that are lighting the skies of Russia.'

When the Empress read Kerensky's speech she demanded that he he hanged as a traitor.

But there were other 'traitors' too. The Labour group of the War Industries Committee issued this proclamation to the Petrograd workers:

On the occasion of the opening of the Duma we must be prepared for a general organization of a demonstration. The entire labouring class of Petrograd, factory after factory, district after district, must march in unison to the Tauride Palace, where the Duma opens, to present the basic demands of the working class and of the democracy. The whole country and the Army must hearken to the voice of the working class.

At a secret meeting in Petrograd of all Left parties, the Bolshevik spokesman Shliapnikov declared that his group could not back the Liberal demand for the creation of a ministry responsible to the Duma. The Bolsheviks would not oppose the planned demonstration, he said, but they would conduct their propaganda with other slogans. They favoured a demonstration on the Nevsky Prospect, 'with our own demands, under the Red flag of Revolution, for the destruction of the Duma and the entire system of Tsarist absolutism.'[3]

In the demonstration on 27 February a large number of officers joined the students in revolutionary songs. The wall between the barracks and the street had begun to totter.

The Duma had been in session a week when Rodzianko heard to his surprise that the Tsar was about to announce the creation of a responsible Ministry. Premier Golitsyn and other members of the Cabinet had been summoned and Nicholas himself promised to appear before the Duma the following day.

Golitsyn's joy was brief, for in the evening the Emperor sent for him again and told him that he was leaving for Headquarters.

'But Your Majesty, what about the responsible Ministry? You planned to go to the Duma tomorrow,' Golitsyn reminded him.

'That's true, but I have changed my mind and am going to Headquarters this evening.'

While Nicholas was floundering, events resolved themselves with sudden speed. On 8 March 1917, the workers of Petrograd went on strike. On 10 March General Khabalov, commander of the Petrograd garrison, sent a wire to the Tsar informing him that workers in many factories were on strike because of the bread shortage and that the populace had become unruly.

The Tsar replied: 'Stop the disorder in the capital at once.' Khabalov ordered the wholesale shooting of the rioters.

To the Empress these rumblings represented nothing more than minor disorders which troops would quickly suppress. On 9 March she wrote her husband:

Yesterday there were riots on the Vasiliev Island and on Nevsky, when the poor raided the bakeries. They demolished the Filipov bakery and Cossacks were sent against them. All this I learned from unofficial sources. The riots increased by ten o'clock, but by one they subsided. Khabalov is now in control of the situation.

The next day she wrote her husband that there was nothing to worry about, provided the Duma caused no trouble.

Her letter began:

The strikers and rioters in the city are now in a more defiant mood than ever. The disturbances are created by hoodlums. Youngsters and girls are running around shouting they have no bread; they do this just to create some excitement. If the weather were cold they would all probably be staying at home. But the thing will pass and quiet down, provided the Duma behaves. The worst of the speeches are not reported in the papers, but I think that for speaking against the dynasty there should be immediate and severe punishment.

On 11 March she confided to her husband that idlers were causing this contretemps:

The whole trouble comes from these idlers, well-dressed people, wounded soldiers, high-school girls, etc., who are inciting others. Lily spoke to some cab-drivers to find out about things. They told her that the students came to them and told them if they appeared in the streets in the morning, they would be shot to death. What corrupt minds! Of course the cab-drivers and the motormen are now on strike. But they say that it is all different from 1905, because they all worship you and only want bread.

On the very eve of open revolution the Empress wrote: 'Monday I read a scurrilous proclamation, but I think everything will be all right. The sun is shining so brightly and I feel so calm and at peace at His grave. He died to save us.' 'He' was Rasputin.

While the Empress was dispatching these letters of comfort, Rodzianko on 11 March wired the Emperor:

The situation is serious. The capital is in a state of anarchy. The government is paralysed; the transport service has broken down; the food and fuel supplies are completely disorganized. Discontent is general and on the increase. There is wild shooting on the streets; troops are firing at each other. It is urgent that someone enjoying the confidence of the country be entrusted with the formation of a new government. There must be no delay. Hesitation is fatal.

This he followed the next day with another wire:

The situation is growing worse. Measures should be taken immediately as tomorrow will be too late. The last hour has struck, when the fate of the country and dynasty is being decided.

'Dissolve the Duma!' replied the Tsar.

Rodzianko's wire advised:

By your Majesty's order, the sessions of the Imperial Duma have been adjourned until April. The last bulwark of order has been removed. The government is powerless to stop the disorders. The troops of the garrison cannot be relied upon. The reserve battalions of the Guard regiments are in the grip of rebellion, their officers are being killed. Having joined the mobs and the revolt of the people, they are marching on the offices of the Ministry of the Interior and the Imperial Duma. Civil war has begun and is spreading. Order immediately the formation of a new government upon the principle submitted in my telegram of yesterday. Revoke your recent order and command the legislative chambers to reconvene. Announce a manifesto to these measures. Your Majesty, do not delay. Should the agitation reach the Army, Germany will triumph and the destruction of Russia along with the dynasty is inevitable. In the name of Russia, I beg Your Majesty to carry out the above recommendation. The hour which will decide your own fate and the fate of Russia has arrived. Tomorrow it may be too late.

General Khabalov sent a wire to the Tsar reporting mutiny among troops in Petrograd and asking for new units from the front to suppress the rebellion.

Nicholas, however, continued to follow his wife's advice. By dissolving the Duma he destroyed the last barrier between himself and the Revolution.

By general agreement an unofficial meeting of the deputies was called on 12 March to decide on a course of action following the Tsar's dissolution order.

Earlier that morning the telephone rang in the apartment house of Vasili Shulgin, a conservative member of the Duma.

'Is that you, Vasili Vitalevich?' asked Shingarev, a Liberal deputy. 'It's time to go to the Duma. It has begun.'

'What are you talking about?'

'It has begun. There is an order to dismiss the Duma; the city is in an uproar. Let's hurry. They are occupying the bridges. We may never get there. An automobile has been sent for me. Come at once to my place, and we will go together.'

As they were driving, Shingarev said, 'That's the answer. Until the last I continued to hope that they would somehow see the light and make concessions. But no, they dismissed the Duma. That was the last opportunity. An agreement with the Duma, no matter what kind, was the last chance to escape revolution.'

When they reached Kamenostrovski Prospect the streets were already thronged. Factories, schools and universities were on strike. As they approached the Neva River, the dense crowd brought their automobile to a standstill.

Shingarev leaned out of the window and said: 'We are members of the Duma. Let us pass.'

A student ran to the window. 'Are you Mr Shingarev?'

'Yes, I am Shingarev. Let us pass.'

'Immediately.'

He jumped on the running-board. 'Comrades, make way! These are members of the Imperial Duma – Comrade Shingarev.' The crowd opened up and the car moved on, with the student still on the running-board. At the Troitski Bridge the road was blocked by a company of soldiers.

'Tell them,' said the student, 'that you are going to the Duma', and with these words he disappeared. In his place appeared an officer who politely apologized for the delay.

'Open up. These are members of the Duma.' As they sped across the deserted bridge, Shingarev remarked: 'The Duma still stands between the people and the government.'

Other deputies came to the Duma, reporting the fast-moving events. Workers were assembling on the Viborg side and were holding an election of some kind – hands raised. A regiment has revolted; apparently the Volinsky. They've killed their commanding officer. The Cossacks have refused to shoot; they fraternize with the people. Barricades have been thrown up on the Nevsky. No one knows anything about the fate of the Ministers. An army of some 30,000 workers, students, soldiers and women is marching on the Duma.

Later there was a meeting of the leaders of all parties in the office of the president of the Duma. Rodzianko presided. To remain in session after the Tsar's order of dissolution meant proclaiming revolution. Rodzianko and the majority did not dare take this step. It was decided to go through the motion of obeying the decree, to meet at once in an informal session. From all sides, from the Right and the Left, came excited speeches. Someone proposed that the Duma refuse to disperse, proclaim itself the acting government, or declare itself a Constituent Assembly. This proposal was not accepted. Another demanded that the Duma declare whether it stood with Nicholas or with the people. Just then there was a commotion at the door, shouts were heard, and an officer rushed into the room.

'Gentlemen of the Duma, I implore your protection,' he cried in a loud, shrill voice. 'I am the head of the guard, your guard, the guard of the Duma. Some unknown soldiers have forced their way in. They have severely wounded my side. They tried to kill me. I barely escaped. Help me!'

At this moment Kerensky spoke up: 'What has just happened proves that we must not delay. I am constantly receiving information that the troops are agitated. They are coming out on the street. I am now going to visit the regiments. I must know what to say to them. May I tell them that the Duma is with them, that it assumes all responsibility, that it will stand at the head of the movement?'

'I do not recall', writes Shulgin, 'whether he received an answer – probably not. But from that moment his figure stood out. He spoke with positiveness, as one having authority. His words and gestures were sharp, to the point; his eyes flashed.

' "He is the Dictator!" I heard a whisper near me.'[4]

The mass of 30,000 marching men and women, soldiers, workers and students had arrived at Tauride Palace. Kerensky addressed the first wave of soldiers to reach the Duma as 'the first revolutionary guard'. The Duma and the revolution were fused in a turbulent union as the people took possession of the building.

On the same day – 12 March 1917 – the workers of the Petrograd factories organized a Soviet of Workers' Deputies, modelled after the Petrograd Soviet of 1905, and elected Chkheidze, leader of the Social Democratic Duma delegation, chairman, with Kerensky as vice-chairman.

The revolting regiments and workers broke into the jails and freed the political prisoners, then marched with the liberated revolutionaries to the Tauride Palace. Here the outstanding figures of revolutionary Petrograd were already assembled. By two o'clock most of the trade-union and co-operative leaders had arrived. Banding together with the Leftist Duma deputies, the leaders of the Labour Group of the War Industries Committee organized the Provisional Executive Committee of the Soviet of Workers' Deputies. It consisted of Socialist Duma Deputies Chkheidze and Skobelev and five other members.

Immediately the committee went into action, calling the first meeting of the Petrograd Soviet of Workers' Deputies for seven o'clock that evening. The appeal was distributed by truck to all factories in the city. Within a few hours the proletariat of Petrograd was organized in a revolutionary assembly. The committee also set up a central staff for the revolutionary armies in the Tauride Palace and took measures to feed the soldiers who were milling in the streets.

The meeting hall of the committee was jammed with workers, soldiers, deputies, intellectuals and correspondents. Long before seven o'clock the delegates began to pour in by the hundreds. They were registered by a crew, representing the committee, grouped around a long table outside the assembly hall.

Men of all the underground Socialist groups flocked to the Tauride Palace. Shliapnikov, the Bolshevik Party delegate, tried to group all his followers around him. Gvozdiov, just liberated from prison, lined up his right-wing Menshevik cohorts. Other Mensheviks gathered around Chkheidze, who frantically answered all their questions with, 'I don't know, comrades, I don't know a thing.' Another group of students, workers and intellectuals centred around the Socialist Revolutionary Vladimir Zenzinov. A Social Democratic lawyer scurried hastily from group to group, arranging the seating and explaining the voting procedure.

At the chairman's table, awaiting the arrival of the Provisional Executive Committee, sat Khrustalev, who had headed the 1905 Soviet, and Sokolov. The latter opened the meeting at nine o'clock and asked for the election of a presidium. When the session began there were two hundred and fifty delegates present, but more and more groups continued to arrive carrying all sorts of mandates and credentials.

The delegates discussed the food situation, measures against developing anarchy, and preparations for the final fight against Tsarism. They then elected a permanent presidium, consisting of Chkheidze as chairman, Kerensky and Skobelev as vice-chairmen, and Gvozdiov, Sokolov, Grinevich and the left-wing Menshevik Pankov as secretaries.

Khrustalev, demanding the floor several times, recalled the experience of 1905. It was clear that he wished to assume leadership. But the delegates were not favourably impressed and he soon disappeared from the scene.

When a group of soldiers asked for the floor, their demand was granted with enthusiasm. Standing on chairs, with rifles in their hands, the soldiers reported what was taking place in their regiments. The account in each case was almost identical but the assembly listened with rapt attention, for their recital spelled the end of Romanov rule.

'We are from the Volinsky regiment . . . from the Pavlovsky regiment . . . from the Litovsky . . . from the Finlandsky . . . from the Grenadiers. . . .'

As the names of the regiments that had turned the bread riots into a Revolution rang out, they were greeted by tremendous bursts of applause.

'We are assembled . . . we were told to say . . . the officers are in hiding . . . in the Soviet of Workers' Deputies we were told to say that we don't want to serve against the people . . . we join our brothers, the workers, in order to defend the cause of the people together . . . we'll give our lives for it . . . our meeting decided to greet . . . Long live the Revolution!'

In a matter of a few moments the delegates decided to unite the revolutionary army and workers in one organization. The assembly now became the Soviet of Workers' and Soldiers' Deputies.

But many regiments were still not represented at the Tauride Palace; there was still danger of a bloody battle between picked Tsarist troops and the revolutionary garrison of Petrograd.

While the Soviet was discussing the situation, a young soldier, waving his rifle above his head, ran in and breathlessly shouted, 'Comrades and brothers, I bring you the comradely greetings of all the soldiers of the Semionovsky Guards. All of us, to the last man, have decided to join hands with the people against the accursed autocracy. We swear to serve the cause of the people to the last drop of our blood.'

Once more the meeting was thrown into a frenzy of enthusiasm. Every member of the audience knew that the Semionovsky Guard had suppressed the Moscow uprising of 1905. The regiment was counted as one of the sturdiest bulwarks of the Tsarist régime. As more and more units rushed their representatives into the hall, revolutionary Petrograd knew that Tsar Nicholas no longer could command the forces to halt the Revolution.

The Soviet published a proclamation telling the people of Petrograd of the formation of this revolutionary assembly, and asking them to maintain order. The proclamation ended with the summons for an elected Constituent Assembly to shape Russia's democratic future.

The document was published in the first issue of *Izvestia*, organ of the Petrograd Soviet, which appeared the next morning. The Soviet also voted that night to allow the daily newspapers suspended by the strikes to resume publication. Nobody challenged the authority of the Soviet to end the press strike, because the powerful Typographical Workers' Union of Petrograd was represented in the Tauride Palace.

The elections to the permanent Executive Committee which followed were largely non-partisan, because the position of each party was not yet clearly defined or familiar to the delegates. Since the underground Socialists were not very well known, writers such as Steklov and Sukhanov, who were contributors to well-known Petrograd and Moscow radical publications, received the largest number of votes. Others elected were the Bolsheviks Shliapnikov and Zalutsky; the lawyer Pavlovich-Krasikov, Dmitrevsky and Sokolovsky. The Executive Committee was also to include the members of the presidium, as well as two representatives of the Central Committees of each Socialist party and of their local Petrograd organizations.

Among those added to the committee the following day were Molotov (who was supplanted by Stalin when the latter returned from Siberia), the Mensheviks Boris Bogdanov and Batursky, the Socialist Revolutionaries Zenzinov and Nicholas Russanov, the Popular Socialists Alexey Peshekhonov and Charnolusky, the Trudoviks Leon Bramson and Nicholas Chaikovsky, the Jewish Socialist Bundists Henrick Ehrlich and M. Rafes (succeeded a few days later by Mark Lieber), and the Latvian and Polish Social Democrats Stuchka and Kozlovsky, both closely aligned with the Bolsheviks.

The majority of the committee were 'internationalists' and Zimmerwaldists, although this majority was shaken slightly by the addition of ten soldiers' representatives.

During the first few weeks not one of the future central figures of the Revolution belonged to the Executive Committee. Some of them were in exile, others still abroad.

In the early days the Soviet set for itself the task of spreading and consolidating the revolutionary gains and fighting military and ideological attacks from the Right. The Soviet was not a conventional parliamentary body. It functioned from day to day, without set rules. Its membership soon reached 2,000; by the middle of March it had 3,000 delegates.

It was to the Soviet that Rodzianko appealed for permission to secure a train to see the Tsar; it was the Soviet that stopped the general strike, reopened the factories and restored streetcar traffic.

At the Duma the situation was still chaotic. No one knew what would happen next. Kerensky and Chkheidze, accompanied by several other Socialist deputies, took a bold chance. They appeared on the streets and made a direct appeal to the soldiers to join the rebellion. The soldiers responded.[5]

With their mandate from the Petrograd Soviet, Kerensky and Chkheidze now persuaded the majority of the Duma to elect a Provisional Committee to take over the reins of government. Both became members of this committee.

The walls of the city were plastered with the first issue of *Izvestia*, calling on the people to complete the overthrow of the Tsarist régime and pave the way for a democratic government.

'The fight must go on to the end. The old powers must be completely overthrown to make way for popular government. All together, with our forces united we shall battle to wipe out completely the old government and call a Constituent Assembly', the proclamation read.

The Tsar's Council of Ministers now offered to disband and to instruct Prince George Lvov or Rodzianko to form a new cabinet. Frantically Grand Duke Mikhail telephoned Chief of Staff General Alexeyev, asking him to make an eleventh-hour appeal to the Emperor to grant a responsible Ministry. The Tsar replied that he was grateful for his brother's advice but would do nothing of the kind. He did not know that the Duma conservatives were already swept into the background by the revolutionary masses of workers and soldiers.

In his imperial train at General Headquarters, near Moghiliev, Nicholas still did not realize what had happened. He would show a firm hand, he thought. He would appoint a dictator to put down the uprising. General Ivanov was chosen for the job. On the night of 13 March Ivanov left for the capital at the head of a detachment of presumably loyal troops. Nicholas gave orders for the imperial train to return to Tsarskoye Selo near Petrograd.

'Went to bed at a quarter past three,' the Tsar recorded in his diary. 'Had a long talk with N. I. Ivanov, whom I am sending with troops to restore order. Slept until 10 a.m. We left for Moghiliev at five in the morning. The weather was fair and frosty.'

In the Tsar's entourage there were those who sensed that the end was near. 'We shall soon hang from the lamp-posts,' said Captain Nilov, a bon-vivant companion of Nicholas. 'We shall have a revolution such as the world has never seen.'

Two trains sped towards the capital. The first carried the Tsar's staff; the second, Nicholas and his personal aides. The passengers on the imperial train slept longer than usual.

At one station it met a detachment of soldiers drawn up on the platform *en route* to the front. When the Tsar came to the window, he heard cheers and the strains of the imperial hymn. For a moment his aide-de-camp Mordvinov felt a glimmer of hope. But his companion, General Narishkin, executive officer of Military Headquarters, whispered into his ear: 'Who knows, perhaps we have heard the last hurrah for the Emperor.'

At two o'clock in the morning the train pulled into the station of Malaya Vishera, where an anxious group was waiting on the platform. It was a clear, frosty night. Nicholas was fast asleep. General Narishkin alighted, followed by Mordvinov.

'Where is the court commandant? Where is the entourage?' Questions were shot at them.

'Everyone is asleep.'

'What do you mean, asleep? Don't you know that Liuban and Tosno have been occupied by revolutionary troops? Haven't you received our wire? We've been ordered to re-route your train straight to Petrograd where there is some kind of a Provisional Government in power.'

Quickly the imperial train started back for Pskov, where General Ruzsky, commander of the northern front, had his headquarters. Perhaps Ruzsky would help.

Nicholas, gazing out of the train window at the changing landscape, had not yet renounced hope that Ivanov's troops would crush the rebellion.

The Empress meanwhile was in Tsarskoye Selo at the bedside of her children, who were sick with the measles. She wrote to her husband:

Things are rotten. I don't know where I can reach you but I firmly believe, and nothing can shake my belief, that everything will be all right. Not knowing where you are, I tried to get in touch with you through Headquarters, as Rodzianko pretended that he did not know where and why you were detained. It is clear that they are trying to prevent you from seeing me before they make you sign some paper, a constitution or some other horrid thing, I suppose. And you, without the support of the Army, caught like a mouse in a trap, what can you do? It is the greatest meanness and vileness, unheard of in history, to detain someone's Emperor. Perhaps by showing yourself to the troops in Pskov and in other places you will rally them around yourself. If you are forced to make concessions, you don't have to feel bound to live up to them because they have been obtained under duress.

Even had Nicholas received these lines in time, there was nothing he could have done. Ruzsky advised him to bow to the will of the Provisional Duma Committee. After more than an hour of argument the Tsar agreed to the formation of a responsible Ministry, headed by Rodzianko. Ruzsky then returned and asked the Emperor to countermand General Ivanov's orders. Nicholas capitulated and wired to Ivanov:

'I hope you have arrived safely. Please take no action until I arrive and receive your report.'

The Tsar made these concessions at half past three on the morning of 14 March. Ruzsky immediately notified Rodzianko by direct wire. But Rodzianko was furious when he received the Tsar's instructions. Had he not recommended this action weeks earlier, when it had been possible? It was too late now. The people now demanded the Tsar's abdication.

At ten-fifteen in the morning Ruzsky once more appeared in the imperial car. Nicholas was expecting a report on Petrograd's reception of his manifesto. Instead, Ruzsky placed before him the tape containing the text of his conversation with Rodzianko. Nicholas asked Ruzsky to read it to him. The communication was long. Then he rose from his chair and walked over to the window. There was a moment of silence. At last Nicholas regained his self-control. He returned to the table and began to talk.

His voice did not betray excitement, but his words were almost incoherent: 'If it is necessary that I step aside for the good of Russia, I am ready, but I am afraid the people will misunderstand. ... Why, the Cossacks will accuse me of quitting the firing line. ... I was born to be unhappy. I bring unhappiness to Russia. ... But the Old Believers will never forgive me for violating the oath I gave on coronation day. ...'

At this point a telegram arrived from General Alexeyev, the Chief of Staff, stating bluntly that the war could be continued only if the Tsar abdicated in favour of his son, under the regency of Grand Duke Mikhail. Every moment lost would lead to further demands by the revolutionists, who now controlled the railroads and supply service for the Army.

Ruzsky read Alexeyev's telegram.

'What do you think about it, Nikolai Vladimirovich?' the Tsar asked.

'The matter is so important,' the general replied, 'that I shall have to ask Your Majesty for a little more time to consider it. Let us hear what the commanding generals on the other fronts have to say.'

At two o'clock Ruzsky called again, this time accompanied by two other generals. None of the Tsar's attendants were in the car. The doors were shut tightly. Nicholas received the three commanders standing, then sat down and asked the callers to be seated. Only Ruzsky accepted the invitation. The other two stood at attention. During the audience the Tsar and Ruzsky smoked incessantly.

Ruzsky reported the latest news. The Tsar's own bodyguards had deserted and marched to the Duma to offer their services; the Empress had expressed a desire to confer with Rodzianko; Grand Duke Cyril Vladimirovich, heading a detachment of troops, had pledged loyalty to the Duma; the military governor of the Moscow District had accepted the authority of the

Provisional Duma Committee; the Tsar's Ministers were under arrest.

At half past two came Alexeyev's wire with the answers of the commanding generals at the various fronts. All favoured abdication.

'But how do I know that it is the desire of all Russia?'

'Your Majesty,' replied Ruzsky, 'circumstances prevent us from sending out questionnaires on this matter. On the other hand things are breaking so fast that the least delay is dangerous.'

There was a moment of silence.

'I have made up my mind,' stated the Emperor, 'I am abdicating,' and made the sign of the cross. The generals did the same.

On telegraph blanks he wrote out two messages. One, to Rodzianko, read: 'There is no sacrifice that I would not be willing to make for the welfare and salvation of Mother Russia. Therefore I am ready to abdicate in favour of my son, under the regency of my brother Mikhail Alexandrovich, with the understanding that my son is to remain with me until he becomes of age.'

The other, addressed to General Alexeyev, declared: 'For the happiness and salvation of our beloved Russia I am ready to abdicate the throne in favour of my son. I request everyone to serve him faithfully and honestly.'[6]

At five o'clock in the morning of 15 March 1917, Duma deputies Guchkov and Shulgin set out from Petrograd for Pskov with a document of abdication for the Tsar's signature.

Shulgin writes:

We arrived at ten o'clock at night. We stepped out on the platform. . . . Someone came up to say that the Emperor was waiting. He led us across the tracks . . . to the car of the Emperor. He appeared in a few minutes. . . . We bowed. . . . He shook hands with us in a friendly way . . . motioned us to a seat. Guchkov began to speak. . . . He was quite excited. . . . He related what was taking place at the capital. . . . He painted things as they were in Petrograd. The Emperor sat there quite composed. . . .

When Guchkov had finished, the Emperor said in a calm and matter-of-fact manner:

'I have decided to abdicate the throne. . . . Until three in the afternoon I thought that I would abdicate in favour of my son Alexei. . . . But at that time I changed my mind to abdicate in favour of my brother Mikhail. . . .'

We did not expect this. It seems to me that after Guchkov raised some objections, I asked for a quarter of an hour to advise with Guchkov ... but this did not take place ... we agreed. ... What else could we do?

The Tsar rose ... and we all stood up. ... Guchkov handed him his outline of the abdication act which the Emperor took, and walked out. After a little while he returned with the text of the abdication, which he handed to Guchkov.

It was then twenty minutes before midnight. The Emperor bade us good-bye, shaking us by the hand ... and his attitude was, if anything, warmer than when we arrived. ... We returned to our car ... and in the morning reached Petrograd.[7]

In Petrograd, the Duma Committee and the Executive Committee of the Soviet had, in the meantime, appointed the members of the new Provisional Government. Heading the Cabinet was Prince George Lvov, President of the All-Russian Union of Zemstvos and Municipalities; Professor Paul Miliukov, leader of the Cadet Party, was named Foreign Minister; Alexander Guchkov, Minister of War, and Alexander Kerensky, Minister of Justice. Most of the other Ministers were prominent Liberal members of the Duma.

Nicholas's abdication in favour of Grand Duke Mikhail came too late. The Soviet of Workers' and Soldiers' Deputies refused to recognize the continuation of the dynasty.

On 16 March, at six o'clock in the morning, Kerensky telephoned the Grand Duke to inform him that the members of the Duma Committee, headed by Rodzianko, wished to talk with him. The Committee had decided upon a course of action the night before. With the exception of Miliukov, all agreed that the Grand Duke should be persuaded to decline the throne. Miliukov's only supporter was Guchkov, who was not yet back from Pskov.

At the home of the Grand Duke, Rodzianko presented the view of the majority. Miliukov then argued that the establishment of order required a suitable symbol of power to which the Russian people were accustomed; namely, a monarch. A Provisional Government without a monarch would be a rudderless vessel which might perish in the sea of popular upheaval. Under such conditions the country would be in danger of falling prey to anarchy before a Constituent Assembly could convene. A Provisional Government alone would not last long, Miliukov asserted.

Kerensky and others replied that the assumption of power by the Grand Duke would not only involve a great risk to his person, but might also lead to a bloody civil war. Miliukov retorted that this risk had to be assumed otherwise they would not be responsible for what might come in the future.

Miliukov advised the Grand Duke to leave Petrograd, where most of the revolutionary troops were stationed, and go to Moscow, where a military force on which the Duma Committee could rely was still available. In Miliukov's opinion, three energetic, popular and resourceful men, one on the throne, another at the head of the Army, and a third at the helm of the government, could save Russia from anarchy.

After several hours of deliberation, the Grand Duke decided, despite Miliukov's pleading, to waive his right to the throne.

'One felt', Miliukov wrote later, 'that the Grand Duke's refusal was inspired not by love for Russia, but rather by fear for his own person.'

Alexandra meanwhile still hoped for a repetition of 1905 when Nicholas, after granting a constitution and civil liberties, had revoked his promise and crushed the Revolution.

She wrote on 16 March:

I quite understand your action, my hero. I know that you could not have signed anything that was contrary to your oath given at the coronation. We understand each other perfectly without words, and I swear, upon my life, that we shall see you again on the throne, raised there once more by your people, and your army, for the glory of your reign. You saved the empire for your son and the country, as well as your sacred purity, and you shall be crowned by God himself on earth in your own land.[8]

The Petrograd Soviet of Workers' and Soldiers' Deputies was now the most important body in Russia. It recognized the authority of the Provisional Government, after the latter pledged itself to carry out eight basic recommendations, framed by the Duma Provisional Committee and the Soviet Executive Committee. These provided full and immediate amnesty for all political prisoners and exiles; freedom of speech, press, assembly, and strikes; the abolition of all class, group, and religious restrictions; the election of a Constituent Assembly by universal secret balloting to determine the form of government and adopt a constitution for Russia; the substitution of the police by a national militia, subject to the local authorities; democratic elections of officials for municipalities and townships; the retention in Petrograd, fully armed, of the military units that had taken part in the Revolution; the extension of civil liberties to the soldiers subject to military discipline while in the performance of duty.

For the moment, the popular idol was Kerensky. Although the only Socialist in the first revolutionary government, he exercised the largest influence because he also represented the Soviet of Workers' and Soldiers' Deputies. Kerensky had been popular for years before the Revolution. Prior to his election to the Duma in 1912, he was known as an eloquent defence attorney at political trials. His investigation into the massacre of the strikers at the Lena gold mines had added to his reputation. He had entered the Duma as a champion of labour and became one of the leaders of the moderate Socialist wing.

Although the first Provisional Government was largely 'bourgeois', it had to bow to the Soviet, whose majority were Mensheviks and Socialist Revolutionaries. Most of these men regarded the Provisional Government with suspicion, as a régime of the propertied classes. The Soviet was determined to steer the Revolution along a course that would bring major social changes as well as political freedom. In March 1917 the Socialist leaders of the Soviet wanted broader freedom for the Russian people than any democracy provided. On 15 March 1917, the Petrograd Soviet issued an order which instructed the troops not to obey orders of their officers unless countersigned by the Petrograd Soviet, and to organize local Soviets in every army unit. This order, aimed at cracking the officer caste system, dealt a death-blow to military discipline.

Kerensky at first served as a link uniting the moderates of the Duma and the radicals of the Soviet. He travelled through the country rallying the people to the support of the new government. He pleaded with them to remember that their freedom could not be consolidated unless a united nation stood behind the government. 'I see', he said, at a meeting of army units in Odessa, 'the great enthusiasm which has swept the entire country. Such miracles as the Russian Revolution which transform slaves into free men happen but once in a century.

'We have suffered enough. And the hearts of all the people of Russia throb with one feeling. Let us throw all our energies into the struggle for peace for the whole world. We believe in the happiness and the glorious freedom of all nations.

'Our slogan shall be "liberty, equality, fraternity". In the name of these things the great miracle has happened, the miracle fashioned out of the blood and sufferings of generations. We are reaping what the best children of Russia have sown with their blood and we are not the owners of the harvest. We are merely its guardians.'

Professor Eugène Trubetskoy, a moderate liberal, wrote:

This revolution is unique. There have been bourgeois revolutions and proletarian revolutions, but I doubt if there has ever been a revolution so truly national, in the widest sense of the term, as the present Russian one. Everybody made this revolution. Everyone took part in it – the workers, the soldiers, the bourgeois, even the nobility – all the social forces of the land.

This was the spirit that animated the March Revolution which overnight transformed Russia into what Lenin, in *Pravda* of 20 April 1917, called 'the freest country in the world'.

Chapter 9
Lenin's Road to Petrograd

The actual news of the Russian Revolution came as a surprise to Lenin and his Bolshevik comrades-in-exile. 'The revolutionary explosion they had so long and so tensely awaited caught them unaware', writes Trotsky. In March 1917 the majority of the Bolshevik leaders were either abroad or in Siberian exile. Zinoviev, Semashko, Lunacharsky, Litvinov, Chicherin, Ganetsky, Radek, Riazanov, Madame Kollontai and Larin had been living abroad for years, some in Switzerland, others in London and Paris. Bukharin was in New York, editing an *émigré* newspaper with Trotsky. Stalin, Kamenev and Sverdlov were in Siberia.

When Bronsky, an old comrade, rushed into Lenin's room early one morning with the breath-taking report from Petrograd, Lenin refused to believe him until the Zurich newspapers confirmed the news. From that moment his whole energy was directed towards one objective: to reach Petrograd as fast as possible. Every hour mattered; out of the fragmentary accounts coming from Russia he had already begun to piece together the new alignment of revolutionary forces. He could see the outlines of the battles ahead, inside his own party and against the others. And he had little faith in the ability of his Bolshevik lieutenants in Russia to steer the right course for the Party until his arrival to assume supreme command.

From all parts of Europe and America, from the wastelands of Siberia and Asiatic Russia, all roads led to Petrograd in the spring of 1917. The army of returning expatriates included men and women of every brand, veteran revolutionists, Liberals, Socialists, peasants, students and radical intellectuals; men who had spent years in Tsarist prisons and at Siberian hard labour; thousands of students and workers who had been swept almost by chance into the earlier maelstrom of 1905. Idealists and shady adventurers, young men and old.

All roads led to Petrograd, by horse-drawn sleigh and freight car, by coach and railroad compartment, by tramp steamer and luxury liner, across the U-boat-infested North Atlantic, by slow ship from San Francisco to Vladivostok, then 6,000 miles across the two continents. All roads led to Petrograd, for the amnesty granted by the Provisional Government was universal. This was Russia's hour of supreme liberty, and Petrograd, shedding its last thin blanket of snow, was the festive tribune of the liberated Russian people.

The first important Bolsheviks to reach Petrograd were Stalin, Kamenev, Muranov and Sverdlov, who completed the long journey from Siberia to the capital before the end of March. They arrived while the political honeymoon was still on, and they became infected with its spirit. But in the offices of *Pravda*, the organ of the Bolshevik Party, which had resumed publication immediately after the fall of the Tsar, they found a different attitude. Molotov and Shliapnikov, the provisional editors of the paper, were attacking the Provisional Government.

Quickly Stalin, Kamenev and Muranov superseded the acting editorial board, the first issue under their direction appearing on 28 March. Under the new triumvirate *Pravda* adopted a concilia- tory attitude towards the government and the other Socialist parties. They urged a fusion between Bolsheviks and the Left Mensheviks and tentative support of the Provisional Government. Furthermore, the new editors condemned the defeatist anti-war slogans being disseminated by some Petrograd Bolsheviks. Still without word from Zurich, they took a line opposed to Lenin's position and to the stand adopted by Trotsky in his New York newspaper. While Lenin and Trotsky, independently of each other, were already summoning the proletariat to war against the Pro- visional Government, and were demanding immediate action to halt the war, Stalin adopted a very cautious position.[1]

On 27 March the Petrograd Soviet unanimously adopted a mani- festo addressed to 'the people of the whole world', which inter- preted the March Revolution as a step towards a democratic peace based on the defeat of Imperial Germany. This manifesto was a far cry from Lenin's interpretation of the war as a purely imperialist struggle between two contending evils. Of this manifesto Stalin wrote in *Pravda* of 28 March:

The mere slogan: 'Down with the war' is absolutely impractical. As long as the German Army obeyed the orders of the Kaiser, the Russian soldier must stand firmly at his post, answering bullet with bullet and shell with shell. . . . It is impossible not to greet yesterday's manifesto of the Soviet of Workers' and Soldiers' Deputies issued to the masses of the world, urging them to compel their governments to call a halt to this wholesale slaughter. ... Our slogan is pressure on the Provisional Government with the aim of compelling it ... to make an attempt to induce all the warring countries to open immediate negotiations. ... And until then every man remains at his fighting post!

Without the benefit of Lenin's instructions, Stalin and Kamenev were trying to carry water on both shoulders. 'All defeatism', wrote Stalin's *Pravda* in March 1917, 'died at the moment when the first revolutionary regiment appeared on the streets of Petrograd.' According to Shliapnikov, when the new *Pravda* hit the streets it threw consternation into the Bolshevik ranks. The Tauride Palace buzzed with news that 'the moderate reasonable Bolsheviks have been victorious over the extremists in their own Party!' In the Executive Committee of the Soviet the Bolsheviks were received 'with poisonous smiles'.

In the factories *Pravda* was greeted with perplexity by Bolshevik workers and with 'malignant satisfaction' by their opponents. The telephone of the *Pravda* office rang all day with inquiries:

'What has happened? Why has our paper turned away from the Bolshevik line?'

In various Bolshevik district headquarters workers met to demand that Stalin, Kamenev and Muranov be expelled from the Bolshevik Party. The following day, 29 March, Stalin told the Petrograd Conference of the Bolshevik Party: 'The Provisional Government, unwilling though it may be, and with wavering and faltering footsteps, has taken upon itself to fortify the gains already won by the revolutionary masses. Such a situation had both its negative and positive aspects. It is not to our advantage to force the march of events and quicken the process of sifting from our midst the bourgeois elements which must later leave our ranks. To the extent that the Provisional Government fortifies the march of the Revolution, we must support it. To the extent that it is counter-revolutionary, we cannot support it.'

At the same meeting Stalin spoke in favour of Tseretelli's proposal for a union of the Bolshevik Party with the Left Mensheviks. The official conference minutes read:

'On the agenda of the day is Tseretelli's proposal for unity.'

Stalin: 'We must agree to this. It is necessary to decide upon our propositions on the question of unity. Unity is possible on the platform of Zimmerwald.'

When Molotov arose to voice his dissent, Stalin replied: 'It is not necessary to anticipate and prevent differences of opinion. As members of one Party our small differences of opinion will fade away.'

That was Stalin's position in March 1917. It was shared by many Left Mensheviks and Bolsheviks. But not by Lenin.

On 20 March, still in Zurich, Lenin wrote the first of his *Letters from Afar*. When it appeared in *Pravda* on 3 April it signalized a complete break with the conciliatory line adopted by Stalin and Kamenev. He attributed the success of the March Revolution largely to 'the British and French embassies with their agents and "connexions" who had been making the most desperate efforts to prevent Nicholas II from concluding "separate" agreements and a separate peace.'

According to Lenin the apparent ease with which the dynasty was overthrown was owing to the 'conspiracy of the Anglo-French imperialists who were pushing Miliukov, Guchkov and Co. to seize power in order to prolong the imperialist war, in order to wage it more ferociously and tenaciously, in order to slay fresh millions of Russian workers and peasants, so as to obtain possession of Constantinople for Guchkov, Syria for the French, and Mesopotamia . . . for the British capitalists, etc.'

On the same day Trotsky wrote in his New York newspaper *Novy Mir*:

'The Tsar's government is no more,' the Guchkovs and Miliukovs are telling the people. 'Now you must pour out your blood for the all-national interests.' But by national interests the Russian imperialists mean the recovery of Poland, the conquest of Galicia, Constantinople, Armenia, Persia. In other words, Russia now takes her place in the joint ranks of imperialism with other European states, and first of all with her allies, England and France.

On 24 March Lenin wrote another *Letter from Afar* summoning the proletariat to organize a militia, 750,000 strong, to combat 'the Guchkovs and Miliukovs, the landowners and capitalists'. The following day he outlined a programme of action for a Soviet of Workers', Soldiers' and Peasants' Deputies. He called for the repudiation of Russia's treaties with the Allies, the publication of all secret agreements, and the proclamation of new peace terms, including the liberation of all colonies and the summons to workers of all countries to depose their governments and transfer all power to Councils of Workers' Deputies.

This was Lenin's summons to world revolution, addressed to the proletariat of all nations.

'The government of Guchkov and Miliukov', he wrote on 25 March, 'is in reality the agent of Anglo-French capital which desires to keep the colonies looted from Germany and in addition to compel Germany to return Belgium and part of France.'

These letters went to Ganetsky in neutral Stockholm. Ganetsky forwarded them to Lenin's sister Maria in Petrograd.

Lenin was still in Zurich and there were obstacles delaying his return to Russia. The Provisional Government offered no objection to the homecoming of its sworn enemy, but the British and French were reluctant to grant him a transit visa and travel facilities. (Similarly, when Trotsky reached Halifax *en route* to Russia, he was detained by the British authorities and was permitted to proceed to Russia only after Foreign Minister Miliukov cabled a demand for his immediate release.)

But Lenin was not in Switzerland for long. If the Allies would not help him return to Russia for the purpose of overthrowing the Provisional Government and concluding peace with Germany, Berlin would.

Ironically enough, it was Martov who first proposed that Russian revolutionists who were on the Allied black-list should return to Russia via Germany in exchange for German prisoners of war in Russian hands. In a cable to the Executive Committee of the Petrograd Soviet, the committee of Russian *émigrés* in Berne warned that if this exchange was not arranged 'the old fighters will consider it only right to look for other ways to come to Russia and fight for international Socialism.'

Lenin seized on this idea without awaiting Petrograd's reply. At first he had thought of paying smugglers to transport him through Germany to Russia, but dropped this plan when told that the smugglers could take him only as far as Berlin. Next he played with the notion of travelling as a mute Swede, but his wife persuaded him that that wasn't very practical.

'That wouldn't do,' said Krupskaya. 'You might dream of the Cadets and curse them in your sleep, and they'd find out you are not a Swede.'

Still, Lenin corresponded with Ganetsky in Stockholm on the feasibility of this bizarre plan. But it was rejected in favour of a deal with the German Government. The precise details of the arrangements with Berlin, which gave Lenin safe passage through Imperial Germany in a sealed train, have since been beclouded by volumes of apologetic double-talk on the part of Soviet historians. Although the broad interplay of personalities and sequence of events which brought Lenin from Zurich to Petrograd have since become clear enough, this significant chapter in Lenin's life story has never been explained in full detail.

Shortly after Martov made his proposal for a Russo-German exchange, Robert Grimm, the Swiss Social Democrat, volunteered his services as an intermediary in obtaining Berlin's consent for the passage of the Russian exiles through German territory. He dropped out of the picture, however, when the Mensheviks refused to act without the consent of the Executive Committee of the Soviet.

When Grimm refused to continue negotiations on this basis Fritz Platten, another Socialist 'internationalist', entered the picture. 'Platten', said the official Bolshevik statement at that time, 'concluded a definite agreement with the German Ambassador in Switzerland, of which the main points were the following: First, that all the *émigrés* should go, irrespective of their attitude towards the war; second, that the train in which they were to travel was to be an extra-territorial one; finally, that all passengers should agitate in Russia for the subsequent exchange of an equal number of Austro-German prisoners interned in Russia.'

That is as far as the official Bolshevik version goes. From the memoirs of General Ludendorff we learn even more. 'Our government, in sending Lenin to Russia, took upon itself a tremendous responsibility', wrote the German Chief of Staff. 'From a military point of view his journey was justified, for it was imperative that Russia should fall.'[2]

General Hoffmann, chief of the German General Staff on the Eastern Front, described the German objective in even more concrete terms: 'We naturally tried, by means of propaganda, to increase the disintegration that the Russian Revolution had introduced into the Army. Some man at home who had connexions with the Russian revolutionaries exiled in Switzerland came upon the idea of employing some of them in order to hasten the undermining and poisoning of the morale of the Russian Army.

'He applied to [Reichstag deputy Mathias] Erzberger and the deputy of the German Foreign Office. And thus it came about that Lenin was conveyed through Germany to Petrograd in the manner that afterwards transpired.

'In the same way as I send shells into the enemy trenches, as I discharge poison gas at him, I, as an enemy, have the right to employ the expedient of propaganda against his garrisons.'[3]

Who was the '*man at home who had connexions with the Russian revolutionaries exiled in Switzerland*'? He was Parvus (Dr Helphand), the former revolutionary Socialist who during the war had become an agent of the German Government. It was Parvus who had suggested to Count Brockdorff-Rantzau, later German Ambassador to Soviet Russia, that the admission of Lenin and the Socialist extremists into Russia could be put to good use by Germany. Parvus's proposal was supported by Count von Maltzan and Erzberger, then the chief of German military propaganda. They convinced Chancellor Bethmann-Hollweg, who accordingly advised the General Staff of Parvus's 'brilliant manoeuvre'.

While Parvus was completing the arrangements through the Wilhelmstrasse, Paul Levi, a German anti-war Socialist who belonged to the Spartacist Union (the forerunner of the German Communist Party), was handling the Berne–Zurich end of negotiations. After conferring with Lenin and Radek in Zurich, Levi requested the Berne correspondent of the *Frankfurter Zeitung* to take up the matter with the German Ambassador in Switzerland. The Ambassador promised to check with Berlin.

The following evening, while Levi was in the People's House, he was called to the telephone. The voice at the other end of the line was the German Ambassador's: 'I've been looking for you all over town,' he said. 'How can I get in touch with Lenin? I expect final instructions any moment regarding his transportation.'

Levi was astonished at the Ambassador's haste. From the tone of his voice he realized that Berlin considered the matter most urgent. When he conveyed the Ambassador's message to Lenin, the latter feverishly began to jot down the terms on which he –

Lenin – would agree to travel through Germany! Lenin dictated the conditions. All of them were accepted. The road to Petrograd was open. But in Lenin's obscure dealings with the German Government the ambiguous figures of Parvus in Berlin and Ganetsky in Stockholm were still to play a large role – a role of which perhaps even Ludendorff and Hoffmann were not completely aware.[4]

In his farewell message to the Swiss workers Lenin told them that the Russian upheaval was merely the prologue to the world revolution. Russia's present role, he said, was that of the vanguard of the revolutionary proletariat.

'It has fallen to the lot of the Russian proletariat', he asserted, 'to begin the series of revolutions whose objective necessity was created by the imperialist world war.

'We know well that the Russian proletariat is less organized and intellectually less prepared for the task than the working class of other countries. . . . Russia is an agricultural country, one of the most backward of Europe. Socialism cannot be established in Russia immediately. But the peasant character of the country . . . may, as was shown by the events of 1905, lead to the development of a democratic-capitalist revolution in Russia and make that a prologue to the world-wide Socialist revolution. . . .'[5]

When news leaked out that Lenin had agreed to travel through Germany, without awaiting the approval of the Petrograd Soviet, it caused an uproar among Socialists in Switzerland and France. At meetings of the Russian *émigrés* Lenin and his followers were denounced. Although professing to disdain these assaults, Lenin was sufficiently concerned with European Socialist opinion to seek Romain Rolland's sanction for his deal with Germany. On 6 April Henri Guilbeaux, a French Socialist who resided in Switzerland, received a telegram from Lenin asking him and Rolland to appear at the railroad station on the day of Lenin's departure. Rolland refused.

'If you have any influence on Lenin and his friends,' the great pacifist writer told Guilbeaux, 'dissuade them from going through Germany. They will cause great damage to the pacifist movement and to themselves, for it will then be said that Zimmerwald is a German child.' When Guilbeaux pressed the matter, Rolland reminded him that Lunacharsky had characterized Lenin as 'a dangerous and cynical adventurer'.[6]

At the station two days later, a large crowd of Russian *émigrés* and Swiss and Italian workers came to see Lenin and his companions off. In his immediate party were Zinoviev, Radek, Krupskaya, Inessa, Karpinsky and several other Bolsheviks. But the party also included some twenty non-Bolsheviks. Lenin had insisted on their travelling with him in order to offset the unfavourable impression produced by his trip under German auspices. Lenin's supporters milled around the waiting train carrying revolutionary banners and singing the 'Internationale'; his enemies, a group of anti-German Socialists, shouted, 'Spies! German spies! Look how happy they are – going home at the Kaiser's expense!'

Lenin stood at the window of his compartment, supporting his chin on the ledge, and shaking his head with a smile. As the demonstration continued, he started to get off the train, but one of his comrades held him back. The angry demonstrators seemed anxious to use their fists. Lenin returned to the car window. His followers on the platform again struck up the 'Internationale' to drown out the catcalls of their opponents. When the train pulled out, police were breaking up the fighting between the two groups.

As the train coiled across the Alps towards the German frontier, Lenin gravely looked out at the receding towers of rock and snow.

'We shall probably never see these mountains again,' said Karpinsky. Lenin continued to stare out of the window.

It was Radek who broke the mood: 'Vladimir Ilyich is imagining himself as Premier of the Revolutionary Government.'

Lenin smiled. As night fell, he and David Suliashvili, a Georgian Bolshevik, settled into upper berths, while Krupskaya and Inessa took the lower ones. Krupskaya complained to Suliashvili: 'What's to be done! Volodya will catch cold without his jacket!'[7]

On 18 April, Ganetsky received this telegram from Lenin:

TRELLEBORG AT 6 P.M. TODAY

Ganetsky met Lenin at Malmø. As they embraced each other, there were tears in Ganetsky's eyes. A few hours later they were in a special car bound for Stockholm. In Lenin's compartment sat Ganetsky, Krupskaya and Zinoviev. They talked late into the night, Lenin pumping Ganetsky for the latest news from Petrograd. Ganetsky was anxious to accompany the Bolshevik leader to Petrograd, but Lenin ordered him to remain at his post in Stockholm. He was to be representative of the Foreign Bureau of the Central Committee of the Bolshevik Party. 'I longed to go to Petrograd with Lenin,' writes Ganetsky, 'but the leader ordered me to remain, and I had to obey.' It was not until four in the morning that Lenin curled up in the corner to get some sleep.

Parvus did not meet Lenin, but conveyed the message that it was urgent to begin working for peace negotiations at once. Lenin replied that his business was revolutionary agitation, not diplomacy.[8]

Chapter 10
Spring Thunder

A great crowd gathered in the twilight of the Finland Station in Petrograd on 16 April 1917. The streets adjoining the station were entirely blocked. Armoured cars moved slowly past the surging masses. Shafts of revolving searchlights pierced the growing dusk. Workers, soldiers, sailors, and representatives of various revolutionary organizations, carrying red banners, made up the milling throng. At last the resounding clang of the first bell was heard, followed by the blinding glare of the locomotive headlight. A moment later the brilliantly illuminated cars glided into view as the train rumbled to a halt.

Lenin was the first to alight. He had not set foot on Russian soil in ten years. With his stooping shoulders and worker's cap, he cut a figure of little distinction, but his piercing grey eyes set him apart from the rest. A group of workers quickly hoisted him on their shoulders and carried him into the 'People's Room' (formerly the Tsar's Room) of the Finland Station. From all sides the crowd surged forward, shouting greetings to the revolutionist who had returned to the liberated capital. Someone handed Lenin a bouquet of flowers.

Carrying this incongruous bouquet in his arms, Lenin strode quickly to the middle of the room, and stopped short before Chkheidze, the chairman of the Petrograd Soviet.

'Comrade Lenin,' said Chkheidze, 'we welcome you to Russia in the name of the Petrograd Soviet and the Revolution. . . . But we believe that the chief task of the revolutionary democracy at present is to defend our revolution against every kind of attack both from within and without. . . . We hope that you will join us in striving towards this goal.'

Lenin stood there as though Chkheidze's words did not concern him in the least. His eyes travelled from one side of the room to the other, taking in the crowd; he examined the ceiling, rearranged the bouquet, which harmonized badly with his rather squat figure and the cap he was wearing, and finally, turning away from Chkheidze and the members of the Executive Committee of the Soviet, addressed the crowd:

'Dear comrades, soldiers, sailors, and workers, I am happy to greet you in the name of the victorious Russian Revolution, to greet you as the vanguard of the international proletarian army. . . . The hour is not far off when, at the summons of our Comrade Karl Liebknecht [the German Spartaçist leader], the people will turn their weapons against their capitalist exploiters. . . . The Russian Revolution, achieved by you, has opened a new epoch. Long live the world-wide Socialist Revolution!'

From the Finland Station Lenin was escorted to the Bolshevik Headquarters in the palace of Kshesinskaya (a former ballet dancer and favourite of the Tsar).

Outside, a throng of soldiers and sailors was waiting. Speaking from the second-storey balcony, Lenin assured them that a series of Socialist revolutions was imminent in Germany, England and France. The Russian Revolution, he said, marked the beginning of an international uprising by the toiling masses everywhere.

Lenin then returned to the large salon where the leaders of the Bolshevik Party were assembled. With a faint smile of contempt, he listened to their speeches, waiting for the last to finish. Then he rose and bitterly assailed them for having given tentative support to the government during his absence in Switzerland.

'No support for the Provisional Government' were practically his first words. Even before his arrival in Russia, he had insisted, in letters to Lunacharsky and Ganetsky, on 'no *rapprochement* with other parties'. To trust Chkheidze or the left-wing socialists Sukhanov and Steklov, he had written, was 'impossible'. Now, his open and complete break with the moderate line taken by Stalin and Kamenev, as editors of *Pravda*, left his lieutenants gasping. Sukhanov, who was present as Kamenev's guest, has described Lenin's first encounter with his Russian party comrades in these words:

'I'll never forget the thunderous speech, startling not only to me, a heretic who accidentally dropped in, but also to the faithful – all of them. It seemed as if all the elements of universal destruction had risen from their lairs, knowing neither barriers nor doubts, personal difficulties nor personal considerations, to hover over the banquet chambers of Kshesinskaya, above the heads of the bewitched disciples.'

After lashing out at his own followers, Lenin disassociated himself from the non-Bolshevik majority in the Soviet, consigning them to the enemy camp. 'That alone was enough in those days to make the listeners dizzy', Sukhanov comments.

'Only the Zimmerwald Left stands guard over the proletarian revolution!' cried Lenin. 'The rest are the same old opportunists speaking pretty words but in reality betraying the cause of Socialism and the working masses.'

Raskolnikov, a Bolshevik leader of the Kronstadt sailors, said that Lenin 'resolutely condemned the tactics pursued before his arrival by the ruling party groups and individual comrades. The most responsible party workers were here. But for them, too, Lenin's speech was a veritable revolution. It laid down a Rubicon between the tactics of yesterday and today.'

While the Bolshevik high command was still reeling under his merciless attack, Lenin restated the basic points of his programme. He minced no words. Many of those present disagreed, but all were impressed by his personal force. Kamenev, who presided, summed up the general Bolshevik reaction to Lenin's speech.

'We may agree or disagree with Lenin's view,' he said. 'We may not follow him in his evaluation of this or that particular situation, but in any case in the person of Lenin there has returned to Russia the recognized leader of our Party and together with him we shall move forward to Socialism.'[1]

Lenin's return to Russia was reported by the entire Russian press, but it failed to ring a bell for the foreign correspondents in Petrograd. Few of them considered the news worth cabling to their newspapers. Lenin himself paid his first visit not to the Tauride Palace but to his mother's grave. No sooner had he settled in the Kshesinsky Palace than he phoned Bonch-Bruyevich for a car and drove out to the cemetery. Reaching the little mound, he stopped in silence, removed his hat, and bowed his head.

Despite the enthusiasm at the Finland Station, when the circumstances of Lenin's return became generally known, it caused resentment among large segments of Petrograd's sailors, soldiers, students and workers. On 17 April the sailors of the Second Baltic Fleet, who had been among the welcoming honour guard, passed a resolution condemning Lenin for accepting German help. In the barracks of the Volinsky regiment, the detachment whose revolt had spelled doom for the monarchy, the question of Lenin's arrest was discussed; among the soldiers of the Moskovsky and Preobrazhensky regiments feeling against Lenin also ran high. Many other soldiers' meetings demanded that the Provisional Government investigate the facts behind Lenin's trip through Imperial Germany.

The union of gymnasium students staged a demonstration against Lenin outside the Kshesinsky Palace, and a delegation of wounded soldiers and sailors appeared with placards reading 'Lenin and company – back to Germany!' These veterans, many of them on crutches, marched to the Tauride Palace demanding that 'the activities of Lenin be stopped by all possible means'. Moreover, they refused to allow Tseretelli and Skobelev to speak in Lenin's defence. Finally, the soldiers' section of the Soviet passed a resolution demanding a 'systematic fight against the Leninists'.[2]

The condition of Russia upon Lenin's arrival was far from a stable one. With the fall of the monarchy Russia experienced a profound psychological shock. The entire population was suddenly swept, in Kerensky's words, by a 'sense of unlimited freedom, a liberation from the most elementary restraints essential to every human society'. At the same time, the people were overcome by a terrible weariness, an utter exhaustion after the strain of the three years of war. The reaction expressed itself in a general paralysis of the will. The workers in the factories ceased to work, the soldiers at the front ceased fighting. 'The people lost the capacity to obey. The authorities were no longer capable of giving directions and issuing commands. . . . In the factories the workers began to roll out in wheel-barrows the especially hateful directors and engineers. In many places the peasants seized the land without waiting for government action. At the front, desertions reached disastrous proportions. The soldiers held meetings from morning till night, and the entire officer corps fell under suspicion. On 13 March the sailors in Kronstadt had killed the commander of the Baltic Fleet and a number of officers. Other officers were arrested and incarcerated. In the cities a wave of lynchings, robberies and lawlessness broke out as the apparatus of local government ceased to function.' It required tremendous effort on the part of the new authorities, the Provisional Government, the Soviet of Workers' and Soldiers' Deputies, and the groups which supported the Provisional Government, to prevent collapse. The prestige and authority of the government and the administrative apparatus were restored somewhat, and the country gradually began to return to some functioning order. The disorders at the front also diminished to some extent.

On the morning following Lenin's return to Petrograd a general Social Democratic conference was held in the Tauride Palace to discuss for the last time the possible union of all factions into a single party. Here Lenin delivered an uncompromising speech, echoing the hard line he had already laid down to his Bolshevik comrades, and putting a quick end to any hope of unity. His vehemence caused a storm of protest. There were catcalls and hisses while Lenin spoke. Alexander Bogdanov, his former close associate, interrupted Lenin by crying out: 'That is the delusion of a lunatic!'

When Lenin concluded his speech, Joseph Goldenberg, a former member of the Bolshevik Central Committee who had just returned from exile, took the floor. He knew Lenin well, had worked with him, and had enjoyed his respect. Containing his anger with difficulty, he declared: 'The place left vacant by the great anarchist, Bakunin, who for many years had no worthy successor, is now occupied. Everything we have just heard is a complete repudiation of the entire Social Democratic doctrine, of the whole theory of scientific Marxism. We have just heard a clear and unequivocal declaration for anarchism. Its herald, the heir of Bakunin, is Lenin. Lenin the Marxist, Lenin the leader of our fighting Social Democratic Party, is no more. A new Lenin is born, Lenin the anarchist.'

Warning that Lenin's programme meant raising the banner of civil war, Goldenberg exhorted his audience to fight against the new danger caused by the arrival of Russia's 'friends from abroad'.

George Steklov, who was to become the editor of *Izvestia* under Lenin's régime, spoke in much the same spirit. 'Lenin's speech', he said, 'consists of abstract conceptions, which show that the Russian Revolution has passed him by. After Lenin acquaints himself with the situation in Russia, he will abandon these theories.'

These unfavourable reactions to Lenin's return and to his first words before the Soviet lulled the leaders of the Provisional Government into a false sense of security. They believed that the very fact that Lenin had been 'imported' into Russia with German assistance would destroy the power of Bolshevik propaganda. On 17 April Skobelev assured the Cabinet that Lenin was a 'has-been who stands outside the ranks of the (Social Democratic) movement'. And Sukhanov, a fairly objective observer, thought that 'Lenin in his present state is so unacceptable to everybody that he represents absolutely no danger.'

This complete miscalculation of Lenin's strength was perhaps best illustrated in the diary entry made by Maurice Paleologue, the French Ambassador to Petrograd, on 18 April 1917. 'This morning', he wrote, '[Foreign Minister] Miliukov told me with a beaming face that "Lenin had completely failed at the Soviets yesterday. He went to such an extreme, so insolently and clumsily defended his thesis on immediate peace, that the hissing forced him to step down and leave. From this he will never recover." ' To which Paleologue wisely added: 'Let us hope so, I told him, but I am afraid lest Miliukov once more be punished for his optimism.'[3]

According to Vladimir Zenzinov, a Socialist Revolutionary member of the Central Executive Committee of the Soviet, only one man – Alexander Kerensky – dissented sharply from the general opinion that Lenin represented no threat to the March Revolution. Zenzinov had been at the Finland Station on 16 April, and had witnessed the reception for Lenin, as well as the change in the wind immediately thereafter. He recalls that within a few days after Lenin's arrival Kerensky told him, 'This man will destroy the Revolution.'

'I tried to convince Kerensky,' said Zenzinov, 'that a single man could not determine the course of events, but Kerensky stubbornly repeated, "No, you understand nothing, this man will destroy the Revolution." '

Even before Lenin had arrived, Kerensky sensed the danger. At a meeting of the Provisional Government, which discussed the growing power of Bolshevik propaganda, Kerensky explained: 'Just wait. Lenin himself is coming. Then it will really start!'[4]

A few days after the stormy meeting in the Tauride Palace Lenin summoned a council of his former Bolshevik colleagues, men who had once stood with him, but whose present attitude was ambiguous. Krassin was among those invited to attend. Lenin was suffering from a sore throat and could barely speak. But this time he had no intention of talking; he wanted to hear what the old Bolsheviks would say. He scarcely uttered a word that evening.

'Lenin', says Sukhanov, 'called in his old marshals, not to discuss the situation and convince them. He wanted to know whether they believed in his new truth, whether they were in accord with his plans and would be useful to him. The marshals spoke. Not one of them expressed his support. . . . Not one proved himself useful for his needs. Lenin silently heard the "traitors" and let them go their way.'

Two days later *Pravda* published Lenin's famous *April Theses*. In this sharp outline of his programme for action Lenin frankly called for civil war as a means of ending the war between nations. The war was caused by the imperialist development of world capital; a democratic peace was therefore impossible without destroying capitalism, he held.

'How shall we end war?' he asked, and replied:

The war cannot be ended by merely wishing for it. It cannot be ended by the desire of only one side. It cannot be ended by just 'sticking the bayonet into the ground', as one soldier expressed it.

The war was not caused by the evil desires of predatory capitalists, although undoubtedly it is to their advantage, since they alone are getting rich from it. The war was caused by the development of world capital for the last fifty years, the millions of threads and filaments that enter into its fabric. You cannot get away from the imperialistic character of the war. It is impossible to make a democratic peace, one that is not imposed by force, without destroying the power of capitalism. It is only by breaking through this front that the proletariat can advance its own interests as a class.

In order to bring permanent end to war, it was essential that the proletariat take power. In Russia the weapon for waging war against capitalism existed in the form of the Soviet of Workers' and Soldiers' Deputies.

The Russian Revolution of March 1917 was the beginning of that process which was to change the imperialistic war into a civil war. This revolution made the first step towards stopping the war. But then a second step is necessary to make the cessation of war permanent, and that is for the proletariat to take over the reins of power. This will serve as the beginning of the world-wide 'breaking through' the front of capitalist interests, and only by breaking through this front can the proletariat free mankind from the horrors of war and secure for it the blessings of a lasting peace. And the Russian Revolution has brought us very close to this chance to break through the capitalist front by organizing the Soviet of Workers' Deputies.

He now supported the Soviet instead of the parliamentary democracy which he had advocated until the March Revolution.

'The parliamentary-bourgeois republic restricts the independent political life of the masses, hinders their direct participation in the democratic upbuilding of the state from bottom to top. The Soviet of Workers' and Soldiers' Deputies docs just the reverse.'

He advocated Soviet control of land, banks and investment trusts of the capitalists, making it clear, however, that this would by no means be the beginning of Socialism.

'The party of the proletariat', he declared, 'can, under no circumstances, assume the task of introducing Socialism in a land of small peasant holdings until the time when the vast majority of the people has come to realize that a Socialist revolution is necessary.'

To emphasize his complete break with the past, Lenin urged dropping the name Social Democratic Party in favour of Communist Party.

'The majority of the "Social Democratic" leaders . . . of the "Social Democratic" parliamentarians and the "Social Democratic" papers which are the means of influencing the masses, have betrayed Socialism, have proved unfaithful to Socialism, and have deserted to the side of their "own" national bourgeoisie.

'The broad masses of the people are indignant over it and feel that they have been deceived by their own leaders.

'And yet they want us to continue this deception, to make it easier for them to cling to the old and antiquated name that rotted away just as did the Second International!

'What we want is to build the whole world over again. We want to end the imperialist war and save the hundreds of millions of people who have been drawn into it and in which billions of dollars have been invested and which cannot be terminated by a general democratic peace without a proletarian revolution – the greatest in the history of mankind!

'And here we seem to be afraid of ourselves. We are holding on to the old dirty apron strings!

'It is time to cast off the old dirty shirt and put on a clean one!'⁵

Lenin's *Theses*, in the words of an old Bolshevik, had the force of an 'exploding bomb'. A few days after their publication the editors of *Pravda* wrote: 'As for Lenin's general scheme, it seems to us unacceptable in that it starts from the assumption that the bourgeois revolution is ended, and counts on an immediate transforming of this revolution into a Socialist revolution.'

The *Theses* met considerable opposition among Lenin's most intimate Party comrades. Lenin's principal opponent in the columns of *Pravda* was Kamenev. Lenin answered his opponents point by point, driving home his views in many articles, pamphlets and speeches. His vigorous line gradually won an increasing number of adherents in the Bolshevik Party.

Adding to Lenin's initial difficulties, the Malinovsky affair now came back to life. In 1915 Lenin's paper had reported that Malinovsky had died. This report was later proved unfounded. Malinovsky himself did not return to Petrograd at this time – that fantastic chapter was to come later – but his record was splashed across the pages of leading Russian newspapers. For when the Provisional Government opened the secret files of the Okhrana, the dossier on Roman Malinovsky was plain enough. He had been an agent of the Okhrana when he first appeared in the St Petersburg Metalworkers' Union and had served the Tsar's political police faithfully until his political eclipse.

A commission appointed by the Provisional Government to investigate the crimes of the Tsarist régime – the employment of *agents provocateurs* was listed as one of its major offences – pieced together the whole story. It questioned all key witnesses, including Lenin and Beletsky, the former director of the Okhrana, and examined all relevant Okhrana documents.

The facts were clear. Malinovsky had worked for the Okhrana under the name of Portnoy. He reported all important Bolshevik meetings, disclosed the identity of Bolshevik leaders who carried false passports, and gave the location of underground Party presses. He was directly responsible for the arrest of the Bolshevik

Central Committee in 1910. He furnished detailed reports on the activities of the editorial offices of *Pravda* and supplied Beletsky with a list of *Pravda*'s financial supporters and subscribers. He was responsible for the arrest of Stalin and Sverdlov, as well as of Troyanovsky's wife. Furthermore, it was at Beletsky's suggestion that Malinovsky became a candidate for the Duma, which had presented certain difficulties because Malinovsky's early criminal record in Poland made him ineligible under the electoral law. This difficulty the Okhrana surmounted by obtaining a false affidavit from the local police chief that Malinovsky had no record. To assure his election, Beletsky arrested his Menshevik rivals on the electoral list.

When Malinovsky was installed in the Duma, the Okhrana chief raised his pay from five hundred to seven hundred rubles a month, in addition to paying him generous bonuses for particularly valuable information. He had a direct wire to Beletsky and met him regularly in the private rooms of the better restaurants of St Petersburg. Malinovsky also furnished the Okhrana with the confidential memoranda of the Social Democratic Duma caucus, as well as advance proof sheets of all *Pravda* articles, which Beletsky personally edited. Chernomazov, the nominal editor of *Pravda*, was no obstacle to these operations. He, too, was an Okhrana agent! The Malinovsky dossier contained two telegrams of congratulation following his election to the Duma, the first from Beletsky, his chief, the second from Lenin's wife. His revolutionary speeches in the Duma were written by Lenin and Zinoviev but they were edited by the Okhrana chief.

Malinovsky's sudden resignation was now explained for the first time. Following a shake-up in the Ministry of the Interior, the new assistant Minister, General Dzhunkovsky, dismissed Beletsky and other top Okhrana officials. When he learned, to his complete surprise, that Malinovsky, the author of the fiery revolutionary speeches in the Duma, was one of Beletsky's agents, Dzhunkovsky was furious. If the fact became generally known, it would create a national scandal and compromise the régime in the eyes of the world. He therefore summoned Malinovsky, paid him six thousand rubles, and ordered him to resign from the Duma.[6]

Confronted with these nasty facts, which established beyond further doubt that his main deputy in Russia, the Bolshevik whip in the Duma and publisher of *Pravda*, was a common stool-pigeon, Lenin admitted that Malinovsky was an Okhrana agent, but explained: 'Malinovsky could and did destroy a number of individuals. But as for the growth of the Party in the sense of increasing its importance and influence on the people by the tens and hundreds of thousands, that growth could not be stopped, controlled, or directed by Malinovsky.'[7]

In the light of Lenin's ferocious attacks on Martov and others, who had demanded years before that Malinovsky be investigated, this was a lame apology, but the concluding chapter was still to be written. Lenin might also have pointed out that other revolutionary parties had also had police spies in high places. The difference, however, was that the others had themselves exposed and purged the traitors in their midst, while Lenin had continued to defend Malinovsky long after there was substantial evidence of his guilt.

Despite the storms, large and small, that raged about him, when the All-Russian Bolshevik Party Conference met from 7 to 12 May 1917, Lenin was in complete command and the main resolutions that were adopted followed his *April Theses*.

Although for the party as a whole this settled the big issues in Lenin's favour, some of the Bolshevik leaders continued to oppose him. Dzerzhinsky, the coming chief of the Soviet secret police, demanded that a dissenting report be heard from the 'comrades who along with us have had the practical experience of the Revolution'. This was meant as a dig at the *émigré* roots of Lenin's doctrines. Kamenev delivered a dissenting report in the defence of the 'bourgeois' democratic state. Kalinin continued to advocate a coalition with the Mensheviks against the Duma Liberals. Smidovich, a Moscow Bolshevik, complained that 'every time we speak they raise against us a bogy in the form of Comrade Lenin's *Theses*'. Stalin remained silent.

Notwithstanding these reservations by leading Bolsheviks, the conference branded the Provisional Government as a 'government of landowners and capitalists', and rejected the proposal of unity with the 'patriotic Mensheviks'. At the same time the conference denied that the Bolsheviks sought or would seek a separate peace with Germany.

'The conference protests', declared the resolution, 'against the

T – H

base slander spread by the capitalists against our Party, that we sympathize with the idea of a separate peace with Germany. Our Party will patiently but persistently make clear to the people the truth . . . that this war can be ended by a democratic peace only through the transfer of all governmental authority, at least in several of the belligerent countries, to the proletariat which is in fact able to put a stop to the oppression of capitalism.'[8]

After this declaration of principles there were some resignations from the Party, including Lenin's old comrade in arms, Vladimir Woytinsky. Kamenev, despite his opposition, did not leave the Party.

The rank and file did not quite understand what Lenin meant by the slogan 'All Power to the Soviets'. To the masses, the Soviets elected by the workers, peasants and soldiers represented the will of the democratic revolution. To Lenin, however, the slogan 'All Power to the Soviets' was the brilliant cover for his real objective: the dictatorship of the Bolshevik Party. While the Petrograd Soviet was packed with Kronstadt sailors and Bolshevik troops, he could hope for that momentary advantage which he would pursue to power. But he did not delude himself as to the ultimate role of this uncertain, undisciplined mass. In democratic elections to the Soviet on a nation-wide basis the Bolsheviks would never receive anything like a majority. In the provinces Socialist Revolutionary sentiment was dominant; in many working-class districts the Mensheviks were still strong. But Lenin not only concealed his aim from the masses who echoed the battle cry 'All Power to the Soviets', but from his own general staff as well.

In May 1917 there were few in Lenin's inner council who realized that the seizure of power in the name of the Soviet would later spell the end of the Soviet as a democratic assembly.

After the conference, the Bolsheviks stepped up their propaganda among workers and troops. By the end of May a large proportion of the workers' section of the Petrograd Soviet was pro-Bolshevik, and a number of units of the Petrograd garrison were also veering towards Lenin.

Lenin's cause among the troops and workers was aided by the major blunder of Foreign Minister Miliukov. On 1 May Miliukov instructed the Russian diplomatic representatives abroad to transmit a note in which he promised that the Russian people would fight on together with their Allies until a 'decisive victory' over Germany had been won.

Miliukov's note immediately aroused a storm of protest among troops and workers in Petrograd. Demonstrations were held demanding Miliukov's resignation. As a result of these protests the Provisional Government published an explanatory declaration, disavowing any Russian desire to annex foreign territories or 'to increase its world power at the expense of other nations'.

The Soviet, determined to continue the fight for peace without annexations, called on the Russian people to rally around the regional Soviets which were springing up all over the country. The Soviet leaders firmly believed that the peoples of all the belligerent nations could compel their governments to begin negotiations for peace without annexations or indemnities.

On 8 May the Executive Committee of the Soviet voted to summon an International Socialist Conference representing all parties and factions of the working class that accepted the proposed peace platform of the Soviet. A delegation representing the Soviet Executive Committee was to go abroad at once to establish contacts in neutral and Allied countries and to meet with delegations of Dutch and Swedish Socialists in Stockholm in order to prepare for the International Conference.

But the storm provoked by Miliukov's declaration of Russian war aims made it clear that there were two governments in Petrograd. And the result of dual power was mounting demoralization at the front and at home. A coalition representing the Provisional Government and the Soviet was essential. On 12 May Guchkov resigned as Minister of War; six days later Miliukov left the Provisional Government. Premier Lvov then called on the Soviet leaders to join in the Cabinet.

On 17 May a new coalition was formed by Lvov with Kerensky as Minister of War and Navy, and five Socialists in the cabinet. Included among them were Victor Chernov, leader of the Socialist Revolutionary Party, and Tseretelli, leader of the Mensheviks. The other cabinet posts went to members of the Liberal parties.

This coalition gave Russia a far more representative régime. The new Cabinet reflected the rising anti-bourgeois tide among the workers and soldiers. But it did not command the strength or authority to govern with a firm hand. The floodgates of revolution were still wide open. Industry and agriculture, dislocated by the stresses of war and corrupt Tsarist mismanagement, were still not producing enough to supply the Army with weapons or the home front with food, clothing and fuel. Moreover, the peasants were dissatisfied with the failure of the Provisional Government to expropriate the land outright for their benefit. Promises that a programme of land reform would be enacted by a democratic Constituent Assembly did not satisfy the impatient villagers. Promises to strive for a peace without indemnities or annexations, while at the same time honouring Russia's obligations as an ally of France, Great Britain and the United States (which had just entered the war), did not appease the restless troops of Petrograd, some 150,000 strong. The mere hint of dispatching these units to the front to relieve the pressure on their hard-pressed comrades was enough to start a new insurrection.

The liberal middle-class intelligentsia, the Socialist and Liberal leadership, and some of the veteran skilled workers of Petrograd, formed the slender dyke of moderation and restraint. Pounding against this dyke was a tidal wave of discontented peasant soldiers, turbulent sailors of Kronstadt, and the peasant masses. These millions distrusted the government's assurances of broad social and economic reforms. They responded to the promise of immediate salvation through still more revolution. The Revolution's need for violence had not spent itself; it was merely stored up, gathering pressure and internal heat. The Socialist leaders of the Provisional Government and of the Petrograd Soviet were trying vainly to mould the furious emotional drive of the revolutionary mass into a pattern of placid democratic faith. After three hundred years of Romanov rule and three years of war and privation they addressed the Russian people in language that would have been more appropriate before an audience of British trade unionists. They reminded them that with President Wilson's declaration of war on 6 April 1917, the character of the conflict had changed; that it was no longer merely a struggle between rival imperialisms; that, together with America, Russia could bring the world a democratic peace, on the basis of principles having nothing in common with the war aims of Tsar Nicholas II. For Wilson, too, wanted a peace without annexations. But to the increasingly demoralized troops at the front and to the hungry villagers these declarations carried little reality. They were abstractions, the fine words of intellectuals.

In Lenin's battle slogans, on the other hand, the restless mass heard its own voice, expressing its piled-up resentment against the whole bourgeois world. In a conversation with Tseretelli in May 1917, Martov ironically shaded the contradictions between 'the political views of Lenin, who regarded the continuation of the war as useful for the revolution, and his demagogic agitation among the masses, to whom he preached the necessity of an immediate end of the war.'

'For Lenin,' Martov said, 'such phenomena as war or peace have no interest in themselves. The only thing that interests him is revolution, and the only real revolution for him is the one in which the Bolsheviks will seize power. I ask myself what Lenin will do if the democracy should succeed in concluding peace. It is quite possible that, in such a case, Lenin would reconstruct the whole of his agitation among the masses and would preach that all the misfortunes of the post-war period were due to the crimes of the democracy, which consisted of having concluded a premature peace and having lacked the courage to carry on the war until the complete rout of German militarism.'

Nowhere was the irrepressible conflict between these cross-currents in the Russian Revolution more vividly expressed than in the debate between Lenin and Kerensky at the All-Russian Congress of the Soviets which opened in Petrograd on 16 June 1917.

It was at this Congress that the fatal dualism, inherent in Russian revolutionary Socialism since the days of Herzen, Lavrov and Bakunin, found its most articulate expression. Arrayed on one side in the Tauride Palace were the Menshevik Social Democrats and the Socialist Revolutionaries, heirs of the traditions of the Decembrists, the People's Will, and the imported democratic rationalism of western Europe. On the other side were Lenin's new Bolshevik followers, the impatient soldiers and peasants who, whether they knew it or not, were the spiritual grandchildren of Pugachev, Nechayev and Bakunin.

Lenin addressed this assembly on 17 June. He began without looking at his audience, his eyes fixed on a distant point at the far end of the hall.

After acclaiming the Soviet as the modern counterpart of the French Revolutionary Convention of 1792, Lenin demanded that the Soviet act at once to wrest all power from the Provisional Government.

'It is not a question of reforms in the future – these are empty words – but of doing something which is needed to be done now. If you wish to appeal to the "revolutionary" democracy, then differentiate between it and the "reform" democracy in a capitalist ministry.

'Tseretelli said that there is not a political party in Russia which would say that it is ready to take all the power into its hands. I say there is. Our party is ready at any minute to do that. [*Applause and laughter.*] Laugh all you want. . . . Our programme in relation to the economic crisis is this – to demand the publication of all those unheard-of profits reaching from 500 to 800 per cent which the capitalists make on war orders; to arrest fifty or one hundred of the more important capitalists and in this way to break all the threads of intrigue. Without such a step, all this talk of peace without annexation and indemnity is worthless. Our next step would be to announce to all the nations, separate from their governments, that we regard all capitalists – French, English, all – as robbers.

'Your own *Izvestia* has become confused. In place of peace without annexations and indemnity, it proposes the *status quo*.

'We believe that the Russian republic should not oppress a single nation – neither the Finns, nor the Ukrainians, with whom the Minister of War is now quarrelling. . . . We cannot make peace without annexation and indemnity until we are willing to give up our own annexations. It is really funny, this play! Every worker in Europe is laughing at it. He says: "They are calling on the people to overthrow the bankers, while they, themselves, send their bankers into the Ministry." Arrest them; lay bare their schemes; find out their intrigues. But you will not do this, although you have the power. . . . You have lived through 1905 and 1917. You know that revolution is not made to order; that in other countries it was brought about through bloody uprisings, but in Russia there is no group or class that could oppose the power of the Soviets. To-day or tomorrow, let us propose peace to all the peoples by breaking with all the capitalistic classes, and in a short time the peoples of France and Germany will agree to it, because their countries are perishing. . . .

'If Russia were a revolutionary democracy, not merely in words, but in deeds, she would lead in the revolutionary movement and not make peace with the capitalists; she would not talk so much of peace without annexation and indemnity, but would put an end to all forms of annexation in Russia, and would announce that she considers every annexation as robbery. If she were to do that, an imperialistic military offensive would not be necessary. . . .'[9]

One Socialist writer, recalling Lenin's speech, reported: 'When he suggested the arrest of fifty or one hundred capitalists . . . he paced the platform like a caged beast, squinted his eyes as if delighting in the imaginary sight of fifty capitalists taken through the streets in cages, and uttered his words rapidly, like one possessed.'

Then Kerensky replied. He warned his audience that the road which Lenin recommended would lead to the end of the Russian people's newly won liberties and to the dismemberment of the country.

'You have been told of 1792 and of 1905. How did 1792 end in France? It ended in the fall of the republic and the rise of a dictator. How did 1905 end? With the triumph of reaction. And now, in 1917, we are doing that which we could have done much earlier. The problem of the Russian Socialist parties and the Russian democracy is to prevent such an end as was in France – to hold on to the revolutionary conquests already made; to see to it that our comrades who have been let out from prison do not return there; that Comrade Lenin, who has been abroad, may have the opportunity to speak here again and not be obliged to flee back to Switzerland. [*Applause.*]

'We must see to it that the historic mistakes do not repeat themselves,' he continued; 'that we do not bring on a situation that would make possible the return of reaction, the victory of force over democracy. Certain methods of fighting have been indicated to us. We have been told that we should not fight with words, not talk of annexation, but should show by deeds that we are fighting against capitalism. What means are recommended for this fight? To arrest fifty Russian capitalists. [*Laughter.*] Comrades, I am not a Social Democrat. I am not a Marxist, but I have the highest respect for Marx, his teachings and his principles. But Marxism never taught such childlike and primitive means. I dare say that it is likely that Citizen Lenin has forgotten what Marxism is. He

cannot call himself a Socialist, because Socialism nowhere re-
commends the settling of questions of economic war, of the war
of classes in their economic relations, the question of economic
reorganization of the state, by arresting people, as is done by
Asiatic despots. . . . You, Bolsheviks, recommend childish prescriptions – "arrest, kill, destroy!" What are you, Socialists or the
police of the old régime? [*Uproar. Lenin: ' You should call him to
order'*]

'You recommend that we follow the road of the French Revolution of 1792. You recommend the way of further disorganization
of the country. . . . When you, in alliance with reaction, shall destroy our power, then you will have a real dictator. It is our duty,
the duty of the Russian democracy, to say: Don't repeat the historic mistakes. You are asked to follow the road that was once
followed by France, and which will lead Russia to a new reaction,
to a new shedding of democratic blood.'[10]

But it was Lenin, not Kerensky, who received an ovation from
the soldiers and sailors who made up the bulk of the audience. A
few days later, however, the Bolsheviks overshot their mark.

While the Congress was in session Bolshevik posters were
plastered on walls of the working-class districts of the capital
summoning the proletariat to demonstrate on the afternoon of 23
June against the 'counter-revolution'. The main slogans were to be:
'Down with the Tsarist Duma!' 'Down with the Ten Capitalist
Ministers!' 'End the War!' 'No Separate Peace with Wilhelm, No
Secret Treaties with the French and British Capitalists!' 'All
Power to the All-Russian Soviet of Workers', Soldiers', and
Peasants' Deputies!' 'Bread, Peace and Freedom!'

On the morning of 22 June Chkheidze told the Soviet Congress
that the demonstration scheduled for the following afternoon had
been secretly planned for days; that a number of military units,
including the First Machine Gun Regiment, would participate;
that unless the demonstration were called off there would be bitter
fighting in the streets of Petrograd. Gegechkori, a Georgian Social
Democrat, read to the Congress the proofs of the next day's issue
of *Pravda*, in which the Bolshevik Central Committee called on
the soldiers and workers to demonstrate against the Provisional
Government.

During this debate before the Soviet neither Lenin, Stalin,

Sverdlov, Kamenev nor Zinoviev was in the Tauride Palace. Nor was Trotsky, who, since his arrival from New York early in May, had been identifying himself closely with Lenin's political line. Krylenko protested against any action by the Soviet Congress in the absence of the Bolshevik leaders. Nevertheless the Soviet voted to rush its delegates to the factories and barracks to cancel the demonstration. The delegates spent the entire night making the rounds of factories and military installations.

When the Soviet Congress convened at eight o'clock on the morning of 23 June, they learned that the Central Committee of the Bolshevik Party had decided, after a night-long discussion, to call off the march. *Pravda* appeared that morning with large white spaces on page one; the Bolshevik proclamation calling on the workers to demonstrate had been pulled out at the last moment.

Trotsky put in an appearance at the morning session of the Soviet, but, despite the demand of many delegates, refused to state his position. It was Kamenev's unpleasant job to speak in the name of the Bolshevik Party. Nervously he protested that the Bolsheviks had had no intention of starting a revolt and claimed that the Party had bowed to the will of the Soviet majority.

Tseretelli, however, rose to deliver an impassioned attack against the Bolshevik Party. For the first time this Socialist leader spoke of the Bolsheviks as conspirators.

'What happened,' he shouted, 'was in fact nothing less than a plot against the Revolution. A plot to overthrow the government and gain power for the Bolsheviks who know that by any other means power will never pass to them. The plot was disarmed the moment we discovered it, but tomorrow it may show itself again. . . . The counter-revolution can only march in through one door – through the Bolsheviks.

'What the Bolsheviks are doing now is no longer theoretical, idealistic propaganda. This is a plot. The weapon of criticism has been exchanged for criticism through weapons. . . . The Bolsheviks must be disarmed.'

Kamenev leaped to his feet with this challenge: 'Mr Minister, if you are not merely casting words to the wind, do not confine yourself to speeches. Arrest me and try me for plotting against the Revolution.'

Tseretelli remained silent. The Bolsheviks walked out of the

Tauride Palace, but not until they had read into the record by their Central Committee charges that Tseretelli had invented the 'plot' in order to disarm the proletariat and reshuffle the Petrograd garrison. The working masses, they warned, would not surrender their rifles and machine guns without battle. If there was to be civil war, the bourgeois and their Socialist 'allies' would be responsible. The Party called on the soldiers and workers of Petrograd to hold fast to the weapons in their hands.

On 26 June *Pravda* ran a story headlined 'The Truth about the Demonstration', labelling Tseretelli's charges against the Bolsheviks a complete lie. Nevertheless, when the details of the proposed demonstration were later revealed, it was learned that the Bolsheviks had actually planned a march on the Mariensky Palace, headquarters of the Provisional Government, led by Bolshevik workers' battalions and pro-Bolshevik troops. Picked groups were to invade the offices of the Ministers, while party orators outside would work up the fury of the crowd. At the proper psychological moment the members of the Provisional Government would be arrested. The Central Committee of the Bolshevik Party, acting in the name of the Soviet, would then proclaim itself the new government of Russia.

It was estimated by the Bolshevik leaders that no more than five to six regiments would oppose them; most of the troops would remain neutral, while the Party could count on the garrison of the Fortress of St Peter and St Paul, several artillery companies, as well as three to four regiments and a number of armed workers' battalions. The commander in chief of the uprising was to have been Nicholas Semashko. In Petrograd, initial success was more than likely. But in June 1917 the Central Committee had grave doubts as to the effect of a Bolshevik *coup d'état* beyond Petrograd. This uncertainty made it hesitate. In the Central Committee debate Stalin favoured immediate armed action. He was supported by Madame Stasova, then the secretary of the Party, while Kamenev and Zinoviev were opposed to making an immediate bid for power. Lenin himself was undecided.

When news of the Bolshevik plan reached the Soviet, Kamenev and Zinoviev, supported by the Central Committee majority, voted to call off the demonstration. Stalin opposed postponement; Lenin did not vote. But the full facts of this abortive Bolshevik plot did not become known until much later. In June 1917 they played the role of offended innocents.[11]

The effect of the June fiasco was to give the Mensheviks and the Socialist Revolutionaries the temporary upper hand in the Soviet. For the moment Lenin's prestige was damaged; his Party had to fall back in retreat under a smoke-screen of alibis and counter-charges. On the other hand, Kamenev had called Tseretelli's bluff. Clearly the Socialists were not prepared to take energetic action against their former comrades. And this was a vital lesson.

Before regrouping his forces for the next move, Lenin left Petrograd for a vacation at the home of his old friend, Vladimir Bonch-Bruyevich, who lived in the village of Neivola on the Finnish railroad. The last three months had exhausted him completely. After ten years as a political *émigré*, the feverish pace of revolutionary Petrograd and the excitement of battle had sapped his strength.

In this quiet countryside, whose landscape was dotted with slender birch trees, Lenin would lie on a blanket for hours in the shade without reading. Sleep and rest gradually restored his frayed health. With his sister Maria, and sometimes with a group of friends, he would stroll down to the lake-shore. Lenin was an excellent swimmer, but his aquatic exploits alarmed his host. He swam far out into the middle of the lake, whose opposite shore was scarcely visible in the foggy distance. Bonch-Bruyevich warned him that the lake abounded in dangerous undertows.

'You say many people were drowned?' Lenin would ask while undresssing.

'Yes, only a short time ago.'

'Well, I won't drown.'

'There are cold currents in it – very disagreeable.'

'I'll warm myself in the sun. You say it's deep?'

'Couldn't be deeper.'

'I'll try to touch bottom.'

Quickly he would run down the sloping shore; a moment later his arms flashed in the air, his body lunged forward, then downward, like a dolphin, under the surface, to come up after a long interval. Then he lay floating on his back, far from the shore.

But Lenin had no opportunity to indulge in these pleasures for long. On 17 July, at about six in the morning, there was a rap on

the window. Bonch-Bruyevich looked out and saw the smiling face
of his party comrade, Savelyev.

'What has happened?'

'There is an uprising in Petrograd.'

Crowds of demonstrators were marching on the Duma and the
Tauride Palace, Savelyev reported; shots were heard in the streets;
there were rumours that the government was mobilizing troops and
an armed clash was awaited at any moment.

Lenin was aroused from his sleep with difficulty.

'I must go,' he said, as soon as he heard the news. He hired a
Finnish cabman to drive him to the railroad station. Perhaps the
decisive hour had come.[12]

Chapter 11
The July Uprising

For weeks preceding the July uprising Russia was being flooded with Bolshevik newspapers and proclamations. Bolshevik agitators were working feverishly among front-line troops, sailors of the Baltic Fleet, the garrison troops in the main cities, and among the peasants. Soldiers were urged to fraternize with the Germans, peasants to seize the land without waiting for the Constituent Assembly. Bolshevik Army newspapers (*Soldatskaya Pravda, Okopnaya Pravda*, etc) distributed at the front and read in the trenches, told the troops to lay down their rifles and go home to their villages.

On 29 June Kerensky, as Minister of War, called on the officers and soldiers of the Russian Army to strike hard at the enemy in a grand offensive on the south-western front; the Central Executive Committee of the Soviets supported Kerensky with an appeal to the armed forces. The main purpose of the drive was to force the Germans to return to the Russian front the divisions which they had diverted to France in preparation for an all-out offensive against the Western Allies. At the same time, the Provisional Government hoped this move would restore the fighting spirit of the Russian Army. The Socialist leaders of the Soviet supported the military offensive. They had been encouraged by a secret letter from three leading German Social Democrats, Kautsky, Haase and Bernstein, who wrote:

Do not be embarrassed by reproaches directed against you from right and left by those who oppose an advance of the Russian revolutionary army. Inactivity on the Russian front only strengthens the militant mood of Germany. The German Government and the Socialist majority supporting it are instilling in the population the hope of a separate peace with Russia, a peace which should help them to win a final victory over the Western Powers. The upsetting of this hope as a result of a Russian advance would only facilitate the struggle against the militaristic policy of the German ruling circles. The strengthening of the Russian front will show that the Revolution does not signify a loss of defensive capacity in the country where it is taking place. It will encourage the revolutionary current in Germany. And the appeals for peace made by the Russian

Revolution will be heeded all the more in the world when it becomes clear that Russia is capable of fortifying these appeals by a show of real strength.

On 1 July 1917, General Brusilov launched an attack on the Galician front. For a short time the Russians scored impressive gains against the Austrian Army, but the Russian offensive soon spent itself. By 19 July the Germans were counter-attacking on a large scale meeting only half-hearted Russian resistance.

Among the troops of Petrograd and the Kronstadt sailors the Kerensky offensive was unpopular from the start, and new revolt was in the air before Brusilov's drive petered out.

On the night of 15 July the Central Committee of the Bolshevik Party held a very stormy meeting. The situation was similar to that of 23 June. An uprising was already under way, and the question was whether to give it full Bolshevik support or yield once more to the decision of the Soviet. Again the Central Committee was divided. It was pointed out that the uprising had begun under highly suspicious circumstances; that nobody seemed to know who was at the head of the movement. There were rumours that German agents were fomenting mutiny among Russian troops.

The Bolsheviks counted most heavily on the sailors of Kronstadt, the Baltic fortress dominating Petrograd. These sailors were expected in the city within a matter of hours, but even their stand was still in doubt. And again the Central Committee could not quite decide how far the revolt would go. If initial successes were attained, had the time come to seize power in the name of the Soviet with the guns of pro-Bolshevik troops, workers and sailors?

The Central Committee debated all night whether the Bolshevik Party should officially assume command of the uprising. In the evening the question was decided in the affirmative and a proclamation to that effect was drafted for publication in *Pravda*. But as incoming reports from various parts of the city indicated that the Provisional Government was taking energetic steps to quell the uprising, the Bolshevik leaders backed down. The *Pravda* proclamation, which had not only been set up in type but also cast, was cut from the matrix. On the following day *Pravda* again appeared with a large blank space on its front page.

The eve of the uprising found Stalin in the editorial offices of *Pravda*. Lenin was still absent from the city, and neither Kamenev nor Zinoviev was on hand. Suddenly the telephone rang. Stalin was wanted on the phone by the Kronstadt sailors' organization. They were in a dilemma: How should they march in tomorrow's demonstration against the government, with or without their rifles?

Stalin had reason to fear that the wires were being tapped and conversations between Bolshevik leaders and their subsidiary organizations recorded. He hesitated. To reply in the affirmative might be playing into the hands of the government. It would expose him to the charge of instigating an armed rebellion.

'I did not take my eyes off Stalin,' related Demian Bedni, the Bolshevik poet. 'I was anxious to know what reply he would make to this telephonic inquiry concerning rifles. Very shrewdly he wrinkled his forehead, smoothed his moustache with his free hand, and responded: "You are inquiring about rifles? You, comrades, know best what to do. We writers, wherever we go, take with us our weapons, our pencils. As to how you conduct yourselves in relation to your weapons – you surely know better yourselves."

'I fell on the divan, bursting with laughter,' continues Bedni. 'The next morning the Kronstadt comrades appeared at the demonstration with their "pencils".'

Although the Central Committee decided to back down, orders for the mobilization of Kronstadt, issued earlier that day, were not cancelled. The armed sailors landed in Petrograd, formed ranks, and marched to the headquarters of the Bolshevik Party. At their head were two Bolshevik lieutenants, Raskolnikov and Roshal.

The arrival of the Kronstadt sailors changed the atmosphere of the capital. Again it seemed that the Provisional Government might fall. Lenin, who had quickly returned to Petrograd, began to waver when he saw the mass of revolutionary sailors outside the Kshesinsky Palace. He went out and addressed them, but his words were non-committal. He did not summon them to revolt, did not tell them in so many words to continue their demonstration. Instead, he delivered a tirade against the Provisional Government and the leaders of the Soviet, whom he called 'social traitors'. He called on the sailors to 'defend' the Revolution and to remain devoted to the Bolsheviks.

At this point Lenin caught sight of Lunacharsky, who was popular at Kronstadt, and told him to speak to the sailors.

Lunacharsky, taking his cue from Lenin, addressed them in about the same language, then placed himself at the head of their column and marched them off to the Tauride Palace.

As the sailors, some 20,000 strong, marched towards the headquarters of the Soviet, they were joined by armed workers; the revolt to which the Bolshevik Central Committee had not dared give official sanction gathered momentum. In working-class districts word was passed around that Red Kronstadt had arrived *en masse* to 'save' the Revolution; that only old men, women and children had remained behind in the island fortress.

On the afternoon of 17 July fighting broke out in various parts of the city; an isolated shot, followed by the rattle of machine-guns, repeated in sector after sector. Dead and wounded piled up in the streets and large-scale looting began. Food, liquor and tobacco stores were raided and quickly emptied by sailors and soldiers. Units of Bolshevik soldiers and sailors 'arrested' well-dressed citizens on the streets.

At about five o'clock the Kronstadt sailors finally reached the Tauride Palace. Belligerently, they demanded to see the Socialist Ministers of the Provisional Government. Victor Chernov, the Socialist Revolutionary leader, was the first to emerge. As soon as he showed himself, cries came from the mob: 'Search him! See if he has weapons!'

'In that case I have nothing to say,' Chernov told the crowd, turning to re-enter the palace. The noise then subsided and Chernov delivered a short address, attempting to pacify the rebels. When he had finished, he was seized by a few strong sailors, forced into an automobile, and placed under arrest as a hostage.

This action threw the crowd into confusion. A group of workers rushed into the palace and warned the Soviet leaders: 'Comrade Chernov has been arrested by the mob! They will tear him to pieces! Save him!'

Pandemonium broke out; the chairman, barely restoring order, quickly told Kamenev, Martov and Trotsky to go out and rescue Chernov from the mob. When Trotsky tried to speak, the mob did not calm down. An eye-witness reported: 'If at this moment a provocative shot had been fired, there might have been a large-scale massacre; they would have torn us all to pieces, Trotsky included.'

Trotsky himself became alarmed at the ugly temper of the crowd. After complimenting the sailors for coming to 'rescue' the Revolution, he shouted above the din: 'You have come here to express your will and to show the Soviet that the working class no longer wants the bourgeoisie in power. Why stain your cause through small outbursts of violence against chance individuals? They are not worthy of your attention. Every one of you is ready to sacrifice his head for the Revolution. I know it. Give me your hand, brother, give me your hand, comrade.'

And he held out his hand to one of the Kronstadt stalwarts. But the latter refused to shake Trotsky's hand. The sailors, however, were somewhat pacified by Trotsky's words and Chernov was finally released. Arm in arm with Trotsky he returned to the safety of the Tauride Palace.

Raskolnikov stood outside the headquarters of the Soviets, still at the head of the Red sailors of Kronstadt, not quite knowing what to do next. From the Bolshevik Central Committee his orders were to act as circumstances indicated. His was still the power to arrest the Executive Committee of the Soviet, but he had no direct orders, and the Trotsky–Chernov episode had confused him. To do nothing was also dangerous, because the men of Kronstadt were in a nasty mood; they might turn against him at any moment.

After an uneasy pause the sailors began to disperse of their own accord. No sooner were they gone, however, than there appeared the pro-Bolshevik 176th Reserve Regiment, which had marched on the Tauride Palace from its headquarters in the suburb of Krasnoye Selo. Their orders, too, were to 'defend' the Revolution. But the Bolshevik leaders were not on hand to give them further instructions. While they milled outside the palace, Theodore Dan, one of the Menshevik leaders of the Soviet, told their commander that their mission was to protect the Soviet against the mob. The regiment was split up into guard details, posted at strategic points in and around the Tauride Palace. Dan was as much in the dark as to the purpose of this regiment as its officers were regarding their march on the Soviet headquarters. It was now seven o'clock in the evening. The first two Bolshevik waves had spent themselves.

A short time thereafter the third wave stormed towards the Tauride Palace – this time a great mass of workers from the giant

Putilov factory. Some of the workers broke into the palace, demanding to see Tseretelli. One of them, armed with a rifle, mounted the tribune and began to shout: 'Comrades! How long are we workers going to tolerate this treachery? You have assembled here and are debating and dealing with the landowners and bourgeoisie. Remember that the working class will no longer tolerate this. We are here, 30,000 strong. We will force our will. We don't want the bourgeoisie! All power to the Soviets! The rifles are firmly in our hands. Your Kerenskys and Tseretellis will not deceive us!'

Chkheidze, who presided, listened calmly to his speech, then handed him the appeal issued by the Soviet to the workers of Petrograd, asking them to return peacefully to their homes. The worker read the document, then stood for a moment in confusion until he was pushed from the tribune. His comrades left the assembly.[1]

The July uprising was over. It had failed chiefly because of hesitation on the part of the Bolshevik leadership and poor coordination among the Kronstadt sailors, the 176th Reserves and the Putilov workers. Whether the Bolsheviks could have exploited the initial success in July to take effective power throughout Russia remains a moot question. Within the next few months the Bolsheviks were to gain strength they did not possess in July. For the moment, however, they were badly defeated, and not the least consequential factor in their defeat was the support of the Government by Cossacks and other local troops.

On 19 July the Provisional Government ordered the arrest of Lenin, Zinoviev, Kamenev, Lunarcharsky, Raskolnikov and Madame Kollontai. The charge: incitement to armed insurrection, with the financial support of the German Government. The Bolshevik headquarters in the Kshesinsky Palace were occupied by government troops.

'Now they will shoot us,' Lenin told Trotsky. 'This is the best time for it.'

'Fortunately,' commented Trotsky, 'our enemies at that time were not consistent enough and did not have the courage to do it.'

Trotsky was right. The Provisional Government, as always, vacillated between a policy of resolute action and fear of offending the non-Bolshevik Socialists, whose notion of civil liberty included the right to preach armed insurrection, mutiny and desertion in time of war. Instead of striking hard, the Provisional Government proceeded with almost dainty caution, while at the same time making premature charges without clinching proof.

The official investigation undertaken by the Provisional Government disclosed the identity of the persons through whom Lenin obtained money, as well as the banks through which the funds passed. The intermediaries were Ganetsky and Parvus in Stockholm and Copenhagen and the attorney Kozlovsky and Madame Sumenson in Petrograd. The money for Lenin went through the Disconto Gesellschaft of Berlin, the Nea Bank of Stockholm and the Siberian Bank of Petrograd.

Early in June 1917 Pereverzev, the Socialist Minister of Justice, received word from a member of the Bolshevik Central Committee that Lenin was in constant communication, through Ganetsky, with Parvus, who was then in Copenhagen. Their correspondence travelled by special courier.

Parvus was conducting German propaganda in various allied and neutral countries through a spurious 'scientific institute' in Denmark. His activities in Copenhagen were exposed by a commission consisting of twenty Russian newspaper correspondents in Copenhagen. Their findings, cabled to the Russian Minister of Foreign Affairs, were published by most Petrograd newspapers on 19 July 1917.

Within a week a letter addressed to Ganetsky, who worked for Parvus, was intercepted. At the end of June two other letters were found, all in the same handwriting, all quite brief, all on a single sheet of stationery. The contents were cryptic, containing only such phrases as 'work is progressing very successfully'; 'we hope very soon to achieve our purpose but material is indispensable'; 'be very careful in letters and telegrams'; 'the material sent to Viborg received; need more'; 'send more material'; 'be super-careful in communicating'. All three letters were from someone in Russia to Ganetsky.

A staff of professional handwriting experts unanimously agreed that the handwriting on all three letters was Lenin's.

Since Russia's complete civil liberty – including freedom to conduct anti-war propaganda – precluded the possibility that Lenin was engaged in smuggling 'illegal' literature, and since he engaged in no business enterprise, it was clear that the 'material' referred to could only be money.

At the same time, on 21 June, Captain Pierre Laurent, a French intelligence officer in Petrograd, gave the Provisional Government the copies of fourteen intercepted telegrams which had been exchanged among Kozlovsky, Ganetsky, Lenin, Madame Kollontai and Madame Sumenson. These telegrams had passed between Stockholm and Petrograd. A few weeks later Laurent delivered copies of fifteen additional telegrams.

These wires, which were easily decoded, told of success in unstated enterprises and requested directions for obtaining and depositing funds. Typical messages read:

PETROGRAD: FUERSTENBERG (GANETSKY), SALTCHEBADEN. STOCKHOLM, NO. 22. BANK RETURNED 100,000 DEPOSIT. IMPOSSIBLE TO COME NOW. ASK TATYANA YACOVLEVNA WHEN SHE RETURNS TO HELP ME THERE. SUMENSON.

FUERSTENBERG, STOCKHOLM, SALTCHEBADEN. NO. 86 . . . . RECEIVED YOUR 123. SENT MY TELEGRAMS 84–85. DEPOSITED AGAIN TODAY 20,000. TOGETHER 70. SUMENSON.

By shadowing Madame Sumenson, it was soon established that she made frequent calls at the Siberian Bank in Petrograd. An examination of the bank's records disclosed that Madame Sumenson had withdrawn 800,000 rubles in two months, and that she still had 180,000 rubles. The money in her account in the Siberian Bank, it was later learned, was sent by Ganetsky from the Nea Bank in Stockholm. Arrested after the July uprising, and confronted with the bank records, Madame Sumenson admitted these facts. She also confessed that she had instructions to give Kozlovsky, then a Bolshevik member of the Soviet Executive Committee, any sum of money he demanded; some of these payments amounted to 100,000 rubles. Letters in Madame Sumenson's quarters made it appear that the money sent from Stockholm by Ganetsky was in payment for medical supplies,[2] but she admitted that she was not engaged in any such enterprise.

All through the year 1917 Parvus was in constant communication with Ganetsky and other Bolshevik representatives in Stockholm. Ganetsky was then a member of the Foreign Bureau of the Bolshevik Central Committee in Stockholm, consisting of himself, V. Vorovsky and Karl Radek. He served as Lenin's confidential agent and handled important confidential commissions for him.

Jacques Sadoul, then French military attaché in Petrograd and later a Communist, referred to the affair in a letter to the French Socialist Minister Albert Thomas, dated 12 November 1917:

Yesterday I visited Joseph Goldenberg, formerly a member of the Central Committee of the Bolshevik Party, a friend of Maxim Gorky and one of the editors of *Novaya Zhizn*. He has just returned from Stockholm and gave me some interesting information about the activities of Ganetsky, Radek, and Parvus in the Scandinavian countries.

In another letter, dated 16 December 1917, Sadoul wrote:

Yesterday I had lunch with Madame Kollontai, Ashberg, and two Swedish Communist leaders in a private dining room. [Ashberg was the director of the Nea Bank.] Our Intelligence Service has reported that Ashberg is serving as the go-between in the transfer of German money to the Bolshevik treasury.

Twenty years later, on 15 April 1937, Ganetsky himself proudly recalled in the Moscow *Evening Gazette* how he had served in Stockholm as Lenin's contact man abroad:

I made use of the diplomatic mail privileges of the government. The old Russian Ambassador, trying to demonstrate his loyalty to the Revolution, turned very liberal and began to express his sympathetic concern with the political *émigrés*. I made use of it and kept on sending sealed envelopes to the Petrograd Soviet through the Embassy. I succeeded in convincing the Ambassador that the Soviet of Workers' and Soldiers' Deputies wields as much power as the government. The Ambassador was compelled to acquiesce, and I used to wire instructions to Petrograd to visit the Foreign Ministry in due time in order to ascertain whether or not my seals had been broken.[3]

Other evidence was supplied by Thomas Masaryk, future President of Czechoslovakia, who was in Russia in 1917. The Czech National Committee had established the Slavic Press Bureau, which actually functioned as an anti-German intelligence organization in Russia. 'We succeeded in establishing the fact that a Madame Simmons [Sumenson] was employed by the Germans as an intermediary in forwarding German funds to some of the Bolshevik leaders', Masaryk later wrote. 'These funds were sent through the German Embassy in Stockholm to Haparanda [a small town on the Finno-Swedish border] where they were transmitted to this madame.' Masaryk gave this information to the Provisional Government.[4]

When Kozlovsky was arrested in July 1917 he protested that there was absolutely no proof of his close association with Ganetsky. But at a preliminary hearing he admitted receiving enormous sums from abroad. He claimed, however, that he, Ganetsky and Madame Sumenson were engaged in smuggling certain articles of contraband feminine toilet into Russia during the war – a statement which Madame Sumenson did not support.

Trotsky, in his autobiography, went so far as to deny the existence of Madame Sumenson. 'No one was able to prove the mere existence of such a person', he wrote.

On 18 or 19 July, exactly at the time of the uprising, Ganetsky was supposed to arrive in Petrograd from the Finnish border. A special committee of the Provisional Government, consisting of Kerensky, Tereschenko and Nekrasov, which had been investigating the relations of the Bolsheviks and the Germans, was aware of this fact and also had reason to believe that Ganetsky carried documents dealing with Lenin's German associations. These Ministers issued an order to arrest Ganetsky immediately upon his arrival.

Pereverzev, the Minister of Justice, however, was not in the confidence of this special cabinet committee and did not know about the Ganetsky trip. He had been gathering his own data on Bolshevik–German relations and, without consulting the Prime Minister, published the incomplete evidence gathered up to that point on Lenin's financial connexions with Germany. When Ganetsky, arriving at the frontier, read the government's declaration in the Petrograd papers, he immediately returned to Stockholm.

Lenin boldly denied all connexions with Ganetsky, Parvus and Kozlovsky. On 26 July he wrote in the Bolshevik paper *Rabochii i Soldat*:

It is not true that Ganetsky played a role in my release from prison in Austria. . . . It is a base lie that I maintained relations with Parvus. In our paper *Sozialdemokrat*, Parvus was called, after the appearance of the the first issue of his magazine *Die Glocke*, a renegade, a German Plekhanov. . . .

The district attorney bases his game on the fact that Parvus is connected with Ganetsky and Ganetsky is connected with Lenin. But this is a real roguish method, because everybody knows that Ganetsky had money dealings with Parvus and we had none with Ganetsky. Ganetsky as a businessman was employed by Parvus.

'Not only did we not participate directly or indirectly in business affairs but in general we did not receive one cent from the above-mentioned comrades [Ganetsky and Kozlovsky], not for us personally or for the Party', Lenin wrote in Gorky's newspaper, *Novaya Zhizn*, on 24 July 1917.

But Lenin's own letters, published by the Soviet Government after the Bolshevik Revolution, refute his statement in 1917 that he had received no money from either Ganetsky or Kozlovsky. In a letter to Ganetsky in Stockholm dated 30 March 1917, released years after the event, he wrote: 'In maintaining relations between Petrograd and Stockholm do not spare funds.'

In a communication dated 12 June 1917, Lenin wrote to Ganetsky from Petrograd: 'Until today we have received nothing, literally nothing from you, neither letters nor packets nor money.' In a third letter, written several days later, Lenin wrote: 'The money (2,000) from Kozlovsky received.'[5]

After Lenin took power, both Ganetsky and Kozlovsky were high in the councils of the Soviet Government. Nine years later, in his *History of the Russian Revolution*, Trotsky devoted a long chapter entitled 'The Month of the Great Slander' to deny that the Bolsheviks received money from German sources. But his defence is merely the refutation of evidence submitted by minor intelligence service agents and rumours published in the reactionary press in 1917. Trotsky discusses the French Revolution, anti-Semitism, Christ, Newton, Marconi and Rasputin in this chapter, and ends triumphantly:

In the assault upon the Bolsheviks, all the ruling forces, the government, the courts, the intelligence service, the staffs, the officialdom, the municipalities, the parties of the Soviet majority, their press, their orators, constituted one colossal unit. . . . You can say without exaggeration that July 1917 was the month of the most gigantic slander in world history.

But he did not attempt to meet the specific evidence presented above or the charges made later by Eduard Bernstein, the German Social Democratic leader, who declared that the money amounted to more than fifty million gold marks.[6] Neither did the official

Soviet historian, Pokrovsky, in his book *The Intelligentsia in the Revolution*, which also devoted many pages to this affair. Nor did the historical seminar of the Institute of Red Professors, whose history of the October Revolution included a chapter on July 1917.

The Provisional Government, on the other hand, bungled the whole affair by releasing just enough facts to the press, before conclusive evidence had been collected, to enable Lenin and Ganetsky to cover their traces and befuddle public opinion.

When the Provisional Government ordered Lenin's arrest on 19 July, he and Zinoviev took refuge in the home of an old Bolshevik worker, Aliliuev, the future father-in-law of Stalin. On 20 July Lenin's sister Maria and Krupskaya visited him there. Lenin hesitated whether to flee or stand trial, and finally decided to escape. 'Let us say good-bye,' he said to his wife. 'Possibly we will never see each other again.'

That evening Lenin's room was searched by a colonel and another officer who took several manuscripts and documents. On 24 July a squad of military cadets ransacked Lenin's apartment, and, not finding him there, arrested his sister Anna, her husband and Krupskaya. But they were released within a day.

Lenin and Zinoviev remained under cover in the house of an old Bolshevik named Emelianov in Razliv, a suburb of Petrograd. Two days after his escape the Bolshevik Kronstadt newspaper *Proletarskoie Delo* ran a letter from Lenin and Zinoviev in which they explained: 'To give ourselves into the hands of the Pereverzevs and Miliukovs would mean to give ourselves up to the enraged counter-revolutionists, who do not wish to know about such constitutional guarantees which exist in the more or less orderly bourgeois countries. . . . Only the Constituent Assembly will have the right to pass on the order to arrest us.'

The next day Trotsky published a letter in the press declaring his solidarity with Lenin's party, and demanding that the order for the arrest of Lenin and Zinoviev include him. He said that his delay in joining the Bolshevik Party was 'explained only by the historical past that has lost all its meaning now'. But at the same time that Trotsky demanded to be placed under arrest, he disappeared from the scene.

At a meeting of the Soviet, Theodore Dan ironically observed that Trotsky asked to be arrested but forgot to leave his address. About a week later, when things quieted down, Trotsky again showed himself in the Soviet and delivered a speech defending the Bolshevik Party.

'It is not true,' he said, 'that the Bolsheviks organized the demonstration on the sixteenth and seventeenth of July. On the eve of 15 July I myself stayed the machine-gunners from action and I did the same at other meetings. Our only slogan was "All Power to the Soviets". This we said then and this I say now. To armed demonstrations, adventures, we issued no call. When the Cadet ministers resigned from the Cabinet, someone's criminal hand staged an attempt to arrest Kerensky and Chernov [*Cries from the floor: "That was done by the Kronstadt sailors!"*]. . . . Whoever was present at this attempt knows that not the sailors, not the workers heard or saw what happened at the columns of the Tauride Palace. At these columns were found a band of scoundrels and Black Hundreds who attempted to arrest Chernov, and when they attempted to do it, I told Lunacharsky, pointing at them, "These are *provocateurs*!" [*Lunacharsky from the floor: "Right".*] and on this libel is built three-quarters of the entire construction of the so-called uprising. . . .'

But on 23 July Stalin told a secret session of the Petrograd Bolshevik organization: 'The uprisings of 16–17 July served to sharpen the crisis. It was Karl Marx who said that every step forward of the Revolution is answered by a step of counter-revolution. Considering the uprisings as a progressive step, the Bolsheviks accept the honour which is ascribed to them by the renegade Socialist. . . .

'The peaceful period of the Revolution has ended. Another period has begun – a period of sharp conflicts and clashes. Life will continue to be turbulent, crisis will follow crisis, the soldiers and workers will not be silent. . . .

'Comrades who say that the dictatorship of the proletariat is impossible because the proletariat comprises a minority of the population evaluate the power of the majority mechanically. The Soviets represent twenty million of the organized elements, but due to their organization, they themselves lead the entire population. If an organized power can put an end to economic chaos and crises the entire population will follow it.

'We cannot count on peaceful pressure on the Soviets. As Marxists we must say: "It's not a question of institution, but which class this institution is promoting". . . . We are unconditionally for those Soviets where we have a majority, and we will try to create such Soviets. But we cannot hand over power to Soviets which ally themselves with counter-revolution.

'To sum up, I repeat: The peaceful path of the Revolution has ended. Since the Revolution has taken a Socialist turn, the petit bourgeois, except the poorest sections of the peasantry, is counter-revolutionary. Therefore the slogan, "All power to the Soviets", is outdated.'[7]

Following Lenin's flight, the Bolsheviks momentarily vanished from the scene. Feeling against them ran so high that for a time Bolshevik leaders who remained in the capital feared to show themselves at public meetings. Steklov, the future editor of *Izvestia*, who was arrested at the home of Bonch-Bruyevich on 23 July, at once declared that he had 'absolutely nothing in common with the Bolsheviks'.

On the same day Shotman met several members of the Bolshevik Central Committee, among them Ordzhonikidze, who instructed him to move Lenin and Zinoviev to a safe place. Ordzhonikidze directed Shotman to one Zof, who in turn took him to a young workman who was to lead him to Lenin's hide-out. Towards evening the two Bolshevik workers boarded a train for Sestroretsk. It was dusk when they reached Razliv. Finally they came to a one-storey building in a side street, inhabited by summer vacationists from Petrograd.

Shotman gave the password, entered, and looked about the two rooms overcrowded with small children. The mistress of the house told him that Lenin and Zinoviev had been moved to the woods for safety. One of the children, a boy of twelve, acted as Shotman's guide. At eleven at night they set out, following a roundabout route to the shore of a bay. Here they got into a boat. By the light of the moon they glided over a sea of weeds to the opposite shore. It took fully a half hour to cross the bay, ten minutes more to walk through boggy brushwood towards a huge stack of hay piled up on a clearing.

When the boy gave the signal, the faint moonlight revealed two figures wrapped in overcoats. There stood Lenin and Zinoviev.

All sat down near the haystack, Lenin showering Shotman with questions. Although it was July, the night effluvia from the marshes made Shotman shiver with cold. Finally the whole party went to sleep in the haystack, where individual 'beds' had been prepared by Emelianov. For a long time Shotman could not fall asleep because of the cold, although he lay between Lenin and Zinoviev, covered with an overcoat.

For the next two weeks Shotman called at the haystack regularly, bringing food and bundles of newspapers from Petrograd. Lenin read the papers, made marginal notes on them, and using a tree stump as a table, wrote his pamphlets *About Our Slogans* and *Can the Bolsheviks Retain State Power?* Here, too, he jotted down in a copybook the outlines of his *State and Revolution*.

For a fortnight Shotman scouted about for a better shelter for Lenin, for it was no secret that Lenin was within reach of Petrograd. In an unguarded moment Sverdlov had told the Sixth Bolshevik Party Congress that, although Lenin was unable to be present, he was nevertheless guiding its work. The statement was picked up by the press, which demanded Lenin's immediate arrest. As a result a redoubled watch was maintained at all frontier points.

Finally it was decided that Lenin and Zinoviev would cross the Finnish border disguised as workers from Sestroretsk, many of whom lived on the Finnish side and carried special permits. The documents were easily obtained. Lenin shaved off his moustache and beard, and put on a wig, while Zinoviev grew a beard and cropped his bushy hair short. Photographs taken in the disguise were then pasted on their false papers.

Lenin, according to the plan, was to travel to Finland, while Zinoviev was to remain in the home of a Finnish worker, Emil Kalske, at Lesnoye, a town near Udelnaya Station on the Finnish railroad.

Shotman and his assistant Rakhia were to accompany Lenin to Finland. A railroad engineer, Ialava, who agreed to take Lenin, was Shotman's childhood chum. When preparations were completed, Shotman and Rakhia went to escort Lenin and Zinoviev from their marshy home.

They arrived in the evening. When Rakhia saw Shotman stop before two men who looked like tramps, he cried in Finnish: 'Why do you stop? Come!'

As the 'tramps' came closer, Rakhia recognized Lenin and Zinoviev. Lenin laughed heartily, pleased that his disguise was so effective. Then they proceeded towards the station.

Emelianov led them down a narrow path into a forest filled with smoke from burning peat. It was difficult to breathe. For a time they were lost, for heavy smoke rose from the ground and darkened the sky. Rakhia was afraid they might sink into the burning bog. They groped deeper into the woods, against the wind and smoke, until they reached a small stream. On the opposite side was a road marked with recent waggon tracks. Quickly they stripped and waded in, holding their clothing overhead. Swollen by spring rain, the water proved to be deeper than they had expected, but they made the other shore safely.

Lenin was in high spirits as they dressed. They carried no compass, but the stars directed them eastward. At last a few houses and a tiny railroad station came into view. With police patrolling the area, Emelianov was sent ahead to scout. He was picked up within a few minutes and held all night. Lenin, Shotman and Rakhia lay in a ditch near the railroad station. They could hear every word spoken by the guards.

Finally Shotman went to the station to inquire when the next train was due; he was also arrested. At last a whistle was heard and a train bound for Belo Ostrov arrived. The station was only dimly lit. As the train halted, Lenin and Rakhia leaped unseen into one of the cars. It was dark inside but soon a conductor entered carrying a green lantern. The conductor knew Rakhia, greeted him, and soon began talking about the latest news in Petrograd.

'This Lenin,' said the conductor, 'is a native Finn. He got two and a half million rubles.'

'For what?'

'That's what I want to know – for what?'

Rakhia explained this was merely gossip, while Lenin sat with his head buried in his hands and said nothing. Finally, they arrived at Udelnaya. As they left the train, Lenin shook the conductor's hand.

They walked in darkness until they reached Kalske's impoverished home, where Rakhia's wife had been expecting them for three days. After eating their bread, Lenin and Zinoviev lay down on the floor, wrapped themselves in newspapers, and went to sleep. It was four in the morning. Later that night Shotman arrived.

The following night Lenin left for the station to meet the train bound for Finland. Clean-shaven and wearing a blond wig, he looked like a genuine Finn. He took his place beside Ialava in the cab, rolled up his sleeves, and started throwing chunks of wood into the firebox.

At each station Shotman and Rakhia jumped off to watch the engine. The train reached Belo-Ostrov, where there was a twenty-minute stop for a border inspection of papers. No sooner did the train come to a halt than Ialava uncoupled the engine and moved it to the water-pump in the darkness. While the frontier officials were examining the papers, Ialava was filling the tank. Just before the third whistle the engineer returned, blew the siren, and was off. Fifteen minutes later all were on Finnish territory. At Terioki horses were waiting to take Lenin fourteen miles inland to a safe refuge.

Leaving Lenin with Rakhia, Shotman took the first available train for Helsinki to arrange Lenin's further journey. Two men brought Lenin to the little town of Lakhit, one hundred and thirty miles from the Finnish capital. With the aid of a member of the Finnish Diet, Shotman arranged for Lenin to live in the home of the Helsinki Police Commissioner. No safer place could be desired.[8]

Chapter 12
The Tide Turns

The first four months of the Revolution witnessed the enactment of a series of basic reforms by the Provisional Government. There was also developed, with the participation of representatives of all parties and social and national organizations, a law to regulate the elections to the Constituent Assembly, based on universal, direct and equal suffrage, and proportional representation. The government seemed to become stronger and better organized, as local Soviets were being superseded by the new organs of municipal and district self-government, elected on the basis of universal suffrage. The Provisional Government was strengthened on 21 July, when Prince Lvov resigned and Kerensky became Prime Minister. Life seemed to be returning to normal.

From the middle of July, when the uprising failed, until September the Bolshevik Party steadily lost ground. Admitting that the July events resulted in a serious setback for the Bolshevik cause, Trotsky later wrote:

In the official Soviet histories it has become the accepted opinion . . . that the July attack on the Party went by almost without leaving a trace. . . . That is utterly untrue. The decline in the party ranks and the ebbing away of workers and soldiers did not, to be sure, last very long, not longer than a few weeks . . . but as the minutes of local party organizations were published, the picture emerged more and more clearly of a July ebb in the Revolution – a fact felt all the more painfully in those days because the preceding upsurge had been uninterrupted.

Yakovleva, then a member of the Bolshevik Central Committee, declared: 'After the July days, reports from every locality described unanimously not only a sharp decline in the mood of the masses, but even a definite hostility toward our party. In a good many cases our speakers were beaten. Membership fell off rapidly, and several organizations, especially in the southern provinces, ceased to exist entirely.'[1]

At the Sixth Bolshevik Congress, with Lenin, Zinoviev and menev absent, only Stalin stubbornly defended Lenin's thesis the Bolsheviks had to prepare for the seizure of power, introducing the following resolution ·'It is the duty of the revolutionary classes to strain every effort to take the power into their own hands, and, in cooperation with the proletariat of the more advanced countries, to lead the country to peace and to a Socialist reconstruction of society.'[2]

But the wane in Bolshevik influence was about to be offset, through a rapid series of events that brought about a decisive breach between the Provisional Government and the Soviets. On 30 July Kerensky appointed Boris Savinkov, former Political Commissar of the Eighth Army, as deputy Minister of War, at the same time naming as Commander in Chief General Kornilov, a man characterized by General Brusilov as 'a man with the heart of a lion and the brains of a lamb'. The son of a Siberian Cossack, General Lavr Kornilov had distinguished himself during the retreat of the Eighth Army in Galicia. After the Revolution, he had briefly commanded the Petrograd garrison. Transferred to the south-western front, he took command once more of the Eighth Army, where he met Savinkov, a right-wing Socialist Revolutionary and former terrorist. On 19 July the Executive Committee of the south-western front had wired Kerensky requesting that the armies of the front 'be placed under the command of a leader capable of uniting and inspiring all the wavering elements and securing a victorious offensive by the sheer force and determination of his will'. The next day Kornilov received the appointment.

Three days later Kornilov demanded an immediate cessation of the offensive on all sectors, in order to preserve the Army, and the introduction of the death penalty for deserters at the front. His demands were met, and within another week Kornilov was Commander in Chief of all the Russian armies.

Kornilov and Kerensky saw eye to eye in military matters, although neither man trusted the other. Both felt that demoralization at the front and growing unrest in the rear would ultimately bring defeat and total chaos for Russia. Kornilov, in addition, wanted to eliminate the influence of the Soviets and 'Bolshevik Petrograd'. For the businessmen and Cadets, who stood on the right fringe of the Revolution, Kornilov represented 'the salvation of the motherland'.

On 19 August Kornilov ordered the transfer of the Third Cavalr-

Corps and the Savage Division (made up of Caucasian and Cossack troops) to within striking distance of Moscow and Petrograd, and still another Cossack division to a region in Finland forty miles from Petrograd. Two weeks later he explained the purpose of this move to his Chief of Staff, General Lukomsky, as follows:

'It's time to hang the German supporters and spies, with Lenin at their head, and to disperse the Soviet of Workers' and Soldiers' Deputies so that it will never reassemble. I am shifting the cavalry corps mainly so as to bring it up to Petrograd by the end of August, and, if a demonstration of the Bolsheviks takes place, to deal with these traitors as they deserve. I want to commit the leadership of this operation to General Krimov. I am convinced that he will not hesitate, if need arises, to hang every member of the Soviet.'[3]

On 28 August the All-Russian State Conference, called by Kerensky, met in Moscow. About 2,400 delegates of all classes and parties, as well as of the armed forces, were present. Included were 488 deputies of the Four Dumas. Despite the demand of the Bolsheviks and Martov's Left Mensheviks that these proceedings be boycotted, the Soviet Central Executive Committee voted to send its delegates to Moscow.

On the day the conference opened, the local Bolshevik organizations called a protest strike, ignoring a vote by the Moscow Soviet against the demonstration. The strike, although not completely successful, was enough to indicate that the conference did not enjoy complete public confidence.

In his keynote address, Kerensky warned all enemies of the Revolution, reactionary and radical alike, that the government would suppress any attempt to overthrow the régime. General Kornilov then delivered a pessimistic report on the Army and demanded that energetic steps be taken to prevent Russia's military collapse. He asked for the suppression of political meetings among combat troops, the dissolution of soldiers' committees at the front, and the restoration of military discipline.

Others who spoke included Plekhanov, Catherine Breshkovsky and Peter Kropotkin. Plekhanov, calling for a united democratic front, said: 'The Soviet leaders themselves admit that they are conducting a bourgeois revolution. Is it then possible to conduct a bourgeois revolution without the bourgeoisie? The capitalist classes, too, must see that a capitalist society cannot exist without the working class and its organizations. Therefore these two classes must join hands and come to an understanding. If this is not done, they will meet the same end as the Kilkenny cats who fought so long that all that remained were their tails.'

Despite much excellent oratory and expressions of good-will, the Moscow Conference accomplished nothing. The Left was alarmed by Kornilov's demands; the Right insisted that it was 'fed up with Kerensky's flowery promises'.

On 3 September the Germans took Riga, threatening the approach to the capital. Immediately afterwards Kornilov asked for direct control over the Petrograd garrison. On 5 September Savinkov arrived in Kornilov's Headquarters at Moghiliev with Kerensky's terms. It was agreed that the Petrograd military district be turned over to Kornilov, but Kerensky insisted that the city itself remain under the control of the Provisional Government. The Prime Minister also asked for the liquidation of the reactionary Union of Officers and the Headquarters political department. Finally, Kerensky requested the dispatch of a cavalry corps to enforce martial law in Petrograd, and 'to defend the Provisional Government against any attacks whatsoever, especially from the side of the Bolsheviks'. Kerensky indicated, however, that he wanted neither the Savage Division, with its Caucasian tribe components, nor General Krimov to be sent to the capital.[4]

On 7 September Kornilov demanded the resignation of the Cabinet and the surrender of all military and civil authority to the Commander in Chief (without naming himself for the role of dictator). On the ninth Kerensky dismissed Kornilov and ordered him back to Petrograd. Kornilov replied by moving his cavalry on Petrograd. It was a bold bid for power, but it collapsed overnight, when the Petrograd Soviet summoned its soldiers and workers to defend the Revolution. Railroad workers refused to transport Kornilov's troops, telegraph operators did not transmit his orders, agitators convinced Kornilov's Cossacks not to fight. The workers of Petrograd formed a militia that was to become the Red Guard of the Bolshevik Revolution. Actually no fighting took place. Kornilov's troops dissolved before they reached the city.

On 12 September 1917, Kerensky became Supreme Commander

and Kornilov was arrested. On 14 September Russia was proclaimed a republic, but on the previous day, the Petrograd Soviet passed a Bolshevik-introduced resolution for the first time.

The Kornilov affair caused the final break between Kerensky and the army leadership as well as the conservative elements. Thereafter Kerensky was at the mercy of the Petrograd Soviet. He had no reliable military forces at his disposal. Under the new conditions, the Bolshevik leaders who had been arrested in July were released. For the Bolshevik cause, Kornilov's unsuccessful *putsch* was a godsend which more than recouped their July losses. Bolshevik influence among workers, soldiers and peasants began to mount swiftly.

From Finland Lenin wrote on 12 September to the Central Committee of the Party:

> The Kornilov revolt was extremely unexpected at such a time and in such a form; it was, one might say, an incredibly abrupt turn in the course of events.
>
> Like every abrupt turn in events, it calls for a revision and alteration of tactics.
>
> It is my conviction that those who are drifting into defencism or into a *bloc* with the Socialist Revolutionaries and into *supporting* the Provisional Government are guilty of lack of principle. It is absolutely wrong and unprincipled. We shall become *defencists only after* the power has passed to the proletariat, *after* peace has been proposed, and *after* the secret treaties and ties with the banks have been broken; *only after all this*. Neither the fall of Riga *nor the fall of Petrograd* will make us defencists. . . . Until then we are for a proletarian revolution, we are opposed to the war, we are *not* defencists.
>
> And *even now* we must not support Kerensky's government. That would be unprincipled. It will be asked: What, not even fight Kornilov? Of course fight him! But that is not the same thing; there is a dividing line. . . .
>
> We will fight and are fighting Kornilov, *just as Kerensky's troops are.* But we do not support Kerensky; *on the contrary*, we expose his weakness. . . .
>
> We must change the *form* of our struggle against Kerensky. While not relaxing our hostility towards him one iota, while not withdrawing a single word we uttered against him, while not renouncing the aim of overthrowing Kerensky, we say: We must *reckon* with the present state of affairs; we shall not overthrow Kerensky just now; we shall adopt a *different* method of fighting him; namely, we shall point out to the people

(who are fighting Kornilov) the *weakness and vacillation* of Kerensky. That was done *before* too. But now it has become *the main thing*. That is the change.

The change, furthermore, consists in this, that *the main thing* now is to intensify our agitation in favour of what might be called 'partial demands' to be addressed to Kerensky; namely, arrest Miliukov; arm the Petrograd workers; summon the Kronstadt, Viborg, and Helsingfors troops to Petrograd; disperse the State Duma; arrest Rodzianko; legalize the transfer of the landlords' estates to the peasants; introduce workers' control over bread and over the factories, etc., etc. These demands must be addressed not only *to* Kerensky, and *not so much* to Kerensky as to the workers, soldiers, and peasants who have been *carried away* by the struggle against Kornilov. Draw them still further; encourage them to beat up the generals and officers who are in favour of supporting Kornilov; urge them to demand the immediate transfer of the land to the peasants; suggest to *them* the necessity of arresting Rodzianko and Miliukov, of dispersing the State Duma, of shutting down the *Rech** and the other bourgeois papers, and of instituting proceedings against them. The 'Left' Socialist Revolutionaries particularly must be pushed in this direction. . . .

And *at this very minute* we must conduct our agitation against Kerensky not so much directly as indirectly, that is, by demanding a most active, energetic and truly revolutionary war against Kornilov. The development of that war alone may put *us* in power, but of this we must *speak* as little as possible in our agitation (all the time remembering that events may any day put the power into our hands, and then we shall not relinquish it). It seems to me that this should be transmitted in the form of a letter to agitators (not through the press), to our agitators and propagandists, and to the members of the Party generally. As to the talk of defence of the country, of a united front of revolutionary democracy, of supporting the Provisional Government, and so forth, we must oppose it ruthlessly as being mere *talk*. This is the time for action.[5]

News of the Kornilov uprising brought in its wake an outbreak of reprisals against officers in many cities. The military section of the Central Executive Committee of the Soviets described such events in Viborg as follows: 'The picture of the lynching was dreadful. First three generals and a colonel, just arrested by the combined Executive Committee and the Army Corps Committee, were dragged from the guardhouse, thrown off the bridge, and shot in the water. Then the regiments took the law into their own hands.

* The leading daily of the Constitutional Democrats.

The troops brought out the commanders and some of the other officers, beat them, threw them into the river, and beat them again in the water. About eleven officers were killed in this manner. The exact number has not yet been established, since some of the officers fled. The murders went on till night.'

According to Podvoysky, a key Bolshevik leader:

The Kornilov revolt had a most unfortunate effect on the military strength of the Army; it also served to attach a final stigma of counter-revolution to the entire officer corps. If the officers had hitherto still managed somehow to retain their position, the rebellion spelled their end. The soldier masses saw clearly that their way diverged from that of their commanders and turned away from them finally and completely.

As a result of the Kornilov revolt, the propaganda of the members of the military organization and pro-Bolshevik soldiers, which had been temporary quelled after the July reaction, now spread with renewed energy among the troops and found a most receptive audience in the nervously exhausted mass of soldiers who refused to wait, who would not consider anything or listen to anyone. . . . Conflicts with the commanding officers became especially sharp and chronic. Bolshevism was gaining ever-widening success and popularity.

But though the Army as such was in its last days, it still held together, if only passively.

The soldiers did not leave their posts, they did not throw down their rifles; fraternizing with the enemy, they nevertheless, in the vast majority of cases, did not allow him to come over to their soil. In the rear, however, the situation was altogether different; army units consistently refused to go to the front; those which reported at the front came greatly depleted in numbers and already entirely demoralized. Such an attitude on the part of the rear depressed the front-line soldiers even more, for they justly felt themselves betrayed, forgotten. . . . Inflamed passions, envy, and the irresistible longing for home which caused mass discontent, combined with total impunity and the disorganization of all supply and transport, undermined still further the already disintegrated front.

The inevitable end was coming. The soldier masses turned away from their commanders, ceased to trust their committees, especially the more important ones, as well as the agents of the government in the person of the military Commissars. Having turned from these, they could no longer be stopped and rapidly followed those who had already long called them to land and freedom and promised to end the hated war.[6]

The mood of the Petrograd working masses was already crystallized long before November. It was predominantly pro-Bolshevik and in favour of the slogan, 'All power to the Soviets'. This was reflected in the composition of the Workers' Section of the Petrograd Soviet and its temper. The correlation of forces among the soldier masses, the regiments, and units of the Petrograd garrison was different. The workers were unarmed, not technically organized as a military force, ignorant in the use of weapons. The garrison soldiers, on the other hand, were numerous, armed, well organized, and most of them had already gone through the school of frontline experience.

The Bolshevik Sadovsky writes:

But the soldier masses were under the sway of the Socialist Revolutionaries and, partly, of the Mensheviks. These influences were predominant and remained so until the middle of September, when a change of mood became evident; at that moment the idea of the seizure of power acquired a realistic foundation. This change was sharply demonstrated during the re-elections to the Executive Committee of the Petrograd Soviet, especially during the re-elections in the Soldiers' Section of the Soviet. Although the latter did not give a majority to the Bolshevik slate, nevertheless nearly 50 per cent of the votes cast for the Bolshevik slate unequivocally showed the shift that had occurred in the mood of the soldier masses, and indicated a crucial change.[7]

In the remaining interval before the general elections to the Constituent Assembly – now scheduled for 25 November – the Provisional Government decided to organize a Preliminary Parliament to function until the Assembly met. This was Kerensky's final effort to reconcile the forces represented in the Soviet with the non-Socialist democratic elements and the peasantry. The conference for the Preliminary Parliament convened on 27 September in Petrograd; all Soviets, zemstvos, trade unions, co-operatives and other democratic organizations were represented. Present, too, were the Bolsheviks.

When Lenin learned that his party was participating, he sent this angry letter from Finland to the Central Committee: 'You will be traitors and scoundrels if you do not at once assign the entire Bolshevik faction to factories and plants, and do not surround the "democratic conference" and arrest all the scum.'

The letter was couched in very strong terms, according to Bukharin, 'and threatened us with dire punishment. . . . We were all astounded. . . . At first everyone was perplexed. Then, after some discussion, we reached a decision. This was perhaps the only occasion in the history of our Party when the Central Committee unanimously decided to burn Comrade Lenin's letter. This incident was given no publicity at the time.'[8]

But Lenin continued to press for the seizure of power. In two letters to the Party leaders, in Petrograd and Moscow, he outlined his strategy:

Having obtained a majority in the Soviets of Workers' and Soldiers' Deputies of both capitals, the Bolsheviks can, and must, take over the power of government.

They can do so because the active majority of the revolutionary elements of the people of both capitals is large enough to carry the masses, to overcome the resistance of the adversary, to smash him, and to conquer power and retain it. For, by immediately proposing a democratic peace, by immediately giving the land to the peasants, and by re-establishing the democratic institutions and liberties which have been mangled and shattered by Kerensky, the Bolsheviks will create a government which *nobody* will be able to overthrow. . . .

Why should the Bolsheviks assume power *now*?

Because the impending surrender of Petrograd will render our chances a hundred times less favourable.

And while the Army is headed by Kerensky and Co. it is not in our power to prevent the surrender of Petrograd.

Neither can we 'wait' for the Constituent Assembly, for by surrendering Petrograd, Kerensky and Co. can always *frustrate* the convocation of the Constituent Assembly. Our Party alone, having assumed power, can secure the convocation of the Constituent Assembly; and, having assumed power, it will accuse the other parties of procrastination and will be able to substantiate its accusations.

A separate peace between the British and German imperialists must be prevented, and can be prevented, but only by quick action.

The people are tired of the vacillations of the Mensheviks and the Socialist Revolutionaries. Our victory in the capitals alone will draw the peasants over to our side. . . .

It would be naïve to wait for a 'formal' majority for the Bolsheviks; no revolution ever waits for that. Kerensky and Co. are not waiting either; they are preparing to surrender Petrograd. The wretched vacillations of the Democratic Conference are bound to exhaust the patience of the workers of Petrograd and Moscow. History will not forgive us if we do not assume power now.

There is an apparatus: the Soviets and the democratic organizations.

The international situation just now, *on the eve* of the conclusion of a separate peace between the British and the Germans, is in *our favour*. If we propose peace to the nations now we shall win.

Power must be assumed in Moscow and in Petrograd at once. . . .

In order to treat insurrection in a Marxist way, *i.e.* as an art, we must, without losing a single moment, organize a *general staff* of the insurrectionary detachments; we must distribute our forces; we must move the loyal regiments to the most important strategic points; we must surround the Alexandrisky Theatre; we must occupy the Fortress of St Peter and St Paul; we must arrest the general staff and the government; against the military Cadets and the Savage Division we must move such detachments as will rather die than allow the enemy to approach the centre of the city; we must mobilize the armed workers and call upon them to engage in a last desperate fight; we must occupy the telegraph and telephone stations at once, quarter *our* general staff of the insurrection at the central telephone station, and connect it by telephone with all the factories, regiments, points of armed fighting, etc.[9]

At the conference, Trotsky, speaking for the Bolsheviks, accused Kerensky of seeking to play the role of Bonaparte. In turn, Tseretelli, who led the fight against the Bolsheviks, declared: 'When you talk to the Bolsheviks you must take along a notary public and two stenographers, otherwise they will later deny everything they said.'

On 3 October the conference gave the Provisional Government a vote of confidence and endorsed the calling of the Preliminary Parliament. On 8 October the Provisional Government was reorganized for the last time with Kerensky as Premier and all Socialist and Liberal parties represented.

The same day Trotsky was elected chairman of the Petrograd Soviet, and Chkheidze, the retiring chairman, Tseretelli, the Menshevik leader, and Gotz, leader of the Socialist Revolutionaries, resigned from the Soviet presidium.

As reports of the pro-Bolshevik surge reached Lenin in Helsinki, he insisted on getting to Petrograd at once, but when Shotman pointed out that the frontier was still closely guarded, the Bolshevik Central Committee voted to postpone Lenin's return.

Impatiently Lenin proceeded to Viborg, intent on reaching Petrograd. Shotman found Lenin at the home of the Finnish writer Latukk. His first question was whether it was true that the Central Committee had vetoed his return to the capital. When

Shotman explained that the Committee had acted in the interest of his safety, Lenin demanded written confirmation. Taking a sheet of paper, Shotman wrote: 'I, the undersigned, hereby certify that the Central Committee of the Russian Social Democratic Labour Party (Bolshevik faction) resolved that V. I. Lenin shall be forbidden to come to the city of Petrograd until further notice.'

Lenin took the paper, folded it carefully, put it in his pocket and with his thumbs in his vest, paced up and down the room, repeating angrily: 'I shall not let it go at that.'

When he had calmed down, he began to show Shotman his figures on the increase in Bolshevik strength among the workers and the lower middle class. Kerensky's complaints about agrarian disorders, argued Lenin, indicated that the countryside was also veering to the Bolsheviks. The time was ripe for the seizure of power.

Shotman argued that the Bolsheviks lacked the experts to run the machinery of state.

'Any worker can learn to run a ministerial office in a few days,' Lenin replied. 'No special ability is needed; the technical part of the work can be handled by the functionaries whom we shall compel to work for us.'

As Shotman continued to quibble over details, Lenin, with more patience than usual, provided the answers. Shotman was particularly disconcerted by Lenin's plan to void the paper currency issued by the Tsar and Kerensky.

'Where will you get new money to replace the old?' asked Shotman.

'We'll start all the printing presses running and print enough bank notes to meet our needs,' Lenin replied.

'Any swindler could counterfeit such currency,' retorted Shotman.

'We'll print it in some special way and type. But why worry about it now? That's the job for technicians. It will take care of itself.'[10]

The basic thing, said Lenin, was to enact the decrees that could convince the Russian people that the power was theirs. As soon as they felt that, they would support the new régime. His first act would be to end the war, thereby winning the support of the front-weary army. The lands of the Tsar, the aristocracy, and the church would be confiscated and turned over to the peasants. The factories and plants would be taken from the capitalists and given to the workers. Who would then remain to oppose the Bolsheviks?

At the end of September Lenin sent a letter to the Central Committee urging immediate preparations for an armed uprising. Comparing the situation before and after the Kornilov affair, he explained that this time the uprising would not fail.

There was no class behind us at that time that could be described as the advance guard of the Revolution; we had no majority among the workers and soldiers of the two capitals. Now we have it in both Soviets; it is due *exclusively* to the attempt to make short shrift of the Bolsheviks and to the Kornilov experience. At that time there was no general revolutionary enthusiasm; now, after the Kornilov affair, there is. . . . At that time there was no *hesitation* of serious political consequence among our enemies and the neither-here-nor-there petite bourgeoisie; now the hesitation is tremendous. . . . Therefore on 3 and 4 July [16 and 17 according to the new calendar] it was physically and politically impossible for us to remain in power, since the workers and soldiers would not have been ready to fight and die for the possession of Petrograd; there was not the ferociousness, the burning hatred. . . . We could not have kept in power on 3 and 4 July [16 and 17] because *before* the *Kornilov affair* the Army and the provinces could and would have marched against Petrograd. Now the picture is entirely different. . . . [11]

Furthermore, Lenin did not consider it advisable to wait for the All-Russian Congress of the Soviets. In a letter on 12 October he wrote: 'To wait for the Congress of Soviets is idiocy, for it would mean losing weeks at a time when weeks and even days decide everything.'

First defeat Kerensky, then call the Congress, Lenin advised.

'The success of the insurrection is now *guaranteed* for the Bolsheviks: (1) we can (if we do not wait for the Soviet Congress) launch a *sudden* attack from three points – from Petrograd, from Moscow, and from the Baltic Fleet; (2) we have slogans that guarantee us support: "Down with the government that is suppressing the revolt of the peasants against the landlords!" (3) we have a majority *in the country*; (4) the disorganization among the Mensheviks and the Socialist Revolutionaries is complete; (5) we are technically in a position to seize power in Moscow (where the start might even be made, so as to catch the enemy unawares); (6) we have *thousands* of armed workers and soldiers in Petrograd who could *at once* seize the Winter Palace, the general staff, the telephone exchange, and the large printing establishments. Nothing will be able to drive us out of these positions, while agitational work *in the Army* will be such as to make it impossible to combat this government of peace, of land for the peasants, and so forth.'

An attack at once, from Petrograd, Moscow, and the Baltic Fleet, would succeed with smaller sacrifice than in July, Lenin said, because the troops would not advance against a government of peace.

> Even though Kerensky *already* has 'loyal' cavalry, etc., in Petrograd, if we were to attack from two sides, and with the sympathy of the Army *on our side*, he would be compelled to surrender.
>
> In view of the fact that the Central Committee has even *left unanswered* the persistent demands I have been making for such a policy ever since the beginning of the Democratic Conference, in view of the fact that the central organ is *deleting* from my articles all references to such glaring errors on the part of the Bolsheviks as the shameful decision to participate in the Preliminary Parliament, the presentation of seats to the Mensheviks in the presidium of the Soviet, etc., etc. – I am compelled to regard this as a 'subtle' hint of the unwillingness of the Central Committee even to consider this question, a subtle hint that I should keep my mouth shut, and as a proposal for me to retire.
>
> I am compelled to *tender my resignation from the Central Committee*, which I hereby do, reserving for myself the freedom to agitate among the rank and file of the Party and at the Party Congress.
>
> For it is my profound conviction that if we 'wait' for the Congress of Soviets and let the moment pass now, we shall *ruin* the Revolution.[12]

In October Lenin completed his pamphlet entitled *Can the Bolsheviks Retain State Power?* More revealing than the contents was the title. The question in his mind was no longer whether the Bolsheviks could seize control but whether they would remain at the helm. If the Tsar could rule Russia with 130,000 members of the nobility and landed gentry, argued Lenin, then the Bolshevik party with 240,000 members was at least as strong.

On 20 October the Preliminary Parliament began its sessions, with the Socialist Revolutionary leader Nikolai Avksentyev, Chairman of the Soviet of Peasant Deputies, presiding. Under Lenin's pressure the Central Committee of the Bolshevik Party passed a boycott resolution. Trotsky read the declaration announcing the Bolshevik withdrawal.

'The bourgeois classes,' said Trotsky, 'while apparently non-political, have set themselves the aim to frustrate the Constituent Assembly [*Clamour from the right, exclamations: 'A lie!'*]. . . . We, the Bolshevik Social Democratic faction, declare: We have nothing in common with this government of national treason. [*Much noise from the right and centre, cries of 'scoundrel'.*] . . . Long live the Constituent Assembly!'[13]

Lenin wrote to Smilga, the Chairman of the Regional Committee of soldiers, sailors and workers in Helsingfors:

> The general political situation troubles me a great deal. The Petrograd Soviet and Bolsheviks have declared war on the government. But that government has the Army and is systematically preparing (Kerensky is at general headquarters. It is obvious that he is considering with the Kornilov men practical measures for crushing the Bolsheviks).
>
> What are we doing? Are we passing resolutions and more resolutions? We lose time, we set 'dates' (Congress of Soviets, 15 November), is it not ridiculous to delay in this manner? Is it not ridiculous to depend on this? The Bolsheviks are not carrying on systematic work to prepare their military forces to overthrow Kerensky.
>
> Events have fully justified the stand I took at the time of the Democratic State Conference, that the Party must work towards an armed uprising. Events force this on us. The question of arms is now the fundamental political question. I fear that the Bolsheviks forget this. They are carried away by 'topics of the day', by details, and by the 'hope' that 'a wave will carry away Kerensky'. Such a hope is quite naïve. It is working 'at random'. Such an attitude on the part of a party of the revolutionary proletariat may prove criminal.

To Smilga he assigned the role of organizing the military and naval forces in Finland for the uprising:

> Now as to your role, it seems to me that the only thing which we can completely have in our hands and which is of military importance is the army in Finland and the Baltic fleet. . . . Give all your attention to preparing the army in Finland and the fleet for the overthrow of Kerensky. Form a secret committee of MOST DEPENDABLE military men; examine with them the question from all sides; collect (and personally verify) accurate information about the composition and disposition of the troops near and in Petrograd, about the possibility of bringing the army in Finland to Petrograd and regarding the movements of the fleet, etc.
>
> Beautifully worded resolutions and Soviets without power make us ridiculous losers. I think that you are in a position to bring together

reliable and military men. Go to the Ino [fortress] and other important points; make a really careful and serious study of the situation; do not be carried away by the boastful phrases which we are too much in the habit of making.

It is quite clear that we must UNDER NO CIRCUMSTANCES permit the removal of the troops from Finland. It is better to risk EVERYTHING on an uprising, the seizure of power – to be handed over to the Congress of the Soviets. I read in today's papers that in two weeks all danger of a [German] landing will be over. It means that you have very little time to get ready.

Furthermore, it is necessary to make use of [your] authority in Finland to carry on a systematic propaganda among the Cossacks who are now in Finland. Some of these, Kerensky and Company, purposely removed from Viborg, for fear they would become tainted with Bolshevism, and stationed at Usikirki and Perkiarvi, which are between Viborg and Terioki, where they would be safely isolated from the Bolsheviks. It is necessary to get full information about these Cossacks and to send among them some of our best soldier and sailor agitators that can be found in Finland. This is most urgent. The same is true in regard to printed matter.

Work among the soldiers and sailors on leave, he urged, and form a block with the Left Socialist Revolutionaries.

'Soldiers and sailors are given leaves of absence. Organize those who have leave to go to the country into propaganda units for systematic agitation. Let them visit villages and counties to agitate in general and for the Constituent Assembly. You are in an exceptionally good position. You can begin at once to form a bloc with the Socialist Revolutionaries of the left wing. Only this move can put real power in our hands in Russia and secure for us a majority in the Constituent Assembly. . . . At the present moment the Socialist Revolutionaries "firm" is doing a thriving business, and you should take advantage of your good luck (for you have Left Socialist Revolutionaries) to form in the villages in the NAME of this firm a bloc of Bolsheviks and Left Socialist Revolutionaries, peasants with workmen, but not with the capitalists.'

Agitation should begin immediately for the transfer of power from the Provisional Government to the Petrograd Soviet, he advised. 'In my opinion, in order to prepare people's minds properly there should be circulated at once this slogan: The power should immediately be placed in the hands of the Petrograd Soviet, which should hand it over to the Congress of Soviets. Why endure three more weeks of war and the Kornilov preparations of Kerensky?'

For his own protection, Lenin instructed Smilga: 'Send me . . . an identification paper (the more formal the better), on the stationery of the Regional Committee, signed by the chairman, with the seal; have it typed or written in a very clear hand, made out to Konstantine Petrovich Ivanov. Have the certificate read that the chairman of the Regional Committee vouches for this comrade and asks all Soviets, Viborg Soviet of Soldiers' Deputies as well as others, to have full confidence in him in every possible way. I need it in case ANYTHING should happen – a "conflict" or "meeting". . . .'[14]

Shortly afterwards Shotman, *en route* to Lenin in Viborg, met Rakhia at the station. There was no need to go to Viborg, said Rakhia with a broad grin. Lenin was back in Petrograd.

Chapter 13
Lenin Seizes Power

Promptly upon his arrival in Petrograd Lenin took over the task of preparing the armed uprising. At a secret meeting of the Bolshevik Central Committee on 23 October 1917, attended by Zinoviev, Kamenev, Stalin, Trotsky, Sverdlov, Uritsky, Dzerzhinsky, Kollontai, Bubnov, Sokolnikov and Lomov, Lenin insisted that the Bolshevik uprising could not wait for the convocation of the Constituent Assembly.

'The international situation is such that we must make a start,' Lenin said. 'The indifference of the masses may be explained by the fact that they are tired of words and resolutions. The majority is with us now. Politically things are quite ripe for the change of power. The agrarian disorders point to the same thing. It is clear that heroic measures will be necessary to stop this movement, if it can be stopped at all. The political situation therefore makes our plan timely. We must now begin thinking of the technical side of the undertaking. That is the main thing now. But most of us, like the Mensheviks and the Socialist Revolutionaries, are still inclined to regard the systematic preparation for an armed uprising as a sin. To wait for the Constituent Assembly, which will surely be against us, is nonsensical because that will only make our task more difficult.'[1]

A long and bitter discussion followed Lenin's summons to insurrection. 'Late at night, probably past midnight, the decision was reached', recalls Yakovleva. 'The meeting lasted about ten hours without a break, until far into the night', Trotsky wrote in 1933. Eleven years earlier, when the details were fresher in his mind, he had declared, 'The meeting lasted all night, people began to leave at dawn. I and some other comrades remained to sleep over.'

The official Soviet version is as follows: 'Lenin proposed the organization of an armed uprising; this proposal was enthusiastically endorsed by all participants, with the exception of Zinoviev and Kamenev. On 7 November 1917, Lenin's plans were translated into action.'

But, according to Trotsky's reminiscences, published in Moscow in 1922, Lenin's proposal for immediate revolt met with very little enthusiasm.

'The debate was stormy, disorderly, chaotic', wrote Trotsky. 'The question now was no longer only the insurrection as such; the discussion spread to fundamentals, to the basic goals of the Party, the Soviets; were they necessary? What for? Could they be dispensed with?'

'The most striking thing', said Trotsky in 1922, 'was the fact that people began to deny the possibility of the insurrection at the given moment; the opponents even reached the point in their arguments where they denied the importance of a Soviet Government. . . .'

In the early hours of the morning Lenin finally won his victory.

'Hastily, with a stub of a pencil, on a sheet of graph paper torn from a child's exercise book, he wrote: "The Party calls for the organization of an armed insurrection." ' The resolution was put to a vote. The official minutes record: 'Votes in favour – 10; against – 2.' But Trotsky claims: 'I do not remember the proportion of the votes, but I know that 5 or 6 were against it. There were many more votes in favour, probably about 9, but I do not vouch for the figures.'[2]

A few days later Lenin again warned that further delay might be fatal. 'The agrarian disorders are increasing, the government is using the most savage measures against the peasants', he wrote. 'Sympathy for our cause in the Army is growing. Ninety-nine per cent of the soldiers in Moscow are with us. The Army and the fleet in Finland are against the government.

'In Germany, it is now clear that the revolution has already begun, especially after the shooting of the sailors. In the elections to the Moscow Soviet the Bolsheviks received 47 per cent of the votes. Together with the Left Socialist Revolutionaries we shall surely command a majority of votes in the country.

'Under the circumstances to "wait" is simply criminal. The Bolsheviks have no right to wait for the Congress of the Soviets. They must seize power immediately. In that way they will save the world revolution, otherwise there is danger that the imperialists of all countries will enter into an alliance against us. . . .

'To defer the question is criminal, to wait for the Congress of

Soviets is juvenile. It is nothing but a formality, a shameful play at formality, and a betrayal of the Revolution.'[3]

Meanwhile, Lenin continued stirring the workers and soldiers against Kerensky. 'Kerensky is praised by the Cadets. He carried out their policy; he consults them and Rodzianko *behind the back of the people*. . . . Kerensky is a Kornilovite who has *accidentally* quarrelled with Kornilov, but remains in a most intimate alliance with the rest of the Kornilovites. . . .

'The Stolypinites, Kerensky and Co., are cajoling the people with the approaching Constituent Assembly elections; as though the people can believe in a *fair* election; under a government which is taking military measures in remote villages, that is to say, obviously *covering up* the arbitrary arrests of thinking peasants and falsifying elections.'

Again and again he promised that when Kerensky – 'this Stolypinite, Kornilovite, and Bonapartist' – was overthrown, the Bolsheviks would 'at once give the land to the peasants, reconstruct democratic liberties and institutions which were maimed and ruined by Kerensky, and set up a government that *nobody* will ever overthrow.'[4]

Some members of the Bolshevik Central Committee still wavered. The majority, however, supporting Lenin, decided on immediate action. On Trotsky's initiative the Petrograd Soviet organized a Military Revolutionary Committee to carry out the *coup d'état*. The Central Committee of the Party, on 5 November, also elected a Political Bureau of seven to make the final technical preparations. But the real leadership in the insurrection was carried out by the Military Revolutionary Committee. In November 1918, when official Soviet historians were not yet deprecating the role of Trotsky in the Bolshevik revolution, Stalin wrote: 'All the work of practical organization of the insurrection was conducted under the direct leadership of the president of the Petrograd Soviet, Comrade Trotsky.'

The Military Revolutionary Committee consisted of two representatives each from the Central Committees of the Bolshevik and Left Social Revolutionary parties, two representatives of their military organizations, two from every soldiers' section of the Petrograd Soviet, and two from the garrison conference. Its membership included Trotsky (as chairman of the Petrograd

Soviet), Dzerzhinsky, Antonov-Ovseenko, Lashevich, Nevsky, Podvoysky and others. Its first elected chairman was Lazimir, but later he was replaced by Podvoysky. Antonov was elected secretary.[5]

In order to gain control of the garrison, the Military Revolutionary Committee appointed a commissar for every army unit in Petrograd and its environs. On the night of 3 November the commissars of the Military Revolutionary Committee were sent to the regiments of the Petrograd garrison. The Military Revolutionary Committee issued an order that 'henceforth all power in Petrograd passes into the hands of the Military Revolutionary Committee'. According to this order, the troops were to obey only the instructions and orders of the Military Revolutionary Committee, which would be transmitted to them through the regimental commissars; all other orders, whatever their origin, were declared counter-revolutionary. This order was in effect the beginning of the armed insurrection, since it brought out into the open the conflict between the Provisional Government and the Military Revolutionary Committee.

In the meantime Lenin, on 6 November, addressed a letter to the members of the Central Committee in which he wrote:

The matter must be decided unconditionally this very evening, or this very night.

History will not forgive revolutionaries for procrastinating when they can be victorious today (will certainly be victorious today), while they risk losing much, in fact, everything, tomorrow .

If we seize power today, we seize it not in opposition to the Soviets but on their behalf.

The seizure of power is a matter of insurrection: its political purpose will be clear after the seizure.

It would be a disaster, or a sheer formality, to await the wavering vote of 7 November. The people have the right and duty to decide such questions not by a vote, but by force; in critical moments of revolution the people have the right and duty to give directions to their representatives, even their best representatives, and not to wait for them.[6]

The bold challenge by the Military Revolutionary Committee showed that the Provisional Government had very small forces at its disposal. The Military Revolutionary Committee thereupon decided not to wait to be attacked but to overthrow the government with the means at its command. A plan was developed for the occupation of the Winter Palace and the arrest of the members of the government. It was proposed to surround the palace while the government was in session, and to encircle it with reliable Bolshevik troops. If the government refused to surrender, it was to be forced to yield by fire from the cruiser *Aurora* and from the Fortress of St Peter and St Paul.

General direction of the operations was entrusted to Antonov, Chudnovsky and Podvoysky. The Winter Palace was to be attacked on the night of 7 November. Headquarters for operations was to be the Fortress of St Peter and St Paul. At the last conference it was also decided that before the assault a delegation be sent to the government with the demand to vacate the palace, yield all arms and surrender to the Military Revolutionary Committee. If no answer came within twenty minutes, the *Aurora* would open fire, the sailors would disembark and the Red Guards would storm the Winter Palace.[7]

On the morning of 6 November Kerensky appeared before the Pre-Parliament and declared that he had in his possession incontrovertible proof that Lenin and his comrades had organized an insurrection against the Provisional Government. The government, he said, was adopting measures for its suppression. It would fight to the end against 'the traitors to the fatherland and the Revolution'. It would unhesitatingly resort to armed force, but success in the struggle required the immediate cooperation of all parties and groups represented in the Pre-Parliament and the help of the whole people. He requested from the Pre-Parliament 'all measures of confidence and cooperation'. Directly after his speech, Kerensky left for Military Headquarters.

The Provisional Government did not have a secure majority in the Pre-Parliament, where Socialists of all shades predominated. The leading figure among them, after Tseretelli's departure to the Caucasus, was Theodore Dan, a Left Menshevik. In reply to Kerensky's speech, he offered a resolution which sharply criticized the Bolsheviks, but at the same time argued that successful action against the Bolsheviks required decisive measures in the struggle for peace, an immediate transfer of landed estates into the hands of the peasants, and the speediest possible convocation of the Constituent Assembly. The projected revolt of the Bolsheviks, declared Dan, speaking in the name of the 'revolutionary democracy', undoubtedly would lead the country to a catastrophe, but the revolutionary democracy would not fight against it by armed force, for 'if the Bolshevik movement is drowned in blood, then, whether the victory is won by the Provisional Government or the Bolsheviks, the real triumph will belong to a third force, which will sweep away both the Bolsheviks, the Provisional Government and the entire democracy.' Dan's resolution placed the responsibility for the impending insurrection both on the Bolsheviks and the Provisional Government, and proposed to entrust the defence of the democratic Revolution to a Committee of Public Defence, to be created from among the representatives of the Petrograd City Council and the parties.

After a long debate, Dan's resolution was passed by 122 votes against 102, with 26 abstaining. After the adoption of his resolution, Dan, accompanied by Abram Gotz, the leader of the Centre Group of Socialist Revolutionaries, departed for the session of the Provisional Government to demand the immediate publication and posting, that very night, of leaflets throughout the city declaring that the government: (1) appealed to the Allied powers that they propose to all belligerent powers the immediate cessation of military action and the opening of general peace negotiations; (2) issued telegraphic orders placing all landed estates under the jurisdiction of local land committees until the final disposition of the agrarian problem; (3) decided to hasten the convocation of the Constituent Assembly.

At the same time, Dan told Kerensky that the representatives of 'revolutionary democracy' were far better informed than he was, that he exaggerated the danger, under the influence of the 're-actionary headquarters'. He said further that the resolution of the Pre Parliament, 'so displeasing to the government's vanity', was extremely useful for a 'break in the mood of the masses', and that the influence of Bolshevik propaganda would henceforth rapidly decline. On the other hand, he said, the Bolsheviks themselves, in their negotiations with the leaders of the Mensheviks and Socialist Revolutionaries, expressed their willingness to 'bow to the will of the majority in the Soviets.' There was much doubt and hesitation among the Bolsheviks themselves on this score, said Dan, and the Bolshevik masses did not want an insurrection. The acceptance by the government of the resolution adopted by the Pre-Parliament, he declared, would strengthen the trend among the Bolsheviks in favour of abandoning the projected insurrection. The purely military-technical measures adopted by Kerensky, on the other hand, merely 'irritated the masses' and hindered the representatives of the Soviet majority from 'successfully negotiating with the Bolsheviks concerning the liquidation of the insurrection'.

'We pointed out', recalled Dan five years later, 'that by its course of action the government was not only ruining itself and the Revolution, but made it impossible for us and for the parties we represented to make common cause with it and render it active support.' According to Dan, Kerensky responded to these arguments with extreme irritation, declaring that 'now is the time for action, not talk'.[8]

In the meantime, the Bolsheviks continued to claim that all assertions concerning 'some alleged Bolshevik plot' were an invention of the 'counter-revolutionaries' and 'the Kornilovist, Kerensky'.

Kerensky had barely finished his conversation with Dan and Gotz when a delegation from the Cossack regiments stationed in Petrograd arrived to see him. The delegates stated that the Cossacks wished to know what forces the government had at its disposal for the suppression of the uprising. Then they declared that the Cossack regiments would defend the government only if he, Kerensky, personally gave them assurances that this time Cossack blood would not be spilled in vain, as it was in July, when the government did not take sufficiently energetic measures for the total liquidation of the Bolsheviks. Finally, the delegation insisted that the Cossacks would fight only at his personal command. Kerensky at once signed an order to the Cossacks to place themselves immediately at the disposal of the district military headquarters and to obey its commands implicitly.

While Kerensky was holding this midnight conversation with the delegates of the Cossack regiments, the Council of Cossack Troops, headed by right-wing Cossack officers, which met all through the night, expressed itself in favour of non-intervention in the struggle of the Provisional Government with the insurgent Bolsheviks.

On 7 November 1917, the very day the Bolsheviks struck, *Izvestia*, the official organ of the All-Russian Central Executive Committee of the Soviets, carried an editorial entitled 'Madness or Adventure', warning that a Bolshevik victory would lead to chaos and a civil war.

It is only three weeks to the Constituent Assembly, only a few days to the Congress of Soviets, and yet the Bolsheviks have decided to stage a new *coup d'état*. They are making use of the wide discontent and great ignorance that exist among the masses of soldiers and workers. They have taken upon themselves the boldness to promise the people bread, peace, and land. We have no doubt whatsoever that they are unable to keep a single one of their promises, even if they succeed in their attempt. . . .

One of the first consequences of the Bolshevik attempt will be to lower the food supplies of the city and Army If the Bolsheviks should really seize power, a state of famine would be reached. A Bolshevik government would never be recognized in the far southern steppes, and the grain which comes for the whole of Russia would be held back. . . .

As regards the land question, the land can be transferred to the toilers in one of two ways, by passing the necessary legislation and proper organization of land distribution, or by the simple method of grabbing by peasants. . . . The best they can possibly do is to issue an order in two words: 'Grab land!' Such an order would lead to agrarian disorders, destruction, which they, to save their face, call agrarian revolts, but under no circumstances can it be called handing over the land to the toilers.

The only kind of peace which the Bolsheviks would get, according to the paper, would be peace on German terms.

By disorganized fraternization, the firing may cease on certain points along the front. . . . One can open the front and give the foe a chance to occupy new territory. In this way, however, peace is not to be had. Only a state can conclude peace. In order to have a peace with some degree of success, it is necessary that the state be united and strong, and have the respect of allies and enemies. The experience of this summer shows that with each German military success the reactionary party in Germany became stronger, the position of Wilhelm improved, and thereby the chances of a democratic peace decreased.

Civil strife would certainly follow the initial success of the Bolsheviks, concluded *Izvestia*.

The Bolshevik uprising can lead only to that. Is it possible that people do not understand that dictatorship and terror are not the way to organize a country? Is it not clear that an attempted uprising, at the time of the preparation for the election of the Constituent Assembly, can be regarded as a non-criminal act only because it is a mad act?

On the morning of 7 November Rakhia told Lenin that the government was planning to open the drawbridges across the Neva. 'Yes, today the thing is going to start,' was Lenin's response.

'Vladimir Ilyich', Rakhia relates, 'was pacing the room, evidently debating something in his mind. Presently he remarked: "It's time to go to the Smolny Institute" [the new Bolshevik and Soviet headquarters located in a fashionable school for girls]. I urged him not to go, pointing out the dangers to which he would be exposing himself. Brushing all arguments aside, he declared: "We are going to Smolny."'

Lenin changed his clothes, bandaged his cheek with a soiled handkerchief, and put on his wig and an old cap. On the way to Smolny they were stopped several times by military patrols. When they reached Smolny the guards at first refused to admit them. After much difficulty the two finally entered the lobby. Lenin sent for Trotsky and Stalin, and the four men retired to a separate room, where Lenin heard Trotsky and Stalin report on the situation.

The newspapers had reported that the negotiations of the Military Revolutionary Committee with the staff of the Petrograd Military District concerning the further fate of the garrison were approaching a favourable end. 'Are you agreeing to a compromise?' Lenin asked Trotsky, with a piercing glance. Trotsky answered that he purposely had given this calming news to the papers, and that it was only a temporary stratagem before the beginning of a general attack.

'That is good!' said Lenin, rubbing his hands and pacing the room. 'That is v-e-r-y good!' he repeated. 'To fool the enemy, to get him to make a fool of himself – was there anything better than that?' remarked Trotsky.[9]

'During this conversation,' relates Rakhia, 'three men came out of the assembly room where the Soviet was in session. One was Theodore Dan, the Menshevik leader. Another took a package out of the coat which was hanging in the room and, opening it, invited the rest to have a bite with him. While conversing, they paid no attention to Trotsky, Stalin, and the third man sitting with them. The lunch was spread out on the opposite end of the table where

Lenin was sitting. Then Dan raised his head and recognized Lenin with the bandage around his cheek. He was very much embarrassed, and immediately left the room with his companions. This incident amused Lenin greatly and he laughed heartily over it.'[10]

Nevertheless, he ordered Bonch-Bruyevich to keep an eye on the Menshevik leader. Bonch-Bruyevich summoned a guard detail and gave them their instructions. They examined their revolvers, hand grenades, and bombs, and then stood silent. Lenin, however, could not sit still. 'When will we begin? . . . What is happening? Where is Podvoysky, Antonov-Ovseenko? Where is he? Send him at once to the Fortress of St Peter and St Paul. Inform him that in the event Podvoysky and the men with him should fall, it will be his duty to take over the command and immediately storm the Winter Palace and bombard the city.'[11]

In the meantime the insurrection spread with incredible speed in the city. Armed detachments of Red Guards occupied the central telegraph office, the post office, and a large number of other government buildings. Armed squads of Bolsheviks surrounded the buildings of the Winter Palace and the Military District Headquarters in an ever-tightening ring. Kerensky, accompanied by Vice-Premier Konovalov, proceeded to Headquarters. It was clear that only the immediate arrival of military reinforcements from the front could still save the situation. Consulting with Konovalov and another Minister, Kishkin, as well as with certain officers at Headquarters, Kerensky decided to move through the Bolshevik lines and personally meet the troops which, they thought, were coming to Petrograd from the front. In an open automobile he drove past Bolshevik patrols, recognized by passers-by and soldiers. The military snapped to attention, from habit. A second later none of them would have been able to explain to himself how this had happened. The automobile now sped on to Gatchina.

The other Ministers were assembled at the Winter Palace. 'After a brief exchange of views,' writes ex-Minister of Justice Maliantovich, the well-known Moscow jurist and Social Democrat, 'we reached the conclusion that the situation was so serious that the Provisional Government would not be true to its duty if it did not remain at the Winter Palace in full force, meeting in continuous session until the final solution of the crisis.'

According to Maliantovich, the general mood of the soldiers

could be described approximately as follows: 'Rather unsympathetic to the Bolsheviks, but also without enthusiasm for the government. A position of neutrality. Will join the victor. . . .'[12]

The All-Russian Congress of Workers' and Soldiers' Deputies was scheduled to open that evening and the Bolsheviks were racing to seize power in order to confront the Congress with a *fait accompli*. Night fell, and the Winter Palace, with Kerensky's Ministers, had not yet been captured. Smolny was in a state of intense agitation.

Meanwhile, in the Petrograd City Council a strange meeting was taking place. The council-men knew that the fighting had reached the square before the Winter Palace. One member delivered an emotional speech demanding that the City Council march in a body to the Winter Palace, 'to die together with Russia's chosen representatives'.

A spokesman for the Soviet of Peasants' Deputies gave his support to this motion, which was adopted with quixotic enthusiasm. With the exception of the Bolsheviks and Left Socialist Revolutionaries, each council-man and peasant deputy rose and declared: 'Yes, I am ready to die.'

The members of the Petrograd City Council and the Soviet of Peasants' Deputies went out into the street and marched towards the Winter Palace, singing the 'Marseillaise'. At the Kazan Cathedral they were halted by a Bolshevik patrol and marched no farther.

When the session of the Second Congress of the Soviets opened in Smolny, Lenin did not appear, remaining in his room. Later someone spread a blanket and two cushions on the floor. 'Vladimir Ilyich and I,' writes Trotsky, 'lay down to rest. But a few minutes later I was called. "Dan is speaking. You must answer him." When I came back, I again lay down next to Vladimir Ilyich, who naturally could not sleep. Every five minutes someone came running in from the auditorium to inform us of what was going on. In addition, messengers came from the city, where, under the leadership of Antonov-Ovseenko, the siege of the Winter Palace was drawing to a close.'[13]

Inside the Winter Palace the isolated, outnumbered defenders were preparing for their last stand. Among them were Socialists and conservatives, a unit of the Women's Battalion, veteran workers, and men of wealth. Of the military defenders, young cadets predominated.

Looking out on the Neva River from the windows of the Winter Palace, the Ministers of the Provisional Government could see the guns of the cruiser *Aurora*, manned by Bolshevik sailors of the Baltic Fleet. The guns were expected to open fire at any moment. In the square, the Bolsheviks were bringing up armoured cars, field-pieces, machine-guns.

Kishkin arrived from Military Headquarters and announced: 'I have received an ultimatum from the Military Revolutionary Committee. I propose that we discuss it.'

The ultimatum demanded surrender within twenty minutes, warning that fire would be opened from the *Aurora* and the Fortress of St Peter and St Paul.

It was resolved to ignore this ultimatum.

The hand of the clock passed eight. The Ministers turned out the overhead lights. Only the electric table lamp on the desk remained lit, its light screened from the window by a newspaper. The room was in half-darkness. Suddenly a loud report was heard, then another. The hands of the clock crawled on till it was past nine. Some of the besieged sat, some reclined, others paced soundlessly over the soft rug that covered the entire floor.

A new sound was heard, muted, but distinct from all others.

'What is that?' asked someone.

'It is from the *Aurora*,' replied the Minister of the Navy Verderevsky.[14]

The earlier noise had been blank shots from the guns of St Peter and St Paul and the *Aurora*. These signalled an intensified exchange of small arms fire which lasted an hour. Then the *Aurora* aimed a six-inch shell which exploded in the palace corridor and spread confusion among the defenders.

Podvoysky writes:

Taking advantage of that, the sailors, Red Guards, and soldiers rushed forward. The savage howling and roar of three-inch and six-inch guns from the fortress fell silent, and the dry, unending rattle of machine-guns was drowned out by the continuous triumphant shouts of 'Hurrah', alternating with other wild, indescribable sounds. An awful, all-engulfing, brief moment that swept one's whole being and fused the heterogeneous mass into a single entity. ... Then a momentary halt before the barricades, and the rapid crackle of machine-guns, rising again above the shouts. . . .[15]

Thirty or forty Bolsheviks, armed with guns and revolvers, broke into the palace. But they were instantly disarmed and arrested. . . . They surrendered their arms without resistance.

Immediately after this, several sailors made their way into the palace, climbed to the upper gallery in the lobby, and dropped two grenades. They were small and poorly made. The sailors were seized and disarmed.

Maliantovich relates:

Suddenly a noise arose somewhere and began to grow, spread, and roll ever nearer. And in its multitude of sounds, fused into a single powerful wave, we immediately sensed something special, unlike the previous noises – something final and decisive. It suddenly became clear that the end was coming. . . . The noise rose, swelled, and rapidly swept towards us in a broad wave. . . . And poured into our hearts unbearable anxiety, like a gust of poisoned air. . . . It was clear: this is the onslaught, we are being taken by storm. . . . Defence is useless – sacrifices will be in vain. . . . The door burst open. . . . A military cadet ran in, drew himself up, saluted, his face excited but resolute.

'What are the orders of the Provisional Government? Defence to the last man? We are ready to obey the orders of the Provisional Government.'

'No, it is not necessary! It is useless! The picture is clear! We want no bloodshed! We must surrender,' they all cried in concert, without discussing the question, merely looking at each other and finding the same feeling and decision in everyone's eyes.

Kishkin came forward.

'If they are here, it means that the palace is already occupied.'

'It is occupied. All entrances are blocked. Everyone has surrendered. This is the only room still under guard. What are the orders of the Provisional Government?'

'Tell them that we want no bloodshed, that we yield to force, that we surrender,' said Kishkin.

There was a noise behind the door and it burst open. Like a splinter of wood thrown out by a wave, a little man flew into the room, pushed in by the onrushing crowd which poured in after him and, like water, at once spilled into every corner and filled the room. The little man wore a loose, open coat, a wide felt hat pushed back off his forehead over his long, reddish hair, glasses. He had a short, trimmed red moustache and a small beard. His short upper lip rose to his nose when he spoke. The eyes were colourless, the face tired. He flew in and cried in a sharp, small, insistent voice:

'Where are the members of the Provisional Government?'

'The Provisional Government is here,' said Konovalov, remaining seated. 'What do you wish?'

'I inform you, all of you, members of the Provisional Government, that you are under arrest. I am Antonov, chairman of the Military Revolutionary Committee.'

'The members of the Provisional Government yield to force and surrender, in order to avoid bloodshed,' said Konovalov.

'To avoid bloodshed! And how much blood have you spilled?' shouted a voice from the mob behind the ring of guards. Many approving exclamations echoed from all sides.

Antonov stopped the outcries.

'Enough, comrades! That's all! We'll straighten all that out afterwards. . . . Now we must draw up a protocol. I am going to write it now. I shall ask everyone. . . . But first I request you to surrender all arms in your possession.'

The military surrendered their arms, the rest declared that they carried none.

The room was jammed with soldiers, sailors, Red Guards, some carrying several weapons—a rifle, two revolvers, a sword, two machine-gun ribbons.

When it was learned that Kerensky had fled, vile oaths were heard from the crowd. Some of the men shouted, inciting the rest to violence:

'These will run off too! . . . Kill them, finish them off, there's no need for protocols! . . .'

'Run them through, the sons of bitches! . . . Why waste time with them! They've drunk enough of our blood!' yelled a short sailor, stamping the floor with his rifle – luckily without a bayonet – and looking around. It was almost a call to action. There were sympathetic replies:

'What the devil, comrades! Stick them all on bayonets, make short work of them! . . .'

Antonov raised his head and shouted sharply:

'Comrades, keep calm! All members of the Provisional Government are arrested. They will be imprisoned in the Fortress of St Peter and St Paul. I'll permit no violence. Conduct yourself calmly. Maintain order! Power is now in your hands. You must maintain order! . . .'

The members of the Provisional Government were then led away towards the Fortress of St Peter and St Paul. Along the way they were met with jeers and threats from the crowds on the streets.

Maliantovich continues:

The mob was growing bolder. The guards increased their pace. . . .
We walked faster and faster. . . . We reached the middle of the bridge.
. . . Our speed no longer helped, it even seemed to provoke the mob.
. . . Another moment, and the guards would be overpowered and thrown
aside. . . . And suddenly!

From somewhere machine-guns opened fire on us. The guards and the
whole crowd flattened down on the bridge. We also threw ourselves
down. There were cries: 'Comrades! Comrades! Stop it! You're firing
on your own!'

Fire was opened from the fortress.

'They've gone crazy – firing from the fortress!' cried someone in our
convoy.

This accident saved the lives of the arrested Ministers.

On the fortress bridge they were met by a small group of soldiers
and escorted inside the fortress.

Antonov began to write the protocol. When he finished reading
it, he raised his head, placed his right hand, palm down, on the
paper, and intoned slowly, almost dreamily:

'An historic document! . . .'

'His face looked transported, enraptured,' writes Maliantovich,
'as if his soul was bursting from its narrow bonds. His gaze was
directed afar. He could not contain himself.'

'Yes,' Antonov continued, 'it will be an interesting social experiment. . . .'[16]

According to Trotsky, Sukhanov firmly believed that, had the
Provisional Government shown initiative on 5 November and
during the night of 6–7 November, it could have captured the Bolshevik Military Revolutionary Committee. 'A good detachment of
five hundred men,' writes Sukhanov, 'would have been entirely
sufficient to liquidate Smolny and everyone there.' Quoting these
words, Trotsky writes: 'Perhaps. But to do this the government
would have required, first of all, resolution and daring. Secondly,
it would have needed a good detachment of five hundred men.
And where was that to be found?'[17]

When news of the arrest of the Provisional Government was
transmitted to Smolny there was a rush to the great hall where the
Soviet Congress was in session. Lenin took off the handkerchief
covering half his face.

'Remove your wig,' whispered Bonch-Bruyevich.

Lenin did so, and his comrades saw the familiar bald head.

'Give it to me; I'll put it away,' offered Bonch-Bruyevich. 'It may come in useful again some day. . . . Who knows?'

When Lenin appeared on the rostrum he received a thunderous ovation. He stood before the packed assembly, hands in his pockets, his head slightly bowed. When the applause subsided, he raised his head and began to speak.

'Comrades, the workers' and peasants' revolution, whose need the Bolsheviks have emphasized many times, has come to pass.

'What is the significance of this revolution? Its significance is, in the first place, that we shall have a Soviet Government, without the participation of a bourgeoisie of any kind. The oppressed masses will themselves form a government. The old state machinery will be smashed to bits and in its place will be created a new machinery of government of Soviet organizations. From now on there is a new page in the history of Russia, and the present Third Russian Revolution shall in its final result lead to the victory of Socialism.

'One of our immediate tasks is to put an end to the war at once. But in order to end the war, which is closely bound up with the present capitalistic system, it is necessary to overthrow capitalism itself. In this work we shall have the aid of the world revolutionary movement, which has already begun to develop in Italy, England, and Germany.

'We have now learned to work together in a friendly manner, as is evident from this revolution. We have the force of mass organization which conquered all and which will lead the proletariat to world revolution.

'We should now occupy ourselves in Russia in building up a proletarian Socialist state. Long live the world-wide Socialist revolution!'[18]

Late that night Lenin went to the home of Bonch-Bruyevich in a state of complete exhaustion. Bonch-Bruyevich made his own bed in the adjoining room, determined to retire only when Lenin was asleep. He locked all doors and prepared his revolvers for instant use. 'Who knows? Someone may come to arrest or murder Lenin,' he thought to himself. 'This is only the first night of our victory. Our success is not yet assured. Anything may happen.'

At last Lenin put out his light. Bonch-Bruyevich was beginning to doze off when he noticed lights go on again. Lenin had risen, tiptoed to the door, and thinking Bonch-Bruyevich asleep, had seated himself at his writing table and began to work.

He wrote, made revisions, and finally prepared a clean copy. The autumn dawn was breaking when Lenin finally went to sleep. When the household was assembled for tea late that morning, Lenin saluted them with: 'Greetings on the first day of the Socialist Revolution.' Then he took out of his pocket the manuscript he had prepared during the night and read his famous decree expropriating the landed estates.

'Now we must see to it that the decree is made public and broadcast throughout the country. Then let them try to take it away,' Lenin asserted. 'No! No power on earth will be able to take away this decree from the peasants and return the land to the nobles. This is the most important achievement of our revolution! Today the agrarian revolution will occur and will become irrevocable!'

'But they will accuse us of having stolen the programme of the Socialist Revolutionaries,' someone remarked.

'Let them say what they will,' Lenin replied with a grin. 'The peasants will understand that we always support their justified demands. . . . We must identify ourselves with the peasants, with their wishes. And if there are fools who laugh at us, let them laugh. We never intended to give a monopoly over the peasants to the Socialist Revolutionaries.'[19]

The immediate question was the form of the new government. What should its members be called? 'Anything but Ministers – that is a vile, hackneyed word,' said Lenin.

'We might call them commissars, but there are too many commissars,' suggested Trotsky. 'Perhaps supreme commissars? No, "supreme" does not sound well either. What about People's Commissars?'

'People's Commissars? Well, that might do, I think,' replied Lenin. 'And the government as a whole?'

'A Soviet, of course – the Soviet of People's Commissars.'

'The Soviet of People's Commissars? That's splendid, savours powerfully of revolution!' said Lenin.[20]

Despite the capture of the Winter Palace, more than one hundred delegates at the All-Russian Congress of Soviets protested against the proceedings of the Petrograd Soviet. Many Army representatives, as well as Socialist Revolutionaries and Mensheviks, walked out of the Congress. When Martov arose to announce the departure of the 'internationalist' Mensheviks, the report of a distant cannon burst into the hall. In the hush that fell, Martov's rasping voice (he was already suffering from tuberculosis of the throat) could be heard: 'That is the funeral of the unity of the working class. . . . We shall not take part in this.' Trotsky rushed to the podium to reassure the hesitant assembly as Martov walked out in silence without looking back. At the exit, a young Bolshevik worker with a black shirt and broad leather belt remarked bitterly, 'And we thought among ourselves that Martov at least would stay with us.' Martov shrugged his head and replied, 'Some day you will understand in what crime you are taking part.' (The worker was Akulov, later secretary of the All-Russian Central Executive Committee in 1935–6, who perished under the terror of Stalin and Yezhov.)

With most of the democratic forces gone from the Congress, the Bolsheviks and their allies (chiefly left-wing Socialist Revolutionaries) passed a formal resolution taking over the government. The Congress promised that 'the authority of the Soviet gives peace, land, the right to soldiers' and workers' control, bread and necessities, the Constituent Assembly and self-development of the nationalities included in Russia.' After warning the soldiers against Kerensky and Kornilov, the Congress adjourned, at six o'clock in the morning of 8 November.

When Lenin and Zinoviev appeared that afternoon before a joint meeting of the Congress, the Petrograd Soviet and members of the conference of the garrison, they were greeted with 'tempestuous and ecstatic applause'. That evening the Congress established what was to be the fundamental law of the Russian Socialist Federated Soviet Republic. Lenin's address to the belligerent nations was unanimously adopted, as well as a decree abolishing capital punishment. The Petrograd Soviet's proposal on land was debated until late into the night, but also was passed. After providing for the formation of Military Revolutionary Committees in all Army divisions, the Congress established the first Soviet Government.

The All-Russian Congress of the Workers', Soldiers', and Peasants' Deputies decrees:

To establish for the administration of the country, until the Constituent

Assembly provides otherwise, a Provisional Workers' and Peasants' Government, which is to be named 'The Soviet of the People's Commissars'. The management of the different branches of life of the state is to be entrusted to Commissariats, the personnel of which secures the accomplishment of the programme announced by the Congress, in close contact with the mass organization of working-men, working-women, sailors, soldiers, peasants, and employees. The governmental authority rests with the *collegium* of the chairman of these Commissariats: *viz.* with the Soviet of People's Commissars.

Control of the activity of the People's Commissars and the right to recall them belong to the All-Russian Congress of the Soviets of the Workers', Soldiers', and Peasants' Deputies and its Central Executive Committee.

For the present the personnel of the Soviet of People's Commissars is as follows:

Chairman of the Soviet of People's Commissars, Vladimir Ulyanov (Lenin)

People's Commissar of the Interior, A. I. Rykov

People's Commissar of Agriculture, D. P. Milyutin

People's Commissar of Labour, A. R. Shliapnikov

War and Navy Committee, V. Antonov-Ovseenko, N. V. Krylenko, and Dybenko

People's Commissar of Commerce and Industry, V. P. Nogin

People's Commissar of Education, A. V. Lunacharsky

People's Commissar of Finance, I. I. Skvortsov (Stepanov)

People's Commissar of Foreign Affairs, L. D. Bronstein (Trotsky)

People's Commissar of Justice, G. E. Oppokov (A. A. Lomov)

People's Commissar of Supply, I. F. Theodorovich

Post and Telegraph, N. P. Avilov (Glyebov)

People's Commissar of Nationality Affairs, J. V. Djugashvili (Stalin)

(Soviet of People's Commissars was later shortened in the Russian to Sovnarcom.)

A vivid picture of the scene at Bolshevik Headquarters during the decisive hours is painted by Trotsky's wife.

'I came into a room at Smolny where I saw Vladimir Ilyich, Lev Davidovich (Trotsky), and I think Dzerzhinsky, Joffe, and some other people. All their faces were greenish grey and sleepy, their eyes bloodshot, their collars dirty. The room was full of smoke. Someone was sitting at the table; around him stood a crowd of people evidently waiting for instructions. Lenin and Trotsky were in the centre of a group. The instructions, it seemed to me, were issued as if in sleep. There was something suggesting sleepwalking in the whole scene. For a moment it occurred to me that I was witnessing a nightmare, and that the Revolution might be lost if "they" did not get a good night's sleep and put on clean collars. Somehow the illusion was closely associated with those dirty collars. I remember the next day I met Maria Ilyichina, Lenin's sister, and hastily reminded her that it was time Vladimir Ilyich changed his collar. "Yes, yes," she laughed. By this time the question of clean collars had already lost its dread significance.'

Trotsky completes the picture:

'The state power has been seized, at least in Petrograd! Lenin has not yet had a chance to change his collar. . . . Upon my haggard face shine the wide-awake eyes of Lenin. He looks at me kindly, with a sort of awkward shyness expressive of an inner affinity. "You know," he says to me haltingly, "to pass so quickly from persecutions and clandestine existence to power" he fumbles for words, then suddenly finishes in German – "*es schwindelt*" [it makes one dizzy] – and swings his hand around his head. We look at each other and smile.'

Kerensky, meanwhile, had reached Gatchina but found no trace there of any troop transports from the front. The same evening he left for Pskov, where he heard only discouraging news from Petrograd. In fact the Military Revolutionary Committee was already active in Pskov itself and it had received a telegram from Krylenko and Dybenko ordering Kerensky's arrest.

General Cheremisov, the Commander in Chief of the northern front, told Kerensky he could give him no assistance. But Kerensky did receive aid from General Krasnov, who commanded a drive against Petrograd. On 9 November Gatchina was taken, despite Bolshevik armed superiority, and the following evening Krasnov's Cossacks entered Tsarskoye Selo.

The victory, however, proved short-lived. Bolshevik agitators and the local troops wreaked havoc among the Cossacks. Krasnov's soldiers were asked 'not to beat up the peasants and workers, as the Tsar and Kornilov had done', and the Cossacks were told they were being led towards 'the return of all power to the land-owners, bourgeoisie and generals'.

The Bolsheviks were aided by reactionary elements who incited hatred against Kerensky for having put down the Kornilov revolt.

Krasnov's small band was thus bombarded with agitation from both the Left and the Right, and demoralization soon set in.

Furthermore, the Vikzhel (All-Russian Committee of the Union of Railroad Employees) threatened to call a general strike if Kerensky did not open peaceful negotiations with the Bolsheviks. On the morning of 13 November Kerensky's military council decided to open negotiations for an armistice in the hope of gaining time. Kerensky insisted on two conditions: (1) that the Bolsheviks must immediately disarm and submit to the reconstituted Provisional Government; (2) the composition and programme of the new government must be determined by the existing Provisional Government, the representatives of all political parties, and the Petrograd 'Committee for the Defence of Fatherland and Revolution'.

Lenin watched every move of Kerensky's offensive, carefully following the counter-operations outlined by Antonov and Podvoysky. He demanded a desk in Podvoysky's office, declaring that he wanted to be kept continually informed and that the Sovnarcom had assigned him together with Trotsky and Stalin to assist Podvoysky. Soon Lenin sent Bonch-Bruyevich and his wife to assist Podvoysky, and then continued sending people every five or ten minutes: someone to help with supplies, another to deal with demobilization, a dynamiter, a flier, an agitator. Gradually Lenin began to issue direct orders, but he still felt that the work was not going so rapidly as it should. . . . 'Several times,' writes Podvoysky, 'I quarrelled with Lenin, protesting against his "helter-skelter" method, until finally, and quite unjustifiably, I demanded to be relieved of my command. Comrade Lenin flared up as never before: "I shall bring you before a party court; we will shoot you. I command you to continue your work and stop disturbing me in mine".'[21]

Krasnov's proposal for an armistice contained the following terms:

'The Bolsheviks will cease all fighting in Petrograd and grant full amnesty to all officers and military cadets who fought against them.

'Until the conclusion of negotiations between the governments, neither side will cross the line agreed on. Should negotiations be broken off, twenty-four hours' notice must be given before the line is crossed.'

Krasnov's Cossack representatives carried this peace offer to the Bolsheviks late in the evening of 13 November.

The next morning the negotiators returned with the sailor representative, Dybenko, a member of the Sovnarcom, who personally accepted the armistice.

'Give us Kerensky, and we'll turn over Lenin to you. Let's trade, ear for car!' he said, laughing.

The Cossacks believed him. They came to Krasnov, demanding that Kerensky be exchanged for Lenin, whom they would immediately string up outside the palace gates.

'Let them bring Lenin here first, then we'll talk to them,' said Krasnov to the Cossacks. But about midday Kerensky sent for him and asked that the Cossack guard at his doors be replaced by a guard of military cadets.

'Your Cossacks will betray me,' Kerensky said bitterly.[22]

Kerensky writes:

Time was fleeting. We waited. Downstairs they bargained. At about 3 p.m. a soldier ran into the room. The trade had been made, he declared. The Cossacks bought their freedom and the right to return home arms in hand, at the price of a single human head! . . . I left the palace only ten minutes before the traitors broke into my rooms. I did not know until the last moment that I would go. Absurdly disguised, I passed under the very noses of the enemies and the betrayers. I was still in the streets of Gatchina when the pursuit began. . . .[23]

In Moscow, meanwhile, the Bolsheviks, led by Bukharin and spurred by a letter from Lenin, voted unanimously for insurrection, and elected a local Military Revolutionary Committee to support the Committee in Petrograd. The centre of opposition to the Bolsheviks in Moscow was found in the City Council. Rudnev, the Socialist Revolutionary mayor, attempted to rally the council in defence of the Provisional Government and on 8 November created an auxiliary 'Committee of Public Safety'.

On 9 November, at 7 p.m., the district commander, Colonel Riabtzev, demanded that the Kremlin, where the Military Revolutionary Committee had installed itself, be evacuated and the committee disbanded. The next morning the Kremlin received news that all Moscow was in Riabtzev's hands, that the garrison had surrendered and was disarmed, that the post office, the telegraph office, and all railway stations were occupied. Crushed by these reports, the Bolshevik commandant of the Kremlin, Berzin, surrendered 'to save the soldiers from being shot'. Berzin and members of the Bolshevik Committee were arrested and the soldiers of the arsenal were shot.

At this point the Vikzhel intervened again, as it had done in Petrograd. It declared that it would permit the transportation of troops which were ready to support the Provisional Government only on condition that the 'Committee of Safety' agreed to the establishment of a homogeneous (*i.e.* a purely Socialist) cabinet. The Committee of Safety yielded to these demands and a temporary armistice was concluded for three days.

On 13 November fighting was resumed by the Bolsheviks, encouraged by the arrival of fresh forces and news of Kerensky's defeat. Two days later a delegation from the Committee of Safety went to the Military Revolutionary Committee to sue for peace.

In the words of an eye-witness, 'Officers, cadets, and students approached the building of the Alexandrovsky school in small squads of ten to twenty men. Amid the general silence of the assembled public, squad leaders reported to the chairman of the commission the names of the squads and the number of men in them. Military cadets, armed with rifles, proceeded into the building, while the officers and students laid down their arms right there on the sidewalk. By twelve only armed soldiers and workers could be seen in the streets.'[24]

The Bolshevik victory in Moscow was complete and final. Both capitals, the new and the old, were now in their hands. The power Lenin had so long sought was now his to be used. To what ends? The Bolsheviks had exploited the war-weariness and land-hunger of peasant sons, calling for immediate transfer of land to the peasants, an immediate 'democratic' peace, immediate convocation of a Constituent Assembly. But these slogans, while highlighting the difficulties of the Provisional Government in the war-torn land, did not constitute a real programme for a party which was soon to be renamed Communist.

According to Sukhanov (whose memoirs Trotsky later described as 'invaluable'), 'The Bolsheviks had no other ideas than the immediate handing over of the land for seizure by the peasants, readiness to propose peace at once, the most confused ideas about "workers' control", and the most fantastic notions of methods of extracting bread with the help of the "sailor" and the "working girl".

Lenin had more "ideas", borrowed whole from the experience of the Paris Commune and Marx's pamphlet on it, and also from Kropotkin. These, of course, included the destruction of the system of credit and the seizure of the banks, the thoroughgoing revision of the whole government apparatus and its replacement by administrators from among the working class (this in peasant, limitless and half-savage Russia!), the liability to election of all officials, compulsory parity between specialists' wages and the average worker's. But all these "ideas" were, first of all, so disproportionately few in comparison with the immensity of the tasks, and, secondly, were so unknown to anyone in the Bolshevik Party, that you might say they were completely irrelevant.'

Sukhanov ascribes the success of Lenin's *coup* largely to the weakness and indecision of the Provisional Government. On the eve of the attack, he says, there 'were in Petrograd loyal elements, if not troops. It might be possible to form a detachment of several thousand from military cadets, the women's services, engineers and Cossacks. A scratch detachment like that might be quite effective. But a firm decision to 'act and attack' had to be made. The General Staff had made no effort to form a scratch detachment.'

On 8 November 1917, the Bolsheviks published a peace decree signed by Lenin and Trotsky and addressed to the belligerent peoples and their governments. It was a well-worded document, calling for a democratic peace without annexations or indemnities, open diplomacy, and the end of secret treaties. The revolutionary spirit behind the decree was indicated by a *Pravda* editorial twelve days later:

The army of the Russian Revolution leans upon inexhaustible reserves. The oppressed nations of Asia (China, India, Persia) await just as passionately the fall of the capitalist régime of violence as do the oppressed proletarian masses of all Europe. To merge these forces into a world revolution against the imperialistic bourgeoisie is the historic task of the workers and the peasants in Russia.

The flame of the October Revolution in Petrograd will inevitably grow into a tempestuous conflagration, which will throw to the ground the authors of this murderous war and will grind into dust the domination of capital.

Lenin's initial formula had been 'Peace Through Social Revolution – peace over the heads of the governments between the peoples that were overthrowing them'. He declared that the aspiration for peace treaties with governments was a 'special kind of opportunism – a bourgeois, pacifist, and clerical position'. Trotsky had said that the idea of a peace without annexations and indemnities was a 'petit bourgeois utopia, because a war completed with revolution must mercilessly destroy all present state borders and create on their ruins a United States of Europe.'

Lenin for his part had previously branded the slogan of a 'United States of Europe' as a 'masked imperialist slogan concealing the plans of the old European capitalist trusts to conquer the rest of the world'.

Once in power, however, the 'petit bourgeois utopian' slogan of peace without annexation and indemnities was adopted as the basis for negotiation. Moreover, Lenin declared that he was ready to consider any other peace terms.

Lenin, Stalin and Krylenko, without awaiting the approval of the Central Committee of the Soviets, issued an order to the soldiers to fraternize with the Germans on the front 'by battalions, by companies, and by platoons'. Many Bolsheviks maintained that this would destroy Russia's capacity for resistance should the German Government turn down their peace offer.

Lenin's ambiguous answer was: 'We appealed for fraternization not by armies but by regiments. We relied in this case on the military experience of Krylenko, who pointed out that such fraternization was absolutely possible.'

Trotsky issued the following order to the Army:

Soldiers! Peace is in your hands. You are not going to allow the counter-revolutionary generals to tear the great cause of peace away from you. You will surround them by a guard in order to avoid the lynchers who are unworthy of the revolutionary army, and in order to prevent those generals from escaping trial. Let the regiments at the front at once elect representatives for an armistice with the enemy. Soldiers! the keys of peace are in your hands. Watchfulness, restraint and energy, and the cause of peace will prevail.

Nevertheless, there was considerable opposition to the Bolshevik programme. Twelve of the fifteen Russian armies did not recognize the new régime, the generals of the Caucasus and of the south-western front allying themselves with the Chief of Staff General Dukhonin. The Petrograd City Council protested that a separate peace would reduce Russia to a German colony; the Municipal Council of Moscow denounced 'a peace imposed by German spies and usurpers'. The General Assembly of the representatives of all state institutions, meeting at Petrograd, called for a general strike against the Bolshevik Government.

But these outbursts did not disturb Lenin. A decree on 1 December ordered new elections to the Petrograd City Council, and two days later the old council was dispersed by sailors and Red Guards. The Socialist Revolutionary mayor and several council-men were arrested.

On the night of 22 November Lenin and Stalin spoke over the direct wire with General Dukhonin, the Chief of Staff, ordering him to cease military operations and open negotiations with the Germans for an armistice. In his account of this episode Stalin says: 'It was a tense moment. Dukhonin and the General Staff categorically refused to obey the orders of the Council of People's Commissars. The army officers were completely in the hands of the General Staff. As for the soldiers, no one could predict what this mass of twelve million men would say, subordinated as it was to the so-called army organizations, which were hostile to the Soviets. In Petrograd itself, as we now know, a mutiny of the military cadets was brewing. . . . I recall that after a pause at the direct wire, Lenin's face suddenly lit up; it became extraordinarily radiant. Clearly he had arrived at a decision.'

Lenin proposed that they go at once to the radio station and broadcast an order dismissing General Dukhonin, and appeal to the soldiers 'to surround the generals, cease military operations, establish contact with the Austrian and German soldiers, and take the cause of peace into their own hands.'

Accompanied by a detachment of sailors and Red Guards, Krylenko departed for Moghiliev to take over command. Dukhonin, who refused to yield his authority, was slain by a mob of soldiers. Krylenko then dispatched emissaries to the German command for preliminary armistice negotiations. On the arrival of these parliamentarians at German Headquarters, Ludendorff telephoned to General Max Hoffmann, German Chief of Staff on the Eastern Front: 'What is your opinion? Should we negotiate with these people?'

General Hoffmann replied: 'Well, doesn't Your Excellency need troops?' Hoffmann referred, of course, to the Western Front.

On 23 November Lenin told the Central Executive Committee of the Soviets: 'A peace cannot be concluded only from above. Peace must be built from the bottom. We don't trust the German generals one iota, but we trust the German people. Without the partipation of the soldiers, a peace concluded by the commander in chief is unstable.'

On 27 November the German Commander in Chief replied to the Soviet Government that he was ready to open negotiations at Brest-Litovsk; and Trotsky proudly declared, 'If the German Emperor is compelled to accept the representatives of Ensign Krylenko and negotiate with them this shows how fast the Russian Revolution has ground under its heel all the ruling classes of Europe.'

The delegation sent by Lenin to Brest-Litovsk had instructions to accept any conditions the Germans laid down. There was little else to do. The Russian Army had virtually ceased to exist after Lenin's peace decree and the order for fraternization. The first peace delegation, headed by Joffe, included a staff of military experts, as well as a worker, sailor, peasant and a woman, who went along for the propaganda effect.

On 30 November Trotsky told a meeting of the Central Executive Committee of the Soviets: 'The German Kaiser spoke to us as his equals.' Two days later he said: 'Sitting at the same table with them [the Germans] we will propose to them categorical questions, without permitting them to avoid answering. Every phase of the negotiations, every word said by them and us, will be transcribed and telegraphed to all the peoples, the judges of our negotiations. Under the pressure of the masses the German and Austrian Governments have consented to sit on the bench of the defendants. You can be sure, comrades, that the prosecutor, in the form of the Russian Revolutionary delegation, will be in his proper place.'

A few days later Trotsky promised: 'If they propose conditions contrary to the fundamentals of our revolution, we will refer these conditions to the Constituent Assembly and say, "Decide". If the Constituent Assembly accepts such conditions, the Bolsheviks will withdraw from the Constituent Assembly and say, "Find some other party to sign such conditions". We will summon all the peoples to our holy war against the imperialism of all nations.'[25]

Chapter 14
Dictatorship

While the street fighting between the Bolsheviks and the adherents of the Provisional Government was still in progress and Kerensky was attempting to retake Petrograd with General Krasnov's troops, the Bolsheviks opened negotiations with the Left Mensheviks and Socialist Revolutionaries for the formation of an all-Socialist cabinet. Kamenev and Rykov headed those Bolsheviks who seriously favoured this coalition, but Lenin urged these negotiations mainly as a cover for military operations against Kerensky's forces.

'Comrade Lenin is of the opinion that the negotiations with the Mensheviks and Socialist Revolutionaries are necessary as a diplomatic move to divert attention from military operations,' the minutes of the Bolshevik Central Committee recorded.[1]

An important part in the fall of the Provisional Government was played by monarchist officers stationed in Petrograd and on the northern front. In remaining aloof during the critical fighting, the monarchists were pursuing their own short-sighted strategy. With Kerensky out of the way, they believed they would quickly dispose of the Bolsheviks as well. Acknowledging the unintended monarchist contribution to the success of the Bolshevik Revolution, Trotsky wrote:

It must be stated that in the beginning of the Bolshevik Revolution the part played by army officers was a noteworthy one. When Lenin and I held special meetings for the officers of the Petrograd garrison where they elected the commanders who were to lead the troops against Kerensky, there were very few of the new commanding officers. They were all former officers of the Tsarist Army and yet the majority of them were with us. It is clear that in most cases they merely wanted to help overthrow Kerensky. Our troops at Pulkovo Hill [near Petrograd] were commanded by Colonel Walden. It was he who surrounded the army of General Krasnov with a large detachment of troops and it was this engagement that decided the fate of Kerensky's march on Petrograd. This Walden was a typical colonel of the Tsarist Army, and just what impelled him to fight on our side I do not know to this day. He was not a young man any longer. It could not be that he sympathized with our aims, for he did not understand anything about them. It was evident, however, that his hatred for Kerensky was so great that for the time being he sympathized with us.[2]

Three days after the Bolshevik *coup d'état*, Plekhanov, from his sick-bed, addressed an 'Open Letter to the Petrograd Workers', urging them to take account of the pitfalls ahead in aligning themselves with Lenin. He wrote:

The reason the events of the last few days pain me so much is not because I do not wish to see the cause of the working class triumph, but, on the contrary, because with all the fibres of my being I wish for the triumph of the workers. The class-conscious elements of our proletariat must ask themselves the question: Is our proletariat ready to proclaim a dictatorship? Everyone who has even a partial understanding as to what economic conditions are necessary for the dictatorship of the proletariat will unhesitatingly answer no to this question.

No, our working class is far from ready to grasp political power with any advantage to itself and the country at large. To foist such a power upon it means to push it towards a great historical calamity which will prove the greatest tragedy for all Russia. . . .

It is said that what the Russian worker will begin the German worker will finish. But it is a great mistake to think so. There is no doubt that in an economic sense Germany is much further developed than Russia. The social revolution is nearer in Germany than it is in Russia. But even among the Germans it is not yet a question of the day. This was well recognized by the various Social Democrats of the Left as well as of the Right wing even before the war, and the war has only diminished the chances of a social revolution in Germany.

That means that the Germans will not finish what the Russians have started, nor can it be done by the French, the British, or the Americans. By seizing power at this moment, the Russian proletariat will not achieve a social revolution. It will only bring on civil war, which will in the end force a retreat from the positions won in February and March of this year.[3]

On 13 November a detachment of Red Guards forced their way into Plekhanov's house in Tsarskoye Selo. Madame Plekhanov explained that her husband was too ill to be disturbed. 'We're searching for weapons. Where's the master of the house?' the leader commanded. Madame Plekhanov took them to her husband's room. That very morning, in reply to her assurances that he would not be molested, Plekhanov had said: 'How little you know these people! They are capable of hiring an assassin to kill me and shedding crocodile tears after my death to arouse the people's emotions.'

While Plekhanov was talking with the Red Guards, a loud knock was heard on the kitchen door and a sailor entered, brandishing a revolver. 'Where is the master? We need the master!' he cried.

The sailor strode over to Plekhanov and putting a pistol to his head shouted: 'Hand over your weapons! If I find them without you, I'll shoot you on the spot.'

Plekhanov replied quietly: 'Killing is easy enough – I have no weapons.'

Plekhanov's calmness pacified the sailor and he prepared to leave when one of his comrades asked Plekhanov what his occupation was.

'I am a writer,' Plekhanov answered.

'What do you write about?'

'About revolution and Socialism.'

'What revolution? . . . Kerensky was also a revolutionary. . . . Are you a Minister of State?' the sailor asked.

'No.'

'Member of the Duma?'

'No.'

'I guess he's not the one,' said the sailor in command.

The following morning a squad of Red Guards again invaded Plekhanov's house. His friends whisked him off in a Red Cross ambulance and transferred him, in the disguise of a wounded soldier, to a French hospital in Petrograd. In the meantime, the news of Plekhanov's treatment had become known; it aroused angry protests. As a gesture of appeasement, Lenin appointed a guard 'to protect the person and property of *citizen* Plekhanov'. He was no longer a 'comrade'.[4]

Many of the old Bolsheviks continued to oppose the *coup d'état* even after its success. Men such as A. A. Bogdanov, Leonid Krassin, Bazarov, Gregory Alexinsky, Professor Rozhkov, Maxim Gorky, and other Bolshevik leaders during the Revolution of 1905 and intimate friends of Lenin, called the Bolshevik seizure of power 'an absurd adventure', the work of people 'in the grip of madness', and Lenin himself 'utterly irresponsible'. They described the Soviet régime as an '*opera bouffe* government, in the throes of an incredible and dangerous delirium'.

On 21 November, two weeks after the Bolshevik rising, Maxim Gorky wrote in his paper *Novaya Zhizn*:

Blind fanatics and unscrupulous adventurers are rushing headlong towards 'social revolution' – as a matter of fact it is the road to anarchy, the ruin of the proletariat and the Revolution.

Along this road Lenin and his aides think it possible to commit all crimes, such as the bloody fight in Petrograd, the devastation of Moscow, the annulment of freedom of speech, the senseless arrests – all the monstrous doing of Von Plehve and Stolypin.

True, Stolypin and Von Plehve acted against the democracy, against all that was sound and honest in Russia, while Lenin has at present the backing of a considerable portion of the workmen, but I trust that the common sense of the working class, the realization of their historical mission will soon open their eyes to the impossibility of fulfilling the promises made by Lenin and the depth of his madness and his anarchistic tendencies, of the Bakunin and Nechayev kind.

The working class cannot fail to realize that Lenin is experimenting with its blood, and trying to strain the revolutionary mood of the proletariat to the limit, to see what the outcome will be.

Of course under the existing circumstances he does not believe in the possibility of a victory for the proletariat of Russia, but perhaps he hopes that a miracle will save the proletariat.

The working-man must know that there really are no miracles, and that he will have to confront hunger, complete disorganization of industry and transportation, prolonged and bloody anarchy followed by reaction no less sanguinary and dark.

That is where the proletariat is being led by its present leader, and one must understand that Lenin is not an all-powerful magician but a deliberate juggler, who has no feeling either for the lives or the honour of the proletariat.

The working class must not allow adventurers and madmen to thrust upon the proletariat the responsibility for the disgraceful, senseless, and bloody crimes for which not Lenin, but the proletariat will have to account.

On 17 November 1917, a number of Bolshevik Commissars, headed by Rykov, resigned in protest against Lenin's refusal to form a coalition government with all the Socialist parties. Simultaneously, Kamenev also resigned as president of the All-Russian Central Executive Committee of the Soviets.

The dissident group issued the following statement:

We hold that it is necessary to form a Socialist government comprising all the Soviet parties. ... We consider that beside this there is only one other path: the maintenance of a purely Bolshevik government by means of political terror. On this path the Council of People's Commissars has entered. We cannot and do not wish to enter it. We see it to lead to the estrangement of the mass proletarian organizations from leadership of political life, to the institution of an irresponsible régime, and to the destruction of the Revolution and the country.

On the same day Austrian Foreign Minister Count Czernin wrote to a friend: 'The German military party – which, as everyone knows, holds the reins of all German policy – has, as far as I can see, done all it could to overthrow Kerensky and set up 'something else" in his place.'⁵

Following Kamenev's resignation, Lenin promptly summoned Sverdlov.

'Jacob Mikhailovich,' he said, 'I want you to become president of the Central Executive of the Soviets. What do you say?'

Sverdlov hesitated, but finally was persuaded to accept.

'Begin at once to create some order,' said Lenin. 'First of all, convene the Bolshevik section of the Central Executive. Then create an organization of non-partisans selected from workers, and, if possible, from the peasants. After that, select the most trustworthy and responsible among our comrades and plant them among the non-partisans. Bring about frequent recesses, and thus give the members of our faction an opportunity to deliberate all the questions with the non-partisans. Above all, they must be able to discover the attitude of every person. We must know what every comrade there thinks. Report to me concerning everything that transpires there. Act immediately, as if you were already president, and we will call a meeting of the Central Committee to whom I will propose that your appointment be confirmed. I believe that the Central Committee will not refuse to confirm you. After that, we will pass it through our faction in the Central Executive of the Soviets and immediately proclaim you president. Count all votes we have in the committee in advance and see to it that all adherents of our faction are present at the meeting.'⁶

Leonid Krassin wrote from Petrograd in a letter to his wife in Sweden:

The Bolsheviks, after smashing Kerensky and occupying Moscow, have failed to reach an agreement with other parties, and they go on issuing new decrees on their own responsibility daily. All work is coming to an end. It means the ruin of production and transport; meanwhile, the armies at the front are dying of hunger. All the leading Bolsheviks, Kamenev, Zinoviev, Rykov, etc., have come around, *excepting* Lenin and Trotsky, who remain as uncompromising as ever and cannot be persuaded to alter their attitude. I am afraid the outlook is black indeed; paralysis of the whole life of Petrograd, anarchy, and probably pogroms.

Two months later he was still of the same mind. He wrote to his wife:

Please do not imagine that I shall join the Bolshevik Party all of a sudden or without thinking it all over very carefully. I told them from the outset that I did not agree with many of their principles, that I considered their tactics to be suicidal, and that I could not even undertake organizing work pure and simple, either for trade, transport, or mobilization as long as the political constitution of the country makes the friendly collaboration of all democratic parties impossible.[7]

Krassin elaborated on this in a conversation with Solomon soon after the latter's return to Petrograd from Stockholm. 'My dear man,' he said, 'this is just a case of staking everything on the immediate introduction of Socialism, that is to say a Utopian ideal pushed to the very limit of folly. All of them here, including Lenin, have lost their minds. Everything that the Social Democrats have been preaching has been forgotten. All our arguments against attempts to make Socialist experiments under present conditions, all our warnings of the dangers which such experiments involve – all these things have been forgotten. The people around here are literally mad. They break up everything, requisition everything, while the confiscated goods are rotting; industry is interfered with, the factories are run by committees composed of ignorant workers who, understanding nothing about their operation, are entrusted with the work of solving all sorts of technical questions.

'Our own plant is also run by a committee of workers. And that is why, you see, they don't allow us to run certain machines. "They are not needed. We can do without them," they say. And Lenin? Why, he is altogether irresponsible. The whole thing is just an incredible and dangerous delirium. We are banking everything not only upon the success of Socialism in Russia, but on the outbreak of a world revolution, regarded from the same Socialist angle, of course. Those who surround him are very diffident to Lenin. They do not say a word against him, and that is how we have actually come back to our old absolutism.'[8]

Vorovsky, later one of the leading Soviet diplomats, was of the same opinion.

Solomon writes:

In the early days following the Revolution Vorovsky told me with heavy sarcasm that I could congratulate him upon being appointed Soviet Ambassador to Sweden. Vorovsky, according to his own statement, did not believe in the permanence of the Bolshevik Government, nor in the ability of the Bolsheviks to do anything sensible, and regarded the whole matter as an absurd adventure, a 'hard nut' on which the Bolsheviks would break their teeth! He mocked his own appointment, and as proof of the lack of seriousness on the whole matter, called my attention to the fact that the Bolsheviks, although they appointed him Ambassador, never thought of supplying him with money to run his office.

'I tell you, it is a farce,' Vorovsky said. 'I hate to be an *opera-bouffe* Ambassador of an *opera-bouffe* government.'

He continued in the service of his firm, at the same time issuing visas to Russia. Shortly thereafter, when we met again, he ironically assured me that the Bolshevik adventure had practically come to a close, as was to be expected, 'for how could Lenin, that nebulous dreamer, do anything constructive? He can destroy all right, that is easy, but to build up, that he cannot do.'

Solomon brought these feelings to an interview with Lenin. 'Tell me, Vladimir Ilyich, as an old comrade of yours, what is going on here? What is this? Is this really a gamble on Socialism on the island of Utopia, only on a more extensive scale? I cannot understand it. . . .'

'There is no island of Utopia,' Lenin replied. 'It is a question of creating a Socialist state. From now on Russia will be the first state in which a Socialist order has been established. I see you are shrugging your shoulders. Well, you have another surprise coming. . . . It isn't a question of Russia at all, gentlemen. I spit on Russia. . . . This is merely one phase through which we must pass on the way to a world revolution.'

Solomon smiled. Lenin squinted his small, narrow eyes and said: 'You are smiling? You mean to say that it is all a fantasy, a dream? I know what you are going to say. I know the whole stock of those stereotyped, threadbare Marxist phrases which in reality are petit-bourgeois futilities which you cannot for a moment discard. By the way,' he suddenly interrupted himself, 'I remember Vorovsky wrote to me about your conversation with him and that you had called it all a dream and all that. Let me tell you, we are past all that. All that has been left behind. All that is nothing but Marxist hairsplitting. We discarded that as one of those inevitable children's diseases which every society and every class must go through and with which they part when they see a new dawn gleaming on the horizon. . . . Don't even attempt to contradict me!' he exclaimed, waving his hands. 'It's no use. You and your Krassin with his theory of natural evolution are not going to convince me. We are turning more and more towards the Left.[9]

'Yes, we will destroy everything and on the ruins we will build our temple! It will be a temple for the happiness of all. But we will destroy the entire bourgeoisie, grind it to a powder.' He laughed. 'Remember this – you and your friend Nikitich [Krassin] – we will stand on ceremony with no one. Remember that the Lenin whom you knew ten years ago no longer exists. He is dead.'

When Solomon protested, Lenin sharply interrupted: 'I will be merciless with all counter-revolutionists, and I shall employ Comrade Uritsky [chief of the Petrograd Secret Police] against all counter-revolutionists, no matter who they are. I do not advise you to make his acquaintance.'

Meanwhile, the job of creating some sort of order out of chaos was proceeding. Requisitions and confiscations were in full swing. But it was necessary to get control of the banks. A decree to that effect was issued. To carry out the seizure, Lenin appointed Menzhinsky Commissar of Finance. 'You are not much of a financier,' Lenin told him, 'but you are a man of action.'

'The appointment was made late in the evening,' writes Bonch Bruyevich. 'Menzhinsky was extremely tired from overwork. In order to put the government's order into immediate execution, he personally, with the aid of one of the comrades, brought a large sofa into the room, placed it by the wall, wrote in big letters on a sheet of paper: "Commissariat of Finance", tacked it over the sofa, and lay down to sleep. He fell asleep at once, and his even snoring spread over the Sovnarcom executive office. . . . Vladimir Ilyich read the inscription, looked down at the sleeping Commissar, and burst into peals of good-natured laughter, saying that it was excellent that the Commissars began by replenishing their energies.'[10]

'Comrade Menzhinsky', relates Petskovsky, an old Bolshevik, 'half-reclined on a sofa, looking tired. The wall over the sofa was graced by a sign: "People's Commissariat of Finance". I sat down near Menzhinsky and began to talk to him. With the most innocent air, Comrade Menzhinsky questioned me about my past and wanted to know what I had studied. I replied, among other things that I had studied at the University of London, where I took up several subjects, among them finance. Menzhinsky suddenly sat up, pierced me with his eyes, and declared categorically: "In that case we shall appoint you director of the State Bank." ' . . . In a short time he returned with a paper which certified, over the signature of Ilyich, that I was director of the State Bank.'

He begged Menzhinsky to cancel the appointment. But the latter explained: 'We need money desperately – at least a few millions. The State Bank and the State Treasury are on strike. We cannot get any money by legal means. The only way is to change the head of the bank and take money.'

Two days later Menzhinsky released him. Petskovsky's career as director of the Russian State Bank was ended. He then decided that the only agency with an opening for him would be the Commissariat of Nationalities. He went to Stalin.

'Comrade Stalin,' he said, 'are you the People's Commissar of Nationalities?'

'Yes.'

'And you have a commissariat?'

'No.'

'I will set up your commissariat.'

'All right. What do you need for it?'

'So far only a mandate.'

Stalin went to the office of the Sovnarcom and returned a few minutes later with a mandate. Petskovsky then wandered through the Smolny Institute looking for office space for the Commissariat of Nationalities. Finally he found a large room where all sorts of committees were in session. Locating an empty table, he placed it near the wall, took a large sheet of paper, wrote 'People's Commissariat of Nationalities' and tacked it on the wall.

'The commissariat is ready,' Petskovsky announced, and returned to Lenin's office.

'Comrade Stalin,' he said, 'come and look at your commissariat.'

Stalin followed Petskovsky through the hall until they came to the 'commissariat'. He muttered something which expressed neither approval nor disapproval, then returned to Lenin's office. Petskovsky ordered blanks and an official rubber stamp, which took all his available cash.

'Comrade Stalin,' he said, 'I haven't a red cent.'

'How much do you need?' asked Stalin.

'Well, for the beginning, three thousand rubles will be enough.'

'Come back in an hour.'

When he returned, Stalin told him to 'borrow' three thousand rubles from Trotsky. 'He has money,' Stalin said. 'He found it in the former Ministry of Foreign Affairs.'

Petskovsky went to Trotsky, gave him a receipt for three thousand rubles, and received the money. Whether the Commissariat of Nationalities ever repaid the Foreign Commissariat is not known.[11]

Incredibly enough, most of the early business of the new Soviet régime was transacted in this manner. While the Council of People's Commissars was enacting decrees which changed Russia's economic and social structure and gave a new course to world history, the main actors were wandering through the corridors of Smolny looking for space, desks, chairs, stationery.

The régime still had no money in its treasury. Summoning the new director of the State Bank, Piatakov, Lenin ordered him to pay out ten million rubles to the secretary of the Soviets. 'Don't return without the money', said Lenin.

N. P. Gorbunov writes:

The State Bank openly sabotaged the government's decrees and demands for funds. All measures undertaken by the People's Commissar of Finance, Comrade Menzhinsky, including the arrest of the bank director Shipov, failed to force the bank to issue the funds needed by the government. Shipov was brought to Smolny and kept there under arrest for some time. He slept in a room with Menzhinsky and myself. During the day the room was used as an office of some bureau (perhaps the People's

Commissariat of Finance). I was obliged, to my chagrin, to yield my cot to him as a special courtesy and sleep on chairs.

Piatakov at first could accomplish nothing. Gorbunov tells how Lenin entrusted him with a decree which ordered the State Bank to waive all rules and formalities and issue to the secretary of the Sovnarcom ten million rubles for government use.

'The money was obtained. Backed by the lower employees and couriers, threatening to bring in the Red Guard, Gorbunov and Osinsky, the State Commissar to the bank . . . forced the cashier to issue the sum required. The reception took place under the cocked guns of the military guards of the bank. There was some difficulty concerning bags for the money. We had brought nothing with us. One of the couriers finally lent us a couple of large old bags. We filled them with money, lifted them on our backs, and dragged them to the car. Driving to Smolny, we grinned happily. In Smolny, we slung them over our backs again and lugged them to the office of Vladimir Ilyich. . . . With special solemnity I submitted them to [him], who accepted them as if it were a matter of course. In reality, however, he was extremely pleased. A clothes closet in the next room was used as the receptacle for the first Soviet treasury; it was protected by a semicircle of chairs and a sentry. A special decree was issued by the Sovnarcom concerning the manner of safe-guarding and use of this money. Such was the beginning of our first Soviet budget.'[12]

A description of the subsequent nationalization of banks is furnished by Bonch-Bruyevich, who prepared the whole undertaking, wrote the orders, organized the transportation, the twenty-eight detachments of sharpshooters, etc. It was necessary to occupy twenty-eight banks, arrest twenty-eight bank directors.

'I requested the commandant of Smolny, Comrade Malkov, to set aside a comfortable room,' writes Bonch-Bruyevich, 'completely private from the public and prepare twenty-eight cots, tables, and chairs. He was also to be ready to feed twenty-eight persons, and to begin with, serve them tea and breakfast by 8 a.m.' The occupation of the twenty-eight banks proceeded without difficulty. It took place on 27 December 1917. 'In the shortest time, the Commissar of Finance appointed new workers to the banks. Many of the directors who had been arrested expressed a desire to continue their work under the Soviet Government, and were immediately released. Commissars were appointed to each bank, and the work continued in so far as it was necessary for the concentration of all funds and operations in the State Bank.'[13]

Lenin's counsel, on the eve of the *coup d'état*, had been: 'Let us seize power, try to nationalize the banks, and then see what to do next. We shall learn from experience.'

He had written to the Central Committee:

We are unanimous in our belief that our first step in the direction of Socialism should be the adoption of such policies as the nationalization of banks and investment trusts. Let us first carry out these policies and then we shall *see* [underscored by Lenin]. After we have nationalized the banks and established control by the workers, we shall be in a better position to judge things, and experience will suggest what new methods to use.

It was on this theory that he now proceeded. The first day after their victory the Bolsheviks published two decrees. One of them disposed of the big landed estates, which were handed over to local agrarian committees, 'pending the decision of the Constituent Assembly'. Another decree ordered the nationalization of banking institutions.

Private property, however, was not abolished. Small land holdings were left untouched and the withdrawal of sums from current bank accounts up to fifteen hundred rubles monthly permitted.

Lenin was still hesitant about the immediate nationalization of the factories. 'Socialism cannot be introduced before the working class learns to lead and assert its authority,' he said, explaining why his measures appeared to be 'incomplete and contradictory'. On 24 January 1918, he declared in a speech at Petrograd:

'Very often delegations of workers and peasants come to the Soviet Government and ask what to do with such and such a piece of land, for example. And frequently I myself have felt embarrassment when I saw that they had no very definite views. And I said to them: you are the government, do as you please, take all you want, we will support you, but take care of production, see that production is useful. Take up useful work; you will make mistakes, but you will learn. And the workers have already begun to learn; they have already begun to fight against the saboteurs. People have transformed education into a fence which hinders the advance of the toilers; this fence will be pulled down.'[14]

Conceiving his dictatorship as merely the advance guard of the world proletarian revolution, Lenin regarded the retention of power as the most urgent problem.

Human nature being what it is, he wrote in *State and Revolution*, it craves submission. Until Socialism was established the proletariat needed the state not to establish freedom, but solely to 'crush the antagonists'.

'We are not Utopians,' Lenin proclaimed. 'We want the Socialist Revolution with human nature as it is now. Human nature itself cannot do without subordination. . . . There must be submission to the "armed vanguard" . . . until the people will grow accustomed to observing the elementary conditions of social existence without force and with subjection.'

In the meantime, the course was quite clear. 'As the state is only a transitional institution which we are obliged to use in the revolutionary struggle in order to crush our opponents forcibly, it is a pure absurdity to speak of a Free People's State. During the period when the proletariat still needs the state, it does not require it in the interests of freedom, but in the interests of crushing its antagonists.' To crush the antagonists was the principal aim of the 'proletarian dictatorship', 'an aim to be attained at any cost'.

On 10 November 1917, the Soviet Government published a decree curtailing freedom of the press, accompanied by the assurance that the repressive measures were only temporary and would become inoperative 'as soon as the new régime takes firm root'.

The Liberal press was promptly silenced with this explanation on 16 November by the Soviet Central Executive Committee:

The suppression of the bourgeois papers was caused not only by purely fighting requirements in the period of counter-revolutionary attempts, but likewise as a necessary temporary measure for the establishment of a new régime in the sphere of the press, under which the capitalist proprietors of printing plants and newsprint would not be able to become autocratic beguilers of public opinion. . . . The re-establishment of the so-called freedom of the Press; *viz.* the simple return of printing offices and paper to capitalists, poisoners of the people's conscience, would be an unpardonable surrender to the will of capital, that is to say, a counter-revolutionary measure.

But it was just as important for Lenin to gag Socialist opinion.

From the first days of Soviet power he insisted on shutting down the Socialist Revolutionary and Menshevik papers. According to Trotsky, at every opportunity Lenin would say: 'Can't we bridle those scoundrels? Tell me, what kind of a dictatorship do you call this?'[15]

Step by step the opposition papers were suspended and shut down. Within a few days after the fall of the Winter Palace Lenin silenced, among the other newspapers, Leonid Andreyev's *Russkaya Volia*, Catherine Breshkovsky's *Volia Naroda*, Plekhanov's *Yedinstvo*, the Left Menshevik organ *Rabochaya Gazeta*, the Socialist Revolutionary *Dyelo Naroda*, the *Narodnoye Slove*, organ of the People's Socialists, and *Dyen*, edited by Lenin's early collaborator, Alexander Potresov.

The printing press of Andreyev's paper was confiscated and *Russkaya Volia* never again appeared. The offices of the *Dyelo Naroda* were guarded by soldiers favouring the Socialist Revolutionaries and the Party managed for a time to issue illegal newspapers at irregular intervals under one name or another. The copies were confiscated as fast as they appeared on news-stands, and the vendors who sold them were subject to severe penalties, in some cases to execution.

Potresov's *Dyen* did not appear for some time. Later in its place came *Polnotch* (Midnight), which was immediately banned for publishing an exposé of Bolshevik Commissar Lieutenant Schneuer, a former Tsarist and German spy who conducted negotiations for an armistice with the German Command.

A few days later *Polnotch* was followed by *Notch* (Night). Then came *V glookhooyou Notch* (In the Thick of the Night), and still later *V tiomnooyou Notch* (In the Dark of the Night). Potresov's brave guerrilla warfare against Lenin's censorship lasted for several months. Plekhanov's *Yedinstvo* reappeared late in December 1917 as *Nashe Yedinstvo*, but it was closed down in January 1918. Thus Lenin settled for all time his *Iskra* arguments of 1903 with Potresov and Plekhanov.

The editor in chief of Catherine Breshkovsky's *Volia Naroda*, Andrey Argunov, one of the founders of the Socialist Revolutionary Party, was imprisoned in the Fortress of St Peter and St Paul and the paper never appeared again. The Socialist Revolutionary *Dyelo Naroda*, the Menshevik *Novy Looch*, and a few others tried returning to life, but on the eve of the Brest-Litovsk Treaty all remaining Socialist newspapers were closed.

At a session of the All-Russian Central Executive Committee of the Soviets on 17 November 1917, Lenin defended the suppression of these publications. 'To tolerate those papers,' he declared, 'is to cease to be a Socialist. . . . The state is an institution built up for the sake of exercising violence. Previously this violence was exercised by a handful of moneybags over the entire people; now we want . . . to organize violence in the interests of the people. . . .

'In answer to the charge made here that we are combating "Socialists" we can only say that in the epoch of parliamentarism the latter have nothing in common with Socialism, that they have rotted away, have become outdated, and have finally gone over to the bourgeoisie. "Socialists who, during the war, provoked by imperialist motives of international robbers, were shouting about defending the fatherland", are not Socialists, but tuft-hunters and bootlickers of the bourgeoisie.'[16]

On 1 December 1917 Lenin outlawed the Cadet Party; on 14 December he assured the All-Russian Central Executive Committee that 'no one, save the Utopian Socialists, ever denied that it would be impossible to triumph without meeting resistance, without a proletarian dictatorship, without putting an iron hand upon the old world', and that 'this iron hand creates while destroying'. And three months later, at the Fourth Congress of the Soviets, to the outcries of the Socialists, *'Our papers have been closed'*, Lenin replied: 'Of course, unfortunately not all of them! Soon all of them will be closed. . . . The dictatorship of the proletariat will wipe out the shameful purveying of the bourgeois opium.'[17]

After the Brest-Litovsk Treaty, when the German Army occupied large Russian territories and Lenin had reason to fear the worst, the censorship was relaxed somewhat, and a few newspapers were allowed to reappear, with the proviso that they were to print on their front page all Soviet decrees and statements by Bolshevik Commissars. In addition, the press was subjected to huge fines for every bit of news that did not please the eye of the censor. Thus Gorky's *Novaya Zhizn* was fined 35,000 rubles for an 'unfavourable' news item.

But even this slight concession did not last long. Early in May 1918 the régime clamped down the lid, closing *Dyelo Naroda*, *Dyen* and *Novy Looch*, and, somewhat later, all the remaining opposition papers, including Gorky's newspaper. Nor was Gorky permitted to resume publication when he made his peace with Lenin.

Since that time there have been no independent newspapers in Russia. The limited rights which the Liberals and Socialists had enjoyed under autocratic Tsarism were denied to all by Lenin. Not only was Russia's press destroyed, but the great organs of Russian culture and ideas, such as the monthly magazines *Vestnik Evropi* and *Russkoye Bogatsvo*, and the daily *Russkiya Viedomosti*, were liquidated. These publications had raised generations of Russian rebels. Their contributors and editors had included the greatest writers and savants of modern Russia: Tolstoy, Dostoyevsky, Turgenev, Ilya Metchnikov, Peter Kropotkin, Nicholas Mikhailovsky, Vladimir Korolenko, Glieb Uspensky, Maxim Kovalevsky and numerous others.

The freedom of speech and press for which generations of Russian revolutionaries had fought since the days of the Decembrists was completely destroyed within a matter of months.

Chapter 15
Lenin Silences the Constituent Assembly

The immediate calling of the Constituent Assembly had been one of Lenin's main slogans from April to November 1917. One of the most serious charges made against the Provisional Government by Lenin, Trotsky, Stalin and the entire Bolshevik Press was that it did not intend to hold elections for this legislative body. Time and again Lenin had promised that when the Bolsheviks took power the Assembly would be speedily convened.

On 5 November 1917, two days before the Bolshevik *coup*, Stalin wrote in *Pravda*:

Having overthrown the Tsar, the people thought that within two or three months the Constituent Assembly would be summoned. But the convocation of the Constituent Assembly has already been postponed once and its foes are preparing for its final destruction. Why? Because in power sit enemies of the people, for whom the timely convocation of the Constituent Assembly is not profitable.

The Bolshevik pledge was plain enough. But the Bolshevik leaders were well aware that the elections, scheduled by the Provisional Government for 25 November, would not give them control of the Constituent Assembly. On the other hand, after having taken power they could not flatly repudiate their promise.

'On the very first day, if not the first hour of the Revolution,' relates Trotsky, 'Lenin brought up the question of the Constituent Assembly. "We must postpone the elections. We must extend the right of suffrage to those who have reached their maturity (eighteen years). We must outlaw the adherents of Kornilov and the Cadets", said Lenin.

'We tried to argue with him that it would not look right. We ourselves had accused the Provisional Government of delaying the elections to the Constituent Assembly.

' "Nonsense," Lenin replied. "It is facts that are important, not words." '[1]

Despite considerable Bolshevik coercion, the election results were even worse than Lenin had expected. In the overwhelming majority of electoral districts, the elections were held on 25 November 1917 – more than a fortnight after the Bolshevik seizure of power. In other districts, the voting took place on 1 and 7 December.

Nevertheless, in a total vote of 41,686,000, the Bolsheviks received only 9,844,000 – less than 25 per cent of the electorate. The Socialist Revolutionaries received 17,490,000; Ukrainian Socialist parties (mostly allied with the Socialist Revolutionaries) 4,957,000; Mensheviks 1,248,000; Constitutional Democrats 1,986,000; candidates of Moslem parties and other national minorities some 3,300,000. Of 707 deputies, the Socialist Revolutionaries elected 370, a clear majority; the Bolsheviks only 175; the pro-Lenin Left Socialist Revolutionaries 40; Cadets 17, Mensheviks 16, national minority groups and others 99. The Russian people, in the freest election in their history, voted for moderate democratic socialism against Lenin and against the bourgeoisie.

From the standpoint of Soviet public relations, no more disastrous result was possible. A 'reactionary' victory would have been easier to handle. But Lenin was prepared, even for this.

On 10 December 1917, the Bolsheviks arrested Pavel Dolgorukov, Fyodor Kokoshkin and Andrey Shingarev, Cadet deputies to the Constituent Assembly. Three days later, they issued a decree proclaiming Cadet leaders 'enemies of the people', subject to arrest and trial by revolutionary tribunals. The decree nevertheless concluded with the statement that 'the country can be saved only by a Constituent Assembly made up of representatives of the labouring and exploited classes of the people'.

In spite of this assurance, a few days later the Bolsheviks arrested a number of prominent Socialist Revolutionaries who had been elected to the Constituent Assembly. These included Nicolai Avksentyev, chairman of the All-Russian Soviet of Peasant Deputies, Andrey Argunov, Alexander Gukovsky, Pitirim Sorokin and others. Many other Socialist leaders escaped arrest only by going into hiding.

Lenin's initial proposal, once the election had proven unfavourable to his régime, was to dissolve the Assembly before it had even convened. But he was compelled to abandon this plan under pressure from the Left Socialist Revolutionaries, whose support the Bolsheviks still needed, and who had joined Lenin's Soviet of People's Commissars only on condition that the Constituent Assembly be convened. Lenin yielded, but demanded that special units of Lett sharpshooters be brought to Petrograd before the Assembly met.

During the month of December, leaders of the Socialist Revolutionary and Menshevik parties devoted themselves to preparations for the opening of the Assembly. They drew up many projects of new laws and formulated policies upon the land question, popular education and foreign affairs, as well as programmes for the daily debates. There were committees for all these subjects and many more. There were numerous meetings at which serious discussion took place, in which experts, specially invited, took part and read prepared reports. The meetings went on in an atmosphere of unreality. Several illusions contributed to this; e.g. that there was no Bolshevik Government; that there was no chance of the dissolution of the Assembly; and that parliamentary life would flow on without friction immediately after the opening ceremony.

The arrangements for this opening had been well thought out. Who should address the Assembly, and on what topics they should speak, who should guide the respective factions – these and kindred problems had already been debated. 'Everything was provided for except – the bands of drunken sailors who filled the galleries of the Tauride Palace and the non-parliamentary cynicism of the Bolsheviks', comments Boris Sokolov, a Socialist Revolutionary delegate. These were not on the agenda, but were quite observable in the proceedings.

After repeated postponements, the date for the opening of the Constituent Assembly was fixed for 18 January 1918. Only small groups in the other parties – principally the Socialist Revolutionaries – properly grasped that the characteristic thing for the Bolsheviks to do was to disperse an Assembly in which they found themselves in a minority. Indeed, some of the Socialist Revolutionaries decided that the assembly stood urgently in need of an armed force to defend it against such an attack, and defence measures were secretly organized, though few members were willing to admit the necessity of these precautions.

Meanwhile, the Bolsheviks were conducting a skilful campaign to to foster a feeling against the Socialist Revolutionaries in the minds of the working people. The astuteness and thoroughness exhibited by the Bolsheviks in their preparation for the November *coup d'état* were exhibited now in their plans for the dissolution of the Constituent Assembly. They left nothing to chance. As they had previously prepared the Army, so now, by assiduous cultivation of a number of regiments of the Petrograd garrison, they secured military support for a fresh attack upon public institutions. To gain the friendly assistance of the workmen was important enough, but the support of a few regiments was absolutely indispensable to overawe thoroughly the Socialist Revolutionaries – even the Red Guard and the Kronstadt sailors might not stand an attack. It was necessary to assure victory by winning over some guard regiments, disorganized and demoralized as they were. The Bolsheviks started with the great advantage of position. Theirs was the only party organization among the soldiers which had survived the November *coup*.

The Petrograd garrison was rendered more formidable owing to the absence of any organized military force on the side of the opponents of the Bolsheviks. Yet a large number of soldiers and sailors were neutral, and few of them wanted to fight. The number upon which the Bolsheviks could actually rely on 18 January, after they had been in power for two months, was, according to Kuzmin, one of the chief Bolshevik commanders in Petrograd that day, not more than 3,000 to 4,000 men – that is, one regiment. They had, in addition, the Red Guard, numbering about 5,000, but Kuzmin did not regard this force as very formidable.[2]

The mood of the workers in the Petrograd region was 'more or less the same' as that of the garrison. The labouring masses, however, had been subjected to a greater amount of propaganda by the Bolsheviks. Though friendly to the Constituent Assembly, the workers' attitude rather inclined to an indifferent scepticism. The large majority of the Petrograd working-men were neutral, not more than 15 per cent having voted for Bolshevik candidates in factory elections.

Sokolov encountered this passive mood. 'The people affected by it seemed ... equally unwilling to rescue the Provisional Government or to join the Bolsheviks.' The numbers of the Bolsheviks were small, but the Party was so compact and so well organized that it could easily withstand the Socialist Revolutionaries and

Mensheviks, whose energies were insufficiently combined and concentrated.

In the early days of January 1918 about 4,000 workers in the government currency plant were addressed by representatives of the various parties. The general feeling was anti-Bolshevik, and the audience would not listen to the Bolshevik speakers. Cries of 'Long Live the Constituent Assembly' punctuated the meeting, which attacked the Bolsheviks' love for power.

At the same time, most of the workers in the Franco-Russian factory gathered to hear the well-known Bolshevik, Smirnov.

'Comrades,' he said, 'we are facing a crisis, facing the possibility of dissolving the Constituent Assembly, because it is obvious already that it is full of bourgeois superstition and that it has a counter-revolutionary tendency.'

Smirnov was answered by a workman named Shmakov: 'No, comrade Bolsheviks . . . You are ruining the prerogatives of all who elected this Constituent Assembly. You must remember that this forcible dissolution will never be forgotten or forgiven by the Russian people or the Russian proletariat.'

The majority of the workers present seemed to support Shmakov, says Sokolov, although they looked upon themselves as Bolsheviks and opponents of the Provisional Government.

The Izmailovsky regiment hesitated for a long time before deciding its course of action. The Bolsheviks conducted a vigorous campaign among the soldiers. A large meeting was held in January in the theatre of the regiment. Krylenko and Piatakov spoke for the Bolsheviks, Fortunatov and Sokolov for the Socialist Revolutionaries. Krylenko and Piatakov delivered the customary onslaught upon the 'imperialistic war', and attacked the Entente, Clemenceau, the 'bourgeois' Provisional Government, etc. Then they spoke of the Constituent Assembly. Immediately the soldiers shouted, 'Don't dare to touch it! Let there be Soviets and a Constituent Assembly! Do you think we elected our deputies for nothing?'

On 16 January Krylenko went to the Semionovsky regiment in order to prepare the ground for the dissolution of the Constituent Assembly by 'clearing away' as he said, 'the heavy atmosphere of counter-revolution which filled the barracks'. He was not favourably received, and was advised to be very careful in what he said, otherwise the soldiers might not listen to him. Shouts were raised by the audience. 'It would not be a bad thing to beat up that fellow. He is getting too conceited.'

Krylenko began, 'Comrades, I have come to talk to you in the name of the Workers' and Peasants' Government ["*What is that government?*" *the soldiers shouted;* "*we do not recognize it.*"] which is very much troubled by the feeling in your regiment. We are advised that the hydra of counter-revolution has a nest here. ["*You are a hydra yourself!*" "*You are a bourgeois yourself! Down with him!*"] I come to you to speak about the so-called Constituent Assembly. Because its bourgeois and counter-revolutionary part has decided to overthrow the Soviet Government. ["*Long live the Constituent Assembly!*" "*Down with the Bolsheviks.*"] I warn you – remember – in the name of the Soviet Government, I declare that if you dare to disobey, you will be punished very severely and without mercy. ["*Your hands are too short.*" "*We are not Dukhonins for you.*" "*The Semionovsky guards you cannot handle so easily.*" "*Enough!*"]'

Krylenko's final words were lost in the clamour that arose from every part of the room. Angrily he went to the regimental committee and threatened: 'If the Semionovsky regiment dare to come out against us you will be responsible. It is very dangerous to jest with me.'

After Krylenko had left, a soldier spoke, amid cheers, of the necessity to defend the Constituent Assembly.

The Socialist Revolutionary Military Committee became aware that the Bolsheviks intended to utilize the sailors of the First and Second Baltic squadrons in the demonstration against the Constituent Assembly. The Socialist Revolutionaries had a small organization among the sailors of the Second Squadron, the chairman of the squadron committee, an intelligent sailor called Safranov, being on the side of the Socialist Revolutionaries. A meeting was held on 16 January, and, after speeches by Safranov and others, an enthusiastic sailor leaped on to the platform and shouted: 'Brothers, comrades, let us swear that we will not go against the People's Assembly.'

'We swear!'

'On your knees, comrades, on your knees!'

And all these thousands of sailors knelt and shouted: 'We swear not to go against the Constituent Assembly.'

This hysterical enthusiasm notwithstanding, nothing further happened. The sailors swore not to go against it – as for defending it, that was another question.[3]

The Assembly was scheduled to open on the morning of 18 January 1918. In anticipation of the long-awaited event, Lenin ordered a detachment of Lettish sharpshooters to Petrograd.

'We cannot depend on the Russian peasant. [That is to say, the Russian soldier.] He is likely to join the other side,' he said. 'We need people with proletarian resoluteness.'[4] Lenin knew that the Lettish troops had no particular sentimental ties with the Russian people and would carry out their orders with the loyalty of a pretorian guard. In the meantime the League for the Defence of the Constituent Assembly – organized by the Socialist Revolutionaries and Mensheviks – decided to greet the opening of the Constituent Assembly by a peaceful procession to the Tauride Palace. This was at once labelled as an attempt at counter-revolution. *Pravda* warned that the bourgeoisie was massing to combat the people, and ordered the inhabitants of Petrograd to remain indoors on the day of the Assembly's opening, as 'no quarter will be given anybody'.

In addition to the Letts, marines were summoned from Kronstadt, and cruisers, supplemented by several submarines, the *Aurora*, and the battleship *Republic*, were brought up along the Neva. Sailors and Red Guards, stationed at the entrance to the Tauride Palace, were instructed to use force to stop unauthorized attempts to enter the building. All passes for the visitors' gallery were issued by Uritsky, chief of the Petrograd political police.[5]

At about eleven o'clock on the morning of 18 January from all sections of the city came large crowds of unarmed workers and students, waving red banners and placards with the inscriptions: 'Proletarians of All Countries Unite!' 'Land and Freedom!' 'Long Live the Constituent Assembly!' They marched to Mars Field, where they were joined by members of the Executive Committee of the Peasants' Soviet.

At Mars Field the marchers stopped before the 'fraternal graves' of those who had fallen in the March Revolution, dipped their banners in tribute, then proceeded to Liteiny Bridge. *En route*, they were joined by new crowds. As the procession was turning into a street leading to the Tauride Palace, it was suddenly met by fire from Bolshevik rifles and machine-guns. The shots came without warning. Another column of unarmed civilians proceeding towards the Tauride Palace from a different direction was also brought to a halt by bullets. All the streets leading to the Constituent Assembly were barred by picked Bolshevik units whose orders were: 'Spare no shells!' One hundred men and women were killed and wounded in Petrograd that day. Comments Bonch-Bruyevich: 'The Mensheviks and Socialist Revolutionaries who came to Smolny on various pretexts asked me, "What will you do if there is a demonstration against the government?"

' "First we will try persuasion. After that we will shoot," I answered briefly.' The shooting began without preliminary 'persuasion'.[6]

A military council had been set up to deal with the population of Petrograd. 'A number of military experts in whom we had absolute confidence were also invited,' says Bonch-Bruyevich. 'These people were organized into an extraordinary military staff and the city was divided into districts. To maintain order in and around the Tauride Palace, I called out the sailors attached to the cruiser *Aurora*. They were supplemented by two companies of sailors from other battleships under the command of the sailor Zhelezniakov, an anarcho-Communist who was a staunch supporter of the dictatorship of the proletariat.

'Provisioning them for several days, and providing each with excellent food rations, I divided the sailors and distributed them in different sections of the city.

'Later I arrived in the Tauride Palace, looked up Uritsky, and advised him to feed the detachment of two hundred dependable sailors and to lead them into the Constituent Assembly in full martial array.'

The Tauride Palace presented a strange spectacle. The halls and assembly room were jammed with heavily armed soldiers and sailors. At each door marines and Red Guards armed with rifles and hand grenades gruffly demanded admission cards. The public galleries were occupied mainly by Uritsky's Bolshevik *claque*.

Instead of opening in the morning, the Assembly did not begin its session until four in the afternoon. The Bolsheviks and Left

Socialist Revolutionaries occupied the extreme left of the house; next to them sat the crowded Socialist Revolutionary majority, then the Mensheviks. The benches on the right were empty. A number of Cadet deputies had already been arrested; the rest stayed away. The entire Assembly was Socialist – but the Bolsheviks were only a minority.

Lenin, accompanied by his wife, sister, and Bonch-Bruyevich, entered through a side door when the Assembly was already filled. They checked their coats in the anteroom and went into a small chamber where they sat, talked, and ate a buffet dinner.

'Since we have really been guilty of such foolhardiness as to promise to call this assembly, we must open it today,' said Lenin with a wry grin, 'but as to the time of its closing, history is still silent.'

Sverdlov entered the chamber and conferred with Lenin on the order of business. Then Uritsky came in, quite excited.

'What's the matter with you?' Lenin asked.

'My fur coat was stolen off my back by bandits,' Uritsky replied. 'I was on my way to Smolny to confer with you, when two bandits attacked me and ordered: "Comrade, take off your coat! You've warmed yourself enough. We are cold! Quick, quick, take it off. You've warmed yourself enough. We are cold!" I was forced to give them my coat.'

A few minutes later Lenin said:

'Well, it is time to begin,' and arising, proceeded through the long corridor to the great hall. When he entered, the session had begun – and it was not proceeding according to Lenin's plans.

'Do you know where our seats are?' whispered Lenin angrily, gripping Bonch-Bruyevich's shoulder.

'Of course I know.'

'Let's go!' He was quite pale, according to Bonch-Bruyevich, his eyes seeming to radiate sparks of fire. He seated himself nervously, folded his hands, and gazed about the entire chamber, slowly turning his head from side to side. The sailors kept their eyes on Lenin, trying to catch his glance, awaiting his orders. On both sides of the platform, in the aisles and corridors, stood armed soldiers and sailors. The galleries were packed with Uritsky's guests and newspaper correspondents. Loaded rifles waited for their chance to speak.[7]

In accordance with custom, the parliament was opened by the oldest deputy. From the Socialist Revolutionary benches rose aged Deputy Shvetzov, a veteran of the People's Will. As he mounted the platform, Bolshevik deputies began slamming their desks while soldiers and sailors pounded the floor with their rifles. Some of the Left Socialist Revolutionaries joined in the clamour. From the gallery one soldier aimed his rifle at Shvetzov. The veteran revolutionist remained calm, vainly ringing the bell to quiet the din. When he placed the bell on the table, it was seized by a man who presented it to Sverdlov as a trophy.

Shvetzov finally found a lull in the noise to say: 'The meeting of the Constituent Assembly is opened.' An outburst of catcalls greeted his words.

Sverdlov then mounted the platform, pushed the old man aside, and declared in his loud, rich voice that the Central Executive Committee of the Soviet of Workers', Soldiers' and Peasants' Deputies had empowered him to open the meeting of the Constituent Assembly. Then on behalf of the committee he read the 'Declaration of Rights of the Labouring and Exploited Masses', written by Lenin, Stalin and Bukharin. The declaration demanded that all state power be vested in the Soviets, thereby destroying the very meaning of the Constituent Assembly. It had been adopted by the Bolshevik-controlled Soviet Central Executive Committee, which had also passed a resolution that 'all attempts on the part of any person or institution to assume any of the functions of government will be regarded as a counter-revolutionary act. Every such attempt will be suppressed by all means at the command of the Soviet Government, including the use of armed force.'

Sverdlov asked the Assembly to decide immediately whether it would accept the programme of the Sovnarcom. Instead, despite the continued tumult, the majority succeeded in moving for the election of a chairman. The Bolsheviks, instead of nominating their own candidate, endorsed Maria Spiridonova, candidate of the Left Socialist Revolutionaries, in the faint expectation of drawing votes from the other parties. Victor Chernov, leader of the Socialist Revolutionary Party, won by a vote of 244 against 151.

In his opening address, Chernov expressed hope that the convocation of the Constituent Assembly meant the end of Russia's nebulous transitional period. The land question was already resolved, he said; the soil would become the common property of all peasants who were willing and able to till it. The Constituent Assembly would pursue an active foreign policy, striving for a democratic general peace without victors or vanquished but would not sign a separate peace with Imperial Germany.

The Constituent Assembly, as the freely elected parliament of the Russian people, was entitled to full legislative power, said Chernov, but it was willing to submit all fundamental decisions to popular referendum. If the Soviets joined hands with the Assembly and respected the will of the people, there would be peace and freedom in Russia; if not, civil war was inevitable.

Under the fire of constant interruptions, Chernov succeeded in finishing his speech. He was followed by Bolshevik orators Bukharin and Skvortsov. Bukharin proposed that the Soviet declaration be passed at the head of the agenda—in order to decide whether the Constituent Assembly sided with the 'factory owners, merchants, and bank directors, or with the grey coats, the workers, soldiers, and sailors.' The reference to factory owners, merchants and bank directors brought ironic laughter from the Socialist majority.

Skvortsov, turning to the Socialist Revolutionaries, said: 'Everything is finished between us. We are carrying the October Revolution against the bourgeoisie to the end. We are on opposite sides of the barricades.'

The Bolshevik speakers were heard in silence by the Socialist deputies. Nor were they interrupted when they used abusive language.

When Tseretelli rose to reply, rifles were pointed at his head and sailors brandished pistols in front of his face. The chairman's appeals for order brought more hooting, catcalls, obscene oaths, and fierce howls. Tseretelli finally managed, nevertheless, to capture general attention with his eloquent plea for civil liberty and his warning of civil war. He was followed by a Socialist Revolutionary deputy who spoke on the peace programme of the Constituent Assembly.

Lenin did not speak. He sat on the stairs leading to the platform, smiled derisively, jested, wrote something on a slip of paper, then stretched himself out on a bench and pretended to fall asleep. Lunacharsky, from his ministerial bench, amused himself by poking his finger into the grey hair of a Socialist Revolutionary veteran. The sailors continued to point their rifles at the Socialist Revolutionaries. The galleries were in an uproar, shouting, whistling, stamping their feet.

Finally Lenin rose and left the hall. In the anteroom he felt the inside pocket of his fur coat, where he kept his revolver. It was missing.

'Who is responsible for order in the Tauride Palace?' Lenin asked Uritsky.

'I am.'

'Then permit me to inform you,' replied Lenin, 'that my revolver has been stolen from my coat, here in the Tauride Palace.'

'That's impossible!' cried Uritsky.

'Yes, it has been stolen. There, you see. Today your fur coat was taken from you in the middle of the street. And tonight robbers stole my revolver. Now do you understand the sort of order that exists among us?'

The Bolshevik spokesmen again pressed for the acceptance of their declaration. After much debate the Constituent Assembly majority rejected the Bolshevik platform and voted to record their stand on the war, the agrarian problem, and Russia's form of government. Thereupon the Bolshevik deputies rose in a body and marched out.

A number of Left Socialist Revolutionary peasant deputies refused to join the Bolshevik walk-out because they had been instructed by their constituents not to leave before the Constituent Assembly adopted a land law. The Left Socialist Revolutionaries were disorganized, some preparing to follow the Bolshevik example and others struggling to remain independent. Finally, having already cast their lot with Lenin, they also left the hall.

Dawn was already breaking when the remaining deputies, representing the elected majority, started to read their decrees. The galleries emptied out and they remained alone with Lenin's sailors and soldiers. The Socialist Revolutionaries and Mensheviks knew their time was short. Chernov was reading the decree on land when a sailor seized him by the arm and said, 'It's time to finish. We have an order from the People's Commissar.'

'Which People's Commissar?' asked Chernov.

'An order – you can't remain here any longer – the guards are tired and we'll turn off the lights,' replied the sailor.

The members of the Constituent Assembly are also tired,' said Chernov, 'but they cannot rest until they fulfil the mandate given to them by the people to decide the questions of peace, land and government.'

Not allowing the sailor an opportunity to continue, Chernov went on reading the decrees. Russia was proclaimed a federated republic with national autonomy for all its constituent peoples. The guards continued to shout: 'Come on, time to finish. We'll turn off the lights.' But the deputies went on with their work, voting for the transfer of land to the peasantry and a democratic peace programme in line with Chernov's speech. When the chair finally recessed the meeting, it was morning.[8]

As Chernov moved towards the door, he was stopped by a middle-aged man who warned him not to use his automobile. A group of assassins were waiting for him, he said. The man told Chernov he was a member of the Bolshevik Party but that his conscience revolted at this action. When Chernov reached his home, his family was surprised to see him. The city was already buzzing with reports that Tseretelli and he had been killed.

Before noon, when the Assembly was slated to reconvene, the deputies found the entrance to the Tauride Palace barred by a detachment of troops with rifles, machine-guns and two field-pieces. On the same day – 19 January 1918, a decree of the Sovnarcom abolished the Constituent Assembly. Newspapers that printed accounts of the 18 January session were seized from the stands and from newsboys by soldiers, and ripped to shreds and burned on piles.

Maxim Gorky's *Novaya Zhizn* wrote:

Yesterday the streets of Petrograd and Moscow resounded with shouts of 'Long Live the Constituent Assembly'. For giving vent to these sentiments the peaceful paraders were shot down by the 'People's Government'.

On 19 January the Constituent Assembly expired – until the advent of happier days – its death foreboding new suffering for the martyred country and for the masses of the people. It is true that at the present moment no death certificate has yet been issued for the Constituent Assembly. But the Prayer for the Dead has already been said over it. The Constituent Assembly is nothing more than a corpse, without life, without soul. It can be resurrected only through a new alignment of forces.

only if the masses of the people come to their senses and soberly realize the impasse to which their own ignorance, cleverly used by a handful of madmen, has brought them.

At the meeting of the All-Russian Central Executive Committee of the Soviet on 19 January 1918, Lenin declared:

'The people wanted the Constituent Assembly summoned, and we summoned it. But they sensed immediately what this famous Constituent Assembly really represented. And now we have carried out the will of the people, which is All Power to the Soviets. We shall break the backs of the saboteurs. When I came from the Smolny, that fount of life and vigour, to the Tauride Palace, I felt as though I were in the company of corpses and lifeless mummies. They drew on all their available resources in order to fight Social-ism, they resorted to violence and sabotage, they even turned knowledge – the great pride of humanity – into a means of ex-ploiting the toiling people. . . .

'To hand over power to the Constituent Assembly would again be compromising with the malignant bourgeoisie. The Russian Soviets place the interests of the toiling masses far above the interests of treacherous compromise disguised in a new garb. A musty spirit of antiquity breathed in the speeches of those super-annuated politicians, Chernov and Tseretelli, who continued tediously to whine for the cessation of civil war. But as long as Kaledin exists, and as long as behind the slogan, "All power to the Constituent Assembly", is concealed the slogan "Down with the Soviets", civil war is inevitable. For nothing in the world will induce us to surrender the Soviet power. And when the Constitu-ent Assembly again revealed its readiness to postpone all the pain-fully urgent problems and tasks that were placed before it by the Soviets, we told the Constituent Assembly that they must not be postponed for one single moment. And by the will of the Soviet power the Constituent Assembly, which has refused to recognize the power of the people, is being dissolved.

'The Constituent Assembly is dissolved. The Soviet Revolution-ary Republic will triumph no matter what the cost.'

That speech was for the record. Privately, after the dissolution decree, Lenin bluntly told Trotsky: 'We made a mistake in not postponing the calling of the Constituent Assembly. We acted very incautiously. But it came out all to the better. The dissolution of the Constituent Assembly by the Soviet Government means a complete and frank liquidation of the idea of democracy by the idea of dictatorship. It will serve as a good lesson.'

And Trotsky reflects: 'Thus with Lenin theoretical considerations went hand in hand with the use of Lettish sharpshooters.'[9]

The night before, a squad of Bolshevik sailors had broken into a hospital and killed two noted Liberals, Professor Fyodor Kokoshkin, a famous scholar, and Dr Andrei Shingarev, one of the leaders of the Liberal opposition in the Duma. Both had been elected to the Constituent Assembly as leaders of the Cadet Party.

When Lenin was told that these murders had brought protest meetings from Socialist Revolutionaries and the Mensheviks he replied: 'Let them protest. Let them boil a little, rage a little, sigh a little, drink a lot of tea, and talk it over until morning and then, believe me, they will quickly go to sleep. That is their actual work. They are not fit for anything else. The Cadets, however, they will undoubtedly begin to organize a counter-revolution. They should be watched with both eyes. With the help of some big general, they can always organize a new Kornilov attempt against the revolutionary power.'

Lenin declared that he had merely followed the advice given by Plekhanov in his fateful speech at the London Congress. The dying founder of Russian Marxism made his last reply to his former disciple: 'The Constituent Assembly dissolved by the People's Commissars represented the labouring masses of Russia. By dissolving the Assembly, the People's Commissars fought not the enemies of the workers, but the enemies of the dictators of the Smolny Institute....

'Their dictatorship is not one of the labouring people, but the dictatorship of a clique. And precisely for this reason they will have to resort more and more to terroristic methods.'[10]

On 22 January, the day of the Petrograd funeral of those who had demonstrated for the Constituent Assembly, Maxim Gorky wrote in *Novaya Zhizn*:

The best Russians have lived for almost a hundred years with the idea of a Constituent Assembly as a political organ which could provide Russian democracy as a whole with the possibility of freely expressing its will. In the fight for this idea, thousands of intellectuals, tens of thousands of workers and peasants have perished in prisons, in exile and penal servitude, on the gallows and under the bullets of soldiers. On the altar of this sacred idea rivers of blood have been spilled – and now the 'people's commissars' have ordered the shooting of this democracy which had manifested in honour of this idea. . . . *Pravda* lies when it states that the January (18) manifestation was organized by the bourgeoisie, the bankers, and so on. . . . *Pravda* knows that the workers of the Obukhov, Patronny and other factories took part in the manifestation, that under the red banners of the Russian Social Democratic party there marched the workers of Vasileostrovsk, Vyborg and other districts. It was these workers that were shot. And however much *Pravda* may lie, it cannot hide this shameful fact.

Lenin, Trotsky and other Soviet leaders later produced many arguments, more and less subtle, to justify the suppression of the Assembly, and the ideal of representative democracy which it symbolized. Perhaps the most candid explanation was given by Lenin in 1919:

'Only scoundrels and imbeciles can think that the proletariat must first win a majority of votes in elections conducted under the bourgeois yoke, under the yoke of hired slavery, and only then seek to win power. . . .

'The proletariat, having assembled sufficiently powerful political and military 'striking forces', must overthrow the bourgeoisie and deprive it of the power of the state, so as to wield this instrument for its own class purposes.

'The opportunists are "teaching" the people that the proletariat must first gain a majority with the help of universal suffrage; then, having gained this majority, it must take over the power of the state; and, finally, on the basis of this "consistent" (or "pure", as it is called now) democracy, it must proceed to organize Socialism.

'We, on the other hand, declare that the proletariat must first overthrow the bourgeoisie and conquer the power of the state, and then use the power of the state, *i.e.* the dictatorship of the proletariat, as an instrument of its class in order to gain the sympathy of the majority of the toilers.'[11]

Lenin's arguments failed to impress Socialists abroad. In a famous critique written in 1918, Rosa Luxemburg declared:

'To be sure, every democratic institution has its limits and shortcomings, things which it doubtless shares with all other human institutions. But the remedy which Lenin and Trotsky have found, the elimination of democracy as such, is worse than the disease it is supposed to cure; for it stops up the very living source from which alone can come the correction of all the innate shortcomings of social institutions. That source is the active, untrammeled, energetic political life of the broadest masses of the people. . . .

'Freedom only for the supporters of the government, only for the members of one party – however numerous they may be – is no freedom at all. Freedom is always and exclusively freedom for the one who thinks differently. Not because of any fanatical concept of "justice", but because all that is instructive, wholesome and purifying in political freedom depends on this essential characteristic, and its effectiveness vanishes when "freedom" becomes a special privilege. . . .'

Socialism, Rosa Luxemburg wrote, 'by its very nature cannot be decreed or introduced by *ukaz*. . . . Only unobstructed effervescing life falls into a thousand new forms and improvisations, brings to light creative force, itself corrects all mistaken attempts. The public life of countries with limited freedom is so poverty-stricken, so miserable, so rigid, so unfruitful, precisely because, through the exclusion of democracy, it cuts off the living sources of all spiritual riches and progress. . . .'

'Without general elections, without unrestricted freedom of press and assembly, without a free struggle of opinion, life dies out in every public institution, becomes a mere semblance of life, in which only the bureaucracy remains as the active element. Public life gradually falls asleep, a few dozen party leaders of inexhaustible energy and boundless experience direct and rule. Among them, in reality only a dozen outstanding heads do the leading and an *élite* of the working class is invited from time to time to meetings, where they are to applaud the speeches of the leaders, and to approve proposed resolutions unanimously – at bottom, then, a clique affair – a dictatorship, to be sure, not the dictatorship of the proletariat, however, but only the dictatorship of a handful of politicians. . . .'

Chapter 16
Brest-Litovsk

The making of an immediate peace with Germany had been one of the main slogans of the Bolsheviks before they seized power. To the war-weary Russian masses this slogan was of tremendous appeal and little thought was given to possible political or economic consequences. Peace at any price was necessary for Lenin in order to consolidate the power of dictatorship. But he also was so convinced of the immediacy of revolution in Germany as well as in the other countries of western Europe that the possible results of a German-dictated peace were without terror for him. He therefore stubbornly persisted all through the period of negotiations in pressing his more wavering colleagues to do anything and everything to achieve peace.

The Soviet peace delegation, headed by Joffe and Trotsky, had been dispatched to Brest-Litovsk at the end of November. On 27 December the Petrograd press published a statement by the Soviet peace delegation claiming that 'the principles of a general democratic peace without annexations are accepted by the nations of the Central Powers', that 'Germany and its allies have no plans whatsoever of territorial aggrandizement, and similarly have no desire to destroy or limit the political independence of any nation.'

This was written at a time when there was no mistake about what Germany really wanted. Scheffer, a deputy in the Prussian Landtag, thus expressed the German interpretation of a 'peace without annexations and indemnities':

'If the British consent to a referendum in India, we will allow the population of Vilna and Grodno to have the same. If they consent to self-determination for Ireland and Egypt, we will do the same for the Baltic provinces.'

But the Bolsheviks persisted in accusing others of the very surrender they were making. 'I am convinced', said Trotsky, 'that if the Right Socialist Revolutionaries were miraculously to come to power once again, they would hurry to conclude a shameful peace in order to free their forces for the strengthening of the bourgeois order in Russia.' Even on his way to Brest-Litovsk, Trotsky told the soldiers that 'the Russian Revolution will not bow its head before German imperialism', and that the Bolsheviks would sign 'only an honourable peace'.

Addressing a meeting of the Petrograd Soviet, Trotsky said: 'We promise you to fight together with you for an honest, democratic peace. We will fight them [the Austro-German representatives] and they will not dare to back up their threats with an offensive.'[1]

On 30 December a representative of the Petrograd newspaper *Dyen* had an interview with Count Hermann Keyserling, head of the German mission which had arrived in Petrograd. At the end of the interview the reporter asked whether it was true that the Germans intended to occupy Petrograd. Court Keyserling replied that for the time being the Germans had no intention of doing so, but that it might become unavoidable if anti-Soviet riots should break out in the capital. On the day following the publication of the interview *Izvestia* printed an official statement in the name of the Commissariat of Foreign Affairs, which declared that the entire story was an invention of the *Dyen*. The Commissariat, it was stated, had placed an inquiry regarding the question with Count Keyserling, and the latter categorically denied having given an interview to anyone. The *Dyen* thereupon sent the same reporter to Keyserling a second time, accompanied by one of the paper's editors who had a thorough command of German. The editor translated the entire interview to Keyserling, asking him to point out any inaccuracies it might contain. Count Keyserling confirmed the correctness of the report. The editor then read to him the statement which appeared in *Izvestia* on behalf of the Commissariat of Foreign Affairs. Count Keyserling replied that a representative of the Commissariat had telephoned him a day earlier requesting, in Trotsky's name, that he deny the interview published in the *Dyen*. However, he had categorically refused to do so. The next day the *Dyen* reprinted its original interview with Count Keyserling, together with an editorial challenging Trotsky to take it to court if there was any falsehood in its statements. Trotsky did not respond to the challenge, but soon afterward the government closed down the *Dyen* together with all the other Socialist and Liberal papers, without resorting to court proceedings.

The Bolsheviks hoped that their speeches at Brest-Litovsk would provoke rebellion in the German Army. On 20 December *Novy Looch*, the central organ of the Russian Social Democratic Labour Party, wrote that 'persistent rumours are circulating about the German intention to undertake a diversion against Petrograd. Important German political and military leaders are at present in Petrograd.' And in the Soviet, Trotsky reported: 'An Austrian officer has received the Sovnarcom's permission to form a detachment from among war prisoners, which is to place itself at the disposal of the Sovnarcom for the work of putting into practice the ideals of the Russian Revolution.' The *Dyen* commented in its issue of 21 December: 'The armed German detachment headed by officers will have no difficulty in carrying into practice Trotsky's ideals in Petrograd. So thinks Trotsky. And Von Lucius [one of the chief diplomats of Wilhelm II] thinks. . . . He also thinks . . . .'

Antonov-Ovseenko subsequently described the reaction of the German war prisoners in Russia to the revolutionary appeals of the Bolsheviks. On one occasion the Bolsheviks had assembled a propagandized German company for review. The company went through military drills with the usual German efficiency. Speaking in German, the Bolshevik commander expressed his praise. In reply, the company replied as one man: '*Hoch*, Kaiser Wilhelm!' 'In general,' concludes Antonov-Ovseenko, 'the German war prisoners turned out to be extremely unsusceptible to our agitation.'[2]

The leaders of the Austro-German peace delegation, German Foreign Minister Von Kühlmann, General Hoffmann and Count Czernin, the Austrian Foreign Minister, although annoyed by Trotsky's revolutionary fulminations, did not overestimate their practical effect.

'There is only one thing for them to choose now – under what sauce they are to be devoured,' remarked Von Kühlmann to Count Czernin.[3]

General Hoffmann pointedly rebuked the Bolshevik emissaries for their attitude. The Russian delegation, said the general, 'talks to us as if it stood victorious in our countries and could dictate conditions to us. I would like to point out that the facts are just the reverse: that the victorious German Army stands in your territory. . . . The Russian delegation demands for the occupied territories the application of the right of self-determination of peoples in a manner and to an extent which its government does not apply to its own country. Its government is founded purely on force, which ruthlessly suppresses all who think otherwise. Anyone with different views is simply declared an outlaw, as a counter-revolutionary and bourgeois.' General Hoffmann then cited the dispersal by force of White Russian and Ukrainian congresses for self-determination and commented: 'Thus do the Bolsheviks apply in practice the right of self-determination.' To the general's assertion that the Bolshevik régime rested only on force the Bolshevik delegation replied: 'Throughout all history no other kind of government has been known.'[4]

When the Soviet delegation heard the German terms, General Skalon, one of the Soviet experts, committed suicide on the spot. Another Soviet delegate, Professor Pokrovsky, said with tears in his eyes: 'How can one speak of peace without annexations if Russia is being deprived of territories equal in size to approximately eighteen provinces?' General Hoffmann did not contradict him.

The majority of the Bolshevik delegation, now headed by Trotsky and Bukharin, were flatly opposed to the German peace terms. This division became so sharp that it nearly precipitated a major split in the Soviet Government.

On 21 January 1918, the Bolshevik Central Committee met with the Bolshevik deputies to the Third Congress of Soviets to discuss the German terms. Lenin spoke in favour of signing peace even at the cost of ceding considerable territory. Trotsky, on the other hand, recommended that war be declared at an end without signing the peace terms. By this device of 'no peace, no war', he hoped that the German and Austrian armies, demoralized by inactivity and revolutionary propaganda, would revolt. The third suggestion was to wage a 'revolutionary war' against Germany and her allies. Fifteen voted for Lenin's recommendation, sixteen for Trotsky's, and thirty-two for 'revolutionary war'.

Three days later the Central Committee again took up the question of peace. Lenin again insisted on immediate acceptance of the German terms.

'The Army,' he said, 'is extremely tired of war. The number of horses is so small that the artillery could not be moved back in case of an enemy advance. The position of the Germans on the islands of the Baltic Sea is so strong that if they ordered an advance they could easily take Reval and Petrograd. To continue the war under such conditions would be equivalent to strengthening German imperialism. Peace would then have to be signed anyway, but its terms would be much worse because we would have no choice in the matter. Undoubtedly the peace which we are now compelled to sign is a rotten one, but if war should break out again, our government would be wiped out and peace would be made by some other government. We must become strongly entrenched in power, and for that we need time. It is necessary that our hands shall be untied.'

Lenin's statement evoked strong objections.

On 24 January 1918, Eduard Bernstein, leader of the anti-war Independent Socialist Party of Germany, published an article in Gorky's *Novaya Zhizn* attacking the Bolsheviks for their dealings with the German militarists:

The German officers are enthusiastic about these wonderful revolutionists. General Hoffmann, who conducted the preliminary armistice negotiations, laughingly tells how he cheerfully answered the Bolsheviks' long declarations of principles: 'Pardon me, gentlemen, but how do your principles concern us?' Once the Bolsheviks not only sacrifice their principles, but at the same time create the impression that Prussian militarism went over to the side of their Social Democratic revolutionary principles under their pressure, once they act this way – it makes no difference whether they do it consciously or through folly – their role is identical with that of the German agents on whom Germany spends countless millions to spread among the people of Allied and neutral countries the ideas of pacifism, anti-militarism, anti-capitalism and revolution.

In German military circles, the success of the negotiations with the Russians is openly interpreted as an indication that all the necessary parties were paid off. As far as we German Socialists are concerned, convinced as we are of the personal integrity of Lenin and Trotsky on the basis of our long associations with them, we stand before an insoluble riddle. Some of us ascribe this riddle to the purely 'business considerations' of the Bolsheviks who originally used German money for their agitation and are now captives of their thoughtless step. The German Socialists are driven to such suppositions, because nobody in Germany can believe that the Bolsheviks are sincerely convinced of the revolutionary consistency of their tactics.

Bernstein concluded his article with the warning that the Bolshevik policies were preparing 'not peace for Russia and for the rest of war-suffering humanity, but the exceptionally cruel triumph of German imperialism, which of course has no thoughts of turning to the Bolshevik faith.'

On 26 January Trotsky returned from Brest-Litovsk to report on the results of the negotiations. He was not optimistic. Still, he wanted to shift the blame to someone else's shoulders.

'The conditions that Von Kühlmann proposed,' said Trotsky, 'received the tacit approval of London; I declare it categorically. England is willing to conclude a compromise peace with Germany at the expense of Russia. The conditions they proposed to us are not only German, but Austrian, French, and English conditions. This is the bill which world imperialism tenders the Russian Revolution.'

At the end of his speech, as though forgetting what he had just said, Trotsky added: 'When it appeared possible that we might break off peace negotiations, the Allied governments one after another proposed recognition of the Soviet power in order that we continue the war. They even offered to pay the salaries of a volunteer army. . . . The Bolsheviks answered with the declaration, "We have withdrawn from the imperialist war, and will never enter it again."'[5]

Many Bolsheviks, still remembering Lenin's slogan of 'a people's peace', were strongly opposed to signing on the terms laid down by the German Imperial Government. To these objections Lenin angrily replied: 'You are worse than chickens. A chicken is afraid to step outside of a chalk circle drawn around her, but she can at least say in her justification that the circle was drawn by a strange hand. But you have drawn with your own hands a formula, and now you look at it instead of at reality. Our formula for a people's peace was supposed to rouse the masses in a struggle against the military and capitalistic governments. Now you wish that we perish and that the capitalistic military governments should emerge victorious in the name of our revolutionary formula.'[6]

Lenin insisted that the German conditions be accepted. He was supported by Sverdlov, Stalin, Smilga and Sokolnikov, but the majority of the Bolshevik Central Committee refused to go along with their chief. And they were supported by many local committees.

Krupskaya writes:

Against Ilyich were the Petrograd Committee and the Moscow Regional Committee. The faction of the 'Left' Communists in Petrograd began to publish their own weekly paper *Communist*, in which they went so far as to say it would be better to relinquish the Soviet power than to conclude a shameful peace. They talked about a revolutionary struggle, not considering their forces. They thought that concluding a peace with the German imperialist government meant the surrender and betrayal of the cause of the international proletariat. To the 'Left' Communists belonged a number of close comrades, with whom we had worked for many years and who had supported us in the gravest moments of our struggle. Around Ilyich there suddenly appeared a void.

Bukharin, as well as Trotsky, Uritsky, Lomov and Dzerzhinsky, declared that to accept Germany's peace terms would be to surrender the entire Bolshevik programme. Finally, by a vote of nine to seven, Trotsky's formula, 'the war is to be discontinued; peace is not to be signed, and the Army is to be demobilized', was accepted.

But they reckoned without Germany. On 16 February General Hoffmann sent an ultimatum to the Soviet Government, and the German Army prepared to resume the offensive. On the receipt of the German ultimatum, the Central Committee called a meeting for 17 February. A group of five, consisting of Lenin, Stalin, Sverdlov, Sokolnikov and Smilga, favoured immediate acceptance of Germany's terms. Six members, Bukharin, Lomov, Trotsky, Uritsky, Joffe and Krestinsky, voted against it. When the question of signing immediate peace or awaiting a German offensive was put to a final vote, it was decided to wait for the results of the German offensive. Perhaps the German soldiers would refuse to fight.

The answer came fast enough. On 18 February the German Army attacked once more. The Central Committee was reconvened and Lenin again demanded immediate signing. Again he had the support of only a minority. Towards evening, as news of fresh German advances came in, the general attitude changed. Lenin, with greater determination than ever, pressed for prompt acceptance. He could not understand the concern of his comrades over ceding 'some Russian territory'. To Lenin the sole important issue was whether or not the German peace terms imperilled the Soviet power.

'If the Germans should demand the overturn of the Bolshevik

T-N

Government, then, of course, we would have to fight,' he said. 'All other demands can and should be granted. We have heard the statement made that the Germans are going to take Livonia and Estonia. We can very well sacrifice these for the sake of the Revolution. If they demand the removal of our troops from Finland, well and good. Let them take revolutionary Finland. Even if we give up Finland, Livonia and Estonia, we still retain the Revolution. I recommend that we sign the peace terms offered to us by the Germans. If they should demand that we keep out of the affairs of the Ukraine, Livonia, and Estonia, we shall have to accept those terms too.'[7]

On a final vote Lenin won seven votes of a total of thirteen. A wire was sent to the German Government announcing that the Soviet Government was willing to accept the peace terms offered at Brest-Litovsk and would reply immediately to any new conditions.

Germany's reply, on 22 February, contained more drastic terms, involving not only surrender of the entire Baltic area, including Finland, but Soviet recognition of a German-sponsored 'independent' Ukraine. When these conditions became known, they created renewed opposition.

The Left Socialist Revolutionaries who were then participating in the government proposed acceptance of Allied aid in order to resist the Germans. On 21 February the French Ambassador, Noulens, telegraphed Trotsky: 'In resisting Germany, you may count on the military and financial assistance of France.' When the question of accepting Allied aid was discussed in the Central Committee of the Bolshevik Party opinion was divided. Some of the members argued as a matter of principle against any negotiations with the 'imperialists', i.e. with the representatives of France and the United States. Others felt that it was admissible, in principle, to make use of aid from 'imperialists', but that it was 'practically inexpedient to accept assistance from the English and French imperialists'. Trotsky and Sokolnikov favoured the acquisition of arms. Lenin was absent from the meeting but sent the following message to the Central Committee: 'Please add my vote in favour of taking potatoes and arms from the Anglo-French imperialist bandits.' However, at the next meeting of the Central Committee Lenin stated that the policy of 'playing with revolutionary phrases' must end.

'If it is to be continued,' he threatened, 'I will resign from the government as well as the Central Committee, and will begin an open agitation against the two. In order to wage a revolutionary war, an army is needed, and we haven't got it. Consequently, we must accept the peace terms.'[8]

A heated discussion ensued. But Lenin's opponents were reluctant to accept his challenge. At the final vote Lenin, Stasova, Zinoviev, Sverdlov, Stalin, Sokolnikov and Smilga voted for the acceptance of the German terms; Bubnov, Uritsky, Bukharin and Lomov voted against it; Trotsky, Krestinsky, Dzerzhinsky and Joffe refrained from voting, explaining that although they considered the peace terms insufferable, they abstained because of Lenin's threat to resign. On 3 March 1918, the Soviet delegates signed the Treaty of Brest-Litovsk.

Those who voted against Lenin's proposal announced that they would not assume responsibility for a decision adopted in fact by a minority and which they regarded as injurious to the cause of the Russian and international revolution. They underscored their opposition by resigning from all positions of responsibility in the Party and in the Soviet. The next day additional resignations were presented by other members of the Soviet. Nevertheless, Lenin could well claim that he had triumphed over his opponents.

At the Bolshevik Party Congress on 6 March Lenin won after a debate lasting a day and a half. A Bolshevik delegate relates how he was impressed by Lenin's calm and good humour:

'With coat unbuttoned, his thumbs in his vest, he strolled back and forth behind the tribune attentively listening to the speeches of the orator. He radiated joy. He was particularly happy whenever the speaker to whom he was listening happened to be an opponent of his. The more vigorous the opponent's remarks, the happier Lenin felt. Often he would break out into loud laughter, holding his sides.'

The next day he told the Congress: 'As every sensible man will understand, by signing this peace treaty we do not put a stop to our workers' revolution; everyone will understand that by concluding peace with the Germans we do not stop rendering military aid; we are sending arms to the Finns, but not military units which proved to be unfit.

'Perhaps we will accept war; perhaps tomorrow we will

surrender even Moscow and then pass to the offensive; if a change takes place in the mood of the people, which change is maturing, for which perhaps much time is required, but which will come, when the broad masses will not say what they are saying now, we will move our army against the enemy. I am compelled to accept the harshest peace terms because I cannot say to myself that this time has arrived. When the time of regeneration arrives everyone will realize it, will see that the Russian is no fool; they will see and understand that for the time being we must refrain, that this slogan must be carried through . . . and this is the main task of our Party Congress and of the Congress of Soviets.'9

Discussing the German popular revolution he had banked on, he declared: 'The revolution will not come as quickly as we expected. History has proved this, and we must be able to take this as fact, we must be able to reckon with the fact that the world Socialist revolution cannot begin so easily in the advanced countries as the revolution began in Russia – the land of Nicholas and Rasputin, the land in which the overwhelming majority of the population was quite indifferent to the conditions of life of the people in the outlying regions. In such a country it was quite easy to start a revolution, as easy as lifting a feather.

'But it is wrong, absurd, without preparation to start a revolution in a country in which capitalism is developed, which has produced a democratic culture and has organized every man. We are only just approaching the painful period of the beginning of Socialist revolution. . . . That is why I think that after history has shattered our hope that the Germans cannot attack and that we can get everything by shouting "hurrah!" this lesson, with the help of our Soviet organization, will very quickly sink into the minds of the masses all over Soviet Russia.'10

Lenin had no illusions as to the terms he had accepted. But since he had no intention of honouring the Draconian conditions for an instant longer than was necessary, he was completely indifferent to the actual details.

'I happened to be in Lenin's room', related Stasova, his secretary, 'when Karakhan brought the draft of the Brest-Litovsk peace treaty. He wanted to unfold it and show it to his chief. Lenin protested vigorously. "What, not only do you want me to sign this impudent peace treaty, but also to read it? No, no, never! I shall neither read it nor carry out its terms whenever there is a chance not to do so."[11]

Two years later Lenin was still attempting to justify his signing the Brest-Litovsk Treaty. In Moscow, on 26 November 1920, he declared: 'It may appear that the result was something like a bloc between the first Socialist Republic and German imperialism against another imperialism. But we concluded no bloc of any kind; we nowhere overstepped bounds, undermining or defaming the Socialist power, but we took advantage of the hostility between the two imperialisms in such a way that in the long run both lost. Germany got nothing from the Brest peace except several million pounds of grain, but brought Bolshevik disintegration into Germany. But we gained time, in the course of which the Red Army began to be formed. . . . We gained time, we gained a little time, and sacrificed a great deal of space for it.'[12]

Brest-Litovsk gave Germany control over the resources of the Ukraine and released many German divisions for the Western Front. But within six or seven months American, French and British troops were on the offensive which cracked the Hindenburg Line and forced Germany to sue for an armistice. The Allied victory compelled the Germans to disgorge the territories they had acquired under the peace treaty which Lenin signed.[13]

Lenin's larger ideological motivations for concluding the Brest-Litovsk Treaty have been clear since 1918. The power of German arms was perhaps conclusive in any case. Yet it has only been in the last decade that historians have been able to understand the powerful non-military influences which Germany was able to exert on Lenin in 1917–18. The understanding is a result of the capture after World War II of numerous secret documents of the German and Austro-Hungarian Empires, which became available to scholars in the mid 1950s.[14]

These documents essentially corroborate the Provisional Government's charges that the Bolshevik Party received money from the Central Powers for the purpose of demoralizing the Russian Army, overthrowing the Provisional Government and preparing a separate peace. These dealings, which began in the autumn of 1914 with a subsidy of some $5,700 to Lenin's newspaper *Sozialdemokrat* by the Austrian-sponsored 'Union for the

Liberation of the Ukraine', reached their height with the activities of Parvus and his Copenhagen Institute, Ganetsky and various German diplomats during the stormy months between the fall of the autocracy and Lenin's *coup*.

German subsidies continued, however, after Lenin had seized power. On 28 November 1917, German Under-State Secretary Busche wired the Minister in Berne: 'According to information received here, the government in Petrograd is having to fight against great financial difficulties. It is therefore very desirable that they be sent money.'

A few days later, State Secretary von Kühlmann telegraphed his liaison officer at General Headquarters: 'It was not until the Bolsheviks had received from us a steady flow of funds through various channels and under different labels that they were in a position to be able to build up their main organ, *Pravda*, to conduct energetic propaganda and appreciably to extend the originally narrow basis of their party. The Bolsheviks have now come to power; how long they will retain power cannot be yet foreseen. They need peace in order to strengthen their own position; on the other hand, it is entirely in our interest that we should exploit the period while they are in power, which may be a short one, in order to attain firstly an armistice and then, if possible, peace.'

Even after the conclusion of the Brest-Litovsk Treaty, Imperial German diplomacy continued to assist the Lenin régime. Count von Mirbach, the German Minister in Moscow, considered the Bolsheviks' hold extremely fragile. On 30 April 1918, he wrote Chancellor Bethmann-Hollweg: 'The supremacy of the Bolsheviks in Moscow is principally upheld by the Livonian battalions, and then also by the large number of motor vehicles requisitioned by the government, which rush continually around the town and can bring troops to danger-spots as required.' On 17 May, von Mirbach cabled his Foreign Office: 'I am still trying to counter efforts of the Entente and support the Bolsheviks. However, I would be grateful for instructions as to whether overall situation justifies use of larger sums in our interests if necessary.'

State Secretary von Kühlmann replied the next day: 'Please use larger sums, as it is greatly in our interests that Bolsheviks should survive. Riezler's funds at your disposal. If further money required, please telegraph how much.'

Two weeks later, on 3 June, von Mirbach cabled again: 'Due to strong Entente competition, 3,000,000 marks per month necessary.' Von Kühlmann on 5 June forwarded to the State Secretary of the Treasury, Count von Roedern, a memorandum by Counsellor Trautmann of the Foreign Ministry. The Trautmann memorandum disclosed that 'during the recent efforts of the Entente to persuade the Soviet of Workers' Deputies to accept the demands of the Entente. . . . Count Mirbach was forced to spend considerable sums in order to prevent any resolution to this effect.' Trautmann continued: 'The fund which we have so far had at our disposal for acquisitions in Russia is exhausted. It is therefore essential that the Secretary of the Imperial Treasury put a new fund at our disposal. In view of the conditions set out above, this fund will have to amount to at least 40,000,000 marks.'

None of the documents discovered thus far has yet to show, of course, that Lenin personally received money from Imperial German officials; he had not, years earlier, participated personally either in the expropriations carried out by Bolshevik strong-arm squads in the Caucasus and elsewhere. Yet the Bolshevik Party rarely took a significant step without his knowledge and approval; and in the long, hard road that brought him from Swiss exile to Brest-Litovsk, it is inconceivable that Lenin was unaware of the timely and substantial assistance provided his movement by the Kaiser's Government. Not that German subsidies altered his views; to the contrary, precisely because of his views he was their ideal recipient.

Chapter 17
Terror and Civil War

The inevitable need of terror as a means of maintaining dictatorial rule had been clear to Lenin before the Revolution. He expounded the theory as early as 1908 at his home in Geneva, relates his old friend Adoratsky. The question was raised as to what should be done by revolutionists when they took power with those who served the old régime. Half in jest, Lenin outlined the procedure: 'We'll ask the man, "Where do you stand on the question of the Revolution? Are you for it or against it?" If he is against it, we'll stand him up against the wall. If he is for it, we'll welcome him into our midst to work with us.'

Krupskaya replied bitterly: 'Yes, and you'll shoot precisely those that are better men for having the courage to express their views.'[1]

Immediately after the Bolshevik *coup*, capital punishment for desertion at the front, reintroduced by Kerensky, was abolished at the suggestion of Kamenev. Lenin was not at the meeting which adopted this measure. When he learned of the decree, he was beside himself with anger.

'Nonsense,' he said. 'How can one make revolution without executions?' Kamenev tried to argue that the new law was applicable only to army deserters.

'That is a mistake,' Lenin protested, 'an unpardonable weakness and pacifist illusion,' and recommended that the order be rescinded immediately. Convinced that this move would make an unfavourable impression, he accepted a compromise: to disregard the new law and shoot deserters.

'In one of our appeals', Trotsky writes, 'it was stated that anyone who gave aid and comfort to the enemy would be killed on the spot. The Left Socialist Revolutionaries protested against this threat.

' "On the contrary," Lenin exclaimed, 'that is just where the true revolutionary pathos comes in. Do you really think that we shall be victorious without using the most cruel terror?"

'That was the period', says Trotsky, 'when Lenin at every opportunity kept hammering into our heads that terror was unavoidable.

'"Where is your dictatorship? Show it to me. What we have is a mess, not a dictatorship. If we cannot shoot a man who sabotages, a member of the White Guard, then what kind of revolution is this?"'[2]

Once, when Lenin heard a report about a series of counter-revolutionary attempts, he grew angry, rose from his chair, paced the office nervously, and exclaimed: 'Is it impossible to find among us a Fouquier-Tinville to tame our wild counter-revolutionists?'[3]

Lenin found his Fouquier-Tinville in Felix Dzerzhinsky. He was fair, slightly round-shouldered, with a short pointed beard and transparent eyes with dilated pupils. There were moments when his friendly smile gave way to icy sternness. At such times his eyes and ascetic bloodless lips revealed a demoniac fanaticism. Rigorous self-denial, incorrigible honesty, and a frigid indifference to the opinions of others completed his make-up. His natural modesty, unassuming air and quiet manners set him apart. He was the great puritan, the 'saint' of the upheaval. Frail and given to occasional fits of melancholy, he sought retirement in unceasing labour behind closed doors, away from the multitude and party comrades alike. For most of the latter he had little respect; nearly all of them came to fear him, some distrusted him, and few mourned him when he died. These few referred to him as 'a chevalier above fear and beyond reproach'. In his bleak asceticism, complete devotion to Lenin, personal unselfishness, and utter lack of feeling towards political opponents, he had no equal.

Like most Bolshevik leaders, Dzerzhinsky did not spring from the working class. He was the son of a rich Polish landowner of the Vilno province. As a student he became a member of the Lithuanian Social Democratic Party, was exiled at an early age, later joined the Polish Social Democratic Party, and spent most of his life in jails and in Siberia. The Revolution released him from a cell in the Taganka prison in Moscow.

Dzerzhinsky himself chose his role as the Grand Inquisitor of the Bolshevik Revolution. Others sought the light of day and the public arena. Dzerzhinsky preferred seclusion and the night.

Upstairs, in the Smolny Institute, Lenin and his lieutenants were drafting the blueprint for a new society. Outside, there was chaos and uncertainty; perhaps tomorrow would bring an end to the daring venture. Lenin had supplied the word, but the sword was needed to consolidate Soviet power. Downstairs, in a small dark corner room at the end of the long corridor, sat Dzerzhinsky. He had just been appointed commandant of Smolny. At his disposal were several detachments of Lettish sharpshooters, whose job was to keep the machine-guns placed in the windows properly oiled. A modest task. The spotlight on the huge yellowish building did not reach the dark corner where Dzerzhinsky sat.

For some days everybody came and went freely in Smolny: workmen in blouses and corduroy trousers, good-humoured soldiers in dirty field-grey, women with bobbed hair, sallow-faced intelligentsia. All were feverishly busy, with important-looking portfolios under their arms, rushing from one floor to another, giving and taking orders, exchanging greetings. Dzerzhinsky, who sat in his guardroom gazing across the broad Neva towards the steeple of the Fortress of St Peter and St Paul, knew that there were many millions outside Smolny who did not like Lenin and his party.

While the Sovnarcom was in session, a polite but firm order came from the commandant's little room, ordering everybody in Smolny to appear for examination. Those who failed to appear were rounded up as they entered or left the building. The guards had been stationed at every entrance and stairway.

'Ah, good day, comrade!' was Dzerzhinsky's quiet greeting to all callers.

There followed a business-like interrogation.

'Who are you?'

'Your full name and address, please?'

'How long have you been in the revolutionary movement?'

'Are you a member of the Bolshevik Party?'

'What is your business at Smolny?'

'How well are you familiar with the place?'

'What references can you give concerning your political reliability?' etc., etc.

Some were subjected to thorough search. The Lettish sharpshooters and Baltic Fleet sailors, quick, obedient, and efficient, did the frisking. Those who aroused no suspicion were supplied with passes permitting them to enter the building. Some were ordered out with the warning not to return. Others found themselves prisoners pending further investigation. Soon a network of espionage enveloped the building which had once been a fashionable school for girls.

On 20 December 1917, Lenin instructed Dzerzhinsky to organize an Extraordinary Commission for Combating Counter-Revolution and Speculation. Under the name Cheka, this Soviet secret police soon became the symbol for a system of terror such as the world had never seen. In later years its name was changed to OGPU, NKVD, MVD, KGB, but its purpose remained the same. Dzerzhinsky became the first head of the Cheka.

In his first address as chief of the Soviet secret police Dzerzhinsky declared: 'This is no time for speech-making. Our Revolution is in serious danger. We tolerate too good-naturedly what is transpiring around us. The forces of our enemies are organizing. The counter-revolutionaries are at work and are organizing their groups in various sections of the country. The enemy is encamped in Petrograd, at our very hearth! We have indisputable evidence of this and we must send to this front the most stern, energetic, hearty and loyal comrades who are ready to do all to defend the attainments of our Revolution. *Do not think that I am on the look-out for forms of revolutionary justice. We have no need for justice now. Now we have need of a battle to the death! I propose, I demand the initiation of the Revolutionary sword which will put an end to all counter-revolutionists. We must act not tomorrow, but today, at once!*'[4]

Then followed a series of uncovered plots, some true, others fantastic, against the Bolsheviks and conspiracies against the lives of the leaders. In his little room Dzerzhinsky was constantly sharpening the weapon of the Soviet dictatorship. To Dzerzhinsky was brought the mass of undigested rumours from all parts of Petrograd. With the aid of picked squads of Chekists, Dzerzhinsky undertook to purge the city. At night his men moved from the dark streets into apartment houses; towards dawn they returned with their haul. Few if any challenged the authority of these men. Their password was enough: Cheka, the all-powerful political police.

Little time was wasted sifting evidence and classifying people rounded up in these night raids. Woe to him who did not disarm all suspicion at once. The prisoners were generally hustled to the old police station not far from the Winter Palace. Here, with or without perfunctory interrogation, they were stood up against the court-yard wall and shot. The staccato sounds of death were muffled by the roar of truck motors kept going for the purpose.

Dzerzhinsky furnished the instrument for tearing a new society out of the womb of the old – the instrument of organized, syste-matic mass terror. For Dzerzhinsky the class struggle meant exter-minating 'the enemies of the working class'. The 'enemies of the working class' were all who opposed the Bolshevik dictatorship.

Furthermore, Dzerzhinsky was conscious that terror was per-haps the only means of making 'proletarian dictatorship' prevail in peasant Russia. In a conversation with Abramovich, in August 1917, he expressed impatience with the conventional socialist view that the correlation of real political and social forces in a country could only change through the process of economic and political development, the evolution of new forms of economy, rise of new social classes, and so on. 'Couldn't this correlation be altered?' Dzerzhinsky asked. 'Say, through the subjection or extermination of some classes of society?'

Dzerzhinsky was the man who directed the actual operations of the Cheka, but Lenin assumed full responsibility for the terror. On 8 January 1918, the Council of People's Commissars set up bat-talions of bourgeois men and women to dig trenches. The Red Guards stationed as their 'surveillants' received the order to shoot anyone who resisted. A month later the All-Russian Cheka de-clared that 'counter-revolutionary agitators' and also 'all those trying to escape to the Don region in order to join the counter-revolutionary troops . . . will be shot on the spot by the Cheka squads'. The same punishment was ordered for those found dis-tributing or posting anti-government leaflets. Not only political crimes were dealt with in this fashion. In Briansk the death penalty by shooting was ordered for drunkenness, and in Viatka the same was ordered for violators of the eight-o'clock curfew. In Rybinsk 'shooting without warning' followed any congregation of people on the streets, and in the Kaluga province those failing to meet military levies in time were likewise ordered to be shot. The same 'crime' was punished in Zmyev by drowning the victim in the Dnie-ster River 'with a stone around his neck'.

On 22 January Krylenko, the Bolshevik Commander in Chief,

instructed the peasants of the province of Moghiliev 'to take the law in their own hands when dealing with perpetration of violence'. When the German offensive of 23 February 1918 began, the Bolshevik Government proclaimed the Socialist Fatherland to be in danger and issued a manifesto which declared that 'Agents of the speculators, gangsters, counter-revolutionary agitators, and German spies are to be shot on the spot.'[5]

Lenin also demanded capital punishment for thieves and hooligans. 'There had not been a single revolution in history,' he declared, 'when people did not . . . manifest salutary firmness by shooting thieves on the spot. . . . A dictatorship is an iron power, possessing revolutionary daring and swiftness of action, ruthless in crushing exploiters as well as hooligans.'

Such was the ideological foundation for an institution which, under Stalin and Khrushchev as under Lenin, continued to be the mainstay of Soviet power and the chief instrument for the control and elimination of all elements considered hostile or dangerous to the established dictatorship.

Lenin, who had preached the need for terror long before the Revolution, often drove other Bolshevik leaders to conduct mass terror even against their will. In a letter to Zinoviev on 26 June 1918, he wrote:

Only today we heard in the Central Committee that in Petrograd the 'workers' wanted to answer the assassination of Volodarsky with mass terror and that you (not you, personally, but the Petrograd members of the Central Committee) restrained them. I protest decisively. We compromise ourselves. Even in the resolutions of the Soviet we threaten mass terror, and when it comes to action, we put brakes on the revolutionary initiative of the masses, who are 'absolutely' right. This is impossible! Terrorists will consider us rags. This is an arch-war situation. We must work up energy and mass-like terror against counter-revolutionaries, and especially in Petrograd, the example of which is 'Decisive'.

The effects of the psychology of terror and the callousness of both Lenin and Dzerzhinsky is well illustrated by an incident described by Naglovsky, who writes:

I recall their silhouettes at one of the meetings with especial vividness; I cannot remember Dzerzhinsky ever sitting through an entire meeting of the Sovnarcom, but he very frequently entered, silently sat down, and left as silently while the meeting was still in progress. Tall, untidy, in huge boots and a dirty shirt, Dzerzhinsky was little liked among the top Bolsheviks. But people were bound to him by fear. And this fear could be sensed even among the People's Commissars.

At meetings of the Sovnarcom, Lenin often exchanged notes with his colleagues. On one occasion he sent a note to Dzerzhinsky: 'How many vicious counter-revolutionaries are there in our prisons?' Dzerzhinsky's reply was: 'About fifteen hundred.' Lenin read it, snorted something to himself, made a cross beside the figure, and returned the note to Dzerzhinsky.

Dzerzhinsky rose and left the room without a word. No one paid any attention either to Lenin's note or to Dzerzhinsky's departure. The meeting continued. But the next day there was excited whispering. Dzerzhinsky had ordered the execution of all the fifteen hundred 'vicious counter-revolutionaries' the previous night. He had taken Lenin's cross as a collective death sentence.

There would have been little comment had Lenin's gesture been meant as an order for wholesale liquidation. But, as Fotyieva, Lenin's secretary, explained: 'There was a misunderstanding. Vladimir Ilyich never wanted the executions. Dzrezhinsky did not understand him. Vladimir Ilyich usually puts a cross on memoranda to indicate that he had read them and noted their contents.' The 'misunderstanding' cost fifteen hundred human beings their lives.[6]

Early in 1918, after Petrograd had narrowly escaped German capture, the Soviet leaders decided that it was no longer a safe capital and determined to transfer the seat of government to Moscow.

An advance party headed by Dzerzhinsky was instructed to take extraordinary security measures along the route and in Moscow. There were rumours that Socialist Revolutionaries intended to blow up the train carrying members of Lenin's cabinet. Lenin himself insisted on secrecy. 'Even in the Sovnarcom,' he asserted, 'there must be no mention of the journey; there may be an accidental slip of the tongue somewhere.'

On his arrival in Moscow with his staff Dzerzhinsky set out to find suitable quarters for his organization. He chose the Rossiya Insurance Company building at 22 Lubianka Street. It was a comfortable structure with plenty of rooms, many side-entrances, spacious cellars, and a broad courtyard. As the main office of the Cheka, 22 Lubianka Street was to become the most notorious address in Russia.

With security preparations completed, the members of the Central Executive Committee were put aboard two special trains. Among them were peasants of various political affiliations as well as Socialist Revolutionaries.

'I carefully studied the party alignment of the Central Executive,' writes Bonch-Bruyevich, 'and so skilfully manoeuvred the seating arrangements that members of all parties were distributed in all the compartments. In the very first compartment I deliberately seated a majority of Socialist Revolutionaries.' Lenin was reassured when he heard of the seating arrangements; the Socialist Revolutionaries were not likely to blow up their own comrades for the sake of killing the Bolsheviks.

At 9.30 on the evening of 10 March 1918, Lenin left Smolny. His automobile stopped at the railroad siding and he entered his unlit compartment. A commissar seated himself in the caboose and gave the signal. Without sounding its siren, the train slowly puffed out of the station.

'What does this mean?' asked Lenin. 'Do you expect us to continue to sit in the dark?'

'I am only waiting until we get on the main road,' replied his aide.

Soon his colleagues were assembled in his compartment drinking tea and discussing plans. Lenin was pleased with the discipline of the Lettish guards, whose commander reported at each station that everything was in order. With military precision the guard detail was changed every two hours.

When the train reached its destination about 7 p.m. on 11 March, it was met by representatives of the Moscow Soviet, who escorted Lenin to his temporary headquarters at the Hotel National.

The following morning, in the bright sunlight which was turning the snow to slush, Lenin set out on a tour of the city. After visiting a friend of his sister Maria, who lived in an outlying district, he left for the Kremlin. When he reached the Troitsky Gate, the guards stopped him. The commandant, fully armed, approached, demanding: 'Who goes there?'

'The president of the Council of the People's Commissars, Vladimir Ilyich Lenin,' crackled his escort.

The commandant, obviously a former officer, took two steps backwards, straightened up like a ramrod, and saluted. The guards did the same. With a smile, Lenin raised his fingers to his round caracul cap.

'Forward!' his escort ordered the chauffeur, and they drove through the old Kremlin gate.

The third-floor apartment chosen for Lenin, formerly occupied by a district attorney, consisted of three small rooms, a kitchen, bath and servants' room. A private telephone system was installed, enabling Lenin to speak by direct wire to all fronts and capitals of the various Soviet republics. A guard commanding a clear view of the third-floor corridor was on constant duty.[7]

Despite Dzerzhinsky's precautions, Lenin ordered a screening of the guards. The Lettish unit which had accompanied him from Petrograd was moved into the Kremlin. 'Every time the Soviet found itself in a critical position, Lenin called in the Letts', recalled P. Stuchka, former Commissar of Justice. 'In his opinion the only segment of the Army that could be relied on was the Lettish division.'[8]

Soon after arriving in Moscow, Lenin told the Seventh Party Congress that private trading had to be abolished. The industrial workers and landless peasants had to help build Communism on the fundamental principles, 'From each according to his capacities, to each according to his needs.'

Production would be guided by social needs, Lenin promised. Communism had to be predicated on the elimination of the middleman. According to Trotsky, Lenin asserted in 1918: 'You will see that within six months we shall establish Socialism in Russia.'

There were special reasons for curtailing private trade. The peasants, unwilling to sell their grain for worthless paper currency, were demanding manufactured goods. In order to secure food for the urban population, the government had to organize a barter system between village and city. Committees were formed in every town with a population of ten thousand to fix local prices. The existing stocks of merchandise were registered. Trading in manufactured goods was placed under state control. But that was not enough.

Lacking sufficient industrial and consumer goods to exchange with the peasants, the Soviet Government, on 10 May 1918, issued an order for the requisitioning of grain from 'rich' peasants. A month later, on 11 June, the so-called 'Committees of the Poor' were created to enforce the decree in every village. An ugly atmosphere of suspicion, espionage and betrayal was created among the peasants. Neighbour spied upon neighbour. Peasants slaughtered their cattle and refused to sow their land, rather than turn over their food supplies to the government. The countryside seethed with local uprisings, which were crushed by punitive expeditions of Cheka troops.

The suppression of civil liberty, the dissolution of the Constituent Assembly, the Cheka terror, and the Carthaginian peace of Brest-Litovsk – which deprived Russia of its richest regions – brought increasing revolt from every stratum of the Russian people. In Rovno, Ryazan, Kostroma, Perm, Tver and Penza, there were clashes between peasants and Red Guards. In Tula, Minsk, Kostroma, Smolensk, Saratov and the Altai, workers and townspeople clashed with the régime. In Petrograd, the workers protested against bread rationing and Brest-Litovsk, despite Cheka arrests of their leaders.[9]

After the dissolution of the Constituent Assembly, all political parties except the Left Socialist Revolutionaries raised the standard of revolt against Lenin's dictatorship. Individual members of the Socialist and democratic parties formed a bloc called the 'League for the Regeneration of Russia', while conservative and reactionary groups organized the so-called 'Right Centre'.

In the spring of 1918 the Right Centre, whose members were always more or less pro-German, entered into secret negotiations with German representatives in Petrograd and Moscow, hoping with German aid to overthrow Lenin and re-establish the dynasty.

The League for the Regeneration of Russia, on the other hand, looked to the aid of England, France and the United States, and made an official request to these countries to restore an Allied front in Russia. Their hope was that in creating a new Eastern Front they could prevent Germany from securing the bread of the Ukraine and from diverting all her troops to the West. By nullifying the Brest-Litovsk Treaty, Russia would be reunited.

Until Brest-Litovsk, the Allies still expected that the Soviet régime would be forced to resume the war against Germany, and some American, British and French representatives entered into negotiations with Trotsky for the extension of Allied military aid in the event of fighting being resumed.

After the Brest-Litovsk peace was signed, the Allies became interested in the proposal of the 'League for the Regeneration of Russia' for the revival of an Eastern Front. The plans of the Allies and Russians conformed but their motives were different. The Allies, in the words of the United States Government, intended to 'make use of Russia rather than serve her'.

At this time a new group, the 'National Centre', was formed, consisting of the liberal and conservative elements who were strongly anti-German and who likewise entered into negotiations with the Allied diplomats in Russia. In June 1918 the Allies, through French Ambassador Noulens, agreed to send military forces to help these anti-Bolshevik forces carry on the struggle against Germany and the Soviet régime.

Earlier, the Japanese had landed several detachments in Vladivostok and other strategic points in Siberia, where tremendous supplies of Allied ammunition and raw material were stored. In Siberia there were also large numbers of German and Austrian war prisoners. Ostensibly the Japanese acted to prevent the Germans from gaining access to these stores and utilizing the prisoners. Actually there was reason to believe that the Japanese intended to remain. British, French and American troops were landed in Vladivostok in July 1918 to counteract the Japanese. Most of these troops remained in the vicinity of the port city. About the same time British and American detachments landed at Murmansk and Archangel. After Brest-Litovsk the Czechoslovak Legion of war prisoners, who had fought as volunteers in the Russian Army, were ordered by the Allied Command to proceed to France via Siberia and the Pacific. Thereupon Berlin informed the Soviet Government that Germany would consider the passage of the Czechs as a breach of the Treaty.

Trotsky, the Commissar of War, ordered the legion disarmed. On 26 May when an attempt was made to carry out this order, the Czechs, then in the Volga region, rebelled and arrested the local Soviet officials.[10]

When Lenin was handed a telegraphic report of the Czech uprisings he became extremely agitated. The cabinet meeting was suspended and Rosengoltz, a strong-armed Bolshevik, was dispatched to the Volga, armed with blanket authority.

On 8 June, workers and soldiers allied with the Socialist Revolutionary Party joined the Czechs. And a Committee of 'Members of the All-Russian Constituent Assembly' was formed which began to organize a volunteer People's Army. Cossacks from the Urals joined forces with the Czechs and the People's Army. Within a short time a vast territory from Samara on the Volga to Vladivostok on the Pacific was in the hands of anti-Bolshevik armies. At the same time the Ukraine and other parts of South Russia were held by German and Austrian troops.

In the Don Region, Generals Alexeyev and Kornilov, former commanders in chief of the Russian Army, organized a White Army. In January 1918 their forces numbered 3,000 men. To crush this force, the Bolsheviks sent an army of 10,000. Since the peasant population of the region was not in sympathy with the programme of the generals, their troops were forced to retreat to the steppes. General Kornilov himself was killed in action.[11]

Two months later the remnants of the volunteer army, numbering only about one thousand men, organized a new offensive and this time found recruits among the Cossacks. In June their number increased to 12,000; in July to 30,000. By October 1918 this Army swelled to 100,000 and occupied a front of two hundred miles, under the command of General Denikin.[12]

On 5 July 1918, a group of officers under the command of Boris Savinkov started a revolt in Yaroslavl, one hundred and fifty miles from Moscow. The Soviet forces sent against him seemed headed for defeat until a detachment of German war prisoners came to their aid. On 21 July Savinkov's officers surrendered to a German war prisoners' commission. Despite their promise to treat the officers as prisoners of Germany, Savinkov's officers were turned over to the Soviet authorities, who executed four hundred and twenty-eight of them.

In the summer of 1918 the Left Socialist Revolutionaries – the only non-Bolshevik political group that had supported Lenin and which had participated in the Soviet Government – also staged a revolt. They submitted a five-point programme to the Congress of the Soviets demanding (1) the abolition of the grain-requisitioning squads; (2) the dissolution of the standing Red Army; (3)

the abolition of Dzerzhinsky's secret police, the Cheka; (4) peace with the Czechoslovak Legion, and (5) a declaration of guerrilla warfare against Germany.

Lenin flatly rejected these demands and ordered the arrest of some leading Left Socialist Revolutionaries. With the connivance of several anti-German Chekists, the Left Socialist Revolutionaries then devised a plan for an armed uprising coupled with terrorist acts against German diplomatic representatives in Russia. On 6 July 1918, Blumkin, a Left Socialist Revolutionary, who was armed with credentials of the Cheka, assassinated Count Mirbach, the German Ambassador in Moscow.

With the support of several squads of soldiers and a rebel Cheka detachment, the Left Socialist Revolutionaries arrested Dzerzhinsky and seized a number of public buildings, including the Moscow Telegraph Office. Telegrams were at once dispatched throughout the country, summoning the people to revolt.

With the telephone system still at his command, Lenin acted swiftly. He mobilized the Communist workers of Moscow, under the command of his loyal Lettish guards, and with their aid order was quickly restored in Moscow. Dzerzhinsky was released unharmed.

In the provinces there was still danger because of the peasant following of the Left Socialist Revolutionaries. To Stalin in Tsaritsyn (later Stalingrad) Lenin sent this message: 'We shall liquidate the revolt this very night, ruthlessly, and tell the people the truth, "We are at a hairbreadth from war. . . . It is necessary everywhere ruthlessly to crush these wretched and hysterical adventurers who have become tools of the counter-revolutionaries."'

To this Stalin replied: 'As regards the hysterical ones, you may rest assured that our hand will not falter. We shall treat the enemies as enemies should be treated.'[13]

The assassination of Count Mirbach brought stern protests from Berlin. The Soviet Government promised an investigation and swift punishment for the assassin, but Blumkin was not caught. In order to appease German wrath, Lenin ordered the execution of about twenty Left Socialist Revolutionary hostages.

'We will make an internal loan from our "comrades", the

Socialist Revolutionaries,' Lenin told Krassin, 'and thus both preserve our "innocence" and promote our interests.'[14]

Meanwhile, in the Urals, Left Socialist Revolutionary Muravyev, who was still nominal Commander in Chief of the Red Army, 'declared war' on Germany in a telegram to Berlin on 11 July 1918, and ordered his troops to advance on Moscow. Before his orders could be implemented, however, Muravyev was killed by a Bolshevik commissar. With his death, this revolt also collapsed. But Moscow and Petrograd were still cut off from most of Central Russia, Siberia, the Ukraine, Crimea and the Caucasus.

While the Czechs and Bolsheviks were fighting in the Urals, ex-Tsar Nicholas and his family were executed in Ekaterinburg on 16 July 1918. They had been placed under arrest immediately after the March Revolution and confined to Tsarskoye Selo. In July 1917, when the Bolshevik trend developed in Petrograd, the Provisional Government had sent them to Tobolsk, Siberia. In March 1918 the Bolshevik organization of the Urals demanded that the former Tsar's family be removed to Ekaterinburg, where they would be in 'safe hands'.

Soon after the arrival of Nicholas, his wife, and children in Ekaterinburg, the leaders of the local Soviet began to discuss their execution. The majority, however, refused to assume responsibility without Moscow's approval. The local Bolshevik leader Goloschokin was sent to settle the fate of the Romanovs.

At first the Central Committee debated the advisability of holding a public trial in Ekaterinburg, but the precarious military situation forced this plan to be abandoned. The Czechoslovak Legion was approaching Ekaterinburg. The verdict was death for Nicholas and his family and the destruction of the bodies 'in order not to give the counter-revolutionaries an opportunity of using the "bones" of the Tsar to play on the ignorance and superstition of the masses.' A special commission was appointed to carry out this order.

'On 16 July', relates Bykov, one of the Ural commissars, 'the persons named to execute the sentence of the Romanovs congregated in the chamber of the Commandant of Ipatyev's house, where the Tsar's family resided. It was decided to bring the entire family into the cellar and there carry out the sentence. Until the very last moment the Romanovs were unaware that they were to be executed. At midnight they were awakened, ordered to dress, and go down to the cellar. In order not to arouse their suspicions, they were told that a 'White' attack upon the house was expected that night. All the other inmates of the house were ordered to assemble in the cellar as well. When they had all congregated, the verdict was read to them and all the eleven members of the Romanov family, Nicholas, his wife, his son Alexei, his four daughters, and the members of his suite were shot on the spot.'

The bodies were wrapped in blankets, loaded on a truck, and driven to a deserted mine shaft several miles beyond the city. There they were temporarily deposited. The next morning the work of destroying them was begun. It was not until the afternoon of 18 July that this task was completed.

The mission was carried out by a detachment of Lettish Chekists, under the command of Yurovsky, a member of the Ural Soviet. The bodies were hacked to pieces with axes, soaked in benzine and sulphuric acid, and burned. The charred remains were dumped into a swamp some distance from the mine, and the soggy ground was raked up and covered with moss and leaves to hide all traces.

'The Soviet power', Bykov later wrote, 'liquidated the Romanovs in an extraordinary fashion. The Soviet power in this incident displayed its extremely democratic nature. It made no exception for the All-Russian murderer and shot him as one shoots an ordinary bandit.'[15]

Official announcement of the execution was made to the Sovnarcom on 18 July by Sverdlov, a day after Lenin had received a full report by direct wire.

The Sovnarcom was in the midst of discussing the draft of a new public health decree. Commissioner of Health Semashko was speaking, when Sverdlov walked into the room and seated himself near Lenin. When Semashko had concluded, Sverdlov whispered something to Lenin.

'Comrade Sverdlov asks the floor to make an announcement,' Lenin said.

'I wish to announce,' said Sverdlov, 'that we have received a report that in Ekaterinburg, in accordance with the decision of the regional Soviet, Nicholas has been shot. Nicholas wanted to escape. The Czechoslovaks were approaching the city. The presidium of the Central Executive Committee has decided to approve this act.' There was no comment.

'Now let us proceed to read the draft point by point,' Lenin resumed. The Sovnarcom returned to the health decree.[16]

On 19 July 1918, *Izvestia* published an official announcement of the execution of the former Tsar which stated that 'the wife and son of Nicholas Romanov were sent to a safe place'. Apparently the extermination of the former Tsarina, the Tsarevich, and his four sisters, was too unsavoury for the public. Moreover, no code of laws, even revolutionary justice, could admit the 'execution' of the former Tsar's physician, cook, chambermaid and waiter.

The night following the death of the former Tsar seven other members of the Romanov family were executed in a town in the Urals. Earlier, Grand Duke Mikhail had been shot in Perm. Trotsky asked Sverdlov who had made the decision to kill the entire Imperial family. 'We decided it here,' Sverdlov replied. 'Ilyich believed we shouldn't leave the Whites a live banner to rally around. . . .' Trotsky commented later: 'Under judicial procedures, of course, execution of the family would have been impossible. The Tsar's family fell victim to that principle which constitutes the axis of monarchy: dynastic succession.'[17]

For Lenin, the wholesale liquidation of the Romanovs was but the fulfilment of what he had written several years before: 'If in such a cultured country as England, which had never known either a Mongolian yoke, the oppression of bureaucracy, or the arbitrary rule of a military caste, it was necessary to behead one crowned brigand in order to teach the kings to be "constitutional" monarchs, then in Russia it is necessary to behead at least one hundred Romanovs. . . .'[18]

Ruthless and violent action against all potential enemies was now the order of the day. 'One becomes ridiculous', wrote the prominent Chekist, Latsis, in *Izvestia* of 23 August, 'when one demands that we adhere to laws which were held sacred at one time. . . . To slaughter all those who were wounded by participating in the battle against us – such is the law of civil war.'

The tone for this action was set by Lenin in his article 'Civil War in the Villages', published in August 1918:

The kulak cherishes a fierce hatred for the Soviet Government and is prepared to strangle and massacre hundreds of thousands of workers.

We know very well that if the kulaks were to gain the upper hand they would ruthlessly slaughter hundreds of thousands of workers, would join in alliance with the landlords and capitalists, restore penal conditions for the workers, abolish the eight-hour day, and once again place the mills and factories under the yoke of the capitalists.

Doubt is out of the question. The kulaks are rabid foes of the Soviet Government. Either the kulaks massacre vast numbers of workers, or the workers ruthlessly suppress the uprisings of the predatory kulak minority of the people against the government of the toilers. There can be no middle course.

These vampires have been gathering the landed estates into their hands; they are once more enslaving the poor peasants.

Ruthless war must be waged on the kulaks! Death to them! Hatred and contempt for the parties which support them – the Right Socialist Revolutionaries, the Mensheviks, and now the Left Socialist Revolutionaries! The workers must crush the kulak revolts with an iron hand, for the kulaks have formed an alliance with the foreign capitalists against the toilers of their own country.[19]

In his orders to his subordinates Lenin minced no words. His directives were brief and demanded action. The following order of 9 August 1918, is a typical example:

It is necessary to organize an extra guard of well-chosen, trustworthy men. They must carry out a ruthless mass terror against the kulaks, priests, and White Guards. All suspicious persons should be detained in a concentration camp outside the city. The punitive expedition should be sent out at once. Wire about the execution of this order.

Chairman of the Sovnarcom, LENIN.

The same day, in a wire to the Nizhnii Novgorod Soviet, Lenin said:

In Nizhni Novgorod there are clearly preparations for a White Guard uprising. We must gather our strength, set up a dictorial *troika* and institute mass terror 'immediately'; shoot and ferret out hundreds of prostitutes who get the soldiers drunk, former officers, etc. Not a moment of delay. It is necessary to act all-out. Mass searches, execution for concealment of weapons. Mass seizures of Mensheviks and other unreliables.

Two days later Lenin cabled again:

In putting down the uprisings make every effort and employ every possible measure to confiscate from their holders all surpluses of bread, to the last grain, carrying this out simultaneously with suppressing the rebellions. To accomplish this, select from every district (do not take, but select by name) hostages from among the kulaks, the rich and the oppressors of their neighbours, and charge them with the duty of gathering, delivering, and turning over to the authorities all surplus bread in the district. The hostages answer with their lives for the speedy and thorough execution of their task.

Chairman of the Sovnarcom, LENIN.[20]

On 20 August, he wired the executive committee in Livny:

Congratulations on the energetic suppression of the kulaks in the district. It is necessary to forge while the iron is hot, and not lose a minute in organizing the poor in the district, confiscate all the grain and property of the rebellious kulaks, hang the instigators among the kulaks, and take hostages among the rich. . . .

And, some weeks later, he cabled the staff of the Fifth Army in Sviazhsk:

Certain that the suppression of the Kazan Czechs and White Guards, as well as the blood-drinking kulaks who supported them, will be of exemplary ruthlessness.[21]

Lenin considered such tactics essential to his ends. 'That we brought civil war to the village', he wrote in a polemic with Karl Kautsky, 'is something that we hold up as a merit.'[22]

Almost from the beginning of Soviet rule there were rumours of plots on Lenin's life, and as his régime adopted increasingly repressive measures, the fears for his safety increased. In January 1918 an unidentified assailant had fired at Lenin's car but missed his mark, his bullet inflicting a slight wound on Platten, the former Swiss Socialist who had joined the Communist Party.

On Friday 30 August 1918, Lenin was to speak at a labour rally in Moscow. Among the late-comers in the hall was a woman who sat close to the platform, resting her elbows on the table, listening carefully to every word that was spoken, while nervously puffing one cigarette after another.

Lenin arrived on schedule and spoke for only a few minutes. Then he descended the platform, put on his hat and coat, and left the hall, preceded by several workers and followed by a large crowd. The chain-smoking woman left at the same time.

Lenin emerged into the open court of the building, where an

automobile was waiting for him. At the door he was accosted by the same woman who asked him some questions. As he walked towards his waiting car Lenin tried to answer her. He had one foot on the running-board when she fired three shots at him, point-blank, from a distance of only a few feet. Lenin dropped to the ground. 'They've killed Lenin! They've killed Lenin!' someone shouted. The excited crowd surged forward, then scattered in confusion. But Lenin got back on his feet and asked to be driven home. With the help of his chauffeur and bystanders, he staggered into his car and took his usual seat. The car sped at breakneck speed to the Kremlin.

'About half-way there,' relates his chauffeur, 'he slumped against the back of the car. He didn't groan, didn't moan, in fact, he made no noise at all. His face was pale. The comrade sitting next to him supported him. Finally we reached the Kremlin. All three of us helped Lenin get out of the car. He stepped heavily, leaning on us and seemingly in pain, but still uttering no words. We asked him: "Shall we carry you in?" He refused. We begged him to let us carry him inside but he wouldn't yield and said: "I will go myself," and turning to me he said: "Take my coat off; I will feel more comfortable."

'I took off his coat and, again leaning on us, he started up a winding stairway to the third floor. While walking up he did not say a word. We came to the door, rang the bell, and they opened the door for us. I led Lenin into the bedroom and put him in his bed. I tried to take his shirt off, but couldn't do it. I had to cut it away.'

His condition was not so grave as it seemed at first, despite the fact that one bullet pierced his neck and another his collarbone.

The woman who had tried to assassinate Lenin was captured a few blocks from the scene. She was leaning against a tree breathing hard. In one hand she held an umbrella, in another a brief-case. She was brought to the Lubianka late that night. At the Cheka hearing she wrote:

My name is Fanya Kaplan. . . . Today I shot at Lenin. I did it on my own. I will not say from whom I obtained the revolver. I will give no details. . . . I had resolved to kill Lenin long ago. I consider him a traitor to the Revolution. . . . I was exiled to Akatoi for participating in an assassination attempt against a Tsarist official in Kiev. I spent eleven years at hard labour. . . . After the Revolution I was freed. . . . I favoured the Constituent Assembly and am still for it. . . . My parents are in the United States. They emigrated in 1911. I have four brothers and two sisters. They are all workers. I was educated at home. I shot at Lenin.[23]

Three days later, on 3 September, the commandant of the Kremlin, Pavel Malkov, a Baltic Fleet sailor, led Fanya Kaplan from a cell in the Kremlin basement and ordered her to march out into the courtyard. 'With twitching shoulders', Malkov later wrote, 'Fanya Kaplan took one step, then another. I took aim. Vengeance was done.' When Malkov asked Sverdlov where she should be buried, Sverdlov replied: 'We will not bury Kaplan. Her remains are to be destroyed so that not a trace remains.'[24]

In Petrograd, on the same day Fanya Kaplan attempted to kill Lenin, a young Jewish student named Leonid Kanegiesser assassinated the chief of the Petrograd Cheka, Uritsky.

The murder of Uritsky and the attempt on Lenin were followed by a period of unbridled terror in Petrograd, as Red Army bands combed the streets in search of bourgeois and intellectuals. Only Communists and important service men felt safe. Arrests were spontaneous; no questions were asked, no quarter given.

Zinoviev could tell the masses of soldiers: 'The bourgeoisie kill separate individuals; but we kill whole classes.' Inflamed by slogans of this sort, the soldiers went about their bloody work with redoubled vigour. Kanegiesser, the slayer of Uritsky, was killed without a trial, and Kronstadt's sailors added fuel to the rising flame of civil war by shooting nearly five hundred of the bourgeois hostages held in the prison of the Baltic bastion.[25]

The Commissar of Internal Affairs, G. Petrovsky, broadcast the following order to all the local Soviets:

. . . Sentimentalizing and laxness must be done away with. All the right-wing Socialist Revolutionaries known to the local Soviet authorities should immediately be placed under arrest. A considerable number of hostages should be taken from bourgeois and officer ranks. The slightest show of resistance or the slightest move made by the White Guardist circles should be met unreservedly by mass executions. The Executive Committee of the local Soviet should display special initiative in this direction.[26]

The Bolshevik press echoed the sentiments of the party leadership in demanding blood. 'For the life of one of our fighters, thousands of our enemies must pay with their lives', cried the Petrograd *Krasnaya Gazetta:* 'Enough! We have been fooling around with them too long! Our enemies are merciless. Let us be merciless likewise! Let us teach the bourgeoisie a bloody lesson to crush out of them, once and for all time, all thought of violence against the living! Comrades, sailors, workers, and soldiers, destroy the remnant of the White Guard and the bourgeoisie, so that nothing is left of them. Death to the bourgeoisie! The slogan of the day shall be: "Death to the bourgeoisie!"'

And the Moscow *Pravda* wrote on 31 August 1918:

Workers! If you do not now destroy the bourgeoisie it will destroy you. Prepare for a mass attack on the enemies of the Revolution. We must eradicate the bourgeoisie, just as was done in the case of the army officers, and exterminate all those who are harmful to the Revolution. From now on the hymn of the working class will be a hymn of hate and revenge, even more terrifying than the hymn of hate that is sung in Germany against England. The counter-revolution, this vicious mad dog, must be destroyed once and for all!

Even before the attempt on Lenin's life, in the 'Catechism of a Class-conscious Proletarian' *Pravda*, on 4 August 1918, had preached mass terror against the enemies of the Soviet régime:

Workers and paupers, grab the rifle, learn how to shoot, be prepared for the uprising of the kulaks and White Guards. Stand up against the wall those who agitate against the Soviet power. Ten bullets to everyone who raises a hand against it! . . .

The bourgeoisie is our eternal enemy, forever boring from within. The rule of capital will die with the last breath of the last capitalist, nobleman, priest, and army officer.[27]

On 2 September forty-six men and women were shot by order of the Nizhnii Novgorod Cheka. 'For every Communist killed or every attempt on the life of a Communist,' pledged the Nizhnii Novgorod *Workers' and Peasants' Gazette,* 'we shall exact the death of the living hostages of the bourgeoisie, for the blood of our murdered martyrs and wounded cries out for revenge.'

In the space of a few days the Petrograd Cheka shot 512 hostages. The *Severnaya Kommuna,* the official organ of the Petrograd Soviet (evening edition of 18 September 1918), reported a meeting of the Soviet of the First Urban District of Petrograd, to discuss the general political situation. In the course of the meeting, Zinoviev, the head of the Petrograd Commune, declared: 'To overcome our enemies we must have our own socialist militarism. We must win over to our side ninety millions out of the hundred millions of the inhabitants of Russia under the Soviets. As for the rest, we have nothing to say to them; they must be annihilated.' After speeches by other members, a resolution was passed which contained the following passages: 'The meeting welcomes the fact that WHOLE-SALE TERROR is being adopted against the White Guards and upper bourgeois classes, and declares that every attempt on the life of any of our leaders will be followed by the proletariat shooting of not only hundreds, as is the case now, but thousands of White Guards, bankers, manufacturers, Cadets and "Right" Social Revolutionaries. . . .' The same paper, under the heading 'The Red Terror', reports: 'In Astrakhan the Extraordinary Commission has shot ten "Right" Social Revolutionaries involved in a plot against the Soviet power. In Perm, in connexion with Uritsky's assassination, and for the attempt on Lenin, fifty hostages from among the bourgeoisie and the White Guards were shot.'

The next number of the *Severnaya Kommuna* (19 September) reported: '*Borisoglebsk*, September 16. For an attempt to organize a movement in opposition to the Soviet authorities, nine Counter Revolutionaries were shot; viz. two rich landowners, six merchants, and the local corn king, Vassiliev. *Yaroslav*. In the whole of the Yaroslav province a strict registration of the bourgeoisie and its partisans has been organized. Persons of manifestly anti-Soviet tendencies are being shot.' (According to *Izvestia*, three hundred persons were shot in Yaroslav.) 'Suspected persons are interned in concentration camps; non-labouring sections of the population are subjected to forced labour.' 'In *Penza*, our comrade Egorov was killed; 152 Counter Revolutionaries were shot for it. . . . Twenty other Counter Revolutionaries (mostly officers and priests) were shot in *Krasnoslobodsk*.' Thus one number reported the executions of 172 persons in two small country towns. *Izvestia* of 19 October, No. 28, contained a report of a meeting of the Conference of the Extraordinary Commission: 'Comrade Bokiy gave details of the work of the Petrograd District Commission since the evacuation of the All-Russian Extraordinary Commission to Moscow. The total number of persons arrested was 6,220. *Eight hundred were shot*.' These were official figures only for the district of Petrograd and for a limited period.

On 23 September 1918, Krassin wrote to his wife:

After the assassination of Uritsky and the attempt on Lenin we went through a period of so-called 'Terror', one of the most disgusting acts of the neo-Bolsheviks. About 600 to 700 persons were shot in Moscow and Petrograd, nine-tenths of them having been arrested quite at random or merely on suspicion of belonging to the right wing of the Socialist Revolutionaries, or else of being counter-revolutionists. In the provinces this developed into a series of revolting incidents, such as arrests and mass executions.[28]

The professed aim of the Red Terror was 'to exterminate the bourgeoisie as a class'. But the term 'bourgeoisie' as interpreted by the Cheka was so elastic as to include, potentially at least, virtually every non-Bolshevik. M. Latsis, one of the chiefs of the Cheka, wrote:

We are exterminating the bourgeoisie as a class. Don't look for evidence of proof showing that this or that person either by word or deed acted against the interests of the Soviet power. The first questions you should put to the arrested person is: To what class does he belong, what is his origin, what was his education, and what is his profession? These should determine the fate of the accused. This is the essence of the Red Terror.[29]

The test was often even simpler, according to Sosnovsky, a Soviet journalist:

I remember a meeting held in the headquarters of the Moscow Soviet in 1918. The question being debated was: 'A Cheka or trial by Tribunal?' Arguments were advanced to show that trial by a tribunal protects the innocent and prevents judicial error. On the other hand, the article of Latsis was referred to to show how unnecessary it was to try the enemies of the Revolution and that it was enough merely to know the name, origin, education, and occupation of the accused to determine his fate.
Then a workman by the name of Muzikin from the Lefertov precinct took the floor and said heatedly:
'Why even ask those questions? I'll just walk into his house and look into his pots. If there is meat in them, then he is an enemy of the people and should be stood up against the wall'.

When Angelica Balabanov protested against the reign of terror she had witnessed in the Ukraine, Lenin intimated with a sardonic smile that her usefulness to the Bolshevik cause was about over.

Later, when she expressed her indignation over the execution of a group of Mensheviks, Lenin replied: 'Don't you understand that if we do not shoot these few leaders we may be placed in a position where we would need to shoot ten thousand workers?'[30]

In an address delivered during this period before the Cheka, Lenin expressed his surprise at the outcries against the shooting of innocent people. We learn from mistakes, he asserted. The important thing was that the Cheka was putting teeth into the dictatorship.

'When I study the activities of the Cheka,' said Lenin in 1918, 'and at the same time hear the numerous criticisms that are made against it, I say that all that is idle talk of the petit bourgeois. . . .

'It is very likely that undesirable outside elements have penetrated the Cheka. We shall drive them out through self-criticism. The important thing to us, however, is the fact that the Cheka is putting into effect the dictatorship of the proletariat, and in this sense it is of inestimable value. Outside of force and violence, there is no way to suppress the exploiters of the masses. This is the business of the Cheka and in this lies its service to the proletariat.'[31]

Two years later Martov, speaking at the Congress of the German Independent Socialist Party in Halle, declared in the presence of Zinoviev:

'In reprisal for the assassination of Uritsky and the attempt on Lenin – two acts organized by separate individuals with, perhaps, the cooperation of a few people – there were executed in Petrograd, the city ruled by Zinoviev, no less than 800 persons, arrested long before and consisting mainly of officers who had nothing to do with these deeds, and who were held not for any counter-revolutionary activity but because of their alleged opposition to the Revolution. [*Commotion in the hall. Cries directed at Zinoviev:* "*Hangman! Bandit!*"]

'A list of these victims was published in *Izvestia* at that time and Zinoviev cannot deny the facts. Among those executed, incidentally, was a member of our party, Krakowski, a metalworker. [*Cries of protest and resentment.*] Nor can Zinoviev deny that similar massacres were carried out in all the cities of Russia upon the direct recommendation of the Central Government in a circular broadcast by Petrovsky, Commissar for Internal Affairs. . . .

'The very fact that the wives of political opponents – even

though these opponents be counter-revolutionists – or their sons are taken as hostages and that on many occasions these hostages have been shot in revenge for the acts of their husband and father is evidence enough of the extent of the terror.'[32]

The Bolshevik *Red Sword* wrote on 18 August 1919:

Ours is a new morality. Our humanism is absolute, for it has as its basis the desire for abolition of all oppression and tyranny. To us everything is permitted, for we are the first in the world to raise the sword not for the purpose of enslavement and oppression but in the name of liberty and emancipation from slavery. We do not wage war against individuals. We seek to destroy the bourgeoisie as a class.

In October 1918 Lenin had blandly denied the charges of terrorism directed at the Bolsheviks. He had declared that Kautsky and 'all the heroes of the Yellow International lie about Soviet Russia on the question of terrorism and democracy'. And at the Seventh Congress of the Soviets he said: 'Terror was imposed upon us. . . . People forget that terrorism was brought forth by the invasion of the world power of the Allies.' The factual record of this period is a refutation of this apology.

Despite the widespread terror, the civil war and the demoralization of the peasantry continued to push Russia farther towards economic ruin. The harvest of 1918 was less than a tenth that of the same area in 1916. On 8 October 1918, the régime nationalized all domestic trade. All shops, great and small, were closed and their inventory used for barter with the peasants.

Lenin also prepared the draft of a decree outlining how he proposed to force all able-bodied men and women to serve the state:

'Every toiler having worked eight hours during the day is obliged to devote three hours to military or administrative duties.

'Everyone belonging to the nobility or the well to do (an income of not less than five hundred rubles a month or has a capital of not less than fifteen hundred rubles) is obliged to obtain a workbook wherein shall be recorded whether or not he has performed his share in military or administrative service. The recording is to be done by the trade union, the Soviet, or the staff of the local Red Guard. The well to do can obtain this book on the payment of fifty rubles.

'Non-workers who do not belong to the wealthy classes are

also required to have such a workbook, which they can obtain for five rubles. For failure to secure such a book or for false entries in it, punishment is to be meted out according to military law.

'All those who possess weapons must obtain a permit for same, first from the house committee, second from the institutions enumerated in paragraph two. Without such permits it shall be unlawful to possess arms. For non-compliance with this law, the offender is to be shot. The same punishment is to be imposed upon all who conceal food.'

This decree, not made public at the time, was published in the Bolshevik press in 1927.[33]

When the decree for the full nationalization of all industrial and commercial enterprises was promulgated, the Soviet state really consisted largely of a few offices in Moscow and Petrograd, whose managers had little practical experience. The 'plan' existed mainly in the brain of Mikhail (Yuri) Larin.

Larin was an old right-wing Menshevik who had lived for many years in Germany as the correspondent of Russian Liberal newspapers. During the war he resided in Copenhagen, and studied the so-called 'military Socialism' of Germany. During the war he thus became an expert in the problems of a planned economy.

When Larin returned to Russia, after the March Revolution, he favoured an immediate separate peace with Germany; because of this he finally joined the Bolshevik Party.

In the summer of 1918 Lenin made Larin the main architect of Socialist construction. He was the author of the decree for nationalization of all industries, large and small. He created, mainly on paper, a system of central institutions for every branch of industry and commerce. All private stores were closed and the merchandise confiscated. With Russia's economy already undermined by war and civil conflict, Larin in effect destroyed the remnants.

When the non-Communist specialist, Lieberman, reported to Lenin on the sad state of the lumber industry as a result of Larin's decrees, Lenin interrupted him with these words: 'Of course we make mistakes, but there are no revolutions without mistakes. We learn from our mistakes, but we are glad we can correct them.'

As for the latest Larin decrees Lenin remarked: 'We are engaged in making revolution. Our Power may not last long, but these decrees will become part of history and future revolutionaries

T-o

will learn from them. They may learn something from Larin's decrees which you consider senseless. We have before us as patterns the decrees of the Paris Commune!'[34]

The population was forbidden to produce or trade, and at the same time the state was not only unable to build new industries but to manage the existing ones. Opening a small factory or shop was prohibited under pain of being shot as a 'counter-revolutionist' or speculator. But there was no trace of state-organized commerce. Economic catastrophe followed. Raw materials disappeared together with consumers' goods and industrial products. The little that remained in private hands vanished from the markets. But although state factories could obtain nothing, there was an active black market where enormous speculation flourished. The result was disastrous inflation. And when the cities were unable to supply the villages with products, the peasants refused to bring their bread and meat to the cities. A great part of the city workers who had come from the villages deserted the hungry cities. The cities were emptied not only of workers but of all who could find food in the villages. Because of the scarcity of labour and materials, hundreds of factories closed down.

To feed at least the essential workers and the administrators, the régime had to send troops to the village to collect bread and grain by force. But the peasants resisted and armed revolts broke out. The peasants in 1918–19 were mostly ex-soldiers who had returned from the front with their rifles, machine-guns and grenades. Thus a war for bread flared in the villages. The city came to take grain but the peasant didn't want to surrender it, because the paper currency had no value. These forced requisitions drove hundreds of thousands of peasants into the arms of the counter-revolution.

The ravaged villages often joined the anti-Bolshevik forces. In the Ukraine one heard that the peasants favoured the 'Bolsheviks' who took the land from nobles, but were opposed to the 'Communists' who sent requisitioning squads. The peasants also replied with sabotage, refusing to produce. Crops dropped to the point where only enough was planted and harvested for local village consumption but nothing for the cities.

At one of the conferences of the Council for Labour and Defence, Lieberman proposed that several tons of bread and oats be designated for the peasants who were to deliver firewood to the cities and railways. One of the Commissars opposed the plan, explaining that this would entail reducing the already meagre bread rations of the city workers.

Alexei Rykov, the vice-chairman of the Sovnarcom, then took the floor.

'We are able, thank God, by dint of our revolutionary pathos, to get our workers and peasants accustomed to working even without bread. But unfortunately we could not get our horses accustomed to it. You may declare the horses to be counter-revolutionary, but you cannot ignore the fact and you must give them oats.'

Turning to Dzerzhinsky, Rykov said: 'Even Felix Edmundovich can do little about it. Let him try to shoot a few dozen horses.'

Lenin closed the discussion and dictated an order to issue bread and oats for the peasants.[35]

In this atmosphere of economic chaos and recurrent civil war, Lenin became more absorbed in the work of the Cheka. At the same time he became increasingly nervous and irritable. According to Naglovsky, 'He frequently lost all self-control at Sovnarcom meetings. This had never happened before. The old conspirator Lenin was clearly wearing out, and this was not because of illness alone. At times, looking at Lenin's tired face, with its contemptuous smile, as he listened to reports or issued orders, it seemed that Lenin saw what mediocrity surrounded him. And his tired grimace seemed to say: "Yes, with such material we'll never emerge from this bog."'

In November 1918 Roman Malinovsky, whom Lenin had reported dead in 1915, suddenly appeared in Moscow. No one was sure what had happened to him after his last conference with Lenin in Cracow following his resignation from the Duma. Badayev, the Bolshevik Duma deputy, writes that he was drafted when the war began and was taken prisoner by the Germans. According to another version, Malinovsky had been in constant contact with Lenin, who entrusted him with the task of carrying on Bolshevik propaganda among Russian prisoners of war.

Now he was brought before a Bolshevik Revolutionary Tribunal to face the very charges Lenin had labelled as slander years before. Malinovsky's trial was held behind closed doors with Lenin present throughout. Malinovsky made no attempt to deny the documented charges brought against him. He told the court that at the time he left the Duma he made a full confession to Lenin. But he tried to convince the court that he was a victim of circumstance. He claimed that serving the Okhrana had been a terrible personal tragedy for him. When arrested for the first time and offered the job of a police agent, he said, he had refused but finally succumbed when the Okhrana threatened to reveal his criminal past. Malinovsky used his full oratorical talents in a six-hour defence speech. 'I am not asking for mercy!' he cried. 'I know what is in store for me. I deserve it.'

'Why did you never forget to receive your monthly pay from the Okhrana?' the presiding judge asked. 'Why did you accept the 6,000 rubles' compensation? You were evidently more interested in the money than in your so-called tragedy.'

'If I refused to accept the money the Okhrana would have suspected me of playing a double game,' Malinovsky answered. 'I had to show that I was faithful.'

'But you had already proved that by delivering our best comrades to the police,' the judge replied. Malinovsky remained silent.

'Despite this pose of sincere self-accusation and penitence,' Badayev writes, 'Malinovsky, at the most decisive moment of his life, told a lie. According to the testimony of the leaders of the Moscow Okhrana, who had no reason to lie, Malinovsky, after his first arrest and first examination by the Tsarist gendarmerie, offered his services as an informer. There is also evidence to prove that two or three years before that first arrest Malinovsky voluntarily supplied the St Petersburg Okhrana with information.

'Malinovsky's life was a series of crimes, his talents, his mind, and his will being used for one purpose: to sell himself at the highest possible price where he could do the most possible harm to the liberation of the working class. He will go down in history as one of its greatest traitors.'[36]

Lenin sat facing Malinovsky, his head bent over a desk while he wrote on a pad. It was obvious, according to Olga Anikst, a Bolshevik witness, that Lenin was undergoing an emotional conflict. He remained in the same position for hours. When the defence counsel said that if Malinovsky had had friends to guide him he would never have become a spy, Lenin stirred, looked up at Malinovsky, and nodded his head many times.[37]

When the verdict of death by shooting was read, Malinovsky began to tremble and his face was distorted by fear. He had obviously expected Lenin's intercession. It is possible that before appearing he had been promised clemency. Lenin himself was undecided. A delegation of Petrograd Bolshevik workers attending the trial demanded to be allowed to witness the execution, apparently fearing that Lenin might commute the sentence of the *agent provocateur* who once enjoyed his full confidence. The next day *Izvestia* reported that Malinovsky had been shot. The minutes of the trial were never published.

In a political report to the Central Committee, Lenin demanded the constant increase of Soviet military strength. 'The existence of the Soviet Republic side by side with imperialist states for a long time is unthinkable', he said. 'One or the other must triumph in the end. . . . And before that end comes, a series of frightful clashes between the Soviet Republic and the bourgeois states is inevitable.'

In May 1919 General Yudenich launched an offensive which soon carried his forces to the gates of Petrograd, cradle of the Bolshevik Revolution. Efforts to organize a workers' militia proved ineffectual, and the fall of the city was expected hourly. Zinoviev, the party boss of the city, was convinced that the Finns would also attack Petrograd.

At that moment when Zinoviev, gathering his staff in Smolny, shouted, 'You shall all remain here! At least for three days! I will not allow anyone to leave!' news came that Trotsky was on his way from Moscow. Meanwhile, Lenin telephoned Ganetsky in the middle of the night: 'Pardon me for awakening you, but there is some highly urgent business. The Council of Defence has an important and secret task for you. The fact is that Yudenich is pressing us very hard in the region of Petrograd, and our blockheads in the city have been unable to organize an adequate defence. We are sending large reinforcements and undertaking decisive measures. But we do not know whether to destroy the State Paper Manufacturing Plant. If it cannot be done in any other way, it will be necessary to blow up the plant.'

This meant cutting off the supply of currency, but Lenin was adamant. The alternative was the risk that Yudenich would get his hands on the plant.[38]

When Trotsky arrived in Petrograd, the atmosphere quickly changed. He summoned the party military leaders, asked for situation reports, and turning to his secretary, whenever their answers displeased him, ordered curtly: 'Record what has been said!'

Trotsky stood in the middle of Zinoviev's office; at the door were his Cheka aide, Pavlunovsky, wearing a cavalry greatcoat, and Komarov, chief of the special section of the Petrograd Cheka. At the table sat the secretary taking notes. And before Trotsky stood the terrified Chief of Military Communications for Petrograd, Araratov.

'How much time is needed for the transfer of troops from the Finland to the Baltic Station?' Trotsky shouted at Araratov.

'About twenty-four hours.'

'What! Sabotage! Record what was said!' Trotsky shouted, and, turning to Pavlunovsky, added: 'Arrest him!'

Pavlunovsky and Komarov were already moving towards Araratov, and if all present had not interceded for him he would have been shot at once. It was explained to Trotsky that it was not necessary to move troops from station to station by train, because they could cover that distance more rapidly on foot.

Before Zinoviev had time to utter a single word, Trotsky turned to Pavlunovsky and said in his resonant voice calculated to reach all present: 'Comrade Pavlunovsky, I command you to arrest immediately and shoot the entire staff for the defence of Petrograd!'[39]

That same night Pavlunovsky carried out the summary execution of the staff. Yudenich did not take Petrograd.

At the same time the dictatorship, supposedly a dictatorship of the proletariat, consolidated its power and was transformed into a dictatorship of the Communist Party. As soon as Lenin had returned to Russia, it is to be remembered, he had insisted that the Bolsheviks change the name of their party to Communist Party and thus disassociate themselves from the now ignominious designation of Social Democrat. A resolution to this effect had been passed on 9 March 1918, at the Seventh Congress of the Bolshevik Party. It is this Communist Party that now gathered all reins of power in its hands and gradually eliminated all opposition parties, groups and movements.

In a formal sense, supreme power was vested in the Sovnarcom and the Executive Committee elected by the All-Russian Soviets of Workers' and Peasants' delegates. But actually the Soviet itself was now an instrument of the Central Committee of the Communist Party. At the Party's Eighth Congress in 1919 Zinoviev declared: 'The fundamental questions of international and internal policy are decided by the Central Committee of our Party. That is the Communist Party, which carries through its decisions through the Soviets. The Central Committee does this skilfully and tactfully, so as not to step on the toes of the Sovnarcom and other institutions. And the Central Committee of the Party has most successfully met this task. Publicly it is the Sovnarcom, but the decisions are made by the Central Committee of our Party.'

Over the Central Committee was its all-powerful Politburo, set up in March 1919, and consisting of Lenin, Trotsky, Kamenev, Bukharin and Stalin.

At the Ninth Congress in 1920 the Politburo was increased to seven members: Lenin, Stalin, Trotsky, Kamenev, Bukharin, Preobrazhensky and Serebriakov. (All of these men, with the exception of Lenin, were later liquidated by Stalin.) The Party Secretariat consisted of three: Krestinsky (executed in 1938), Preobrazhensky and Serebriakov.

The relationship of party and government was thus described by Lenin in 1920:

We are afraid that the Party will be too large because to a ruling government inevitably gravitate careerists and scoundrels who only deserve to be shot. The Party is led by a Central Committee of nineteen people. The current work is done in Moscow by a small collegium, by the Organizational Bureau and by the Politburo. . . . Out of this emerges a 'real oligarchy'! Not one important political or organizational question in our state institution is decided without the direction of the Central Committee of the Party.

In his report to the Eleventh Party Congress, Zinoviev, then president of the Comintern, defined the role of the Communist Party as follows:

'I am speaking concerning the fact that we constitute the single legal party in Russia; that we maintain a so-called monopoly on legality. We have taken away political freedom from our opponents; we do not permit the legal existence of those who strive to compete with us. We have clamped a lock on the lips of the Mensheviks and the Socialist Revolutionaries. We could not have acted otherwise, I think. The dictatorship of the proletariat, Comrade Lenin says, is a very terrible undertaking. It is not possible to ensure the victory of the dictatorship of the proletariat without breaking the backbone of all opponents of the dictatorship. No one can appoint the time when we shall be able to revise our attitude on this question.'

Chapter 18
In The Kremlin

On 1 May 1918 Lenin stood on the Kremlin wall, where Napoleon once had watched Moscow burning, and gazed down at the May Day demonstration in Red Square.

'The most important thing is not to lose constant contact with the masses,' he told his companion. 'One must be in touch with the life of the masses.' And he asked what the crowd was saying, what their mood was, was their demonstration spontaneous or artificial?[1]

Settled under the same ancient bulb-shaped cupolas and church walls where centuries of Russian autocrats had been crowned, the new master lived a very frugal existence. The rooms adjoining his apartment smelled of cats and carbolic acid. Sharing the apartment were Krupskaya, his sister Maria, and their maid. They ate out of the Tsar's silver and china, but their food was rather tasteless and often insufficient. Despite their red caviar, occasional butter, cheese, and jelly, it was poor fare compared to the table of an ordinary citizen before the Revolution. There was never enough firewood to heat the rooms properly, nor sufficient teaspoons for their guests.

'We are good revolutionists,' said Lenin, 'but I don't know why we feel obligated to prove that we also stand on the heights of foreign culture. As for myself, I don't hesitate to declare myself a barbarian.'

Lenin enjoyed incognito contact with the common people of Moscow, talking with the man on the street, the common labourer and peasant, to get their honest opinions on the Bolshevik cause. He often rode beyond the city to chat with plain people. Once, when hunting in the woods near Moscow, he was approached by an old man who was picking mushrooms. 'How are things, Grandpa?' asked Lenin. 'Have you found enough mushrooms?'

'To the devil with the Bolsheviks!' answered the old man. 'Under their rule even mushrooms don't grow.'

'What's the matter? Don't you like the new government?'

'Why should I? They've stolen and destroyed everything.'

'Wait, wait, old man,' replied Lenin, 'when we build our factories we will have enough.'

Korotov, who was Lenin's secretary at the time, describes how Lenin attempted to 'educate' his commissars. When one of them bungled a job, he was summoned by Lenin, who asked him point-blank: 'Do you admit being in the wrong?' If he did, Lenin handed him pen and paper, ordering him to 'write a reprimand to himself'. The worker would compose the text and Lenin would endorse it: 'To be published as an order.'

Lenin's day began at 11 a.m. and often ended at six the next morning. He rose at ten. At eleven he was at his desk reading the papers. Interviews and conferences followed according to schedule. A blackboard in his office recorded all his conference appointments for the day; a time limit was set for all interviews.

Promptly at five each evening Lenin left his office for dinner. He always dined at exactly the same hour and trained all his associates to do likewise. 'One can work and rest at any time,' he would say, 'but dinner must be eaten regularly at the same hour!' He saw to it that Krupskaya, who held the post of Deputy People's Commissar of Education, also dined at the proper time. Every day Lenin sent his chauffeur to pick her up, instructing him: 'Do not wait until she comes down, but go up to her office and insist on her coming home to dine at once.'

At 7 p.m. Lenin was back in his office for cabinet conferences. But many times he interrupted his meal to telephone his secretary:

'How about it, Comrade Dmitriev? Are the Commissars there?'

'So far only three of them have shown up.'

'Not enough. It is five to seven. We must hustle!'

When the meetings of the Sovnarcom ended, usually at one or two in the morning, Lenin was generally the last to leave, and always with the same parting message, 'If there is something important, call me up.' Back in his apartment, he continued working until five or six in the morning.

Lenin was a skilful chairman who did not allow debates to turn into a discussion of unnecessary detail. Not more than ten minutes was allowed per speaker to discuss even the most important matters. But if a particularly significant point came up he would begin to make notes rapidly.

The key words in his notes were always underscored two or

three times and the final decision in a vertical line. Suddenly he would stop the speaker and begin to read what he had jotted down: his draft of a resolution or decree or an amendment to the law that was being discussed.[2]

Work was a stimulant to Lenin's strength. It was he, Mstislavsky, recalls, who soothed the frayed nerves of his colleagues. He cites meetings of the Defence Council, where the members, after a hard day's work on perhaps sixty items of an economic and military nature, 'would frequently show signs of fatigue and exasperation, and that, of course, was reflected in the character of the debate. The fresh, contagious laugh of Lenin usually served as a tonic on such occasions. He enjoyed the fun of those meetings and seemed anxious not to miss the slightest opportunity for laughter. His joviality immediately communicated itself to the other members and the tenseness of the atmosphere was relaxed.'

The men around Lenin who were intent on remaking the world were sometimes treated as though they were in a classroom.[3] Smoking was forbidden because Lenin could not tolerate it. But since smoking was a necessity for some, 'the smokers were allowed to use a venthole, one at a time,' says Mstislavsky. 'If any foreigners had been present at these meetings, they certainly would have been amused to see the People's Commissars go up to the venthole with their cigarettes, like schoolboys smoking in secret, take a few puffs, and then return to their seats. Sometimes there would be several men waiting in line to use the venthole and a conversation in whispers would begin, which naturally interfered with the meeting. In the end, Lenin had to disperse the line of smokers.'[4]

While Lenin was a devoted son and brother, he judged his family with the same detachment as he did his friends and colleagues. Only towards his martyred brother Alexander, and his sister Anna, was love coupled with respect. Of Anna he often said: 'Here is a woman with a head on her shoulders. As the peasants say: "She is a regular man." However, she committed an unforgivable folly in marrying that clumsy Mark [Elizarov]. Naturally she treads him under foot.

'As for Manya [Maria], she'll never set the world on fire,' he confessed. As to his younger brother Dmitri, Lenin once remarked to a friend: 'Do you remember how Yershov in his fairy tale characterizes the third brother?

' "The eldest was a wise boy.
' "The middle one was so-so.
' "The third was simply a fool." '

When Dmitri was appointed to a high post in the Crimea, without Lenin's knowledge, he was very much annoyed and told Krassin: 'The idiots evidently wanted to ingratiate themselves with me by appointing Mitya [Dmitri]. They did not notice that although we both answer to the same name, he is simply an ordinary fool, only fit to nibble at literary sweets.'[5]

Lenin's sister Anna often visited him with her husband and children. He always welcomed them warmly and tried to keep them with him as long as possible. On occasion they would go to the woods to pick mushrooms, go boating or play croquet.

It was Anna who would accompany Lenin to visit Krupskaya when Lenin's wife was recuperating from exhaustion and overwork at a sanatorium not far from Moscow. Krupskaya's physician had prescribed two weeks of rest, but she had gone on working. Lenin, as head of the government, officially ordered 'Deputy People's Commissar of Education, Comrade Krupskaya, to take a half month's rest.'

Lenin went to visit her almost every day, and sometimes brought a bottle of milk. Sometimes he walked, but more often he went by car. One Sunday, the car in which Lenin and Anna were riding to the sanatorium was stopped by two men. 'Your money or your life,' they demanded. 'I am Ulyanov-Lenin,' the victim protested. The robbers were unimpressed and repeated, 'Your money or your life.' Lenin had no money. He got out of the car, took off his coat and, without surrendering the bottle of milk, proceeded on foot.[6]

In February 1920, Inessa Armand, who had been an active Bolshevik since her return to Russia with Lenin in April 1917, fell ill. After the Bolshevik Revolution Inessa had become a member of the Soviet Executive Committee, the head of the Moscow Soviet for National Economy, and later chief of the department of women workers in the Bolshevik Central Committee.

When Lenin heard of Inessa's illness, he wrote: 'Please write me what is the matter. The times are bad: typhus, influenza, Spanish flu, cholera. I am just out of bed and do not go out. . . .

What is your temperature? "Don't you need anything" for a cure? I beg you very much to write me frankly. Get well. Your Lenin.'

Later, he wrote her again: 'To leave the house "with fever" is plain insanity. I urgently beg you not to leave the house and tell your daughters "from me" that I beg them to watch and "not let you out" (1) until the complete restoration of normal temperature, and (2) until the doctor permits it.'[7]

In August, Lenin arranged for Inessa to be transferred to a sanatorium in the North Caucasus, at Kislovodsk. Inessa's condition appeared to improve; she played the piano for her friend Polina Vinogradova, who came to visit. But then Inessa had suddenly to be evacuated. A defeated detachment of White soldiers was coming down from the mountains to surrender at Kislovodsk, and the local authorities, fearing disorders, decided to evacuate the patients to Nalchik. *En route* Inessa contracted cholera, and died within a few days.

'At three o'clock in the morning of 11 October', Vinogradova writes, 'I was awakened by the telephone ringing. I did not have time in my sleepy state to grasp what was happening before I heard Lenin's voice on the wire: "Forgive me for wakening you. . . . The coffin with Inessa Armand's body is just arriving at Kazan Station. Are you ready?" '

Lenin, Krupskaya, Inessa's children, and a delegation of women workers including Vinogradova stood by the lead-sealed coffin at Kazan Station. Although Lenin and Krupskaya were invited to get into a car to follow the funeral carriage, they refused.

'We shall follow the coffin on foot,' Lenin said. It was a long journey across Moscow, from the Kazan Station to the House of the Trade Unions.[8]

Angelica Balabanov, who saw Lenin at the funeral, writes: 'I never saw such torment; I never saw any human being so completely absorbed by sorrow, by the effort to keep it to himself, to guard it against the attention of others, as if their awareness could have diminished the intensity of his feeling. . . . Not only his face but his whole body expressed so much sorrow that I dared not greet him, not even with the slightest gesture. It was clear he wanted to be alone with his grief. He seemed to have shrunk; his cap almost covered his face, his eyes seemed drowned in tears held back with effort. As our circle moved, following the movement of the people, he too moved, without offering resistance, as if he were grateful for being brought nearer to the dead comrade.'

Alexandra Kollontai corroborates these observations. Years later she told her friend Marcel Body: 'When Inessa's body was brought from the Caucasus and we accompanied her to the cemetery, Lenin was unrecognizable. He walked with closed eyes; at every moment we thought he would collapse.' Kollontai thought that Lenin 'was not able to go on living after Inessa Armand. The death of Inessa hastened the development of the sickness which was to destroy him.'

In the hectic days of war and civil war, when it seemed at times that all Russia and all the world were against him, Lenin the man retained an interest in his political opponents which seemed at variance with his sharp public speeches. About Martov, his old comrade in exile, he remained privately solicitous to the very end, even when Martov was dying in exile. But Lenin also showed sensitivity to the views of older figures in the Russian democratic movement and tried in his way to gain, at least temporarily, their good-will. These efforts – and the chasm which had opened between Lenin and the older revolutionaries – were well illustrated in the cases of Prince Peter Kropotkin and Vladimir Korolenko.

By the time of the Russian Revolution Kropotkin had been a world figure for three decades. Geologist, explorer, historian and revolutionary anarchist, he had won international renown with his *Memoirs of a Revolutionist* in 1889. He had, early, greeted Liberal, Social Democratic and Socialist Revolutionary foes of the autocracy as allies, but was quick to see the danger of sectarianism presented by 'professional revolutionaries'. In 1909, he wrote:

Every revolutionist dreams about a dictatorship, whether it be a 'dictatorship of the proletariat', *i.e.* of its leaders, as Marx said, or a 'dictatorship of the revolutionary staff', as the Blanquists maintained. . . . They all dream about a revolution as a possible means of destroying their enemies in a legal manner, with the help of a revolutionary tribunal, a public prosecutor, a guillotine. . . . All of them dream of capturing power, of creating a strong, all-powerful, totalitarian state which treats the people as subjects and rules them with thousands of millions of bureaucrats supported by the state. . . . Thinking, say many revolutionists, is an art and a science which is not devised for common people.[9]

When Kropotkin arrived in Petrograd on 10 June 1917, after forty-one years of exile, he was greeted by a crowd of 60,000 people who had waited for him until two in the morning. Moved as he was by 'that crowd of intelligent, bold, proud faces', Kropotkin soon began to feel the war-weariness of the Russian people. The democratic revolution in Russia had made Kropotkin a passionate believer in the Allied cause; and he took part in the Moscow State Conference of August 1917, pleading for a federative system, hailing the coming elections to the Constituent Assembly.

In Moscow, in November 1917, when Kropotkin heard the first cannon volleys of the Bolshevik uprising, he exclaimed: 'This is the burial of the Russian Revolution.' And, shortly after Brest-Litovsk, he described the Bolsheviks to an American observer in this manner:

'They have deluded simple souls. The peace they offer will be paid for with Russia's heart. The land they have been given will go untilled. This is a country of children – ignorant, impulsive, without discipline. It has become the prey of teachers who could have led it along the slow, safe way. . . . There was hope during the summer. The war is bad – I am the enemy of war – but this surrender is no way to end it. The Constituent Assembly was to have met. It could have built the framework of enduring government.'

All this time Kropotkin lived in the small town of Dmitrov, outside Moscow. He kept aloof from politics, although – much as he opposed the Bolsheviks – he disapproved the foreign military intervention once it had become clear that the aims of England, France and Japan were so largely territorial.

On 10 May 1919, however, Kropotkin felt compelled to speak to Lenin. An old friend and colleague was being held as a hostage, earmarked for execution, and Kropotkin went to the Kremlin to plead for his life. The conversation, which took place in the apartment of the old Bolshevik Vladimir Bonch-Bruyevich, soon developed into a long discourse on the Revolution and Russia's future.

Kropotkin tried hard to influence Lenin to abolish the entire system of taking hostages and shooting people in reprisal for opposition activity. He reminded Lenin of the Committee of Public Safety, which had killed so many outstanding leaders of the French Revolution. Kropotkin noted that later, one of its members was discovered to have been a judge under the Bourbons. 'I scared him a little,' Kropotkin later told his friend Dr Alexander Atabekian.

Lenin showed Kropotkin considerable respect at this meeting. The two men talked about Bolshevik methods, about the co-operative movement, about the development of bureaucratism in the Soviet state. Lenin tried briefly to sketch his own ideal conception of future Soviet development. Kropotkin listened attentively and then told Lenin: 'You and I have different points of view. Our aims seem to be the same, but as to a number of questions about means, actions and organization, I differ with you greatly. Neither I nor any of my friends will refuse to help you; but our help will consist only in reporting to you all the injustices taking place everywhere from which the people are groaning.'

Lenin took up the offer. He asked Kropotkin to send him information about injustices, which the veteran revolutionist did on several occasions. On 4 March 1920, Kropotkin described the miserable condition of the countryside and the sodden attitude of the local population.

'At every point', he wrote, 'people who don't know actual life are making awful mistakes for which we have to pay in hundreds of thousands of human lives and the ruination of whole regions. . . . If the present situation should continue much longer, the very word "socialism" will turn into a curse, as did the slogan "equality" for forty years after the rule of the Jacobins.'

Nine months later, Kropotkin returned to the subject of hostages: 'Is it possible that you do not know what a hostage really is – a man imprisoned not because of a crime committed but only because it suits his enemies to exert blackmail on his companions? . . . If you admit such methods, one can foresee that one day you will use torture, as in the Middle Ages. . . . The rulers of countries where monarchy still exists have abandoned long ago the means of defence now introduced into Russia with the seizure of hostages. . . . What future lies in store for Communism when one of its most important defenders tramples in this way on every honest human feeling?'

Before his death on 7 February 1921, Kropotkin wrote Lenin

other letters, as yet unpublished. Lenin was enraged. He told Vladimir Obukh, an old Bolshevik: 'I am sick of this old fogey. He doesn't understand a thing about politics and intrudes with his advice, most of which is very stupid.'

Lenin had as little success with the great humanist Vladimir Korolenko, whom Maxim Gorky once described as 'the most honest of Russian writers, a man with a large and vigorous heart, a rare man in the beauty and steadfastness of his spirit.' A revolutionary in his youth who had spent years in Siberian exile, Korolenko had been a Populist, critical of Marxism as early as 1897. During the Revolution, he had supported the Provisional Government and the Allied war effort. On 5 December 1917, he addressed the Bolsheviks in the Petrograd Socialist Revolutionary newspaper *Dyelo Naroda*.

You are celebrating your victory, but this victory is fatal for a section of the people who won the victory together with you, even fatal perhaps for the Russian people as a whole. . . . For a time you have stifled freedom, but you have not vanquished it. It is no victory if the thoughts of the people, its literature, are all against you. Your triumph is evil and terrible. . . . Power (based on a false idea) is doomed to perish as a result of its own arbitrary acts.

During the civil war, Korolenko protested equally against the pogroms and outrages of both Whites and Reds. Lenin was impatient with the venerable writer. 'They are all the same,' he told Bonch-Bruyevich. 'They call themselves revolutionaries, socialists and even "of the people" but have no notion of what the people need. They are prepared to leave the landowner, the mill owners and the priests, all of them, at their old posts, as long as they have the possibility of chattering about this or that right in any gathering. . . . There is little hope that Korolenko will understand what is now happening in Russia, but for the rest, we should try to give him all the details. . . . He should at least know the motives for all that is happening. Then, perhaps, he will stop judging us and will help us in the matter of affirming soviet authority where it is established.'

In June 1920, Lenin sent Lunacharsky, the people's commissar for education, to talk with Korolenko in Poltava. The young commissar and the old writer had a long conversation and then Lunacharsky went to attend a meeting at the town theatre. Soon afterwards, Korolenko was visited by the relatives of some men condemned to be shot for 'speculation in bread'. Asked to intervene, Korolenko came to the theatre and asked Lunacharsky: 'Prove that you feel strong. Show that you will mark your visit here by an act of mercy rather than one of cruelty.' Lunacharsky promised to do what he could, but next day sent a note informing Korolenko that the death sentence had been carried out 'before my arrival'.

In the next few days, Lunacharsky and Korolenko met again, and agreed that Korolenko would outline his views about the Revolution in a series of letters, which Lunacharsky would have printed, with his comments, in *Izvestia*.

'In his letters to Lunacharsky,' writes a contemporary Soviet scholar,[10] 'Korolenko spoke his mind with the directness and frankness characteristic of him. . . . Korolenko believed neither in the utopia of the past, nor in the utopia of the future.' However, neither Lunacharsky nor Lenin ever saw fit to publish Korolenko's letters, which were sharply critical of Communist actions. None of the six has yet been published in Russia.

Korolenko's own views emerge clearly from these letters, as well as those he wrote to Maxim Gorky. To Gorky, he wrote on 20 November 1920, for example, that the killing of the two liberal Constituent Assembly deputies, Shingarev and Kokoshkin, was 'the same sort of atrocity as the murder of Rosa Luxemburg and Karl Liebknecht, and the fact that it has gone unpunished leaves the same indelible stain.' In his last letter to Gorky, written a few months before his death in December 1921, Korolenko wrote:

Some day history will note that the Bolshevik Revolution used the same means against sincere revolutionaries and socialists as had the Tsarist régime, that is, strictly gendarme methods. . . . It is not surprising that we have made mistakes which only demonstrate how social revolution *should not be made*. This is, of course, also a service to the social revolution in general. But poor Russia will pay for these 'model experiments' in such a way that her example will perhaps discourage other countries. For a long time, perhaps, they will say: 'We've seen it, we've seen it from the Russian example.'

By this time, however, Lenin himself had begun to witness the effects of the Bolshevik experiment on revolution, socialism and democracy in other countries.

Chapter 19
Comintern

On the day World War I ended Lenin was convinced that prospects were favourable for the proletarian revolution which, a year earlier, he had described as 'never so close at hand as now'.

'The International World Revolution is near', he wrote on 11 November 1918, 'although revolutions are never made to order. Imperialism cannot delay the world revolution. The imperialists will set fire to the whole world and will start a conflagration in which they themselves will perish if they dare to quell the Revolution.'

The Bolsheviks began to prepare for world revolution soon after they seized power. On 24 December 1917, the Sovnarcom had allocated two million rubles to 'the foreign representatives of the Commissariat of Foreign Affairs for the needs of the international revolutionary movement'. In an order signed by Lenin, Trotsky, Bonch-Bruyevich and Gorbunov, and published in *Izvestia* two days later, the Sovnarcom declared that it considered it necessary 'to come to the aid of the Left Internationalist wing of the working-class movements of all countries with all possible resources, including money, quite irrespective of whether these countries are at war or in alliance with Russia, or whether they occupy a neutral position.'

Despite the fact that Russia was in the midst of civil war, Lenin did not for a moment lose sight of his goal of triumphant Marxian revolutions all over the world. Conditions in central and eastern Europe following the armistice were chaotic; soldiers returning from the front were weary, disillusioned and embittered. In Germany and Austria-Hungary the monarchies were overthrown, the Austro-Hungarian Empire collapsed; Poland and the Balkans were in a state of ferment. Workers in Allied countries were also restless. The soil seemed fertile for Communism.

Germany was the first country outside Russia in which the Bolsheviks began to further their aims of world revolution. Revolutionary propaganda, leaflets, and other such material were brought in by the Soviet diplomatic representatives. Joffe, the Soviet

Ambassador to Germany on the eve of the German Revolution, later subsequently claimed that 'the Russian Embassy had collaborated with the German Socialists in the preparation of the German revolution'.[1] Neither the government of Prince Max of Baden nor the Socialist government installed after the Revolution, however, were eager for close relations with the Soviet régime. A movement for the institution of soviets similar to those in Russia spread through many of the industrial cities of Germany, and a Congress of Soviets was held in Berlin to which Russian representatives were invited. The Bolsheviks sent a delegation consisting of Joffe, Rakovsky, Radek, Bukharin and Ignatov. The delegation was barred by the German military, however, and only Radek, in disguise, succeeded in getting to Berlin.[2]

Radek's first appeal was to the powerful Independent Socialist Party. In the name of Soviet Russia he denounced the Social Democratic Government headed by Ebert and Scheidemann and called for a real revolutionary government. This government, said Radek, would unite with Russia at the Rhine to declare a new war on the imperialist Allies.[3]

Soon afterwards Radek was instructed to conclude a secret pact with Karl Liebknecht, the Spartacist leader. Under the agreement Lenin promised to furnish funds for Spartacist propaganda and weapons, and to recognize Liebknecht as the president of the German Soviet Republic. In January 1919 the Spartacists staged a revolt in Berlin, which was quickly suppressed, and Liebknecht and Rosa Luxemburg were killed.

After the Communist Revolution in Hungary, Lenin concluded a similar agreement with Béla Kun, the Communist dictator, in March 1919. This agreement provided that Russia and Hungary would extend economic and military aid to each other.

Lenin realized the weakness of the Hungarian dictatorship; much smaller than Russia, Hungary could 'more easily be throttled by the imperialists'. Nevertheless, two months after Béla Kun had nationalized industry and the banks, Lenin advised him as follows:

'Be firm. If there are waverings among the Socialists who came over to you yesterday, or among the petty bourgeoisie, in regard to the dictatorship of the proletariat, suppress the waverings mercilessly. Shooting is the proper fate of a coward in war.'[4]

When Radek was arrested at the Bolshevik Propaganda Bureau in Berlin on 12 February 1919, the police found in his possession the draft of a plan for a general Communist offensive in central Europe, scheduled for that spring. A German Communist revolt was to be synchronized with a Red Army march through Poland to Germany.

A number of Bolshevik leaders later referred to this plan in their memoirs. One of these was Antonov-Ovseenko, the besieger of the Winter Palace, who was then the commander of the Ukrainian Red Army. Writing about the ebb period in White attacks, he declares:

Considerable forces were freed and we prepared to send them to the aid of Red Hungary. We prepared for this on the basis of the direct instructions of the Centre (Central Committee of the Party), because the Centre has never countermanded for us the order to break through and unite with Hungary – a project which was confirmed by the Commander in Chief in his directive of May 5.

Even before 5 May, however, Antonov-Ovseenko had received an order from Commander in Chief Vatzetis declaring that 'direct, close connexions with the Soviet troops of Hungary' was one of the aims of the Ukrainian campaign.[5]

Moreover, Professor Paul Miliukov, the historian and former leader of the Cadet Party, quotes the following statement by one of the Hungarian Communist leaders immediately after the short-lived Soviet dictatorship was proclaimed in Budapest:

Within three weeks we shall have an army of 150,000 well-drilled men, fully equipped. We are surrounded on all sides by discontented people. We shall begin with Czechoslovakia. Then will come Rumania, then Yugoslavia. Three months later Italy will join us. On the eighth of April there will be a meeting of the Soviet of Workers' and Soldiers' Deputies in Berlin. We have absolutely trustworthy information that Germany is going Bolshevik. Under the circumstances, how will France be able to stay out much longer? Then England's turn will come. Everything is in readiness as far as Czechoslovakia, Rumania, Bulgaria, Italy, France and England are concerned, up to the last piece of paper. No country will be able to resist us.

Late in 1918 word reached Moscow that the British Labour Party had issued a call for an international Socialist and Labour conference to be held in Paris or Berne. To Lenin this signalized the revival of the hated Second (Socialist) International. Moreover, Lenin was certain that the conference would condemn his dictatorship. He countered by calling a conference of his own. The purpose was to outlaw Socialists everywhere as 'counter-revolutionists' and 'traitors' and to proclaim his offspring as the true heir of the First Workers' International.

Furthermore, the reaffiliation of the left-wing elements with the Second International had to be prevented at all costs. Even though a representative international congress could not be held in Russia at this time, it was necessary that a preliminary meeting be summoned to offset the effect of the British Labour Party's move.

In January 1919 Lenin addressed an open letter to the workers of Europe and America urging them to found the Third International. On 24 January Soviet Foreign Minister Chicherin sent out invitations for an international congress to meet in Moscow early in March. The conference proposed by the British Labour Party was denounced as a 'gathering of the enemies of the working class'; all 'friends of the Third Revolutionary International' were instructed to stay away.

When the Berne Conference of European socialist parties decided to send an international commission headed by Kautsky to investigate conditions in Soviet Russia, the need for a Communist counter-move became more urgent. Lenin, Zinoviev, Trotsky, Rakovsky and Angelica Balabanov, former Secretary of the Zimmerwald Union, were among the most active in the preparations for the creation of a new International, which could denounce the Berne parties and assume the mantle of the pre-war Second International.

According to 'Comrade Thomas', who was active in these preparations, some twenty-four invitations were sent by special courier – former prisoners of war in Russia who were sent home, at Soviet expense, with secret letters sewn in the linings of their hats or trousers and instructed to deliver the letters to various of Lenin's sympathizers abroad. Because most of the prisoners had no political interests whatever, only three or four of the letters were actually delivered.

The First Congress of the Communist International (Comintern) was opened in the Kremlin on 2 March 1919. Most of the thirty-five delegates and fifteen guests had been hand-picked by the Bolshevik Central Committee from the so-called Communist parties in the small nations which had belonged to the Russian Empire, such as Estonia, Latvia, Lithuania and Finland. Others were war prisoners or foreign radicals who happened to be in Russia at the time. Holland, the Socialist Propaganda League of America (made up mainly of Slavic immigrants), and the Japanese Communists, were all represented by a Dutch-American engineer named Rutgers, who had once spent a few months in Japan; England by a Russian *émigré* named Feinberg who had served in the Soviet Foreign Office; Hungary by a war prisoner who later escaped with a large sum of money. Jacques Sadoul, who had come to Russia during the war with the French military mission and remained to throw in his lot with Lenin, had been suggested as a French representative, but another delegate was produced. When word was received that Guilbeaux, the anti-war French editor, was on his way to Russia, a special train was sent to the border to pick him up and rush him to Moscow in time to vote for France. As the so-called representative of the French left wing he was given five votes.

'I was astonished and disgusted at this news,' says Madame Balabanov, 'but after my previous conversation with Lenin on the subject of Guilbeaux, I knew it would be useless to protest.' [Guilbeaux later became a Fascist.]

The Swiss delegate was Platten, who had helped arrange Lenin's return to Petrograd, had accompanied him through Germany, and had been in Russia ever since. Boris Reinstein, of the American Socialist Labour Party, who had also come to Russia in 1917, declined to act as an American delegate, except in a fraternal capacity, on the ground that he had no credentials from his party. In fact, the only duly-elected delegate from beyond the Russian orbit was Hugo Eberlein, who represented the German Spartacist Union. He had been chosen partly because of his known stubbornness, and instructed to oppose the foundation of a new International. The Spartacists believed that there was no point in creating an International when genuine Communist parties had yet to exist. Eberlein held to his resolve, although at the last moment he failed to protest when the decision to launch the International was announced, and was followed immediately by an ovation and the singing of the *Internationale*.

The Congress was an unusually impromptu affair. There had been no prior consultations, reports or discussions. Lenin's theses were not given a preliminary reading. The Manifesto was drafted in an anteroom by Trotsky during the sessions, and made public immediately without consultation or debate. (It concluded: 'Under the banner of Workers' Soviets, of the revolutionary struggle for power and the dictatorship of the proletariat, under the banner of the Third International, workers of all countries unite!')

At one point, in the midst of a rather tedious speech, the door was flung open and a bearded man in Austrian uniform burst into the hall, proclaiming, 'I'm the delegate of the Austrian Communists!' He then pulled out a knife and began to cut open his soldier's greatcoat, from which he produced his mandate, and related what he had gone through in making his way to Moscow through the Ukrainian front. This was Hubert Steinhardt, and when he had finished, someone from the presidium whispered to him, 'Hail the Congress of the Communist International.' Steinhardt did – the first time these words were spoken in public.

At another point Lenin sent Madame Balabanov a note.

'Please take the floor and announce the affiliation of the Italian Socialist Party to the Third International.'

She replied on the same scrap of paper, 'I can't do it. I am not in touch with them. There is no question of their loyalty, but they must speak for themselves.'

Another note came back immediately:

'You have to; you are their official representative for Zimmerwald. You read *Avanti* and you know what is going on in Italy.'

This time she merely looked at him and shook her head. When the Congress adjourned at the end of the third day's session, she decided to return to the Ukraine immediately. Meeting Trotsky as she was leaving the hall, she bade him goodbye.

'Goodbye? What do you mean?' he asked. 'Don't you know that you are to be the secretary of the International? It has been discussed, and Lenin believes that no one but you should have this position.'

'I heard', relates Balabanov, 'that Radek was organizing foreign sections of the Communist Party with headquarters in the Commissariat of Foreign Affairs. When I went there to investigate, I found that this widely heralded achievement was a fraud. The members of these sections were practically all war prisoners in Russia. Most of them had joined the Party recently because of the privileges which membership conferred. Practically none of them had any contact with the revolutionary or labour movement in their countries, and knew nothing of Socialist principles. Radek was grooming them to return to their native countries, where they were to work for the Soviet Union. Two of these prisoners – Italians from Trieste – were about to return to Italy with special credentials from Lenin and a large sum of money. I understood that they knew nothing of the Italian movement, or even of the elementary terminology of Socialism. I decided to take my protest directly to Lenin.

'Vladimir Ilyich,' said the first secretary of the Comintern, 'I advise you to get back your money and credentials. These men are merely profiteers of the Revolution. They will damage us seriously in Italy.'

'For the destruction of Turati's [Socialist] Party,' Lenin replied coldly, 'they are quite good enough.'

A few weeks after this conversation word came from Italy that Lenin's two emissaries had squandered the money furnished to them by the Soviet Government in the cafés and brothels of Milan.[6]

By 1920 the Comintern was able to check effectively a movement for democratic government in Italy. The Fascists were not yet a strong factor in Italy but former Premier Francesco Nitti recognized the serious danger posed by royal and military influences, and he proposed the overthrow of Victor Emmanuel and the proclamation of a democratic republic. He approached the Italian Socialist Party, which consisted at the time of a right wing led by Turati, a Maximalist faction under Seratti, and the Communists. The Turati group stood solidly for Nitti's proposal, while the Maximalists wavered. The decision was in the hands of the Communists.

To Vladimir Diogot, Lenin's personal emissary to Italy, came Bombacci, secretary of the Central Committee of the Socialist Party, with two Communist comrades:

'Nitti has proposed the deposition of the King and the proclamation of a republic,' Bombacci explained. 'Seratti almost agrees. Tomorrow the question must be decided at the Central Committee. I would like your opinion to convey to the committee.'

'In the name of the Comintern,' Diogot replied, 'you can tell the Central Committee of the Party that participation in such a *coup d'état* represents the betrayal of the working class. . . . It matters little who is on the throne – Nitti or the King. We must rather stir up the revolution from below more energetically, so as to destroy both the King and Nitti. . . . Then *we* shall proclaim *the dictatorship of the proletariat*.'[7] Diogot, speaking for Lenin, thus killed the Nitti proposal. The Socialist Party, then Italy's largest single party, consistently refused to enter a coalition and attacked all coalitions formed by other democratic groups. After the Party had split in January 1921 at Livorno, the Communists concentrated all their attacks on the other Socialist factions. In May they completely dismissed the Fascist menace, asserting that a temporary white reaction was necessary to destroy the influence of the Social Democrats. The elections held that month they called 'a trial of the Socialists'. In October 1922 Benito Mussolini provided the Communists with their 'temporary white reaction', which lasted a generation.

The Comintern was organized to fulfil the historic role of carrying into effect the dictatorship of the proletariat, wrote Lenin. The Russian Socialist Republic was firmly established. And if such success could be achieved in backward Russia the coming revolution in other more advanced countries would accomplish even more.

'The First International (1864–72) laid the foundation for the international organization of the workers for the preparation of a revolutionary attack upon capital', Lenin explained. 'The Second International (1889–1914) was the international organization of the proletarian movement whose growth was extensive rather than intensive, and therefore resulted in a temporary drop in the revolutionary level and in a temporary increase of opportunistic tendencies, which finally led to the shameful downfall of this International. . . .

'The Third International took over the work of the Second International, cut off its opportunistic, social-chauvinist, bourgeois and petit-bourgeois rubbish, and began to carry into effect the dictatorship of the proletariat.

'The international union of parties heading the greatest revolution in the world, the movement of the proletariat for the overthrow of capital, now rests upon the firmest ground; namely, the existence of several Soviet republics, which are putting into practice, on an international scale, the dictatorship of the proletariat, its victory over capitalism.

'The history of the world inevitably tends towards a dictatorship of the proletariat, but it proceeds by devious ways, not always simple or smooth.

'Soviet or proletarian democracy was born in Russia. The second most far-reaching historical step of world-wide significance after the Paris Commune has been made. The Soviet Republic of proletarians and peasants was the first stable Socialist republic in the world. At this very moment it no longer stands alone in the field.

'In order to carry on the Socialist work of reconstruction, in order to bring it to a successful conclusion, much is yet needed. Soviet republics in countries with a higher degree of civilization, whose proletariat has greater social weight and influence, have every prospect of outstripping Russia as soon as they start upon the road of proletarian dictatorship.'

Lenin savagely attacked the Socialist International as a 'handmaiden to the bourgeoisie', and bourgeois democracy was dismissed as having outlived its purpose.

The most democratic bourgeois republic was never more than an instrument for the suppression of the workers by capitalists.

'Liberty in the bourgeois republic always meant liberty for the rich. The proletarians and the toiling peasants did and had to utilize this republic to prepare themselves for the task of overthrowing capital, of overcoming bourgeois democracy. . . .

'For the first time in the world Soviet or proletarian democracy has created a democracy for the masses, for the toilers, for the workers, and the poor peasants. . . .'[8]

Gregory Zinoviev was chosen president of the new International. Its actual head, however, was Lenin, and in the Comintern, as in the Bolshevik Party, he enforced iron discipline.

Lenin was convinced that the Soviet régime could not survive unless it provided the spark to ignite the fires of revolution in other parts of Europe.

Previously when Madame Balabanov, in Stockholm representing the Zimmerwald Union, had complained to Lenin about irregularities in the distribution of the Bolshevik news service, Lenin had replied:

'Dear Comrade: The work you are doing is of the utmost importance and I implore you to go on with it. We look to you for our most effective support. Do not consider the cost. Spend millions, tens of millions, if necessary. There is plenty of money at our disposal. I understand from your letters that some of the couriers do not deliver our paper on time. Please send me their names. These saboteurs shall be shot.'

Madame Balabanov replied that she could not see why the propaganda campaign on behalf of Russia or the world revolution required such sums. Nevertheless large sums of money began to arrive, most of which was to be paid out to agents who were setting up Communist cells throughout the world.[9]

But Lenin's hopes of early European revolution failed to materialize. The march of the Red Army on Poland and Latvia was stopped at the very outset. The three Communist uprisings in Germany were suppressed. Béla Kun's dictatorship in Hungary lasted only a few months. 'The Hungarian dictatorship', says Bukharin, 'was opposed by the majority of the population, both in the cities and rural districts.' Likewise the Communist uprisings in Vienna and Czechoslovakia were speedily crushed. But these setbacks did not change Lenin's fundamental theories of world revolution. When the Polish Army was driven out of the Ukraine in 1920, Lenin ordered the ill-fated Red Army march on Warsaw. Perhaps this was the opportunity to carry Soviet revolution to western Europe. Lenin advocated 'feeling out the Poland of the bourgeois and landowners with bayonets', according to Trotsky.

'We all know now that the march on Warsaw which we undertook at Lenin's suggestion was a mistake for which we paid dearly', Trotsky wrote. 'This error not only brought us to the peace of Riga, which cut us off from Germany, but it also helped the bourgeoisie of Europe to fortify itself. There is no doubt that in Poland itself the revolution would have developed more successfully if it had not been for our intervention and its failure.'[10] Lenin later also admitted that the march on Warsaw was a mistake.

Despite reverses and civil war, Lenin continued his intimate contact with the work of the Comintern. Preparations for the

Second Congress were entrusted to a personally organized Comintern bureau in western Europe. The Dutch Communist, Rutgers, was summoned at 3 a.m. on 14 October 1919, for detailed instructions on the work of the Western European Bureau.

Although constantly interrupted by calls from the front which informed him of Denikin's march on Orel, Lenin made careful inquiries as to Rutgers' comrades and work. He told Rutgers, 'If you hear on your way [back to Holland] that Tula is captured, you can tell our foreign comrades that we may possibly be compelled to move to the Urals.'[11]

In June 1920 the Second Congress of the Comintern opened in Petrograd. Later it moved to Moscow, where its sessions continued until August. This time there were delegations of Communist and left-wing Socialist groups from thirty-seven countries.

Acting on the programme submitted by Lenin, the Second Congress laid down the methods to be employed for spreading Communist propaganda throughout the world. It evolved the plan of organizing secret Communist centres in every country, for the purpose of fomenting revolutions, while at the same time Communist parties, wherever possible, were to engage in legal political action.

The parliamentary tactics of the Communists were succinctly defined by the International: '*No Parliament can under any circumstances be an arena of struggle for reforms, for betterment of the conditions of the working class. . . . The only question can be that of utilizing bourgeois state institutions for their own destruction.*'

One of the keystones of Communist policy throughout the world, this declaration could only be regarded as, in effect, a candid admission that the Communists were fundamentally opposed to democracy.

The only organizations admitted to Comintern membership were those which subscribed without reservation to the complete programme of the Third International and were ready to follow the tactics laid down for international Communism by Lenin.

To strike at the colonial sinews of imperialism was essential for victory over world capitalism.

'European capitalism draws its chief strength not from industrial countries of Europe, but from its colonial possessions,' declared the Second Congress. 'The surplus income received from colonies is the chief source of wealth of modern capitalism. The European working class will therefore be able to overthrow the capitalistic system only when this source has finally dried up.'

Under Lenin's aegis, the Second Congress adopted its famous 'Twenty-one Points'. They bear Zinoviev's signature, but the author was Lenin, and the document is included in the third edition of Lenin's collected works.

The most significant of the Twenty-one Points specified:

1. Political parties that wish to affiliate with the International must completely, and as soon as possible, end all associations with the reformist or centrist movements in Socialism.

2. The parties must strive to remove from all important posts in the labour movement (party organizations, editorial offices, trade unions, parliamentary groups, etc.) members of reformist or centrist groups and appoint in their place true Communists, even if at first ordinary workers have to take the place of experienced 'opportunists'.

3. Parties which have not radically altered their tactics must make sure that not less than two thirds of their Central Committees and other executive bodies shall consist of individuals who, prior to the Second Congress, openly and unequivocally declared themselves in favour of joining the Third International.

4. Parties that have kept their old Social Democratic programme must change it immediately to a Communist programme, adapted to local conditions. All such programmes must receive the approval of the Congress or of the Executive Committee of the Communist International.

5. All parties entering the Communist International must change their name and call themselves 'Communist Parties' in order that their differentiation from the old Socialist parties may be clear to everybody.

6. All parties must be organized upon the principle of 'democratic' centralization and iron discipline. The Executive or the Central Committee of the individual party must be the final authority and possess broad powers, subject only to the decision of the Comintern.

7. The Communists must not rely on 'bourgeois legality', but establish everywhere, along with their overt organizations, a secret apparatus which in time of revolution will be of great aid to the party. All parties which enjoy a legal existence must periodically sift their membership and purge their ranks of all 'petit-bourgeois' elements .

8. Decisions of the Congresses and the Executive Committee of the Comintern are binding on all parties affiliated with the Communist International. Members who oppose the terms and instructions of the Comintern must be expelled from the party at once.

9. Each party is obligated to wage an active campaign against the Amsterdam Trade Union International, against non-Communist trade unions, against 'social patriotism' and 'social pacifism', against the belief in the League of Nations, disarmament, and arbitration as a means of averting war.

10. Each party obligates itself to conduct an energetic propaganda within the trade unions, co-operatives, and other workers' organizations and to organize within these bodies Communist cells which must subordinate themselves to the party.

11. The Communist parties are under special obligation to conduct vigorous propaganda in the army. In countries where such propaganda is prohibited by law, it must be conducted by secret means.

12. The party press must be under the control of the Central Committee. All important documents of the Executive Committee of the Communist International must be published in the leading party organs.

The subsequent Congresses of the Communist International elaborated on these basic points. Thus the Third Congress instructed the Executive Committee to work out precise regulations concerning the organization of Communist cells in the factories, trade unions, Army and Navy.

In July 1921 the Comintern Executive Committee issued an order that national congresses of member parties were to be held after the Comintern congresses, as assurance that the decisions of the local parties would be in line with the edicts of the Comintern.

The Fourth Congress ruled that in the future all delegates to the Comintern should come to Moscow uninstructed, without any definite mandate from their party as to how to vote on issues that were expected to arise. This assured that control would remain on top.

Lenin, as the author of these Comintern provisions and instructions, was forging all over the world rigidly centralized and disciplined Bolshevik parties, modelled after his Bolshevik Party and led by small groups of professional revolutionists, who were subject to the supreme authority of the Central Executive Committee of the Comintern.

On 15 October 1920, the German Independent Socialist Party met in Halle in order to vote on the question of affiliation with the Communist International.

Martov, Lenin's old *Iskra* associate, made the trip from Moscow to Halle and presented his indictment against Lenin's régime and the Comintern. Comintern President Zinoviev and Russian Communist representative Lozovsky, who had gone to Halle to state the case for the Communist International, were rather surprised when Martov made his appearance on the platform.

His speech came shortly after the Red Army's drive on Warsaw had been turned back and Lenin's effort to carry Soviet rule to the German border had ended in defeat.

Martov reminded the delegates that when the Russian Army was approaching Warsaw, 'the organized workers of England and other countries, remembering the solemn promises of the Soviet Government to conclude peace with Poland the moment the latter repudiates its aims of conquest, developed with maximum energy their efforts to force the Entente to abandon its aid to Poland and thus compel her to make a peace proposal. Finally, this was accomplished.

'But the Red Army continued its advance on Warsaw, crossed the Vistula, occupied Soldau, while Soviet diplomacy openly sabotaged the beginning of negotiations and, when these finally began, presented demands tantamount to the abdication of the Polish Government; *i.e.* demands deliberately calculated to provoke a rejection. And all this was done after a gala meeting of the Petrograd Soviet, presided over by Zinoviev, where the resolution was adopted: "no peace with Poland until her bourgeoisie is overthrown and a Soviet government established in that country." In addition a Revolutionary Committee composed of Polish *émigrés* imported from Russia took up the duties of a Provisional Polish Government in the areas occupied by the Red Army.

'Zinoviev has told you,' said Martov, 'that the Bolsheviks did not seek to provoke Germany into a war with the Entente. That is a lie! It was none other than Trotsky who at the height of the Russian victories in Poland declared in a speech: "We will give battle to the Entente on the Rhine!" In Soldau officers and commissars of the Red Army declared repeatedly in addresses before enthusiastic meetings of German nationalists that Russia would return West Prussia to the German Fatherland. In order to strengthen this touching alliance between the German nationalists and the Bolsheviks, the commander of the Army made a public announcement that in view of the agrarian character of that province there would be no Soviet introduced there.

'I need not tell you how the *Rote Fahne* [German Communist organ] and the Communist orators during all that period were agitating for war, for the utilization of the Red Army's advance towards the borders of Germany as a means of nullifying the peace of Versailles. This you know yourselves only too well.

'Zinoviev had the temerity to declare here that after the defeat of Denikin executions were discontinued in Russia,' Martov continued. 'He forgot to add that that was for a short time only, and that soon after, despite the most solemn promises, they were renewed and are now continuing on an appalling scale. According to an official statement in *Izvestia*, 800 men were executed during the month of July by military courts-martial alone!

'But the system of terror is not confined to murder only. There are mass arrests, the suppression of all freedom of press and assembly, imprisonment under forced labour without trial, daily punishment for strikes or for any kind of collective action by the workers, the prohibition of election to the Soviets of certain parties and, finally, according to Zinoviev's own admission, exile of workers belonging to the Communist Party for daring to criticize their leaders. This terror is approved by the Third International as a system of government admissible for Socialists.'[12]

Martov was followed by Rudolf Hilferding, who, after Kautsky, was generally regarded as the leading theoretician of Marxism. Hilferding, who was to be slain in a French prison under Hitler, declared: 'When we beheld on this international platform our Comrade Martov, we realized from his very appearance and that of Zinoviev that we had before us the representative of the oppressed, one of those Socialists, flesh of our flesh and bone of our bone, against whom the Bolshevik terror is applied. There could have been no sharper protest against this terror than the wan and worn face of Comrade Martov when he suddenly stepped on the platform.

'It is clear to us that Bolshevism is but a system of opportunist, imperialist policy, flatly contradicting the fundamental principles of Marxism.

'Between us and the Bolsheviks there is not only a wide

theoretical difference but an impassable moral gulf. We realize that they are people with quite a different morality and ethics.'[13]

Martov's reply to Zinoviev and the speeches of Hilferding, Arthur Crispien, Georg Ledebour, Wilhelm Dittmann and other spokesmen of German left-wing Socialism contributed greatly to the subsequent bolt of the Independents from the German Communists and to their declaration of open war against the Comintern.

For Martov, the Halle Conference marked his last great battle in the war against Leninist doctrine which he had been waging since the London Congress in 1903. Lenin's party of professional revolutionists, which Martov had opposed in 1903, had destroyed democratic Socialism in Russia; it was now reaching out, through the Comintern, to undermine it everywhere.

The strategy and tactics of the Communist parties must be as flexible as possible, the parties must learn to utilize all methods of struggle, from armed insurrection to infiltration in the most 'reactionary' trade unions and parliaments, said Lenin. They must be able to combine legal and underground activities; they must be able to attack boldly and fearlessly, but must also be able to retreat in an organized manner, to enter into practical compromises 'even with the devil and his grandmother'. They must be able to take advantage of the friction, conflicts and quarrels in the bourgeois camps, and quickly and unexpectedly substitute one form of struggle for another when circumstances demand it.

Lenin personally issued the instructions directing the work of the Comintern in each country, as the reams of his memoranda to party associates clearly indicate.

In reply to the British Labour Party's protest against the Bolshevik occupation of the Georgian Socialist Republic – after a Soviet guarantee of Georgian independence – Lenin wrote in a memorandum, dated December 1921, 'We must take immediate measures of a two-fold character':

1. We must come out in the press with a series of articles signed by different names, ridiculing the views of the so-called European democracy on the question of Georgia.

2. Some caustic journalist should be instructed at once to prepare the draft of a note in reply to the British Labour Party in the politest terms. In

this note it should be made thoroughly clear that the proposal to evacuate Georgia and to conduct a referendum there might be a reasonable suggestion coming from sensible people who have not been bribed by the Entente, providing the same measure were applied to all nations of the globe. More particularly, in order to suggest to the leaders of the British Labour Party the great importance of modern imperialist relationships in international politics, we respectfully propose that the British Labour Party favourably consider the following measures:

First to evacuate Ireland and conduct a popular referendum there; second, to take the same steps in India; third, to apply the same measures in Korea; fourth, to take the same action in all countries where armies of any of the great imperialistic powers are kept.

The note should emphasize in the politest terms possible that those willing to reflect on our proposals on the system of imperialistic relations existing in international politics will also be capable of appreciating the implications of the suggestions made to us by the British Labour Party. The purpose of the note, extremely polite in form and popular style (so as to appeal to the intelligence of ten-year-old children) should be to ridicule the idiotic leaders of the British Labour Party.[14]

Lenin's policy towards his opponents on an international scale in 1921 was a logical extension of his bitter attacks on Party opponents in 1907. The tactics advised by his memoranda are reflected by a plethora of Communist stratagems since its writing.

No important business that concerned the Comintern escaped Lenin's personal attention. On 3 February 1922, *Pravda* published a story to the effect that the International Metalworkers' Union was introducing a proposal at their coming International Congress for a general strike of all organized workers in the event of war.

In a memorandum to Bukharin and Zinoviev the very next day Lenin suggested the Comintern line on this proposal:

Regarding yesterday's dispatch from Hanover about the recommendations of the Metalworkers' Union to include among the questions to be discussed their proposal to call a general strike as a measure against war, I suggest the following.

1. To publish in *Pravda* and *Izvestia* a series of articles explaining at length the whole childishness and social-patriotic character of the sentiments expressed by the metalworkers.

2. To bring up this question at the next enlarged session of the Executive Committee of the Comintern to consider measures against war, and to adopt an appropriate resolution, making it clear that only a

revolutionary party, experienced and prepared in advance, with a well-working illegal machinery, can successfully conduct a fight against war; and explaining also the way to wage this fight is not through a strike against war but through the formation of revolutionary cells in the fighting armies and through training and preparing for a revolution.

Lenin was not only the author of the basic Comintern plans and programmes, but also the frank advocate of a system of 'revolutionary morality' which justified the use of subterfuge and lies in political struggle. He wrote:

> The Communists must be prepared to make every sacrifice, and, if necessary, even resort to all sorts of cunning, schemes, and stratagems to employ illegal methods, to evade and conceal the truth, in order to penetrate into the trade unions, to remain in them, and conduct the Communist work in them at all costs.

> The struggle against the Gomperses, the Jouhaux, the Hendersons [American, French and British labour leaders] ... who represent an *absolutely similar* social and political type as our Mensheviks ... must be waged without mercy to the end, in the same manner as we have done it in Russia until all the incorrigible leaders of opportunism and of social chauvinism have been completely discredited and expelled from the trade unions.

The Austrian Socialist Government revealed that vast sums had been sent by Moscow to its agents to overthrow that government. To which Eduard Bernstein, German Social Democratic leader, added in 1921: 'If we recall the uprisings in the Ruhr, in central Germany, and Bavaria, all of which were partly instigated by the Bolsheviks, then the estimate of several millions sent by Moscow will not be exaggerated. The same held true for other countries.'[15]

The Comintern, after Lenin's death, expanded its operations and vastly increased its international network of agents. But the long-range strategy and tactics remained largely those which Lenin had laid down.

Chapter 20
Kronstadt

Kronstadt was the proudest bastion of the Bolshevik Revolution. The sailors of the island fortress off Petrograd had marched against Kerensky in July 1917 and had stormed the Winter Palace in November to install Lenin in power. Later, when Red Petrograd was threatened by General Yudenich, the Kronstadt sailors had rallied to the defence of the Soviet régime.

On 1 March 1921, the sailors of Kronstadt revolted – against Lenin. Mass meetings of 15,000 men from various ships and garrisons passed resolutions demanding immediate new elections to the Soviet by secret ballot; freedom of speech and the press for all left-wing Socialist parties; freedom of assembly for trade unions and peasant organizations; abolition of Communist political agencies in the Army and Navy; immediate withdrawal of all grain-requisitioning squads, and re-establishment of a free market for the peasants.

The Kronstadt revolt came as the climax of a series of rebellions, disturbances and protests embracing large areas of Russia. As a result of 'War Communism', Russia in March 1921 was on the verge of economic collapse and new civil war in which foreign intervention played no part. The White Armies had been decisively defeated in the autumn of 1919, and were no longer a factor after the capture and execution of Kolchak and the departure of Denikin early in 1920.

In 1919 and 1920, famine, disease, cold and infant mortality had claimed some nine million lives – apart from the military casualties of the civil war. In the Urals and the Don region, the population had been reduced by a third. The living standard of the Russian worker had sunk to less than a third of the pre-war level, industrial output to less than a sixth of 1913 production. The prices of manufactured goods sky-rocketed, while paper currency dropped in value until, in January 1921, a gold ruble was worth 26,529 paper rubles. Nearly half the industrial work force deserted the towns for the villages.

The requisitioning of grain continued with increasing demands on the peasants, while the government, owing to the collapse of industry, was unable to make payment in kind. The peasants refused to plough their land, because there was no incentive for cultivating more than was needed for immediate village consumption. By 1921 cultivated land had shrunk to about 62 per cent of the pre-war area, and the harvest yield was only 37 per cent of normal.

A series of peasant uprisings began. The first, led by the Communist commander of a Red Army cavalry division, began in Samara in July 1920. Later came new armed uprisings in the lower Volga and Altai–Omsk regions. The most serious arose in Tambov province in Central Russia – and was quelled only by the force of special Red Army and Cheka detachments and by Lenin's order, on 14 February 1921, to discontinue grain requisitioning in the area.

By this time the mood of rebellion was gaining force in the cities, and within the Communist Party itself. In the Party the resistance came from the so-called 'Workers' Opposition', led by former Labour Commissar Shliapnikov and Alexandra Kollontai, later Russian Ambassador to Mexico and Sweden.

This opposition had developed partly from conditions inside the Party, which a large number of opportunists had joined in order to entrench themselves. Lenin had declared: 'At every step one finds that purely petit-bourgeois elements fall into the category of workers. It seems as if the proletarian character of our Party does not really guarantee it against a possible predominance, within a very short time, of petit-bourgeois elements.'

At the same time, the Workers' Opposition reflected the estrangement of Communist trade-union chiefs, caught between Kremlin policies and the rising discontent of the workers. In a famous pamphlet, Mme Kollontai complained: 'The workers ask – who are we? Are we really the prop of the class dictatorship, or are we just an obedient flock that serves as a support for those who, having severed all ties with the masses, carry out their own policy and build up industry without any regard to our opinions and creative abilities under the reliable cover of the party label?'

The Workers' Opposition had little sympathy for non-Communists, but demanded greater prerogatives for trade-union leaders as against the party apparatus. The workers of Petrograd, who began rising in mid-February 1921, went a great deal farther.

On 24 February, strikes were called in the government munition works, the Trubochny and Baltiiski mills and the Laferm factory. Next day, workers of the Admiralty shops and Galernaya docks joined the strikers. The régime proclaimed martial law, sent Red Army cadets to disperse the demonstrations, and locked out the Trubochny strikers. On 27 February, a strikers' proclamation declared:

'A complete change is necessary in the policies of the Government. First of all, the workers and peasants need freedom. They don't want to live by the decrees of the Bolsheviks; they want to control their own destinies. Comrades, preserve revolutionary order! Determinedly and in an organized manner demand: Liberation of all arrested Socialists and non-partisan workingmen; abolition of martial law; freedom of speech, press and assembly for all who labour. . . .'

Thus the Soviet régime now faced rebellion by the very masses of workers, soldiers and sailors who had been won by Lenin's slogans of 'peace, bread and land'.[1]

Zinoviev, the party boss of Petrograd, sensed that the disturbances in his city might lead to full-fledged insurrection. He ordered the cadets of the military schools to occupy all the bridges of Petrograd. Workers were crossing the ice to the island fortress of Kronstadt. A revolution within the revolution was developing.

Zinoviev telegraphed Lenin and Trotsky, asking for reliable troops. Trotsky immediately sent the former Tsarist officer, General Tukhachevsky, to Petrograd. At the same time, Lenin dispatched Mikhail Kalinin, the president of the Soviet Union, to talk to the Kronstadt sailors. Kalinin called a meeting and tried to pacify the men, but his words were drowned out by loud protests.

'Why are our fathers and brothers in the villages shot? You are sated; you are warm; the commissars live in the palaces.'

The military commissar accompanying Kalinin was shoved off the platform as the sailors lifted in his place one of their own speakers who, waving his cap, cried: 'Comrades, look around you and you will see that we have fallen into a terrible mire. We were pulled into this mire by a group of Communist bureaucrats, who, under the mask of Communism, have feathered their nests in our republic. I myself was a Communist, and I call on you, comrades, drive out these false Communists who set worker against peasant and peasant against worker. Enough shooting of our brothers.'

The men shouted their approval as sailor Petrechenko leaped on the platform and denounced the shooting of workers in Petrograd and the executions of peasants in the villages. He attacked the régime for surrounding itself with Tsarist generals. Then he proposed a resolution against the Soviet dictatorship. It was carried by acclaim. 'Arrest them!' shouted sailors, pointing to Kalinin and the commissar who came with him. But they were not arrested. Kalinin and his staff were allowed to leave Kronstadt in peace. Some minor commissars were placed under arrest.[2]

On 2 March, an order signed by Lenin and Trotsky called the sailors 'tools of former Tsarist generals' and branded their movement 'the work of Entente interventionists and French spies'. At the same time, Zinoviev organized a state of siege in Petrograd, ordered Communist regiments to disperse all crowds and to crush any demonstrations with machine-gun fire. Hundreds of suspected Socialist Revolutionaries and Mensheviks were arrested. To reduce tension among the workers, they were allowed to go into the countryside for food and were issued extra allocations of meat, shoes and clothing.

On 5 March 1921, the Kronstadt sailors formed a revolutionary committee of fifteen men – nine sailors, four workers, a male nurse and a school director. The chairman of the committee was the sailor Petrechenko. By the next day, General Tukhachevsky was already speeding by special train from Moscow to organize the suppression of the rebellion. He massed 60,000 picked men consisting of Cheka troops, Communist military cadets, and other dependable forces. To prevent rebellion in Petrograd, he ordered the regular garrison there disarmed. Decrees signed by Trotsky and Tukhachevsky declared:

To the garrison and population of Kronstadt and the rebel forts: The Workers' and Peasants' Government has decided that Kronstadt and the naval ships should at once be turned over to the Soviet Republic and therefore I order all those who raise their hands against the Socialist Fatherland to lay down their arms immediately. Those who refuse must be immediately disarmed and surrendered to the Soviet officials. The arrested commissars must be released at once. Only those who surrender unconditionally can hope for the mercy of the Soviet Republic. Simultaneously I also gave an order to prepare for the suppression of the rebellion and the destruction of the rebels by armed forces. The responibility for all the misfortune that will fall on the peaceable elements will be on the heads of the White Guard rebels. This warning is the last one.

Signed, Chairman of the Revolutionary Military Council of the Republic, TROTSKY.[3]

At Kronstadt the officers advised the sailors to begin an offensive against Petrograd at once, otherwise they would be lost. But the sailors said they would not 'shed needless blood'. They would only defend themselves if Trotsky dared to spill the people's blood.

Trotsky did not wait. He issued an order to the effect that if the rebels did not surrender they would be shot singly, 'like ducks in a pond'. The sailors refused to yield. On the evening of 6 March Tukhachevsky's planes flew over the Gulf of Finland to bomb the houses and forts of Kronstadt.

Trotsky and Tukhachevsky realized that in three weeks the ice would melt and their troops would be unable to attack the island fortress. Moreover, the warships manned by Kronstadt sailors could steam to Petrograd. On 7 March Tukhachevsky began to bombard the forts with heavy artillery. The Revolutionary Committee of Kronstadt then dispatched this radio message to the world:

The first shot has thundered. But the entire world knows of it. The bloody Field Marshal Trotsky who stands up to the waist in the fraternal blood of the workers was the first to open fire against revolutionary Kronstadt, which rebelled against the government of the Communists in order to re-establish the real power of the Soviets. We will rise or fall under the ruins of Kronstadt, fighting for the bloodstained cause of the labouring people. Long live the power of the Soviets! Long live the world Socialist Revolution![4]

The ultimatum expired and the sailors still did not yield. Tukhachevsky then ordered an assault against the fortress. In the early morning, when the ice was still blue, the advance of the Cheka and Communist troops began. The Communist military cadets were out front, clad in white robes to blend with the snow. They were followed by picked Red Army troops, behind whom were Cheka machine-gunners to prevent any desertions. The sailors returned Tukhachevsky's artillery fire with the guns of the fort and the ice-locked warships.

In the nearby city of Oranienbaum several Red Army regiments mutinied and refused to fight the sailors. Cheka units rushed to the scene and shot every fifth soldier.

The Kronstadt sailors resisted so fiercely that Tukhachevsky demanded that the Bolshevik Party leaders come to the front to raise the morale of his forces. From Moscow the Tenth Congress of the Communist Party rushed 300 high-ranking officials to the scene. At the same Party Congress, on 8 March 1921, Lenin said in the course of a speech: 'I have not yet received the latest news from Kronstadt, but I have no doubt that this mutiny, which quickly revealed the familiar figures of the White Guard generals, will be liquidated within the next few days, if not within the next few hours. There can be no doubt about this.'

On the night of 16 March Tukhachevsky redeployed his forces in squares in preparation for storming the fortress. At the same time, his batteries increased their bombardment. The battleships returned fire. The next evening Tukhachevsky sent all available planes to bombard the fortress.

Trotsky kept his word. Thousands of sailors were shot like ducks in a pond. Tukhachevsky later said: 'I was in the war for five years, but I cannot remember such a slaughter. It was not a battle; it was an inferno. The blasting of the heavy artillery continued all night and was so powerful that in Oranienbaum all the windows were shattered.

'The sailors fought like wild beasts. I cannot understand where they found the might for such rage. Each house where they were located had to be taken by storm. An entire company fought for an hour to capture one house and when the house was captured it was found that it contained two or three soldiers at a machine-gun. They seemed half-dead, but they snatched their revolvers and gasped, "Too little did we shoot at you scoundrels." '[5]

On 17 March Tukhachevsky reported to Moscow that Kronstadt was silent. Thousands of sailors and soldiers lay dead in its streets.

Some of the sailors succeeded in escaping to Finland. But the majority of those captured alive were shot by Cheka firing squads, and the rest were exiled to remote prison camps.

Lenin discussed the revolt a month later. On 21 April 1921, he wrote:

The most characteristic feature of the Kronstadt events was precisely the vacillation of the petty-bourgeois element. There was very little of anything that was fully formed, clear, and definite. We heard nebulous slogans about 'liberty', 'free trade', 'emancipation from serfdom', 'Soviets without the Bolsheviks', or new elections to the Soviets, or relief from 'party dictatorship', and so on and so forth. Both the Mensheviks and the Socialist Revolutionaries declared the Kronstadt movement to be 'their own'.

The bourgeoisie is really a class force which inevitably rules under capitalism, both under a monarchy and in the most democratic republic, and which also inevitably enjoys the support of the world bourgeoisie. But the petty bourgeoisie, *i.e.* all the heroes of the Second International and of the 'Two and a Half' International, cannot, by the very economic nature of the case, be anything else than the expression of class impotence; hence the vacillation, phrases, and helplessness.[6]

With the guns of Kronstadt still resounding, Lenin realized that the time had come for compromise if the Bolsheviks were to retain power. Despite 'Left' objections, he introduced a New Economic Policy (NEP) in the spring of 1921.

In 1918 Lenin had regarded private enterprise as anathema. Now he admitted that private trade was indispensable for restoring Russia's economic health. The wage system was restored and peasants' property rights in their produce was recognized. The 'civil war in the villages' was brought to an end. On 15 March 1921, at the Tenth Congress of the Party, Lenin declared: 'We must try to satisfy the demands of the peasants who are dissatisfied, discontented, and legitimately discontented, and cannot be otherwise. . . . In essence the small farmer can be satisfied with two things. First of all, there must be a certain amount of freedom of turnover, of freedom for the small private proprietor; and, secondly, commodities and products must be provided.'[7]

Following the introduction of the New Economic Policy, economic efficiency rather than Communist theory became the chief objective of the Soviet industrial experts and technicians. Workers were paid in accordance with the value of their services.

In his address before a conference of Moscow Communist organizations in October of 1921 Lenin frankly admitted that the attempt to introduce Communism at this stage had been a mistake.

He placed the onus for his compromise with pure Communist principles on the failure of the peasants to supply the workers with enough bread.

'I regret it,' he stated, 'because our experience, which is not very long, proves to us that our conception was wrong. Our New Economic Policy means that in applying our former methods we suffered defeat and had to begin a strategic retreat. Let us retreat and construct everything in a new and solid manner; otherwise we shall be beaten. The defeat we suffered in the spring of 1921 on the economic front was more serious than that we had ever before suffered when fighting against Kolchak, Denikin and Pilsudski. The system of distribution in the villages and the immediate application of Communist methods in the towns held back our productive forces and caused the great economic and political crisis we met in the spring of 1921.'

Lenin recommended that the return to private enterprise be applied first to agriculture and then to small industry. Basic industries and transportation as well as foreign trade would remain under government control. He therefore foresaw no danger of a capitalist revival as the result of the New Economic Policy. To the new system Lenin gave the name of 'State Capitalism'.

'Riding the wave of enthusiasm which swept the people first in the political and then in the military field, we hope to utilize this enthusiasm in achieving economic reforms equally far-reaching in nature', Lenin explained.

'We hoped through the decrees of the proletarian government to found state industries and organize the distribution of state products upon a Communist basis in a country that was petit bourgeois! Life has shown that we made a mistake. A succession of transition periods such as State Capitalism and Socialism was required to prepare, through many years of preliminary work, the transition to Communism. Not upon the foundation of this enthusiasm but with the aid of such enthusiasm born of the Revolution, upon the basis of personal interest, personal participation, upon the basis of economic purposefulness, you must attempt first to build small bridges which shall lead a land of small peasant holdings through State Capitalism to Socialism. Otherwise you will never lead tens of millions of people to Communism.

This is what the objective forces of the development of the Revolution have taught.'[8]

A year later Lenin was confident that Russia, under the NEP, was advancing on the road to Socialism.

'Socialism is no longer a question of the remote future. We have brought Socialism into everyday life,' he wrote. 'No matter how difficult the problem may be, no matter what the obstacles that must be overcome or how many difficulties it may involve, we shall achieve it, not tomorrow, it is true, but surely in the course of the next few years, in such a way that the Russia of the NEP will be transformed into Socialist Russia.'[9]

A short time afterwards, however, he was not nearly so confident. 'We have not even completed the foundation for a Socialist economic order', he declared. 'The hostile forces of dying capitalism may yet take everything away from us. This must be clearly understood and frankly admitted, for nothing is so dangerous as illusions. On the other hand, there is nothing alarming, nothing to give the slightest reason for falling into despair because we recognize this truth. We have always taught and have always preached that to assure the victory of Socialism it is necessary to have the united forces of the workers of several highly developed countries.'[10]

Early in the summer of 1921 Lenin appeared before the Third Congress of the Comintern to define the platform to be adopted in relation to the NEP. He assured the foreign delegates that the NEP was necessary for the advancement of world revolution.

'The development of international revolution which we predicted is progressing,' he explained. 'But this advancing movement is not as direct as we had expected. . . . The fact must be taken into account that now, unquestionably, there has been reached a certain balance of forces. Consequently we must take advantage of this brief breathing space in order to adapt our tactics to this sort of zig-zag of historical development.'

By the end of 1921 Lenin could point to a general economic revival, particularly in the transportation system, mining, and small trade, as the result of the new policy.

The NEP, however, came too late to avert the famine resulting from crop failures and the lack of reserve supplies, caused by Communist policy towards the peasants since 1918. On 26 June

1921, *Pravda* revealed that 'about 25,000,000 people' were suffering from famine. Despite large-scale relief organized by the American Relief Association under Herbert Hoover, starvation took the lives of no less than five million people in 1921 and 1922.

Moreover, although peasant revolts, industrial strikes and the Kronstadt uprising had forced Lenin to revise Russia's economic structure, he made no political concessions. On the contrary, the last vestiges of political opposition were ruthlessly stamped out. 'The place for Mensheviks and Socialist Revolutionaries, open or disguised, is in prison', Lenin wrote. '. . . Terror cannot be dispensed with, notwithstanding the hypocrites and phrasemongers.'

Some time later Lenin declared: 'When the Menshevik says, "You are now retreating; I was always in favour of retreat, I agree with you, I am your man, let us retreat together," we say in reply that for the public advocacy of Menshevism our revolutionary courts must pass sentence of death, otherwise they are not our courts, but God knows what. . . . The sermons which Otto Bauer, the leaders of the Second and Two-and-a-Half Internationals, the Mensheviks and Socialist Revolutionaries preach express their very natures: "The Revolution has gone too far; we have always said what you are saying now; permit us to say it again." And we say in reply, "Permit us to put you up against the wall for saying that." '[11]

At the Tenth Party Congress, Lenin also dealt with the Workers' Opposition within the Party. To their demand for greater 'workers' control' of industry, he replied: 'If the trade unions, nine-tenths of whom are not Party members, appoint the administrators of industry, then what need is there of the Party?' Lenin told the Congress that 'the whole syndicalist absurdity must be thrown into the waste-basket.' Lenin ordered the disbanding of the Workers' Opposition group and all other dissident groups within the Party, under threat of expulsion. A resolution of the Tenth Congress, 'On Party Unity', drafted by Lenin, forebade Party members to organize, agitate or prepare platforms – even within Party circles – against decisions of the Central Committee.

'It is necessary,' Lenin declared, 'that everything should be subjected to the Soviet power and all the illusion about some kind of "independence" on the part of detached layers of population or workers' co-operatives should be lived down as soon as possible.

. . . There can be no question of independence on the part of separate groups.' Consequently, 'there can be no question, now that the world is threatening to strike at the root of capitalism, of the independence of individual parties.'[12]

The trade unions became an appendage of the Party machine and the independent workers' co-operatives were completely eliminated. At the same time, Lenin's political police perfected a system of internal espionage that blanketed Russia with a network of agents far more efficient than the Tsarist Okhrana. Ironclad censorship imposed silence on all criticism of Lenin's policies. The press, radio, cinema and theatre became, for the first time in history, an exclusive instrument of state propaganda. And the prisons and concentration camps were filled with far more prisoners than under any of the Tsars. Kronstadt had marked the last great revolt of the Russian people. Henceforth, Lenin's dictatorship was secure. The totalitarian state was coming into being.

Chapter 21
Dictator Without Vanity

Lenin might well have said: 'I created the Bolshevik Party. I was the brain of the November Revolution. Several times, when our power seemed about to crumble, I saved it by bold improvisation, by signing an unpopular peace in 1918, by introducing the NEP in 1921. I created the Comintern and gave it the revolutionary theory and strategy through which Russian Bolshevism became a world force.' Lenin could rightfully have said all this, but never did, for no dictator in history was less vain. In fact he was repelled by all attempts on the part of the men around him to set him on a pedestal.

When the Moscow Committee of the Bolshevik Party staged a celebration on his fiftieth birthday he refused to listen to the eulogizing speeches. In order not to offend the audience, he appeared for a moment, but only after the barrage of idolatry was over.

'Comrades,' he said, 'I must thank you for two things: for today's greetings and even more for excusing me from listening to the anniversary speeches.'

The fulsome praise constantly heaped on him by the Soviet newspapers disturbed him even more. 'What is it for?' he asked Bonch-Bruyevich, showing him some of the headlines. 'I find it difficult to read the papers. Wherever you look, they write about me. I consider this completely un-Marxist emphasis on an individual extremely harmful. It is bad, entirely inadmissible, and unnecessary. And these portraits? Everywhere! What is the purpose of all this?'

In reply to a Comintern question whether he spoke any foreign language fluently, Lenin wrote 'none', although he spoke at the Comintern's Third Congress in very good German, only occasionally being at a loss for the precise word he wanted. 'What are your specialities?' asked the questionnaire of the Tenth Party Congress in 1921. 'None', replied Lenin.

When the sculptor Nathan Altman was working on his bust, Lenin refused to assume a pose because he thought it would look unnatural. 'Work as much as you must, Comrade Altman,' said Lenin. 'I shall not disturb you.'

Maxim Gorky vainly tried to resolve the riddle posed by the vast contradiction between the man and the political leader.

'A passion for gambling was part of Lenin's character', says Gorky. 'But this was not the gambling of a self-centred fortune seeker. In Lenin it expressed that extraordinary power of faith which is found in a man firmly believing in his calling, one who is deeply and fully conscious of his bond with the world outside and has thoroughly understood his role in the chaos of the world, the role of an enemy of chaos.

'He could with equal enthusiasm play chess, study a volume on the *History of Dress*, debate for hours with his comrades, fish, walk along the stony paths of Capri, hot and glowing in the southern sun, admire the golden colours of the furze bush and the dirty children of the fishermen.

'In the evening, while listening to the tales of Russia or the villages, he would sigh with envy.

' "After all, how little I know of Russia! Simply Simbirsk, Kazan, Petersburg, exile, and that's about all."

'He enjoyed fun, and when he laughed, his whole body shook, really bursting with laughter, sometimes until tears came into his eyes. There was an endless scale of shade and meaning in his inarticulate "Hm" – ranging from bitter sarcasm to cautious doubt, and there was often in it the keen humour given only to one who sees far ahead and knows well the satanic absurdities of life.

'Squat and solid, with a skull like Socrates and the all-seeing eyes of a great deceiver, he often liked to assume a strange and somewhat ludicrous posture: throw his head backwards, then incline it to the shoulder, put his hands under his armpits, behind the vest. There was in this posture something delightfully comical, something triumphantly cocky. At such moments his whole being radiated happiness.

'His movements were lithe and supple and his sparing but forceful gestures harmonized well with his words, also sparing but abounding in significance. From his face of Mongolian cast gleamed and flashed the eyes of a tireless hunter of falsehood and of the woes of life – eyes that squinted, blinked, sparkled sardonically, or glowered with rage. The glare of those eyes rendered his words more burning and more poignantly clear.'[1]

Yet the same Lenin capitalized on ignorance to weave fantastic charges against his political opponents. Thus when a few days after the Bolshevik Revolution unruly soldiers and sailors of Petrograd broke into the wine cellars of the city, Lenin did not hesitate to charge that the raid had been organized by the Central Committee of the Constitutional Democratic Party.

To discredit his enemies in the eyes of the Russian people, everything was permissible. Martov was branded by Lenin as a 'traitor' and 'renegade', and yet when Lenin was ill he remarked 'with sorrow' to Krupskaya, 'And Martov, too, they say, is dying.' To Gorky he complained, 'What a pity Martov is not with us. What a wonderful comrade he is!' He burst into laughter when he heard of Martov's remark that there are only two real Communists in Russia – Lenin and Madame Kollontai (the latter for her advocacy of sexual freedom). His laughter ended with a sigh: 'What a wise man Martov is!'

Shortly before his own death, Lenin inquired about Axelrod and Martov, pointing to their names in a paper and stuttering, 'What?' He asked Krupskaya to call Kamenev and inquire about Axelrod's health, then listened to her report of the telephone conversation.

For Martov, the lifelong foe of Bolshevism, Lenin retained more personal affection than for his most devoted lieutenants. In 1916, he had written that Lunacharsky (future Commissar of Education) and Manuilsky (future head of the Comintern) were 'without heads', Radek, he wrote, 'conducts himself like an impudent, impertinent, stupid huckster. . . . If Radek did not understand what he was doing, he is a little fool. If he understood, he is a scoundrel.' In the same letter, he wrote that Piatakov 'doesn't have a particle of brains; he's like a little pig'. After a quarrel with Piatakov and Bukharin, he wrote in November 1916, 'I have done everything possible for a "peaceful" settlement. If you don't like it, I'll smash your faces and show you up as little fools before the whole world.' In February 1917, reacting against manoeuvres among the Russian *émigrés* in New York, he wrote, 'Trotsky arrived and that scoundrel at once palled up with the right wing of the *Novy Mir* against the Left Zimmerwaldists! That's how it is! That's Trotsky! Always himself. Wags his tail, cheats, poses as a left-winger, helps the "right" wingers as long as possible.'[2]

Lenin did not allow personal feeling to influence his actions.

According to Gorky, he reduced everything to the following formula:

'Whoever is not with us is against us. People who are independent of history are only imaginary. Even if we grant that at some period in the past they did exist, they certainly do not exist now and cannot. They would be useless. Everybody, down to the most unimportant man, is drawn into the vortex of reality tangled as it has never been before.'

'You say I simplify life too much? You think this simplification threatens culture with destruction?'

Then followed his ironic, characteristic sound, 'Hm . . . Hm. . . .'

Lenin constantly preached that all notions of morality had to be harnessed to class interests.

'We repudiate all morality which proceeds from supernatural ideas or ideas which are outside class conceptions,' he told a gathering of Young Communists. 'In our opinion, morality is entirely subordinate to the interests of class war. Everything is moral which is necessary for the annihilation of the old exploiting social order and for uniting the proletariat. Our morality, then, consists solely in close discipline and in conscious war against the exploiters. We do not believe in external principles of morality and we will expose this deception. Communist morality is identical with the fight for strengthening the dictatorship of the proletariat.'

The problem of religious faith was reduced to the same formula. Lenin wrote long before the Revolution:

Religion is one of the forms of spiritual oppression which everywhere weigh upon the masses of the people crushed by continuous toil for others by poverty and loneliness. The weakness of the exploited classes in their struggle against their oppressors inevitably produces a belief in a better life after death, just as the weakness of the savage in his struggle with nature leads to faith in gods, devils, and miracles. Religion teaches those who toil in poverty all their lives to be resigned and patient in this world and consoles them with the hope of reward in heaven. But the exploiters are urged by faith to do good on earth because in this way they hope to win a cheap justification for their existence and a ticket of admission to heavenly bliss. Religion is the opiate of the people, a sort of spiritual liquor, meant to make the slaves of capitalism drown their humanity and their desires for a decent existence.

As an expert political strategist, Lenin had little compunction about shifting his ground to meet changing conditions. Once, when he found Karl Radek reading a collection of articles he had written in 1903, Lenin laughed heartily. 'Isn't it interesting to read what fools we were then!'[3]

His literary and artistic tastes were conventional and unperceptive. The apostle of political and social revolution rejected revolutionary experimentation in music, poetry and painting. There is no record (as Louis Fischer has noted) that Lenin ever visited the Louvre in Paris, the National Gallery in London, or any other art museum or gallery in London, Paris, Berlin, Munich, Switzerland or, for that matter, St Petersburg or Moscow. He attended few concerts.

He regarded modern poetry as generally decadent. 'Some sound all right,' he told Berzin, 'but there is very little sense in it.'

For Turgenev he had high regard; in fact he even contemplated writing an analysis of his works. But his favourite novel was Chernyshevsky's *What Is to Be Done?*, a tendentious work of slight literary merit. He admired Victor Hugo, chiefly for his novel, *Ninety-three*. Among the poets he preferred Nekrasov, who was known as 'the Russian Robert Burns', and Tiuchev – despite his Slavophile tendencies – for the spirit of elemental revolt that pervaded his writings. Dostoyevsky was a 'reactionary, albeit a genius', and while Lenin admired Tolstoy as an artist, he rejected his social and ethical doctrines.

He wrote in 1908:

The inconsistencies in the works, the opinions, the teaching, and the school of Tolstoy are glaring. On the one hand, he is an author of genius who has produced incomparable classical pictures of Russian life for world literature. On the other hand, we have the landowning aristocrat and the saintly fool. Here the most sober realism, the tearing off of all masks; there the preaching of the most infamous thing in the world – religion – the attempt to replace the official priest by priests of moral conviction, and thus to cultivate a refined and hateful form of parsondom.

Yet the same man told Gorky, after hearing a Beethoven concert, 'I know nothing more beautiful than the "Appassionata". I could hear it every day. It is marvellous, unearthly music. But I cannot listen to music often. It affects my nerves.'

Lenin did not attend the theatre more than a dozen times during his life in the Kremlin. One evening he witnessed a performance of *The Flood* and was so pleased that the next day he went again, this time to see Gorky's *Lower Depths*.

'Despite his liking for Gorky, he was critical of the play,' says Krupskaya. 'And after his experience that evening he gave up the theatre for a long time.'

The last play Lenin saw was Dickens's *The Cricket on the Hearth*, presented by the Moscow Art Theatre, but he could not sit through the performance. 'Ilyich was bored after the first act,' recalls Krupskaya. 'Dickens's middle-class sentimentality began to get on his nerves, and when the dialogue commenced between the old toy seller and his blind daughter, Ilyich could stand it no longer and walked out in the middle of the act.'

Experimental theatre was incomprehensible to Lenin. Krupskaya tells of his disconcerting experience at a performance arranged for Red Army men. Lenin was seated in one of the first rows. The actress Gzovskaya recited a Mayakovsky poem:

> '*Our God – the advance*
> *Our heart – the drum.*'

As she spoke the lines she advanced straight towards Lenin.

He sat there bewildered by her unexpected gesture. When Gzovskaya was followed by an actor who read Chekhov's *The Evildoer*, he heaved a sigh of relief.[4]

'Why worship the new,' Lenin asked Clara Zetkin, the German Communist leader, 'merely because it is new? That is nonsense, sheer nonsense. I have the courage to recognize myself to be a barbarian; I cannot extol the products of expressionism, futurism, cubism and the other "isms" as the supreme revelations of artistic genius. I do not understand them and they give me no pleasure.'[5]

The man was at once a theoretician and folk leader, Utopian and realist. His Utopia was the world revolution, but in everyday politics he was hard-boiled and extremely practical. He was a dogmatist, yet a clever enough tactician to reject no compromise that advanced his purpose. Throughout his career Lenin was backtracking on slogans he had previously preached as gospel. He favoured the Constituent Assembly as long as that made an effective slogan against Kerensky. When that body went against him he dissolved it. When it appeared that even in the Soviet he had no secure majority, he established the dictatorship of the Bolshevik Party which finally became the dictatorship of the Politburo. He readily appropriated the ideas of his opponents and used them to new advantage. Yet in a large sense he remained always true to a single idea and a single aim. From the moment he became a 'professional revolutionist' he devoted his entire life to the cause of the proletarian revolution – as he understood it. But like Nechayev and Tkachev, Lenin never looked for harmony between ends and means. All the means that led towards the goal were justified. The end was far more important than the path to it.

He had tremendous admiration for Tkachev and Nechayev, the apostle of 'terrible, complete and unsparing destruction'. As early as 1904 he told Bonch-Bruyevich that Tkachev 'was unquestionably closer than others to our point of view', and he carefully studied Tkachev's writings. After the Revolution, according to Bonch-Bruyevich, 'he attributed very great importance to Tkachev urging everyone to read and study him.'

'People completely forget,' Lenin said, 'that Nechayev possessed unique organizational talent, an ability to establish the special techniques of conspiratorial work everywhere, an ability to give his thoughts such startling formulations that they were forever imprinted on one's memory. It is sufficient to recall his words in one of the leaflets, where Nechayev, replying to the question, "Which members of the reigning house must be destroyed?" gives the succinct answer, "The whole great responsory" [prayer for the Imperial House]. This formulation is so simple and clear that it could be understood by everyone living in Russia at a time when the Orthodox Church held full sway, when the vast majority of the people, in one way or another, for one reason or another, attended church, and everyone knew that every member of the Romanov house was mentioned at the great responsory. The most unsophisticated reader, asking himself, "But which of them are to be destroyed?" would see the obvious, inevitable answer at a glance: "Why, the entire Romanov house." But this is simple to the point of genius!'[6]

He studied Clausewitz carefully, often echoing his maxim that war was a continuation of politics by other means. In the margin of Clausewitz's book he wrote: 'A good leader.'

He was no social dreamer in the ordinary sense. Russia was his laboratory for testing Communism on a grand scale; the immediate welfare of the Russian people was secondary. The enormous sacrifices which his great experiment required were inescapable and irrelevant. Mercy was a bourgeois virtue. The man who loved children, animals and nature seldom lifted a finger to save human beings from Cheka firing squads. Gorky, who often burdened him with pleas for men and women who were condemned to death, felt that his intercession aroused almost contempt. 'Don't you see you are wasting our time on mere trifles?' asked Lenin. 'You are compromising yourself in the eyes of our comrades, the workers.'[7]

But although he had no mercy for his enemies, he tolerated the worst scoundrels provided he could make use of them. 'There are no morals in politics,' he often said; 'there is only expediency.'

Against the background of his contemporaries Lenin is sharply distinguished by the fact that although he was a truly Russian phenomenon, he was at the same time completely free of narrow national bonds. Hence he could say with full sincerity: 'The interests of world Socialism are above national interests.' In the Soviet Government he relentlessly fought Russian nationalism.

As an orator, Lenin had a brilliant grasp of mass psychology and a virility of language that captivated audiences. In his mind, the entire political world revolved on the axis of force. The first step was the seizure of power, the next was to retain it. Suppression of all civil liberties and mass terror were the only reliable means. The ultimate goal – a classless society – would be reached someday.

There is no clue whether Lenin in his last days still expected that this state he had created would some day dispense with its all-powerful instruments of suppression. Reducing world politics to the irreconcilable struggle between Sovietism and capitalism, he regarded society as in a continual state of war pending the victory of the world revolution. And as long as there was war, dictatorship was necessary.

Lenin had no staff of secretaries to prepare his material, and never quite mastered the art of dictation to a stenographer. In fact, Radek declares, 'he even looked at a fountain-pen much as a Don peasant regards the first automobile he encounters.'

In his hours of leisure Lenin was an excellent companion, instigating practical jokes, suggesting entertainment, and otherwise enlivening the atmosphere. 'His humour, *joie de vivre*, bubbling energy,' says Semashko, 'could be felt everywhere. He was always surrounded by gay laughter.'

The children of his comrades always awaited his visits with joyous expectation, for he would talk very seriously with each of them and invent games to play. Even in his Kremlin days he found time for them.

Berzin, one of Lenin's closest friends, describes how, in the hectic days of the first winter in power, Lenin still remembered his little daughter Maya, and asked that she visit him. When the visitors arrived, Lenin became the playmate of the seven-year-old girl.

'Vladimir Ilyich entered into a long and quite serious conversation with the girl. Both of them spoke with great animation. I don't know what they talked about. Then they began to play hide-and-seek, and this was the picture I saw before me.

'Nadezhda Konstantinovna [Krupskaya] and I were sitting at the table talking; a seven-year-old girl was standing in the corner with her eyes closed, and Vladimir Ilyich was walking around in search of a place to hide.

'At first they played rather quietly, hiding behind the cupboard, closet, or the drapes. But soon all the obvious hiding-places were exhausted.

'The girl was looking everywhere but could not find her partner. Then she saw his shoes sticking out from under the sofa. She jumped up and began pulling "uncle" from his lair. There was a loud childish scream, and the ripple of jolly, happy laughter from Vladimir Ilyich.'

When he drove through near-by villages, his sister Maria relates, a crowd of tow-haired peasant youngsters would come racing up to our car and beg us for a ride. Vladimir Ilyich would ask [the chauffeur] to stop, and the car would be filled to overflowing with a boisterous, exultant crowd of children. When we had gone a kilometre or so, the children would get out and with happy shouts run back to the village.'[8]

His favourite relaxation during his first years in the Kremlin were Sunday trips to the country. 'Farther away from city noise, farther from Moscow!' he would say to his chauffeur, Gill, each Saturday, as he selected the spot for an excursion. They would leave Saturday night and drive fifty or sixty kilometres beyond the city. In the spring they hunted woodcocks and grouse. In the summer they bathed, wandered through the woods, rested on the grass. In the fall they hunted again, usually rabbits and grouse. After the spring of 1919 he was often accompanied by his brother Dmitri or sister Maria. Travelling incognito, they would stop for the night with some peasants. After supper and talk with the hosts, Lenin would say, 'And now to bed! We'll rise at dawn and be off to the woods! Show us the hayloft!'

On these jaunts Lenin would not sleep anywhere but in the hay-loft. When offered bedding, Lenin resolutely refused. 'No, please don't do anything! We'll sleep right here on the hay. No bedding! There won't be the same feeling, the same pleasure.' He would cover himself with his coat or a thin blanket. Early in the morning he would go to the river or the well to wash. It was a day of move-ment, hunting, lying on the grass, and running races. On Monday morning he would leave the woods, the village, or river, renewed and refreshed.

On one excursion out of Moscow Lenin came upon an old peasant who was picking mushrooms in the woods. Soon the two men were engaged in warm conversation. As they parted, the peasant sighed:' They say a certain Lenin rules Russia these days. If that Lenin were like you things would really start moving.'9

Chapter 22
The Testament

Towards the end of 1921 Lenin's health became seriously impaired. Sometimes, during his work, he would clasp his head and remain immobile for several minutes. He complained of increasing insomnia and weariness, and his headaches became more frequent. At the beginning of 1922 he developed spells of vertigo which forced him to catch hold of the nearest object to keep from falling. When his physicians assured him that this was a trifling ailment caused by overwork, he brooded and observed moodily, 'No, I feel this is the first sign.' No one was able to dispel his pessimism. 'Remember my words,' he said to his friends. 'I will end in paralysis.' He began to study his symptoms in medical books.

Early in December he went to his home in the village of Gorki, leaving a note to the members of the Politburo: 'Despite the fact that I have diminished my work and extended my rest, my insomnia has increased devilishly. I am afraid that I will be unable to report either at the Party Congress or at the Congress of the Soviets.' From the village of Gorki he still dictated Soviet policies. When Foreign Commissar Chicherin proposed that the Soviet Government agree to certain changes in its constitution in return for economic 'compensations' from Europe and America, Lenin replied angrily: 'I think that Chicherin should be immediately sent to a sanatorium, and there should be no negligence about it.'

The Eleventh Party Congress in March 1922 was the last Lenin attended. It was after this Congress that the Central Committee elected Stalin General Secretary of the Communist Party.

The leading medical specialists of Russia and Germany were summoned to examine Lenin. In March 1922 the doctors still found no organic affliction in his nervous system. On 23 April, an operation was performed to extract one of the two bullets remaining in his body as a result of the attempted assassination in 1918; the doctors supposed that the deterioration of his health might be due to the effects of metal oxidation. The operation was successful, and the stitches were removed four days later. But Lenin's health did not improve. Early in May he suffered his first stroke. For a short time he lost his speech and the ability to move his right hand and leg. Within a few weeks he could no longer speak or walk. Then he began to suffer attacks that lasted from half an hour to two hours. After these attacks he felt somewhat better. He asked the doctors to tell him if this was the end. If so, he had to leave special orders. The doctors felt reasonably sure that the end was not yet in sight. But Lenin was now an invalid. While his understanding remained unimpaired, he could no longer express himself clearly, even with signs.

The supervision of his medical care was in the hands of the Central Committee of the Party, but in all matters of importance the doctors dealt through Commissar of Health Dr Semashko. Through Dr Semashko the doctors questioned Lenin on delicate questions to reach a proper diagnosis, questions which they were afraid to ask Lenin directly. 'In such circumstances,' tells Semashko, 'the doctors chose me as the intermediary between them and Vladimir Ilyich. I realized that my mission was not liked by Vladimir Ilyich, but it was necessary for his recovery, and Vladimir Ilyich was often angry and dissatisfied.'

Lenin was nursed by his sister Maria, while Krupskaya taught him to write with his left hand and to articulate words aloud. Her experience as a former teacher was very useful now and Lenin, like an apt schoolboy, exercised himself in reading and writing.

Driven by his indomitable will, Lenin's body made a terrific effort to recover its normal state. His brain, which had lost the faculty of associating letters with sound, gradually recovered. In the long winter nights he would lapse into a sort of pensive doze. At such moments he wanted to hear music. Piatakov, who was an excellent pianist, would be summoned and would play various selections by Chopin, Brahms and Bach. While playing, Piatakov often noticed that Lenin's face would completely change, become calm, simple and childishly earnest. The usual cunning gleam in his eyes disappeared entirely.

Lenin's convalescence at Gorki, after his first stroke, had begun on 28 May. Within a few weeks he was allowed to see his close associates, but only on condition that they did not talk business. 'Under those conditions,' he said, 'it's better not to have permission at all.' He asked the doctors for things to do. 'If I don't do anything, I shall of course start thinking about politics. Politics is a most engrossing thing, and only something even more engrossing could deflect me from it, but there is no such thing.'

Lenin was amused when he heard that the official medical bulletin on his stroke had referred to an intestinal disease affecting the blood circulation. 'I thought the best diplomats were at The Hague,' he said, 'but it seems they are in Moscow – they are the doctors who have composed this bulletin about my health.'[1]

By July, Lenin was again on his feet. He began playing each morning with a young Irish setter named Aida, and hoped to go hunting in the future. These were stormy days in Moscow for his colleagues. From 8 June to 7 August, there took place the trial of twenty-two leaders of the Socialist Revolutionary Party, charged with organizing an uprising against the Soviet power in 1918 (despite the amnesty granted by the Soviet Government to SR members on 25 February 1919). Lenin had been concerned with this trial from the beginning. When, at the futile Berlin 'conference of the three Internationals' (Social Democratic, left-wing Socialist and Communist), Bukharin and Radek agreed that there would be no death sentences and that representatives of the Socialist Internationals could attend the trial, Lenin protested fiercely in *Pravda* of 11 April 1922:

Radek, Bukharin and the other representatives of the Communist International acted improperly in making concessions without assuring for themselves corresponding concessions by the other side. This need not, however, lead us to the conclusion that the agreement should be nullified. Such a conclusion would be wrong. We must simply draw the lesson that in this case the bourgeois diplomats proved themselves more skilful than our own and that we must learn to manoeuvre and act more skilfully in the future.

A number of Western Socialists, including Emile Vandervelde of Belgium and Theodore Liebknecht of Germany, came to Moscow to defend the Socialist Revolutionaries. They were greeted by hostile demonstrations on arrival – with Bukharin personally egging the crowd on. In the course of the trial, there were further demonstrations. Defence witnesses and documents were not admitted. The Western defence attorneys finally withdrew from the case, and had to stage a twenty-four-hour hunger strike in order to leave Moscow. Vandervelde summed up the trial itself as follows:

The Bolsheviks brought four indictments against the Socialist Revolutionaries:

1. The Socialist Revolutionaries defended the Provisional Government with arms in their hands. The Socialist Revolutionaries admit this fact and are proud of it.

2. The Socialist Revolutionaries defended the Constituent Assembly with arms in their hands. The Socialist Revolutionaries admit this fact and are only sorry that they did not succeed in carrying this to a successful conclusion.

3. The Socialist Revolutionaries waged an armed struggle against the Soviet Government. The Socialist Revolutionaries admit this as an undeniable historic fact.

But all these three accusations must be ruled out of court, for the Soviet Government had issued an amnesty covering all these actions and even legalized the Socialist Revolutionary Party.

4. The Socialist Revolutionaries took part in Volodarsky's assassination and in the attempt on Lenin. There is not a shred of evidence nor a single witness to support this charge. . . .

The Soviet Government was torn between the agreement it had made in Berlin, the determination to discredit the Socialist Revolutionary Party, and the open defiance of the defendants. Lenin was thinking ahead to possible future cases of this kind. In a note to D. I. Kursky, Commissar of Justice, in connexion with the discussions in May 1922 of a new Criminal Code, Lenin wrote:

In my opinion it is necessary to extend the application of execution by shooting to all phases covering activities of Mensheviks, Social Revolutionaries and the like; a formula must be found that would place these activities in connexion with the international bourgeoisie and its struggle against us (bribery of the press and agents, war preparations, and the like).

By a strange irony, this note was first published (in the Moscow *Bolshevik*) on 15 January 1937, at the height of Stalin's Moscow Trials of Old Bolsheviks. Among those who then perished were Piatakov, the judge in the SR trial; Krylenko, the prosecutor; Bukharin, who had incited the crowds against the defence attorneys; and Kamenev, who had produced the eventual 'solution' to the Bolshevik dilemma.

In his closing address, Krylenko declared, 'Blood must flow here in order that it may not flow again.' But then, after demanding the death penalty, Krylenko suddenly offered the Socialist Revolutionaries acquittal and freedom provided they 'repented' and disavowed their party.

'There can be no question of repentance or disavowal,' replied Eugène Timoffeyev, one of the SR leaders, who had served twelve years at hard labour in Siberia under the Tsar. 'From these benches you will never hear anything like that.'

On 7 August, the court condemned twelve of the defendants to death, the others to prison terms – and submitted the verdict for the examination of the Bolshevik Party conference. Here a large group urged that the sentences be commuted to permanent banishment outside the U.S.S.R. Trotsky, Stalin and Bukharin opposed such mercy; they urged giving the defendants twenty-four hours to reconsider a disavowal of their party and principles, in which case the sentences would be reduced; otherwise, the verdict was to be carried out at once.

Lenin was undecided. Finally, Kamenev proposed that the death sentences be confirmed, but that the executions be held in abeyance. In the event of any overt act against the Soviet régime deemed to be the work of Socialist Revolutionaries, the executions would be carried out at once. In fact, the Socialist Revolutionaries, after long years in prison and concentration camps, were liquidated by Stalin during the Great Purges without any overt act by Socialists.

As a result of his convalescence in Gorki, Lenin improved to such an extent that on 2 October 1922 he was able to return to Moscow.

The doctors permitted him to work from eleven to two and from six to eight, on the condition that he rest two days a week. He again began to preside over the Politburo and Sovnarcom, and to talk for hours on the telephone and with visitors, to dictate letters and articles, and issue secret instructions to Communist agents in other countries. He even took the risk of appearing at the Fourth Congress of the Comintern. He came into the hall, accompanied by his usual group, and went directly to the platform. Delegations of various countries all rose and began to sing the 'Internationale', each in its own language. Lenin stood silent, his head inclined to one side. Then he began to talk slowly, conserving his strength. Soon, however, he began to talk louder and faster. Unable to find the appropriate German word, he snapped his fingers by way of appeal. From the first rows and table came promptings, not always correct, and these he waved away impatiently. He summoned the Communists abroad to greater activity and promised them Soviet support.

'Depend on us. We have broad shoulders. Prepare yourself solidly. Don't accept the battle too early. Gather strength and strike the bourgeoisie as is necessary. Strike it only in the chest when you are sure of victory.'[2]

In the middle of the speech Lenin's strength began to give way. His voice grew weaker, he snapped his fingers more frequently, and when he finished he was covered with perspiration. Clara Zetkin ran up and kissed his hand. Lenin gallantly returned the gesture.

In the second half of November, Lenin began suffering again from painful headaches and insomnia. Lydia Fotyieva, his principal secretary, kept a record of his illness and noted that he continued work despite doctors' objections. On 25 November she reported: 'Today the physicians prescribed absolute rest.'

From that day on Lenin's regular work routine ceased. He did not come to his office regularly, did not receive so many people. On the other hand, he read more than ever.

Lenin at this time no longer said, as he had in 1918, that Socialism was 'already being realized in fact'. On the contrary, he now wondered: 'Is it not clear that in a material, economic, industrial sense we are not yet at the threshold of Socialism?'

As for Larin, the author of the sweeping nationalization decrees of 1918, Lenin dispatched him to London 'for his health', advising Krassin, the Soviet Ambassador to London:

'1. Keep him (Larin) in London as long as possible.

'2. If you believe even one of his statistics, we'll kick you out of the service.

'3. Take care of his health. Cure him. Select a *responsible* doctor.

'4. Keep him busy with protracted literary work in the German and English materials. (If he doesn't know it, teach him the English language.)

'Points 1, 3, and 4 are to be carried out with particular diligence and *particular tact*. Point 2 is triply important.'[3]

He now dubbed the policy of prohibiting the development of private trade as 'stupid and suicidal'. And he embarrassed orthodox Communists with the order: 'Learn to trade'. Lenin was restoring the monetary system and explained: 'If we succeed in stabilizing the ruble, we have won.'

Lenin no longer wanted to set up compulsory collective farms and to establish the communal tillage of soil.

'We have done many stupid things with regard to collective farms. The question of the collective farms is not on the order of the day. We must rely on the individual peasant; he is as he is and will not become different within the near future. Peasants are not Socialists, and building Socialist plans in the same way as if they were Socialists means building on sand. The transformation of the peasant's psychology and habits is something that requires generations. The use of force will not help. The task before us is to influence the peasantry morally. We must give consideration to the middle peasant. The *efficient peasant* must be the *central figure* of our economic *recovery*.'[4]

In December 1922 a second stroke came, this time more severe. By a mighty effort Lenin again fought off this illness. His physicians insisted on complete rest, complete cessation of all mental effort. A few weeks later, ignoring their advice, he began to work on an article about the role of co-operatives in the Soviet economic system. He defined Socialism as 'an order of civilized co-operators in which the means of production are socially owned'. Parallel to this, Lenin noted that 'the political and social revolution in Russia preceded the cultural revolution.' The greatest attention should now be directed towards instilling culture among the masses. 'The transition to Socialism requires complete transformation of thinking, a whole period of cultural development.' A month later, to the astonishment of many, he added: 'We could do for the start with some genuine bourgeois culture.'

These were his last articles; on 12 December Lenin sat at his desk for the last time in his life. The following day he began to wind up his affairs preparatory to a rest in the country. For two or three days he dictated letters, issued various instructions, and received comrades. Worried about the interruptions in his work, he often reiterated that he was in a hurry to liquidate it properly, as he might be taken ill suddenly.

To Stalin he dictated a well-known letter:

'I have now finished liquidating my affairs and can depart in peace. There remains only one circumstance which disturbs me very strongly – that I cannot take part in the Congress of the Soviets. . . . To forego it I would consider to be a great inconvenience to myself, not to put it more strongly.'

After consultation with his doctors, Lenin had to abandon hope of attending the Congress of Soviets, which opened on 16 December. He was reluctant to go to Gorki again, for the trip by aerosleigh was exhausting and there was too much snow to go by automobile. He also developed an acute toothache. To the Politburo in connexion with the Congress, Lenin – disturbed by various troubles among the non-Russian nationalities, particularly the Georgians – sent a brief note:

I am declaring a war not for life, but to the death, against Great Russian chauvinism. As soon as I rid myself of my damned tooth, I shall eat it with all my strong teeth. One must *absolutely* insist that the united Central Executive Committee be presided over in turn by:

A Russian
A Ukrainian
A Georgian, and so on.
Absolutely.

On 23 December he began dictating a 'Letter to the Congress' to a stenographer, M. A. Volodicheva. The doctors objected, but Lenin argued that either he would be allowed to dictate or he would not follow the cure. At a conference between the doctors and several Politburo members the next day, it was agreed that Lenin could dictate for five or ten minutes a day. On 25 and 26 December, in four sessions, he dictated the letter which was to become known as his 'Political Testament'.

As Lenin had become increasingly incapacitated, a struggle for power had developed between Zinoviev, Trotsky and Stalin. Zinoviev was the president of the Communist International and of the Petrograd Soviet; Trotsky the chairman of the Military Revolutionary Council and Commissar of War; and Stalin the General Secretary of the Party.

When Lenin relinquished his work, the leadership of the Party went to the triumvirate of Zinoviev, Kamenev and Stalin. By April 1923 a silent fight for control had developed between Zinoviev and Stalin. Trotsky, for his part, began to campaign against the triumvirate. His post of chairman of the Revolutionary Council was an honorary one and he was not given any key work in the party machine. At the Bolshevik Congress in 1923 Trotsky hinted that he was being side-tracked, and that his abilities were not being sufficiently utilized.

For a time the dominant figure in the Politburo was Zinoviev. He had a majority in the Central Committee, whose members felt that under Zinoviev each would be able to broaden his sphere of influence. Of the six members of the Politburo apart from Lenin, Trotsky was opposed by all, and Tomsky played only an insignificant role. Thus Zinoviev, Kamenev and Bukharin constituted a majority against Stalin. But neither the majority of the Central Committee nor of the Politburo ever thought of elevating Zinoviev to leadership, for the recognition of leadership required control of the Party Congress. And here Stalin loomed large. Slowly but surely he gradually planted his men as secretaries all through the Party organization, stopping at nothing to gain control of the Party machine.

By the end of 1922, when it became clear that Lenin's condition was hopeless, Stalin began to work out a series of changes in the governmental structure. Stalin himself did not deny that he had made extraordinary advance preparations for the Twelfth Party Congress, which met in March 1923. 'For the last six years,' he said, 'the Central Committee never prepared for the Congress as at this moment.'

In the 'testament' which he dictated on 25 and 26 December 1922, and in a postscript added on 4 January 1923, Lenin undertook to evaluate the various Bolshevik leaders, endeavouring to find the man or men capable of succeeding him. He concluded by recommending the removal of Stalin as General Secretary.

Lenin wrote:

Comrade Stalin, having become general secretary, has concentrated enormous power in his hands, and I am not sure that he always knows how to use that power with sufficient caution. On the other hand, Comrade Trotsky, as was proved by his struggle against the Central Committee in connexion with the question of the People's Commissariat of Transport and Communication, is distinguished not only by his exceptional ability – personally, he is, to be sure, the most able man in the present Central Committee – but also by his too far-reaching self-confidence and a disposition to be far too much attracted by the purely administrative side of affairs.

These two qualities of the two most able leaders of the present Central Committee might, quite innocently, lead to a split. If our Party does not take measures to prevent it, a split may occur unexpectedly.

I will not further characterize the other members of the Central Committee as to their personal qualities. I will only remind you that the October episode of Zinoviev and Kamenev was not, of course, accidental, but that it ought as little to be used against them as the 'non-Bolshevism' of Trotsky.

Of the younger members of the Central Committee, I want to say a few words about Piatakov and Bukharin. They are, in my opinion, the most able forces (among the youngest). In regard to them it is necessary to bear in mind the following: Bukharin is not only the most valuable theoretician of the Party, as he is the biggest, but he also may be considered the favourite of the whole Party. But his theoretical views can with only the greatest reservations be regarded as fully Marxist, for there is something scholastic in him. (He never has learned, and I think never fully understood, the dialectic.)

And then Piatakov – a man undoubtedly distinguished in will and ability, but too much given over to the administrative side of affairs to be relied upon in serious political questions.

Of course both these remarks are made by me merely with regard to the present time, or on the supposition that these two able and loyal workers may not find occasion to supplement their knowledge and correct their one-sidedness.

25 December, 1922.

Postscript: Stalin is too rude, and this fault, entirely supportable in relation to us Communists, becomes insupportable in the office of General Secretary. Therefore I propose to the comrades to find a way to remove Stalin from that position and appoint to it another man who in all respects differs from Stalin only in superiority – namely, more patient, more loyal, more polite, and more attentive to comrades, less capricious, etc. This circumstance may seem an insignificant trifle, but I think that from the point of view of preventing a split and from the point of view of the relation between Stalin and Trotsky, which I discussed above, it is not a trifle, or it is such a trifle as may acquire a decisive significance.

4 January 1923.
LENIN

The 'rudeness' of Stalin, to which Lenin referred, had been manifested in a telephone conversation with Krupskaya on 22

December. In a letter to Kamenev next day, Krupskaya had complained:

> Because of a short letter which I had written in words dictated to me by Vladimir Ilyich by permission of the doctors, Stalin allowed himself yesterday an unusually rude outburst directed at me. This is not my first day in the Party. During all the thirty years I have never heard from any comrade one word of rudeness. The business of the party and of Ilyich are not less dear to me than to Stalin. . . . I beg you to protect me from rude interference with my private life and from vile invectives and threats. I have no doubt as to what will be the unanimous decision of the Control Commission, with which Stalin sees fit to threaten me. . . .

Two and a half months later, on 5 March 1923, Lenin sent Stalin the following letter:

> You permitted yourself a rude summons of my wife to the telephone and a rude reprimand of her. Despite the fact that she told you that she agreed to forget what was said, nevertheless Zinoviev and Kamenev heard about it from her. I have no intention to forget so easily that which is being done against me, and I need not stress here that I consider as directed against me that which is being done against my wife. I ask you, therefore, that you weigh carefully whether you are agreeable to re-tracting your words and apologizing or whether you prefer the severance of relations between us.[5]

Trotsky has called this the last surviving Lenin document. The morning after its dictation, Lenin asked his secretary, Fotyieva, to deliver it personally to Stalin and await his reply. But that very day Lenin's condition took a sharp turn for the worse. On 9 March he suffered his third stroke.

Professor Rozanov found Lenin in a very grave state, running a high fever and suffering from complete paralysis of the right extremities as well as aphasia. Lenin's entire vocabulary consisted of a few words such as 'Lloyd George', 'conference', 'impossibility', and several others. Helplessly he sought to convey a variety of meaning by the inflexion of his voice and by gestures. His gesti-culations, although insistent, were not always comprehensible. This so greatly agitated the patient that in tense excitement he would motion everyone out of his chamber – physicians, nurses, attendants, all.[6]

There was no hope of recovery. All that could be done was to make Lenin comfortable. In the middle of May he was taken from the Kremlin to Gorki again. Towards the end of July he improved slightly and could be taken out into the garden in a wheel-chair. His spirits and appetite improved. Later he could even walk across the room, supported by a cane or the arm of his wife or sister. Once more he began to interest himself in politics and to practice speaking. He had lost the ability of uttering complete words. He knew the word he wanted to use but could not articulate it completely. He would say 'Rev-rev-rev-vo-vo-vo-lu', for 'revolution'. Krupskaya prompted him by making him repeat the first syllable, then the next, and the next. Lenin tried with all his power to learn but with little result.

In the autumn his condition seemed to improve still more. In October 1923 a miracle appears to have taken place. As if rising from the dead, Lenin was again on his feet. On 10 October an event took place which was related to Valentinov in three versions. He does not know which is the correct one.

On this day, to the consternation of his wife and doctors, Lenin suddenly sent for his car, declaring that he had to go to Moscow. Attempts were made to dissuade him, but he commanded imperiously, and no one dared to disobey. Lenin went to Moscow. According to one version, he was accompanied only by Krupskaya. According to another, his doctor was also with them. The third places still another person in the car. Throughout the drive, as if sensing that life was granted him for the briefest time, he urged the chauffeur on: 'Hurry, hurry!'

In Moscow he went to his office in the Kremlin. This is again described in three versions. Silently, with hands folded behind his back, Lenin walked around his office, as if taking leave of the place from which he once guided the destinies of Russia. That is one version. Another has it that Lenin took a certain document from his desk and put it in his pocket. This second story is contradicted by a third: he looked for the document; not finding it there, he became furious and shouted incoherently.[7]

His illness, meanwhile, progressed according to its own laws, with the brain deteriorating. To cheer the patient, he was taken on auto or sleigh rides in good weather. On 24 December his wife set up a Christmas tree and called in the peasants. Lenin was cheerful.

On 20 January 1924, however, according to Dr Semashko's

official report, Lenin 'felt unwell. He awoke out of sorts, complained of headache and had no appetite. The next morning he
awoke with the same feeling, refused food, and only at the insistent request of those around him was he persuaded to eat a little
at breakfast and a little at dinner. After dinner he lay down to
rest. Suddenly, the members of his household noticed that his
breathing was heavy and irregular. At 6 p.m. on 21 January 1924,
a severe attack set in. Lenin lost consciousness. His breathing became worse and worse. His face grew deathly pale. His temperature
rose rapidly. Within fifty minutes, he died of a haemorrhage of the
brain which resulted in paralysis of the respiratory organs.'

The body was embalmed after a thorough macro-and-micro-
scopic pathological examination. The examination revealed mul-
tiple and extensive areas of softening in the left and partly in the
right hemispheres of the cerebrum and a fresh haemorrhage in
the region of *corpora quadrigemina*. Interpreting these objective
findings, the official autopsy report gave as the basis of his disease
and death very marked sclerosis of cerebral vessels as a result of
excessive cerebral activity combined with a hereditary pre-
disposition towards arteriosclerosis.

According to a German specialist who was present at the
autopsy, Lenin's brain 'shrank in its material composition' to
about 'one quarter' of the normal size of the cerebral mass.

'When we opened him up,' writes Professor Rozanov, 'we found
a massive sclerosis of the cerebral vessels and sclerosis only. The
amazing thing was not that the thinking power remained intact in
such a sclerotic brain, but that he could live so long with such a
brain.'[8]

Professor Foerster, who attended Lenin until the moment of his
death, explained that 'the illness lasted two years. It came on unnoticed and developed gradually. After a period of comparative
improvement, which awakened the hope of recovery, a sudden
attack, which lasted an hour and affected the respiratory organs,
brought on the end.

'Lenin's malady was occasioned by inner causes,' he concluded.
'It developed according to inner laws, independent of external
factors, with merciless inevitability.'[9]

From the snow-blanketed village of Gorki the news of Lenin's
death reverberated throughout Russia. A long procession of

friends and disciples from Moscow and its environs filed past the coffin. On 23 January the body was carried by his Communist disciples to the railroad station for transportation to Moscow. The entire route from Gorki to Moscow, thirty miles long, was lined with people as the train bearing the body of Lenin passed on its way. In Moscow the body lay in state in the House of the Trade Unions. A procession of hundreds of thousands came to pay their last tribute.

On the day of the funeral a large black flag draped the building. At four o'clock in the morning soldiers of Lenin's military guard silently met in front of the house. From afar came the dull, continuous rumble of cannon in Moscow saluting the memory of Lenin. The soldiers of the guard raised their rifles and fired three volleys in salute.

It was very cold that morning as most of Moscow turned out for the funeral procession. The coffin was carried by the members of the Politburo. The entire day endless delegations of workers and Red Army units, delegations of foreign Communists, passed by the bier and left wreaths. Only at four in the afternoon was Lenin's body placed in a crypt to the accompaniment of all the factory whistles of Moscow.

His body was not buried or cremated like the remains of other revolutionary leaders, but was embalmed and lodged in a rich mausoleum in Red Square, decorated with the five black letters of Lenin's name.

Lenin, who detested hero worship and fought religion as an opiate for the people, was canonized in the interest of Soviet politics and his writings were given the character of Holy Writ.

Five days after Lenin's death, on 26 January 1924, Stalin delivered a speech before the Congress of the Soviets in which he said:
'In departing from us, Comrade Lenin bequeathed to us the duty of holding aloft and guarding the purity of the great title of member of the Party. We vow to you, Comrade Lenin, that we will fulfil your bequest with honour.

'For twenty-five years Comrade Lenin reared our Party and finally raised it into the strongest and most steeled workers' party in the world. . . .

'In departing from us, Comrade Lenin bequeathed to us the duty of guarding the unity of our Party like the apple of our eye.

We vow to you, Comrade Lenin, that we will also fulfil this bequest of yours with honour. . . .

'In departing from us, Comrade Lenin bequeathed to us the duty of guarding and strengthening the dictatorship of the proletariat. We vow to you, Comrade Lenin, that we will spare no effort to fulfil also this bequest of yours with honour. . . .

'Lenin told us more than once that the respite we have gained from the capitalist states may be a short one. More than once Lenin pointed out to us that the strengthening of the Red Army and the improvement of its condition is one of the most important tasks of our Party. . . . Let us vow then, comrades, that we will spare no effort to strengthen our Red Army and our Red Navy.

'Our country stands like a huge rock surrounded by the ocean of bourgeois states. Wave after wave hurls itself against it, threatening to submerge it and sweep it away. But the rock stands unshakeable. Wherein lies its strength? Not only in the fact that our country is based on the alliance between the workers and peasants, that it is the personification of the alliance of free nationalities, that it is protected by the strong arm of the Red Army and the Red Navy. The strength of our country, its firmness, its durability, lies in the fact that it finds profound sympathy and unshakeable support in the hearts of the workers and peasants of the world.

'Lenin never regarded the republic of Soviets as an end in itself. He always regarded it as a necessary link for strengthening the revolutionary movements in the lands of the West and the East, as a necessary link for facilitating the victory of toilers of the whole world over capital. Lenin knew that only such an interpretation is the correct one, not only from the international point of view, but also from the point of view of preserving the republic of Soviets itself. Lenin knew that only in this way is it possible to inflame the hearts of toilers of all countries for the decisive battles for emancipation. That is why this genius among the great leaders of the proletariat, on the very morrow of the establishment of the proletarian dictatorship, laid the foundation of the Workers' International. That is why he never tired of .expanding and consolidating the union of the toilers of the whole world, the Communist International . . .

'In departing from us, Comrade Lenin bequeathed to us the duty of remaining loyal to the principles of the Communist

International. We vow to you, Comrade Lenin, that we will not spare our lives to strengthen and expand the union of the toilers of the whole world – the Communist International.'[10]

For many years, the oath that Stalin took at Lenin's bier continued to guide the destinies of the Soviet Union. Stalin went considerably beyond Lenin: in executing dissidents and potential rivals even among Communists, in accusing Party and Red Army leaders of being Fascists, in cancelling Lenin's New Economic Policy and proceeding with forcible collectivization of agriculture, in encouraging anti-Semitism and the dification of his own person. After Stalin's own death, his heirs proclaimed a 'return to Leninism', but in its first decade even this return was only partial. The historical issues posed by Lenin's ideas and actions remained to be faced.

In 1930, a right-wing Communist named Syrtzov wrote that what the Party leaders termed 'experience' was in reality but the expression of self-confidence on the part of men who did not know what they were doing. 'They are acting according to the rule: Let us see what comes out of it, and if life should punch us on the head, then we shall become convinced that we should have acted otherwise.'

Stalin and, later, Khrushchev urged Russia to overtake the advanced nations of the West; Lenin in 1917 had banked on the International Communist revolution. A half-century after Lenin's *coup*, neither has come to pass; nor is either in sight. Leninism lives on, but with each passing year it becomes increasingly an anachronism – not least in Russia.

Appendix
Essentials of Leninism

The following excerpts from Lenin's writings and speeches furnish a master guide – in Lenin's own words – to the ideology which continues to inspire Communist actions in the world today.

Dictatorship and Soviet Democracy

Capitalism cannot be defeated and eradicated without the ruthless suppression of the resistance of the exploiters, who cannot at once be deprived of their wealth, of their superiority of organization and knowledge, and consequently for a fairly long period will inevitably try to overthrow the hateful rule of the poor; secondly, a great revolution, and a socialist revolution in particular, even if there were no external war, is inconceivable without internal war, *i.e.* civil war, which is even more destructive than external war, and implies thousands and millions of cases of wavering and desertion from one side to another, implies a state of extreme indefiniteness, lack of equilibrium and chaos. . . .

(*Selected Works*, Russian Edition, Vol. 2, pp. 277–8)

Only the dictatorship of the proletariat is able to liberate mankind from the yoke of capital, from the lies, the sham, the hypocrisy of bourgeois democracy, which is a democracy *for the rich*; it alone is able to establish democracy for the *poor*, *i.e.* to make the benefits of democracy *really* accessible to the workers and the poorest peasants, whereas at the present time (even in the most democratic-*bourgeois* republic) the benefits of democracy are actually inaccessible to the overwhelming majority of the toilers.

(ibid., Vol. 2, p. 300)

Proletarian democracy is a million times more democratic than any bourgeois democracy; Soviet government is many millions of times more democratic than the most democratic-bourgeois republic.

Only a deliberate flunkey of the bourgeoisie, or a political corpse who does not see real life from behind the dusty pages of bourgeois books, who is thoroughly imbued with bourgeois-democratic prejudices, and thereby objectively becomes the lackey of the bourgeoisie, could have failed to see this. . . .

(*Collected Works*, Vol. XXIII, 1929 Edition, p. 350)

We said to the bourgeoisie: 'You, exploiters and hypocrites, talk about democracy while creating at every step a thousand-and-one obstacles to prevent the oppressed masses from taking their part in politics. We now take you at your word and in the interests of these masses we demand the extension of your bourgeois democracy in order to prepare the masses for a revolution with the purpose of overthrowing you, the exploiters. And, should you exploiters attempt to offer resistance to our proletarian revolution, we shall turn you into pariahs and mercilessly suppress you; we shall do more than that, we shall not give you any bread, for in our proletarian republic the exploiters will have no rights, they will be deprived of fire and water. . . .'

(ibid, Vol. XXII, p. 375)

If we are not anarchists, we must admit that the state, i.e. coercion is necessary for the transition from capitalism to socialism. The form of coercion is determined by the degree of development of the given revolutionary class, and also by special circumstances, such as, for example, the heritage of a long and reactionary war and the forms of resistance put up by the bourgeoisie or the petty bourgeoisie. Hence, there is absolutely no contradiction between Soviet (i.e. Socialist) democracy and the exercise of dictatorial powers by individual persons.

(Selected Works, Russian Edition, Vol. 2, p. 280)

The Soviet Socialist Democracy is in no way inconsistent with the rule and dictatorship of one person: that the will of a class is at times best realized by a dictator who sometimes will accomplish more by himself and is frequently more needed . .

(Collected Works, 1923 Edition, Vol. XVII, p. 89)

Civil Liberties

. . . We are not going to let ourselves be deceived by such high-sounding slogans like freedom, equality, and the will of the majority, and those who call themselves democrats, the partisans of pure democracy, consistent democracy, directly or indirectly opposing it to the dictatorship of the proletariat – those people we class with Kolchak's accomplices.

We declare that we are fighting capitalism as such, the free, republican, democratic capitalism included, and we realize, of course, that in this fight the banner of freedom will be waved defiantly at us. But our answer is . . . 'every freedom is a fraud if it contradicts the interests of the emancipation of labour from the oppression of capital'.

(ibid., 1923 Edition, Vol. XIV, pp. 80–1, 203–4)

Dictatorship is a state of acute war. We are precisely in such a state. There is no military invasion at present; but we are isolated. On the other hand, we are not entirely isolated in so far as the whole of the international bourgeoisie is not in a position to wage open war against us, because the whole of the working class, even though the majority is not yet Communistic, is sufficiently conscious to prevent intervention. The bourgeoisie is already compelled to reckon with the temper of the masses even though the latter have not yet entirely come over to Communism. Therefore the bourgeoisie cannot start an offensive against us, although the latter is not precluded. Until the final issue is decided, the state of terrible war will continue. And we say: *A la guerre comme à la guerre;* we do not promise any freedom nor any democracy.

(ibid., Vol. XVIII, p. 336)

Ideological talk and phrase-mongering about political liberties should be dispensed with; all that is just mere chatter and phrase-mongering. We should get away from those phrases.

Propaganda to be carried on among workers and peasants should be only of the following kind: The 'freer', or more 'democratic', a bourgeois country is, the more fiercely does the capitalist gang rage against workers' revolution; this is exemplified by the democratic republic of the United States of America.

(ibid., 1923 Edition, Vol. XVIII, pp. 100, 375)

World Revolution

Uneven economic and political development is an absolute law of capitalism. Hence, the victory of socialism is possible first in a few or even in one single capitalist country taken separately. The victorious proletariat of that country, having expropriated the capitalist and organized its own socialist production, would rise against the rest of the capitalist world, attract to itself the oppressed classes of other countries, raise revolts among them against the capitalist, and, in the event of necessity, come out even with armed force against the exploiting classes and their states. For 'the free federation of nations is impossible without a more or less prolonged and stubborn struggle of the socialist republic against the backward states'.

(Lenin and Zinoviev.
Against the Stream, Lenigrad, 1925, p. 156)

Modern capitalism cannot fight against us, it could not even if it were a hundred times stronger than it is, because over there, in the advanced countries, the workers disrupted its war yesterday and will disrupt it even more effectively tomorrow; because over there the consequences of the war are unfolding themselves more and more.

(*Collected Works*, Vol. XVIII, p. 181)

As long as capitalism and Socialism remain, we cannot live in peace. In the end one or the other will triumph – a funeral requiem will be sung either over the Soviet Republic or over world capitalism. This is a respite in war.

(ibid., Vol. XVII, p. 398)

Wilson's glorified republic proved in practice to be a form of the most rabid imperialism, of the most shameless oppression and suppression of weak and small nationalities. The average democrat in general, the Menshevik and the Socialist-Revolutionary, thought: 'Who are we even to dream of a superior type of government, a Soviet Government? We'd be thankful for at least an ordinary democratic republic?' And, of course, in 'ordinary', comparatively peaceful times such a 'hope' would have lasted for many a long decade.

But now . . . there is no *other* alternative left: *either* the Soviet Government triumphs in every advanced country in the world, or the most reactionary imperialism triumphs, the most savage imperialism which is out to throttle the small and feeble nationalities and to reinstate reaction all over the world. This is the Anglo-American imperialism which has perfectly mastered the art of using for its purposes the form of a democratic republic.

One or the other.

There is no middle course.

(ibid., Vol. XXIII, p. 292)

War, National Defence and Peace

An imperialist war does not cease to be imperialistic when charlatans or phrase-mongers or petty-bourgeois philistines proclaim sentimental 'slogans'; it ceases to be such only when the *class* which is conducting the imperialist war and is bound to it by millions of economic threads (or, rather, ropes), is *overthrown* and is replaced at the helm of state by the really revolutionary class, the proletariat. There is no other way of getting out of an imperialist war, or out of an imperialist predatory peace.

(ibid., Vol. XXIII, p. 377)

The Frenchman, the German, or the Italian who shall say: 'Socialism is opposed to violence against nations, *therefore*, I defend myself when my country is invaded', *betrays* socialism and internationalism. For *he only thinks of his own* 'country', he puts 'his own . . . bourgeoisie' above everything else and forgets about the *international connexions* which make the war an imperialist war, and *his* bourgeoisie a link in the chain of imperialist plunder.

(ibid., p. 380)

The trade unions, for example, the reformist trade unions, are passing resolutions against war and threatening to call a strike against war. Recently, if I am not mistaken, I read a telegram in the newspapers to the effect that an excellent Communist in the French Parliament made a speech and pointed out that the workers would prefer to rise in revolt rather than go to war. The question cannot be put in the way we put it in 1912, when the Basle Manifesto was published. The Russian re-volution alone showed how it was possible to emerge from war, and what efforts this entailed; what it means emerging from a reactionary war by revolutionary methods. Reactionary imperialist wars are inevitable in all parts of the world; and humanity cannot forget, and will not forget, in solving problems of this sort, that tens of millions were slaughtered at that time and will be again.

(*Selected Works*, Russian Edition, Vol. 2, p. 614)

To recognize defence of one's fatherland means recognizing the legiti-macy and justice of war. Legitimacy and justice from what point of view? Only from the point of view of the socialist proletariat and its struggle for emancipation. We do not recognize any other point of view. If war is waged by the exploiting class with the object of strengthening its class rule, such a war is a criminal war, and 'defencism' in *such* a war is base betrayal of socialism. If war is waged by the proletariat after it has conquered the bourgeoisie in its own country, and is waged with the object of strengthening and extending socialism, such a war is legitimate and 'holy'.

(*Selected Works*, English Edition, Vol. 7, p. 357)

The Socialist, the revolutionary proletarian, the internationalist, reasons differently: 'The character of the war (whether reactionary or revolution-ary) is not determined by who the aggressor was, or whose territory the "enemy" has occupied; it is *determined by the class* that is waging the war, and the politics of which this war is a continuation. If a given war is a reactionary imperialist war, that is, if it is being waged by two world coalitions of the imperialist, violent predatory, reactionary bourgeoisie, then every bourgeoisie (even of the smallest country) becomes a participant in the plunder, and my duty as a representative of the revolutionary proletariat is to prepare for the *world proletarian revolution* as the *only* escape from the horrors of a world war. I must reason, not from the point of view of "any" country (for this is the reasoning of a poor, stupid, nationalist philistine who does not realize that he is only a plaything in the hands of the imperialist bourgeoisie), but from the point of view of my share in the preparation, the propaganda, and in the acceleration of the world proletarian revolution.'

(*Collected Works*, Vol. XXIII, p. 380)

What would have saved us still more would have been a war between the imperialist powers. If we are obliged to tolerate such scoundrels as the capitalist thieves, each of whom is preparing to plunge a knife into us, it is our direct duty to make them turn their knives against each other. When thieves fall out, honest men come into their own.

I have pointed to one imperialist antagonism, one of which it is our duty to take advantage, the antagonism between Japan and America. Another one is the antagonism between America and the rest of the capitalist world. Nearly the whole of the capitalist world of 'victors' emerged from the war with tremendous gains. America is strong, everybody is now in debt to her, everything depends on her, she is being more and more hated, she is robbing everybody, and she is robbing them in a very original way. . . . We must take this trend of circumstances into account. America cannot come to terms with Europe – that is a fact proved by history.

(ibid, Vol. XVII, pp. 391–2)

The world has been divided up; Japan has seized a colossal number of colonies, Japan has a population of fifty million, and she is comparatively weak economically. America has a population of a hundred and ten million, she has no colonies, although she is several times richer than Japan. Japan has seized China, which has a population of four hundred million and the richest coal reserves in the world. How can this plum be retained? It is absurd to think that the stronger capitalism will not deprive the weaker capitalism of everything the latter has plundered. Can the Americans remain indifferent under such circumstances? Can strong capitalists be left by the side of weak capitalists and think that they will not try to seize what they can? What would they be good for in that case? But in such a state of affairs, can we remain indifferent and merely say as Communists: 'We shall carry on propaganda for Communism in these countries.' That is true, but that is not all! The practical task of Communist policy is to take advantage of this hostility and to incite one against the other. . . . Of course to support one country against another would be a crime against Communism. But we Communists must use one country against another. Are we not committing a crime against Communism? No, because we are doing so as a socialist state, which is carrying on Communist propaganda and is obliged to take advantage of every hour granted it by circumstances in order to gain strength as rapidly as possible.

(ibid., pp. 386–7)

Socialism victorious in one country does not by any means at one stroke preclude all war in general. On the contrary, it presupposes wars. The development of capitalism proceeds with the greatest unevenness in the various countries. This cannot be otherwise under commodity production. It inevitably follows from this that socialism cannot be victorious first in one or in several countries while the others will for some time remain bourgeois or pro-bourgeois. This ought to give rise not only to friction but to an outright endeavour by the bourgeoisie of other countries to crush the victorious proletariat of the socialist state. In such event war on our part would be legitimate and just. It would be a war for socialism for the liberation of other peoples from the bourgeoisie.

(ibid., Vol. XIX. Quoted by Joseph Stalin in his book, *The October Revolution*, New York, 1934, pp. 166, 167)

We are living not only in a state, but in a system of states, and the existence of the Soviet Republic side by side with imperialist states for a long time is unthinkable. One or the other must triumph in the end. And before that end comes, a series of frightful clashes between the Soviet Republic and the bourgeois states is inevitable.

(ibid., Vol. CVI, p. 102)

Communist Tactics and Strategy

The proletariat, having assembled sufficiently powerful political and military 'striking forces', must overthrow the bourgeoisie and deprive it of the power of the state, so as to wield this *instrument* for its *own* class purposes. . . .

The proletariat must first overthrow the bourgeoisie and conquer the power of the state, and use the power of the state, *i.e.* the dictatorship of the proletariat, as an instrument of the class in order to gain the sympathy of the majority of the toilers. . . .

In the first place, the proletariat can achieve this aim not by restarting the old machinery of state power, but *by smashing it to atoms* and not leaving a stone of it standing (heedless of the howls of the panic-stricken petty bourgeois and of the threats of the saboteurs). It must then create a new apparatus, this new apparatus which is adapted for the dictatorship of the proletariat and for its struggle of proletarian toiling masses.

(ibid., Vol. XVI, p. 448)

Universal suffrage provides an index of the state of maturity of the various classes in the understanding of their tasks. It shows how the various classes are *inclined* to solve their problems. But the *solution* of the problems is effected not by means of the ballot, but by the class struggle in all its forms including civil war.

(ibid., p. 455)

It is essential that the party of the revolutionary proletariat should participate in bourgeois parliamentarism for the purpose of educating the masses by means of elections and the struggle of parties within parliament. But to confine the class struggle to the parliamentary struggle, or to regard the latter as the supreme and decisive form of struggle, to which all other forms of struggle are subordinate, means practically to desert the proletariat for the bourgeoisie.

(ibid., p. 456)

No parliament can in any circumstances be for Communists an arena of struggle for reforms for betterment of the situation of the working class. . . . The only question can be that of utilizing bourgeois state institutions for their destruction.

(ibid., Vol. XXV, p. 566)

Participation in bourgeois-democratic parliaments even a few weeks before the victory of the Soviet republic, and even after that victory, not only does not harm the revolutionary proletariat, but makes it easier to prove to the backward masses why such parliaments should be dispersed, makes it easier to disperse them, and facilitates the political extinction of bourgeois parliamentarism.

(ibid., Vol. XVII, p. 149)

In any capitalist country the strength of the proletariat is incomparably greater than its numerical strength in proportion to the total population. This is due to the fact that the proletariat economically dominates the centre and nerve of the whole economic system of capitalism, and also because under capitalism the proletariat economically and politically expresses the *true* interests of the vast majority of the toilers.

For this reason the proletariat, even when it forms a minority of the population (or when the class-conscious and truly revolutionary vanguard of the proletariat forms a minority of the population), is capable of overthrowing the bourgeoisie and of then gaining numerous allies from among the mass of semi-proletarians and petty bourgeois, who otherwise would never in advance favour the rule of the proletariat, would not have understood the conditions and aims of the rule of the proletariat, and who only by their subsequent experience become convinced that the dictatorship of the proletariat is inevitable, proper, and legitimate.

One of the essential conditions for preparing the proletariat for victory is a prolonged, persistent, and ruthless struggle against opportunism, reformism, social-chauvinism, and similar bourgeois influences and tendencies which are inevitable as long as the proletariat acts under capitalist conditions. Without such a struggle, without a preliminary complete victory over opportunism within the working-class movement there can be no hope for a dictatorship of the proletariat.

(ibid., p. 458)

A Communist must be prepared to make every sacrifice and, if necessary, even resort to all sorts of schemes and stratagems, employ illegitimate methods, conceal the truth, in order to get into the trade unions, stay there, and conduct the revolutionary work within. . . .

(ibid., Vol. XVII, pp. 142–5]

Is there such a thing as Communist ethics? Is there such a thing as Communist morality? Of course there is. Often it is made to appear that we have no ethics of our own, and very often the bourgeoisie accuse us Communists of repudiating all ethics. This is a method of shuffling concepts, of throwing dust in the eyes of the workers and peasants.

In what sense do we repudiate ethics and morality?

In the sense that they were preached by the bourgeoisie who declared that ethics were God's commandments. We, of course, say that we do not believe in God, and that we know perfectly well that the clergy, the landlords, and the bourgeoisie spoke in the name of God in order to pursue their own exploiters' interests. Or instead of deducing these ethics from the commandments of God, they deduced them from idealistic or semi-idealistic phrases, which were always very similar to God's commandments.

We repudiate all such morality that is taken outside of human class concepts. We say that this is deception, a fraud, which clogs the brains of the workers and peasants in the interest of the landlords and capitalists.

We say that our morality is entirely subordinated to the interest of the class struggle of the proletariat. Our morality is derived from the interests of the class struggle of the proletariat.

And what is this class struggle? It is – overthrowing the Tsar, over-throwing the capitalists, destroying the capitalist class. . . . We sub-ordinate our Communist morality to this task. We say: 'Morality is that which serves to destroy the old exploiting society and to unite all the toilers around the proletariat, which is creating a new Communist society'.

(ibid., Vol. XVII, pp. 321–3)

Notes

Prologue

1. *Alexander Ilyich Ulyanov i Dyelo Pervavo Marta 1887 goda (Alexander Ilyich Ulyanov and the Case of March 1, 1887)*. Moscow, pp. 342–3. Also: Viktorovski, N. G., *A. I. Ulyanov*. Moscow, 1927, pp. 15–30.
2. Govoryukhin, O. M., *Pokusheniye na Imperatora Alexandra III (The Attempt on the life of the Emperor Alexander III)*. '*Golos Minuvshavo*'. Prague, 1926. No. 3, pp. 224–7, 230–4.
3. Yakovenko, B. V., *O Vtorom Pervoe Marta, 1887 goda (About the Second March 1, 1887)*. '*Istoriko-Revolyutzionnyi Vestnik*'. Moscow, 1927. No. 32, pp. 9–11.
4. Ilyinski, L., *Semeistvo Ulyanovykh (The Ulyanov Family)*. *K Godovshchine Smerti N. I. Lenina – Sbornik*. Leningrad, 1925, pp. 78, 82–3.

Chapter 1

1. '*Dekabristy*', *Neizdannyye Materialy i Stati (The 'Decembrists' –* unpublished materials and articles). Moscow, 1925.
   Also: Bazilevski, B., *Gosudarstvennyya Prestupleniya v Rossii v xix Vyekye (Political Crimes in Russia in the Nineteenth Century)*. Stuttgart, 1903. Vol. I, pp. 6–10, 81–5, 113–15.
2. Plekhanov, G., *Sochineniya (Collected Works)*. Moscow, 1925. Vol. XX, pp. 94, 102, 104, 105.
3. Burtzev, Vl., *Za Sto Lyet (For a Hundred Years)*. London, 1897, pp. 15–24.
   Also: Thun, A., *Istoriya Revolyutzionnyhk Dvizhenii v Rossii (The History of the Revolutionary Movements in Russia)*. Geneva, 1903, pp. 1–13.
4. Burtzev, Vl., ibid, pp. 29–30, 45–6.
   Also: Lemke, M., *Dyelo M. I. Mikhailova 1861 Goda (The Case of M. I. Mikhailov, 1861)*. '*Byloye*', St Petersburg, 1906. No. 1.
   Also: Lemke, M., *Protzess Velikorostzev (The Trial of the Velikoross Group)*. '*Byloye*', St Petersburg, 1907. No 7, pp. 81–6.
5. Thun, A., *The History of the Revolutionary Movements in Russia*, pp. 29–32.
   Also: Burtzev, Vl., ibid., pp. 90–7.

Also: Zasulich, V., *Vospominaniya* (*Reminiscences*). '*Byloya*', Petrograd, 1919. No. 14.

Also: Zasulich, V., *Nechaievskoye Dyelo* (*The Nechayev Case*). *Gruppa Osvobozhdeniya Truda*. Moscow, 1924. Sbornik No. 2, pp. 31–5, 42–9, 57, 62, 63, 68.

Also: Deitch, Lev, *Byl li Nechaiev Genialen?* (*Was Nechayev a Genius ?*). ibid., pp. 77–9.

6. Lavrov, P., *Nasha Programma* (*Our Programme*). '*Vperiod*', Zurich, 1873. Reprinted in Burtzev's *For a Hundred Years*, pp. 106, 107, 108, 110, 111, 112. Anenskaya, A., '*Yiz Proshlikh Iyet*', *Russkoye Bogatstvo*, No. 1, 1913.

7. *Materialy dlya Biografii Tkacheva* (Materials for the biography of Tkachev). '*Byloye*', St Petersburg, 1907. No. 7/19, p. 162.

Also: '*Nabat*'–*Sbornik Stateiiz Zhurnala* '*Nabat*' *za 1875–1879 Gody*. (A collection of articles from Tkachev's magazine *Nabat* for the years 1875–9.) Geneva. Quoted by N. Zhordaniya in his book *Bolshevism* (Russian). Berlin, 1922, pp. 9, 10, 11.

Also: Karpovich, Michael, *A Forerunner of Lenin – P. N. Tkachev*. *The Review of Politics*. Vol VI, No. 3, July 1944, pp. 336–50.

8. Lavrov, P., *Russkoi Revoluytzionnoi Molodiozhi – Redaktor Zhurnala Vperiod* (*To the Russian Revolutionary Youth from the editor of Vperiod*). London, 1874, pp. 40–3.

Also: Gertzen (Herzen), Alexander, *Sbornik Posmertnykh Statei*. (A collection of posthumous articles.) Geneva, 1870, pp. 284–6.

Also: Gertzen (Herzen) A. I., *Polnoye Sobraniye Sochinenii* (*Complete Works*). Petrograd, 1919 1923. Vol. XX, p. 132.

9. Morozov, N., *Vozniknoveniye Narodnoi Voli* (*The Origin of the 'People's Will' Party*). '*Byloye*'. St Petersburg, 1906. No. 12, pp. 1–22.

Also: Tuhn, A., pp. 131–4.

Also: *Pismo Ispolnitelnavo Komiteta k Alexandru Tretyemu* (*Open Letter of the Executive Committee of the 'People's Will' Party to Alexander III of March 10* (*22*), *1881*). *Literatura Partii Narodnoi Voli*, Paris, 1905, pp. 903–8.

10. Figner, Vera, *Polnoye Sobraniye Sochinenii* (*Complete Works*). Vol. I, pp. 162–6.

11. *Narodnaya Volya*, St Petersburg. No. 6, 23 October 1881, p. 1.

12. *Literatura Partii Narodnoi Voli*, p. 950.

13. Burtzev, Vl., *For A Hundred Years*, pp. 226–9.

Also: Martov, L., *Istoriya Rossiiskoi Sotzial-Demokratii* (*The History of the Russian Social Democratic Labour Party*). Moscow-Petrograd, 1923, pp. 9–15.

Chapter 2

1. Lenin, V. I., *Pismak Rodnym* (*Letters to Relatives*), with a preface by Maria Ulyanova. Moscow, 1930, p. 11.
2. Ulyanova-Yelizarova, Anna, *Vospominaniya ob Ilyiche* (*Reminiscences about Lenin*). Moscow, 1934, pp. 18, 21.
   Also: Ulyanov, Dimitri, *Iz Lichnykh Vospominanii o Vladimire Ilyiche*. (*Personal Reminiscences about Vladimir Ilyich*.) In the miscellany *On Lenin*. Moscow, 1925. Vol. IV, p. 51.
   Also: *Pravda*, (Moscow) 21 January 1941.
   Also: *Lenin's Mother* (English Edition). Moscow, 1934, pp. 20–1.
3. Ulyanova-Yelizarova, Anna, *O Zhizni Vladimira Ilicha v Kazani* (*On Lenin's Life in Kazan*). *Molodaya Gvardiya*. Moscow, 1924, Nos. 2–3.
4. Lepeshinski, P., *Zhiznennyi Put Lenina* (*The Life Road of Lenin*). Leningrad, 1925, pp. 9–10.
5. Ulyanova-Yelizarova, Anna, *Reminiscences about Lenin*, pp. 29, 34.
6. *Leninskii Sbornik* (*Lenin-Miscellany*). Moscow, Vol. XXXIII, pp. 15–16.
7. Vodovozov, V., *Moyo Znakomstvo s Leninym* (*My Acquaintance with Lenin*). *Na Chuzhoi Storone*. Prague, 1925. No. 12, pp. 176–7.
8. Ulyanova-Yelizarova, Anna, *Reminiscences about Lenin*, pp. 43–57.
9. Krupskaya, N., *Vospominaniya* (*Reminiscences*). Moscow, 1926. Vol. I, pp. 12, 18–21.
   Also: Potresov, A. and B. Nikolaevsky, *Sotzial-Demokraticheskoye Dvizheniye v Rossii* (*The Social Democratic Movement in Russia*). Moscow-Leningrad, 1928, pp. 356–7.
   Also: Potresov, A., Lenin. *Geselleschaft*. Berlin, 1927. No. 2.
10. Martov, L., *Zapiski Sotzial-Demokrata* (*Notes of a Social Democrat*). Berlin-Moscow. Vol. I, pp. 263–4, 268–9.
11. Lunacharski, A. V., *Lenin i Plekhanov* (*Lenin and Plekhanov*). *Prozhektor*. Moscow, 3 June 1928. No. 23.
    Also: Semashko, N., *Klochki Vospominanii* (*Bits of Reminiscences*). Moscow, 1930, pp. 60–4.
12. *Perepiska Plekhanova s Axelrodom* (*Correspondence between Plekhanov and Axelrod*). Moscow, 1925. Vol. I, pp. 269–75.
13. Lenin, V. I., *Letters to Relatives*, pp. 40–3.

Chapter 3

1. Ulyanova-Yelizarova, Anna, *Reminiscences*, pp. 57–72.
   Also: Krupskaya, N., *Reminiscences*. Vol. I, pp. 22–5.

2. *Vladimir Ilich v Ssylke* (*Vladimir Ilyich in Exile in Siberia*). *Proletarskaya Revolyutziya*. Moscow, 1929. Nos. 2–3, pp. 220–1. 225, 233, 234–6.

3. Krupskaya, N., *Reminiscences*. Vol. I, pp. 28–35.
   Also: Ulyanova-Yelizarova, Anna, *Reminiscences*, pp. 79–84.
   Also: Drizdo, Vera. *Nadezhda Konstantinovna*. *Novy Mir*. No. 2, Moscow, 1957.

4. Krzhyzhanovksaya, Z. *Neskolko Shtrikhov iz Zhizni Ilicha* (*A Few Features of Lenin's Life*). *Molodaya Gvardiya*, Moscow, 1924. Nos. 2–3.
   Also: Krzhyzhanovsky, G., *Iz Vospominanii o Lenine* (*From My Reminiscences about Lenin*). Moscow, 1925. *On Lenin*, Vol. IV, pp. 18–19.

5. Ulyanov, Dmitrii, *Iz Moikh Vospominanii o Vladimire Iliche* (*From My Reminiscences about Vladimir Ilyich*). *On Lenin*. Vol. IV, pp. 48–9.
   Also: Ulyanova-Yelizarova, Anna, *Vozvrashcheniye Ilicha iz Ssylki* (*Lenin's Return from Siberian Exile*). *Kommunist*, Moscow, January, 1926. No. 21, pp. 88–9.

6. Eldelman, B., *Pervyi Syezd R.S.D.R.P.* (*The First Congress of the Russian Social Democratic Labour Party*). *Proletarskaya Revolyutziya*. Moscow, 1924. No. 1, pp. 59, 63, 64, 96–8.

7. Lepeshinski, P., *Zhiznennyi Put Ilicha* (*Lenin's Life Road*). Leningrad, 1925, pp. 24–5.
   Also: Martov, L. (J.), *Istoriya Rossiiskoi Sotzial-Demokratii* (*The History of the Russian Social Democratic Party*). Moscow, 1922, pp. 53–7
   Also: Keeps, J. L. H., *The Rise of Social Democracy in Russia*. Oxford, 1963.

8. Kudelli, P. F., *Arest Lenina v 1900 Godu v Peterburge* (*Lenin's Arrest in St Petersburg in 1900*). *Krasnaya Lyetopis*, Leningrad, 1924. No. 1 (10), p. 46.

9. Kudelli, P. F., *Lenin i 'Iskra'* (*Lenin and 'Iskra'*). *Krasnaya Lyetopis*, Leningrad, 1926. No. 1, pp. 10–19.
   Also: Lenin, V. I., *Selected Works* (English Edition). Vol. 4, Book 1, p. 30.
   Also: Martov, L., *The History of the Russian Social Democratic Party*, pp. 56–7.

Chapter 4

1. Liadov, M., *Rasskaz Saratovskavo Delegata* (*Report of the Saratov Delegate*). *Staryi Bolshevik*. Moscow, 1933. Nos. 3–6, pp. 181–2.

456 Notes

Also: Pyatnitzki, O. A., *Zapiski Bolshevika* (*Reminiscences of a Bolshevik*). Moscow, 1933, pp. 22–5, 50–1.

2. Obolenskaya, P., *Propaganda i Agitatziya v Period 'Iskry'* (*Propaganda During the 'Iskra' Period*). *Staryi Bolshevik*. Moscow, 1933. Nos. 3–6, pp. 108–13, 116–21, 123, 126–33, 135.
   Also: Buchbinder, N. A., *Epokha 'Iskry'* (*The 'Iskra' Epoch*). Moscow, 1927, pp. 20, 24–5.

3. Lenin, V. I., *Izbrannyia Stati i rechi* (*Selected Articles and Speeches*). Moscow, 1924, p. 180.

4. Krupskaya, N., *Vospominaniya* (*Reminiscences*). Vol. I, pp. 67–9, 72.

5. Alexyev, N., *V. I: Lenin v Londone v 1902–1903 g.g.* (*Lenin in London in 1902–1903*). *On Lenin*, 1925. Vol. IV, pp. 67–9.

6. Lenin, V. I., *Pisma k Rodnym* (*Letters to Relatives*). pp. 107–9.

7. Krupskaya, N., *Reminiscences*. Vol. I, pp. 80–2.
   Also: Trotsky, L. D., *O Lenine* (*On Lenin*). Moscow, 1924, pp. 5–24.
   Also: Ziv, Dr G. A. (Siff, H. A.), *Trotsky* (*Russian*), *Reminiscences*. New York, 1921, p. 48.

8. Ilyin, V. (Lenin), *Za Dvenadtzat Lyet* (*For Twelve Years*). St Petersburg, 1906. Vol. I, pp. 205–6, 212–13, 246.

9. Zhordaniya, N.N., *Bolshevizm*. Berlin, 1922, pp. 6–8.

10. Potresov, A., *Posmertnyi Sbornik Proizvedenii* (*Posthumous Miscellany of Works*). Paris, 1937, p. 296.

11. Takhtarev, K. M., *Lenin i Sotzial-Demokraticheskoye Dvizheniye* (*Lenin and the Social Democratic Movement*), Reminiscences. *Byloye*. Leningrad, 1924. No. 24, p. 22.

12. Varentzova, O. A., *Raznoglasiya v Srede 'Iskry'* (*Dissensions in the 'Iskra' Group*). *'Staryi Bolshevik' 1933*. Nos. 3–6, pp. 67–72, 80–7.
   Also: Potresov, A. and B. Nikolaevsky, *Sotzial-Demokraticheskoye Dvizheniye. v Rossii*, pp. 299–302.
   Also: Krupskaya, N., *Reminiscences*. Vol. I, p. 88.

13. Shotman, A. V., *Zapiski Starovo Bolshevika* (*Reminiscences of an Old Bolshevik*). Moscow, 1932, pp. 89–95, 97.
   Also: Krupskaya, N., *Reminiscences*. Vol. I, pp. 89–98.
   Also: Lenginik, F., *Vtoroi Syezd Partii* (*The Second Congress of the Party*) *Staryi Bolshevik*, 1933. Nos. 3–6, pp. 163–71.
   Also: Martov, *The History of the Russian Social Democratic Labour Party*, pp. 76–85.

14. *Protokoly Vtorovo Syezda R.S.D.R.P.* (*Minutes of the Second Congress of the R.S.D.L.P.*). Geneva, 1904, p. 169.
   Also: Plekhanov, G., *Sochineniya* (*Collected Works*). Moscow, 1925. Vol. XIII, p. 385.

15. *Minutes of the Second Congress of the R.S.D.L.P.*, p. 133.

16. Plekhanov, *Sochineneniia*. Vol. 13, p. 90. Trotsky, N.(L.D.), *Nashi*

Politicheskiya Zadachi (Our Political Aims). Geneva, 1904, pp. 95, 102.

17. Krupskaya, N., *Vospominaniya o Lenine (Reminiscences about Lenin).* Moscow, 1932, pp. 74–8.
Also: Pyatnitski, O., *Zaposki Bolshevika (Memoirs of a Bolshevik),* pp. 55–8.
Also: Trotsky, *On Lenin,* p. 46.
Also: Martov, *The History of the R.S.D.L.P.,* pp. 87–90.

18. Lenin, V. I., *Sochineniya (Collected Works).* Vol. XXVIII, pp. 389–90.
The first edition of Lenin's works was published in Moscow in twenty volumes between 1922 and 1924. This edition contained all of Lenin's published writings and speeches, with lengthy and valuable expository notes on the events and people mentioned by Lenin.

The second edition, published in thirty-two volumes between 1926 and 1929, included many of Lenin's unpublished articles, notes and letters to comrades and co-workers. The editorial explanatory notes were enlarged. The first twenty-six volumes were edited by Bukharin, Molotov and Skvortsov-Stepanov; the last four by Molotov, Adoratsky and Savoliev. This was, until very recently, the authoritative edition, and is the edition referred to unless otherwise indicated.

A so-called third edition, published in 1932, was merely a reprint of the second.

Under Stalin, in 1938, an official pronouncement condemned the 'crude political errors of a damaging character in the appendices, notes and commentaries to some volumes of the works of Lenin,' Accordingly, the Marx-Engels-Lenin Institute began publication in 1941 of a fourth edition, in thirty-eight volumes, which was finally completed in 1958. This contained a few previously unpublished letters, but also failed to contain many letters previously published; furthermore, it did away with most of the notes and commentaries of previous editions.

Starting in 1960, a fifth edition began to appear, with fifty-five volumes scheduled. This newest edition contains additional letters, notes and drafts of articles by Lenin.

In addition to these editions of the *Sochineniya (Collected Works),* a group of Lenin's more important works were published in 1939 in two large volumes entitled *Izbrannyya Proizvedeniya (Selected Works).* An English edition of the *Selected Works* contained only a small part of Lenin's writings and speeches. Finally, a large volume entitled *Lenin-Stalin-1917, Selected Writings and Speeches* was published in English in Moscow in 1938. The quotations from Lenin's works in this book are taken mostly from the various Russian editions of the *Sochineniya* and are indicated in the notes as *Collected Works*. Wherever the quotation is taken from the English Edition it is marked *Selected Works*. Those taken from the *Izbrannyya Proizvedeniya* are indicated as *Selected Works* (Russian Edition).

Also: Krupskaya, *On Lenin*, pp. 78–83.

19. Lenin, V. I., *Collected Works*. Vol. XVII, p. 89.
20. Valentinov, *My Talks with Lenin. Forward*, New York, January 1948. Nikolai Valentinov, the Socialist author of many books on economic and philosophical problems, joined Lenin after the split in the R.S.D.L.P., but later parted with him. Lenin mentions him in several articles and letters. In a footnote to Lenin's *Letters to His Relatives* (Russian Edition, Moscow, 1931, p. 325) Valentinov is described as 'a Social Democrat – a Menshevik who in 1917 left the Menshevik Party. Lately works in the *Torgovo-Promyshlennaya Gazeta* (Organ of the Supreme Economic Soviet). Of his philosophic works are known: *Marx and Marxism*, (Moscow, 1908, *The Philosophical Construction of Marxism* (Moscow, 1908), and others'.

Valentinov, one of the authors of the original Soviet Five-Year Plan, left Russia a few years before World War II and lived in Western Europe. His reminiscences were first published, in part, in the New York *Daily Forward* in 1948; then, in full, in New York under the title *Vstrechi s Leninym* (*Meeting With Lenin*) in 1953. He died in Paris in 1964.

21. Ilyin, V. (Lenin), *Materializm i Empiriokrititsizm* (*Materialism and Empiriocriticism*). Moscow, 1909, p. 257.

Chapter 5

1. Argunov, A., *Iz Proshlavo Partii Sotzialistov-Revolyutzionerov* (*From the Past of the Socialist-Revolutionary Party*). *Byloye*. St Petersburg, 1907. No. 10–22, pp. 94–112.

   Also: *Pamyatnaya Knizhka Sotzialista-Revolyutzionera* (*A Remembrance Book of a Socialist Revolutionary*). Paris, 1911. Vol. I, pp. 1–8.

   Also: Dan, Theodor, *Proiskhozhdeniye Bolshevizma* (*The Origin of Bolshevism*). New York, 1946, pp. 300–6.

   Also: Alexinsky, G., *La Russie Revolutionnaire*. Paris, 1947, pp. 64–6.

2. Polovtzev, A. A., *Dnevnik* (*Diary of A. A. Polovtzev*). *Krasnyi Arkhiv*, No. 46.

3. Dan, *Proiskhozhdeniye Bolshevizma*, pp. 309–12.

4. Kranikhfeld, V. P., *Krovavoye Voskresenye* (*The Bloody Sunday*). *Mir Bozhii*, St Petersburg, 1906. No. 1.

   Also: Rutenberg, P., *Dyelo Gapona* (*The Case of Gapon*). *Byloye*. Paris, 1909. No. 2, pp. 29–38.

Also: *Iskra*, Geneva, 1905, Nos. 84–6.

Also: *Vperiod*, Geneva, 1905, Nos. 4–7.

Also: '*Osvobozhdeniye*', Paris, 1905, Nos. 64–7.

5. *Doklad Witte Nikolayu Vtoromy* (*Witte's Report to Nicholas II*). *Krasnyi Arkhiv*. Nos. 11–12, pp. 51 ff.

6. *K Dvadtzatiletiyu Revolyutzii 1905 Goda* (*On the 20th Anniversary of the Revolution of 1905*). *Byloye*. Leningrad, 1925. No. 4, pp. 31–5, 37, 124–5, 130–2, 135–44.

Also: Kirpichnikov, S. D., *Litugin i Soyuz Soyuzov* (*Litugin and the Union of Unions*). *Byloye*. Leningrad, 1925. No. 6.

Also: Witte, S. Yu. *Vospominaniya* (*Memoirs*). Berlin, 1922. Chapter 23.

7. Tskhakiya, M., *Iz Lichnykh Vospominanii o Vladimire Iliche* (*From Personal Reminiscences about Vladimir Ilyich*). *On Lenin*. Moscow, 1925. Vol. I, pp. 56–7.

Also: Krupskaya, *Reminiscences about Vladimir Ilyich* (Russian). 1932, Part I, pp. 92–7.

Also: Martov, *History of the R.S.D.L.P.*, pp. 118–21.

8. Lenin, *Selected Works* (English Edition). Vol. 3, p. 113.

9. Lenin, *Collected Works*. Vol. VIII, pp. 325–6.

10. Martov, *History of the R.S.D.L.P.*, pp. 146–7.

Also: Dan, *Proiskhozhdeniye Bolshevizma*, pp. 396–7.

11. *Lenin v Deistvitelnosti Yevo Roman s Yelizavetoi K.* (*Lenin's Romance with Elizabeth K.*). *Illyustrirovannaya Rossiya*. Paris, 31 October 1936. The story of Lenin's affair with Madame K. appeared in the French magazine *Intransigeant* and the Paris Russian weekly magazine *Illyustrirovannaya Rossiya* (*Illustrated Russia*), on 31 October, 7, 14 and 21 November 1936. The Editorial Committee of the latter magazine included the famous Russian writers Ivan Bunin, Dmitri Merezhkovsky, Boris Zaitzev and Zinaida Gippius. The identity of Elizabeth K. was not revealed by the editors. But the story was copyrighted by Gregory Alexinsky, a former close friend and associate of Lenin for many years. He was the leader of the Bolshevik deputies in the Second Duma. Both he and his wife Tatyana lived with Lenin for a number of years, first in Finland, later in Switzerland and Paris. During World War I, he became a bitter enemy of Lenin. He is the author of a number of works on Russia and the Russian Revolution, published in French and in English. Elizabeth K. mentioned meetings and conversations with a few other well-known Bolsheviks, who were still living in Moscow. None of them denied her story. She also published photostatic copies of excerpts of letters to her from Lenin, written clearly in Lenin's handwriting. While it is quite possible that Alexinsky or the editors

of her memoirs have added or glamorized portions of her story, the author accepts as authentic those parts of her testimony, quoted in this book, that tally with the published memoirs of other associates of Lenin, and with what the author has learned over a period of years about Lenin's life and views from people who were close to him at various times.

12. Lenin, *Collected Works*. Vol. VII, Part 2, pp. 57–66.

13. *Illyustrirovannaya Rossiya*, 31 October 1936.
    Also: Alexinskaya, Tatyana, *Miting v Paliustrove* (*The Meeting in Paliustrov*). *Rodnaya Zemlya*. Paris, 1926. No. 1, p. 6.

14. Lunacharsky, A., *Vospominaniya o Lenine* (*Reminiscences about Lenin*). Moscow, 1933, p. 21.

15. *Illyustrirovannaye Rossiya*, 7 November 1936.

16. Martov, *History of the R.S.D.L.P.*, pp. 178–9, 182–3, 191–2, 199, 201–2.
    Also: Dan, *The Origin of Bolshevism*, pp. 413, 420.

17. Lenin, *Dve Taktiki* (*Two Tactics*). *Selected Articles and Speeches* (Russian Edition). Moscow, 1924, p. 401.

18. ibid., pp. 385–6, 402–3, 409–11.

19. Gorky, M., L. B. Krassin. *Izvestiya*. Moscow, 19 December 1926.
    Also: Rudnev, V., *Gorky-Revolyutzioner* (*Gorky the Revolutionist*). Moscow, 1929, p. 54.

20. Gorky, *Novaya Zhizn*. 2 May 1918. Litvinov, M. M., *Transportirovaniye Oruzhiya v Rossiya* (*The Transportation of Arms to Russia*). *Pervaya Boyevaya Organizatztiya Bolshevikov*- Miscellany. Moscow, 1934, pp. 104–11.

21. Ruzer, L., *Iz Vospominanii ob Iliche* (*From My Reminiscences about Ilyich*). *On Lenin*. Vol. II, pp. 121–5.

22. Lenin, *Collected Works*. Vol. XI, p. 220
    Also: Abramovich Raphael, *In Tzvei Revolyutziyes* (*In Two Revolutions*) (Yiddish). New York. Vol. I, pp. 290–1.

23. Balabanov, M., *Tzarskaya Rossiya Dvadtzatavo Veka* (*Tsarist Russia in the Twentieth Century*). Moscow, 1927, pp. 88–9.
    Also: Woytinsky, V., *Delo Sotzial-Demokraticheskoi Fraktzii Vtoroi Dumy* (*The Case of the Social Democratic Faction of the Second Duma*). *Letopis Revolyutzii*. Berlin, 1923, pp. 122–4.
    Also: Martov, *History of the R.S.D.L.P.*, pp. 219–21.

24. Martov, *History of the R.S.D.L.P.*, pp. 222–5.
    Also: Resolutions of the London Congress, Lenin, *Collected Works*. Vol. VIII, pp. 524–48.
    Also: Dan, *The Origin of Bolshevism*, pp. 430–3.

25. Lepeshinski, P., *Zhiznennyi Put Ilicha* (*The Life Road of Lenin*). pp. 41–2.

26. Krzhyzhanovskaya, Z., *Neskolko Shtrikhov iz Zhizni Ilicha. On Lenin.* Vol. II, p. 48.
27. Krupskaya, *Vospominaniya*, p. 121.

Chapter 6

1. Bibeinishvilli, B., *Kamo. S. predisloviyem M. Gorkavo (Kamo. With an introduction by Maxim Gorky).* Moscow, 1934, pp. 118–23, 129–37, 141–3.
2. *Pisma P. B. Axelroda i J. Martova (Letters of P. B. Axelrod and J. Martov). Russkii Revolyutzionnyi Arkhiv,* Berlin, 1924, pp. 184–7. Also: Krivosheina, Yevgeniya, *Stranitzy o Kamo (Pages about Kamo). Staryi Bolshevik.* Moscow, 1934. No. 19, pp. 124 ff.
3. Medvedyeva-Ter-Petrosyan, S. F. *Tovarishch Kamo (Comrade Kamo). Proletarskaya Revolyutziya.* Moscow, 1924. Nos. 31–2, pp. 127 ff.
4. *Pisma P. B. Axelroda i J. Murtova,* p. 175.
5. Lenin, *Collected Works.* Vol. X, p. 88.
6. Martov, *Sotzialisticheskii Vestnik.* Berlin, 1922. No. 16.
7. Martov, *Spasiteli ili Uprazdniteli ? (Saviours or Nullifiers ?).* Paris, 1911, pp. 3, 17–18, 21–8.
   Also: *Pisma P. B. Axelroda i J. Martova,* pp. 188–90.
   Also: Shesternin, S., *Realizatziya Nasledstva Shmidta i Moll Vstrechi s Leninym (The Realization of Schmidt's Legacy and My Meetings with Lenin). Staryi Bolshevik.* Moscow, 1933. No. 5 (8), pp. 147, 150–7.
8. Woytinsky, Vl., *Gody Pobed i Porazhenii (The Years of Victories und Defeats). Reminiscences.* Berlin, 1922. Vol. II, pp. 102–3.
   Also: Volsky, Stanislaw. *Dans le Royaume de la Famine et de la Haine La Russie Bolsheviste.* Paris, 1920, p. 26.
   Also: Charasch, A. *Lenin. Mit einem Vorwort von Paul Axelrod.* Zürich, 1920, p. 12.
9. Solomon, G., *Lenin i Yevo Semya (Lenin and His Family). Reminiscences.* Paris, 1931, pp. 62–8.

George Solomon joined the Social Democratic movement before the turn of the century and was a close friend of the Ulyanov family. In 1903 he joined the Bolshevik faction, taking an active part in the Revolution of 1905. Exiled to Siberia in 1906, he escaped to Belgium, where he renewed his contact with Lenin. In 1913 Solomon returned to Russia, and was active in the March Revolution. Although a member of the Bolshevik Party, he did not agree with Lenin. During the November Revolution, he was in Stockholm. Like his friend Krassin, he later held various high posts in the Soviet Government. He was

Soviet Consul in Hamburg in 1918, later first Assistant Commissar of Foreign Trade and afterward Director of the Arkos (Soviet Trade Mission) in London. In August 1923, seven months before Lenin's death, Solomon resigned from his post and became an *émigré*. Six years later his memoirs were published in Paris.

10. Krupskaya, *Vospominaniya o Lenine*, p. 134.

11. *Pisma Lenina k Rodnym*, pp. 802–4

12. ibid., pp. 344–5.

13. *Illyustrirovannaya Rossiya*, 28 November 1936.

14. Krupskaya, *Vospominaniya o Lenine*, pp. 161–2.

15. Krzhyzhanovskaya, *Neskolko Shtrikhov iz Zhizni Lenina. On Lenin.* Vol. II, p. 49.

16. *Illyustrirovannaya Rossiya*, 28 November 1936.

17. Krupskaya, *Vospominaniya o Lenine*, p. 165.

18. *Bolshaya Sovetskaya Entziklopediya* (*Large Soviet Encyclopedia*). Vol. II, p. 389.

19. Krupskaya, *Vospominaniya o Lenine*, pp. 198–9.

20. Lilina, Z., *Lenin kak Chelovek* (*Lenin – the Man*). *On Lenin.* Vol. II, p. 68.

21. Badayev, A., *Bolsheviki v Gosudarstvennoi Dume* (*The Bolsheviks in the Dumá*). Leningrad, 1929, pp. 84–90.
Also: Krupskaya, *Vospominaniya o Lenine.* pp. 210–11.
Also: Troyanovsky, A., Telegram to Plekhanov. *Yedinstvo*, Petrograd, 23 April 1917.
Also: *Pisma P. B. Axelroda i J. Martova*, p. 229.
Also: Sumsky, S., *Troyanovsky. Poslyedniya Novosti*, Paris, 1 and 2 January, 1934.

22. Badayev, *Bolsheviki v Gosudarstvennoi Dume*, pp. 263–4.

23. ibid., pp, 169–70, 176–7, 194.

24. ibid., pp. 230–5, 242–6, 254–5.
Also: Samoilov, F., *Po Sledam Minuvshavo* (*In the Footsteps of the Past*). Reminiscences of an old Bolshevik. Moscow, 1934, pp. 341–7.
Also: Rodzyanko, M., *Iz Vospominanii* (*From My Memoirs*). *Byloye*, 1923. No. 21, pp. 248–9.

25. Bukharin, N., *Pamyati Ilicha* (*In Memory of Ilyich*). *Pravda*, Moscow, 21 January 1925.

26. Gilbeaux, Henry, *Vladimir Ilyich Lenin*. Leningrad, 1925, p. 152.

27. For Lenin's instructions, *Collected Works*, Vol. XXXV, pp. 108–10; Vol. XX, pp. 463–502. On Inessa Armand, here and elsewhere, the basic sources are – in addition to Lenin's works and the Moscow *Leninskii Sbornik* – Krupskaya, *Sbornik Pamiati Inessyi Armand* (Moscow 1926) and *Vospominanyia o Lenine* (Moscow 1957); Valentinov, op. cit.; Marcel Body, 'Alexandra Kollontai' (*Preuves*,

Paris, April 1952); and Bertram D. Wolfe, 'Lenin and Inessa Armand', *Slavic. Review*, March 1963.

Chapter 7

1. *Leninskii Sbornik (Miscellany on Lenin)*. Moscow, 1924. No. 1, p. 131.
2. Kautsky, Karl, *Sozialisten und Krieg (Socialists and War)*. Prague, 1937, pp. 370–3.
   Also: Scheidemann, Philip, *Memoirs of a Social Democrat*. London, 1929. Vol. I, pp. 185–7.
   Also: Zinoviev, G., *Lenin, His Life and Works* (English), p. 34.
3. Ganetzki, Ya., *Vospominaniya o Lenine (Reminiscences about Lenin)*. Moscow, 1933, pp. 16–18, 27–32, 34.
   Also: Karpinski, V., *Dva Sluchaya (Two Occurrences)*. *On Lenin*. Vol. II, pp. 148–9.
4. Litvak, A., *In Zurich and in Geneva during the First World War*. Reminiscences. *Collected Works* (Yiddish). New York, 1945, pp. 244–6.
5. Krupskaya, *Vospominaniya o Lenine*, p. 217.
6. Litvak, *In Zurich and Geneva during the First World War*. Reminiscences. pp. 246–7.
7. *Izvestiya*, Moscow, 1 August 1934.
   Also: Shklovsky, G., *Bernskaya Konferentziya 1915 Gods (The Berne Conference of 1915)*. *Proletarskaya Revolyutziya*. 1925. No. 5 (40), pp. 134–59, 167, 179–85.
8. Krupskaya, *Vospominaniya o Lenine*, pp. 219–20.
9. ibid., pp. 224–5.
10. Safarov, G., *O Tovarishche Lenine (About Comrade Lenin)*. *On Lenin*. Vol. I, p. 78.
11. Zinoviev, G., and V. I. Lenin, *Protiv Techeniya (Against the Tide)*. Moscow, 1925, p. 29.
12. Litvak, A., *In Zurich and in Geneva During the First World War*. Reminiscences, pp. 252–6.
13. Badayev, *Bolsheviki v Gosudarstevennoi Dume*, pp. 338–42, 347–50, 374–83.
14. *Proletarskaya Revolyutziya*. Moscow, 1936. No. 7, p. 167.
15. Lenin, *Collected Works*. Vol. XXIX, p. 167.
16. Balabanov, *Tzarskaya Rossiya Dvadtzatavo Veka. Kharkov*, 1927, pp. 55–6, 61, 106–7, 126–30, 171–3.
17. Balabanov (Balabanova), Angelica, *My Life as a Rebel*. New York, Harper & Bros., 1938, pp. 134–41.
    Also: Lenin, *Collected Works*. Vol. XX, p. 637.
    Also: Zimmerwald-Kintal, *Sozial-demokrat*, 10 June 1916, No. 54–5.

Also: Shklovsky, G., *Zimmerwald. Proletarskaya Revolyutziya,* 1925, No. 9 (44), pp. 85–106.

18. Zinoviev, and V. I. Lenin, *Protiv Techeniya,* pp. 324–5.
19. *The Letters of Lenin* (English). New York, Harcourt, Brace & Co., 1937, pp. 355–6.
20. Krupskaya, *Vospominaniya o Lenine,* pp. 243–4, 256.
21. Balabanov (Balabanova), Angelica. In oral conversations with the author.
22. Lenin: *A Brief Sketch of His Life and Activities* (English). Moscow, Marx-Engels-Lenin Institute, 1942, pp. 178–9.
23. Zinoviev and V. I. Lenin, *Protiv Techeniya,* p. 522.
24. Filiya, M., *Iz Davnikh Vstrech* (*From Past Meetings with Lenin*). *On Lenin* (A collection of articles published by *Pravda*). 1927, pp. 73–4.
25. Solomon, *Lenin i Yevo Semya,* pp. 76–8.
26. Lenin, *Collected Works.* Vol. XIX, p. 357.

Chapter 8

1. Balabanov, *Tzarskaya Rossiya,* pp. 77–9, 127–9, 171–2.
   Also: Mstislavski, S., *Gibel Tzarizma* (*The Wreck of Tsarism*). Leningrad, 1927, pp. 41–6.
   Also: Melgunov, S., *Na Putyakh k Dvortsovomy Perevorotu* (*On the Roads Towards a Palace Revolution*). Paris, 1931, pp. 127–8. Sergei Melgunov, Russian historian and radical, edited for many years the outstanding Moscow historical monthly *Golos Minuvshavo* (*Voice of the Past*) until the magazine was suppressed by the Bolsheviks. He later continued to publish the magazine in Prague. He is the author of many historical works dealing with the Russian liberation movement and various phases of the Revolution.
2. Rodzyanko, M., *Krusheniye Imperii* (*The Fall of the Empire*). *Arkhiv Russkoi Revolyutzii.* Berlin. Vol. XVIII, pp. 153–69.
   Also: Guchkov, A. I., *Iz Vospominanii* (*From My Memoirs*). *Poslyedniya Novosti.* Paris. Nos. 5644, 5647, 5651.
   Also: Shchegolev, P., *Poslednii Reis Nikolaya Vtorovo* (*The Last Voyage of Nicholas II*). Moscow, 1928, pp. 14–18, 20–2.
3. Shliapnikov, A., *Semnadtzatyi God* (*The Year 1917*). Moscow, 1925. Vol. I, pp. 40–4.
   Also: Melgunov, *Na Putyakh k Dvortsovomu Perevoroty,* pp. 206–9, 212–15.
4. Shulgin, V., *Dni* (*Days*). Moscow, 1925, pp. 102–8
5. Sukhanov, N., *Zapiski o Revolyutzii* (*Notes on the Revolution*). Berlin-Moscow, 1922. Vol. I, pp. 86–8, 123–6, 128–34, 179–83. Nikolai Sukhanov, a left-wing Socialist and Zimmerwaldist, is

described in the footnotes to Vol. XXVII of Lenin's *Collected Works* (Second Edition, p. 592) as a 'non-partisan Social Democrat, Internationalist . . . one of the editors of the internationalist magazine *Letopis* during the war and after the March Revolution an editor of *Novaya Zhizn'* (Maxim Gorky's Petrograd newspaper in 1917–18). The footnote also said he was one of the leaders of the Executive Committee of the Petrograd Soviet in the early months of the Revolution, that he published a seven-volume *Notes on the Revolution*, and that he later was a member of the Communist Academy in Moscow (from which he was withdrawn in 1930, because his views were 'not in accordance with the aims of the Academy'). The same volume of Lenin's work also contains two articles by Lenin about Sukhanov's Notes. Lenin criticized Sukhanov's thesis that Russia has not reached 'the high development of productive forces under which Socialism is possible', but Lenin did not dispute the accuracy of the historical facts of the Revolution as related by Sukhanov. Trotsky's *History of the Russian Revolution* quotes extensively from Sukhanov's *Notes*. Lenin, writes Trotsky (Vol. I, p. 166), described Sukhanov as 'one of the best representatives of the petty bourgeoisie'. In his book *Stalin* (p. 194), Trotsky calls Sukhanov's *Notes* 'invaluable'.

Also: Mstislavski, *Gibel Tzarizma*, pp. 82–4, 106–7.

6. Shchegolcv, *Poslednii Reis Nikolaya Vtorovo*, pp. 40–88.
7. ibid., pp. 99–105, 115–17.
8. Balabanov, *Tzarskaya Rossiya Dvadtzatavo Veka*, pp. 238–9.
   Also: *Pisma Alexandry Feodorovnoy ik Nikolayu Vtoromu* (*Letters from Alexandra Feodorovna to Nicholas II*). *Krasnyi Arkhiv*. Moscow. 1923. No. 4, p. 219.

Chapter 9

1. Shliapnikov, *Semnadtsatyi God*. Vol. II, pp. 179–88.
   Also: *The Letters of Lenin* (English). p. 425.
2. Ludendorff, Erich, *Meine Kriegserrinerungen* (German) (*My War Reminiscences*). Berlin, 1919, p. 407.
3. Hoffmann, Max, General, *Der Krieg der Versaumeten Gelegenheiten* (German) (*The War of Missed Opportunities*). Munchen, 1924, pp. 174–89.
   Also: Scheidemann, *Memoirs of a Social-Democrat*. Vol. I, pp. 333–4
4. *K Istorii Plombirovannova Vagona* (*The History of the Sealed Train*) – an interview with Paul Levy. *Poslyedniya Novosti*, Paris, 2 March 1930.

5. Lenin, *Collected Works*. Vol. XX, p. 68.
6. Guilbeaux, Henry, *La Fin des Soviets* (*The End of the Soviets*). Paris, 1937, p. 30.
7. Anikst, Olga, *Vospominaniya o Lenine* (*Reminiscences about Lenin*). *On Lenin*. Vol. IV, pp. 92–3.
   Also: Karpinski, *Dva Sluchaya*. *Mologaya Gvardiya*, Moscow, 1924, Nos. 2–3.
   Also: Suliashvili, D. *Vstrechi s Leninym v emigratsii*. *Neva* (Leningrad), No. 2, 1957.
8. Parvus, *Pravda Glaza Kolet* (*The Truth Strikes the Eye*). Stockholm, 1918. Quoted in Prof. Melgunov's *Zolotoi Nemetskii Klyuch Bolshevikov* (*The Golden German Key of the Bolsheviks*), p. 69.

Chapter 10

1. Sukhanov, *Zapiski o Revolyitzii* (*Notes on the Revolution*). Vol. III, pp. 7–25.
   Also: Raskolnikov, F., *Priyezd Lenina v Rossiyu* (*Lenin's Arrival in Russia*). *On Lenin*. Vol. III, pp. 87–9.
2. *Rech* (Petrograd liberal daily), 17 (30) April 1917.
3. Bonch-Bruyevich, *V. I. Lenin v Rossii* (*V. I. Lenin in Russia*). Moscow, 1925, pp. 26–8.
   Also: Sukhanov, *Zapiski o Revolyutzii*. Vol. III, pp. 50–4.
4. Zenzinov, Vladimir (Told to the author in 1927 and later confirmed by Kerensky).
   Also: Nabokov, Vladimir, *Vremennoye Pravitelstvo* (*The Provisional Government*). *Arkhiv Russkoi Revolyutzii*, Berlin. Vol. I, p. 75.
5. Lenin, *Collected Works*. Vol. XX, pp. 76–81.
6. Badayev, *Bolsheviki v Gosudarstvennoi Dume*, pp. 257–65.
   Also: Tsiavlovsky, M., *Bolsheviki po Dokumentam Moskovskavo Okhrannavo Otdeleniya* (*The Bolsheviks According to the Documents of the Moscow Okhrana*). Moscow, 1918, pp. 14 ff.
7. Badayev, *Bolsheviki v Gosudarstvennoi Dume*, p. 268.
8. Lenin, *Collected Works*. Vol. XX, p. 613.
9. *Izvestia*, Petrograd, 19 June 1917.
   Also: Pinontkovski, S., *Khrestomatiya po Istorii Oktyabrskoi Revolyutzii* (*A Chrestomathy of the History of the October Revolution*). Moscow, 1930, pp. 133–41.
   Also: Tseretelli, I. G. *Memoirs of the February Revolution*. Paris, 1964.
10. *Izvestia*, Petrograd, 20 June 1917.
11. Lenin, *Collected Works*. Vol. XX, pp. 526–7, 629–30, 671–2.
    Also: Sukhanov, *Zapiski o Revolyutzii*. Vol. IV, pp. 367, 452.

Also: Danilov, S., *Vladimir Ilyich. On Lenin*. Vol. III, pp. 144–5.
12. Bonch-Bruyevich, *Lenin v Rossii*, pp. 68–70, 85–6.

Chapter 11

1. Sukhanov, *Zapiski o Revolyutzii.* Vol. IV, pp. 470–80.
   Also: Miliukov, P., *Istoziya Vtoroi Russkoi Revolyutzii (The History of the Second Russian Revolution)*. Sofia, 1921. Vol. I, pp. 237–48.
   The secret letter from Kautsky, Haase and Bernstein was published for the first time by Irakli Tseretelli in his *Vospominanii o fevralsky revolutsii,* Paris, 1963, Vol. I, p. 233.
2. Melgunov, S., *Zolotoi Nemetskii Klyuch Bolshevikov (The Golden German Key of the Bolsheviks)*. Paris, 1940, pp. 98–101, 104–11.
   Also: Nikitin, B., *Rokovyye Gody (The Fateful Years)*. Paris, 1937, pp. 109–77.
   Colonel Nikitin headed Petrograd Military Intelligence after the March Revolution, and was in close contact with Allied Military Intelligence. Part of his memoirs was published in 1936 in Professor Paul Miliukov's Paris newspaper, *Poslyedniya Novosti*, and appeared in book form the following year. The documents quoted in this book from Nikitin's memoirs were all in the possession of the Provisional Government; none of its representatives who investigated the case ever doubted their authenticity.
   Also: Kerensky, Alexander, *The Crucifixion of Liberty*. New York, John Day Co., 1934, pp. 321–9.
   Also: Lenin, *Collected Works*. 1928 Edition. Vol. XXI, pp. 11, 29–32, 46–7.
3. Ganetsky, Ya., *Ot Fevralya k Oktyabryu (From February to October)*. *Proletarskaya Revolyutziya*, Moscow, 1924, No. 1 (24).
   According to a statement made to the author by Alexander Kerensky, the Russian Ambassador in Stockholm acted in this manner under specific instructions from the Provisional Government, enabling it to keep track of Ganetsky's operations. Ganetsky was unaware of this.
4. Masaryk, Thomas, *The Making of a State*, London, Allen & Unwin, 1927, p. 243.
5. *Neizdannyye Pisma Lenina (Lenin's unpublished letters) Proletarskaya Revolyutziya*. Moscow, 1923. No. 9 (21), pp. 229–31.
6. Bernstein Eduard, *Ein Dunkles Kapitel (A Dark Chapter)*. *Vorwaerts*, Berlin, 14 January 1921.
   'From the Entente side,' wrote Bernstein, 'it has been asserted and still is maintained that Lenin and his comrades had been supplied at that time with large sums of money by Imperial Germany in order

that they might carry on more effectively therewith their disruptive agitation in Russia.

'Lenin and his comrades have indeed received sums from Imperial Germany. I learned of this as early as the end of December 1917. Through a friend I made inquiries of a person who, owing to his connexion with official quarters, was in a position to be well informed and I received a reply confirming this. I was not able, however, to find out how large the amounts were or the name or names of the intermediaries. Now I have learned from reliable sources that the sums in question were almost incredibly large, certainly amounting to more than 50 million gold marks. In other words, the sums were sufficiently large to remove all doubt as to their origin in the minds of Lenin and his comrades. The matter is therefore of no small interest in the evaluation of their political morality. Nor is it without value in judging the methods employed by Imperial policy.

'Of this we shall treat in a separate article. I am sure of the arguments which, from the viewpoint of military expediency, could seem to justify the financing of the Bolshevik *coup*. The officer who first mentioned this matter to me quoted a leading member of Parliament of one of the Allied Powers, with whom he had official contacts, as saying that this was 'a master stroke on the part of Germany'. Indeed one cannot blame Lenin and his comrades for the final outcome. One of the results of their action was Brest-Litovsk and no doubt Trotsky and Radek still remember the arrogance of the German Military Command. General Hoffmann who then negotiated with them had them doubly under his thumb, and never failed to let them feel it.'

On 20 January 1921, Bernstein published another article in the *Vorwaerts* on this matter. 'My bringing to public attention the fact that Lenin and his comrades had received more than 50 million gold marks from the German Imperial Treasury for the furtherance of their activities,' he wrote, 'has elicited from the *Rote Fahne* [official organ of the German Communist Party] a threatening note against me. It demands that I name my informers so that these "unscrupulous slanderers" might be given the opportunity to prove their assertions before a court. And as a docile pupil of Moscow it writes in the same gracious tone: "Should Herr Eduard Bernstein not heed this demand we will then call him not only an old idiot but also brand him publicly as a shameless slanderer and we will see to it that Herr Eduard Bernstein never comes before the public without the charge of shameless and unscrupulous slanderer falling upon his head. . . . We still hope that Bernstein is only an old feeble-minded gossip and that he will name his witnesses. We are waiting."

'My reply can be very short. . . . As author of the article I am responsible for its assertions and am therefore entirely ready to support them *before a court*. The *Rote Fahne* need not set in motion its alarm-and-cudgel guards against me. Let it bring charges against me or let it get a legal representative of Lenin's to do this and it may rest assured that I will do my best to dispose of all the difficulties that might stand in the way of a thorough-going investigation of this affair.'

They never did.

7. Yelov, B., *Posle Yulskikh Dnei* (*After the July Days*). *Krasnaya Letopis*. Leningrad, 1923. No. 7, pp. 95, 109–10, 117–18.

8. Shotman, A., *Lenin v Podpol'ye* (*Lenin in Hiding*). *On Lenin*. Vol. III, pp. 102–11.

   Also: Yemelyanov, Nikolai, *Tainstvennyi Shalash* (*The Mysterious Tent*). *Krasnaya Letopis*. Leningrad, 1922, No. 4, pp. 133–9.

   Also: Rovia, Gustav, *Kak Lenin Skryvalsya u Gelsingforskavo Politzmeistera* (*How Lenin Hid in the House of the Helsinki Police Commissioner*). *Krasnaya Letopis*. Leningrad, 1922. No. 5, pp. 308–9.

Chapter 12

1. Trotsky, *The History of the Russian Revolution*. New York, 1923. Vol. II, pp. 252, 254, 256.

2. *Protokoly VI-vo Kongressa R.S.D.R.P.* (*Bolshevikov*). (*Minutes of the Sixth Congress of the Bolshevik Party*), 26 July–3 August 1917. Moscow, 1934.

3. Lukomsky, A. S., General, *Vospominaniya* (*Reminiscences*). Vol. I, pp. 228, 229.

4. Kitayev, P., *Savinkov i Kornilov* (*Savinkov and Kornilov*). *Byloye*. Leningrad, 1925. No. 3 (31), p. 179.

5. *Lenin-Stalin-1917, Selected Writings and Speeches* (English Edition). Moscow, 1938, pp. 396–8.

6. Podvoisky, N., *Voyennaya Organizatziya Tze-Ka Bolshevikov* (*The Military Organization of the Central Committee of the Bolshevik Party in 1917*). *Krasnaya Letopis*. Leningrad, 1923. No. 9, pp. 34 5.

7. *Proletarskaya Revolyutziya*. Moscow, 1922. No. 10, pp. 72–3.

8. ibid., pp. 318–19.

9. Lenin, *Selected Works*. Vol. V, pp. 215–17.

10. Shotman, *Lenin on the Eve of October*. *On Lenin*. Vol. 1, pp. 116–18.

11. Lenin, *Selected Works* (Russian Edition). Moscow, 1939. Vol. 2, p. 90.

12. Lenin, *Collected Works*, 1928 Edition. Vol. XXI, p. 241.

13. *Rech*. Petrograd, 21 October 1917.

14. *Leninskii Sbornik*. Vol. IV, pp. 335–9.

Chapter 13

1. *Proletarskaya Revolyutziya*, Moscow, 1922. No. 10, p. 462.
2. ibid., p. 58.
3. ibid., pp. 464–5.
4. Lenin, *Collected Works*. Vol. XXI, pp. 60–1, 213, 273.
5. *Proletarskaya Revolyutziya*, Moscow, 1922, No. 10, pp. 72–3, 75, 77.
6. *Lenin-Stalin-1917*, *Selected Writings and Speeches* (English Edition), p. 609.
7. Podvoysky, *Voyennaya Organizatziya R.S.D.R.P. Krasnaya Letopis*. Leningrad, 1923. No. 8, pp. 15–18, 23.
8. Dan, F., *K Istorii Poslednikh Dnei Vremennovo Pravitelstva* (*The History of the Last Days of the Provisional Government*). *Letopis Revolyutzii*. Berlin, 1923. No. 1, pp. 171–5.
9. Trotsky, *On Lenin*, p, 74.
10. Rakhia, *Moii Vospominaniya o Vladimire Iliche* (*My Reminiscences about Lenin*). *About Lenin*. Moscow, 1927, pp. 43–7.
11. Bonch-Bruyevich, *On the Fighting Posts of the Revolution*, p. 114.
12. Malyantovich, P., *V Zimnem Dvortze 25-26-vo Oktyabrya, 1917 Goda* (*In the Winter Palace October 25–26* [*Nov. 7–8*], *1917*). *Byloye*. Petrograd, 1918. No. 12, pp. 117–19.
13. Trotsky, *On Lenin*, p. 77.
14. Malyantovich, *VZimnem Dvortze*, pp. 125–6.
15. Podvoysky, *Voyennaya Organizatziya Tze-Ka Bolshevikov*, pp. 28–9.
16. Malyantovich, *V Zimnem Dvortze*, pp. 130–4, 136–7, 140–1.
17. Trotsky, *The History of the Russian Revolution* (Russian). Vol. II, Pt. II, p. 321.
18. *Izvestia*, Petrograd, 8 November 1917.
19. Bonch-Bruyevich, *On the Fighting Posts of the Revolution*. pp. 123–7.
20. Trotsky, L.D., *Moya Zhizn* (*My Life*). Berlin, 1930. Vol. II, pp. 58–9.
21. Nikolayevsky, Boris. '*Stranitsi Proshlogo*'. *Sotsialisticheskii. Vestnik*, July–August 1958. Podvoysky, *Voyennaya Organizatziya*, pp. 38–9.
22. Krasnov, P., *Na Vnutrennem Fronte* (*On the Internal Front*) in *Oktyabrskaya Revolyutziya*. Miscellany. Moscow, 1926, p. 80.
    Also: Kerensky, A., *Izdaleka* (*From Afar*). Paris, 1922, pp. 194–203.
23. Kerensky, A., *Gatchina*, in *Oktyabrskaya Revolyutzia*. Moscow, 1926, pp. 201–2.
24. Miliukov, P., *Nizverzheniye Vremennovo Pravitelstva* (*The Downfall of the Provisional Government*) in *Oktyabrskaya Revolyutziya*, pp. 252, 253, 260–5, 270.

Also: Pyatnitsky, O., *Moskovskiye Bolsheviki v Oktyabrskiye Dni 1917 Goda* (*The Moscow Bolsheviks in the October Days of 1917*). *Bolshevik*. Moscow, 1933. Nos. 20–1.
25. *Izvestia*, Petrograd, 9 December 1917.

Chapter 14

1. *Protokoly Tze-Ka R.S.D.R.P.* (*Bolshevikov*) (*Minutes of the Central Committee of the Bolshevik Party August 1917–February 1918*). Moscow, 1929, p. 152.
2. *Proletarskaya Revolyutziya*. No. 10, 1922, pp. 61–2.
3. *Yedinstvo*. Petrograd, 28 October (10 November) 1917.
4. Plekhanov, G., *God na Rodine* (*A Year in the Native Land*). Paris, 1921. Vol. I, pp. xiii–xiv.
5. Czernin, Count Ottokar, *In the World War*. London, Cassell & Co., 1919, p. 216.
6. Bonch-Bruyevich, *On the Fighting Posts of the Revolution*, pp. 175–6.
7. *Krassin, Liubov*, Leonid Krassin, *His Life and Work*. London, Skeffington & Son, 1929, p. 64.
8. Solomon, G., *Sredi Krasnykh Vozhdei* (*Among the Red Leaders*). Paris, 1930. Vol. I, pp. 13–14.
   Also: Solomon, G., *Lenin and His Family*, pp. 88–90.
9. ibid, pp. 12–13.
10. Bonch-Bruyevich, *On the Fighting Posts* . . ., p. 10.
11. *Proletarskaya Revolyutziya*, 1922. No. 10, pp. 101–3.
12. Gorbunov, N. P., *Lenin* (*Reminiscences*, English Edition). Moscow, 1934, pp. 6–14.
13. Bonch-Bruyevich, *On the Fighting Posts* . . ., pp. 200–1.
14. Lenin, *Selected Works* (English Edition). Vol. 7, p. 278.
15. Trotsky, *On Lenin*, p. 102.
16. Lenin, *Collected Works*. 1922 Edition. Vol. XV, p. 176.
17. Lenin, *Collected Works*. 1928 Edition. Vol. XXII, pp. 69–73, 77, 583–4.

Chapter 15

1. Trotsky, *On Lenin*, pp. 91–2.
2. Sokolov, Boris, *Zashchita Uchreditelnavo Sobraniya* (*The Defence of the Constituent Assembly*). *Arkhiv Russkoi Revolyutzii*, 1924. No. 13, p. 41.
3. ibid., pp. 50–4.
4. Trotsky, *On Lenin*, p. 93.

5. Bonch-Bruyevich, *On the Fighting Posts* . . ., p. 246.
6. ibid, p. 240.
7. ibid., pp. 254–6.
8. Vishniak, Mark, *Vserossiiskoye Uchreditelnoye Sobraniye* (*The All Russian Constituent Assembly*). Paris, 1932, pp. 98–116.
   Also: Sokolov, *Zashchita Uchreditelnavo Sobraniya*, No. 13, pp. 67–8.
   Also: Chernov, Victor, *Russia's One-Day Parliament*, New Leader (New York), 31 January 1948.
9. Trotsky, *On Lenin*, p. 94.
10. Plekhanov, *God na Rodine*. Vol. II, p. 267.
11. Lenin, *Collected Works*. Vol. VXI, p. 336.
12. Luxemburg, Rosa, *The Russian Revolution* (English Edition), Michigan, 1961, pp. 62–71.

Chapter 16

1. *Bolsheviki u Vlasti* (*The Bolsheviks in Power*). A collection of articles published by the Socialist Revolutionaries. Moscow, 1918, p. 55.
2. Antonov-Ovseenko, V. A., *Zapiski o Grazhdanskoi Voine* (*Reminiscences about the Civil War*). Moscow, 1924. Vol. I, p. 227.
3. Czernin, Ottokar, *In the World War*, p. 259.
4. *Proceedings of the Brest-Litovsk Conference*. Washington, 1918, p. 82.
5. *Bolsheviki u Vlasti*, p. 56.
6. Radek, K., *V. I. Lenin*. In *25 Years of the Bolshevik Party*. A collection of articles. Tver, 1923, p. 242 f.
7. Lenin, *Collected Works*. Vol. XXII, pp. 198–9, 258, 607.
8. *Pravda*. Petrograd, 23 February 1918.
9. Lenin, *Selected Works* (English Edition). Vol. 7, pp. 303–4.
10. ibid., pp. 294, 295.
11. *On Lenin*. Vol. II, p. 16.
12. Lenin, *Selected Works* (English Edition). Vol. 7, pp. 282–3.
13. According to Rudolph Hilferding, a leading German Independent Socialist in the years 1918–21, the Bolsheviks sought at that time to have the war continued under any conditions. They were afraid, first, that the Allies would attack Russia after having triumphed over Germany; secondly, they hoped that the continuation of the war would lead to successful world revolution.
    Writing in the *Neue Vorwaerts* of 2 September 1939, under the pseudonym of Richard Kern, Hilferding declared:
    'Lenin signed the treaty of Brest-Litovsk in order to prolong the war between Germany and Austria on the one hand, and Great Britain and France on the other hand, and in order to secure peace

Notes 473

for himself. He did it at the risk of bringing about a victory of the
reactionary Habsburgs and Hohenzollerns over the western demo-
cracies, and against the opposition of Trotsky, who fully realized the
possibility that a German victory might result from the Brest-
Litovsk peace treaty. The intervention of the United States, of
American "capitalism", as the foolish "vulgar Marxists" used to say,
intervention which could hardly be foreseen at that time, saved him
from this danger. But Lenin may at that time still have counted on a
world revolution after the war, and the most important thing to him
was to gain time. At any event, since the end of the war, Russian
dictatorship had only one aim in view: to *drive Germany into a war
against the Western Powers*, and, if possible, to stay out of the war
itself. That is why Moscow *urged* Haase, immediately after the
armistice (November 1918), to continue resistance on Russia's side.
Later Radek was sent to Berlin in order to bring about a rejection
of the Versailles Treaty. At that time contacts were established with
the national-Bolshevik and German nationalist groups who were the
precursors of National Socialism. At the same time the German
Communists were transformed into fiery patriots within twenty-four
hours. When the Monarchist Kapp organized his *putch* (13 March
1920) Moscow forbade the German Communists to participate in
the general strike proclaimed by the Socialist parties and the Free
Trade unions, and the Moscow *Izvestia* revealed the true reason for
this when it wrote that the Bolsheviks would rather come to terms
with an honest German nationalist government than with the Social
Democratic traitors.'

14. The German Foreign Ministry archives, containing documents relating to German foreign policy from 1867 to 1920, were found by
the U.S. Army in five castles located in the Harz Mountains. Among
these documents were thousands of reports, letters and telegrams
concerning relations between the Bolsheviks and the Government of
Wilhelm II. Selections of these documents have been published in
International Affairs (London), 1956; in *Die Welt* (Hamburg) and
the Social Democratic *Vorwaerts* (Bonn) in the course of 1957;
in *Lenins Ruckkehr nach Russland 1917*, edited by Werner Halweg,
published in Leyden, Holland, also in 1957; and in *Germany and
the Russian Revolution*, edited by Z. A. B. Zeman, Oxford, 1958. In
addition, a number of documents of the former Austro-Hungarian
Empire have been examined by Stefan T. Possony and reproduced in
his *Lenin: The Compulsive Revolutionary*, New York, 1964.

Chapter 17

1. Adoratsky, *Vospominaniya o Lenine* (*Reminiscences about Lenin*) Moscow, 1939, pp. 66–7.
2. Trotsky, *On Lenin*, pp. 101–5.
3. Bonch-Bruyevich, *Na Boyevykh Postakh Revolyutzii* (*On the Fighting Posts of the Revolution*), p. 195.
4. ibid, pp. 198–201.
   Also: Zubov, N., *Dzerzhinsky*. Moscow, 1933, pp. 9–11, 49–57.
5. *Znamya Truda* (daily), Moscow, 23 February 1918.
6. Iks. [Naglovsky, A.] *Krasnyye Vozhdi* (*The Red Leaders*). Reminiscences. *Sovremennyya Zapiski*. Paris, No. 61, pp. 441–2.
   Alexander Naglovsky, who joined Lenin soon after the split in the Social Democratic Party, withdrew from party activities during the years of reaction and became a successful engineer. Although he opposed Lenin's tactics after the March Revolution, he rejoined the Bolshevik Party and after the October Revolution occupied several high government posts. In the late twenties, while a member of the Soviet mission in Italy, he resigned and became an *émigré*. In 1937 he sent the author several chapters of his memoirs in the hope of having them published in the United States. Part of this manuscript was later published in the Paris Russian quarterly *Sovremennyya Zapiski*. Naglovsky died in France at the beginning of World War II.
7. Bonch-Bruyevich, *Na Boyevykh Postakh Revolyutzii*, pp. 330, 335, 339, 343, 346, 347, 348.
8. Stuchka, P. *The History of the Lettish Army Regiments. Vechernaya Krasnaya Gazeta*. Leningrad, 23 February 1928.
9. Abramovich, R., *The Soviet Revolution*. New York, 1962, Chapter 9. The details are largely based on *Novaya Zhizn*, January–June 1918.
10. Lenin, *Collected Works*. 1929 Edition. Vol. XXIII, p. 545.
11. Parfenov, P., *Grazhaanskaya Voina v Sibiri* (*The Civil War in Siberia*). Moscow, pp. 25–6.
12. Miliukov, P., *Rossiya na Perelome* (*Russia at Crossroads*). A History of the Revolution. Paris, 1927, Vol. II, pp. 17–21, 33–4, 41–3, 60–2.
13. Lenin, *Collected Works*. Vol. XXIII, pp. 549, 551, 554–6.
    Also: *Bolshevik*. Moscow, 1936. No. 2, p. 74.
14. Solomon, *Sredi Krasnykh Vozhdei*. Vol. I, p. 83.
15. Bykov, P., *Posledniye Dni Romanovykh* (*The Last Days of the Romanovs*). Moscow, 1926, pp. 114–21.
    For a detailed report of the killing of the Tsar and his family see Sokolov, N., *Ubiistvo Tzarskoi Sem'i* (*The Murder of the Imperial Family*). Berlin, 1925.

16. Milyutin, V., *Stranitzy iz Dnevnika* (*Pages from a Diary*). *Prozhektor*. Moscow, 1921. No. 4.

17. *Trotsky's Diary in Exile, 1936*, New York, 1963, pp. 81–2.

18. Lenin, *Collected Works*. 1923 Edition. Vol. XI, Part 2, p. 429.

19. Lenin, *Selected Works* (English Edition). Vol. 8, pp. 1929–31.

20. Bosh, Yevgeniya, *Vstrechi i Besedy s Vladimirom Ilichem* (*Meetings and Talks with Vladimir Ilyich*). *On Lenin*. Vol. III, pp. 80–1.

21. Lenin, *Collected Works*. Vol. XXXV, pp. 275–97.

22. Lenin, *Collected Works* (Russian Edition, 1923). Vol. XV, p. 507.

23. Bonch-Bruyevich, *Tri Pokusheniya na Lenina* (*Three Attempts on Lenin's Life*). Moscow, 1930. pp. 3–5, 78–80.
    Also: *Proletarskaya Revolyutziya*. Moscow, 1933. No. 7, pp. 275–84, 285.

24. Malkov, P., *Zapiski Kommendanta Moskovskog Kremly*, Moscow. 1959, pp. 160–1.

25. Smilg-Benario, *Na Sovetskoi Sluzhbe* (*In Soviet Service*). *Arkhiv Russkoi Revolyutzii*. 1921. No. 3, pp. 149–50.

26. '*Yezhenedel'nik Ve-Che-Ka*' (*Weekly of the Cheka*), Moscow, 1918, No. 1.

27. *Pravda*, Moscow, 4 August 1918.

28. Krassin, Lyubov, *Leonid Krassin, His Life and Work*, p. 98.

29. *Krasnyi Teror*, Moscow, 1918, No. 1, 1 October.

30. Balabanov Angelica, *My Life as a Rebel*, p. 188.

31. *Yezhenedel nik Chrezvychainoi Kommissii* (*Weekly of the Cheka*), Moscow, 1918, November–December.

32. Martov, J., *Das Problem der Internazionale und das Russische Revolu-zion* (*The Problem of the International and the Russian Revolution*). In 'The Minutes of the Extraordinary Congress of the Independent Socialist Party in Halle', Germany, 1920, pp, 216–17.

33. *Komsomol'skaya Pravda*, Moscow, 22 December 1927.

34. Liberman, S.I., *Diela i Lyudi* (*Events and Men*), New York, 1944, p. 80.

35. ibid., p. 112.

36. Badayev, *Bolsheviki v Gosudarstvennoi Dume*, pp. 266–8.

37. *On Lenin*. Vol. IV, p. 47.

38. *Izvestia*, Moscow, 21 January 1937.

39. Naglovsky, *Krasnyye Vozhdi, Sovremennyya Zzpiski*. Paris. No. 61, pp. 445–7.

Chapter 18

1. Bonch-Bruyevich, pp. 398–400.

2. Dmitriyev, N., *Lenin v Melochakh-K Godovshchine Smerti Lenina*

(*Lenin in Small Things – On the Anniversary of His Death*). Moscow, 1925, p. 172.

3. Iks (Naglovsky), *Krasnyye Vozhdi. Sovremennyya Zapiski.* Paris, No. 61, pp. 441–2.

4. Danilov, S., *Vladimir, Ilyich. On Lenin.* Vol. III, pp. 149–50.

5. Solomon, *Lenin and His Family*, pp. 28–9.

6. Balabanov, A., *Impressions of Lenin.* University of Michigan Press, Ann Arbor, 1964.

7. *Leninsky Sbornik*, Vil. XXXV, pp. 131–2.

8. *Izvestia*, 8 May 1964.

9. Quoted by Volin in *Internatsionalnii Sbornik* (Russian), *P.A. Kropotkin i ego utcheniye.* Chicago, 1931, p. 59.

10. Georgi Mironov, *Korolenko, Molodaya Gvardia,* Moscow, 1962, pp. 351–2.

Chapter 19

1. *Pravda*, Moscow, 2 February 1921.

2. Radek, K., *Noyabr* (*November*). Reminiscences of November 1918. *Krasnaya Nov.* Moscow, 1926. No. 10, pp. 139–75.

3. Heilmann, Ernst, *Die Noske Garde* (*The Noske Guards*). Berlin, 1920, p. 63.

4. Lenin, *Collected Works.* Vol. XXVI, p. 229.

5. Antonov-Ovseenko, V., *Vospominaniya o Grazhdanskoi Voine* (*Reminiscences about the Civil War*). Moscow. Vol. IV, p. 330.

6. Balabanov, Angelica, *My Life as a Rebel*, pp. 209–17.
   Also: Borkenau, F., *The Communist International.* London, Faber & Faber, pp. 161–70.

7. Diogot, Vladimir, *V Svobodnom Podpolye* (*In the 'Free' Underground*). Reminiscences about underground work in the years 1919–21. Moscow, 1923, pp. 28–9, 38.

8. *The Third International and Its History.* Reprinted in *Pravda,* 3 March 1929.

9. Balabanov, Angelica, *My Life as a Rebel.* pp. 175, 188, 235.

10. Trotsky, *On Lenin*, pp. 87–8.

11. *Istorik-Marxist.* Moscow, 1935. No. 2–3, p. 90.

12. *Minutes of the Extraordinary Congress of the Independent Socialist Party in Halle, Germany.* Berlin, 1920, pp. 212–13.

13. Hilferding's speech. In *The Minutes of the Extraordinary Congress of the Independent Socialist Party in Halle, Germany*, pp. 180–204.
    Also: *Freiheit.* Berlin, 29 October 1920.

14. Reprinted in *Bolshevik*. Moscow, January 1939.

15. Bernstein, Ed., *Ein Dunkles Kapitel. Vorwaerts.* Berlin, 14 January 1921.

Chapter 20

1. Abramovich, R., *The Soviet Revolution*, pp. 189–95.
   Also: Lenin, *Collected Works*. Second Edition, Vol. XXVI. p. 300. Schapiro, L., *The Origins of the Communist Autocracy*. Oxford, 1956.
2. Gool, Roman, *Tukhachevsky*. Berlin, 1922, pp. 159–61.
3. *Pravda*. Moscow, 8 March 1921.
4. *Pravda o Kronshtadte* (*The Truth about Kronstadt*). A collection of documents, published by the Socialist Revolutionaries abroad in 1921, p. 20.
5. Gool, *Tukhachevsky*, pp. 173–4.
6. Lenin, *Selected Works* (English Edition). Vol. 8, pp. 97, 194–6.
7. ibid., pp. 110–11.
8. Lenin, *Collected Works*. 1922 Edition. Vol. XVIII, p. 369.
9. Lenin, *Collected Works*. Vol. XX, Pt. 2, p. 487.
10. Lenin, *Collected Works*. Vol. XIII, Pt. 2, p. 108.
11. Lenin, *Selected Works* (English Edition). Vol. 8, p. 343.
12. Lenin *Collected Works*. Vol. XV, pp. 585–7.

Chapter 21

1. Gorky, M., *Vladimir Lenin*. Leningrad, 1924, pp. 12–21.
2. Lenin, *Collected Works*. Fourth Edition. Vol. XXXV, pp. 189, 202–3, 231.
3. Radek, *V. I. Lenin*. In *Twenty-Five Years of the Russian Communist Party*. Tver, 1923, p. 234.
4. Krupskaya, *Vospominaniya o Lenine*, pp. 179–83.
5. Zetkin, Clara, *On Lenin*. Vol. IV, pp. 147–8.
6. Bonch-Bruyevich, V., *Tridtzat Dnei* (Monthly), 1934, No. 1.
   Also: Bonch-Bruyevich, *Biblioteka i Arkhiv R.S.D.R.P. v Zheneve* (*The Library and Archives of the R.S.D.L.P. in Geneva*). *Krasnaya Letopis*. No. 3, 1932.
7. *Pravda*, Moscow, 21 January 1937.
8. Ulyanov, D. and M. *O Lenine* (*On Lenin*). Moscow, 1934, p. 92.
   Also: *Isvestia*, Moscow, 21 January 1930.
9. Gil S., *Shest Let s V. I. Leninym* (*Six Years with V. I. Lenin*). Reminiscences of Lenin's personal chauffeur. Moscow, 1947, pp. 22, 24–6, 34, 70.

Chapter 22

1. Fotyieva, L., 'Lenin in 1922'. *Ovtyabr* (Moscow), No. 4, 1963.

2. Lenin, *Collected Works*. Vol. XXVIII, pp. 344–9.
3. *Leninskii Sbornik*. Vol. XXXV, p. 318.
4. Lenin, *Collected Works*. Vol. XXVI, pp. 37, 48, 241, 243, 246–7, 305.
5. Fotyieva, op cit. The Testament and other Lenin documents dealing with Stalin were confirmed at the Twentieth Congress of the Soviet Communist Party in February 1956. Earlier, their existence had been made known directly by supporters of Trotsky and indirectly by Stalin (in *Speeches About the Opposition*, Moscow 1928).
6. *On Lenin*. Vol. III, pp. 134–5.
7. Valentinov, *My Talks With Lenin*. Forward. New York, January 1948.
   Also: *V. I. Lenin: A Brief Sketch of His Life and Activities*. Moscow, 1942, p. 317.
8. *On Lenin*. Vol. IV, p. 207 and Vol. III, p. 136.
9. Foerster, O., *Vospominaniya o Bolezni i Smerti Lenina* (*Reminiscences about Lenin's Illness and Death*). *On Lenin*. Vol. IV, p. 207.
10. *Pravda*, 27 January 1924.

Index